THE

Annals of Newberry

IN TWO PARTS

PART FIRST
BY
JOHN BELTON O'NEALL, LL. D.

PART SECOND
BY
JOHN A. CHAPMAN, A. M.

97 - 1278

Yours truly
John Betton O'Neill

THE

Annals of Newberry

IN TWO PARTS

PART FIRST
BY
JOHN BELTON O'NEALL, LL. D.

PART SECOND
BY
JOHN A. CHAPMAN, A. M.

COMPLETE IN ONE VOLUME

CLEARFIELD COMPANY

Originally Published
Newberry, South Carolina
1892

Reprinted
Genealogical Publishing Co., Inc.
Baltimore, 1974
Reprinted for
Clearfield Company, Inc. by
Genealogical Publishing Co., Inc.
Baltimore, Maryland
1995

Library of Congress Cataloging in Publication Data

O'Neall, John Belton, 1793-1863.
    The annals of Newberry, in two parts.

    Reprint of the 1892 ed. published by Aull & Houseal, Newberry, S. C.
    1. Newberry Co., S. C.—History. I. Chapman, John Abney, 1821-
II. Title.
F277.N505 1974   975.7'39   73-17361
ISBN 0-8063-7992-8

Reprinted from a volume in
the George Peabody Branch,
Enoch Pratt Free Library,
Baltimore, Maryland
1974

Made in the United States of America

PART FIRST.

INTRODUCTION.

My predecessor and master in this field of labor closed his work amid the mutterings of a gathering storm, which was soon to burst in fury over the country. It passed, leaving in its track many ruins of fortunes and many wrecks of men. It was the purpose of this writer to record the names of all who took an active part in that great struggle and bore the fury of that storm. After that to collect and arrange such other matter, biographical, religious, literary and anecdotical as might properly be included in the Annals of Newberry.

It has also been thought well to include in this volume the portraits of the representative men of Newberry of the times past in which they lived and moved. This has been done so far as it was possible to obtain their likenesses. All that could be obtained the artist has reproduced here.

The wo. k is now done, and I close my labors with the closing days of 1892 in the midst of profound peace at home and abroad, with the prospect, so far as man can tell, of a long continuance.

God grant that the prospect of peace and prosperity may not be delusive.

JOHN A. CHAPMAN.

December 19th, 1892.

THE

ANNALS OF NEWBERRY

HISTORICAL, BIOGRAPHICAL AND ANECDOTICAL

BY

JOHN BELTON O'NEALL, LL.D.

TO

THE PEOPLE

OF NEWBERRY DISTRICT

THE ANNALS OF NEWBERRY,

HISTORICAL, BIOGRAPHICAL AND ANECDOTICAL,

ARE RESPECTFULLY DEDICATED,

AS THE OFFERING OF A SON TO HIS MOTHER,

BY

JOHN BELTON O'NEALL.

INTRODUCTION.

The work which is now about assuming the shape of a book, was begun in 1850, without any such purpose. The object is truly stated in the opening number. As the work progressed, material accumulated, their value was perceived, and an effort was made to so mould them as to give character to their publication. Public attention was fixed upon it, and a general desire has been expressed that it should assume some permanent form. That is now attempted, and it is hoped that it will constitute some contribution to the history of the State, and will preserve the names of many worthy men, which would otherwise be lost.

The Appendix contains some account of the great flood of August, '52, the injury to the Greenville and Columbia Railroad, the memoir of William Spencer Brown, the Engineer who was drowned in it. These seemed to me to be germain to the history of Newberry, and well worth preserving. The sentence on Motley and Blackledge, and the notice of Gov. Johnson, and the letter of Mr. Pope, may be considered as matters which I was much interested in preserving.

JOHN BELTON O'NEALL.

May 31st, 1858.

NEWBERRY ANNALS.

NO. 1.

One who is heartily tired of the incessant war of politics, and who is sick at heart with the intestine divisions by which this best of all governments is threatened to be rent asunder and cast to the winds, proposes, as far as time, information, and opportunity may serve, to discharge the duty of preserving much in relation to the district of his birth, which might otherwise perish.

Whence the name *Newberry* is derived it is impossible with certainty to say. I have heard some assert, it was called Newberry County, after a captain of that name, in Sumter's State troops, but whether there was such an officer, I have never been able to ascertain. Certain it is, that a family of that name once lived beyond Pedee, in that section now called Marlborough district. Lately it has been my privilege to make the acquaintance of a preacher of the name of James Newberry, and therefore it may be that the tradition is true. Others have supposed that it was called after some place in England or the United States; but it is to be remarked that the names of similar sound elsewhere are spelled Newbury, while our district name is uniformly spelled Newberry, and pronounced with the accent on the second syllable. Others have supposed it was a fancy name, from the beautiful appearance of the country—covered with the oak, hickory, walnut, pine, elm, and poplar forests, intertwined with grape and muscadine—the ground carpeted with the rich covering of pea-vine, and studded all over with fruit-bearing shrubbery. It is hence supposed that the first settlers, enchanted with the prospect, might have said it was pretty as a new berry—and hence it was called Newberry! I like this notion best. It better accords with Colonel Rutherford's enthusiastic expression: "South Carolina is the garden-spot of the world, and Newberry the garden-spot of that garden-spot." It began to be settled before 1752, when Duncan's settlement, on the creek now bearing his name, was made. It must have been pretty well settled by 1762, for in that year Kelly and Furnas opened their store, at Kelly's old store, Springfield. The description given by Samuel Kelly then, of the face of the country, is still remembered. He said that "it was in the spring the most beautiful scene his eyes ever beheld. The open woods presented no obstruction to the view. The hills and vales were covered with pea-vine and maiden cane; the former in bloom made it look like a garden."

Newberry lies in the parallel of 34° north latitude, and almost due west from Columbia. The town is 34° 16' 37" north, and 41' west. Its bearing from Columbia is north 68, west 36¼ miles. It is bounded northeast by Broad River; east by a line running from the ferry known before the Revolution as Shirer's, afterwards as Dawkins' and Ruff's, now Hughey's, south 17 west, to a point just above the mouth of Buffalo Creek, on Saluda River; thence south by Saluda River to the Island ford; thence west by the old road, called the Ninety-Six road, to Odell's ford, on Enoree; thence northwest by the road to Crenshaw's ford on Tiger; thence north, down the Tiger River to its junction with Broad River. Its western border on Laurens is about thirty-one miles; its eastern, on Lexington, is about sixteen. From Parkin's, now Croft's ford, on Saluda, to Hendrix's ford, now Tucker's bridge, on Enoree the north and south, or meridian line of the district, passing directly through the town, is about twenty-six miles. Its length, on a line east and west passing through the town, is about the same. I suppose what is said in Mill's Statistics, p. 641, is true, that the average extent of the district is equal to about twenty-four miles square, and that it contains about 368,640 square acres, which would make the territorial wealth of the district, at an average of five dollars per acre, (which is much too low,) equal to nearly $2,000,000. This is soon to be doubled, and perhaps quadrupled, by the Greenville and Columbia and Laurens Railroads, and possibly the Spartanburg Railroad crossing from the mouth of Fair Forest direct to Newberry Court House, may add another million to the value. How much has Newberry contributed to these great works? *Altogether not $130,000.*

This body of 368,640 square acres, constituting the district of Newberry, presents the most unbroken body of cultivable land in any portion of the State. There are not 10,000 acres in the whole which have not been cultivated, or which may not, by proper agricultural industry, be brought into cultivation. A great deal—I think nearly 100,000 acres—are still in forest; another hundred thousand may be regarded as waste from improvident culture. About 168,000 acres are in cultivation, and according to the census of 1840, supported 18,350* persons, equal to about one soul for every nine acres of cultivated land. This population ought to be doubled by doubling the cultivated land, which could easily be done; and should be quadrupled, by improving the cultivation, and proper attention to manufactures. That same census tells us we then made 57,350 bushels of wheat, 1,129 of barley, 73,185 of oats, 708 of rye, 635,634 of corn—making a total of our grain crop of 768,006 bushels, not quite forty bushels to every soul. This is entirely too small for our wants. I hope the census for 1850† will show that it is at least doubled. The cotton crop is put down at 3,105,107 pounds. If this be of picked cotton, as I presume was intended, it may constitute an approach to the present crop of Newberry, 30,000 bales; assume this to be true, and the annual income of the district is nearly a million of dollars. *This is soon, I hope, to be doubled.*

The town of Newberry stands upon lands originally granted to John Jones. It had passed from the memory of every one that such a man ever lived *there*, when there appeared, about 1819, among its inhabitants, a very old stranger, apparently between 70 and 80—an idiot—who said his name was James Jones; that his father once lived thereabouts. It was apparent from his knowledge of localities, such as Kelly's old store (Springfield,) and the old inhabitants, that it was true as he stated. For instance, stepping into the old house at Springfield, in the lifetime of its venerable occupant, Hannah Kelly,

---

* The census of 1850 gives the aggregate of the population of Newberry district 20,143—making about one person to every eight acres.

† By the census of 1850, the product of wheat had increased to 79,375 bushels, barley had fallen off to 1,081, oats had increased to 99,798, corn to 664,058, rye had fallen off to 696 bushels—making our aggregate grain crop in 1850, 845,008 bushels.

The cotton crop is, I see, set down at 19,894 bales, of 400 pounds each, making a total of 7,954,690 pounds.

and sitting down for a moment, this poor wandering stranger said to her as he rose, he believed he would step over to Billy Coate's, and walked towards the north door, which had been closed, and the steps removed, for more than a quarter of a century. The old lady said that that was once the familiar way of passing out of the house to the elder William Coate's who lived and must have died between 1762 and 1796. This strange being, after lingering for a few days in the neighborhood, and talking of persons long dead, as of yesterday, disappeared, and was heard of no more. He probably returned to Georgia, from whence he said he came. Many were incredulous, but on looking to the mesne conveyances it was found that John Jones, whom he claimed as his father, was once the proprietor of the town of Newberry. When the court house was located, it belonged to John Coate, (commonly called little John); his settlement was originally at the Cedar Spring, south of the grave yard. But when the court house was located, he lived in a house on the lot now owned and occupied by Dr. Thompson. The north end of Coate street is about opposite to the site of the old house. It was then called Coate's shop. The location was accidental, or perhaps I should say capricious. The strongest sections of the district were then the Enoree and Little River settlements. The Enoree settlement desired the court house to be fixed at Col. Rutherford's, (now Bauskett's or Wadlington's); the Little River wished it at Kelly's old store, (Springfield). Between the two, the county court Judges would not decide. They determined to run the transverse lines of the district, and where they intersected, *there* the court house should be builded. This was accordingly done; the lines intersected in a millpond, (Duren's,) on the branch running by or through John Garmany's old place, near the road to Ashford's ferry. Carnes, (Peter,) the County Attorney of facetious memory, insisted that it would be a capital notion to build the court house, like a tub-mill, over the pond. The county court Judges, however, demurred to the argument, and after a regular *"curia advisare vult"* determined to build the court house at Coate's shop, and accordingly there it was builded; and here was the beginning of the town of Newberry. When that was, and other matters, in the following number.

NO. 2.

In 1783 an ordinance was passed, appointing commissioners to divide the districts of Charleston, Georgetown, Cheraw, Camden, *Ninety-Six*, Orangeburg, and Beaufort, into counties "of a convenient size, not more than forty miles square." In Ninety-Six the commissioners were Andrew Pickens, Richard Anderson, Thos. Brandon, *Levi Keysey*, (Casey,) *Philemon Waters*, Arthur Simpkins, and Simon Berwick. Under this ordinance, I presume that Edgefield, Abbeville, and Newberry were laid out. For in the Act of 1785, "For laying off the counties therein mentioned," &c., Abbeville, Edgefield, and Newberry *are* spoken of as existing counties. Laurens, Spartanburg, and Union are not only laid off, but also named in the Act. It is to be observed that in this last Act, this district's name is spelled Newbury. The boundaries are the same as those given in No. 1, except that the ford on Enoree, called in it Avery's, is in the Act called Anderson's; that on Tiger, called in No. 1 Crenshaw's, is in the Act called Hill's; and the county is extended below the line, now existing eight miles on Broad River, and thence across to the mouth of Bear Creek on Saluda. In the Act of the same year (1785) "establishing county courts," &c., the true spelling of the district name "*Newberry*," is resumed. It is worthy of observation, how the commissioners to lay off the district of Ninety-Six into counties were scattered. General Pickens, Richard Anderson, and Judge Simpkins were south of Saluda River. General Pickens in the county afterwards called Abbeville; Richard Anderson near the line between it and Edgefield; and Judge Simpkins in the latter, and near the present court house; Col. Waters and Gen. Casey were between Broad and Saluda rivers, and in Newberry; Col. Brandon north of Enoree, in the county afterwards called Union; and Simon Berwick in Spartanburg. This is the gentleman who was murdered by outlaws on his return from the seat of government, probably in 1783.

The Act of 1785 (ratified 22d of March) commonly called the County Court Act, and drawn, as is generally understood by Judge Pendleton, provides for a court to be held in every county, once in three months, by seven Justices of the Peace, to hold their commissions during good behavior, and to be elected, first, by a joint nomination by the Senate and House of Representatives; vacancies among them, afterwards occurring, were to be filled by themselves; any three of the said Justices were a quorum to hold the said courts. The number of Justices was increased two by the Act of 10th of March, 1786, and by the Act of 17th March, 1787, was further increased to eleven.

The Justices of the Peace first appointed to hold the County Courts for Newberry, were, as appears from the records of 1785 and 1786, Robert Rutherford, Robert Gillam, George Ruff, Levi Casey, John Lindsey, Philemon Waters and Levi Manning. The first County Court was held at the house of Col. Robert Rutherford, 5th of September, 1785. The Justices present were Robert Rutherford, Robert Gillam, Geo. Ruff and Levi Casey. The Clerk and Sheriff were, by the County Court Act, to be appointed by a majority of the County Court Judges. From the entry made in the records, it appears that Thomas Gordon had been appointed by the Justices before their meeting as a court, Sheriff of Newberry, and commissioned by the Governor, William Moultrie, for two years, the term of Sheriff's office according to the Constitution of 1777. At the first meeting, William Malone was appointed Clerk, and held his commission during good behavior. He continued Clerk, and discharged the duties of his office by his deputies, Thomas Brooks Rutherford, Major Frederick Nance and William Sattrewhite, to May term, 1794, when, on his resignation, Major Frederick Nance was appointed in his stead.

It appears that at the September court, 1796, held at the house of Colonel Robert Rutherford, (Justices present, Robert Gillam, Robert Rutherford, Philemon Waters, Levi Casey, John Lindsey, and William Caldwell,) the following entry in relation to the court house was made: "Pursuant to law the Justices proceed to situate the court house of this county at John Coate's, (little) or within one mile and a half of that place, as future circumstances may direct, pointing out the most advantage that may be derived to the publick in situating the same." It is to be observed that this is the first time that William Caldwell appeared on the bench as one of the County Judges.

This was the first step to the settlement of the controversy about the location of the court house. The court was, notwithstanding the order of September, '86, held March term, 1787, at Colonel Rutherford's. At June term the court assembled at the same place on the 4th of the month. present Robert Rutherford, Levi Casey, Philemon Waters, George Ruff, John Means, William Caldwell and Robert Gillam, Justices. They adjourned to meet the next day, "at John Coate's, on the north side of Bush River, agreeable to the order of September, 1786." At this court, Robert Gillam, who had been previously appointed, produced his commission and assumed the duties of Sheriff. At the September court (7th), present, Philemon Waters, George Ruff, Levi Manning, Levi Casey, John Means and John Hampton, Justices, the following entry was made: "William Caldwell, Esq., and Mr. Joseph Wright are appointed to run the line agreed on by the Justices to fix the public buildings by, and that they return their survey to the Justices on the 4th Monday in this month, at the house of John Coate's, and the surveyors sworn." The survey was made, and resulted as stated in No. 1; no entry, however, is made about it until the September term, 1787, when the Clerk was ordered to pay to William Caldwell and Joseph Wright, "surveyors of a line across the county, in order to settle the place for the public buildings of the said county, the sum of £2 16s. each, and £3 10s. to the chain carriers." The matter remained under the order of September, '86, until September, '88, when at a court wherein Philemon Waters, Levi Casey, Robert Rutherford, William Waddlington and John Lindsey, Justices, presided, an order was made, reciting the order of '86, and stating that since it, that part of the county below the Orangeburg line had been taken off, and therefore the court house and other public buildings should be erected on the lands of Samuel Teague, near the Tea Table rock, and commissioners were appointed to buy two acres for for the same from Mr. Teague, and to have the buildings erected. By the Act of 1788, (29th January) the eight miles below the Ninety-Six or Orangeburg district line, (now our district line, as described in No. 1,) added to Newberry County by the Act of 1785, were taken off and included in Lexington County.

At March court, 1789, present, Robert Rutherford, James Mayson, Jacob Roberts Brown, Philemon Waters, William Caldwell, Mercer Babb and Thomas W. Waters, Justices, it appears from an entry that John Coate "made a present to the county of two acres, on which to erect the public buildings," which was accepted by the vote of all present except Robert Rutherford, who objected "by reason the place was not *centrical.*" Col. Philemon Waters and William Caldwell were directed to lay out the two acres thus given; which they did, and returned a plat. It is embraced by the parallelogram made by Caldwell Street on the east; Pratt Street, south; McKibben Street, west; Boyce Street, north. Titles were made, and Mr. Coate was called into court and received the thanks of the Justices for this liberality.

One of his grandsons now lives in the town thus begun, and will, it is hoped, always receive patronage and respect, *for that* his grandfather gave to public use all that beautiful square described.

In 1791, (19th of February) an Act was passed, constituting, as it were, a new era in the County Courts. The number of Judges were reduced to three, "to be elected by joint nomination by the Senate and House of Representatives." The Judges elected for Newberry County were James Mayson, Jacob Roberts Brown and George Ruff. Col. Mayson lived in Abbeville, but owned the place called Peach Hill, in Newberry. The grand jury, at the July term, presented, as a grievance, that one of the Judges lived in another county, and it, with the other presentments, were at October term, ordered to be entered on the minutes, and Judge Ruff "was directed to send them to the next Legislature." Nothing resulted from this, for Colonel Mayson continued, to the dissolution of the county courts, a Judge, and a most excellent one too, for Newberry. At July term, 92, Judge Ruff resigned; Levi Casey was appointed in his place. The Act of '98 curtailed very much the jurisdiction of the county courts; that of '99, by its 9th clause, ended the whole matter by abolishing (most happily) the county courts. Newberry was, I think, most fortunate, even in her county court administration. Yet I have no doubt there were many abuses, and certainly there are a good many rather humorous anecdotes arising out of it.

NO. 3.

As this number will be principally devoted to the preservation of some county court anecdotes, I will venture to commence it, by relating a matter, the sequel to which is given in the minutes of the county court, now before me.

In November, '86, at the election of members of the General Assembly, a gentleman, living then on the Beaverdam, or Bush River, was a candidate. He was particularly obnoxious to the Enoree settlement. It was found, at the poll, at Col. Rutherford's, (the *quasi* court house,) which was I presume, then the only one, in the district, that he was receiving such a number of votes, as would insure his election. To defeat it, a rather heady young man, (afterwards, and to his death, in 1816, a good and respectable citizen,) seized the bag containing the votes, tore it up, and trode the votes in the mud, so that it was impossible any return could be made. At March court, 1787, the following entry appears on the journals: "Aaron Cates came into court, and confessed himself guilty of a breach of the peace, in disturbing the election held in this county, in November last for members of the General Assembly, and threw himself on the mercy of the court, and begged forgiveness for his offence, and prayed a bill of indictment might not go to the grand jury—the court took his case into consideration, and proceeded to fine him one shilling," &c. This is, indeed, an unheard of proceeding, and judgment, in a court of justice: and yet, perhaps, the times and state of society excused it.

The pleading, in the county court, is remarkable for its singularity and brevity. I cite the case of Daniel McElduff *vs.* Elizabeth and William Turner—debt. The record is as follows: "Came the plaintiff by James Yancy, Esq., his attorney, and the defendants, by Chas. Goodwin, gentleman, their attoney came and defend and say they are not indebted to the plaintiff, as he in his declaration sets forth, and of this they put themselves on the country, and the plaintiff does likewise the same. Therefore, the parties join issue for the trial of the cause at the next court."

Some of my friends, who once figured at the Lexington bar, must have taken pattern by this, when such a plea as

the following was pleaded: "The said defendant comes and
defends, &c., and says, that he, does not owe the said plaintiff
one cent, but on the contrary, he oweth him considerable."

In the practice of the court, the power of the court to
punish for contempt was, I see, freely exercised. On one
occasion, one of the Judges and the County Attorney were
each fined £5 for contempt, very probably for blows stricken,
in the presence of the court, and were bound to keep the
peace. At the succeeding term, acknowledgments were made,
and the fines *remitted*. But a most extraordinary proceeding
is mentioned in February term, 1797. Wm. McGlamery,
Hugh McGlamery and Patrick Bradley, (I give the names, as
they appear in the minutes—the true names of the two first
are Wm. and Hugh Montgomery,) had been arrested for an
assault and contempt of the court, (probably fighting in the
court yard,) and having broke custody, the Brigadier General,
(Casey, I presume,) issued his orders for their apprehension.
They were retaken and brought before the court and fined,
the two first $60 each, the other $20. This was raising the
posse comitatus with a vengeance!

I have heard some other instances of summary punishment,
one of which shows the rude manners of the day. In '87
or '88, or thereabouts, a cake baker, known better by the
nickname of Billy Behold, than his real name, William
English, was engaged in an affray, in front of Coate's house,
where the court was in session, the Sheriff and his *posse* of
constables were sent out to suppress it. They seized Billy
Behold, and dragged him in. Unable to get him through the
crowd, thronging around the temporary bar, they lifted him
up over the heads of the people, and threw him down among
lawyers. He was ordered to gaol. Next morning he made his
peace by telling their worships, "behold, behold," he said,
"may it please your worships, I was a little *teddivated*." A
strange word, but perhaps a pretty good one to describe
drunkenness.

Another instance of the familiarity, and of the want of
respect with which the court was treated, may be given.
Paddy Bradley, mentioned in the second paragraph above, on
a court day, had taken "a wee drap too much," and had
mounted himself up on one end of the long bench occupied

by their worships, who were engaged in an earnest discussion about the ways and means to pay for building a bridge. It was urged, one would think, very conclusively, that they had not the money, and therefore could not build it. But Paddy's drink and Irish propensity to blunder, made him think otherwise, and induced him to intrude his advice, "Egad," he said, "gie them trust for pay!" Whether they took his sage advice or not, I am not informed, but it is more than possible they did.

A scene between Peter Carnes, a well-known lawyer of that day, and Judge Mayson in Court, is worth recording. It was at June or July term, Carnes made his appearance, in his shirt sleeves. Judge Mayson, who was a Scotchman, said to him, "Mr. Carnes, the coort don't know you!" "Humph," said Carnes, "don't know me, ha!" Turning upon his heel, and walking out of court, he purchased a blanket, and cutting a hole in it, he thrust his head through, and drawing it around him, walked into the court room, and presenting himself to their worships, he demanded, "Does the court know me' now!" The effect may be imagined—an universal laugh excused the contempt. Carnes' argument was, that although the rule of court required a lawyer to wear a gown, it had not prescribed the color, and therefore his blanket was a sufficient gown!

One of Judge Mayson's judgments is remembered. It was characteristic of the man and of the court. The case was assault and battery. Timothy Goodman *vs.* John Tune. Goodman was celebrated for card playing, and Tune, as a bully. Goodman, it appeared, cheated Tune at cards, and he whipped him. Mayson, for himself and his brethren, said "as Mr. Goodman was a carder, and Mr. Tune a fighter, the judgment of the court was, that each party should pay his own costs, and go without day."

Carnes and Shaw were rival lawyers, at the county court bar of Newberry—Carnes was a very large man—Shaw a very small one. Carnes was remarkable for his wit and good humor—Shaw for his pride and petulance. The latter when irritated could make no argument. On one occasion, in a case of some consequence, Carnes had made the opening speech, and sat down. Shaw arose and commenced his argument alongside of Carnes. When standing, the lappel of the coat of the former was just even with that of the latter. Large buttons, and straight-breasted coats were then the rage. Carnes buttoned a button or two of Shaw's coat into his, snatched up his hat, jumped up in a great hurry, and walked to the door, dragging, apparently without noticing it, poor Shaw after him. At the door, he affected to have discovered it, for the first time, and looking down at him with apparent surprise, he exclaimed, "Brother *pop corn*, what mischievous rascal hitched you to me ?" The *ruse* had the effect intended. Shaw, when released, was so enraged he could not make his speech.

Carnes' comment on Robert Starks' first speech in an assault and battery case at Newberry, and Starks' practical reply are too good to be lost. Neither Starks' exterior nor speech had impressed Carnes with any favorable notion of his learning or talent. He said to the Judges he did not believe the young gentlemen knew what an assault and battery was. Starks was instantly on his feet, shaking his fist in Carnes' face, he said, "*that* is an assault," and drawing back, and striking him a full blow in the face with his fist, sufficient to have felled an ox, he said, "*there is battery.*"

Carnes sat down, rubbing his forehead, and exclaiming, "*I did not think the fellow had so much sense !*"

So much for the present. In our next, I propose to go back, and look over the population of Newberry in groups, before and after the revolution; and in connection with such a survey, some matters of history and anecdote may be related.

In attempting to sketch the population of the district in
groups before and after the revolution, much must depend
upon tradition, until we come within the last forty years;
then, indeed, we may speak from some knowledge of our own.
Previous to this time, which, in legal language we may call
within the memory of man, there may be occasional inaccuracies. When any such are discovered, it would be
regarded as a singular favor, that they should be pointed
out.

Newberry was settled very much by three classes of people,
Germans, Irish, and emigrants from our sister States, North
Carolina, Virginia, and Pennsylvania.

The Germans, (*i. e.* the Summers, Mayers, Ruffs, Eigle-
bergers, Counts, Slighs, Piesters, Grays, DeWalts, Boozers,
Busbys, Buzzards, Shealys, Bedenbaughs, Cromers, Berleys,
Hellers, Koons, Wingards, Subers, Folks, Dickerts, Capple-
mans, Halfacres, Chapmans, Blacks, Kinards, Bouknights,
Barrs, Harmons, Bowers, Kiblers, Gallmans, Levers, Hartmans,
Fricks, Stoudemoyers, Dominicks, Singleys, Bulows, Paysingers,
Wallerns, Stayleys, Ridlehoovers, Librands, Leapharts, Hopes,
Houseals, Bernhards, Shulers, Haltiwangers, Swigarts, Meetzes,
Schumperts, Fulmores, Livingstons, Schmitz, Eleazers, Drehrs,
Loricks, Wises, Crotwells, Youngeners, Nunamakers, Souters,
Eptings, Huffmans,) settled almost in a body, in the Fork, be-
tween Broad and Saluda Rivers; and their settlement extended
from the junction of the two rivers, opposite to Columbia
to within three miles and a half of Newberry Court House.
Much more of this settlement was included in the original
county of Newberry, when the line extended from a point
eight miles below Hughey's ferry, on Broad River to the
mouth of Bear Creek, on Saluda River, than is embraced
in the present district. Such a line would bring, within
Newberry, the whole of the old settlement of Springhill,
west of Mrs. Veal's present residence. In speaking of Newberry, we shall consider it proper to speak of it as
embracing this rich portion of Lexington as well as its
present limits.

The German settlement, headed by Adam Summer. the father of Col. John Adam Summer, began in 1745, and was called the Dutch Fork. Notwithstanding this name, very few of the Dutch proper, (Hollanders,) settled in Newberry. Some of the settlers were either Palatines, or their descendants. To relieve the people of England from the support of the poor Palatines, who had been, by the oppression of their own government in religious matters, and the invasion of a foreign enemy, driven from Germany, and had in large numbers come over to England, under the proclamation of Queen Anne, and were quartered in tents and booths in the vicinity of London, measures were taken early to send them off to North Carolina and South Carolina. For in 1710, "the inviting, and bringing over the poor Palatines of all religions, at the public expense," was pronounced by Parliament "to be an extravagant and unreasonable charge to the kingdom, and a scandalous misapplication of the public money, tending to the increase and oppression of the poor, and of dangerous consequence to the constitution in Church and State, and that who ever advised their being brought over was an enemy to the Queen (Anne) and the kingdom." After such a resolution. the removal of the Palatines was, as might be expected, pressed and hastened in every possible way. Commissioners were appointed by the Queen to collect and receive money for their use, and to provide them with settlements. The commissioners allowed £5 per head to transport them; and each of them who had received 20 shillings of the contributions for their use, placed *that* in the hands of Christopher DeGraffenreid* and

---

* This gentleman, Christopher DeGraffenreid, commonly called and known in the histories of America, as Baron DeGraffenreid, was a native of the Canton of Berne, Switzerland, and hence the settlement of his colony was called New Berne, and this gave rise to the name of the town, now known as Newburn, in North Carolina. It is said in Williamson's History of North Carolina, that he abandoned the Palatines, and returned to Switzerland. If this be so, he must have, at a subsequent time, returned to the United States, or he must have left his family behind him, when he returned to Switzerland, or his family must have afterwards come to America, for his descendants, Christopher and Allen DeGraffenreid, lived in Union and Chester districts to their deaths. The former had in his possession, as I have

Lewis Mitchell, who undertook, and did transport 650, (about 120 families,) to North Carolina. A few found their way to South Carolina. For them, the township of Saxe Gotha on the south side of the Congaree, and in the immediate vicinage of Granby, was directed to be laid off. Before 1746, I learn from the case of the State vs. Starke, 3d Brev. 106, about twenty settlers answering the description of the persons for whom the township was laid out, had settled in it. But they could not long have maintained their footing, for it was subsequently granted and recovered by the late Robert Starke, Esq. On the trial of the case above cited, one of the witnesses for Starke, the defendant, was Frederick Boozer, (the father of our late worthy fellow-citizen, David Boozer, who recently, so strangely destroyed himself.) After the death of the said Frederick in 1816, it was found he had in his possession a grant for a part of the said township to his father. Hence, I conclude, *he* was one of the Palatines. Busby, who died in Edgefield, at an age said to be greatly above 100, was another one of the witnesses, and proved on the trial the building of the fort for the protection of the settlers. He was also, I suppose, a Palatine.

From Dr. Hazelius' excellent work, "The American Lutheran Church," I learn, that the original German settlers were generally from the neighborhood of the Rhine, Baden and Wurtemburg. This accords with what is said in Williamson's History of North Carolina. We are told in his first volume, page 176, that the Palatines were from "Heidelberg and its vicinity on the Rhine."

Many of the German settlers, other than the Palatines, as well as the Irish, hereafter to be spoken of, received grants of land, on what was called the King's bounty; that is,

---

understood, the grants to his ancestor for a large body of land in North Carolina. It is said in Williamson's History of North Caro-lina, that five thousand acres were granted to DeGraffenreid on his paying 20 shillings for every 100 acres, and six pence quit rents, and that he complied with these conditions, and thus became Baron DeGraffenried. The lands for the Palatines were also granted to him. He mortgaged them to Polock: never paid the debt, and thus the Palatines lost their land, which is now owned by the Polocks.

child. These were, also often called *Head Rights*. Many of
the German and Irish settlers, in consequence of their
gratitude to the King for this bounty, adhered to him in
emigrants obtained bounty warrants (if I recollect right) of
100 acres for the head of a family, and 50 acres for each
the revolution. Some few of the Germans, such as Col.
John Adam Summer and Major Frederick Gray were ardent
and devoted whigs. I have been often told, that on the
field of Stono, Col. John Adam Summer, then a private,
was one of the men, who, under the command of Philemon
Waters, (then, perhaps, only a captain,) brought off an
American field piece, after it had been abandoned by its
officers and men. Of Maj. Gray's services, I know nothing,
certain. His father's family were divided: part adhered to
the King: he alone, I think, was a whig. In some of the
partisan affairs, with which the war abounded, he was
wounded, but he recovered, lived long in Newberry, at the
places where James Maffett and Thomas Chandler now live.
He was major of one of the battalions of the now 39th
regiment; he was also a member of the State Legislature;
he removed, when he was an old man, to Abbeville, and
there died, full of years, surrounded by his numerous highly
respectable descendants.

The German population of Newberry have been at all
times remarkable for their thrift. Previous to 1804 they still
occupied, almost without exception, the original settlement,
the territorial limits of which have been herein before
described, Their farms were generally small. The German
language was spoken and taught; and it was sometimes with
difficulty that German women could be induced, (if they
were able,) to speak to a stranger in English.* Since then,

---

* It is a singular fact in Natural History that until within the last
thirty or thirty-five years, in all that tract of country lying on Bush
River, and generally west of a line from the mouth of Bush River
to the mouth of Indian Creek, the night bird, whose cry sounds
"Whip-poor-Will" was that generally heard: now and then a solitary
"Chuck-Will's-Widow" commonly called the *Dutch " Whip-poor- Will,"*
enlivened the night. The former bird is now never heard in any part of
the district, where I have had the opportunity of observing. It
sometimes salutes me, like on old acquaintance, about Laurens. The
latter bird is now universal with us. The popular notion, was that

however, their settlements have been gradually extended, until they have pretty much lost their nationality, which before distinguished them. They are *now* intermingled with the other population of the district. They are now as remarkable for their love of improvement, as their ancestors were for honest acquisition and industry.

An intimate knowledge of, and acquaintance with the German people of Newberry, enable me to say, that for honesty, hospitality, untiring industry, fidelity in the discharge of every duty, public and private, devoted and unchanging friendship, intelligence and a desire for education, they are *now* unsurpassed. In the beginning of the 19th century, they were little disposed to indulge in speculation of any kind. I have often heard it said, that any one in whom they had confidence, could by riding to three or four houses in the Dutch Fork, have borrowed $1,000 in silver. Their small gains had been carefully hoarded, and were willingly loaned to any safe borrower. But in a few years, raising cotton, and the spread of intelligence gave them all the means of entering successfully, as agriculturists, merchants, mechanics, lawyers and doctors, in the race for wealth and distinction, and nobly, in hundreds of instances, have they succeeded.

Their hospitality has been always remarkable. Perhaps I could say, with truth, nothing delights a German, (a Dutchman, as we familiarly call him,) more than to have a traveler stop with him; and certainly nothing delights his wife more than to crown the table with enough and to spare of good and well cooked provisions. Often have I looked with amazement at the cheerfulness with which I have seen the ladies of the Fork, toiling day after day, and night after night, to make their husband's guests comfortable.

Among the German population, until education and improvement pervaded the mass, there was much superstition, such as belief in ghosts, witches and charms.

---

it traveled westward with the Germans. I presume, however, the true solution is that the "Whip-poor-Will" proper is a more solitary bird, and as the forest falls, and settlements become more dense like the buffalo, it passes on, and the latter bird, less solitary, takes its place.

A German of the name of Kinard, (not, however, related to my worthy friend, Capt. Martin Kinard,) was particularly remarkable for his belief in all such foolish and absurd notions. He told many extravagant stories of ghosts, who, he affirmed, were allowed to walk in certain limits. One is remembered. He said, that he and an unbeliever were riding after night, and were approaching a ghost's walk, when his companion, using a very unseemly word, said, "there is where one of them —— was sworn in." Kinard said, "I do assure you, the word was hardly out of his mouth, when spang a hand takes him on the side of the head, and comes mighty nigh knocking him off his horse." "Aha!" said Kinard, "may be he was not still after dat!"

A good old lady, belonging to the Irish settlement in the Stone hills, near to where he lived, Kinard affirmed to be *a witch.* "Ah," said he, "may be she does not milk the dish rag!" On being challenged for proof he said, he milked a great many more cows, and "we churns, and churns, and at last we get a little bit of butter, not so big as mine fist. She churns a little and gets a geat big bit, so big as mine head." Poor simpleton, the old lady's witchcraft consisted in feeding and taking care of her cows.

A description which he gave of a Dutch doctor physicking himself, tragical as it turned out to be, is too good to be lost. He said he was sick, and he went out into the woods, and he got "yerbs and roots, and he boiled and boiled, until it was as black as tar, and drank a cup full of it, and I assures you, it take four men to hold him down till he die!"

I have often heard the Germans of the Fork charged with such belief in witchcraft, that at each house, at the door step, and nailed to the sill, might be found a horse shoe, as a charm against it. But I have never seen any thing to justify such an assertion. Indeed, *now,* I believe, they are as free from such foolery as most people. In 1812, Henry Hampton, more celebrated for his wit than his law knowledge, in arguing File's case, at Newberry, thought proper to attack the good old man, whose horse had been stolen, Geo. Crotwell, and to say of him and all his brother Germans, that they all believed in witchcraft, and had each a horse shoe nailed beneath his door. The slander traveled ahead of him, and so indignant were the Forkers, that on his way to Columbia, he could not get lodging for the night.

Many among the Germans once believed in *using*, that is the cure of disease by cabalistic words, and passing the hand of the operator over the part of the body or limb affected. Many well authenticated cures have been found in *the Fork*. Since *mesmerism* has become fashionable, and is believed by many intelligent, well-educated men, I confess I cannot see why *using* should not also be. It is but another name for *mesmerism*. I fancy, Dr. Koon* can present as many claims to be believed, as Drs. Webster and Trotter, and if a college of instruction in mesmerism was to be established in this State, I think Dr. Koon has more claims to be President than any man within my knowledge.

In general, Germans are remarkable for truth. They have not as much imagination as the Irish, the English, the French, or the Native Americans. They are, therefore, not as liable to lie. Notwithstanding this, one of the greatest lies I ever heard was ascribed to *a Dutchman*. He was reported to have said, "I was minding my tadda's sheeps, inside of de field, among dem was a crate pig fighting ram sheep. Along, outside of de fence, comes anoder crate pig fighting ram sheep; they tid make signs mit their heads at one anoder through de fence. I tid let de fence down, and they tid come together, ram, jam, and deir horns did make the fire fly, so that it did set fire to de woods, and burnt up mine tadda's fence—and may be he wash not mad !'"

So much, and perhaps too much, for the present. Hereafter, I hope to be able to speak more at large of Col. John Adam Summer, and other highly meritorious Germans. In the next number, it is proposed to treat of a class of the early inhabitants, who have, as a body, entirely disappeared. I allude to the *Friends*, commonly called Quakers.

---

* The doctor died soon after this was written.

The Quaker settlement was on Bush River and the Beaverdam. It extended from three to four miles on each side of the river. A line drawn from the Tea Table Rock, by the place once owned by Wm. Miles, now the property of Mathias Barr, to Goggan's old field, now Washington Floyd's, would be about the northwest limit. The settlement was prolonged down the river to the plantation, formerly the property of Col. Philemon Waters, now of Chancellor Johnston. No finer body of land can be found in South Carolina, than that embraced within those limits.

When the settlement commenced, or whence came the great body of settlers, it is out of my power to say with certainty. Certain it is that Wm. Coate, before '62, lived between Spring Field and Bush River, and that Samuel Kelly, a native of King's County, Ireland, but who came to Newberry from Camden, settled at Spring Field in '62, John Furnas at the same time, and adjoining, made his settlement. David Jenkins, about the same time, or possibly a few years before, settled on the plantation where major Peter Hare resides. Benjamin Pearson and Wm. Pearson lived on the plantation, once the property of John Frost, now that of Judge O'Neall, as early as '69. Robert Evans, who settled the place now owned by Sampson Marchant, came also from Camden, probably between '62 and '69. John Wright, Jos. Wright, Wm. Wright, James Brooks, Joseph Thomson, James Patty, Gabriel McCoole, John Coate, (Big) Isaac Hollingsworth, Wm. O'Neall, Walter Herbert, Sr., Daniel Parkins, Daniel Smith, Samuel Miles, David Miles, William Miles, Samuel Brown, Israel Gaunt, Azariah Pugh,* William Mills, Jonathan and Caleb Gilbert, John Galbreath, James Galbreath, James Coppock, John Coppock, Joseph Reagin, John Reagin, Abel and James Insco, Jesse Spray, Samuel Teague, George Pemberton, Jehu Inman, Mercer Babb, James Steddam, John Crumpton, Isaac Cook, John Jay, Reason Reagen, Thomas and Isaac Hasket, Thos. Pearson, the two Enoch Pearsons, Samuel Pearson, Nehemiah Thomas, Abel Thomas, Timothy Thomas, Euclydus

---

* The ancestor of Senator Pugh, of Ohio.

Longshore, Sarah Duncan, Samuel Duncan, and John Duncan, were residents of the same tract of country before or during the revolution, and were Friends or were ranked as such by descent.

The Friends had three places of meeting, one, the oldest and principal, at Bush River, where their house of worship still stands, neglected, but not desecrated. Within the grave yard, south of it, sleep hundreds of the early settlers of Bush River. Often have I seen more than five hundred Friends, women and children, there gathered together to worship God in silence, and to listen to the outpouring of the spirit, with which some of the Friends, male and female. might be visited. In imagination, often can I see the aged form of the elder David Jenkins, sitting immediately below the preacher's bench, on the left of the southern entrance to the men's meeting, leaning on the head of his staff, his large protruding lower lip, the most remarkable feature of his face. Alongside of him might be seen the tall form and grey hairs of Tanner Thomson, as he used to be called. Scarcely could the sacred stillness of Friends' meeting keep him from snapping his thumb and finger together, as if feeling a side of leather. Just here I recall the person of Isaac Hollings-worth. His was a stalwart form, more than six feet high. He sits the picture of firmness, and ever and anon, throwing up the ample brim of his flapping beaver, he looks as if he was restless for execution. He it was of whom youngsters, who did not know the meaning of "turning out of meeting" used to suppose the duty was demanded of leading an erring member to the door, saying to him, as he applied his foot to the seat of honor : "Friends have no further use for thee." A little further to the right or lower down, might be seen the pale features of that excellent man, Joseph Furnas ! Near to him was to be seen the tall, erect form, florid com-plexion, clear, blue eye, ample forehead, and grey hair of John Kelly, Sr. ; just alongside of him might be seen Isaac Kirk. Friend Kirk, as he used to be called, was a true Quaker. He was plain and simple as a child, kind and for-bearing in every thing. No better heart was ever covered by a straight-breasted coat. He had his peculiarities : one, that in reading, he read as if he was singing the passages—an.

other, that when talking to any one his foot had always to
be in motion. It was, therefore said, when he called on a
debtor to dun him, his mission was known by his kicking
the chips, sticks, and stones all around. In this vicinage
might be seen the person of Samuel Gaunt, dressed with all
the precision of a Quaker, but neat as a pin. A little above
him might be seen the tall form and gray hairs of James
Brooks. A little lower might be seen the brothers, Abijah,
Hugh, William, John, Henry, and Thomas O'Neall. Some
description of some of these may be afterwards attempted, but
here will not now be given.

In the women's meeting, on the preacher's bench, under
their immense white beavers, I recall the full round faces
and forms of the sisters, Charity Cook and Susannah Hollingsworth. Both wives, both mothers of large families, still
they felt it to be their duty to preach "Jesus and him crucified." The first, Charity Cook, was indeed a gifted woman.
She traveled through the States extensively. Twice visited
England and Ireland. When her husband drove his stage
wagon into Rabun's creek, at a time when it was high,
drowned two horses, and only escaped drowning himself by
riding a chunk to land, she swam to the shore, and thus
saved herself. Her sister, Susannah Hollingsworth, was not
so highly gifted. Henry O'Neall, and other young Friends,
used to affirm, that when Aunt Suzey, as she was called,
began to pray, they could always keep ahead of her by
repeating the words she was about to say. Just below the
preacher's bench, the once round and graceful form (afterwards bent by 82 winters) of Hannah Kelly, once Hannah
Belton, a native of Queen's County, Ireland, might be seen.
No more intelligent, kind, or benevolent face ever met the
upturned gaze of her juniors. Well might it be said of her,
that she was indeed "a mother in Israel." Her eye of blue,
her long straight nose, high cheek bones, and clear Irish
complexion, can scarcely ever be forgotten by those who saw
her. Their other places of meeting were Rocky Springs, now
a Baptist meeting house, and White Lick, on the land where
Robert Burton now lives. They were much junior to that of
Bush River, and therefore they are not necessary to be
further described.

Every thing relating to Friends *here* is now a novelty. Their very dress, the broad-brimmed, low-crowned hats, straight-breasted, collarless coats; breeches without suspenders, and of the plainest color, is strange to us *now*, but was and is defended upon the ground that they seek no change—it is comfortable, and as they found society dressed in the time of George Fox, so it is with them now. The dress of the females, was equally plain, and defended on the same ground. White beavers, with the mere indentation for a crown, with a brim around it of full six inches every way, secured on the head by a plain white ribbon passing through loops, or perfectly plain silk bonnets called hoods ; caps as plain as possible ; long-waisted gowns or wrappers and petticoats, constituted the *tout ensemble* of a Quaker lady's dress. Their language 'thou,' to a single person, or 'you' to more than one, was grammatical, and free from all personal idolatry, and therefore they used it. It is true, that it was corrupted, and 'thee' the objective instead of the nominative case of the personal pronoun was used.

They met to transact business and worship on the fifth day (Thursday,) weekly, and on the seventh day, (Saturday,) monthly. There were also quarterly and yearly meetings of delegates. The meeting for worship was every first day (Sunday) at 11 o'clock. At that hour all entered the house, and sat covered and in silence for an hour, unless the spirit moved some Friend to speak. Any Friend may speak under the influence of the spirit, but in general only those speak in public whose gifts have been approved. If prayer be made, then the Friend who prays, uncovers himself, and kneeling down, utters the petitions which the spirit prompts. The congregation rise and the men are uncovered during prayer. As soon as it is closed, all take their seats covered. At the end of the hour, the elder members grasp one another by the hand, walk out and every body starts for home.

Just here, I may be pardoned for stopping and relating an anecdote. John Wright, the father of Charity Cook and Susannah Hollingsworth, was a very aged man at the time of which I am about to speak, but principally accustomed to walk to and from meeting. He was living with his daughter, Susannah Hollingsworth; something prevented her from going to meeting; she induced the old man to ride her mare. This he did; but after meeting, he walked out of the meeting house, and home as usual. As he entered the door, his daughter said to him, "Father, where is the mare?" "Dads me, Sue, I forgot her," was the old man's prompt reply. This old gentleman before his death, assembled his sons, his sons' wives, his daughters, his daughters' husbands, his grand children, and their respective wives and husbands, and his great grand-children. When all were assembled, they numbered one hundred and forty-four. Did he not deserve well of the Republic? Where can such a family now be found?

A pair of young people about to marry are said to pass meeting by their purpose being announced at one monthly meeting, when a committee is appointed to inquire if there be any objections. At the next, if their report be favorable, Friends assent to the marriage, and on the succeeding fifth day (Thursday) it takes place by the man and woman standing up and holding one another by the right hand, and repeating the ceremony. The man says about as follows: "I take this my friend to be my wedded wife, whom I will love, cherish and her only keep, until it shall please the Lord to separate us by death." The woman says: "I take this my friend to be my husband, whom I will love, honor and obey until it shall please the Lord to separate us by death." I may not be accurate in the words. I am sure I am in substance, although I never saw but two marriages of Friends, one of Robert Evans and Keren Happuch Gaunt in 1806; and the other of Joseph Stanton and Sarah Hollingsworth in 1807. As soon as the ceremony is repeated, they sit down; a Friend, most generally the clerk of the men's meeting, reads a certificate of the marriage, which is signed by Friends present. The meeting then proceeds, as usual, to its close. I ought to have mentioned before, that there is a clerk of both the men's and women's meeting. Every thing of importance is regularly entered upon their books, such as business transactions, marriages, births and deaths. Every child born of parents who are Friends, is by descent a Friend. The same result follows, if the mother alone be a Friend. No beggar or pauper was ever known among Friends. They take care of all such. Their meeting of Sufferings provides for these and all other wants.

The Quaker community of Bush River was a most interesting one. Small farms, enough and to spare, among all, was its general state. Hard working, healthy, yet an honest, innocent and mirthful, though a staid people, make up altogether an interesting picture. It is true, among them were many hickory, or formal Quakers; now and then some wet, or grog-drinking Quakers; and now and then some cheating Quakers. But these are now no more—of each I would only say, *"requiescat in pace."* The only valid objection which I know to the practice of Friends is, that they do not generally sufficiently attend to the religious education of their children and the reading of the Scriptures. In this respect, there are, I know, many, very many illustrious exceptions; and I believe their rules require the Scriptures to be read, and their children to be religiously instructed. In other points, I think no religious community can present better claims for respect, and even the admiration of men.

In the beginning, Friends were slave owners in South Carolina. They however, soon sat their faces against it, and in their peculiar language, they have uniformly borne their testimony against the institution of slavery, as irreligious. Such of their members as refused to emancipate their slaves, when emancipation was practicable in this State, they disowned. Samuel Kelly, who was the owner of a slave or slaves in '62, when he came from Camden, refused to emancipate his, on the grounds that he had bought and paid for them : they were therefore his property ; and that they were a great deal better off as his property, than they would be if free. He was therefore disowned. His brother's children manumitted theirs. Some followed them to Ohio ; others have lived *here* free, it is true, but in indigence and misery, a thousand times worse off than the slaves of Samuel Kelly and their descendants. For the far-seeing old gentleman took good care in his last will, that the bulk of his slaves who were left to his widow, should not be emancipated, by giving her the power to dispose of them at her death, provided

1   C

it was to some member of or among his family. Friends are
opposed to war; they therefore hold everything which apper-
tains to it to be contrary to their discipline. Hence, Generals
Greene and Brown were disowned. Still, however, they never
entirely forgot their duty to their country. I have before
me now the soldier's song, on the receipt of the Quaker's
present of 10,000 flannel shirts, to the army marching from
England into Scotland, against the Pretender:

> "This *friendly* waistcoat keeps my body warm,
> Intrepid on the march and free from harm,
> A coat of mail, a sure defender,
> Proof against the Pope, the Devil, and Pretender.
> The Highland plaid of no such force can boast!
> Armed thus, I'll plunge the foremost in their host,
> With all my force, with all my strength, with all my might,
> *And fight for those whose creed forbid to fight!*"

After the bloody battle of Guilford, gladly did Friends obey
the call of him, whom, although disowned, they gloried in
claiming as a Quaker, Nathaniel Greene, and rushed in throngs
to take charge of the wounded Americans and Britons!

Between '97 and '99, Abijah O'Neall and Samuel Kelly, Jr.,
bought the military land of Jacob Roberts Brown, in Ohio;
the great body of it was in Warren County, near Waynesville.
Abijah O'Neall visited, located the land, and in '99, in the
language of Samuel Kelly, Sr.:

> "Beyond the mountain and far away,
> With wolves and bears to play,"

he commenced his toilsome removal to his western home.
When about starting, he applied to Friends for his regular
certificate of membership, &c. This they refused him, on the
ground that his removal was itself such a thing as did not
meet their approbation. Little did they *then* dream that in
less than ten years they would all be around him in the then
far West!

Abijah O'Neall was about five feet eight inches high, stout,
round-shouldered, light brown hair, eyes grey, nose Roman,
mouth protruded slightly, his face had the appearance of
great firmness. Such was his character. He came up to the
Latin description, *"ver bonus tenax propositi."* Every body
knew this, as may be better illustrated by a little anecdote:

a young man boarding with him, disposed to play off a joke on an old family negro, who had been manumitted, but who still lived with Miss Anne, (as he called Mrs. O'Neall,) seized the old man on his way to mill, and said to him, "Jack, I'll carry you off and sell you." "You can't do dat," said Jack; "de bery Bije (the usual abbreviation of the name Abijah) can't do dat." He had some strange peculiarities. For many years before his death, he would not sleep on a feather-bed; he must have a straw bed. Again, he cut his hair as close as possible, and had at least two windows in the crown of his hat. This was to keep his head cool. He drank neither tea nor coffee. He was a surveyor, and after he went to Ohio spent much of his time in the woods as such, and as a hunter in the pursuit of game. He believed firmly that this State would, in time, become as sterile as the deserts of Arabia. Such at least were his words in 1810, when I last saw him.

But it will be asked, what became of the Friends? Between 1800 and 1804, a celebrated Quaker preacher, Zachary Dicks, passed through South Carolina. He was thought to have *also the gift of prophecy*. The massacres of San Domingo were then fresh. He warned Friends to come out from slavery. He told them if they did not their fate would be that of the slaughtered Islanders. This produced in a short time a panic, and removals to Ohio commenced, and by 1807 the Quaker settlement had, in a great degree, changed its population. John Kelly, Sr., Hugh O'Neall, John O'Neall, Henry O'Neall, James Brooks, Isaac Kirk, Walter Herbert, William Wright, Samuel Gaunt, William Pugh, and Timothy Thomas alone remained. Land which could often since, and even now after near forty years cultivation in cotton, can be sold for $10, $15 and $20 per acre, was sold then for from $3 to $6. Newberry thus lost, from a foolish panic and a superstitious fear of an institution, which never harmed them or any other body of people, a very valuable portion of its white population. But they are gone, never to return! It is our business to repair the loss, by better agriculture, more attention to the mechanic arts, and more enterprise. Thus acting, our wasted fields will yet blossom like the rose, our streams will resound with the music of machinery, and our hills will be vocal with the songs of industry and peace.

NOTE TO NO. 5.

The screw auger was invented in Newberry by a Quaker, Benjamin Evans, who lived on a place now owned by Gillam Davenport, and who removed with other Friends to Ohio. Joseph Smith and John Edmondson learned the trade with him, and followed it; the first until he was unable to follow it longer; the latter until he secured an independence. Many a box of screw augers have I seen sent by wagons to Charleston, between 1800 and 1807. I think Samuel Maverick,* who now resides near Pendleton, then in Charleston, shipped some to England. Some one will ask, what sort of auger was previously used? The barrel, auger, with a mere bit to enter the wood.

In rummaging some old papers, I found the following:

"Camp at Brooks' Plantation, 5th, January, 1781.

"This is to certifiy that James Galbreath has supplied the first Battalion 71st Regiment, with one hundred dozen sheaves of Oats, and ten bushels Indian Corn.

"COLIN CAMPBELL, Q. M. 1st Bat. 17th Reg."

"Brooks' plantation" is where Clement Nance, Esq., formerly lived, near Bush River. James Galbreath was a Friend, and was never paid for his oats and corn. The 71st Regiment was part of Tarleton's command, which was then in pursuit of Morgan, and which twelve days afterwards fought the battle of the Cowpens, and were made prisoners. Tarleton marched from Cornwallis' camp at Winnsborough, Fairfield District, across Broad River, thence to incercept Morgan, who made an apparent move on Ninety-Six. In the direct line to reach that place, or strike Morgan between there and Hammonds' old store, he arrived at Rush River; one battalion of the 71st he threw across the river, and encamped it on its southwestern bank, at Jacob Chandler's, (now James Tinn's,) the other, with the main body of Tarleton's command, was encamped on the northeast side of the river, at Brooks' planta-

---

* Mr. Maverick died since this was written.

tion. In the night a great fall of rain took place, and made the river impassable; there was no bridge across it, except at William O'Neall's mills (now Bobo's) five miles below Chandlers'. To unite the 2d Battalion with the 1st, it had to descend the river, and after encamping for one night, at least, at William O'Neall's, it crossed at his mills, and united with the main body near Coate's shop, (Newberry Court House,) and encamped at the Tea Table Rock. Thence the march was directed, with little variation, for Morgan's camp, at the Grindall Shoals on Pacolet, and afterwards to the Cowpens. I suppose a delay of several days, perhaps three or four, occurred about Bush River. This, at the outside, would have brought Tarleton to the Tea Table Rock by the 9th January; from it to the Cowpens does not exceed seventy-five miles. How eight days could have been spent between these points, is to me inconceivable, especially when Tarleton is represented in history as rushing on his flying foe with his infantry mounted behind his cavalry. This discovery of the true date of his encampment at Bush River, shows that he approached the old wagoner with slow and cautious marches.

From Tarleton's Campaigns in the South, now before me, it seems that on the 2d January, 1780, Lord Cornwallis, still at Winnsboro', directed Tarleton, then west of Broad River, "If Morgan is still at Williams'," (in the lower or eastern part of Laurens District, and not far from Ninety-Six) "or anywhere within your reach, I should wish you to push him to the utmost." Morgan never was at Williams'; a detachment from his command, commanded by Cornet Simmons, had previously captured Williams' Fort.

On the 4th of January, Tarleton, writing to Lord Cornwallis, thus speaks of the country around Brooks', his encampment: "My encampment is now twenty miles from Birely's, in a plentiful forage country, and I can lay in four days' flour for a move."—*Tarleton Campaign. Notes F. and G.* 244–5.

I annex three bills of goods bought in Charleston: one without date, and one in '83, and made out in South Carolina currency, 7 for 1; the other is 1777, and is made out in the same currency, and appears to have been paid in current bills, issued probably in the State from 1774 to 1783. These three papers will give a better idea of the difficulty of the times than any description.

MR. WM. O'NEALL

Bo't of ROWL'D RUGELEY

1 Paper Pins 3s9d; 1 pr Woms Hose 17s6.....................£	1 : 1 : 3
1 Pr Woms Hose 17s6; 2 lb Allspice 10s......................	1 : 12 : 6
14 yds Green Callimanco, a 10s.....................................	7 : :
4 yds Red Durant a 15s is 60s....................................	3 : :
20 Bushels Salt a 17s6...	17 : 10 :
4 Wool Hats a 13s9 is 55s; 2 yds Callo is 35s..............	4 : 10 :
1 Pc Tape 7s6....................................	7 : 6
2 lb Coffee is 15s...	15 :
8 Copperas a 2s6 is 20s; ½lb Ginger 5s......................	1 : 5 :
1 India Silk Handkf 62s6...	1 : 12 : 6
187 lbs Bar Iron a 7£...	13 : : 9
55 lbs Ax Barr a 2s6..	7 : :
30 lbs Brown Sugar...................	5 : 12 : 1
39 Wire Sieve, 35; 5 gallons Molasses a 12s6 is 62s6.........	4 : 17 : 6
v2 Quire Paper 7s6...	0 : 15 :

£69 : 19 : 6

Deduct 1 gall molasses.......................   12 : 6

£69 : 7 : 0

Rec'd of Mr. O'Neall
  2 Barrls Flour ; Gro 606
          R   60

          446 a 95......................... 25 18 6
  2 Ferkins Butter 184 R 34 is 150 a 2s9......... 20 12 6
  1 Ferk   Do   94 R 16   78 a 18.......... .. 5 17 -

52 : 8 : 0

16 : 19 : -

Mr. WILLIAM O'NEALL
1783   th   Bo't of PARKER & HUTCHINGS
January 12, 2   Pewter Dishes and 2 Basons ; ro't 11¼ lb
                  at 19s..£ 5,,12,,5
            1   Hoe 17s6 ; 2 Doz'n fish Hooks 5s................ 1,, 2,,6
            1   Sad Iron 15, Scarlet Cloak 90s................... 5,, 5,,-
            1   Pr Spurs, 15s; 1 in tacks 12s7; 1 in ditto 15s... 2,, 2,,6
            3   in Pd Nails at 37s6 and bag 5s6................. 5,,15,,-
            1   fur Hat 57s6 ; 1 Doz'n knives and forks 30s... 4,, 7,,0
            1   Sett Bosses 5s ; 10 yds Camblet £5.............. 5., 5,,1
            7   yds Greece Calimanca at 11s3................... 3,,10,,9

1	Blk Silk hhkf 32s6 ; 1 Iron Pott 20s............	2,,12,,6
1	Tin Kettle 30s, 16¾ lb Steel at 3s9.............	4,,12,,9
4	yds Girth Webb 15s ; 1 lb pepper 15s.........	1,,10,,-
1	Doz'n Cups and Saucers, 10s : 1 Tea Pott 6s3..	,,16,,3
6	Plates, 4 Bassons and 1 Dish ; ro't 13¼ lb...	6,,12,,6
5	pds Black Lasting at 27s6; 1 Frying Pen 26s6.	8,, 5,,*
23	lb Sugar, at 3s9...	4,, 6,,3
2	lb Yeller Oaker.....ᴄ....................................	-,,10,,-
23	yds Coat Binding at 1s3..............................	1,, 8,,9
1	Candle Moto 20s ; 6 lbs of Iron at £7 10s...	5,,11,,6
1	Pr Salts 7s6 ; Sticktwist 3s9........................	-,,11,,3
1	Scain Silk 3s9 ; 3 yds Donlas 33s9..............	1,,15,,6
2	Dozen Buttens 7s6 ; 3 Large do 2s6...........	-,,10,,-
1½	yd Blk Shalloon 26s3 ; 1 ps Cheek 23 23 ds at 10s........ ....ᴠ...........................	12,,16,,3
1½	yds fine Swan Skin at 15s............................	1,, 2,,6
½	Doz'n Tin Cups.....................................	-,,15,,-

$$£87,, 6,,9$$

By 1340 lb nt Tobacco................................ 67,,—,,-

Bal'ce due P. & H............. 20,, 6,,9

Mr WILLIAM O'NEALL   CHA's TOWN, agt 20th 1777.
                                    Bo't of THO's BOURKE

20½	Bushels Salt a 77s6 and 5 Bbble 20.......................£95 : 8 : 9
100	Iron a £17 10s....................................... 17 : 10 :
1	Gallon Rum £5.. 5 : — : -
11	lbs Steel a 9s... 1 : 19 : -
4	Gallons N. Rum a 75s .... 15 : — : -
3	pints Rum... 2 : — : -
3	lbs Coffee............. .... 2 : 5 : -
4	lbs. Brimstone a 5s................................... 1 : — : -
3	Hatts a £4.................................. .... 12 · — : -

£155 : 2 : 9

Received of Mr. Wm. O'Neal Twenty-Eight Pounds Currency, in full of all account as under.

                                    THOMS BOURKE.

Error in the above 20 Busls Salt £15—being over cost in mistake.
Cash rec'd this 23 May, 1778........ 13

£28

NO. 6.

The Irish settlers of Newberry did not locate themselves in one body. Some, the Thompsons, McQuerns, Drannans, Youngs, Fairs, Carmichaels, and Hunters, settled in the Stone Hills, or just in the west margin of that tract. The descendants of many of them are still residents of the district. The place now called Stony Battery was the residence of two of the Thompsons, Daniel and William. Samuel McQuerns was a blacksmith; honest, industrious, and persevering, he succeeded in securing a competence. His shop stood at the spot where the old Congaree road, now called the Rush River road, turns off from the Lee's ferry road. He was a man of remarkable physical powers, but could not compare with his father, who, when a laborer, in Ireland, said, he did two men's work in a day, and had two men's allowance. Sam'l McQuerns had been impressed as a sailor, in the British navy. He was present at Spit Head when the Royal George, of 110 guns was sunk. His description of the scene was awful. It was pay-day on the ship; most of the sailors had their women on board. He represented that 300 such were drowned. He usually closed that portion of his account by saying "there was a brave slaughter of w——s, till you." He was one of the boat's crew sent on the perilous duty of the rescue of many of the drowning men. The officer of his boat observing a man pick up a goose, knocked him down instantly, saying, "d——n y're eyes, will you offer to snatch a goose when men are drowning all around you?" The sinking of this noble ship is matter of history. The gallant Admiral went to the bottom, in her cabin, seated in his chair, apparently overwhelmed in an instant by the rushing flood. It seems that the accident occurred by running her metal to one side, and thus careening her until she shipped the sea, which in an instant filled her immense bowels, and sunk her in that element over which she had floated the symbol of "Britannia rules the waves."

These settlers were Seceders, now called Reformed Presbyterians. Their meeting house, Prosperity, is still in the place where first worshipped the emigrants.

As a body, none better deserved the character of good citizens than they did. In hard and industrious labor, as mechanics and agriculturists, they laid the foundations of that competence which they respectively acquired. Few of the original settlers survive. William Fair is the only one of them now living, near the original Irish settlement, called the Stoney Hills.* He is now a very aged man, approaching to eighty, but still retaining much of the activity of his younger years. He may often be seen on a sale day, walking the streets of Newberry, slender, tall, and straight, as if time had made a slight impression upon him. By continual industry and temperate habits, he has raised and educated a large family, and provided an ample inheritance for them all. His sons, Jas. Fair, Esq., of Abbeville, Archibald Fair, of Florida, Col. Simeon Fair, of Newberry, Dr. Samuel Fair, of Columbia, Gen. E. Y. Fair, of Montgomery, Alabama, and Dr. Drury Fair, of Selma, Alabama, are the best proofs which can be offered of their ancestor's worth. Another, William Hunter, the oldest son of good old Nathan, is, I presume, still alive.† Two years ago I saw him at the Court House, and he said to me, (if I remember right,) that he was then in his eighty-sixth year. Everything about him seemed to me to say, that the stout constitution of the Irish weaver might carry him safely beyond ninety. Most fervently do I wish it may! For none better deserve the blessing of length of days than such an honest, pure-hearted, laborious mechanic, as he has always been.

Another settlement of the Irish commenced just about Frog Level, and extended along the Charleston road, north and west to Crotwell's old place. In this section were found the Boyds, (not the family of our Ordinary,) McClelands, Greggs, Wilsons, Conners, Neals, McNeils, Camerons, Flemings. Some of these were as remarkable for their thrift as the Stoney Battery settlers, but this was not the case in general.

---

* Since writing the foregoing, he died, Monday, 15th December. 1851, in his 82d year.

† This was written in 1850. Since then he has been gathered to his fathers.

One of the men mentioned here, James Fleming, was the subject of lynch law, in the time of the Regulation, 1764. The tree, the great oak, on the south side of the road, and opposite to the spring, at Springfield, is the only surviving witness of the transaction. An incident connected with his subsequent life may better illustrate the character of the inhabitants than anything else which I can give. He was chopping, (*i. e.* cutting down a tree,) some distance from his house. In its fall, his leg was caught under it, or some of the smaller trees broken down by its fall; he managed to extricate it, and sat down on the log; his cry for assistance brought to his aid a neighbor, Thos. Reagan. When he came, James was swinging his broken leg from side to side, and said to him, as he walked up with his axe on his shoulder, "take your axe, Tammy, and chap it off." But this the stout farmer would not do. He shouldered poor Jamie, and carried him home. The leg was so shattered, and the bone protruded so far through the skin, that the skill of the neighbors was unavailing to set it. A Dutch doctor was sent for and before he could perform the operation, it was found, as he thought, necessary to cut off a part of the shin bone. To do this, a hand saw was the only instrument. For this painful operation, he was held by John McCleland, commonly called "*Wee Jack.*" To him, Jamie said "och, Johnny, I canna thoult," "but ye maun thoult," was Jack's answer. On being asked by a "*Friend,*" "did not he (Jamie) complain mightily?" Jack replied, in his short quick manner, "he gurned a wee bit." "How could thee hold him, Jack?" was the next inquiry. "I could have haud him down till he wud have been sawed a two of the meddle," was Jack's fierce reply. Notwithstanding this rough practice, Jamie got well, and lived many a *suspected* day afterwards.

Just at the upper end of this settlement, called "Mullexander," lived William Gregg, remarkable for his honesty and many virtues. On being solicited to subscribe to pay the preacher, he said, "no, faith, I'll no subscribe, I'll just gie sax pence for every sermon I hear him preach." At this good man's house lived for a time two Irish emigrants of a later day, but long citizens, and worthy citizens, too, of Newberry. I allude to Samuel McCalla and Samuel Spence.

The life of the first would furnish in some of its details materials for a romance, and yet be true! He was one of the Irish Rebels, as they were called in England, here, we should say Irish Patriots of '98. He was captured I presume, in the disastrous route of Vinegar Hill. He owed his life, as I have often heard him say, to a lady, who pulled the epaulette off his shoulder, and the feather from his hat, not five minutes before he was taken. He was marched day after day, to the place of execution, and witnessed the "short shrift" of many of his companions, Ireland's murdered sons. At last he was given his choice, to serve his Majesty seven years, or be transported from the kingdom. He chose the latter, and as he used to say, he put in leg bail in the West Indies, and sought his future home in Newberry. Here he pursued, first, the business of a stone mason and brick layer, afterwards that of a hatter, till he had enough and to spare. But during the long period, from '98 to 1818, he was separated from his wife and child. He often paid their passage to America, but until 1818, he was not allowed to fold them to his anxious bosom. He was then a Justice of the Peace for Newberry; but only a few years was left him for happiness. His constitution, broken by repeated attacks of fever, gave way, and in the fall of '24, he passed from this transitory world.

Samuel Spence, tailor Spence, as he used to be called, who does not remember? His wit, industry, honesty and virtue commend his memory to all his surviving acquaintances. Ever on his board, until he secured competence, and more than competence, he could say with truth to his countrymen, *work*, and you cannot fail to succeed. Many and many an unfortunate Irishman, he fed, clothed, and found employment, until he could do better. Few men will be found hereafter among us, who will so well fill the place of the good citizen and honest man.

The Irish of this settlement, like that below, were also generally Seceders. Their place of religious meeting was Cannon's Creek. Here still their children, who remain, worship God as their fathers did. Scattered through the Black Jack section of Newberry were the Montgomerys, Sloans, Spences, Wrights, Caldwells, Wilson, (Thomas and James).

Another family of the Caldwells was located in the Dutch Fork. Of this last family was Chancellor Caldwell. His father, Dan Caldwell, died in the great epidemic of 1816.* He died early, but his life was such an one, that he had no enemies! For he was, indeed, a man without spot. James Wilson lived to be, I think, almost an hundred years old. One of his grandsons, Joe Caldwell, is now one of the most successful planters of Newberry, and pushing his interests in Florida. In the Long Lane, Gilder's and King's Creek's settlements, lived the Glenns, Chalmers, McMorries, Glasgows, McCrackens. Higher up, between Indian and Duncan's Creeks, and Duncan's Creek and Enoree, might be found the Boyces, Marshalls, McKees, Gordons, McCreless, John Boyd, of Ballamena, the Mars, Madigans, and the Hughes.†

Col. Glenn, the father of my worthy friends, (two of Newberry's best citizens,) Col. John and Dr. George W. Glenn, was a revolutionary soldier.

William Chalmers, the father of such respectable men as Capt. James, David and Dr. Alexander W. Chalmers, here began his struggle for competence, which a long life of industry enabled him to realize.

Capt. John McMorries, the father of the worthy citizens of our town and district, of that name, was born in Fairfield District on the 5th January, 1769, in a few months after the landing of his parents in the United States from Ireland.

---

* Since writing this passage, which was originally prepared "of this family, is Chancellor Caldwell," the melancholy intelligence of the death of James J. Caldwell, a Chancellor of the State, has reached me; probably while writing it he was breathing his last. Truly are we constantly in the midst of death! His age, not more than fifty, promised many years of usefulness in his distinguished position; but God, who sees not as man sees, thought it best that his labors *here* should end. His pure spirit released from its earthen tenement on the 11th of March, 1850, is, I trust, at rest, in everlasting happiness. Well has he performed his part ; and by death his page of glory has been secured from any possible stain which a longer life might have made.

† James Hughes lived to the great age of one hundred and ten years. My informant says : "I have known him myself to ride to Capt. Mc.'s store, after he was one hundred years old, to get a bottle of old Jamaika." This was bad business for a centenarian ; it was, however, the result of early habit.

He married Nancy Morgan,* the daughter of Major Spencer Morgan, who once lived in the neighborhood of Spring Hill, and who was a cousin of the lion-hearted old wagoner, Gen. Daniel Morgan. He removed to and settled in Newberry. His first place of business, as a merchant, was at the place now known as McCreless' old store. He removed thence to Poplar Grove, where he did business for many years, and where he died. Of his "highly useful life" little remains which can now be collected. He was known for his virtues, and universally respected for the good which he did. He was the Senator from Newberry District in the State Legislature from 1808 to 1812. Elected over such men as Willliam Caldwell and Maj. John Hampton, soldiers of the Revolution, constitutes in itself the · best evidence of his excellence and worth. It is, however, right to say, that in the midst of the poll one of his opponents, Maj. John Hampton, died. Still Mr. McMorries' majority was such as to show, that the life of his talented opponent, who was thus removed, would not have altered the result. He declined a re-election in 1812, and spent the balance of his life in virtuous and useful retirement. I remember Mr. McMorries attended, and I think presided in the first anti-tariff meeting held in Newberry District.

To it was submitted the memorial of the Charleston Chamber of Commerce prepared by their Committee, the Hon. Judge Richardson, Jeremiah Yates, Elias Horry, R. J. Turnbull, Christopher Jenkins, James Adger and James Ferguson. The meeting was a small one, for the matter was then little understood, and the oppression was not then felt. He had, however, the merit to perceive the remote consequence of the beginning of legislation afterwards found to be too oppressive to be patiently borne. When this was, I do not remember, and cannot now ascertain.

Mr. McMorries, many years before his death, became a member of the Baptist Church at Bausketts.

John Boyce, the elder, I never saw; he, however, is better known by his sons, Robert Boyce, John Boyce, David, Boyce, Alexander Boyce, Ker Boyce, and James Boyce, than any

---

* This lady, in '58, is still living in the town of Newberry, in excellent health.

sketch could make him. All of these are men who have made themseles known in Newberry, Laurens, Union, and Charleston. He lived in that section called Mollyhorn. He was a merchant, and drove on a farm, and everything else from which money could be made. Often have I heard his son Ker relate the circumstance of starting a drove of cattle from his father's for Charleston, among which was an ill-natured steer, which could neither be led nor drove. The young men were afraid of him. The old man hooted at them for their cowardice, and charged upon the ox on his pony, but he found no flight in the animal; then it became his turn to run, and putting his nag to the top of his speed, he presented this scene: the steed in full pursuit, he himself leaning forward in his saddle, lashing with furious energy his flying pony, his gray locks streaming in the wind. It looked to be *a rather ticklish affair, and indeed so it proved,* for the steer ran him so close, that in one of his lunges he stuck his horn under the saddle, and dragged it off from under Mr. Boyce, but he escaped unhurt. His house was built with one upper or garret room, which opened with a door on the road. In this room, the old man Marshall, who had been tasting a drop of dram, was put to sleep, and in the night he awoke, and getting up opened the door, and walked out. When he struck the ground, he turned about, and with great wonder said, "Johnny Buice, you make yer steps very high of this country." This gentleman, Marshall, was the father of James, George,* Samuel, Hugh and Joseph, the four last of whom are now, I believe, residents and highly respectable citizens of Abbeville, having removed from Newberry many years ago. James was a native of Ireland, and had some very peculiar notions and expressions. I recollect his once telling me when a candidate for the Legislature, "shew me a lawweer wi hair in the palm of his hand, then I'll believe he is an honest man!" This he said to a lawyer, to a man with whom he was friendly, and for whom, I presume, he voted.

Capt. Geo. McCreless, twice a member of the House of

* George, since this was written, died.

Representatives from Newberry, was not one of the original settlers; though he lived in the village and district with short intervals of absence from 1803 to his death. An intimate personal knowledge justifies me in saying that no more firm and honest man ever lived. He commanded the Newberry Artillery Company, in the celebrated Camp Alston expedition in 1814. Just beyond his place, on the north bank of Patterson's Creek, lived James Gordon, a celebrated stone mason, and an equally celebrated Free Mason. Of him is reported the anecdote, that he was foreman of a jury who tried a man for assault and battery, and who, in their hearing, offered to plead guilty, but for some cause retracted, and went on trial; and notwithstanding his confession, they returned a verdict of "not guilty." Judge Grimkie, in amazement said, "How could you return such a verdict, after his confession?" "Why," said the foreman, "he has always been such a liar we could not believe him." On the 14th of July, 1815, he was at his neighbor, Capt. Mc-Creless' *still house*, on the south side of Patterson's Creek; an immense fall of rain took place; he left the still house after night, but *never reached his house*. It was supposed he attempted to walk a log across the creek, tottered off, and was drowned. His body was found next day in the creek!

Robert McKee lived midway between Indian and Duncan's Creek. His house still stands on the margin of the road, and when I ride by, I often look for the venerable form and gray hairs of my good Irish friend. But in a good old age of more than eighty years he has been gathered to his fathers. The White Church, at the Long Lane, once called, I think, "King's Creek Church," "Gilder's Creek"; and that of more recent origin, "The Head Spring," constituted the places of worship to which these settlers, who were either Presbyterians or Seceders, resorted.

John Boyd, of Ballamena, John Boyd, (called Johnny Buckles) and David Boyd, Sr., (the last two lived between Gilder's Creek and Bush River), were Covenanters. Like the Quakers, they set their faces against slavery; yet, if I remember right, John Boyd was the owner of slaves at his death. I know that David Boyd, Sr., the father of our excellent Ordinary,

Hugh K. Boyd, manumitted his, but was compelled, from their want of thrift, to gather them all home, and take charge of them as if they were his slaves. David Boyd, Sr., was a Revolutionary soldier, and deserves a fuller notice than is here given. John Boyd's celebrated expression, when advised to settle a law suit, in which he was ultimately successful, is worth remembering. "I'll mak a spoon, or spile a horn."

Many others, Irish, were scattered through the Bush River, Little River, and Saluda settlements, such as the Kellys, O'Neall's, McConnells and Nelson's. It is proposed in future numbers to speak more at large of Samuel Kelly and Hugh O'Neall, and his father, William O'Neall, and therefore here I pass them over, and will close this number, already too long, by two Irish anecdotes.

An Irishman and credulity are very often synonymous terms. Robert Nelson and his sons settled between the Beaverdam and Saluda, near to the place where Esquire Walter Herbert now lives.* John was at work for Wm. Gould, (better known as old Bill Gould.) Ears of green corn (called in the upper country roasting ears, in the lower country, mutton corn,) boiled, were on the table at dinner. Jack was helped to an ear, and after eating off the grain, as he saw the others do, holding the cob in his hand, he looked at Gould and said, "Billy what do ye do wi the stecks? Do ye ate them, too?" "Oh yes!" was the reply, and Jack masticated the cob!

Jo. McConnel, who afterwards went to Ohio, lived for a time between Beaverdam and Saluda. He lost his cow, and after many days of search, going down "a brae," he fancied he heard some one crying out, *"here is yer coow mon!"* He said he went "his way" and when he came to the place "sure enough there was his coow in the mire," and "there stud a green shouthered angel on a tussock—when he stud up he sat down, and when he went he went by jirks!"

---

* Since dead.

NO. 7.

Many of the Friends came from Pennsylvania, some from Virginia, and a few from North Carolina. The other settlers, who belong neither to the Friends, the Germans, nor the Irish, were also emigrants from the States mentioned. Some few came from Maryland.

Of these, William Turner was one of the earliest. He was a native of Maryland. The tract of land granted to him, on which he probably settled, as early as 1751, was granted in 1752. It lies on the east side of Little River, near its mouth, at Long's bridge.

In 1760, began that fresh outbreak of the Cherokees, which followed on the heels of Governor Lyttleton's treaty at Fort George, in 1759, and which preceded the two expeditions, successively commanded by Cols. Montgomery and Grant. The last was in 1761, and has given the name of its commander to the war with the Indians. It has been usually called Grant's war! But it was in 1760, that the Cherokees, burning with rage for the murder of the hostages at Fort George, and which had been caused by the murder, by one of the Indian Chiefs, Occonostota, of the commander of the fort, Capt. Cottymore, and the wounding of Lieuts. Bell and Foster, rushed upon the defenceless settlements on Long Cane, Saluda and Little River.

On that occasion, Turner's house was used as a place of defence for himself and his neighbors; (a block house or station, as such places were called,) and was surrounded by a stockade. Rising early in the morning, he found a paper stuck in the fork of a peach tree, before his door, with a stone laid upon it. Opening and reading it, he was told, the Indians were on their way, and would soon be in that neighborhood. Whence came the information, he never knew; but it gave him such warning, that by closing the approaches through the stockade, and shutting every body within the house, the danger, imminent and threatening as it was, was

1   D

escaped. For, as expected, the Indians came, surrounded, and repeatedly fired upon the house; but the height of the stockade compelled them to fire so high, that although their balls penetrated the house, yet they injured no one. The balls in the logs of the house, afterwards called Long's Old House, remained as a testimony. until it was not many years since taken down. My friend who informed me of these particulars, told me they were shewn to him by the venerable widow of Wm. Turner, (who I presume, died in 1810,) and from whom he received the traditions now here embodied.

On this place, lived until her death, within the last five years, the grand-daugher of the first settler, Mrs. Mary Gaskins, the wife of John Gaskins, now of Winter Seat,* Edgefield. Her mother, Mrs. Priscilla Long, was the daughter, and I think, youngest child of William Turner. She, and her daughter, Mrs. Gaskins, were both born on this place. The grand-mother, Mary Turner, the mother of Priscilla Long, and the daughter Mrs. Gaskins, then Mary Long, afterwards the wife of Henry Coate, and after his death, of John Gaskins, all lived on it.

At Springfield now lives the grand-son of Samuel Kelly, who there settled in 1862. The dwelling is now within one hundred yards of the spot where he settled. The old house then built, and afterwards occupied by the family, until the death of the present resident's grand-mother, in 1820, (June) is still, although removed and repaired, standing in the yard, and the family of the grand-son now use the noble fountain of water from which Samuel Kelly and his family drank. Often *here*, from 1820, to October, 1848, was seen the rare spectacle of four generations of people living under the same roof. Can any other instances of similar kind be given in Newberry? If so, glad shall I be to hear of them; for I love *that fixedness* with which families linger around their ancestral homes. The very walnut, locust, and oak, at Springfield, feel to me almost like relations, for beneath their shade have passed my grand-father, grand-mother, father, mother, uncles, and aunts, all of whom, with one very near

---

* Since dead.

and dear exception,* have gone, and their place "shall know them no more."

My friend, F. R. Higgins, from whom much of what I have stated was gathered, tells me that he thinks there is a grant on Enoree, (probably of the tract of land now owned by Richard Sondley,) to Pennington, older than that to William Turner, hereinbefore mentioned, and which I had thought was the oldest in the district, except some grants to the Germans. This agrees with what is said in Mills' Statistics, that John Duncan, a native of Aberdeen, Scotland, but an emigrant from Pennsylvania to South Carolina, settled on Duncan's Creek in 1752, and that Jacob Pennington, living on Enoree, ten miles below, was his nearest neighbor.

Assuming this to be true, I think it may be considered as pretty certain that the parts of Newberry first occupied and settled by the white man, were as follows: the Dutch Fork in 1745; the east side of Little River, near its mouth, (Turner's settlement,) in 1751; the Canebrake, on Enoree, (Pennington's grant,) 1751, or possibly earlier; and Duncan's Creek, (Duncan's settlement,) in 1752.

The fort called Pennington's, which was, I presume, erected as a protection against the Indians in 1760, is at Colonel Duckett's, on Indian Creek; the remains may, I have been told, still be traced. This place was probably first settled by Pennington; but it has been, for the last fifty or sixty years in the possession of one family, Thomas Duckett, his son, Jacob Duckett, and his son, Colonel J. W. Duckett, and through all that time has been remarkable for the care and thrift with which it has been managed.

It is difficult to so classify the remaining settlers of New-berry, who were neither Germans, Friends, nor Irish, as to speak of them in a body. It will, however, be attempted to give a sort of bird's-eye view of the other parts of Newberry and its inhabitants, running down from its earliest periods to those within the memory of man, in its legal sense, to wit: within the last twenty years.

In the Enoree and Duncan's Creek settlements, including under this general head the settlements on Indian, Gilder's,

---

* Since writing this, in October, 1850, my mother, to whom it alludes, died.

and King's Creeks, lived the Lyles, Kellys, Malones, Wadling-
tons, Gordons, Rutherfords, Calmes, Maybins, Sims, Caldwells,
Hendersons, Kenners, Littletons, Vessels, Valentines, Flanagans,
Hendricks, Hills, Odells, Duncans, Ducketts, Roberts, Whit-
mires, Herndons, Parks, Dugans, Caseys, Bonds, Starkes,*
Tinneys, Speakes, Hustons, Lindseys, Fords, Grastys, Cham-
bers, Crenshaws, Finches, Shells, Eppes, Hattons, Browns,
Murrays, Wells, Kings, Powells, Williams, Gillams.

Of these, as a class, I can say little, Their habits presented
nothing peculiar. Some were Baptists, some Presbyterians;
and at a time subsequent to the Revolution, many became
Methodists. In this entire section the inhabitants were whigs.

Colonel James Lyles was an inhabitant of the Fork,
between Enoree and Tiger. He was, I have no doubt, in
General Williamson's expedition against the Indians, in 1776,
although in the memoir of Maj. McJunkin, published in the
Magnolia, the Col. Lyles engaged in that duty is called
John, yet I think it is pretty clear that Col. James Lyles
was thereby intended. He was also in the affair at Hanging
Rock, 7th August, 1780. I presume he was at Blackstocks,
as he was part of Sumpter's command. Whether he was at
King's Mountain in October, '80; at the Cowpens in January,
1781, and at the seige of Ninety-Six, I have no means of
knowing. He returned to his family after the capture of
Fort Granby on the 14th of May, 1781, and died leaving

---

* Thomas Starke was a revolutionary soldier. He was remarkable for
dry, and what would be now called, coarse humor; but an instance of
that kind may give a better idea of the man, of the state of society, than
anything else which I could give. John Speake, Esq., once Sheriff of
Newberry, was thought by some, and especially by Mr. Starke, to be a
little too fond of show. Dining with him on some occasion, when there
were persons present, before whom Mr. Speake desired to show to the
best advantage. Coffee was about to be served, and Starke was asked if
he would take some? "Give it to me, Jacky, in a tin, may be I might
break the vessel," was the reply. Old Tom Starke, as he was called,
drank to great excess. He never visited Newberry Court House or
Latham's store (Springfield) without getting drunk, and being left on
the ground. About 1805 or 1806, he visited Newberry, bought a pound
of powder; it was wrapped up in paper. and in his pocket; he got
drunk; lay down before the fireplace, at night, in the tavern; his clothes
took fire, the powder exploded; he was awfully burned, and in a few
days died. Thus from drunkenness perished a revolutionary soldier.

a family of three daughters, one of whom, Mrs. Elizabeth Maybin, the wife of Col. Benjamin Maybin, survives.*

James Kelly was a lieutenant in the Revolution, and served through the whole war. His brother Edmund, was a soldier; he died within the last seven or eight years at the great age of more than an hundred years.

Anthony Parks was one of the first settlers of Newberry District. He is mentioned in a note to Ramsay's History of South Carolina, 1 vol. p. 208, as having traveled in 1758, a few hundred miles among the Indians to the west of the Alleghany mountains. His half brother, Col. Thomas Dugan, lived just at the confluence of Gilder's and Indian Creek. He was a soldier in the Revolution; he was I think, one of the gallant men who triumphed at King's Mountain. Two of his brothers, with Anderson, and one of the Fords, were hewn to pieces in the Revolution by the Turners, as a retaliatory act of vengeance for the death of their brother, who had been slain by a party of whigs. He commanded, after the organization of the militia, the Enoree regiment. He lived to be an old man, and raised a large family; all of whom, as well as himself, have paid the great debt of nature.

In this section of the district was one of the earliest classical schools in the upper part of the State. To the Methodists, and I see from Ramsay's History of South Carolina, to the Rev. Mr. Dougherty, (called in it Dorothy) we are indebted mainly for that fine institution of learning, the Mount Bethel Academy. Elisha Hammond, the father of Gov. Hammond, and Josiah P. Smith were its principal teachers. It gave to the country such men as Judge Crenshaw, his brothers, Dr. Crenshaw and Walter Crenshaw, Chancellor Harper, John Caldwell, Esq., Dr. George W. Glenn, John R. Golding, Gov. Richard J. Manning, John G. Brown, Dr. Thomas Smith, of Society Hill, N. R. Eaves, of Chester, and Thomas Glover, of Orangeburg. Chancellor Caldwell owed a sort of divided allegiance to the Newberry Academy and that at Mount Bethel. For at both places he

---

* A fuller account of this gentleman, (Col. Lyles,) is given subsequently.

received parts of his academical education. The Mount Bethel Academy furnished the first students and graduates of the South Carolina College.

In connection with this part of the subject, I may be pardoned for recalling to the memory of the people of Newberry, the names of two of the founders and patrons of the Academy, Charles Crenshaw and Edward Finch. Both of the names are extinct in Newberry; a grand-son of the latter, is however, still in the immediate neighborhood of his ancestral home.

Charles Crenshaw, (Mr. Grainger, as he was most generally called,) lived and died at Long Lane. From a very early day, until 1812, he was the Tax Collector of Newberry. No more obliging and correct public officer lived. His sons, Archy Crenshaw, Dr. Abner Crenshaw, Judge Anderson Crenshaw, Walter and Willis Crenshaw, Esqs., are now too well remembered in Newberry, to make any further mention of his claims to respect necessary.

Of his neighbor, Edward Finch, I know little. He was a Methodist, and a stern, uncompromising Christian. He was a magistrate; many a blasphemer was made to pay a shilling for each profane oath uttered in his presence. The old law, under which he acted so well for the assertion of good morals, still exists, and if it was now and then enforced by our worthy magistrates, it would go far to drive out the odious and inexcusable sin of *taking the name of God in vain.*

His son, Dr. Ivy Finch, was the friend and companion of many who now survive. Cut off in the morning of his life, in an instant of time, he was not permitted to unfold those powers which promised so much for his country, himself and his friends. He left Columbia in December, 1815, in company with a large party of friends. He understook to drive a horse, the property of his friend, Judge Crenshaw; his vicious properties were well known. At the fork of the roads, just beyond Butcher town, where the road to McGowen's ferry, now the Broad River bridge, turns off from the road to Winnsboro', the horse took fright, and ran away. In his flight he carried his sulky to the left of the road, over the high stumps of some hickory saplings, and thus threw him out of the sulky; in falling, he was caught by his leg between the shaft and foot board, and in that position, the left side of his head was brought in contact with the wheel, and he thus probably received his death wound. He was, however, carried in that position more than an hundred yards, when his head struck against the sharp knob of a stump in the road, which seemed to have followed the sutor of the skull all around, dividing it perfectly. Just at this place, where the road from Mr. Guignard's, afterwards Judge Gantt's house, comes into the road above described, the horse kicked loose from the sulky, and left the lifeless body of Dr. Ivy Finch! Alas! alas! how true is it, that in the midst of life we are in the midst of death! Of the nine persons, who were in the company, and who surrounded his dead body, four* survive!

No. 7 Continued.

The Baptist settlement extended from the borders of the Enoree and Duncan's Creek settlements, (through which we have passed,) southwest towards Saluda. It was mainly located on Bush River and Little River. It extended on Bush River from the line traced in No. 5 as the northwest boundary of Friends to the old Ninety-Six road, the western line of the district; through it were scattered many Presbyterians, and after the Revolution many Methodists. In it were to be found the Grays, Coles, Crows, McCraws, Beltons, Coats, Williams, Reeders, Pitts, Mangums, Davis, Neals, McAdams, Ritchies, Thomas, Dalrymples, Griffins, Floyds, Clelands, Davenports, Leavells, Newmans, Pages, Carwiles, Jones, Burtons, Gibsons, Crosswhite, Eastlands, Petersons, Speers, Stewarts, Stevens, Kellys, Goggans, and Spearmans.

The settlement occupying the fork between Little River and

---

* Now only one.

Saluda, and covering Mudlick Mill and Page's Creek, constituting the southwest portion of the district, was composed of the Caldwells, Williams, Gillams, Dysons, Cunninghams, Satterwhites, Grisbys, Neelys, Chappells, Wells, Hills, Moons, Paynes, Rudds, Smiths, Watkins, Burgess, Boazmans, Paylors, Wallaces, Turners, Proctors, Swift, Phillips, Jamieson, Adams, Vaughan, Barlow, Younghusband, Moores, Ritchies, Goodmans, Farrows, Walker, Goldings, Creswells, Browns, and Halls.

The Baptist settlement anciently had but one place of meeting, Bush River; out of that have arisen three others, Cross Roads, Mount Zion, and Mount Olive. I hope to be able in some future number to give a full account of it, and of many of its leading inhabitants. For the present I defer it, in the hope of being permitted to consult, and glean much from the records of the old Bush River Baptist Church.

In connection, however, with some of the family names mentioned, in the limits of the Baptist settlement, I must relate an incident, which though small, as the tribute of ship money demanded of John Hampden and other martyrs of liberty in the time of Charles I., is remarkable, as giving rise to one of the guards of liberty constantly observed now in our courts I mean the Act of December, 1811, "to prevent any citizens of this State from being sent to goal until he be heard by himself or counsel."—Acts of 1811, page 32. At October term, 1807, (I speak without reference to the records,) Judge Grimke presided; Major Benjamin Long was Sheriff, acting under a *pro tem.* appointment in the place of P. B. Waters, (deceased;) David Stevens, David Peterson and Gabriel McCoole were constables in charge of the doors of the courthouse. They were reported by the Sheriff as absent from their posts, without leave; the Judge, without any enquiry, ordered them to goal. This constituted one of the articles of impeachment prepared in 1810 against the venerable Judge; but the whole impeachment, for the want of a constitutional majority was refused to be presented by the House of Representatives in 1811. The Act of 1811 was passed at the same session to prevent a similar exercise of arbitrary power. For in that case if the Judge had heard the excuses of the respectable men who then condescended to fill the office of constable, he never would have imprisoned them. The answer of one of them to one of the committee, who prepared the articles of impeachment, was mentioned by Mr. Thomas Hunt, the chairman of the committee, in the debate on the articles of impeachment in 1811, as an instance of a freeman's indignation, at a false imprisonment: "I had the disgrace," said he, "of looking through the grates of Newberry gaol."

The settlement, in the fork, between Little River and Saluda, furnished three of the members of the first Provincial Congress, John Caldwell, John Satterwhite and James Williams; two of these, Caldwell and Williams, were distinguished officers in the Revolution, and sealed their devotion of liberty with their blood. It furnished also many other noble soldiers of liberty; among them will be found Maj. Robert Gillam, Robert Gilliam, Jr., Joseph Goodman, John Wallace, William and James Caldwell. In it too lived Robert Cunningham, a general in the British army. His residence was Peach Hill. He was mistaken in his duty; but never have I heard it alleged or supposed that he did any act which reflected on his character as a man or an officer.

I am promised materials, which I hope will enable me in a subsequent number to give biographical sketches of John, William and James Caldwell, of the two Robert Gillams, father and son, and of the wife of the latter, the venerable lady, Mrs. Elizabeth Gillam, of Joseph Goodman, and of John Satterwhite, the elder. I shall avail myself speedily in some number of the opportunity to republish a memoir of Col. James Williams. I, too, would gladly, if I could avail myself of the materials, do justice to General Cunningham, by giving some account of him. I hope, too, to be able to do some sort of justice to the memory of Dr. Jacob Roberts Brown. For the present, I confine myself to sketches brief, as may be expected from general knowledge and tradition, of two of the inhabitants who have passed away.

The name Younghusband, will be seen as mentioned among the inhabitants. He came into the settlement subsequent to the Revolution. Many, I have no doubt, never heard of him. He lived on the place where Mr. John Barlow afterwards lived, and which possibly, after his death, belonged to Edward Pitts. He had been an English sea captain. He undertook to live like an old English Baron, in his castle. His log house was furnished with loop-holes; he had a good stand of arms. His gate was an hundred yards or more from his house; as soon as any one entered it, his spy glass was to his eye; if he did not like his appearance, his man Dick was ordered to warn him to leave. He had conceived a great dislike to Claiborn Goodman; he had more than once warned him not to walk through his fields Discovering him on some occasion inside of his gate, he sallied out upon him, with his negroes, seized him, and threw him down to tie him. Goodman had rode to the gate, and had his spurs on; when thrown, he used them upon Younghusband's man Dick, who was holding him down, with such good effect, that he sprang from him. Younghusband said to him "Sirrah, how dare you let the rascal go?" "Lord, Massa, he spur me?" was poor Dick's reply. But notwithstanding the spurs, and a gallant resistance, Younghusband and his *"nagurs"* tied Goodman, and left him tied, to get some means of taking him to prison. While they were gone, he extricated one hand, got his knife, and cut his cords into fragments, and was *"non est"* when his captors returned. What became of Younghusband I do not certainly know. I have been told he died at the place of which I have spoken.

The name Moon, mentioned above, is also subsequent to the Revolution. Dr. M. W. Moon lived long and to much good purpose, in the fork between Little and Saluda Rivers. He was a physician of much eminence and practice. He was an able and acceptable Methodist preacher. His estimable son, Dr. Peter Moon is all of his immediate family who remain in the settlement.

For many years after the Revolution, this settlement was foremost for intelligence, patriotism and moral worth. That it has ceased to be as prominent, as it once was is deeply to be regretted. It is now one of the richest sections of the district, and yet judging from some recent indications, I fear there is not so much liberality, as once characterized it. I trust, however, that this reproach, (if it be true,) will not long characterize it, especially when I remember *there* is the home of so much intelligence, worth and liberality as belong to Dr. Peter Moon.

Passing from the mouth of Little River down Saluda to

Waters' ferry, which, before 1804, might be considered the western boundary of the German settlement on the river, thence turning north along the Charleston road to the Irish settlement and thence along it to the Quaker settlement, and skirting its border of the mouth of Bush River, and following its southwestern border to the Baptist settlement on Little and Bush Rivers, we shall find the Turners, Longs, Edwards, Stevens, Thomas, Taylors, Coxes, Clarys, Darnells, Duns, Allisons, Caradines, Hatchers, Nelsons, Higgins, Martins, Rileys, Worthingtons, Wests, Blacks, Arnolds, Cothrans, Larks, Mills, Conwills, Goulds, Kings, Jones, Lesters, Musgroves, Bemounts, Morgans, Dennis, Johnsons, Palmers, Ganters, Waters, Bates, Rials, Spillers, Morris, Langfords, Calks, Lindseys, Bielers, Waits, Mannings, Banks, Hares, Richardsons, Presnells, Cain, Baldres.

I have already spoken of William Turner. I may hereafter have occasion, in connection with revolutionary incidents, to speak of his sons, Dick and Ned, two of Cunningham's well tried "*braves*" and two well known tories. I have lately heard, with astonishment, that Ned Turner is still alive in Florida. If so, he must be verging on to 100. Wonderful indeed will it be, after his many hair breadth escapes in and since the Revolution, if God should spare him to be a centenarian.

William Stevens, John Edwards and Benjamin Long were sons in-law of William Turner. The two first I never saw. David and Edward Stevens, two of our worthy and respectable citizens are his sons. Judging of the father, by them, we shall have no further occasion for description or remark. The whole family of Edwards is extinct in Newberry; the children of Edward Edwards, a son of John Edwards, returned, I think, after his death, to Virginia. John S. Edwards, a grandson, removed to and died in Pickens.

Maj. Benjamin Long lived at Turner's place, (ever since my recollection, called Long's bridge.) He married Priscilla, the youngest daughter. She had been twice previously married, first to James Cheney, second to Isaac King. She had children by neither of these marriages. Benj. Long was a native of Union. In the battle of the Cowpens, he belonged to Brandon's regiment, and was sabred by one of Tarleton's dragoons in the beginning of the fight. Two of the wounds thus received left large scars on his face. He was major of the Saluda battalion of the upper militia regiment in Newberry District, and for a short time Sheriff. He died in 1816. Of his children, numerous as they were, few survived him. Of those who did survive him, none now remains. One of his grandsons, Mr. John Coate, resides at the town of Newberry. Great and sad have been the mortality and changes among the families above given. The neighbors, James Thomas, Benjamin Taylor, Jacob Crosswhite and Thomas Eastland.are remembered, as living on or near Little River. Where are their families? Gone, scattered, removed or dead!

Cornelius Cox, the maternal grand-father of my friend F. B. Higgins, Esq., left four sons, George, James, John, William. He, and they after him, lived on the place just below Higgins' ferry on Saluda. They are all no more. The name is now unknown in that section of the district. George Cox gave rise to the saying "like Cox's snake and cat." When a boy, carrying a cat in his arms, just as he was in the act of crossing a fence, he discovered a snake in its coil, and threw the cat upon it, exclaiming, "devil to devil."

William Cox must have been a singular man from some of his queer remarks which I have often heard repeated. He was observed in a very dry time ploughing closely a very grassy piece of corn; the observer said to him: "Bill you will kill your corn!" "Well," he said, "I want it to die an honorable death!" On a cool day in October, some one remarked in his hearing, there would be frost the succeeding night; he said, "No, I was to-day in the Saluda bottom, and the kuckleburs are not ripe yet; there will be no frost till they are ripe." His death was most probably occasioned by an injury received by him, in an affray between him, John Turner, Jr., and James Coate, (son of big John.) Coate fled the country: John Turner, Jr., was convicted of the assault with the intent to kill and murder, and was sentenced at March Term, 1807, by Judge Trezevant to stand two hours in the pillory, and underwent the punishment. Had it not been for covering him with an umbrella, and the supports of his friends in holding him up, he must have died in the pillory!

A little lower down the river, lived Col. Daniel Clary. He was a tory Colonel in the Revolution; but notwithstanding this

great error, few men were more beloved. At the battle of
Musgrove's Mills, on Enoree, in which Col. Williams, (perhaps
Col. Shelby,) defeated Col. Innis, Clary was present as a
British Colonel commanding the militia; and in the *melee* of
defeat, his horse was seized at the same moment by the cheeks
of the bridle by two whig soldiers. He escaped captivity, by
exclaiming "damn you, don't you know your own officers."
After the peace, he performed well all the duties of a good
citizen, and was peacefully gathered to his fathers, leaving a
respectable family, all of whom are gone, with the exception
of a grandson, Col. Clary, now living in Edgefield, and a
great grand-daughter.

In their immediate vicinity, lived John Worthington, quiet,
moral, inoffensive and industrious; few men deserved more as
a parent and a neighbor. From 1804 to 1808, he far exceeded
any man I knew, in the quantity of cotton which he raised
in proportion to the number of hands he employed. Wealth
flowed in upon him apace, and at his death, probably in 1826
or 1827, he still had, after providing for his large family,
who had previously married, a very considerable estate. Where
are now his sons, or their descendants? All are gone, so
far as my knowledge extends, with the exception of one
grand-son, Dr. Worthington. Two of his daughters, Mrs.
Samuel Chapman and Mrs. Frank Spearman, survive; another,
his eldest daughter, Mrs. Hunter, is long since dead, but is
represented by several descendants. The only survivor of the
settlers in this settlement, prior to 1804, is Hezekiah Riley,*
(if he indeed be still spared,) for last October, at Anderson,
I saw him beyond four-score, stretched upon the bed, which
I feared was to be his bed of death. An honest, good, but
impatient man, he has passed beyond the ordinary limit of
life, and has seen his numerous progeny go down to the

---

* When I speak of Mr. Riley as the only survivor of this settlement, I
mean the Saluda settlement proper. For of the Beaverdam settlement,
Esquire Walter Herbert still remains. He has passed his three-score and
ten, and has filled with credit to himself, and advantage to his country,
the offices of captain in the militia, a Magistrate and Representative in
the Legislature. He is now adorning an old age of usefulness, by presenting an example of total abstinence from all which can intoxicate.
Both have died since this was written.

grave, with one solitary exception, and he, I fear, is far from being any comfort to his aged parent.

Passing beyond the Beaverdam, and standing on the rocky hills, between Bush River and Saluda, I ask, as I look around, where are the numerous families of the Goulds, Conwills and Mills? All are gone, with the exception of Benj. Conwill, son of old Benjamin, and Mrs. Dicy Myers, daughter of Joe Conwill. Old Bill Gould lived to the left of the road leading to Hewitt's ferry within two or three hundred yards of Esquire Walter Herbert's present residence, and within one hundred yards of the old ford on the Beaverdam Creek.* He lived to a great age, probably beyond ninety. He was the leading man among the Goulds, Conwills, Blacks, Kings and Wests. He loved mischief like a feast, and hence anything which occurred to terrify an ignorant people, generally had its origin with him. The ignorance around him may be judged of by this fact. Many of the young men of the families named were at different times his croppers. If he offered a third of his crop for compensation, it was generally refused as too little; while a fourth would be greedily accepted, as being more. His brother Harry was almost idiotic. He was always to be seen with his rifle, shot bag, and big coat, and graced with leggins and green garters!

Joe Conwill lived to the left of the road, leading from O'Neall's, now Bobo's mill, on Bush River by the crab orchard to Parkin's ford, (now Crofts') on Saluda. His widow Sophia Conwill, who at an age of more than fourscore,h as, within a few years died, was too good and useful a woman to be forgotten. Her husband has been dead more than thirty years. He was a pale, sickly looking man; but possessed of much activity, spirit and firmness. His unhealthy appearance arose, as it was said, from being bitten by a mad dog. He was just married to her, of whom I have spoken as his widow, Sophia Goodwyn. Hunting racoons, (as was then the practice,) his dog treed one, while the tree, on which the coon had taken refuge was falling under the axes of his companions,

---

* Here was the first Methodist meeting house in the Beaverdam and Saluda settlement, and possibly in the district. The first preacher *there* (located perhaps) was Daniel Earp, (pronounced Harp. I think he removed to and died in Pendleton District before its division.

he held his dog, which, struggling to get away, bit him. The next day, the dog was found to be mad. In a few days, Conwill and his young wife went to the Pine House, Edgefield, to obtain the services of Dr. Swearingen, in the cure of the former. Swearingen, whose reputation, as possessing the secret of curing hydrophobia, extended far and wide, undertook the case, and after a few day's prescription, having as he supposed, sufficiently guarded, by his medicine, against a paroxysm, left home for a few hours, leaving Conwill at large. In a short time, he was discovered to be exhibiting the usual appearances of hydrophobia. He was fortunately in the yard; the women took refuge in the house, and barred the door; he made repeated attempts to break in; at last, he took the road towards Augusta, at a dog trot; tongue protruding from his mouth, and the saliva dripping from it. In a short time, Swearingen returned home; being told what had occurred, he pursued Conwill on horseback. When he overtook him, he leaped off his horse, cut his bridle reins from his bridle; tied Conwill therewith, drove him home before him, *and cured him.* He lived I presume, at least thirty years afterwards; but he always affirmed, that at the full and change of the moon, he felt the effect of the bite! What has become of Swearingen's remedy? Did it die with him? Has he not a son still living near the Pine House?

John West, the father of the Wests, who lived on the Beaverdam, lived beyond an hundred years. When he said he was an hundred, or close in its neighborhood, he was found in the woods hunting squirrels, and said he could then see to shoot a rifle, as well as he ever did. He died after 1804.

No. 7 Concluded.

John Musgrove, (Col. Musgrove, as he, as well as his brother Edward, was called,) lived on Saluda. Of him, I have no personal knowledge, nor do I know the precise spot where he lived. At his place, the Regulators and Scofelites, in 1764, met in battle array; happily, however, no actual battle occurred; flags were exchanged, and they agreed to separate, and petition the Governor to redress their grievances. This was done, and the result was, that after the great delay of five years, the Circuit Court Act of 1769 was passed. This quieted all domestic dissension by bringing justice home to the people. Although no actual battle was fought between the Regulators and Scofelites, yet I have always understood there was some firing. The following humorous anecdote shows *that* must have been the case. A rather windy gentleman, who lived on the Beaverdam, joined the Regulators, and talked a great deal about the fighting he would do. As the parties were nearing one another, guns were fired; he took the alarm, fled, and wearing a long tailed coat, with a lead inkstand in the skirt pocket, as he jumped a gully, it flew up and struck him on the back part of the head; he fell forward, exclaiming "I am shot! I am a dead man! quarters, gentlemen! quarters, gentlemen!"

The man Scofel, who was made a colonel by Lord Charles Greville Montague, the Governor of the Province, and is called Scoveil, in Ramsay's History, must have been a great scoundrel, fit only to command the thieves and disorderly persons with whom, as might be expected, the upper country, without any court higher than Charleston abounded, and to suppress whom the Regulation was instituted by Thomas Woodward, Joseph Kirkland and Barnaby Pope. For I have often heard it related by one, (whose memory I never found at fault,) that Scofel, after the Circuit Court Act went into operation, was tried at Ninety-Six for stealing chickens. The proof was, that there were 38 chickens stolen; Scofel swore "it was a *dom'd* lie, there were only sax and thirty, for I eat the guzzards."

John Musgrove, from whom I have wandered off to give some particulars attending the Regulation, or growing out of it, was a tory colonel in the Revolution; the only known act of his command was the encampment of his forces on the Knoll, beyond the saw mill, at Bobo's mill, on Bush River, and his precipitate flight *thence*, on hearing a false report, that the whigs, under Casey, were about attacking him. He must have been a man of considerable substance. For, many years after the Revolution, a large number of horses called "heretics" were wild in the Stone Hills, and were said to be the issue of his stock turned loose in the range.

Passing for a moment out of the immediate range of country through which we have been sweeping, and sliding within the bounds assigned in No. 5 for the Quaker settlement, we meet with the only relics of the Dunkers or Dunkards, within my knowledge, in this State. Their settlement was mainly on the Palmetto Branch, north of Bush River. Of this persuasion were originally the Chapmans, Summers, Lynches, Prathers and Martins. David Martin, the father of the family here named, lived on Saluda, near Hewitt's ferry. Among these Dunkers, and the Quakers, without any definite participation in either, lived the Elmores, Mills, Hawkins, Brooks, Atkins, McKinseys, Larges, Gillilands, Abernathys, Coates, Downs, Hilburns, Thweatts, Sheppards, Ramages, Nances, Gillams, Coopers, Cates, Myers, Juliens, Rileys, Elsmores, Barretts, Curetons, Harps, Hays.

The Dunkers are baptized by immersion: they kneel in the water, and are thus plunged three times under it; they neither shave their heads or beards. Most of the leading Dunkers, in the settlement to which I have alluded, became Universalists, but not to the extent now held by that body of Christians. Many retained the long flowing beard. Often have I seen the patriarch of that settlement, the good old man, Joseph Summers, with his white beard, extending to and resting on his breast. He was a native of Maryland. He introduced the wheat called the Yellow Lammas, by bringing, as much as he could, in a stocking leg, from that State. It was perfectly white, when it was first brought. In a few years it became yellow, and was much valued. I fear in the many changes we have undergone, this valuable variety of wheat has been entirely lost.

My venerable friend, Giles Chapman, the great preacher of what was called Universalism, until within the last twenty years, certainly, always preached the Dunker faith. For I see "they deny the eternity of future punishment"; and such unquestionably was always his teaching. He, like his father-in-law, Joseph Summers, wore his beard.

Giles Chapman was a native of Virginia; he was born in 1748; his father, on immigrating to this State, first located

1   E

himself for a season, at the place of our town. Giles Chapman was a saddler by trade. He married a daughter of Joseph Summers. From my earliest recollection, 1799 or 1800, he lived at the place where his worthy son, Samuel Chapman, Esq., now lives, and there he lived until his death, in, I presume, 1819.

He began to preach in 1782. Often have I heard his discourses. He was beyond all doubt an eloquent and a gifted preacher; and seemed to me to be inspired with a full portion of that holy and divine spirit, which taught *"God is Love."* His education and means of information were limited, yet his mighty Master spake by him, as he did by the fishermen "in words that burn, and thoughts which breath." His ministry was much followed, and in recurring to his spotless life and conversation, his continual zeal to do good, his kind and benevolent intercourse with men, and the meek humility with which he bore the railing of the sects of Christians, who differed in opinion with him, I have never entertained a doubt, that whether right or wrong, in abstract matters of faith and theology, he was indeed a disciple of *Him who came into the world to save sinners.*

I can see him *now* as plainly in my mind's eye, as I have seen him hundreds of times, as well in all the various pursuits and intercourse of life as in the pulpit; and yet I find it difficult to give of him a life-like description. He was rather above the ordinary size; grey hair and beard, not very long, but worn; his dress very much that of Friends; a face of the most placid and benevolent expression.

He married more persons than any other clergyman; he never would have more than $1 for his service; "that was as much as any woman was worth," was his laughing reply to the question "how much do you charge?" This was his jest. For no man ever appreciated more highly woman, good virtuous, suffering, feeble woman, than he did, and none had ever more cause to value her; for certainly none better as wife and mother was to be found than his "ain gude wife."

As a husband, father, master, neighbor and friend, none was ever more justly beloved than Uncle Giles, as he was familiarly called by the country all around him.

The old Dunker meeting house stood near, and I think in

the graveyard just at the edge of the Charleston road, a little north of east from Esquire Samuel Chapman's residence.

Recurring to the more immediate settlements, or rather sections of the district from which I passed to indulge myself in some recollections of the Dunker settlement, and to pay a just tribute to old friends and neighbors, I will, without further particularizing, say that until 1804, there were many of the inhabitants of the Stone Hills who belong to that class called the pioneers of civilization, and who live more by hunting and fishing than work. Of these, I remember very well the Rialls who, between 1800 and 1804, removed to the far West. Among them occurred a swap of wives. One fancied the wife of his neighbor, and proposed an exchange; it was agreed to, and executed on the delivery of a jug of rum as boot.

Many will yet remember John and Thomas Downs: *they were both hunters and fishermen.* John was also, however, a hard-working man, but Tommy never loved either "the warm side or cold side of a corn field." Of him was told the story, that as soon as blackberries were ripe, he skinned with the bark entire, except on one side, two hickory saplings, and casing his legs in the bark thus obtained, he entered the briar patches for his living, exclaiming "I would not give thank-ye, for meat and bread."

It must not, however, be supposed, that the schoolmaster was not in the south side of Newberry District. Three very good primary schools were on Bush River; James Howe, whose remains are in Chapman's graveyard, taught south of Bush River, for many years, on the plantation where Abijah O'Neall once lived, between the old brick house and Thomas Lake's, and in sight of the road leading to Mendenhall's mill. This gentleman was a relation of General and Admiral Lord Howe; he was a Londoner; he left England in consequence of some incidents attending his wife's death, which utterly disgusted him, and made him a recluse and a hermit. His penmanship I have never seen excelled. Under his direction the writer of this sketch, and many others, received the first impulses of that learning, which has made him and them, whatever he or they ever has or have been. No better, kind-hearted pedagogue ever ruled with or without "*an ickory*" the youths of Bush River. Another school north of the river was headed by Richard Clegg, also an Englishman, who wrote a good hand, and understood arithmetic well; but he *loved liquor*, and at home or in his school, he *was like each and all of its votaries, tyrant*. He removed and died in Ohio. The third school was taught by John B. Mitchel, a soldier of the Revolution, who being captured and made a prisoner by the British, probably in New Jersey, accompanied their armies to the south, I think as a servant to one of the officers. He *here* remained. He was a preacher of the Methodist denomination for the last forty or fifty years of his life. He was an excellent teacher; many of the inhabitants of Newberry were taught by, and well remembered "Master Mitchell." He lived far beyond four score, and died in Edgefield District, within the last six or eight years.

The Newberry Academy, built by voluntary subscriptions, went into operation, at the village, now town of Newberry, in 1806. Its most palmy days were when taught by the Rev. John Foster and Charles Strong. Many of the men of Newberry, among whom are Chancellor Johnston, F. B. Higgins, Esq., Judge O'Neall, Drayton Nance, Esq., there received their academic educations. Its value to the community can only be sufficiently estimated by those who have experienced its benefits. It is hoped, under its present teacher, Mr. Williams, it will rival and even excel its past brightest days.

This number has carried me greatly beyond the usual limits; but I hope the information which it embodies may excuse its length. In our next, Mr. Editor, we will run hastily over the settlers of the original town of Newberry, give some account of matters connected with its history—notice briefly the public officers connected with the administration of justice, whose offices are kept at the town: and then in the succeeding number, if we can obtain the materials, we will indulge in a hasty glance at the old Bush River Baptist Church and settlement.

———

REV. CHARLES STRONG.

The righteous shall be held in everlasting remembrance. The memory of the just is blessed; but the name of the wicked shall rot. In estimating the relative value of human character, there is a vast difference between the standard adopted by the Bible, and that which obtains among men. On the page of profane history, the names of warriors, statesmen, and politicians, occupy a prominent place, and their exploits constitute the theme of eulogy; but in the Bible we have a record of the names, and a history of the deeds of those who while in the world were not of the world. And the example of those who have walked with God is exhibited for our imitation, that we may be stimulated to follow them who through faith and patience are inheriting the promises. Some of the most interesting and instructive portions of the Bible are those in which we have a delineation of the life and character of those who in the midst of a crooked and perverse generation, did shine as lights in the world. And this scriptural example would seem to recommend the propriety of preserving a faithfml record of the lives of those who were a blessing to the age and the country in which they lived. But not unfrequently it happens that the most useful men are so constantly employed in an unostentatious way, in works of faith and labors of love, that they have had neither leisure nor disposition to preserve a record of passing events with which they were identified. And hence the biographer searches in vain for such materials, as would enable him to do anything like justice to their memory. This dffiiculty is very sensibly experienced at the present moment, while I undertake to give a brief sketch of the life of a dear friend, who was removed from the scene of his earthly labors in the vigor of his days, and in the midst of his usefulness.

The Rev. Charles Strong, son of James and Letitia Strong, was born August 4th, 1788. The offspring of Christian parents, he enjoyed the unspeakable advantage of a good religious education in early life. By the diligence and care of his pious parents, he was, while yet a child, made familiar with that admirable summary of Christian doctrine which is contained in the Westminster standards. And in addition to the religious training which he enjoyed under the parental roof, it was his privilege to enjoy the pastoral care of that thorough theologian, and that devoted minister of Christ, Rev. John Hemphill, D. D. Of the time when he was brought to submit to the yoke of Christ, and of his early Christian experience, the writer of this brief sketch has no definite information. All that is known with certainty is, that profiting by the religious instruction which he received, he was kept from running into those follies and irregularities into which so many of our youth are precipitated; and while he was yet young, he began to seek after the God of his father; and at an early period of life, made a public profession of the name of Christ. While yet a child, being distinguished for a sprightly and teachable disposition, and manifesting a fondness for books, his worthy father resolved to give him a good education, with a view to qualify him for usefulness in the church of God. Accordingly he entered the academy at Monticello, which was under the care of the Rev. James Rodgers, an institution somewhat famous in its day, and in which many of our distinguished professional men in the South received the rudiments of their education.

Having acquired that classical and scientific knowledge necessary to an entrance upon the study of a profession, Mr. Strong, deeply impressed with a sense of his obligation to redeeming grace, and anxious to make known to others the Saviour who was precious to his own soul, resolved to devote himself to the work of the ministry. Accordingly having made known his intention to the first Presbytery of the Carolinas, he was received as a student of theology; and in the autumn of the year 1811, he repaired to New York and entered the Theological Seminary, which was under the care of Rev. John M. Mason, D. D., that prince of American theologians, and first of pulpit orators. Under this able instructor, Mr. Strong devoted four years to theological studies, the usual term required in this institution. Having completed the preparatory course of study with honor to himself, he returned to his Presbytery and after performing with acceptance the usual exercises of trial, was on the 13th of July, 1815, licensed to preach the Gospel, as a probationer for the holy ministry. For the term of something more than a year, according to the custom of the church, he exercised his ministry among the vacant congregations under the care of the Presbytery. And being received with favor, he was soon urged to accept of a pastoral charge. And having accepted a call from the united congregations of Cannon Creek, King's Creek and Prosperity, he was ordained to the office of the holy ministry, and was installed November 8th, 1816. Here during the short period of his ministry, he discharged the duties of a Christian pastor with much acceptance, securing the confidence and esteem of the people over whom the Holy Ghost had made him an overseer.

In accordance with the arrangements of Divine Providence for the good of society, Mr. Strong selected as the partner of his joys and of his sorrows, Miss Nancy Harris, daughter of John and Martha Harris, to whom he was united in marriage February 13th, 1817. In the person of this lady, the Lord provided for Mr. Strong a wife of singular excellence, distinguished for piety and prudence, and one admirably qualified for the responsible station which she was called to fill.

Occupied in an extensive and interesting field of labor, enjoying the respect of the community and the warm affections of the people of his charge, Mr. Strong seemed to have before him the prospect of usefulness and comfort. Possessing a vigorous constitution, and enjoying a good degree of health, the church was promising herself the long continued enjoyment of his valuable services. But how mysterious are the dispensations of Him whose way is in the sea, whose path is in the great waters, and whose footsteps are not known! In the short space of eight years, the work assigned to this faithful servant in the church below was finished; and he was removed from his field of labor and usefulness on earth, as we trust, to the enjoyment of his reward on high. On the 20th of July, 1824, this young, ardent and devoted laborer in the vineyard of the Lord rested from his labors. His amiable partner remained behind, to mourn her irreparable loss, for the space of eighteen years; and on the 8th of November, 1842, was called, as we trust, to join her husband in the happy world where sorrow never comes.

The fruits of the happy union of this beloved pair, were five children, four daughters and a son. Of the four daughters, the youngest, who was the wife of Mr. A. L. Patterson, of Burke County, Georgia, has already been called to follow her worthy parents. Three, who yet survive, have been called to occupy stations similar to that which their excellent mother adorned, and are the wives of respectable ministers of the Associate Reformed Church. The only son, John Mason Strong, devoted himself to the healing art, and occupied a respectable position in the medical profession.

Mr. Strong was in person of the middle size. In a prepossessing countenance, mildness and benevolence were blended together; and these attractive qualities were lighted up by a peculiarly piercing eye. Gentle and unaffected in his manners, he was a most agreeable companion. Easy of access and familiar in his intercourse, he was always a welcome visitant among his parishioners. Unassuming, and at the same time, dignified in his deportment, his presence commanded respect. In the pulpit, free from everything like pharisaic austerity on the one hand, and levity on the other, his appearance was solemn and impressive. Possessing a voice clear, soft and harmonious, he was always heard with interest. Deeply impressed with a sense of the great importance of holding fast the truth as it is in Jesus, he determined in the exercise of his ministry not to know anything save Jesus Christ and Him crucified. Disregarding matters of curious speculation, as unworthy of a place in the pulpit, it was his aim to preach the Gospel, not with enticing words of man's wisdom, but in demonstration of the Spirit and of power. His preaching consequently was not of that character which is adapted to amuse the curious; but which is suited rather to alarm the careless, to encourage the anxious enquirer, to comfort the mourner in Zion, and to build up the believer in faith and holiness. But well qualified as this good minister of Jesus Christ was to be a successful laborer in the vineyard of the Lord, and greatly needed as his services seemed to be, it pleased God to remove him thus early from the toils and the conflicts of the church below, to enjoy, as we doubt not, the reward of the faithful servant—Blessed are the dead who die in the Lord—they rest from their labors.

————

THE REV. CHARLES STRONG.—Twenty nine years have passed since the author of the following tribute to the memory of the Rev. Charles Strong saw him; still to-day, it seemed to him, as if he saw him, as he had seen him hundreds of times!

He was of a common size, five feet eight or nine inches high; hair black; growing back, and divided above his temples, so as to expose his noble, intellectual forehead; eyes black; teeth good; face well formed, and rather ruddy, betokening health; his disposition was cheerful and happy, and this was seen in his lively, pleasant countenance.

He, with Joseph and James Lowry, entered the South Carolina College, among the first students, probably, in 1805 or 1806. Their necessities compelled them to board themselves; this they did by furnishing their own provisions, and cooking for themselves, in a room of the College near to their dormitories and study, which they were permitted thus to use.

Notwithstanding this difficulty, by which many of the present youth would not only be startled, but would be turned back from the pursuit of an education, these clever young men pursued their studies with unabated ardor, and graduated, in December, 1808, good scholars, and prepared to be useful men. All these afterwards became ministers of the Gospel, teachers and preachers of their mighty Master's word.

Charles Strong, immediately after his graduation, took charge of the Newberry Academy, and there taught until the summer of 1812, with great ability and success. His school was a large one, and beyond all doubt fully remunerated him for his labors.

No better teacher could *then* have been found, his pupils showed *then* and *since* that they had been well taught. Gen. James Gilliam, Judge O'Neall, and F. B. Higgins, Esq., are three of his surviving pupils.

In 1812 he left Newberry, and went to New York to enter upon his ministerial course of study. At the end of three or four years he returned home, married Miss Harris, of Mecklenburg, N. C., and took charge of the Associate Reformed Presbyterian congregations of Prosperity, Cannon's Creek, King's Creek and Head Spring, in Newberry. When his services *there* began is not certainly known; he was, however, thus employed before 1818; he settled among his people, within about six miles of Newberry C. H., on the road leading from the Black Jack, by William Spence's to the Long Lane, and there lived in great comfort and happiness, dispensing benefits and blessings all around him, until the summer of 1824. In the latter part of July, or the first days of August, he was called from his labors *here* to his everlasting rest! He was attacked with a high grade of bilious fever, and died in a few days, leaving a wife, four daughters and a son surviving him.

On the first Monday of August, in the town of Newberry, in the presence of a great many auditors, Judge O'Neall, the President of the Newberry Bible Society, auxiliary to the American Bible Society, delivered before them, in an extra meeting called for that purpose, the following address. It was the outpouring of the heart of a pupil and intimate friend, when his memory and virtues were fresh, and is therefore more to be depended on as faithful than anything which could now be given:

Fellow-Members: It has become my duty to announce to the Society the mournful event which causes it to meet. The death of our late President, the Rev. Charles Strong, was a circumstance so deeply affecting our interest and feelings as to justify an extra meeting. It has always been regarded by all bodies, whether civil or religious, as proper to bestow some mark of respect upon the memory of departed worth. It is true, it cannot be of any value to the dead, but it is of vast importance to the living. It sanctifies all our feelings of love, affection and respect, and in the language of Ossian, "It is like the memory of joys which are past; pleasant, yet mournful to the soul." The effect of such a tribute of respect, in exciting individuals to be also worthy, is manifest and striking. If the good and great men were permitted to descend to the tomb without any observation or comment, all the effects of their virtues would be lost with their names. Society might mourn in silent sadness the loss, but no voice would arise from the tomb, bidding the survivors to "go and do likewise."

To those who knew our deceased brother eulogy is unnecessary! His life spoke the good man in every sense of the word! His virtues were proclaimed in every act of his life, whether public or private! And, were it reasonable for me, in the present state of affairs, to seek for the name of an individual on whom there was neither spot nor blemish, I should exultingly place my finger upon that of the Rev. Charles Strong! It has been my good fortune to know him long, and to know him intimately; and whether in the relation of a teacher or of a friend, he was alike the object, not only of my respect, but also of an attachment which nothing but death could have terminated. The principal public duties of Mr. Strong's life were those of a teacher, a minister of the Gospel, and a founder of this Society. As a teacher, no individual could have boasted more of uninterrupted success; and no person of his age enjoyed in that capacity a more extended fame. Many of his pupils are now before me, and with me they will bear witness to the value of his instructions; and with me they will say, "We owe him a debt of gratitude which can never be extinguished." As a preacher Mr. Strong never pretended to the highest claims of eloquence. He taught lessons of Christianity in the plain language of honesty and truth. He addressed the understandings of his hearers with the arguments of reason and piety, and like the dews of heaven they descended, spread over and adhered to every mind. One might have thought it strange that people could listen to him without feeling the necessity of worshiping God in spirit and in truth! He sought not to make converts by terror, but by love! He did not hold out God as an object of terror, but of love unto his congregations! Although possessing great learning himself, he never sought to array his sermons with its pedantry; they were delivered in plain, unornamented language, suited to the feelings and capacities of his hearers; and as such he rendered them practically useful; and hence he became, not one of the most eloquent, but one of the most useful ministers of the Gospel. That he was in earnest in his calling, and that he endeavored to teach others to be what he really was, the good Christian, needs no demonstration. His congregations, his friends, his acquaintances, and even those who never saw him but once, will bear witness to it. From the time he was ordained a preacher of the Gospel, he was "the vigilant watchman on the tower," proclaiming at all times the approach of the enemy. Temporal, when contrasted with eternal things, were considered as trash; and as one of the shepherds of Christ's flock, His staff and His scrip were preferred by him. His eyes were turned to the living God, whom he worshiped in spirit and in truth; and to His throne and the mercy-seat of Christ he diligently called the attention of all people to whom his ministry extended.

Mr. Strong was the founder of the Newberry Auxiliary Bible

Society. He was not only its founder, but also its support. His exertions prevented it from sharing, in common with many other good undertakings, an untimely fate. His unwearied attention to it, and his virtues, carried it triumphant through all its past difficulties. As being the means of distributing the word of God to the poor and needy, the ignorant and uninformed, the bond and the free, he cherished this society. It is, and it ought to be, a living record of his Christian worth. The relations of life, whether those of neighbor, friend, husband or parent, were all discharged by Mr. Strong in that way which will endear his memory to every one. When the tomb closed upon his body, it did not spread the pall of darkness upon his name. His neighbors, his friends, his wife and his children will shed, it is true, many a tear of regret over his grave, but yet sorrowing and in tears, they will say he was a good neighbor, a steadfast friend, and an affectionate husband and parent!

Such, fellow-members, is a brief outline of our founder, former President, and fellow-member. His death, while yet in early life, has deprived us and society in general of his valuable services. For such a loss and deprivation we must grieve; but that grief ought to be tempered and restrained by a pious resignation to the will of Divine Providence. We should say with Job, "The Lord gave and the Lord hath taken away, blessed be the name of the Lord!" And our tears should be dried up with the recollection of our deceased friend and brother, in the exchange of time for eternity, has entered upon that happy state, "Where the wicked cease from troubling, and the weary are at rest." But notwithstanding the consolations of religion may dry up our tears, yet a sincere grief for his loss, a just and a virtuous attachment to his memory, and the claims of society, require of us a last tribute of respect.

"Hic saltem accumulem donis, et fungar, inani munere."

NO. 8.

In approaching the fulfillment of the promise given, at the close of No. 7, I think it necessary to say a word or two more as to the location of the town of Newberry. It is situated immediately between the north and south branches of Scott's or Scotch Creek, and about a mile above their junction. The name of the creek is, in my estimation, doubtful. For, although the pronunciation most general is Scotch creek, yet I have never been able to see the slightest reasons why it should be so called. The other name may be traced to an old settler, Thomas Scott, who lived near the south branch.

The town was originally entirely confined to the space between Harrington, Adams, Boundary and McKibbin streets. It was subsequently extended east as far as Chancellor Johnston's homestead. The corporation now extends a mile, every way, from the court house, and I hope, in less than five years, all this space will be fully occupied by an active, enterprising population. The streets are entirely too narrow, being only 33 feet wide; they were thus granted by the proprietors, John and Henry Coate. They are generally described in the deeds "with the privilege of a street 33 feet wide, all around an acre square." If any of them should ever be abandoned as streets, then, instead of belonging to the lot owners, they will revert to the heirs of the proprietors. It is proper to remark, that in all the lots recently laid off in connection with the extension of the town west, they have been laid out 40 and 50 feet wide. The Greenville and Columbia Railroad now soon thus far to be completed, passes around the south and western parts of the village.* The depot is immediately between the extension of Pratt and Friend streets. It stands upon an elevation which overlooks the whole of the old town, which lies east of it. The town of Newberry, when it comes to be well built up east, south, west and north of the depot, will be a very

---

*In March, 1851, it reached Newberry, and with all its branches (164 miles) was finished December, 1853. The town of Newberry is now a beautiful, prosperous one; it contains 1,800 inhabitants.

beautiful one. The north branch of Scott's Creek will run through it, just at the base of the depot hill; along its southern margin will run the extension of Harrington until it intersects Drayton street. Newberry may, like old Rome, boast of being built on her seven hills, and may even point to the creek winding its way through her clustering houses, as her Tiber. But if this dream, as many of our *wise ones* will no doubt call it, should ever be realized, I hope that the town of Newberry will never be disgraced by civil dissensions, immoral practices, or that most hateful and disorganizing of all business, *the dram shop;* but on the contrary, that she will be blessed by a harmonious, honest, working, sober, patriotic and religious people. If this be so, I shall proudly point to the town where much of my life has been spent, and to the prosperity of which I have devoted many of my energies, as worthy of all praise and imitaiton.

It may not be amiss, too, to remark that the supposition that the town is unhealthy is entirely without foundation. There was once good reason to say that it was so; but since the removal in 1831, of Farnandis' mill pond on the north fork of the creek, and since the Town Council have bestowed a *little care*, on the cleanliness of the streets, there is no local cause for disease; and accordingly, for several years past, it may challenge comparison for health, with any of the towns of the interior.

There are two meeting houses in the town.* The Baptist was built in 1832, for the church which grew out of the great revival of 1831. This extraordinary outpouring of the Spirit took place under the preaching of Elder N. W. Hodges, assisted by Messrs. Barnes, Chiles and Furman. The church thus gathered together, where none before existed, has had the services of Elders Barnes, Hodges, Mangum, Lindsey, Frean, Gibson, Landrum, Barnet, and has now those of Elder Brantly. Mr. Hodges was a native of Abbeville, and a graduate of the South Carolina College. He lived from December, 1831, to 1835, in the village. Under his care the church grew and multiplied greatly. He was afterwards the agent of the Baptist State Convention and resided at Greenwood for

---

*There are now six, besides those mentioned in the text, are the Presbyterian, Episcopal, Seceders, and Lutheran.

several years, until he was transferred to the Furman Institute, and took charge of the classical school. In 1842 he finished his useful labors and was gathered to his rest. His second wife preceded him by a few weeks; their children have been cared for by their brethren and sisters. Thomas Frean united himself to the Baptist Church, at Newberry, on leaving the Methodist connection, in which he had been a local preacher. He was ordained, and occupied the place of Pastor of the church for a few years; indeed, until he was elected Surveyor General, and removed to Columbia. He is an Irishman; he has fine talents, and has very faithfully improved them. He still lives in Columbia. Long may he be spared to his family and to usefulness. The other meeting house is the Methodist. It was built about 1833. A very respectable body of Methodists and pious Christians there worship God. The Presbyterian house of worship called Aveleigh is about one and a half miles from the town.* John Coate, (little) the original proprietor of the town, and of course the first resident, did not live within the first village, as laid off by himself. Indeed it was not extended beyond his dwelling, (on the lot now owned by Dr. Thompson,) until after the death of his son, Capt. Henry Coate. I have no distinct recollection of John Coate. He must have died between 1802 and 1804. He was represented as a very skilful mechanic, capable of executing almost anything, as a blacksmith, or as a silversmith. He left many children, two of whom, Henry Coate and Marmaduke Coate, lived at different times in the village, and had much to do with its prosperity.

Henry Coate was the deputy of Sheriff John Speake, the first District Sheriff of Newberry, who was elected in December, 1800, and entered on the duties of his office in February, 1801. Most of the business of the office was conducted by the deputy, who was a man of business, and every way worthy of the trust. He performed the disagreeable duty of executing the first man hanged at Newberry, William Tate, otherwise called and better known as William Tannyhill, who was convicted at March Term, 1802, and executed for horse stealing. In connection with this unfortunate man's fate may be stated a circumstance which created much excitement at the time:

* Removed to the town.

Two physicians, (one of whom was afterwards a man of much distinction,) determined on possessing themselves of the body. The poor culprit, at his request, was decently interred, and he had also made arrangements to have his grave inclosed.

The doctors succeeded in disinterring the body, and dissecting it. One of them, who, then lived at Dr. Biellers, (now Chancellor Johnston's plantation, at the mouth of Bush River,) put the bones in a bag, and actually carried them home, more than ten miles, at night. Just as he reached Geo. McKinsey's (now Dr. Bobo's present residence,) his bag became untied, and he lost a part of the skeleton; he roused McKinsey from his sleep, got a light, and to the horror of the stout farmer gathered up the *disjecta membra*, (the scattered bones,) and pursued his homeward way. The report got out, that he boiled the bones in Bieller's still, and many a whiskey drinker turned with loathing from the after runs of whiskey there made. The doctors were indicted for this sacriligious invasion of the rest of the grave; one, the most guilty, fled the country, the other remained, and against him the prosecution was allowed to fall.

After this episode, which is longer than the main discourse, I must be allowed to return to Capt. Coate. He commanded for many years the company of cavalry, originally raised by Maj. William Craig and Frederick Nance, and finally commanded by Capt. John Cappleman.* He was the surrogate of the Ordinary, Samuel Lindsey, Esq., (except a brief interval, which was filled by John Gould,) to his resignation, in

---

* This company, originally a very fine one, dwindled down to a very poor troop. The horses and accoutrements of the troopers were very remarkable for their lack of every thing to constitute cavalry. I remember very well to have seen the squadron reviewed in 1808, south of the Academy. One of the men belonging to Cappleman's troops was McCart; he had neither cap nor other cavalary equipment, except a long dragoon's sword; he rode a very small pony. In one of the charges he was fully 100 yards in the rear, accompanied by a dog, nearly as large as his charger. One of the students defeated McCart's file coverer by throwing a stone at, and hitting the poor dog, and sending him yelping from the field. It was on that occasion that the reviewing officer drawing up his command in line before the Academy, said to Cappleman's company, "Gentlemen, if I was in your places I would be ashamed of riding such little rat tail ponies, which I could take by the tail, and sling over the Academy at one jerk."

1815. He was also the deputy of Sheriff Long, in his brief sheriffalty of 1807. After his marriage to his first wife, Elizabeth Long, he ceased to reside in the then village. After her death, he married her sister, Mary. He died in 1827. Of him, I may well say, that he had many, very many excellent qualities.

Maj. Frederick Nance was, I presume, the first settler at and within the limits of the village of Newberry. He was a native of Amelia County, Virginia; he was born the 13th day of August, 1770, and died the 10th of February, 1840. He lived in the house now owned by his daughter, Mrs. Dorothy B. Pratt.* He married Elizabeth Rutherford, the daughter of Col. Robert Rutherford. Maj. Nance was the deputy of Wm. Malone, the first County Clerk of Newberry, from May term '91, till February, '94, when he ceased to be the deputy and Wm. Satterwhite was appointed in his place. At May term, '94, Wm. Malone resigned, and Maj. Nance was appointed County Clerk in his place. When the County Courts were abolished in January, 1800, and the Circuit District Courts established in '98 and '99, went into operation, he was recommended and appointed by the Governor, Clerk of Newberry, and continued in office until 1807, when he resigned, and Y. J. Harrington, Esq., our present excellent Clerk, succeeded him.† The writer had not that sort of knowledge in 1807, which would enable him to speak with accuracy of the discharge of the duties of Clerk by Maj. Nance; but judging from his records, and *then* reputation, it is due to him to say that no one could have better discharged the duties. Indeed, few men had the influence which he had while in that office; he was pretty much the legal adviser of all the citizens.‡ The process of arraignment of a criminal is a very imposing one, when properly carried out. The fine person of Maj.

---

* Mrs. Pratt is no more.

† Mr. Harrington died fall of 1850.

‡ He was also a merchant and laid the foundations of the wealth which he realized in the successful pursuit of that business. His direction to Y. J. Harrington, who was in 1799 his clerk, and who then had little acquaintance with the people trading at Newberry, is so creditable to our German population that it ought to be generally known. He said to him, "Whenever a Dutchman asks for credit, you need not hesitate about it, and without consulting any one, you may give the credit asked."

Nance, and his full knowledge of, and correct arraignment of a prisoner, made, in the spring of 1807, a deep impression on the writer, who, as a country boy, looked upon and listened to that ceremony when James Toland was put to the Bar. How he acquired the title of major ought perhaps to be stated: he was the lieutenant of the company of cavalry raised by Craig and himself. When Craig became the major, he rose to be captain. Prior to his promotion, Henderson and Williams, lieutenants in other companies, junior to him, became captains. On Craig's abdication of the command of the squadron, by leaving the country, Col. Creswell, who commanded the regiment, held under the law providing for promotion by seniority, that as Frederick Nance was the oldest lieutenant in the squadron, although the junior captain, he was entitled to the command of the squadron. He accordingly commissioned him major, and as such he commanded, at one regimental or squadron muster. Captains Henderson and Williams protested against Colonel Creswell's decision, and a Court of Inquiry reversed it. The consequence was that Frederick Nance and John Henderson both resigned, and James Williams became the major. After Major Nance's resignation of the clerkship, he was a candidate for Congress to fill up General Casey's unexpired term; he was defeated by Capt. Joe Calhoun; but he received an almost unanimous vote in Newberry. He was elected Lieutenant-Governor, December, 1808, and qualified with the Governor, John Drayton. In 1812, he was elected Senator in the State Legislature from Newberry, and served two terms. In 1816 he was appointed the Elector of President for the Congressional District, consisting of Newberry, Fairfield and Laurens, and voted for James Monroe, President, and Daniel D. Tompkins, Vice-President. Having served for two years, as a Representative, while Major Nance was Senator, enables me to say that Newberry never has had a more faithful and useful servant than he was. The deafness, which was creeping on him, induced him to decline a re-election in 1820, and he ever after lived a private man. He was twice married: his first wife I have already named. The death of this excellent lady took place in 1829; her many virtues endeared her not only to her own family, but also to her many friends. None, however, felt her loss like her husband. In 1831, he married Mrs. Theresa Ruff, who survived him. By his first marriage, he had eleven children, nine of whom, Robert R., Dorothy B., Drayton, Amelia, Frederick, Sarah, Frances, Alfred and Laura, lived to be men and women; by his last marriage, he had one daughter, Martha, now Mrs. Calmes.*

Major Nance was a useful man. He was a good neighbor, a firm friend, a devoted husband and father. Having known him from my childhood to his death, it is right and proper that I should say he well deserves to be remembered, when Newberry presents her most respectable and worthy citizens.

I think, at one time, Samuel Lindsey, Esq., lived in the village, and occupied as a tavern the old house, which stood on the ground, where the brick hotel now stands. This gentleman was a soldier of the Revolution; he, with his brothers, John, James, Thomas and Col. John Adam Summer, under the command of Col. Philemon Waters, brought off a field piece at the battle of Stono, which had been abandoned by its officers and men. From '99 to 1815 he was the Ordinary of Newberry District, and I regret to be compelled to say, that his office was neither well kept, nor its duties well understood. In 1813 an attempt was made by John Gould to have him impeached; this was pursued until December, 1814, when, after a regular hearing before a committee, of which Samuel E. Kenner was chairman, it was recommended that articles should not be preferred against him; this was concurred in by the House; and thus the matter ended. He was an intelligent, venerable looking man; he wrote a good hand but never understood anything of accounts. He drank intoxicating drinks to excess for many years before 1815; in the beginning of that year, he was struck with paralysis, which deprived him of the power of speech, and the use of his right hand, so that he could not write. In this miserable condition, he, by his surrogates, John Gould and Henry Coate, discharged the duties of his office until November 1815, and actually made his mark to many an official paper. His resignation, in November, 1815, was sent to the Legislature, and James Farnandis, Esq., very much to the honor and advantage of Newberry, succeeded him.

* Of these nine only two, Frederick and Laura, in '58 survived.

Samuel Lindsey lived many years after the sad visitation of Providence, to which I have alluded; in his old age, and laboring under this grievous infirmity, he experienced a change of heart, and was united to the Baptist Church. He lived to be an old man, beyond three score and ten. He died probably in 1826 or 1827.

Here I may be permitted to remark, that with this exception, and possibly Sheriff Speake, Newberry, from 1785 to this time, has never had *a bad public officer. Never has a surety of a Sheriff, Ordinary, Tax Collector, Clerk, or Commissioner in Equity, been compelled to pay a cent for any default, in any one of these public offices! This is high praise*, but it is true; and hence the unexampled prosperity of Newberry. Such a thing as ruling a Sheriff *here* to compel him to pay money which he has collected, and about the application of which there is no dispute, *is, ever has been, and I hope ever will be, unknown.*

No. 8 CONTINUED.

The old tavern occupied by Captain Lindsey, as he was often called, was afterwards occupied and kept by Nicholas Vaughan for a short time. There was nothing remarkable in his life upon which I can put my finger. His sons, by his first marriage, Drury, James and Walter V., were very well known in Laurens and Newberry. His second wife was Nancy Lee, the widow of Andrew Lee, of Lee's ferry, on Saluda. (Of her and her first husband, when I come to speak of the Revolution, I may detail an anecdote.) By his second marriage he had one or more children. He died on Saluda, I think, about 1804 or 1805.

William Satterwhite, (commonly called Buck Satterwhite,) who was the deputy of William Malone, County Clerk from February, '94 to May, '94, and who was the Sheriff of the County from '98 till 1801, kept tavern in the house above described. It is probable he preceded Nicholas Vaughan. During the time he kept this house, his wife eloped with Maj. Wm. Craig, leaving behind her, her infant child. Strange to say, she and Craig lived in Florida and Georgia, as man and wife, happily and respectably. Maj. Craig was an United Irishman of 1791, the object of which Society was, as stated in the address of '93, "universal enfranchisement and a real representation of the people in Parliament." Like Rowan and others, he had to fly from his country, where I have always understood he left a wife and children. He was a merchant at Newberry, and did business in a house which stood where the house now occupied by Mr. Jones as a cabinet maker's shop stands, and which was burnt. My impression is, he built in its place the house now standing, and there did business, until he fled from Newberry, taking with him the wife of his landlord and friend, in 1799.

This was a death blow to the injured husband; his habits of drink. which were verging to excess before, now became confirmed, and opened to him an early grave !

John Anderson, the third person buried in the village graveyard, kept tavern at Newberry. My impression is, he kept tavern, in 1802, in the house now owned and occupied by Hugh K. Boyd as a kitchen, afterwards in the house occupying the site of the brick hotel. A celebrated wag, (John Gould) has often told, that at that period, "the various boarders at Mr. Anderson's hotel, each morning paraded on the hill, where the Courthouse stands, before breakfast; when the horn blew, each started at the top of his speed; if any one stumped his toe, he turned back, well knowing before he could get in all would be eat up."

The house (Boyd's) was afterwards occupied by Jacob Lewis, who was dubbed by the mischievous wags "Chewwink," after a little bird having a cry somewhat resembling that name, and remarkable for its habit of bobbing up and down on a limb.

Poor Jake was a good natured, honest man utterly unfit for such a business; and to use a cant expression, "he was soon used up." While living in Newberry, his niece was supposed to have taken laudanum. Jake was seen posting early in the morning to the doctors; "Where are you going, Jake?" was the inquiry, "I am going after the doctor, that d——d nephy of mine has taken lodamy draps," was the answer.

Among the early settlers of Newberry was Dr. Samuel Todd, who was a sojourner for a short time; he subsequently moved to, and died in Laurens, possessed of great wealth. Of him, during his sojourn at Newberry, a most laughable anecdote was told by John Thweatt. The Doctor was an Irishman, fresh from the *sod.* He had heard a great deal about bees; in a plum orchard, near the village, he fancied he had found a swarm; running into the house, he communicated the fact to his wife, who, like himself, was from Ireland: "Och, Dr. dear, and how shall we know our baes from Maj. Nance's baes?" was her anxious response. "Och, child," said the Dr., "our baes can be kenned well enough, they are as ba faced and as white-legged as our sorrel mear." He procured Peter Julien to hive the bees for him, and sadly to the cost of both, they found, instead of a swarm of bees, a large hornet's nest.

Peter Julien, better known as Esquire Julien, was long a magistrate, and afterwards the Coroner of Newberry District. He often lived in the village, and finally killed himself, where the old road leading through Chancellor Johnston's possessions by Frank Aikins old place into the Charleston road, near Esquire McCalla's residence, turned off from the Columbia road. This fatal deed was performed by hitching the trigger of a shot gun on the limb of a bush and holding the gun to his breast, and pulling it forward. He was an old man, full of years, when he thus foolishly and madly cut short his career.

John Thweatt! who does not remember John? beyond doubt one of the most witty men who ever lived in this land. He was a native of Virginia. He lived often in the village. He was as remarkable for his good humor as his wit; yet to him was left the honor of beating the bullies of the Fork, and the Chinquepins, and thus making them very peaceable men. I allude to Honorius Sheppard and Wm. Montgomery, (commonly called Billy McGlamery.) John's usual occupation was wagoning. It is impossible to embody in such an article as this, the innumerable anecdotes in which he was concerned. I mention one with a view to follow it up, by showing in his after life, that impenitence did not follow and close it up against hope. Driving his wagon on a warm day, in the spring, on a return trip from Charleston, along the old road, above Orangeburg, he came opposite to a clearing, in which a man and his sons had been engaged in burning the logs. They were as black and dirty as lightwood smoke and sand could make them; as soon as John saw them, he leaped from his horse, and kneeling down, he prayed in a loud voice "Great God, be pleased to send a shower to wash these poor people, for I have often heard that nothing unclean shall enter into the kingdom of heaven, and if they should now be cut off in their present unclean condition, they never *there* can enter!" The amazement of his auditors may be imagined, it cannot be described.

He left Newberry for Georgia, where I think he now lives, a member of, and I have heard, a preacher of the Methodist denomination. Thus, indeed, although he began to pray in ridicule, he now, like Saint Paul, may be pointed out as a convert, for *"lo! he prayeth!"*

The "L" house, owned and occupied by Dr. Long, was built by Major Thomas W. Waters in '99 or 1800. Its first occupants (whom I remember) were John, George and Lewis McCreless. The latter was killed soon after he came to the village near the mile stone on the Columbia road, by his horse running away with him, and throwing him against a tree. He was the first person buried in the village graveyard. Miss Bond, the daughter of John P. Bond, of Lexington, and niece of John McCreless, was the second.

Of George McCreless, I have already spoken. John McCreless was a very remarkable man. Few men surpassed him in his capability to discharge any business. His information, for the time he lived at Newberry, between '99 and 1806, was rather above the common standard. He composed pretty good poetry. A friend, from memory, has furnished me with the following:

> "Billy McGlamery is come to town
>   To empty cups and glasses!
> He takes the taverns, in a line,
>   And drains them as he passes.
> He robs the flies of what is their right,
>   And leaves them not a taste, sir,
> I warrant you he stays all night,
>   To see that nothing wastes, sir!"

He sold out his possessions to Mr. John Johnston, the father of Chancellor Johnston, and removed from Newberry. I next met with him in 1811, as a tavern keeper at Spring Hill, Lexington District. He was subsequently elected the Clerk of the Court for that district, removed to or near Granby, and discharged the duties of Clerk, Register of Mesne Conveyances, Commissioner of Locations and Ordinary, until the Court was removed from Granby to Mrs. Corley's, the present seat of justice, Lexington Court House. This was about 1820. The last I knew of him was in the neighborhood of Columbia, in 1829. Since then I have lost sight of him; whether he be dead or not, I cannot say, though I presume he is.

Daniel Brooks, Esq., was another of the early settlers of Newberry. He lived on the lot where Dr. Harrington lived in 1850; he built the house which Vincent V. Pope removed from it. Brooks was a saddler by trade and a man of much intelligence; he wrote a good hand; he was long a magistrate of Newberry. He lived a few years since in the neighborhood of Due West Corner, Abbeville. His son John was one of the brave men, who went out from Newberry as a volunteer in the Mexican campaign, and returned, after treading, in victory and triumph, the streets of Mexico. Since, he madly put an end to his life.

Samuel Ker, Esq., was the first lawyer who ever resided in Newberry; he was *here*, I know in 1804; how much earlier he occupied the ground I do not certainly know, probably in 1803. He lived in the house just spoken of, he had a fine practice; but was not, I think, a very well educated lawyer. Connected with his name and family is another very interesting reminiscence. His wife and her sister were from the West Indies. The latter, on the voyage thence to Charleston, was engaged to McNeill, of the firm of Sherman & McNeill, of Charleston. He alleged that the engagement was a mere piece of badinage on his part, but she made it earnest. They were married; the firm failed. McNeill, after sojourning for a time at Newberry, left for his place of nativity, Caswell County, North Carolina. He had contracted habits of intoxication, which soon carried him to his grave. One child was the issue of the marriage. In 1815, I saw his widow, she, who had once revelled in wealth, who had been the associate of taste, fashion and refinement, in a cabin, not 15 feet square, in the wild woods of a very remote part of Caswell County, every tittle of furniture about the house was not worth twenty dollars. At her feet were children born in her widowhood. Her child by McNeill was in the care of a highly respectable gentleman, James Yancey, Esq. How sad are the consequences of intemperance! Ker removed about 1806 from Newberry to Louisiana, possibly to New Orleans.

Simon T. Sherman, of the firm of Sherman & McNeill, Charleston, though not an inhabitant of the village, yet was the son-in-law and surrogate of Samuel Lindsey, Esq. He lived near the ford of the creek, on the road from Newberry to Higgin's ferry. He lies buried somewhere near the place where he lived, in that part of the plantation of Judge O'Neall on the creek, and above the ford but where, though often sought for, cannot be ascertained. He died between 1811 and 1812, leaving, notwithstanding the failure of his firm, a considerable property in the possession of his widow; but a large debt of the firm to Hugh Patterson, for Penman, Shaw & Co., was set up after his death, and although compromised at a great deal less than was due, swept off the great bulk of his property.

George Schoppert settled in Newberry in '99. He went there as a mechanic, in the employment of his' brother-in-law, Thomas W. Waters, who was engaged in building the jail, the courthouse, and out of the refused timber for these public buildings, his "L" house herein before spoken of. Mr. Schoppert was an industrious house carpenter; he soon made out to buy the western quarter acre of the lot now belonging to Dr. Harrington. Here he lived from "99 to 1826, when he died. Here he raised his children, Precious, Philip, Joseph and Elizabeth; all of whom, except Philip, are no more. Mr. Schoppert built most of the houses in the Village and its vicinity from '99 to his death. He was the ensign of the Newberry Artillery Company, and served the tour of duty at Camp Alston in 1814. He came to this State from Maryland, but I think he was a native of Pennsylvania. He was a soldier in the army embodied to put down the Whiskey Insurrection, and when in his cups, used to take great delight in singing an old soldier's song, beginning "We are the boys who fear no noise." The Dutch dance, "Hoop so saw" was another of his favorites, when he had a taste too much of the "overjoyful." He was of German descent, and was as hard working, honest, industrious a man as ever the sun shone upon. From great poverty, he struggled on to rather more than competence, notwithstanding an expensive family. His widow Catherine survived him. She was an universal favorite in the mirth-loving village of Newberry. Caty Chopper, as she was usually called, and her snuff-box were synonymous with *fun*, until 1819, when she became a member of the Methodist Church. Her husband soon followed and died 1825. She died about 1829. Their child, Joseph, died before either of them, I think in 1817 or 1818. Precious married Dr. Thomas Shell, whom she survived; Elizabeth married Joel Stevenson, who survived her; Philip is now an inhabitant of Eutaw, Alabama. Like his father, he was a house carpenter; he partook much of his mother's temperament; he loved mischief and fun, and was rarely surpassed at either. No man has spent a more laborious life, and no one has more signally failed in securing even competence. He, like his parents, is a Methodist, and is, I believe, a Christian. If my good wishes could change the adverse current against which he has been rowing, he would have *them* now as he has ever had, with now and then a little more substantial than good wishes.

John Speake, the Sheriff from February, 1801, to February, 1805, never lived at the court house. He was a soldier of the Revolution, and died, I presume, since 1828. The office of Sheriff had not many duties in his time; such as they were, he had but little to do with them. He, however, whipped the first man I ever saw whipped for the violation of the law. At October Term, 1802, John Sloan (calling himself Col. John Sloan,) a stranger in our community, was indicted before Judge Brevard, at Newberry, and convicted of passing, knowing it to be counterfeit, a counterfeit double guinea which was not current coin, and therefore not within the statutes against counterfeiting the current coin or passing such counterfeited current coin, knowing it to be counterfeit. I see, on looking to the indictment, he was indicted merely for passing a counterfeit double guinea knowing it to be counterfeit. I apprehended on such an indictment, no judgment could have been awarded, if the matter had been properly canvassed. I presume from the sentence passed; it must have been awarded under the statute, 3 H. 8. c. 1, "against them that counterfeit letters, or privy tokens to receive money or goods in other men's name," and which provides punishment for such as be thereof convicted, "by imprisonment of his body, setting upon the pillory or other corporal pain, (except pains of death"). The culprit was tied to the hickory, which once stood east of the old shoe store. He received 39 on his bare back; and every stripe upon his fair and fat back might have been counted by the marks, none of which cut the skin. He said that "it put him into such an exceeding good humor, he seemed as if he loved the world."

No. 8 Continued.

Sheriff Speake was succeeded by P. B. Waters, the son of Col. Philemon Waters, of revolutionary memory, who was elected December, 1804, and entered on the duties of Sheriff in 1805. He married shortly before, or soon after he was elected, Sarah, the daughter of Robert and Elizabeth Gillam. He and his wife lived in the house herein before described, built by Daniel Brooks, Esq. He removed from his plantation on Bush River to the house now owned and occupied by Major John B. McMorries, but did not live to complete it.*

---

* David Gunn, after the removal of Major Cureton, hereafter to be spoken of, lived in this house to his death, in '27 or '28. He was a native of North Carolina, neighborhood of Fayetteville. He came to Newberry about 1811 or 1812. He was a wheelwright: he made gigs and Windsor chairs; he had very little competition, and must have made money. He worked first where Hugh K. Boyd lives; after he bought Cureton's lot, he built a shop on the corner, just opposite to L. J. Jones' dwelling. He

Mr. Waters was a surveyor, and a very good and successful one. The duties of Sheriff he was very competent to perform, and most faithfully did he discharge them. Mr. Waters was the librarian of the Library Society, which was raised about 1803, and consisted of the villagers, and many of the people of the country around. They had a pretty good selection of books, and much good did it do, by placing the means of information within the reach of many who could not otherwise have obtained it. But like many other good things, after a while it began to languish, and "languishing did live" until 1811, when it died, by the members ordering all the books to be sold. I am almost tempted to say, shame upon such folly! Such an institution, *now* in the town of Newberry, would be worth more than thousands of dollars divided amongst its inhabitants. Many an one, with the opportunity of thus getting books, would be found reading instead of bending his elbow at that celebrated place called "Juliu's."

Sheriff Waters died in 1807, (February,) he left two children, and a third was born soon after his decease. His daughter, Mary, is the wife of Philip Schoppert. Robert, his eldest son, emigrated to Texas, was a soldier in the Texan war against Mexico; was captured at Mier, and was long a prisoner in Mexico; was at length released, at the instance of Gen. Thompson, while minister to that republic. In the war of the United States with Mexico, he was one of the Texan Rangers, and died between Matamoras and Monterey. Philemon, his youngest son, emigrated to Alabama, and there died.

No better man ever lived in Newberry than Sheriff Waters He was a well-educated, honest, high-minded man, faithful in the discharge of all his duties, and all the relations of life; he was the worthy son of a worthy sire.

---

was a violent Federalist, and when he came to Newberry he was in the midst of Republicans, and had, therefore, a very uncomfortable time as to politics, for years. For generally he was in a minority of one. He, however, worked constantly, and people overlooked his political errors, on account of his industry. He was a bachelor; when prosperity came to him, it brought in its train habits of drink, which not amounting to drunkenness, yet shortened his days, and wasted his means; he died with little more than paid his debts and the expenses of administration.

The house now occupied by Pope and Farrow,* once stood in the rear of Steele's store house, now General Hunt's; it was then kept by John Gould, as a billiard house. He subsequently was associated with P. B. Waters, as a merchant, and did business in Henry Coate's house, which stood where Steele's store stands. He, in 1814, 1815 and 1816, kept tavern in the "L" house, then the property of James Farnandis.

This gentleman (John Gould) was the nephew of old Bill Gould (the Beaverdam King). He received a pretty good English education; wrote a good hand, and was often employed as a clerk by Capt. Daniel Parkins, Hugh O'Neall, and other merchants. At the sale of the personal estate of Capt. Daniel Parkins, in February, 1803, which extended through a week, he was clerk of the administrators. At that time he got the nickname of "the tongs." He was remarkable for very long and slim legs! A little bird had been caught in the snow, which then for several inches in depth covered the whole country, and given to the youngest child of the deceased, Mark, then an infant; it had fluttered out of his hands, and took refuge under a corner cupboard. Every body was anxious to retake the bird for the weeping child; among the rest, Gould had been in anxious pursuit, and when it took refuge under the cupboard, he got down on all fours, and was reaching under to seize it. Old Billy Mills sitting by the fire, and looking on, observing Gould, said to the company, "Never mind boys, *the tongs* will get it."

Mr. Gould was also a teacher, and along the Beaverdam taught the young idea how to shoot. His frequent residences at Newberry made him the participant in and the maker of many a joke. An example is all which I can give.

Walking one night through the orchard, where Mooney's shop and brick house now stands, he heard some one praying, and walking up to the sound, he found a house carpenter and joiner, Dixon, with his neck handkerchief tied around his neck, and fastened to the limb of an apple

* Since removed to make room for the Newberry Bank and Jones' Law Office.

tree, and him on his knees. Gould said to him, "what are you doing here?" "I am going to Heaven!" was the foolish answer. Gould replied, "everybody will be in bed and asleep before you get there." He untied the handkerchief from the limb, shouldered Dixon, carried him to the fence and threw him over it into the road, and that broke the love charm which was leading the old fool on to suicide. He afterwards married the *mother of the woman* for whom he was then about hanging himself. No man delighted more in mirth and a frolic, than did Gould. He married Charity Lindsay, the daughter of Thomas Lindsay; he had three children by her, one of whom, the youngest daughter, is, I think, married and living in the Dutch Fork. His wife died, and is buried in the village graveyard. After her death he removed to Georgia, and thence to Louisiana. There he was for a long time confined in goal for debt; he was released by an act of the Louisiana Legislature. He was last heard of in Natchez soliciting the charity of his Masonic brethren, and there he died.

No man had higher natural talents; these properly cultivated, directed and sustained by moral principle, would have made him any where, a first-rate man. As it was, early vicious association and habits made him a *free thinker*, and gave a loose rein to his appetites and passions, and when to this was added a continual growing and increasing propensity to drink, it is not wonderful that he did not live out half of his days, and that his life was closed in poverty and suffering.

James Caldwell, Esq., was elected in December, 1807, Sheriff of Newberry in the place of Sheriff Waters; he entered on his duties in February, 1808. He never lived in the village; the active duties of his office were devolved on his deputies, James Farnandis and William Caldwell. I shall have, I hope, hereafter, better means of doing justice to the memory of this good man, who bore upon his face the marks of Cowpen's well-fought field, and therefore for the present I will pass him by.

James . Farnandis was a native of Union District, and came to Newberry about 1805; he was first employed as

the deputy of Major Frederick Nance, then the Clerk of
Newberry. He was one of the deputies of Sheriff Caldwell,
and had charge of the books. His accuracy was then as
manifest, as it subsequently became well known. He married
Sarah, the daughter of John Johnston, about 1810. In
1815, he was elected the Ordinary of Newberry, and set
about the Herculean task of arranging the papers, and
settling on just principles the accounts of the executors,
administrators and guardians, who were accountable to his
jurisdiction. He laid the foundations of that system, which
has, under the successive administration of Cureton, Wilson,
Boyd and Lake made the Ordinary's office, what it ought
to be, the certain security of, and means of redress, for
widows, orphans, and creditors. I know perfectly well that
few men possessed the intelligence or the energy which was
necessary to bring order and right out of the chaotic confusion which then pervaded the Ordinary's office; yet Mr.
Farnandis, in less than three years, accomplished that task;
he resigned in 1818, and was temporarily succeeded by
Robert R. Nance. Thomas T. Cureton was, however, elected
in 1819. Mr. Farnandis from 1812 till 1824 lived about a
mile from the village, on the Higgin's ferry road.* From
1824, to his removal to Mississippi, in 1838, he occupied

---

* At or near this place once lived James Daugherty. *He was a character*, and if I could transfer him to paper, it would well repay that
trouble; but the hope is vain ! He was an Irishman; he always kept bar,
as it was called, for Major Nance, in time of court; that is he sold spirits
for cash; he never gave change; he always made it his rule that the
change should be taken in drink. He was also the Sexton of the burying
ground of Friends at Bush River. He dug a grave for a female acquaintance; by mistake, he put the head, where the feet should have been. Her
sister complained and, said "Jamie, how could thee serve her so?"
"Done it on purpose: she never was like any body else, if you were to
die, I'll dig your grave cross ways," was 'he reply. He was a thriving
farmer, always had corn to sell or give away: a poor man, Robin Perkins,
came to Jamie for a grist; it was freely given, and while shelling it, dinner
came on; Robin was invited in to take "pot luck." When seated, he said
to Jamie, "May I say grace ?" "Yes, say grace, poor soul." He began
and continued, until Jamie's stock of patience was exhausted; he broke
in upon Robin's lengthened petitions, by saying, "Hoot toot, man cut it
short !" Jamie's wit and love of liquor brought him to poverty before
life closed. He died an old man, full of years, near to the plantation of
his friend, John Kelly.

and kept the brick hotel, of which he was part owner.
He was also a merchant for many years, associated first
with Y. J. Harrington. They built in 1815, the brick store
house, where Mr. Robert Stewart has for many years successfully followed the same business. He was afterwards
associated in business with Y. J. Harrington, Birt Harrington
and Alexander Chambers. Mr. Farnandis was one of the
best farmers in Newberry District; he cultivated less to the
hand than most persons, but his plantation looked more
like a garden than corn and cotton grounds. He deserves
to be noticed, too, as a slave owner. His negroes were
well-housed, well-clothed, well-fed, never over-worked, and
whenever an overseer exercised any cruelty on his people,
he was instantly dismissed. When he removed to Mississippi,
his slaves were ready to, and some of them did, abandon
wives and children, (of their own will) rather than be sold,
left here, and thus be separated from their master. This
is as it should be. I would have every Southern planter
like him, and then, indeed, might we say to Abolition
vaunting "Cease vipers, you bite a file." Mr. Farnandis
died in Mississippi about 1843; he left his wife and five
children, to wit: Caroline, John, Henry, Mary and Sarah,
surviving him.

Mr. Farnandis was a firm, unflinching man; he looked
neither to the right hand nor to the left in the discharge
of duty. He was a zealous and devoted friend; he bore
suffering and misfortune with more uncomplaining fortitude
than belongs to most men; he was an honest, just man,
who loved and practiced truth and sincerity. He became a
Campbellite Baptist before his death; and whether there be
error or not in that form of faith, it is not for me, either
now to discuss or praise. Of one thing I am certain, from
my knowledge of Mr. Farnandis, that he firmly believed
his profession to be right, and that he is now in the
blessed company, whose robes have been washed and made
clean in the blood of the Lamb!

No. 8 Continued.

William Caldwell, son of James, (better known as Long

Billy) was one of the deputies of his father,' from 1808 to 1812; he married first the only child of Col. Jas. Creswell, deceased. His second wife was the interesting and intelligent lady, Harriet McDowell. He was the captain commanding the company of cavalry belonging to Col. Tucker's command in the Camp Alston expedition of 1814. Often have I looked upon him, at the head of his well mounted, well-uniformed troop, and have heard his stentorian voice, commanding a charge, and in imagination have contrasted him with Kleber, who, like him, was heard higher than his fellow men, and concluded, if the times had served, his sabre would have led, and pointed many a column to victory. He was elected in 1816, Sheriff of Newberry, and continued in office till February, 1820. He died in 1825; his second wife survived him; he left two sons by his first marriage, James and William. No more noble and generous man ever lived.

The Hon. Ker Boyce mentioned in No. 8, as one of the citizens of the then village, now town of Newberry, has since fulfilled his course and been gathered to his fathers, after a life of honor and usefulness, and it is now altogether proper that the surviving friends of his youth, manhood and age, should give some fuller account of him. He was born 8th of April, 1787, in that portion of Newberry now called Mollohon; he was the fifth son of John Boyce and Elizabeth Miller his wife.

His father was an industrious, thriving Presbyterian Irishman. His sons were taught to live as he did, "whatever his hands found to do, to do it with his might."

The consequence was that they all began with *little*, but that *little* soon became *much.*

Ker Boyce was the clerk, in his commencement, with the late John McMorries. He delighted in recurring to this period of his life, and narrating the many laughable circumstances in which he then bore a part. The impossibility of transferring to paper his mirth-loving and mirth-moving anecdotes, as he was in the habit of narrating them, prevents the attempt.

He subsequently settled at Newberry, where he played deputy Sheriff for a time, and took part in everything calculated to produce fun. Many were the predictions that such a

1   G

mischievous *chap*, as he was, would never be of any account.

But such prophecies were soon shown to be altogether wild.

In 1814 he bought the square lying between Adams and Caldwell and Friend and Pratt Streets, in the town of Newberry, from his future father-in-law, Mr. John Johnston, with his stock of merchandise in the store which he then occupied. This was, as people supposed, the finishing blow for the "*mad cap*," Ker Boyce. An old store, and ruin for a young merchant are regarded as synonymous. But *here* again they were at fault. Mr. Boyce soon shewed that he knew perfectly well what he was about. His business prospered daily.

In December, 1812, he was elected the Tax Collector of Newberry by the Legislature. His description of his electioneering by fun and wit would be worth preserving, but it can not be fully done. One of his opponents had secured, as was supposed, the interest of a leading and excellent member from Greenville, Philemon Bradford. Mr. Boyce boarded at the same hotel and slept in the large room, where Mr. Bradford and his colleagues also slept. Mr. Boyce insisted he must sleep with Mr. Bradford, it was conceded, and by his attentions, wit, and good sense, he so won upon him that in a few days, noticing his (Boyce's) opponent mixing his morning toddy, he said to him "you drink too much, I can not vote for you, I intend to vote for my young friend Boyce." Was not that a good temperance lecture for 1812? How many members of the Legislature of 1854–5 will do so likewise?

Mr. Boyce, finding the duties of his office inconsistent with his mercantile interests, resigned in 1814.

In the year 1813 he began to trade, overland, with Philadelphia. Cotton was hauled from Newberry and goods brought back by wagons. He and the late Thomas Pratt annually mounted their horses and rode to Philadelphia, purchased their goods, and each thus laid the foundation of their respective fortunes.

In 1815 they visited Amelia Island on horseback, purchased a stock of goods, which they understood was there for sale, and transported it to Newberry by wagons.

In this year, perhaps June, he married his first wife, Miss Nancy Johnston, the third daughter of Mr. John Johnston. No more lovely woman ever blessed a husband.

In 1817, finding Newberry to be too narrow a field for his enterprise, he and his brother-in-law, Samuel Johnston, formed a copartnership, and commenced business in King Street, Charleston. Subsequently, they transferred their business to the Bay and became factors and commission merchants. Mr. Johnston was the most perfect man of business with whom 1 ever was acquainted; this added to an excellent judgment of his own as well as his partner's, with the latter's tireless energy and activity, made the firm certain of success, and accordingly they realized large profits. But the hand of death was on Mr. Johnston; he never had fully recovered from a mismanaged attack of bilious fever, in Caswell County, North Carolina, in 1815. Consumption exhibited itself, and remorselessly hunted him down. Before his death, Mr. Henry was associated with them: the firm at his death, I presume in 1822, stood Boyce, Johnston & Henry. Here the writer may be indulged in dropping a tear on the tomb of Samuel Johnston, Jr., and saying he was good, virtuous and worthy of a friendship, which never was broken.

In 1823, Mr. Boyce sustained the first great misfortune of his life, his never enough admired lady died at the house of his brother-in-law, James Farnandis, Esq., and she sleeps the sleep which knows no waking, in the town graveyard of Newberry. Their children, John, Samuel and Mary, now the wife of Wm. Lane, of New York, survived her.

In 1825, was one of the great commercial revulsions, which South Carolina has again and again experienced. Mr. Boyce, on that occasion, trembled in the balance; nothing saved him from ruin, but the assets of his deceased partner, Johnston. He and Mr. Boyce had realized about $50,000; this sum was in Mr. Boyce's hands as surviving partner. He put the whole of it in requisition to save himself from ruin. Then it was, that the friendship of the late Mr. Blackwood, President of the Planters & Mechanic's Bank, stood him in great stead. He had observed Boyce's previous great industry, and when he thought, notwithstanding the assets of Mr. Johnston, he must fail, Mr. Blackwood said to him, he could have funds, to any extent he needed, from the Bank over which he presided. This carried him through.

In, I think, 1826, he had the singular good fortune to

replace the wife which he had lost, by her sister, equally lovely, Amanda Caroline, the sixth daughter of Mr. John Johnston. Mr. Boyce continued most successfully in the firm, first of Boyce & Henry, and then of Boyce, Henry & Walter.

In 1830 began the great Nullification struggle. Mr. Boyce was, *I know*, opposed to this dangerous experiment; but, like many other good men, he was forced by circumstances into the ranks of that party, who for years pressed upon South Carolina the fearful issue of a contest, either with the General Government or between the hostile parties of the State.

When the late Wm. Aiken was unfortunately killed, in March, 1831, the question was debated by the Union party of Charleston, who should be his successor, as a representative from Charleston. The writer was deputed to wait on Mr. Boyce, ascertain his sentiments, and he was told, if you can vouch for him he will be nominated. This was done, in both respects, and yet the Union party, by some strange fatality, nominated another. Gen. Hamilton was too good a tactician to suffer such a blunder to pass unimproved; he fastened upon Mr. Boyce, and with great adroitness, drew him in to go with him and his party, without, as he assured him, requiring any sacrifice *of principle*.

This blunder of the Union party secured the triumph of Nullification. For Mr. Boyce's many business friends scattered all over the State took very much his lead.

Although the writer and Mr. Boyce were, by his siding with Nullification, placed in opposite political ranks, yet it never disturbed their friendship.

When the Bank of Charleston was chartered Mr. Boyce secured a large amount of the stock, and in so doing realized a great deal of money.

In 1837 occurred another great commercial revulsion. In it Mr. Boyce was supposed to be much shaken. After it passed over, he told the writer that "he had to pay $180,000 for his friends and customers; but" said he, "I was taught a lesson in 1825, for no man was I liable who was not in visible property worth more than my liability for htm." To meet this payment he had to sell a large amount of Charleston Bank stock, I think he said not less than $150,000. This he then thought a great misfortune, but it was directly to the contrary. For he sold at a great advance, and in a short time the stock receded below par.

Mr. Boyce was concerned in the greatest improvements of the city. The Charleston Hotel and the Hayne-street buildings are mainly to be ascribed to him.

After the risk which he ran in 1837, he determined to retire from the factorage and commission business, which he accordingly did, and devoted himself to other sources of increasing his great wealth. For the last seventeen years of his life, whatever he touched seemed to realize the fabulous account of becoming gold.

He was President of the Charleston Bank for several years, and Senator for St. Phillip's and St. Michael's for at least two terms.

Between 1836 and 1840 he lost his second wife; no purer Christian, no better wife and mother ever descended to the grave. Mr. Boyce felt the loss was irreparable. He never married again. She left five children, the Rev. James P. Boyce, Nancy, the wife of Mr. Tupper, Rebecca, the wife of Mr. Burckmeyer, Ker and' Elizabeth.

Mr. Boyce's eldest son John died in Florida about '48; his other children still survive.

For many years Mr. Boyce was a private citizen; his family and his estate demanded and received all his attention.

He died at the house of his son, the Rev. James P. Boyce, in Columbia, 19th March, 1854, having nearly completed his 67th year.

He made no profession of religion, although he attended regularly worship at the First Baptist Church of Charleston, of which his second wife was a member, and of which his son, the Rev. James P. Boyce, and several of his other children were subsequently members.

Mr. Boyce, though no professor, felt, I have no doubt, the power of religion in his heart. He was a perfectly moral man. If he ever swore it has escaped the recollection of the writer. He was habitually temperate; when others drank to excess, and it was considered no disgrace, he was sober. He was for many years a member of the Charleston Total Abstinence Society.

Mr. Boyce was a man of high character in every respect;

he was scrupulously honest and punctual; he always demanded his own; if he ever was guilty of a mean thing, it is a matter which to me, who knew him better than most men, is unknown.

He was an ardent and devoted friend. This is not mere. praise, it is a justice, which many of his former friends in Newberry if now alive would vouch, as well as does the writer. One distinguished man in South Carolina was saved by him from utter ruin. It is true he was prudent in succoring his friends; he could and did say "no" at the proper time.

In the circle of his family my opportunity of observing him enables me to say he was the kindest of husbands and fathers. His wife and children met and enjoyed him as their best friend and companion.

At his death he left an immense estate, probably reaching to near two millions. Out of it he devoted $50,000 to charitable education, and if he had been spared a few days longer, it is believed he would have been the liberal and venerated patron of the Furman University. But God, who sees not as man sees, called him from earth, and left to his noble-minded son, the Rev. James P. Boyce, to pour out his wealth upon the cherished institution of his denomination.

The death of such a man is necessarily to be mourned by those who loved or knew him; and yet standing by his tomb we are consoled by reflecting that he lived long, well, and prosperously, and hoping that he is now enjoying more than this world could ever give.

Thomas Taylor Cureton was elected Sheriff in 1812; he, therefore, succeeded James Caldwell, and preceded William Caldwell. Mr. Cureton was, I think, a native of Virginia; his mother Hannah's maiden name was Thweatt; she was the sister of John Thweatt, herein before spoken of. She was from 1804 a very infirm widow. The principal care of her and her daughters devolved upon Thomas T. Cureton, and certainly no son and brother ever discharged his duty better. He was the clerk of Hugh O'Neall in 1807; he was subsequently in the employment of Elisha Hammond, who carried on the mercantile business at Stoney Battery; he purchased out his stock and carried on the business on his own account afterwards. He was elected major of the upper batallion of the now 39th regiment, in 1810. When elected Sheriff, it was very much against the predilection of the villagers, who preferred James McMorries, Esq. Major Cureton was remarkable for his easy good nature. It was therefore predicted by almost every one that he would be ruined by his office. But he employed Anderson Crenshaw, Esq., late Chancellor Crenshaw, of Alabama, and he went through his office by his advice, and therefore without loss. He resigned his commission as major, when he removed to Laurens, about 1817; he was appointed by General Tucker, Deputy Assistant Inspector General of the 9th brigade. He returned to Newberry, and was elected January, 1819, Ordinary of Newberry District, and continued in office till 1827, when he resigned, removed to Georgia, and soon afterwards died. He resigned his brigade staff appointment in 1819. He married soon after he was elected Sheriff, Mary Manning, the youngest daughter of Levi Manning, one of the first County Court Judges. He left several children. Major Cureton for many years before his death was a member of the Methodist Church. He was an honest, conscientious, good man; he wrote a good hand, and understood accounts and book-keeping very well. He discharged with scrupulous exactness and fidelity the duties of his offices, when left to himself; his want of self-reliance sometimes made him yield too ready an ear to designing men. An instance of this kind occurred in the administration of Robert Cates, (deceased,) and had it not been for a plainly mistaken judgment of the Court of Appeals, would have injured him seriously. Their mistake saved a good man from heavy loss; as the opinion has never been published, and the error is not likely to be perpetuated as a matter of law, it may very well be classed as one of those chances where good comes out of wrong. Major Cureton lived in the house now owned and occupied by Major J. B. McMorries.

JOHN S. CARWILE.—The death of this really good man has made a great void in the social circle in which he lived and moved. To the writer he was as an elder brother, and as such he mourns him, but not with a grief which cannot be comforted. For in its midst he feels constantly that he is now an angel of light, life and glory.

John S. Carwile was the son of Zachariah Carwile, a soldier

of the Revolution, who lived to the great age of more than 90 years. He was born on the 17th day of February, Anno Domini 1786, in Laurens District. His early life was spent in laborious occupations; still he managed to obtain a good English education. Few men wrote a better hand or had a more perfect knowledge of figures. He taught school in the Pitt's settlement, Newberry District, for many years. He married on the 20th day of December, 1809, Elizabeth Williams, his amiable and excellent lady, who preceded him to the tomb. They raised seven children, Mary, now the wife of Dr. Richard C. Griffin, Zachariah Carwile, Sarah, now the wife of Hillary Gary, John B. Carwile, Richard C. Carwile, Elizabeth and Caroline. Their eldest child, Stephen, a most interesting boy, died when young, to the great grief of his father, who had intended him to be trained for the profession of the law by his friend who now drops a tear on his tomb. Richard, mentioned above, was among the patriotic youths who composed company L, and, under the command of Captain (now General) Williams, marched to Mexico, and there perished from disease. This was the source of great and just grief to the parents, but in his excellent life they had their greatest consolation. To their other children, good, amiable and affectionate, they could, and did, turn with the feeling that God had further greatly blessed them. On the 9th of November, 1811, John S. Carwile was received as a member of the Bush River Baptist Church.

In December, 1815, John S. Carwile was elected by the Legislature Tax Collector of Newberry District. He was one of the party who, returning from Columbia, was present when Dr. Ivy Finch was killed by his horse running away with him at the forks of the road in Butcher town. All of that party of ten are now, with the exception of one, in the silent grave.

In January, 1820, he was elected Sheriff of Newberry District, and entered on his duties in February of that year, and served out his term of four years. In 1828 he was re-elected Sheriff and served another full term. The writer has had occasion to notice carefully for thirty-eight years, the manner in which Sheriffs in the State have and still do perform their duties; and he has no hesitation in saying Mr. Carwile was the best Sheriff who has ever come under his observation. His books are in the Sheriff's office at Newberry, and they are worthy of any counting-house in the State. Every transaction in his sheriffalties can be traced without difficulty. He never used the money of a party; he never was told to collect any money and failed to do it. If he chose to befriend a debtor, he paid the money to the creditor, and thus was both kind and just. He was never ruled save to settle questions of contested right. The writer recollects, while he was at the Bar, he had occasion to say, "Mr. Carwile, I must rule you in the case of A *vs.* C D." Nothing ever before or since excited an angry feeling on his part towards the writer. But it required "a soft answer" on that occasion to satisfy him; he had to be told it was merely a rule to settle who was entitled to the money.

On the 11th of October, 1817, he succeeded Stephen McCraw as the Clerk of the Bush River Baptist Church. This office he retained until the 11th of October, 1829, when he resigned, and was succeeded by Gen. John K. Griffin. On the 6th of October, 1831, he and James Divver were dismissed from the Bush River Baptist Church to become the founders of the Newberry Baptist Church, which was about being gathered and constituted out of the converts in the great revival of September, 1831. Having been a Deacon in the Bush River Baptist Church, he became also Deacon in the Newberry Baptist Church. In this church he was appointed, and continued to be the Clerk, until about a year before his death, when his feeble health caused his resignation.

He was for many years a delegate, first from Bush River, and then from Newberry, to the Association. He was also for many years the Clerk of the Association. The Circular of 1844, on "the daily reading of the Scriptures," was prepared by him. It is a short, simple, but beautiful *expose* of a Christian's thoughts on this interesting subject. The various duties he performed with a zeal and fidelity never surpassed.

After he ceased to be the Sheriff he became the assistant of his brother and friend, Y. J. Harrington, as Clerk and Register of Newberry. This office he filled to November, 1850, when he was called to follow the remains of his friend to his last resting place. Subsequently he was appointed by the

Governor, Clerk *pro tempore*. He steadily refused to be a candidate for the vacant office. In discharging his duties as Assistant Clerk, and Clerk *pro tempore*. It is but justice to say he was fully equal to his friend, Y. J. Harrington, who was *"primus inter pares."*

Mr. Carwile was a member of the Board of Commissioners of Free Schools for Newberry District for many years, and was Clerk and Treasurer. He introduced the rule that teachers should keep a day-book, in which should appear the exact time in which the poor children of the district attended school. None save the poor had the benefit of the Free School Fund.

In 1836 he became a member of the Newberry Baptist Bible Society, and its Treasurer and Secretary. For fifteen years, without money and without price, he discharged the duties of that office. In every part, at every meeting, as the Society traveled over the district, he was seen alongside of his friend and brother, the President. At length disease compelled him, in 1851, to vacate the office.

Mr. Carwile was executor, administrator, guardian, and trustee in many, very many, instances. Under his management every thing was done right and exactly as it should be. Hence no one ever complained or thought hard of him in the discharge of his delicate trusts.

He became a teetotaller many years before his death, and no man was more sincere or devoted. He was a member of the Newberry Agricultural Society; and to him we are indebted for the recipe which relieved us and the country from *smut in wheat*.

For forty-one years he was a member of the Baptist Church. None ever lived a more consistent and orderly life. He was a noble, firm, self-sacrificing Christian, "full of mercy and good fruits." The place where he and his brother, Y. J. Harrington, formerly sat in the house of worship belonging to the Baptists at Newberry, is now entirely vacant. *No one ever occupies it.* And the eyes of the members, as they fall upon it, see the fulfilment of the Scriptures, "the place which once knew them shall know them no more forever."

In all the relations of life he was faultless; as a citizen, no duty was ever demanded of him that he was not ready to fulfil; as a friend, he was faithful and sincere; as a son, his aged parent experienced fully his grateful attentions; as a husband, father and master, he was among the kindest. His now deserted home has been moistened by the tears of friendship, filial affection, and servile attachment. Few and far between are the visits of such men to earth.

He was of medium size, hair black, his eyes dark hazel, nose Roman, features regular, mouth and chin well formed. His temper was originally quick, but he had it completely under his control. His disposition was a lively, cheerful one; he loved society and partook fully in the pleasures of friendship. In his family circle he had great delight; his children were to him in his widowed state his greatest solace.

Ill health, which had often admonished him, "be ready," confined him to his chamber for several months, until Monday, the 8th ultimo, when, after much suffering, his pure spirit was released from its tenement of clay, and, on wings of faith, flew away, and is at rest.

> "Far from affliction, toil and care,
>   That happy soul is fled,
> The breathless clay shall slumber here,
>   Among the silent dead !
> Now he resides where Jesus is,
>   Above this changeful sphere,
> The soul was ripened for that bliss,
>   While yet he sojourned here."

In 1824 Col. Samuel Cannon was elected Sheriff. This clever and good man was descended from the earliest settlers of Newberry. The creek near which he was born, raised and died, was called after one of his ancestors "Cannon's Creek." He was a major in Col. Tucker's regiment, which marched in 1814 to Camp Alston, between "Garden's Corner and Pocotaligo" in Beaufort District. He was one of the court consisting of all the officers of the regiment, who advised Col. Tucker to disobey the Governor's (Alston's) order to detail two companies to throw up, under Col. Youngblood's direction, as engineer, *a tete du pont* on Port Royal Island. On his return from *that senseless campaign* of six weeks, he participated largely in the popularity of the colonel, who was blessed by the men as having, at great personal hazard, relieved them from a position where military defence was wholly unnecessary, where no laurels could have been gathered, but where many a cypress would have been nurtured to weep over soldier's graves by the malaria of swamps and rice fields. He was soon after his return made the colonel of the 8th, now the 39th regiment. He was elected to the House of Representatives in December, 1816, and continued to be elected until October, 1822, when I think he was not a candidate. After the expiration of his term as Sheriff he was a private man. He died in '49, having passed beyond three score and ten, leaving numerous descendants, children and grand-children. He was a surveyor and teacher, and in these, as well as his more public capacities, he did his duty, and did it well. He was a member of the Methodist Church. He deserved the respect and confidence of his fellow-citizens.

Robert Rutherford Nance, the eldest son of Major Frederick Nance, was elected Sheriff in January, 1832; he resigned and removed to Alabama in 1835; he was born 2nd of November, 1795; he graduated in the South Carolina College in December, 1813, in the class of which George McDuffie and John G. Creagh received the 1st and 2nd honors; he was principally engaged, until his marriage, in the mercantile business as a clerk in the firm of Pratt & Nance, in the house now occupied by Julius B. Smith. In 1817, he married Mary S. Pope, the second daughter of Capt. Sampson Pope, of Edgefield. He then entered upon the business of a merchant, as a partner in the firm of which his father had been previously a member! On the election of Judge O'Neall in August, 1817, to the command of the 8th, afterwards the 39th regiment, he was appointed by his early friend, fellow-student and roommate in college, adjutant; he served until after the election of General Wright to the command of the 10th brigade; he was then appointed Deputy Assistant Inspector General in the place of T. T. Cureton, who had resigned upon his election to the Ordinary's office. This office he retained until about 1825, when he resigned. On the resignation of James Farnandis as Ordinary, in 1818, he was appointed by the Governor to fill the office *pro tem.* until a successor was elected by the people. The election resulted in favor of T. T. Cureton; if Maj. Nance had stood upon his legal rights, under the exposition given to the constitution in the case of the State *vs.* Wm. M. Hutson, 1st M. C., 240, he would have been entitled to hold the office during good behaviour. But he knew he had in fact only been temporarily appointed, and therefore cheerfully pursued the right way, and yielded the office to his more popular rival. He was elected by the Legislature Tax Collector for Newberry, in the place of J. W. Tinsley, Esq., who resigned in 1824. This office he retained for two terms, and gave it up to become Sheriff of Newberry. In 1831 or '32 he became a convert to the truth, and united himself to the Baptist Church at Newberry. As has been already said, Mr. Nance removed to Alabama, in 1835. He found the Sheriff's office a barren field, for it had been thoroughly harvested and gleaned in the preceding sheriffalties. In his term there was little debt existing in the district, and therefore little to do in the Sheriff's line. He thought it was necessary to remove to provide better for his family: *it was a sad mistake.*

The duties of the offices which he had from time to time held were well, faithfully and honestly filled. He was an honest, intelligent, conscientious man, who "knowing the right, still the right pursued." He died in July, 1846, leaving his wife and six children surviving; two of his sons, Rutherford and Frederick Sampson, went out as volunteers in the war with Mexico, in the Newberry company, and were in the various battles of Contreras, Cherubusco, Chapultepec and the Garita de Belin, and returned *unscathed* to their mourning mother.

One who knew Robert R. Nance as the writer of this sketch knew him may be pardoned in saying he deserved more than he ever obtained, *prosperity.* No purer man ever lived, no better citizen could, in his day, have been found; no more sincere relative and friend has ever been known by me. As a husband and father, if he had a fault, it was that he was too kind, too indulgent. *He was a Christian*, not known by profession merely, but by works—works evidencing the good, merciful and pious heart.

He was succeeded by Reuben Pitts, and he by General H. H. Kinard, and he by his brother, John P. Kinard, and at this time the office is held for the second term by Gen. Kinard, who has thus been placed by the people alongside of Mr. Carwile, as worthy of being twice Sheriff of Newberry. These

several gentlemen are still in the midst of life and usefulness.*
It would therefore be improper that I should undertake to do
more in reference to them than to say they have well and
faithfully discharged all their public duties, and deserve well
all the honors heretofore conferred upon them. That they
each may live to adorn a long life by many, very many acts
of virtue, usefulness, prosperity, and happiness, is the wish
of a native citizen of Newberry.

Having now run through the Sheriff's office from 1797 to
the present time, and intending hereafter as I may have the
means, to give some account of the County Court Sheriffs from
'85 to '97, I turn to the Clerk's office. I am unable to say
anything more of the first Clerk, Wm. Malone, than that from
the records; it appears that he did the duties of Clerk entirely
by his deputies, and that, as is said by my worthy friend, Col.
Benjamin Maybin, "he was a worthy and respectable citizen."
Of Major Nance, his successor, I have fully spoken.

Young John Harrington, Esq., was the successor of Major
Nance. Although several months have come and gone since
the excellent man whose name is at the head of this paragraph was suddenly called away, it cannot be amiss or unin-
structive to sketch imperfectly his life and character. He was
born in Union District, on Thicketty Creek, on the 5th of
April, 1784. He was the son of John Harrington, who died
early; his mother, Frances, married Col. Robert Rutherford, of
Newberry, in the year 1795, and with her family removed to
his residence, nine miles below the town.

His mother was a member of the Methodist Church, and
remarkable for her many domestic virtues and exemplary piety.
Her second husband, Col. Rutherford, performed a father's part
in many respects to her children. His habits of industry led
him to demand from his step-children similar habits. Young
John *here* probably acquired much of that singular activity of
character and devotion to business which was so conspicuous
in his after life. The first cotton gin ever put in motion in
Newberry belonged to Col. Rutherford; it was attended to by
his step-son, Young John. Often has the writer of this heard
him describe the quantities of cotton brought to be ginned in
small parcels. This demanded of him unceasing attention, and

---

*Since this was written Mr. Pitts has been called to his Father's house.

here he probably learned the useful lesson of life, *to be accommodating and agreeable to all.* He was at one time put to learn the wagon making business with one of the McClelands; he, however, remained *there* a very short time.

He came to the village of Newberry in '99. It was then a place of only three or four houses. He was the clerk of Maj. Frederick Nance, who was the then Clerk of the Court, and a merchant in extensive business. Young John became the general manager of the store; his age then was a little more than fifteen. His devoted attention and activity claimed and received the entire confidence of his employer. While thus engaged he performed, on a wager made hy Major Nance and Benjamin Long, Esq., the then almost incredible feat of picking out 100 lbs. of cotton from the pods in one day.

He married early, probably in 1804, his excellent lady, (now his mourning widow) Nancy Calmes; and settled permanently in the town of Newberry.

Young and active and cheerful, they brought into life the combined qualities of energy and concert, which made their lives so successful and useful.

With his step-father he was associated in mercantile business; this he followed successfully, till he was appointed Clerk in place of Major Frederick Nance, who resigned in 1807.

This office he retained until a week before his death, in November, 1850. For forty-three years, therefore, he was Clerk; and if in that great period of near half a century he ever failed in the discharge of his duties, it is what never came within my knowledge. Indeed, he was a *pattern Clerk*, worthy of imitation in everything. Kind, attentive, well informed and intelligent, he was equal to every duty arising in the correct administration of the complicated affairs of his office. He wrote a good hand,—he wrote with great facility and accuracy; hence the ministerial business of his office was most correctly carried out. He was often called on as Clerk, or as ex-officio, a Commissioner of Special Bail, to decide legal questions; this he did with singular promptitude and accuracy for one not educated as a lawyer.

In term time if a criminal was to be arraigned, juries or witnesses to be sworn, there was no necessity to appeal to forms, or to be prompted through a stammering ungraceful performance of the duty demanded. It was done as well and gracefully as it could be done. The writer has seen every clerk in the State in the discharge of his duty, and never has he seen any one who could or did surpass Young John Harrington.

He was a merchant for many years in the village of Newberry. The profits thus acquired, added to his other means, made him comparatively a wealthy man.

In 1831 he with his wife was buried in the liquid grave with Christ his Saviour, and rose to newness of life as *a Christian.* He was one of the members who composed the Newberry Baptist Church. With Thos. Pratt, he was ordained a deacon, and so continued till his death. No church member ever passed a more consistent life; always at his post, always ready to act in the discharge of any duty, well may the church mourn her loss. Indeed, it will be hard to make its members forget his well-remembered face and active form. Often does the eye falling on his vacant seat turn away in sadness, and bedimmed with a tear, while the heart speaks *"he was, and is not."*

He was from a very early day a warm and devoted member of the Temperance Reform. He belonged to the Head Spring Temperance Society, and only ceased to be its President at the annual meeting preceding his death.

He was sorely tried in the death of and removal of his children: his second son, his third and fourth daughters were called from their families to the bosom of their Father and God! His eldest son and eldest daughter removed far from him. Still he bowed with unwavering meekness and humility to his mighty Master's will. He was still the same cheerful man he had ever been. He felt and wept, as a parent ever will —but as he looked upon his dying children, or clasped *their* orphan children to his bosom, he could only say of the dead as King David did: "I shall go to them, but they shall not return to me."

The breaking, however, of these natural bonds prepared him for the loosening of the "silver cord" of life;—for some time he was strongly impressed with the belief that his days were numbered. He set about the preparation of his affairs; "he set his house in order"; but before all earthly things were ready the dread mandate came. On the 11th of November, 1850, he was kept within his house

by rain; in the evening he said he must visit the town; (his residence being within the corporate limits, but some distance from the business part,) he accordingly rode over, —nothing unusual was remarked; he was cheerful and happy as usual; he failed to arrange the business which he desired—he returned home, ate his supper, conversed with his family, called them around the family altar, and poured out his soul before God. He retired to rest, and in a short hour ceased to be numbered with the sons of men. A disease of the breast, called by physicians apoplexy of the lungs, with which he had been often threatened, came down upon him like an armed man and summoned him to his Master's presence. May we all be like him, ready for so sudden a summons.

He left his affectionate wife and partner of his days, and seven children, to mourn their loss. Great indeed is it; but still to them it ought to be a constant consolation that he has exchanged earth for heaven, trials for joys, tears for smiles, misery for happiness, and poor frail mortality for immortality.

His character may be drawn in a few words. He was a good man, a good citizen, a good officer, a good husband, a good father, a good master, and a good friend. In all these relations he did his duty, and the tears shed over his grave, and the respect testified for his memory by all, both friends and foes, constitute the only eulogy necessary. On his tomb let it be written, "he lived to die, and he died to live forever and ever, in mansions of bliss."

―――

No. 8 Continued.

Major Cureton was succeeded as Ordinary by Mr. William Wilson, a native of Edgefield District, long and advantageously known as a merchant before his election. As Ordinary he discharged the complicated duties of his office with unexampled fidelity and rare intelligence. Though not bred to the law, he soon possessed himself of the principles necessary to the adjudication of the difficult questions occurring in his

1   H

forum, and certainly decided them with great correctness.
He was one of the converts of the great Baptist revival at
Newberry in 8831, and became a member of the Baptist
Church.

He died very suddenly, indeed almost instantaneously, in
1845. His wife, Charlotte, the daughter of Francis Higgins,
had preceded him by many years to the tomb. He left two
children him surviving, James Wilson, of Spartanburg, and
Sarah Anne, the wife of Burr Ramage, Esq.

Mr. Wilson was rather a reserved man, and after the death
of his wife excluded himself more from general society than
is perhaps advisable. But as an officer and a man he deserved
the confidence and respect of all who knew him.

He was succeeded by Hugh K. Boyd, the present Ordinay,
who had been the Tax Collector from 1836 to 1844. Of him,
as of the surviving incumbents, Newberry has great cause to
be proud, and in pointing to their officers and lives she may,
like the mother of the Gracchi, say "these are my jewels."*

The Commissioner's office (in equity) was first filled by
F. B. Higgins, Esq., who graduated in the South Carolina
College, December, 1813. He was elected December, 1817,
and continued to December, 1826. Mr. Higgins is an attorney
at law, and has filled many important public positions, in all
of which he has received the unqualified approbation of all
who have been called on to notice his course. Knowing
him from childhood to the present hour, and having had much
to do with him in most of the relations of life, I may, I
trust, be permitted to add my testimony of his life, that it
has been characterized by educated intelligence, undeviating
honesty, purity of purpose and great usefulness. His second
son, John C., was one of the young men who volunteered and
served out his entire Mexican campaign, receiving only a
slight wound in the various battles in which he was engaged;
he went out a private, he returned a lieutenant.

Mr. Higgins was succeeded by Drayton Nance, Esq., the
second son of Major Frederick Nance, and a graduate of the
college in the class of 1821. Mr. Nance is also an Attorney
at Law. He declined a re-election in December, 1838. Mr.
Nance has ever since chosen a private instead of public life.

---

* Mr. Boyd is now numbered with the dead.

With the single exception of the place of director of the Greenville and Columbia Rail Road Company, he has sedulously avoided public employment. To that great work he has, however, from the beginning given all his energies.

Of Mr. Nance, who is yet comparatively a young man, it may be indelicate for one who has known him from his birth to undertake to speak of him as he deserves. He is a clearheaded, well-informed, virtuous, good man. He does not give to himself that sweep of public usefulness which he could and will, I trust, yet do.*

He was succeeded by Thomas H. Pope, Esq., in December, 1838; he resigned in 1840; he is the eldest son of Captain Sampson Pope; he also is a lawyer of extensive practice and well known reputation. He has served one term in the Legislature. He possesses a clear head and an honest heart, and is, I trust, to be long an useful man and virtuous citizen.† The present incumbent, Lambert J. Jones, succeeded him. He is the son of Elijah Jones, once the clerk of Hugh O'Neall, on Bush River, and afterwards well known as a man of business, for the few years he lived. He died young, and left two children, Whitfield B. and Lambert J., who were infants.

Mr. Jones is a graduate of Brown University Rhode Island. He is a lawyer of growing practice and reputation. By the energy which he has displayed in overcoming the difficulties of his early life, there is much to hope from the future. Glad shall I be to see him favored by length of days, virtuous and honored prosperity.

Of the Tax Collectors of Newberry, several have been already mentioned. After the resignation or death of Charles Crenshaw, in 1812, Ezekiah Eastland, under a *pro tem.* appointment, discharged the duties of the office. He was the son of Thomas Eastland, of Little River, and was a member and Deacon of the Bush River Baptist Church. He was a man much prized by his friends and associates for the many sterling qualities which he possessed. He lived a short time in the village; he removed to Tennessee or North Alabama about 1818.

---

* In September, 1856, Drayton Nance was cut off by apoplexy.

† Vain was the hope, for in February, 1857, Mr. Pope ceased to be numbered among the sons of men !

After Mr. Boyce resigned in 1815, George Dugan held the temporary appointment. He was a son of Col. Thomas Dugan; he afterwards did business as the clerk of Boyce & Harrington, and Birt Harrington & Co., and was subsequenly the partner of Birt Harrington in the firm Harrington & Dugan. He lived many years in the village and was an universal favorite. He died unmarried about 1827 or 1828. Recalling him to memory: he stands before me, the friend of my youth, rejoicing in hopes never realized. He seemed to deserve length and happiness of days; but God who knows all things, and orders all things for the best, called him *home* early.

Major James W. Tinsley succeeded John S. Carwile as the Tax Collector. This gentleman was the son of James Tinsley, one of the few Whigs spared at the massacre at Hay's Station, and a grandson of old King's Mountain Jim, (Col. James Williams.) He was a soldier in the war of 1812, and was the sergeant of the company enlisted and commanded by Major George Butler. He was elected major of the 38th regiment, commanded then by General John K. Griffin. A most ungenerous charge made against him by a personal enemy of embezzlement of the public funds, supported by an appearance of truth, arising out of slight neglects, drove him to the verge of madness, and certainly was the means of cutting short the life of his amiable lady, and finally led to his resignation soon after entering on his second term in 1824. The writer settled Major Tinsley's accounts as Tax Collector in the Treasury at Columbia, and it is due to his memory that he should state here what he did then, that there was not the slightest foundation to believe that there was any wilful or corrupt default. He had as acts of favor to the people frequently received taxes when his books were not present, and in some instances of small amounts had mislayed the memoranda or forgotton to enter them on his books. The whole deficit, after being subject to the scrutiny *of a malice which never tired*, did not amount to $100.

Major Tinsley remained in Newberry a few years, married a second time, removed to Georgia, and there became a man of wealth and considerable distinction. He died in 1846.

Alexander Chambers succeeded Robert R. Nance as Tax Collector in '32, and continued till December, 1836. This gentleman was of the mercantile firm herein before mentioned in the sketch of the life of James Farnandis. He lived in the village of Newberry for many years. He lives now in the State of Alabama. Good, honest, just and true in all the relations of life, may, and ought to be written on the stone which will not, I hope, for many years be placed over his mortal remains.

Of James Bonds, who succeeded H. K. Boyd as Tax Collector, and Jacob Kibler, the present incumbent, it need only be said that they have walked in the steps of their predecessors; they have in every respect shown themselves worthy public servants. Having now closed a review of the public officers of Newberry District, the uniform plaudit of "well done" which has accompanied each and all, may seem to strangers like indiscriminate praise, *but it is not.* Nothng has been awarded which was not merited. Well may Newberry challenge comparison with her sisters in the State, and say "shew me such a body of men as the local officers of whom sketches have been herein given, and I will give place, but not till then."

Much, however, still remains to do justice to the village and its inhabitants. I shall speak of a few of the old inhabitants who have not as yet been noticed before. I briefly notice the resident attorneys and physicians, past and present.

Mr. John Johnston (the father of Chancellor Johnston) came to Newberry about the year 1806. I first remember business being carried on by him and a gentleman of the name of Bones,* in the house occupying *then* the present site of Steele's storehouse. Whether Mr. Johnston then lived in the village, I am not certain. The latter part of 1806, or beginning of 1807, he and his family lived in the L house. Mr. Bones soon left the concern, and Mr. Johnston did business alone in the house where the brick hotel stands. He owned much of the land west of the creek

---

* This gentleman was said to have been a major in the army of the Irish Patriots of '98, and like McCalla, owed his life to an escape more than mercy.

now belonging to Judge O'Neall. Mr. Johnston was an Irishman, and like many others, began life poor and by industry closed it in wealth. The writer knew him well from 1815 to his final removal from Carolina, and has great reason to say he was a most kind, hospitable and good man. He had a large family, for each of whom he amply provided. He removed to Alabama about 1840, and died there, in a few years afterwards full of years, being beyond four score.

The first courthouse, when that which preceded the present was finished, was sold, and purchased by Robert and John Boyce, and was by them removed and converted into a tavern. It stood east of the printing office, and was successively occupied by Robert and John Boyce, Nathaniel Durkie, Robert Boyce, Henry Stringfellow, Robert McCullough and others!

Robert Boyce was the eldest son of John Boyce spoken of in No. 6; he lived at Newberry from 1802 to 1816, when he removed to Charleston, and there died about 1838. He married Lydia Waters, the daughter of Philemon Waters, (commonly called Ferry Phil.;) she was a most intelligent, well educated lady, energetic, and capable of managing any business; she well deserved, what she did not attain, a happy old age. She died in 1829!

Mr. Boyce was a singularly cheerful, mirth-loving man. If he ever injured or wilfully pained another, it was not, I am sure, intended. He left two sons, John and William, him surviving; the latter is a highly promising lawyer of Fairfield.* John Boyce, the second son of John Boyce, was a more energetic man than his brother Robert; his disposition was, however, a stern, uncompromising one. "Whatever his hands found to do, he did it with his might," the consequence was, that he died one of the wealthiest citizens of Laurens District.

Nathaniel Durkie I knew by sight, but had no acquaintance with him. He had the reputation of a speculating, failing tavern keeper.

Henry Stringfellow, (called by the youngsters of Newberry, Old King Cole,) was a native of Chester. He lived at

---

* William W. Boyce is now a member of Congress.

Newberry from about 1811 to 1821. He was a kind-hearted, honest man. He removed to Alabama, and there died, leaving three children, Frances, William and Thornton, him surviving.

Robert McCullough succeeded him as the owner of the hotel. Mr. McCullough is still alive, and lives, I presume, still in Edgefield. His life and residence in our town was accompanied by many difficulties, but he passed through them all, bearing, and justly bearing, the reputation of an intelligent, industrious, virtuous man.

Thomas Pratt came to Newberry as the clerk of Y. J. Harrington, in 1806. By patient, untiring industry and perseverance as a merchant, he became one of the wealthiest and best citizens of the town.

He and Ker Boyce, during the difficult periods of the war in 1813 and 1814, visited more than once Philadelphia, on horseback, laid in there their stocks of goods, and wagoned them overland to Newberry. So, too, they once paid a visit to Amelia Island, and there succeeded in purchasing goods, and in the same way transported them to Newberry. When the war ceased, he pursued the same business through the ordinary channels, to his death in 1837. He married in 1816 the eldest daughter of Major Frederick Nance, the amiable and excellent lady now Mrs. Dorothy Brooks Pratt. He and she were converts of the great Baptist revival in 1831. Messrs. Harrington (Y. J.) and Pratt, were the first Deacons of, ordained and set apart as such, by the Newberry Baptist Church. He left nine children, William, Robert, Simeon, Priestly, Amelia, Mary, Carolina, Virginia, Angelina, all of whom are still in our midst, except Priestly, who went out as a volunteer, and died in Mexico, at Puebla.* Sad, indeed, was his fate, and that of the other young men, Summers, Stewart Cole and Carwile, who left homes of ease and abundance, and died upon the fields of Mexico from that wasting disease which seldom released its hold upon its victims ! Home, parents, brothers, sisters and friends, were ever before their sick and failing eyes, never, alas, to be "in reality beheld." Often have I looked with a bleeding heart

---

* Amelia has since died.

upon the daguerrotype of Stewart, Pratt and Summers, taken in a group while in Augusta, on their way to Mexico. They stood together like brothers; two, Summers and Pratt, died in Puebla; Lieut. Stewart, after he had left the City of Mexico, on his return home.

Thomas Pratt deserves a much fuller notice than even an intimate friend is able to give from memory. His modest worth never challenged observation; but still in every respect he deserves all which honesty, virtue, piety and intelligence can demand.

William Pinchback, was one of the old inhabitants of Newberry. He built the corner house on Caldwell and Boyce Streets, now occupied by Mr. Bierfield as a hotel. Before he built upon it, the law office of Samuel Farrow, Esq., stood upon the corner. Mr. Pinchback came to Newberry from Chester, in, I presume, 1810 or 1811. He was a cabinet maker, and drove on an immensely profitable business in that line. He subsequently became a hotel keeper and merchant. He, like Pratt and Boyce, made one or more trips North, carrying out cotton and returning with merchandise. On one of his trips he brought back a large quantity of oil stones, which had been thrown out of the ditches cut at Baltimore to throw up the intrenchments to protect the city from the invasion of the British, at the time Washington was burnt, in 1814. He was much laughed at about his cargo of *Whetstones*, but I have no doubt he made money thereby.

He removed to Charleston and there did business as a cotton speculator, and realized a fortune in 1825; he afterwards lived many years in Abbeville District, and there owned a large and valuable plantation. He finally removed to Mississippi, and there died in '48, leaving neither wife nor children. His large estate descended to, and has been divided among his collaterals, of whom our worthy townsman, John Holman, is one.

————

No. 8 CONTINUED.

John B. Davidson, a native of Newberry, lived in the town of Newberry from 1805 to his death in 1828. He was a house carpenter and joiner by trade, but he loved to play "*gentleman of elegant leisure, and to sharpen his wits by grog*" too well to succeed by work. Instead of supporting his wife, as is the duty of every man, he was supported by her. Mary Anne Davidson, by her needle, realized competence, and yet maintained a drinking husband.

Many an incident in his life, spent in such a village as Newberry, afforded much merriment to the standers by of the time, and could I transfer them to paper, would make many a one clasp their sides to prevent bursting from the laugh which would attend their narration. This cannot, however, be done, and I beg to refer my readers to the 22nd No. of the Drunkard's Looking Glass, pp. 176 and 180–1, of the Permanent Temperance Documents, for a better summary of these matters than any which I can now give.

Marmaduke Coate, the youngest son of John Coate, (little) lived in Newberry from 1812 to 1828. He was a surveyor of much experience and intelligence. He married Mary Coate, the daughter of James Coate, of Edgefield, about 1816, who died in 1827; he afterwards married Nancy Rotton, of Edgefield, and finally emigrated to Alabama, where I hope he still lives. He made the surveys of New-berry, Lexington and Richland, in 1820, under the authority of the Legislature, for the purpose of making an accurate map of the State. His surveys will be found in Mills' Atlas; they are remarkable for their fullness and accuracy; he built and occupied till 1829, the house now occupied by Mr. Seybt.

Duke (as he was usually called,) from his youth was like Falstaff, not only full of humor himself, but the cause of mirth and humor in other people.

This made him the boon companion of every idle man, in a village (*which has been always remarkable for the great encouragement it afforded to loafers;*) the consequence was, he contracted habits of drink, which led on to neglect, and finally to ruin.

No more honest and good-hearted man was ever an inhabitant of Newberry. It is sad to think of the ruin which has come down like a rolling wave from the storm-stirred mighty deep upon many such a man.

Lieut. Col. Birt Harrington long lived in the town of Newberry. Indeed he might have been said to have "grown with its growth, and strengthened with its strength." He was for a time clerk in a merchant's store; then he wrote in the Clerk's office; again he studied law; but all at last yielded to the better business which he long pursued at Newberry, that of a merchant. He married in 1819, Harriett, the third daughter of Samuel Johnston, of Farfield. He was successively the lieutenant and captain of the Newberry Artillery Company, the major and lieutenant colonel of the 39th regiment.

He removed to North Alabama about '39, where he still lives, and there I hope he is long to live, useful and happy. Newberry in him, as in many other instances, has to regret the loss of an excellent, intelligent man, from continual desire to change which has so long pervaded our community. Indeed, Newberry District is to this State, Georgia, and the Western and Southwestern States a sort of Northern hive. Go where you will, *you find a New-berry man*, everywhere such an one has made some impress on the society of which he is a member.

Messrs. John Holman and Robert Stewart are among the oldest surviving inhabitants of our flourishing town. They both have carved out for themselves the road to fortune. Both deserve everything which honesty, perseverance and virtue ought to expect. But they are in our midst, and of them there is no necessity for me to write. The same may be said, and deservedly said, of the younger men, John Coate, John B. McMorries, E. Y. McMorries,* Vincent B. Pope, Joseph Mooney and G. T. Scott, who may be classed among the next oldest inhabitants of the town.

Hiram Hutchison, President of the Bank of Hamburg, and John I. Gracy, of Columbia, were merchants of Newberry. Mr. Hutchison, I think, began business at Newberry in 1819, and Mr. Gracy in a short time afterwards. They both removed to Columbia about '28 or '29 Mr. Hutchison in 1831 sold out his stock as a merchant, and became the first Cashier of the Commercial Bank; he resigned that

---

* E. Y. McMorries died suddenly of apoplexy in '54.

post and transferred his position to Cheraw,—there he was blessed by uniting to his growing fortunes the amiable and accomplished lady, Miss Collins. He afterwards became Cashier and finally President of the Bank of Hamburg; he lives now in Charleston a man of fortune. Long may he enjoy the fruits of his labors, which, directed by intelligence and perseverance, have so fully succeeded. Mr. Gracy has steadily pursued his business as a merchant, until now he is one of the first merchants in Columbia. He married the excellent lady, Miss Bratton, of Fairfield, but had the misfortune to be early called upon to follow her to the grave; she left him, however, three little ones to receive his care. Mr. Gracy is one of the kindest and purest men with whom I have ever associated. It is gratifying to every just principle of our nature to see such a man prosperous and happy. May his life be continued to an honored old age, and be crowned ·with every blessing.*

Having thus sketched some of the other inhabitants of Newberry, I now propose to give some account of the lawyers who once were there.

James McKibben, Esq., was at Newberry in 1804, and here remained until 1811. He was a lawyer not remarkable for learning, but unquestionably possessed of very considerable abilities. He did not trim the midnight lamp, nor did he undergo the twenty years lucubrations which Sir John Fortescue affirms to be necessary for a Judge; nor, indeed, even that commended by Justice Blackstone, in the introductory chapter to his first volume of the Commentaries, and the perusal of which I would commend to my young friends of the Bar at Newberry and every where.

Mr. McKibben was a member of the House of Representatives from 1806 to 1810. He there acquired, and deservedly, the reputation of a very useful member.

Indeed, his turn of mind was better calculated for deliberative assemblies than the rough and tumble of the Bar. In 1811 he removed to Union and there followed his profession. He was a candidate for Congress in 1814 and was defeated by Wilson Nesbit, Esq. In December of that year he was elected major of the brigade of State troops,

---

* Mr. Hutchison died in New York in 1856.

for which provision was made by the Legislature, and of which Judge Huger was elected general.

Mr. McKibben was the Senator from Union to the State Legislature from 1818 to 1826. He died suddenly in 1827. He never was married; this with him, as with most men, took from him every noble motive to eminence and success,

No more convivial and social man belonged to any society than he was in the beginning of life. Long before his death he felt like he was a solitary and recluse—and as such he was little disposed to mingle in the societies which he once loved so well.

David T. Milling, Esq., a native of Fairfield, settled at Newberry in 1807 or 1808. He was a diligent practitioner for many years; he understood practice very well, and often availed himself of his knowledge of technicalities to overwhelm his more careless rival, (McKibben.) But he never could or would make a speech. On one occasion he was commended by his client, who had non-suited his adversary on account of some slip which Milling detected: "Give me," said old Tom Lindsey, "a dumb lawyer." He married Maria Latham and removed to Georgia, where he died some years ago.

In 1809 (November), Judge Crenshaw and John Caldwell, Esq., were admitted to the Bar, and settled at Newberry. Both were graduates of the South Carolina College, and both were very far from being dumb lawyers.

Anderson Crenshaw was the first graduate of the South Carolina College; he graduated in 1806; studied law with Judge Nott, of Columbia, and came to the Bar with a most accurate knowledge of his profession.

His cases were always well and properly made up in the pleading, and thoroughly prepared, he went to trial with great probabilities of success. His arguments were replete with good sense, but were never remarkable for eloquence. To him, more than any one else, may be ascribed the character of the Newberry Bar for legal knowledge and industry. He presented the example which has had effect, good effect, for forty years.

Mr. Crenshaw, however, lacked judgment; he often failed in cases where less learned men would have succeeded. He married in 1815 Miss Mary Chiles, of Abbeville; he removed to Alabama in 1819; there he became a Judge of the circuit law courts, and of the court of appeals, and subsequently a Chancellor. He died in 1848, full of years, usefulness and honors.

John Caldwell, Esq.. never pretended to the learning of his rival, Judge Crenshaw; indeed, he was not like him bred at the feet of Gamaliel. He studied law with Samuel Farrow, Esq., and kept an office for him at Newberry a year or two before he was admitted to the Bar. Mr. Caldwell had in many respects greatly the advantage of his rival; he had been thoroughly educated, theoretically and practically, for a merchant; he was an accomplished surveyor; he commanded one of the first troops of cavalry in the upper country; he was one among the most active young men of his day; and he possessed an easy elocution, and a quick and ready perception of both law and fact. These great natural advantages were often sufficient to carry him through all the defenses of his rival; but now and then his Parthian agility was unequal to the measured tread of the Macedonian phalanx of his adversary.

He and Judge Crenshaw were elected together to the House of Representatives in 1812; in that year Mr. Caldwell voted for the Bank and became a Director in that institution, and thereby lost his seat; he was elected the Cashier of the Branch Bank in Columbia, to which place he removed in 1814. In 1813, with Chancellor Harper, he was elected a Trustee of the South Carolina College. They were the first graduates honored with that high distinction. He remained in Columbia until after the death of his first wife in February, 1816. Elizabeth Caldwell, daughter of Judge Hunter, most amiable and excellent of women, on thy tomb should be written:

> "Beneath this stone doth lie
> As much of virtue as could die;
> Which when alive did vigor give
> To as much goodness as could live!"

He resigned his cashiership, returned to Newberry, and married Abigail O'Neall, the eldest daughter of Hugh O'Neall. He has been the Representative of Newberry in the State Legislature for at least three terms since. He retired from the Bar several years ago.

He has been grievously afflicted for many years; but still he is spared; and would that it could be so, that his infirmities might be overcome, and that in comfort and happiness he might enjoy a green old age.*

Of Judge O'Neall, Chancellor Johnstone, Solicitor Fair, Messrs. Bauskett, Col. P. C. Caldwell, Pope, Heller, Jones, DeWalt, Ramage, Crosson, Williams, Garlington and Baxter, it is not my purpose to speak.

I may be pardoned to recall the memories of John G. Brown, Simon P. Gray, Robert Dunlap, James J. Caldwell, Dennis L. Moon and George F. Eppes, and to mention another who has ceased to belong to our State, Spencer C. Harrington.

John G. Brown was the eldest surving son of the Revolutionary officer and soldier, Dr. Jacob Robert Brown, who was also one of the County Court Judges of Newberry. He graduated in the class of 1811, in the South Carolina College, and received a high distinction. He studied law with Judge Crenshaw at Newberry, and was admitted to the Bar in January, 1814; he practiced law at Newberry to his election, in December, 1815, to the office of Secretary of State. In 1817 he was elected with Judge O'Neall and Warren R. Davis, Trustees of the South Carolina College. They were the second set of graduates who received the honor of being set over the destinies of their Alma Mater. He was subsequently a member of the House of Representatives from Newberry. Judge O'Neall, John Caldwell, John G. Brown and Benjamin Maybin were the Representatives elected in 1824. Soon after the expiration of that term, he removed to Columbia. He was one of the members of the Convention of 1830, which was the result of our Nullification difficulties. He had been previously elected President of the Branch Bank of Columbia. He married in 1818 or 1819, Rebecca, the daughter of Governor Taylor; he died at the Limestone Springs in 1839.

John G. Brown was a man of very excellent abilities; indeed, I might, in one sense, say he was a man of genius. He was a wit; possessed great colloquial powers; told an anecdote as well as (if not better than) any body else.

---

* He died 15th of January, 1856, in the 71st year.

He wrote well, but never could speak extemporarily. He was the loved and cherished companion of his acquaintances.

Simon P. Gray graduated in the same class. He was the eldest son of George Gray; studied law with Judges Nott and DeSaussure in Columbia in 1812 and 1813, and he was admitted to the Bar, I think, in December, 1813, and practiced for a short time at Newberry. He soon, however, either became disgusted with his profession, or found a better and more profitable employment in his firm.

He removed from Newberry District to Alabama about 1819; married there, and died, I think, in 1835. He was never capable of speaking eloquently, though he always spoke with good sense. He was a companionable, pleasant acquaintance and friend.

Robert Dunlap was the second son of Major Wm. Dunlap, of Laurens; he graduated in the class of 1817; he studied law with Judge O'Neall, and was admitted to plead and practice law, December term, 1820. He married first Amelia, the second daughter of Major Frederick Nance, and afterwards Sarah, his third daughter.

Mr. Dunlap was elected in '26 to the House of Representatives. He removed to Alabama about 1833, and there died in 1836. His wife and three children survived him; only two of his children now remain.

He was a clear-headed, well-read lawyer; he never had any elocution; he spoke sensibly but with some hesitation. He had many virtues calculated to make his memory dear to those who knew him.

James J. Caldwell (Chancellor Caldwell) was a native of Newberry; he was the only son of Dan Caldwell. He studied at the Newberry Academy part of 1813, while Judge O'Neall was the teacher; after he ceased to teach, he prepared himself for college at Mount Bethel; he entered college in the Junior Class just as it rose in December, 1815; his father and mother both died in the great epidemic of January, 1816. He graduated in December, 1817, and began the study of the law with Judge O'Neall. The latter part of 1818 he took charge of the Edgefield Academy, where he taught about a year. He was admitted to the Bar in December, 1819, or May, 1820. He entered upon the practice of the law at Newberry Court House, and single-handed, toiling on year after year, he at last reached the front ranks of his profession. He married in 1826, Nancy McMorries, the eldest daughter of James McMorries, Esq. He was elected to the Legislature in 1830, and continued a member until his election to the Solicitorship in December, 1835. In December, 1833, he was elected Brigadier-General of the 10th brigade. In 1844, he removed to Columbia; in December, '46, he was elected Chancellor, in the place of Chancellor David Johnson, who was then elected Governor; he died Monday, 11th March, 1850, leaving· his wife and five children him surviving.

This gentleman shewed what could be accomplished by good manners, patience and untiring industry. He possessed talents of high order; he spoke and wrote well. If he had a fault in these respects, it was that he was too diffuse. In all his public elections before the people, it is due to his memory to say *he never treated to a drop of intoxisating drink.* He possessed more equanimity than most men. Seldom, very seldom, did he lose this balance. He was a good man, a virtuous lawyer, a faithful Representative and a just Judge. Greater men have certainly been in the service of the State, but none of purer purpose.

Dennis L. Moon, Esq., a son of Dr. M. W. Moon, studied law at Newberry with Chancellor Caldwell; was admitted to the Bar in '25 or '26. In 1827 he managed the case of Meek *vs.* Atkison, 1st Bail. 84, and deserved to have gained it. Judging from his effort in that case, I think if he had been spared, he would have made a very respectable lawyer. But life to him was a mere morning; he died in a short time afterwards. His principles and disposition were such as must have given him the respect and esteem of society.

George F. Eppes, Esq., was also a native of Newberry District; he was the second son of Mr. Daniel Eppes. Mr. Eppes graduated at Randolph, Macon College, Va. He studied law and was admitted to the Bar in '42. He commenced the practice forthwith at Newberry Court House, and was rapidly rising to eminence when death, like an armed man, entered upon him, and bore him away. He died in September, 1846, after a few days' illness. He died unmarried, leaving his mother and only brother him surviving.

He was a Methodist, and died in the full triumph of Christian faith. His talents, good humor, patience, industry and good habits would have made him anything which he desired to be. No man's death caused deeper regret, or produced more profound humility to the chastening hand of God, than his.

Spencer C. Harrington, the eldest son of Y. J. Harrington, Esq., was admitted to the Bar in the spring of 1828; he studied law with Judge O'Neall, and was his partner from his admission until the latter was elected to the Bench, December, 1828. He then was the partner of Drayton Nance, Esq., until he abandoned the practice. He was for some time a merchant; he owned the house now belonging to L. J. Jones, Esq. He and his wife were members of the Baptist Church, Newberry. He removed about '36, and lives now in Mississippi.* He is another of the native citizens who have been unfortunately carried from us by the fancied *El Dorado* of the Southwest. Such removals have drained us of many of our best young people. It is to be hoped the drain is now stopped, and hereafter, instead of going from us, they will begin to return.

Mr. Harrington is a good man. His talents were not of that order to make him a distinguished .man, but were calculated to make him, what is far better, an useful man. If it were so that South Carolina could offer him sufficient inducements to return, none would hail such event with heartier welcome than the friend who writes this sketch.

No. 8 Concluded.

The physicians of Newberry village deserve a more thorough knowledge to portray their skill and character than I possess. Of the living, Drs. Thompson, Ruff, Long, Harrington, Caldwell, Pratt and James, I may not speak; they must speak

---

* He has been also cut off.

for themselves in their lives and conversations. But of the dead, Drs. Waldo, Adams, Shell, Dobson, and the absent, Drs. Johnston, Mendenhall and Benjamin Waldo, I may venture to speak.

Dr. Joseph W. Waldo was a native of Connecticut; he came to Charleston, taught school for a short time, and then came to Newberry, where he settled himself in 1800, at the house of his friend, John McMorries, to practice medicine. He said, when he landed in Charleston, he had but a single dollar. He soon attained eminence and distinction as a physician; he settled at Newberry Court House in 1803, and here, with occasional sojourns in Charleston and elsewhere, for nearly thirty years he practiced medicine with singular and unvarying success. Few men understood as well as he did the nature of Southern disease.

In 1812 he was for a short period deprived of his reason; this probably was mania-a-potu. During the prevalence of this disease, he attempted to kill himself. He escaped from the house and care of his friend, Y. J. Harrington, Esq., saddled his horse, and riding to the place where Lewis McCreless was killed; he fancied the demons, who were driving him on, ordered him to dismount and kill himself; he obeyed and made the attempt. His friend, Harrington, who pursued him the instant he knew his escape, found him walking up and down the road, bleeding from both arms; he told him he had opened the main arteries of his arms, and run his lancet into his side in the region of his heart as far as he could push it for the handle. But he was mistaken, he had in his hurry only opened the veins of his arms; and the lancet in his side had struck a rib and run around on it. His friend bound up his arms and brought him back to his house. He got well, but the visions which haunted *then* his imagination, ever after adhered to it. He became deeply impressed with his awful impenitent condition; after awhile he experienced a work of grace, and attached himself to the Baptist Church.

In 1814 he married Elizabeth, the widow of his early friend, Luke Smith; by her he had two children, Benjamin and Elizabeth.

He removed to Connecticut, leaving his wife behind him in

1829. He died in Connecticut, at his residence, in 1838.

I have never known a man who had such a fixed and stubborn purpose, and who possessed so much real kindness of heart. He had great intelligence, and great knowledge of his profession. Certainly on religious and domestic matters his mind was greatly diseased from 1812 to his death. Yet I have no doubt, with all his eccentric thoughts and actions, he was really and truly a Christian.

Dr. Freeborn Adams, a native of Massachusetts, married Judith Finch, the daughter of Edward Finch, and settled at Newberry Court House in 1806. He was a most patient and untiring attendant on a sick bed. That he gave general satisfaction, as a physician, was fully shewn by the flood tide of prosperity which he experienced. A friend said to me a few days ago, he was the most industrious man he ever saw. While other professional men would have been idle for want of something to do in their immediate vocation, he was engaged in any work which needed to be done about his improvements. He lived first in a house built by Dr. Waldo, north of the brick house, owned now by Joseph Mooney, and at the eastern termination of Boyce Street. He subsequently built the brick house just spoken of, and had opened it as a tavern and boarding house a short time, when he took sick and died in September, 1813. He left his wife and three infant children, a son and two daughters, him surviving. Dr. Adams was a good man and well deserves to live in the memory of the people of Newberry, and for that purpose the street running north and south, in front of Mooney's brick house, is called Adams Street.

Dr. Thomas Shell was a native of Newberry; he studied medicine with Dr. Johnston; he married in 1816, while he was yet a student, Precious Schoppert. In the fall of 1816 and beginning of 1817 he attended the Lectures at Philadelphia, and on his return commenced practice at Newberry, which he continued to his death in 1826.

Dr. Shell was a man of plain good sense, of great honesty and morality. He was a good physician; his family was expensive and lived beyond his means; he died therefore insolvent, leaving his wife and three little ones to struggle with all the evils of poverty.

Dr. Daniel Dobson was a native of North Carolina, and I think a graduate of the North Carolina University of Chapel Hill. He taught school near Dr. Glenn's and at Newberry for several years. He was beyond doubt one of the best teachers whom I have had occasion to observe for many years. He studied medicine, and graduated at the Charleston College in 1845. He practiced, but did not obtain that full measure of business which his talents and acquirements entitled him to expect. In 1848 he visited Mexico for the purpose of bringing home the mortal remains of the gallant young man, Lieut. John W. Stewart, the son of his friend and patron Robert Stewart. He succeeded in his purpose, but died soon after his return, July 6th, 1848.

Worthy, talented and well educated, well may we deplore the loss of such a young man; but our loss is his gain; *he died a Christian.*

Dr. Burr Johnston, the son of Samuel Johnston, of Fairfield, was a student of the Newberry Academy in 1807 and 1808; he entered the College in 1809, and graduated in 1811; he studied medicine with Dr. Waldo at Newberry C. H. in 1812 and 1813; the latter part of 1813 and beginning of 1814 he visited Philadelphia, attended the lectures; on his return he commenced the practice at Newberry C. H., and unremittingly continued it until 1840, when he removed to Alabama, where he now lives, and where long may he live with all the blessings of life around him. In 1818 he bought the plantation of Y. J. Harrington, where Col. Fair now lives; he married his first wife; Harriet Foote, the same year.

Dr. Johnston was an experienced, safe physician, a firm friend, a good neighbor and patriotic citizen. Everybody regretted his removal, and even now gladly would he be welcomed back by his old friends.*

Dr. M. T. Mendenhall is a native of Guilford County, North Carolina; his wife is the only child of the good man, Isaac Kirk, spoken of in No. 4. Both are descended from friends, on paternal and maternal lines; both were born in the Society; both are now members of the Baptist Church, Charleston.

Dr. MARMADUKE THOMAS MENDENHALL—Dr. Mendenhall is no

---

*In the last year this eminently good man died.

more, was a sad announcement to him who writes, when on Wednesday, 5th November, 1852, at Camden, it first fell on his ear. Still it presents itself to recurring thoughts in enduring sadness. Farewell, friend, brother and co-laborer ! This world has been passed, and your journey to other and brighter worlds on high has been completed. May we there, in God's appointed time, meet in never ending joy.

To die as to live in well remembered honor and glory, is the just reward of him who has lived in usefulness and virtue. This great meed has been earned and won by him whose home is above. Few men lived to better purposes than he did.

Dr. Mendenhall was born in Guilford County, North Carolina, in the Society of Friends, on the 18th day of December, 1798. His father, James Mendenhall, is an elder in the Society of Friends; he still survives at the great age of eighty-two years. His mother, Miriam, was an eminent and gifted speaker among them; she died in 1845, aged seventy-one years. He received a tolerably good classical education, and having selected medicine as his pursuit, he graduated at Philadelphia, in February, 1822. Soon after he became acquainted with Phœbe Kirk, the only child of Isaac Kirk, (deceased,) of Bush·River, Newberry District, South Carolina, who like himself was born and raised a Friend. They were married on the   day of March, A. D. 1824, and soon after he removed to, and settled on, his wife's fine real estate, four miles south of Newberry. The mills on Bush River he thoroughly rebuilt, and made them merchant mills indeed. He here practiced medicine for several years successfully. Here were born their only two children, Pauline Eliza and James Kirk. In February, 1830, he removed to the town of Newberry, and there he and his wife became the subjects of converting grace, and in September, 1831, were immersed, and became members of the Baptist Church at Newberry, which was constituted in the October following out of the many converts under the preaching of Elder Hodges and his assistants, Furman, Barnes and Chiles. He there resided until 1837, practicing medicine and aiding in every good word and work. In 1835 he was set apart as a Deacon.

In 1837 he removed to Charleston to engage in the mercantile business, under the firm of Fort, Townsends & Mendenhall. The beautiful brick building in Granite Row, corner of Hayne and Meeting Streets, was their house of business. They did a large and extensive business. Fort, the Georgia partner, died the second year, and the firm, thus reduced to the Townsends, of New York, and Mendenhall, of Charleston, pursued the business. He became, while thus engaged, a Director of the Bank of the State, and had the entire confidence of its President, the late Judge Colcock, for several years. Upon the dissolution of the firm Dr. Mendenhall retired a considerable loser, and entered upon a new field, that of a commission merchant. He was sustained by many friends, and apparently fortune smiled upon him. But confidence in a broker, who removed to New Orleans, and a participation in his large hazardous speculations, and securityship for a brother Director in the Bank, an apparently well doing man, but who suddenly disappeared from South Carolina, compelled him to close his doors in 1846.

Notwithstanding that bankruptcy thus came down upon him suddenly, and like a strong man bound him, yet he neither lost the confidence of his creditors, nor his self-respect. He soon burst the shackles which were around him, and in pure and virtuous honesty was taken by the hand, and sustained by the community in which he lived. He was elected, on the resignation of Mr. Lehre, to the Ordinary's office. At the expiration of his term he was re-elected. The duties of that great office he performed admirably well. Although having no knowledge of the law when elected, he soon made himself master of all those points which usually were made in his office. His decisions on contested questions were remarkable for the clearness and perspicuity with which he stated and argued the case. The lawyers of Charleston often spoke of him as an accomplished Ordinary.

He joined, on removing to Charleston, the First Baptist Church, and became a Deacon in it. He sustained Dr. Brantley in the trying circumstances attending a portion of his ministry. He has been the intimate friend of Mr. Kendrick since he had the charge of the church.

In 1842 or '43 he became a member of the Charleston Total Abstinence Society, and on the retirement of Benj. G. Howland, its first and never enough admired President, he became his successor. For several years he discharged most faithfully the duties of President. He early became a Son of Temperance, and in October, 1849, he became the G. W. P. He was from first to last an ardent, working and eminently useful *Teetotaller.* He was from its organization the President of the Southern Baptist Publication Society, and contributed much to its success.

Upon the resignation of A. J. Lawton he became the Treasurer of the Baptist State Convention. He was from an early day a member of the Board of Trustees of the Furman Institution, and from the beginning of the Furman University. He was a liberal contributor to every good work both in money and labor. He performed faithfully his various duties in the offices to which he gave himself in the promotion of religion and temperance. He lived to educate and to see his children settled for life. Pauline married Benj. Scott, Esq., and lives near Chattanooga in the enjoyment of the independent comforts of a farm. James Kirk Mendenhall is the Pastor of the Camden Baptist Church. His father attended his ordination in October, and soon after his return to Charleston was struck down with country or yellow fever, and in a few days closed his useful life. He died on Tuesday evening, the 2nd of November, 1852.

With good old Jacob he could have exclaimed, "Few have been the days of my pilgrimage *here.*" Yet, notwithstanding he was cut down while yet the summer of life was upon him, he was ripe for the harvest. His life had been one of active pious usefulness, and he was to be gathered early as rich fruits into the garner of everlasting righteousness and peace.

Weep not parent, wife, children and friends, although dead he lives, yea *lives here,* and *lives in eternal life.* He has experienced the value of the great scripture truth, "Blessed are the dead who die in the Lord," and his survivors will realize that "his works do follow him." No man has died in South Carolina whose death has excited more real sorrow. Every body was ready to drop a tear on his tomb, and say "a good man has been gathered to his fathers."

Dr. Mendenhall was rather less than the common size, his hair was sandy, his complexion ruddy, his eyes blue, and his features regular and betokening great intelligence. He was a

kind hearted benevolent man. His purpose was to do good,
and he gave himself up to carrying it out. His disposition
was social; he enjoyed his friends and family. Hospitality
was a part of his nature. At his house his brethren and
friends always found a hearty welcome. He was an exact
and ready accountant. He wrote a good hand. He composed
and wrote easily; his letters and other compositions were
remarkable for their perspicuity and force. He spoke plainly,
forcibly and well. He made no pretensions to oratory; but
yet he never failed to secure an attentive auditory whenever
he chose to speak. In all the relations of life, as a friend,
child, parent, husband and master, he was good, just and
true. As a citizen and an officer he was never found wanting.
Few, very few, such men live or have lived amongst us as Dr.
Mendenhall. His death has made a great void—still we must
not mourn. With the poet let us say:

> "Servant of God well done;
>   Rest from thy loved employ,
> The battle fought, the victory won,
>   Enter thy Master's joy."

Dr. Benjamin Waldo, the son of Dr. Joseph W. Waldo,
graduated in the Medical College of Charleston in 1836; he
settled at Newberry in 1838, and with increasing reputation
and usefulness pursued his business to the fall of 1847, when
he removed to Florida. He married Sarah, the daughter of
John Lipscomb, of Edgefield. Few men ever were greater
favorites in Newberry, as was shewn in his election to the
Legislature in 1844.

James Divver lived after 1828 in the house built by Marmaduke Coate, until December, 1833, when he removed to
Charleston.

The life of this gentleman is romantic enough to gratify
the morbid taste of the present age for the wonderful, if we
had space to give it. He was an Irishman. He landed in
New Brunswick, and there became a member of the Baptist
Church; his wanderings thence I cannot trace; he came to
Newberry District in 1819, with his bundle on a stick, and
taught a common country school until the fall of 1820. In
the summer of that year he began the study of the classics

at the Newberry Academy, and at a school near James Mc-
Morries, in Laurens, he completed his Academic education.
He entered the Junior Class of the South Carolina College,
by the bounty of the Clariosophic Society, incorporated in
December, 1822. He was in 1823 elected Treasurer of the
College, with a salary of $400; he graduated December, 1824,
and was elected at the same time tutor of mathematics in the
South Carolina College, with a salary of $1,000. Such unex-
ampled success attending the course of a stranger indicated
rare qualities of the head and heart. Such had James
Divver; he was one of the best mathematicians ever graduated
at the South Carolina College: he was a true Irishman,
generous and devoted. But an unfortunate habit, too much
indulged in, of using intoxicating drink, made it necessary
for him to resign. He came to Newberry, and took charge of
the Academy in 1828, (January;) he married in February,
Sophia Coppock.

From 1833, Mr. Divver's arrival in Charleston, till 1845, he
taught school for a great time with unexampled success.
About that time he took charge of the Merchants' Hotel,
King Street, Charleston; he died December, 1847, leaving a
widow and nine children. Misfortune after misfortune crowded
on his latter years, and he died largely insolvent; but his
family were not left destitute; a provision which a friend
induced him to make soon after his marriage for his wife and
children saved them from poverty. From '42 to his death,
Mr. Divver was a member of the Total Abstinence Society,
and never tasted intoxicating drink. James Divver was a
simple, pure minded, good hearted Irishman, an excellent
teacher, the best of husbands and fathers.

David Boozer, (Big Dave, as he was usaully called;) was
an inhabitant of the town of Newberry, until Sunday, 10th of
February, 1850, on which day, he blew out his own brains,
and rushed into the presence of his mighty Maker. He was
a native of Newberry. The writer knew him well from 1808
to his death: he was possessed of great energy of character;
had generally a great flow of spirits, and until within a few
years had been attended by unexampled prosperity. The
change in this respect, although he was still surrounded by
an ample estate, unsettled his reason, and led to the rash,

mad act, which he committed. He left a widow, his second wife, and an adopted child to mourn their great loss. His aged mother, of more than four score years, still survives; sad and awful indeed was it to see her bending over his mangled remains, and lamenting her first born son only as a mother can lament. He was an honest, good man. How frail, however, is poor humanity, at all times, and never more sadly illustrated than in the case of David Boozer's suicide.

The Newberry Agricultaral Society, constituted in 1838, is a district institution, but holding here its annual meetings, may be briefly noticed in connection with the town. Beginning with 1841, the annual meetings have since been numerously attended. Premiums were awarded for stock and various other matters *then* and since. One hundred persons now belong to it. The annual meeting brings them together to impart to one another the benefits of each year's observation and experience. They dine together, with cold water as their only beverage, and with improved and improving friendships they meet and separate. The reports from various committees are always interesting, and have given a high character to the Society. Newberry has improved under the influence of such a Society more than the most sanguine dared to hope. The officers of the Society are John Belton O'Neall, President; Dr. George W. Glenn, 1st Vice President; Simon Fairar, 2nd Vice-President; Silas Johnston, Recording Secretary, and W. B. D'Oyley, Treasurer. I trust I may be allowed to express the hope, that this Society may increase in numbers and usefulness, until Newberry shall be cultivated like a garden, and all her resources shall be fully developed.

There has been a Female Academy, with occasional interval, in operation for many years. Lately the Trustees of the Academies, male and female, have applied a portion of their funds, derived originally from escheated estates, granted by the Act of 1828, to the purchase of a lot between Johnston and Boundary Streets, and have erected on it a beautiful and commodious brick house. There is a fine school now in operation under the charge of a well educated, intelligent and Christian teacher, Mr. DuPre,* It is to be hoped that New-

---

* Now under the care of Mr. Hood and Mrs. Anderson.

berry will not suffer herself, in the education of her daughters, to be behind any district in the State; and that the school will be such as to justify its teachers's permanent settlement among us.

Reader, before you is the village or town of Newberry from its earliest days. May it hereafter far surpass and exceed what it ever has been.

NO. 9.

In No. 8, by some strange forgetfulness, the names of Henry Summer, Esq., and Dr. Benedict Mayer were omitted among the professional gentlemen now living in the town of Newberry. Both of them have too much merit, both as men, and in the law, and in physic, to be omitted when Newberry is remembering her children.

Nicholas Summer, Esq., once well known in the town and district of Newberry as a young man of talent and a lawyer of promise, deserves to be chronicled among her past worthies.

He was the eldest son of Capt. John Summer, of Pomaria, formerly of Lexington, now of Newberry District. He was born 27th of October, 1804. In 1826, he applied to Judge O'Neall to study law, who advised him to graduate before he attempted the study. He accordingly entered the South Carolina College in December, 1826, and graduated with the first honor of his class in December, 1828. He studied law and was admitted to the Bar in December, 1830. He settled at Newberry, and successfully pursued his profession as the partner of Robert Dunlap, Esq., and after his removal, alone, until February, 1836, when he and a younger brother, John, volunteered in Col. Goodwyn's regiment of mounted volunteers in the Florida campaign against the Seminole Indians. He was the orderly sergeant of Capt. Hargrove's company, and on the 30th of March was badly wounded by a ball fired by the Indians in an ambuscade, as the company filed into a swamp, which shattered his thigh bone. In this wounded condition he was carried to Tampa Bay, where he languished until the 13th of June, when he was released from pain and suffering here, and entered upon an everlasting state. His brother who accompanied him, and who had been constantly by his bed side, in a few days after his death sickened and died. Of them I may be permitted to say in the beautiful, inspired language of King David, when lamenting the fall of Saul and Jonathan, they "were lovely and pleasant in their lives, and in their death they were not divided." Sad, however, is the reflection, whenever we contemplate the bed of glory as the bed of death, and remember how many noble men have been sacrificed, uselessly sacrificed, in such a war as that waged against the Seminoles.

Nicholas Summer was a well educated man, capable of being eminently useful! He spoke well, and there can be little doubt, had he been permitted to live, he would before this have occupied the front rank of his profession. As it was, he only gave the promise of the fruit by the richness of the flower.

Having discharged the pleasing, yet mournful duty of a just tribute to a young friend, I turn now to the more appropriate business of this number, the Bush River Baptist Church. Their house of worship is near the river whose name it bears, and is about twelve miles southwest of Newberry. This venerable religious body, was constituted in 1771 by Elders Philip Mulkey and Samuel Newman. It consisted of nine members, one of whom, Samuel Newman, became the Pastor. It is remarkable, that with one exception, this church, from its constitution, in 1771, to the present time, has called its Pastors from its own members. Of Elder Newman, I have been unable to obtain any satisfactory accounts; his descendants, until very recently, lived near to the church, perhaps some may still remain. He died suddenly in, I presume, '73; as in that year, Elder Thomas Norris, a licensed preacher of the Baptist Church of Little Saluda, in Edgefield District, was called to the care of the Bush River Baptist Church, and accepted the call. He was ordained the same year by Elders Philip Mulkey and David Rees; and became the Pastor of the Lord's little flock of Bush River.

Elder Norris was a peculiar man, and endeavored to walk in the primitive manner of the Apostles. He visited his people and friends on foot, and as he entered a house, he said, in the language of his Master, (Luke 10:5) "peace be to this house." He practiced the washing of the feet of his brethren, as taught in John 13 chap. 4, 5. His pastorship was in the troublesome times of the Revolution. He taught the doctrine of *non-resistance;* for his boldness in thus preaching he was shut up in the prison of old Ninety-six. His liberty was offered him again and again, if he would cease to teach and preach as was his wont. In the martyr spirit of Christianity, he refused to accept his liberty on any such condition. He was at length released without condition, and in his pure, humble and guileless way, continued to preach and teach "Jesus and Him crucified," until 1780, when he, too, like Elder Newman, was suddenly called home.

In 1781, John Cole, Sr., a member of the church, was called to be their Preacher; he entered upon the duties thus laid upon him; and in 1783, was ordained and set apart to the work of the Gospel Ministry by Elders Joseph Burson and John Web. The church, under his care, grew and increased daily, until 1791, when the church was first represented in the Bethel Association. At this time Michael Landers was appointed the clerk, and a regular record of the proceedings of the church began to be kept. In '94 it appears that that good man, David Mason, was one of the messengers to the Association. For more than forty years, I presume, he was a member of this church, and engaged in the blessed work of reconciliation and peace, which so much characterized him during my knowledge of him for the last twenty years of his life.

In 1802 was that great revival of religion, which may have been several times since equalled, but has certainly never been surpassed. It seemed as if the spirit of the living God was pervading the whole community, and that all were rising up and crying out "men and brethren, what shall we do to be saved?" That many extravagancies were enacted, and much which, to us of a more sober day, seems to be no work of the gentle spirit of Christian grace, was present is true. The falling of many, and the spasmodic action of others, called "the *jerks*," occurred under the preaching of the ministers, who then and there proclaimed their Master's word. Whether such things be or be not the fruits of the Spirit, it is not for such an one as I to say. Still I would venture to suggest, that there is much more of human sympathy and terror than repentance in such scenes. But still many were truly converted, and became bright and shining lights in the Lord's house. From the 22nd of August to the 30th of October, inclusive, ninety-four persons were received and baptized on a profession of faith. On the 4th of September,

Charles Crow was received and baptized. This gentleman, as will be hereafter seen, was "a chosen vessel" of the Redeemer, destined to bear the word not only to his neighbors, but to a distant land.

On the 9th of July, 1803, Charles Griffin, Esq., was received and baptized. Mr. Griffin was first appointed a Justice of the Peace for Newberry in 1798, and continued as such, and as a Justice of the Quorum till his death in 1820. At his appoint ment, and for many years after, it was no small honor to be a Justice of the Peace. None but the most intelligent and virtuous members of the community were then appointed. Mr. Griffin was a member of the House of Representatives of South Carolina in 1810 and 1811. No man better deserved the affectionate regard of his neighbors; for he was indeed *a good man*, and *verily his works follow him.*

On the 13th of October, 1804, Stephen McCraw was appointed the clerk of the church in place of Michael Landers, deceased. Mr. Landers I never knew, and cannot, therefore, speak of him further than to say he seems to have been capable of writing a good hand, and keeping in very decent order the records of the church.

He died childless; his widow was the wife of John Gooch; and his adopted son, John Demony, after her death, was, by his will, entitled to his land.

Stephen McCraw was an active, bustling, intelligent little man, who, soon after the close of the war of 1812, was seized *with the mania* of bettering his fortunes in the southwest, and emigrated to Alabama.

On the 8th day of March, 1806, I find the following query was propounded to the church; "Is it a matter worthy of censure for brethren *to carry or send spirituous liquors to public places to sell by the small?*" The answer was: *"We think it a practice beneath the dignity of a disciple of Jesus, and that it is not sanctioned by the Gospel!"* This was indeed the glimmering light of that better day of Total Abstinence which is now so radiant every where. Especially does it delight me that this venerable church, now near eighty years of age, should have been, forty-four years ago, permitted to testify against *the abominable traffic in intoxicating drink.* Brethren, may I not ask you to ponder well upon this ancient action of your own church, and inquire whether it is not your duty, one and all, to be alongside of your present worthy pastor in his war against strong drink?

On the 8th of August, 1807, two gifted brethren of the church, James Teague and Charles Crow, were called to the work of the Gospel Ministry, and Elders Palmer, Shackelford, Lilly and King were appointed to ordain them. On the 29th of August, Elders Palmer and King attended, and in the presence of the church, ordained them. On the 9th of November, 1811, John S. Carwile, heretofore spoken of in No. 8, was received as a member. In 1817, 11th of October, he became the clerk of the church in the place of Stephen McCraw, resigned, which place he retained until 11th October, 1829, when he resigned and was succeeded by John K. Grffiin. On the 6th October, 1831, Mr. Carwile and James Divver were dismissed from the Bush River Church to become the foundation of the church at Newberry, which was about being gathered and constituted out of the converts of September previous.

————

No. 9 CONCLUDED.

James Teague was not permitted to labor long in his Master's Vineyard; he died young.

John Cole, Sr., the third Pastor of the Bush River Church, died full of years and pious usefulness, in 1816. For thirty-five years he had been the Pastor; he had seen the church begin as a little flock, grow, increase, and become as a great army. Every where his praise was in all the churches; and yet there is no record of him from which a fuller and better account can be given of his life and services. He lies in the quiet church yard of Bush River, in the midst of his flock and family. His glorified spirit is in the presence of Him whom he loved, honored and served so well here on earth.

On the 9th of October, 1816, Elder Charles Crow was called to, and took upon himself the pastoral care of the church. Never was any religious body confided to abler and better hands. Few preachers were better endowed with grace from on high; few men in or out of the ministry presented more loveable lives than Charles Crow. He continued to discharge the duties till 1825, when, like many of his brethren, he thought it to be his duty to his family to seek his home in the Southwest. There he has been permitted ever since to preach most acceptably his Master's Kingdom, and long may he be continued, faithful, able and venerable, as he is, to labor in that great work.

On the 12th of January, 1822, Daniel Mangum was received as a member. On the 9th of April, 1825, David Peterson, a member of the church and an ordained minister, was called to the care of the church; he accepted the sacred trust, but in a few months he was removed from usefulness below to glory above. Mr. Peterson was no common man. He had experienced a full share of the vanities of this world. Like Solomon, he had tasted the falsely called pleasures of the world; and like him he could have exclaimed "vanity of vanities; all is vanity." Like him, he had learned wisdom in the courts of experience, and like him he had turned to the living God! He had a limited education; but he possessed a great flow of words, not without ideas, but the just representatives of them. If he had lived, it is probable he would have been eminently useful. But God does not see as men see! He called him from his post; his hour of watching was past, and he was allowed to enter upon his rest!

Elder Daniel Mangum, Pastor of the Bush River Baptist Church, Newberry District, is no more! This good man and faithful preacher of his Master's Word literally died in his work. He preached at the Reedy River Baptist Association, Hurricane Church, Laurens District, on Saturday, the 18th ult., he was taken sick, was unable to reach his home, and died at the house of one of his relations and brethren, Dr. Rock, on Saturday the 26th, at about half-past 6 P. M., in the 65th year of his age, leaving a widow and several children to mourn their irreparable loss.

No man has better performed his part in this world. No man was better prepared to enter upon his everlasting rest!

He became a member of the Bush River Baptist Church, 12th January, 1824; on the 3d of November, 1825, he was

1 J

set apart by the church for the work of the ministry; he was ordained as a preacher and evangelist on the 7th January, 1826; on the 12th of May, he became the Pastor of the church. This position he retained till his death. For twenty-six years he labored incessantly in that church as its Pastor, to lead his friends, relations and neighbors to righteousness and peace. Eminently were his labors blessed! Many precious and great revivals took place under his ministry. Perhaps the greatest was that of '31–'32, when 145 were added to the church. Scarcely a year has, however, passed away without some in-gathering.

He was for many years also the supply of the Cross Roads, Rocky Spring and Mount Zion Churches. He was the supply of the Newberry Baptist Church for over two years. Other churches he also attended, and faithfully led the people along the way of truth and righteousness. He was, from its organization, a member and one of the Vice-Presidents of the Newberry Baptist Bible Society. He was a Teetotaller, having early become a pledged man, and with undeviating fidelity, maintained his position as a friend of temperance. He was elected Moderator of the Reedy River Baptist Association in 1851, and again in '52. Of him, the friend and brother who pens this imperfect sketch had occasion in 1850, to say: "Mr. Mangum has been now for twenty-four years constantly and laboriously engaged in preaching. Few men can point to more fruits. Indeed, few men have had the physical ability to undergo the labor which he has performed. In the midst of constant preaching he has not failed to seek and obtain knowledge. He has improved a limited education to very good purpose. Often have I listened to his discourses and found them replete with arguments, wisdom and piety. Sometimes I have been delighted with bursts of genuine eloquence. He has taken a part, a noble part, in all the benevolent operations of the present day of Christian Light, Missionary, Bible and Temperance. I call his part a noble one, because he has often been called to sustain these good causes against the ignorance and prejudice of brethren whom he loved." This which was said as living, may be now repeated as posthumous praise, with the addition of two years spent in the same good way.

Mr. Mangum was not only a preacher of righteousness and a philanthropist; he was a good citizen, neighbor and friend. In all these relations he was never found wanting. Occasionally he taught the young children of his neighborhood to enter upon the duties of life! Every public duty demanded of a citizen he discharged! The bed of sickness, and the chamber of death in and out of his congregation, never failed, when within his reach, to have his presence, services and sympathy! He began life a poor man, but by patient industry, aided by his excellent wife, he attained to competence. He could have said to his people, as Samuel did to Israel, "Behold, here I *am*; witness against me before the Lord, and before his anointed: whose ox have I taken? or whose ass have I taken? or whom have I defrauded? whom have I oppressed? or of whose hand have I received any bribe to blind my eyes therewith?" He was an honest, pure, good man, full of mercy and good work. Blessed with an even good temper, a cheerful, social and happy disposition, when these came also to be purified by religion, he became indeed worthy of the great love and respect which he received from all who knew him.

Mr. Mangum was about six feet high, of a large and powerful frame. His voice was one of great power. It was often tasked to its utmost by preaching to large congregations in and out of doors. For years his friends remarked his failing physical powers, but notwithstanding he must have known that he was wearing away, the work was before him, "the fields were white for the harvest," and he could not, and would not hold back.

In the pulpit he sang, prayed and preached, with the power and zeal of the early Apostles. "Repent, and be baptized every one of you, in the name of Jesus Christ, for the remission of sins," fell from his lips with no ordinary power, on the ears of hundreds of believing, trembling sinners! He was indeed a man of God, and as such he entered upon his great and everlasting rest.

The loss is ours, the gain is his. His wife, children, brethren, sisters and friends may and will mourn as human nature demands, but their tears should be dried by remembering—he lived a man, he died a Christian, and he lives now a saint in everlasting glory.

On the 6th of October, 1826, General John K. Griffin, Esq., was received as a member; on the 8th of November, 1828, he was ordained a Deacon, and on the 11th of October, 1828, he was appointed Clerk, and continued in the discharge of its duties until his death in 1841.

The various duties of Member, Deacon, Clerk, and Messenger to the Association, were most exemplarily performed by General Griffin.

General Griffin was born 13th of August, 1788; married very young, I think when about nineteen, the daughter of Col. John Simpson; she died, I think, about 1828; he married, in '36 or '37, Sarah Dunlap, the widow of Robert Dunlap, Esq., and third daughter of Major Frederick Nance.

In 1814, John K. Griffin, then captain of militia, was marched under the command of Major Jason Meadow to the neighborhood of Georgetown, where he performed a tour of six months in the regiment under the command of Col. Alston. He returned from that expedition a very popular man. He retained his popularity, thus beginning, to his death. In October, 1816, he, with George W. Glenn, John B. O'Neall and Col. Samuel Cannon, was elected a member of the House of Representatives; he was again elected in 1818; in 1820, he was elected Senator in place of Major Frederick Nance, and continued to be re-elected, '24 and '28. In 1830 he was elected to Congress in the place of his friend, Gen. Starling Tucker, who declined a re-election.

He was re-elected, '32, '34, '36 and '38. In 1840 he declined a re-election. In 1825 he was elected Brigadier General in the place of his friend, John B. O'Neall, who had been promoted to the rank of Major General of the 5th division.

In 1829 he was elected Major General in the place of John B. O'Neall, who in December previous, had been elected a Judge. In 1833, December, by that Act of the Legislature which vacated all the military commissions in the State for party purposes, and which better deserves the brand of "unrighteousness" than any ever passed, he ceased to be a Major General. On the 1st of August, 1841, he closed his useful life in the full triumph of Christian faith.

General Griffin was a good man, and a faithful public officer; he possessed plain unpretending good sense, with a great deal of practical, useful knowledge. He approached his various public trusts with great diffidence; but he never failed by persevering industry to make himself fully equal to the duty demanded.

His brother, Col. Bluford F. Griffin, was received by the Bush River Baptist Church as a member on the 12th of November, 1831; on the 6th of August, 1841, he succeeded his deceased brother as Clerk, and is now 'in the discharge of its duties.

Having now glanced' hastily over the history of this ancient church, it may be permitted to observe that from her have proceeded Mill Creek, (now Cross Road's Church) which was constituted in 1801; Mount Zion and Mount Olive, constituted, I presume, since 1831.

Bush River Baptist Church is not only the oldest Baptist Church in Newberry, but probably in the upper country. She is one of the largest and most powerful among all her sisters. She has been heretofore signally blessed, in being provided constantly with a shepherd to lead the flock, and in the continual out-pouring of the spirit of all grace.

May her present worthy pastor long be spared to her May she continue to grow and increase and multiply until she shall far exceed her former self.

NOTE.—Charles Griffin, Esq., herein before spoken of, was born 23d June, 1763; he died 9th of August, 1820. He was born in Virginia. He was a soldier of the Revolution, and wounded just above the left hip joint. This occurred at Musgrove's Mills on the Enoree. He was taken at Hay's Station. How he escaped, or other particulars of his Revolutionary service, cannot now be ascertained. He was appointed a magistrate in 1798—(not 1738.)

NO 10.

In this number I propose to give some further and fuller account of the Fork, that is, the tract of country lying on Broad River, between Enoree and Tiger, and separated from Union by the district line from Avery's Ford on Enoree to Hill's (now Crenshaw's) on Tiger, which is about equal to six miles square. This section of Newberry possessed, and still possesses, many great natural advantages. The rich rolling land lying between the rivers was once as fertile and productive as could be desired. Improvident culture has made many of the hills bare—still good husbandry, as illustrated on many farms, has shewn that although wasted they were not impoverished. The Broad, Enoree and Tiger Rivers furnish a navigation for mountain boats, whereby most of the produce raised sought, and still seeks, a market.

The original settlers were the Lyles, Jones, Sashal Grasty, the Kellys, Chandlers, Bonds, Gorees, Fergusons, Hills, Hancocks, Stewarts, Gordons, Curetons, Dicksons, Nolands, Avereys, Andersons, Caldwells, Wadlingtons, John Clarke, James Murphy, the Littletons, Greens, Robisons, Shadrack Vessels, Daniel Mackel Duff, the Maybins, (William and Matthew,) Thomas Wilson, Thomas Perry and John Walker. They were generally immigrants from North Carolina and Virginia, except the Maybins, who came from near Ballamena, Antrim, Ireland.

Before I enter upon the account of the other inhabitants of the interesting section, I trust I may be pardoned for first speaking of the family of my friend, Col. Benjamin Maybin, and himself. From him the materials for the sketch of the old inhabitants of the Fork, and the incidents of the Revolution, were principally obtained. Since he communicated them he has been gathered to his fathers, and of him, therefore, I may venture to give as perfect an account as my means will permit.

William Maybin, the father of Col. Benjamin Maybin,

with his wife and one child, his wife's mother and sister, and a younger brother, Matthew Maybin, landed in Charleston in 1771, thence passed on to the place whereon the Colonel lived, at his death, well known as Maybinton, and there settled. He and his family were Presbyterians, and like all of that class, took the side of liberty. In 1776 he was in Williamson's memorable campaign against the Cherokees, in a company commanded by Capt. Cureton, and in the regiment commanded by Col. John Lyles, and was beyond doubt present, and participated in the ring fight and other affairs leading to the complete overthrow of the Cherokees. A full account of this expedition will be found by the curious in the memoir of Major McJunkin, published in the second volume of the Magnolia, at page 32.

After the fall of Charleston in May, 1780, William and Matthew Maybin, Shadrack Vessels and others, joined Sumter, either in North Carolina or on the Catawba, in this State. They were present on the 7th of August, 1780, at the battle of Hanging Rock, in which Col. Maybin stated Vessels was killed, his father taken prisoner, and that his Uncle Matthew made his escape. In this there must be some inaccuracy. For at Hanging Rock Sumter was victorious, and although it is possible that Vessels was there killed, yet it is not likely that a prisoner was taken by the vanquished party, or that there was any necessity for any of the victors to escape. It is most likely that William Maybin was taken prisoner at, and that his brother Matthew escaped from, Sumter's surprise by Tarleton at Fishing Creek, on the 18th of August, 1780, eleven days after the battle of Hanging Rock, and this is made almost certain by a subsequent part of Col. Maybin's narrative, in which he speaks of Vessels' death taking place at Sumter's defeat at Hanging Rock. William Maybin was taken to Charleston, and died on board a prison ship, *that charnel house of liberty*, to which British pride, tyranny and cruelty consigned so many of the gallant spirits who fought and bled for Carolina. He was *here* before his death found by his wife's brother, Benjamin Duncan, who was a soldier in the British army. He prevailed on his officers to permit the ·soldier of liberty, William Maybin, to be brought on shore, and interred in his mother earth. He sleeps in what was then called Potter's field.

Benjamin Duncan then visited his bereaved sister, and after some stay with her, returned to his duty, but promised, as soon as possible, to come back, and take care of and provide for her and his other single sister, and as a pledge, left with Mrs. Maybin his watch and other things. It was soon reported among the tories that Mrs. Maybin's brother had left with her his gold watch; it, however, was magnified by rumor, as usual, for it was only a silver one. Spoil, spoil, ever first in the thoughts of many of those guilty traitors, who were hurling the most deadly blows at their bleeding country, soon brought two of this band of marauders to the house of the widow and orphans; they demanded the watch, accompanied by threats that they would take the lives of the women, Mrs.. Maybin and her sister and the children, if it was not delivered. Mrs. Maybin, with a mother's feeling predominating for the safety of her children, fled to the woods, leaving her sister to contend with the ruffians. The watch was hid under the head of the bed; she succeeded in baffling their cupidity; they found it not. It descended to, and was worn, preserved and valued as a precious relic by the late Col. Benjamin Maybin; doubly endeared to him as a memento of his uncle, and the sufferings and fortitude of his mother and aunt.

The family of William Maybin, after his death, suffered the usual privations of the Revolution. When Rawdon's army pursued Green on his retreat from Ninety-Six, they encamped about a week at Col. Glenn's, now Brazleman's, Mills on Enoree; they then marched through the Fork, and crossed Broad River at Lyle's Ford. On this march the soldiers plundered everything in their way! The only piece of meat left for the food of the family of Mrs. Maybin, and which she had hid on the *wind beam* of her house, was found and taken. A small grey mare called, *Dice*, her only beast, was also borne away, though she afterwards fortunately recovered her. Such a *foray* is so disgraceful to a regular army, that I am reluctant to conclude that it could have had the sanction of the commander, *an Irishman*, (Lord Rawdon), afterwards the celebrated

Earl of Morra. But his command, which followed him from Ireland, was made up very much from the gaols; and, therefore, it may be very well supposed that they were a set of accomplished rascals, capable of stealing even the last morsel from the widow and orphans.

On another occasion, a tory visited Mrs. Maybin's cabin, and finding a piece of homespun in her loom, he cut it out and bore it off as prize. What a fiend must such a man have been, who could look upon the almost naked children of a poor lone woman, and take from her the means of a scanty covering? He, however, did not escape. For little Ephraim Lyles afterwards meeting with him, and finding the cloth upon his legs in a pair of leggius, inflicted upon him a severe drubbing, and made him give up the cloth. This was justice, nobly and happily administered, and if little Eph. (as he was usually called) had never done any other good deed, his memory deserves to be cherished and respected for *this, so characteristic of a generous Carolinian.*

The family, as I have before said, were Presbyterians, and worshiped as often as they could, at King's Creek, where lies Col. Maybin's maternal grand-mother. Benjamin Maybin was born 10th of February, 1775; he was, therefore, a mere infant during the dark days of the Revolution. He was born where he lived and died.

Of his early life I know but little. He had, I have no doubt, to struggle with many difficulties; but the same unconquerable spirit, which carried him unbent through many of the trials of his subsequent life, enabled him to triumph over *them.* He obtained a pretty good English education. He was for many years a merchant, and by patient industry accumulated a handsome fortune, and made his homestead on the main road from Henderson's bridge on the Enoree to Buncombe, a pretty little village bearing his name.

He commanded during the war, the 8th, afterwards, 38th regiment of militia. He resigned, when General Starling Tucker was elected Brigadier, in 1815. He was twice a member of the House of Representatives. He died the 27th of May last.

The last twenty-four years of his life were spent in
retirement. He was twice married. By his first wife he
had a large family, none of whom survived him except his
son, Major William Maybin, of Columbia. He with two
grand-children, the children of John Maybin, (deceased,) are
his only lineal decendants. His second wife, the youngest
and now the only surviving child of Col. James Lyles, was
the widow of Capt. John Henderson when she became his
wife. One son, the only fruit of this marriage, a fine
promising boy, was cut off, while pursuing his collegiate
course. Mrs. Maybin survived her husband, and is now
(March, 1850,) in the 69th year of her age. Any one
who looks upon her, will see at once that she is the descendant of a *race of heroes*, and that she could, and would
if necessary, play the part of the Spartan mother, when
she said to her son, as she delivered his shield, "return to
me victorious, or be borne upon this shield!"

Having known Col. Maybin intimately for thirty-five years,
it is a duty which I discharge with pleasure (if there can
be pleasure in speaking of a deceased friend) to do something like justice to his memory.

He was a well informed man in most of the matters
affecting his own rights or those of his country. In private
life no man maintained what was due to himself with
more unflinching firmness. Many undertook to oppress or
overcome him. *None ever succeeded.* The poor unaided
orphan boy maintained his foothold among the Lyles,
Gordons, Wadlingtons and Malones; and after many years
stood *"primus interpares."*

As a public officer, he discharged his duties in the most
faithful and exemplary way. Ever at his post, and ever
ready to do what duty demanded, he deserved more than
he ever obtained, *unceasing popularity.* He was *too honest,*
too sincere to be always popular. His opinions he never
disguised. Such as they were, popular or unpopular, the
people knew them. The consequence was he could not
always be elected to the Legislature, when he desired to
be. He was a Union man, when the storm of Nullification
scowled over the sky of South Carolina. To be in such a
minority tried the nerves of a man. As a husband and

father, he was all which affection ever demanded. He was often called to stand by the bed of death; his first wife and his many children were borne from him. Still he was seen like King David, rising from the affliction, and exclaiming "I shall go to *them*," but they "shall not return to me!"

Col. Maybin was a man of violent passions; but I never knew him do a mean act to gratify them. He had enemies, who hated and pursued him with a vengeance which seemed never to tire. Such he met with a similar spirit, and it may be, that on such occasions, his passions may have carried him too far, and that in striking at his enemies, he may have touched those, who until then, were not his foes.

In reference to one matter of his life, the children of his last wife by her former marriage, I can speak with great certainty. No man ever exhibited a greater desire to treat them with a parent's kindness than he did. When they, as was natural, looked at him with the jealousy with which children generally regard a step-father, well do I know that his heart was wrung by it; and that he was ready, always ready, to bestow upon them a father's care and a father's blessing. After the death of his youngest son, this disposition was fully shewn, in a division among them of what he considered their mother's estate.

He is gone! His earthly course is closed; he has entered upon his everlasting state. Full of years, full of usefulness, he has been gathered to his fathers. May those who are his descendants imitate his virtues, and be like him, entitled to have written on the tomb which covers his remains: "He had his faults, but they were specks on the beautiful snow white drapery of a virtuous, honest, good life."

Ephraim, John and Williamson Lyles were brothers. Ephraim settled on the east side of Broad River; he was the father of Col. Arromanus Lyles, Col. James Lyles, Big Bill, Big Eph, Henry and John; all of whom settled, except Col. Arromanus, west of Broad River; all were actively engaged in the Revolution. Their father, Ephraim, was shot in his own house before the war commenced, (as is stated by Col. Maybin,) but this I presume, means before the fall of Charleston, in 1780. For, until then the upper country scarcely knew the war.

John Lyles, the brother of Ephraim, was elected colonel, and may have served in the campaign called the snow camps, beginning in November, '75, and taking its name from the great snow which fell upon the encampment of the army at Hollingsworth's now Simpson's Mills, Rabun's Creek, Laurens District, on the 24th of December, at night. A full account of this expedition, will also be found in the memoir of Major McJunkin, 2nd Magnolia, 31.

Col. Lyles commanded in the expedition of the subsequent year against the Cherokees, to which allusion has already been made. In No. 7, I was mistaken in supposing Col. James Lyles had the command. The memoir of Major McJunkin was right. Who was present at the battle of Hanging Rock is uncertain. Col. Maybin states that Col. John Lyles was too old to take part in the revolutionary struggle subsequent to the fall of Charleston. Col. James Lyles, it seems from his statement, died at Chester, 1st July, 1780; he could not, therefore, have been present. I presume it was John Lyles, the youngest son of Ephraim, who, as Col. Maybin says, commanded the Fork company, and which we know was in that action on the 7th of August. It was nothing unusual for a captain commanding an independent detachment to be called colonel in accounts of the Revolution.

James Lyles, the second son of Ephraim, was appointed colonel, on the resignation of his uncle, John, after his return from the Cherokee expedition in '76. He commanded and bore part in all the partisan affairs, until the fall of Charleston.* Retreating then before the enemy, he was taken with the small pox, and was borne by his troops and friends on a litter to Chester Court House, where, on the 1st of July, he died, leaving a widow (afterwards Mrs.

---

* In Tarleton's Campaign in the South, '93, he speaks of one Lisle who was from the district between Enoree and Tiger Rivers, being banished to the Islands, returning, he took place in the regiment formerly commanded by Col. Nash, then by Col. Floyd, in the British interest, and carried it all off and joined Sumter. Who the *Lisle* spoken of by Tarleton may be is uncertain.

Goree,) and three infant daughters; the youngest and only surviving one of whom is Mrs. Elizabeth Maybin, herein before spoken of. At his death, his youngest brother John probably succeeded to his actual command; not more than a company proceeded on, and joined Sumter on the Catawba, and fought the battle of Hanging Rock.

John Lyles after the war became major of the lower battalion of the Enoree regiment, by seniority, and removed to Georgia.

Williamson Lyles, the youngest brother of Ephraim and Col. John Lyles, was also too old to undergo the hardships of the war, after 1780; he had only one son old enough to take part in the bloody struggle for liberty. Ephraim Lyles, (commonly called little Eph.) was that son, and gallantly did he perform his part. Like most of his compeers, little can be told of what he did or suffered.

No. 10 CONTINUED.

Sashal Grasty was a good whig, but too old for active service, when the tide of war rolling from the sea-board overwhelmed the whole interior, he was seized by the British, or tories, with five or six negro slaves and marched to Ninety-Six gaol, where being imprisoned with others who had the small pox, he caught that fatal disease and died. He left children, one of whom, Patsy, was the first wife of Samuel E. Kenner, Esq., another, Mrs. Susan Lyles, widow of Col. Arromanus Lyles, died within the last twenty years at Maybinton; her descendants are in that neighborhood. Her life, if it could be gathered together, would shew that truth is sometimes more marvellous than fiction.

James Kelly was a soldier in the regiment raised in the beginning of the Revolution, called Thompson's Rangers. He was on Sullivan's Island at the memorable repulse of the British fleet, 28th July, 1776. From the names of the officers actually in the fort, given in Moultrie's Memoirs, 1st vol. pp. 183, neither Col. Thompson nor any of his officers seem to have been *there;* but from the vote of thanks by Congress, to be found at the same page, it is manifest Col. Thompson's regiment had a part in that glorious affair. It is probable, as they were riflemen, that they were stationed to prevent the landing of the British on the Island. This service they performed while Moultrie and his gallant compeers were comparing the strength of Palmetto logs, manned by Carolinian hearts, with the wooden walls of old England, sustained by her noble tars, who had victoriously unfurled their master's flag on every sea, and *hitherto* against every power.

He was appointed a lieutenant in the militia service; he was present at, and bore a part as a good soldier, in the capture of Fort Granby, on the 14th of May, 1781. Of his other services I am uninformed. He lived long after "wild war's rude blast was blown," and enjoyed the precious fruits of *constitutional liberty*, which his services contributed so much to obtain, and died, leaving a posterity to inherit the glorious estate thus won—and which may they, and all of South Carolina, and the other people of the United States, ever enjoy unmarred by *disunion, or any sectional parties or factions.*

Mordecai Chandler belonged to Capt. John Lyles' company which was scouring the country below the Saluda. (This must have been in December, 1780, or January, 1781.) They (that is the company) found two men in the woods, unarmed. On being questioned, they professed to be whigs who had escaped from the British fort at Granby, and were endeavoring to make their way to General Morgan's camp, at the Grindal Shoals, on Pacolet. Mordecai Chandler and George Reddin were detailed to conduct them to *the old wagoner.* They proceeded some distance, at some point in Union, having encamped for the night—while Chandler and Reddin were asleep, the pretended whigs rose on their escort, seized their arms, and in the conflict which ensued, wounded Chandler severely in the head, and finally made both him and Reddin their prisoners, and marched them to Ninety-Six and delivered them to the commander, Col. Cruger, by whom they were kept as prisoners until that post was evacuated. Chandler was thence taken to Dorchester, where he remained until he was exchanged near the close of the war.

In the war of the Revolution, both whigs and tories guarded the passes of the great rivers, especially the fords. Noah Bonds was one of the guards stationed west of the Broad River, at the Fishdam ford. The tories held the eastern bank. They often taunted the whigs with banters and opprobious words across the river. It is at the ford about a quarter of a mile wide. Noah, unwilling to bear such abuse, determined to try *his big rifle.* He levelled her at a tory, who was exposing his rear to an attack, and, strange to say, lodged the ball in the back part of his thigh! My informant, (Col. Maybin,) says the ball struck the water before it reached the eastern bank. The aim and direction, however, being true, the rebound carried it home. The colonel remarked, "it was said the man was not killed, *but he did not appear there again.*" One dose of American lead was quite a sufficient one for him.

Major Thomas Gordon, it is supposed, was elected major under the command of Col. John Lyles, and served with him in snow camps, and in the expedition against the Cherokees. He took an active part in the revolutionary struggle; but, like many another, the details of his services cannot be now obtained. He was the *first Sheriff* of Newberry, entering on his duties at the first county court, held at the house of Col. Robert Rutherford, 5th September, 1785. His term of office was two years, according to the constitution of 1778. The duties of his office were correctly performed; and as such, I am proud to say, they have ever since been performed. His descendants are still, I presume, to be found in the Fork.

Captain Curenton (or *Cureton,* perhaps, for I know this name was often pronounced Curenton,) commanded the company to which William Maybin belonged, in the expedition commanded by Williamson, herein before spoken of. David Dixon was his lieutenant.

John Caldwell, Esq., (father of Esquire John Caldwell and Joseph Caldwell, of Enoree, and therefore grand-father of Davis and John Caldwell, of Columbia, and Robert

Caldwell, of Charleston,) was captain of one of the revolutionary whig scouts. He was killed in the Dutch Fork.

John Clark settled on the Enoree, near the place now called Clarke's ford; he was a zealous, staunch whig during the war. In a skirmish, at Clarke's ford, under the command of Capt. Jones, he was shot through the leg, and escaped to a bluff a mile distant. To this place the enemy traced him by his blood—took him prisoner. His mother furnished him with a little salve and some cloth to bind up, and, afterwards to dress his wounds. His captors compelled him to mount a very poor horse, and thus to ride him, with nothing to separate him from his sharp backbone, except an old quilt his poor mother took from her scanty bed covering, and gave to him. With his feet bound under *this garron*, he was compelled to ride in great increasing agony to old Ninety-Six, more than forty miles. There he was in his wounded condition cast into prison, in the very midst of persons suffering under a virulent type of small pox. Nine of his fellow prisoners died. He was the tenth—and most marvellously got well; he was liberated, made his way home, and lived long after the Revolution. His descendants are still to be found in Newberry District. Capt. Jones, under whom Clarke served, was killed in the skirmish, and lies now on the bank of the river; near the ford. Johnson, not an inhabitant of the Fork, a brother-in-law of Clarke, was taken in the skirmish, and hanged on a tree just above the ford. Charles Littleton, (father of Mark and Charles,) was taken prisoner, carried to Ninety-Six gaol, where he also contracted the small pox, and died before he reached home. William Greer was a staunch whig and did good service; he was shot and killed by a tory in his own house.

Shadrack Vessels, heretofore spoken of as falling in Sumter's defeat at Fishing Creek, was, like his father, a firm, devoted whig. Charles Vessels, his father, lived at Snow Hill, (I presume now known as Liberty Hill,) opposite Augusta, Ga. Charles Vessels was a boat builder. While the British were in possession of Augusta, a sentinel was posted on the bank of the Savannah opposite to, or so as to be seen from, the boat yard. Vessels conceived the possible notion of killing the poor sentinel on his post. He swam up the river, with his butcher knife in his mouth, crept upon the sentinel and killed him. *This was murder;* it belonged not to war.

Charles Vessels was afterwards taken by the British. They were altogether uninformed of his murder of the sentinel; if that fact had been known, he would have been hanged, and justly hanged, on the first tree. He was considered as a mere prisoner. On account, however, of his turbulent disposition and stubborn spirit, he was put in irons and shipped for England. On the voyage the ship sprang a leak: the captain proposed to liberate him if he would assist in stopping it. He swore he would not; and wished they might go to hell together. The leak was, however, stopped without his assistance. He returned after the war, and if my memory be not at fault, I heard of his chopping off the head of a sleeping or drunk Indian with his broad-axe, at a place where he was building a boat, or flat, on the Ogechee. It is stated by my friend Col. Maybin, that he, Charles Vessels, after his return from England, took charge of the two sons of his son, Shadrack Vessels, whom he raised to nearly man's estate, when he died. Is it not a mysterious providence, that such a man of blood should die in his own bed? The scriptures are generally literally fulfilled in that "the violent man shall die a violent death." Daniel Mackel Duff, a celebrated partisan, was also taken prisoner, and, with Vessels, sent to England, where he remained until the war terminated; he then returned. He married a daughter of Col. William Farr, of Union. He was well known as a claimant for losses and pensions, during the Revolution, in the State Legislature.

No. 10 Continued.

Col. Ferguson after Cornwallis' victory of the 6th of August, moved from Camden at the head of the 71st

1   K

regiment, with the view of visiting the tory settlements of the upper country, training their young men, and afterwards rejoining the army. In the execution of this plan, he passed through Fairfield, crossed Broad River at Shirey's, (now Hughey's ferry,) and camped in the Dutch Fork, on Heller's Creek, near the late residence of that good citizen, David Hentz, who was called from us by his mighty Master about the same time that Col. Maybin obeyed the same awful summons! He here remained encamped for several days. Resuming his march, he crossed the Enoree at Kelly's ford, and encamped in the Fork, at the plantation of Col. James Lyles, deceased. He thence marched by John Robison's, plundered his house, and continued his march towards the mountains. Little did this accomplished officer, but ferocious enemy of American liberty, dream that he was marching to rouse the mountaineers, and that they, like the Highlanders of his own native land, would be gathered to his overthrow by the fiery and bloody cross, which he was preparing by oppression to light and wet with blood, and which, though not to be borne from hand to hand, as in Scotland, was to be seen and heard from, until the whole mountain region of South Carolina, North Carolina and Virginia, should be in arms. *But so it was.*

In less than two months, he and his men, regular and militia, were hunted to the death by the hardy mountaineers. On King's Mountain, he gallantly met his fate; there he and Col. Williams, of the Americans, lie with no other monument than the naked mountains, and no other requiem than the cry of the eagle, as he nightly seeks his mate.

In January, 1781, Matthew Maybin, James Chandler, Mark and Charles Littleton, little Eph. Lyles, and others living in the Fork, left their homes to unite with Morgan before the battle of the Cowpens. That glorious battle was fought and won; and the news reached them on the way. Still they were able to do good service. They fell upon a part of Tarleton's baggage train at Love's ford, near Gov. Johnston's plantation, and captured it; horses, negroes, wagons, and all other property, they managed to get safely into the block house on Pacolet, where the whole was divided among the captors. Seven negroes thus captured, were part of the spoil to which our friends of the Fork were entitled.

It is a highly important fact, and worthy of being especially recorded, that the inhabitants of the Fork were more united in their devotion to liberty, than any other settlement in the upper country. When the British regarded South Carolina as a conquered province, a proclamation was issued, inviting all the friends of the King to remove below their line of posts, extending from Ninety-Six by Granby to Camden, and that they should be protected; only one man from the Fork availed himself of the ignoble privilege, and sad was it for him that he did so, for the whigs afterwards caught and killed him.

Heavy, however, were the calamities with which the Fork was visited—plantations were wasted, families were in poverty and want; and last but not least, nine heads of families, in the six miles square, had been forever removed. Five were killed; two died in Ninety-Six gaol; one on a prison ship at Charleston; and one, Col. James Lyles, who had to be carried from home in a litter, with the small pox on him, got wet crossing Broad River at the Fish Dam ford, and died at Chester. Nine widows and their orphan children in the narrow compass of six miles square, is indeed a sad memorial of even a war waged for liberty. How slowly and fearfully should we approach a war, which is to make our happy homes desolate, our wives and children, widows and orphans, and liberty itself *a thing which was!*

The inhabitants of the Fork at the Revolution were more generally under the influence of religion than, perhaps, most of the other settlers, with the exception of the Friends. Many of the patriots, herein before mentioned, were members of the church. All of them (except the Maybin family,) were Baptists. The Baptist meeting house of that day was called Littleton's meeting house; it stood on the bank of the Enoree at Littleton's ferry, and in the plantation now belonging to Major Jesse Maybin. It has undergone two removals, and is now located near the village of Maybinton.

After the Revolution, Samuel E. Kenner, the Hendersons, Sims, Hardys and others, immigrated to the Fork; and some of the old settlers, Wadlingtons, Littletons, Gordons and Lyles', moved south and west. Samuel E. Kenner was the step-son of Maj. Spencer Morgan; he was a man of great native talent. Few men of my acquaintance possessed a clearer head and sounder judgment than Samuel E. Kenner. He had considerable information; he had traveled and observed faithfully. He had been the super-cargo of one of the slave ships employed or owned by Gen. Hampton. He was twice a member of the Legislature—first in 1810; then in 1814. He was universally respected; and his popularity was such that he could at any time have been elected. He was a magistrate for many years. His first wife was Patsy Grasty, the daughter of Sashal Grasty; by her he had five children, all of whom, although living to be men and women, are now in their graves. His second wife was Lucy Goree, the half sister of Mrs. Elizabeth Maybin, by whom he hal eight children, all of whom, except two, are numbered with the dead! He himself, after attaining to a good old age, died in 1844. His widow still survives, and resides where he lived and died.

John Henderson (commonly called Capt. Jack Henderson) lived at the place on Enoree, where his son Thomas Henderson now lives. He was the son of David Henderson, and was a married man when he came from Virginia, between '90 and '94. He had then three children. Capt. Henderson was a worthy, bold, frank man. When he was a friend, he was one indeed; and when he was an enemy, it was equally well known—concealment was no part of his character. He raised and commanded a fine troop of horse; the same afterwards so well commanded by Capt., afterwards Col., John Glenn. He gave up his commission in consequence of the dispute about the majority between himself, Maj. Nance and Col. James Williams, spoken of in No. 8.

He was elected to the Legislature in 1812 and 1814. In this last year, when the detachment of troops under Col. Means and Maj., afrerwards Gen., Dawkins marched from Spartanburg and Union to Charleston, they were quartered for a night at Hend rson's. His house and barns were opened for their accommodation; his beeves slaughtered, and his flour and meal baked for their food; and all without money or price. This was exactly in character with his life—he was generous to those whom he loved.

He died 1st January 1816, in the great epidemic of 1815-'16, which was then, for a second time, experienced in Newberry District, and accompanying its ravages went up the universal wail of death! Mr. Henderson left a numerous family, all of whom survive, except his son D. Waltour Henderson, who died in a few days after him, leaving an only child, now Mrs. Elvira Nance, of Newberry. None more seriously lamented the death of Capt. Henderson than the writer of this sketch. He had been his friend when he needed friends; and he felt and knew that in him, if his life had been spared, he still would have been, as he had been. But to that, as all other chastenings, he has been able to say, "God's will be done!"

NO. 11.

The office of Historiographer, when the materials are scattered everywhere, and when tradition more than written authority must be appealed to, is far from being an agreeable one; yet the task of the Biographer, when everything depends upon the memory of the writer, or of others is still more difficult, and still more disagreeable. In short biographical sketches of men of other times, there is, however, a rich vein, worth—well worth—being explored. This task is about being undertaken, with very imperfect materials; still, such as they are, they will afford great interest and may lead some one better informed to do greater justice.

A much valued friend has furnished me with the facts which will enable me to speak of a revolutionary soldier at present little known, and at the same time to speak of another instance in the History of Newberry, where the third generation is in his ancestral home! Maj. Micajah Harriss, one of our best citizens, now in his 53d year, lives upon a tract of land granted to Jeremiah Williams, 20th June, 1753, lying on Heller's formerly called Williams' Creek, which was conveyed by him to the grand-father of the present occupant, Burr Calvert Harriss, 19th January, 1773; he occupied it until his death; his youngest son, Micajah Harriss, succeeded him, and lived upon it until his death, in 1814; his widow continued the possession to her death, in 1819; she was succeeded by her youngest son, Maj. Micajah Harriss, who has ever since occupied, and long may he, in honor and usefulness occupy, *his patrimonial acres!* This is another instance where the descendant of an original settler is still looking upon the scenes, treading the soil familiar to his ancestors, and drinking from the same noble fountain from which they drank; *here* too repose the ashes of of the grand-father, grand-mother, father and mother of the present owner. How can such an one do otherwise than exclaim,

"This is my own, my native land !"

Burr Calvert Harriss was an immigrant from Virginia, and is supposed by his grand-son to have been of English extraction. His son, Micajah, was a soldier in the Indian war, supposed by my friend to have been Grant's, (but this could not have been, as that took place in 1761, and Burr Calvert Harriss came from Virginia about 1773). It is probable, he, Micajah, took part in the wars with the Cherokees in 1776, under the command, probably, of Col. John Lyles, in General Williamson's campaign. Micajah Harriss was an active soldier of the Revolution, and on the 12th January, 1780, was commissioned by Gov. John Rutledge, *lieutenant;* his commission to that effect is still preserved, as a precious relic, and is in possession of his son. It should be framed and hung up in his parlor, like that of Gen. Marion, which is thus preserved in the drawing-room of one of Charleston's noble sons, who married the relative of the great Carolina hero! Micajah Harriss afterwards became captain. His services *in the times which tried men's souls* were, beyond doubt, arduous and full of trials; but the remembrance of them has perished generally. A single instance of the spirit of self-sacrifice of that glorious era can be given. He with his wife's brother, James Sheppard, were taken prisoners by a tory scout, and were carried to some halting point, on King's or Indian Creek, where it was proposed to put them to death.

When a halt was ordered, one of the tories proposed to another to shoot them; he offered the unwelcome duty to a third, and he to another, until the whole scout declined the bloody work. They then offered to the prisoners, if either would shoot the other, he should be discharged. This was indignantly rejected, Sheppard then said to the captors: "If one life would satisfy them, he was single; his brother-in-law, Harriss, was a married man, and had one or two children; let me, therefore, be the victim." This alternative Harriss would not consent to accept. "If one has to die, let us both die together," was his manly reply. The tories, struck by the self-sacrificing spirit exhibited by their prisoners, discharged them *on parole;* but that they should not depart entirely from their usual vocation of blood and plunder, they kept Captain Harriss' fine mare which he rode, and sent him home on foot.

In 1781, a party of whigs, under the command of Col.
Hays, passed in the neighborhood of Coats' shop, (Newberry
Court House,) to Jacob Brooks', (now the plantation of Harrington Pope.) Two of the party, James Tinsley and John
Campbell, a lad, son of Captain Angus Campbell, of Laurens,
and brother of the present Dr. Robert Campbell, diverged
from their direct route to have a horse shod at Coats' shop,
at the Cedar Spring, just below the village graveyard. Having
accomplished this, they started to rejoin their companions at
Brooks'. They were fired upon just about where the barn of
Drayton Nance, Esq., now stands, on Higgins' road. One
ball took effect in the bridle arm of Campbell; his mare
jumped from under him, and accompanied Tinsley in his flight
to Brooks'. There the command turned out, and retracing
Tinsley's steps, they found Campbell dead. The persons, whoever they were, who had wounded him, had completed the
work of death. His companions bore him to Coats' shop. On
the margin of Scott's Creek he was buried; and there he
slept the sleep of death until, in 1849, the excavations for the
railroad laid bare the remains. They were collected, with
pious care, by his excellent brother, Dr. Robert Campbell, and
buried in the family burying ground.

Shortly before the close of the Revolution, at the Shop
Spring, about half a mile south of Bobo's Mill, on Bush River,
a similar thing occurred. A whig scout, commanded by Capt.
John Sloan, from whose expression about the lock of his
musket, that it was "stiff of the frizzen," came the saying,
"stiff of the frizzen, like Sloan's musket," passed the mills,
called _then_, after their proprietor, O'Neall's, (now Bobo's.) In
his command was a man named Ichabod Wood. He was a
New England man and a sailor. In an almost famished condition he had, years before, attached himself to the wagon of
William or Henry O'Neall, in the neighborhood of Charleston,
and with one or other of these gentlemen had come into the
interior. He lived much with William O'Neall, and was
remarkable for his inoffensive disposition and industrious
habits. He was always averse to fire arms, and especially to
shooting them. He had been married but a short time, and
was either living on the land of his early patron and friend,
Wm. O'Neall, or very near to it, when he was summoned to

do duty in Sloan's scout. He, Sloan, and the rest of the party, were seen to ride into and through Bush River, at the old ford below the mills, by William O'Neall and his son, Hugh. Soon afterwards they started to walk to dinner at the residence of William O'Neall, south of Bush River, and west of the mills about half a mile. In their way, they were nearer to the Shop Spring than at the mills. A gun was heard to fire, and William O'Neall said to his son, Hugh, "That was sorely against poor Ichabod's will"; alluding to his known dislike to a gun being fired. In a few moments, however, a messenger came to tell them that indeed it was "sorely against poor Ichabod's will," for *Ichabod Wood was shot*. It seemed that he and Sloan rode to the Shop Spring for water, and were fired upon from the thick wood around the spring. The ball was no doubt aimed for Sloan. It, however, passed through the lungs of poor Ichabod, who in a few hours ceased to live. He lies in the quiet yard of Friend's burying ground, near Mendenhall's Mills, Bush River. The assassin never was discovered.

No. 11 Concluded.

I propose to close this number with some slight account of the former proprietor of the plantation, now owned by the Messrs. Crofts, Capt. Daniel Parkins. Whether his father settled the place, I do not certainly know. The family came from Winchester, Va., and, I think, consisted of the brothers and sisters. I remember to have heard this anecdote in relation to the graveyard at that place: One of Capt. Parkins' sisters was the wife of Hugh O'Neall, who settled at, and owned the mills, on Little River, at the place now called Milton, Laurens District. One of his brothers, Thomas O'Neall, died at Parkins', and while the family were debating the question where he should be buried, a ball of fire. as they called it, a meteor, as it really was, passed over the house, and was seen to fall where the graveyard is. They regarded it as a divine intimation where the dead was to lie—he was accordingly there buried, and thus began the graveyard called Parkins'.

Capt. Parkins was born in 1758. He was therefore a man fully grown before the tide of war reached the interior. Like many other good and mistaken men, he was supposed to be a loyalist in principle. He, however, took no active part. The principles in which he had been raised and educated were those of Friends. He owned a mill on Saluda, just below the ford (Parkins'.) He was usually employed in attending the grist mill and in preparing meal for the country around him. A party of whigs from Indian Creek, to whom he was obnoxious, was on their way to capture, or kill him. Their approach was discovered by one of his sisters, while they were yet several hundred yards from the dwelling house, which was two or three hundred yards from the mill. She started in a run to inform her brother of the approach of his enemies. They seeing her, and guessing her purpose, put their horses in full speed to anticipate her. As soon as she discovered this, she began to halloo, so as to attract her brother's attention; the noise of the machinery of the mill prevented him from early hearing the outcry. The leading horse soon came along side of her; she seized his bridle, pulled it off his head and turned him into the woods, and continued her race; the second she served the same way. By this time her brother was aware of what was going forward; leaping out of the mill, with his gun in his hand, into Saluda, he pursued the shoal until he was enabled to reach the island now called Pope's, then a dense forest. There he was safe, for the party knew not how to reach it; and if they had been able to do so, they never could have found him in its impenetrable thickets.

He married Jane Caradine, the daughter of Abraham Caradine, who lived below him on Saluda, at Caradine's ford. Soon after his marriage the house was surrounded at night by a party of whigs, probably the same who had attempted to surprise him at his mills. There was only one manner of escape, that was by boldly dashing through the surrounding party. Caradine and Parkins sprang from their beds, the former snatched down a musket and throwing into its barrel a handful of powder and shot, and priming in the same

hurried way, he threw open the door and fired upon the party, killing one who sat upon the fence just before the door. Both took advantage of the confusion, and sprang out the house and ran for their lives. Parkins made good his escape. Caradine was an elderly man and ran heavily; he was shot in one of the corn rows of his field; when the party came to where he lay, he enquired "if the rascal he shot at was dead?" and being told that he was, he quietly remarked "he was satisfied." and soon was himself in the silent house of death.

Capt. Parkins, after the Revolution, was regarded by all as a virtuous, good man. He had particularly the friendship of that gallant old soldier of liberty, Col. Philemon Waters, his near neighbor. Either at, or soon after the re-organization of the militia, he was elected captain of the Saluda company, in the 8th (now 39th) regiment of militia. In '96 he was appointed a Justice of the Peace; in '98 he was re-appointed; in '99 he was appointed, with Robert Rutherford, Edward Finch, Isaac Kirk and Hugh O'Neall, a Commissioner of Public Buildings. He discharged all the duties appertaining so these respective appointments in that faithful way which insured him the respect of every one. He was a merchant of extensive business—at first on his own account, afterwards as the senior partner of Capt. Sampson Pope, in Edgefield, and Hugh O'Neall, on Bush River, Newberry. He also did an extensive business in Greenville, under the management of Mr. Beverly Borum. He, by these various pursuits, realized a handsome fortune. He was a rich man, but this did not stay the approach of the fell destroyer? Many of his children had been taken from him in their early life. As early as '99, 1800, 1801 and 1802, Capt. Parkins' place was regarded as a sickly one. Fever and ague was every year a visitant of his household. But, in 1802, the angel of death, in the great epidemic of that year, entered his house. On Sunday night, the 7th of November, his eldest son, Abraham, a noble young man, thoroughly trained and educated for a merchant, died. On Wednesday, the 10th, his third son, John, a fine, promising lad, died. On Thursday, the 11th, his excellent wife, Jane, in the 41st year of her age, died; and on Friday, the 12th, the sad drama was closed by the death of the husband and father! On Saturday, the 13th, in the presence of an immense multitude, he and his wife were placed in the same grave, and his son, John, alongside of them. During the sickness of his family, he had exhibited no particular disease; but as one after another died, it seemed as if cord after cord, which bound him to this life, was breaking. On the death of his wife he announced to his friends that he could not live. He desired to provide for two of his widowed sisters, (the Mrs. McDaniels) and a nephew, Daniel Parkins. He directed notes for $300 each, to be drawn payable to his sisters; these he signed. He then called for his pocket book, and out of it directed $100 to be taken and given to his nephew, and after cautioning the attending physician, Dr. Moon, to give him nothing to blunt his faculties, he gradually sunk and passed away as peaceably as if falling asleep. He left four sons, Charles, Isaac, Allen R. and Mark. Charles died in 1807; Isaac in 1809; Mark in 1817—all unmarried. Allen R. became therefore the heir and possessor of the fine estate of his father, which had rapidly accumulated during his infancy, and had been further increased by the addition of his brother Charles' estate. He married in 1816, a most amiable and excellent lady in Greenville, Miss Paul. He soon sold his fine estate in Newberry to Mr. Edward Croft. He resided to his death, in 1837, in Greenville District; he left a widow and several children. His eldest son, Daniel, recalls to my mind, each time I see him, his grand-father. Capt. Daniel Parkins was under the common height, but he was remarkable for his large compact body and limbs. Few men possessed as much strength and activity. I well remember to have seen him once throw down and literally strip a man twice his size, who had treated him rudely and torn his clothes. His complexion was sallow, arising, I suppose, from his frequent sickness. His eyes, of black, were full of intelligence and energy. No kinder man, better neighbor, affectionate father, husband or brother, ever lived. No firmer man, in all his public or private relations, lived in Newberry. Cool in danger, undaunted in execution, he passed through life as he died, without quailing at danger.

His character, in this respect, may be better understood by a circumstance of great danger, in which he acted a bold, fearless and successful part. In passing to old Ninety-Six, for many years after the war, it was the custom in passing

from O'Neall's mills, on Bush River, to cross Saluda River, at Parkins' Ford, and go up the old Charleston road. Plank was then hauled from Bush River to Ninety-Six, as it now is from the piney woods to Newberry C. H. A wagon and team belonging to Mary O'Neall, and driven by her son John, (a lad 17 or 18,) and another belonging to and driven by John Jay, were engaged in this business. In one of their trips, on reaching Saluda, the stream was found to be swollen; a consultation was had, and it was concluded it could be passed. The team of Mrs. O'Neall's was in front, and attempted the passage before that of Jay. As soon as the wagon reached the deep water it floated; as might have been expected from its load, (plank.) The consequence was, that down the stream went horses, wagon and driver. The latter made every effort to extricate his team by cutting them loose, but he either failed by losing his knife, or, in the excitement, by not cutting his hame-strings. Jay attempted to swim to the rescue, but was seized with the cramp and had to get upon a rock to save himself from drowning. Parkins hearing the noise ran to the river, and seeing the dangerous position of the young driver and his team, plunged in and swam to their rescue. He cut the lead mare loose, and attempting to cut another loose, in the struggle the knife was knocked out of his hand—he sprang upon the mare cut loose, swam her to land, got another knife, swam her back, cut loose the other horses and saved them, driver and Jay.

The great epidemic of that year, 1802, called afterwards the cold plague, was then first experienced in Newberry, in 1815–'16; it again returned, again and again it has since re-visited us. But for the last several years it has disappeared; and, it is hoped, never to return. Fearful indeed has been the judgments of God in this behalf! May we avert them by humbling ourselves in His mighty presence.

NO. 12.

Col. Robert Rutherford, as one of the early settlers and prominent citizens of Newberry District, deserves a prominent place in the sketches which we are now attempting. Would that I had the honor of knowing him intimately, then I might have done something like justice to his name. A friend who knew him intimately, and who felt for him all the esteem which gratitude creates, has given to me the benefit of his recollections. Still our united endeavors will present a very imperfect *picture* Such as it is, it is better than none, and therefore it is presented.

He was born in April, 1734, in the State of Virginia, and served his apprenticeship to the carpenter's trade, at Hobb's Hole, in the neighborhood of which place he married his first wife, Dorothy Brooks. How long he resided in Virginia is not known; he removed to Chatham County, N. C., where he became colonel of the county, and this gave him the title which he bore to his death.

Before the Revolution, or perhaps before 1780, he removed to South Carolina, and settled in Newberry District, nine miles east of the town, at a place which he called Liberty Hill. What part he bore in the Revolution is not known; that he was a whig, and perhaps an active one, is shown from the position which he maintained in society after its close. He was for many years a member of the Legislature. He was appointed a County Court Judge at the very beginning of the system in 1785, and continued to act till 1791.

In 1791, or 1792, he was called upon to experience that greatest misfortune which can befall a man in this world—the death of his wife and the mother of his children. He had a large family of children by her, one of whom was Mrs. Elizabeth Nance, heretofore spoken of; and another, William Rutherford, long well known as a citizen of the eastern part of the district. In 1795, he married the widow, Frances

Harrington, of Union; by her he had no children. *Her* children, however, received a father's care and attention.

In 1796, he started one of Whitney's Cotton Saw Gins; this is believed to have been the first put in motion in the upper part of South Carolina. This great invention is what has made cotton the subject of universal trade, and the commercial agent which now very much governs the monetary affairs of the world. Before the discovery of the saw-gin, cotton was separated from the seed by the slow process of the fingers, or the roller-gin. It was therefore little regarded, except for domestic consumption. But when it was found that by the saw-gin thousands of pounds of seed-cotton could in the day be picked and baled up for market, it became matter to which industry could be profitably applied. The cotton saw-gin has given to the Southern States the supremacy which they now enjoy as producers. In a day of sectional hatred, it ought to be remembered—gratefully remembered— *that Whitney, the inventor of the cotton saw-gin was a Yankee.* Great as was his invention, it benefited him little; his patent was violated and justice denied to him everywhere, *except in South Carolina; here he was paid by the Legislature for his invention, and his patent made free to the people.* This model gin stood in the Secretary of State's room until after 1820.

About 1809, Col. Rutherford built in the neighborhood of the town of Newberry, where his step-son, Y. J. Harrington, Esq., afterwards lived, and there he died in 1814, *in his eightieth year.* Col. Rutherford was, I should think, about five feet eight; more remarkable for his ponderous heavy grey eye brows, than any other feature which is remembered.

He was a man of great energy of character—"whatever his hands found to do, he did it with his might." This was shown by the success which attended him during life; he succeeded in whatever he undertook. As a merchant, planter, and public undertaker, he was tried and not found wanting. He was one of the first cotton planters in Newberry, and an eminently successful one. He was one of the Commissioners of Public Buildings with Daniel Parkins, Edward Finch, Isaac Kirk and Hugh O'Neall, appointed in 1799. Under their direction and jealous supervision, was constructed the court house and gaol, which preceded those now in use. In 1805 he built the Newberry Academy; to this institution he was a large subscriber.

The friend whose pen gave me the benefit of a short sketch of the colonel's life and character, says: "He had a heart open as day to melting charity, which he never withheld from any, (except a drunkard, or a lazy person.) Those gentlemen of elegant leisure, he utterly abominated. *"Work Sonny,"* was his injunction to such. One of his observations may here be very well chronicled: He said people often said "it was too dry or too wet to work." God, he said, gave the seasons—it was man's duty to work—"work dry, work wet"—and he never failed to find that "God gave the increase." When a poor woman, Mrs. Myers, was left with a house full of little children, in very difficult, if not destitute circumstances, by the death of her industrious husband, John Myers, *the rope maker*, the colonel sent his negroes, horses and ploughs, and cultivated her crop. To deserving young men, especially his step-sons, he extended a helping hand in placing them in situations to live and do well.

His last wife was a very pious lady, who belonged to the Methodist communion. The colonel made no profession of religion; yet he was always seen at meeting with his excellent lady, although he had no great liking for the shouting and other violent excitements, which were perhaps more common *then* than *now*. On some occasions, about the commencement of the last war, he was at a camp meeting, and just as a good deal of excitement was getting up, and as a popular preacher was about to offer to sinners the opportunity of asking for pardon, the colonel, who occupied a seat in the midst of the congregation, rose to make his way out. The preacher seeing this, called on all who felt that they were sinners and needed a Saviour's pardoning love, to come forward and kneel down. The colonel was still receding; again he invited Christians to kneel down, still the colonel was erect; at last, said he, "let all who are Republicans kneel." This, as the story goes, brought the old gentleman down! He could not bear to be counted as an enemy to the country, under whose glorious stars and stripes he had grown to competence and honor, and had been blessed with countless blessings. Might not many an one, at the present time, imitate the colonel, and bending down in the presence of the King of kings, ask him in mercy to avert *that worst of all evils—Disunion.*

I propose next to speak of another of the old settlers of Newberry District—William Calmes. He was born near Winchester, Va., about the year 1761. At twelve years of age, he accompanied his father to South Carolina, who purchased the tract of land before spoken of, granted to Pennington, known as the Canebrake on Enoree, and now the property of Richard Sondley, eleven miles east of the town. He returned with his father to Virginia, and at sixteen years of age, volunteered in the army of the Revolution. He served for some time as a private; he was promoted to the rank of lieutenant, in which capacity he served under the command of the Marquis De La Fayette, in those brilliant manœuvers which baffled the skill of the greatest captain of the English army, Lord Cornwallis, and finally cooped him up at Yorktown, and delivered him and his fine army captives to the great American General, Washington; thus making "Cornwallis," in the language of a Virginia negro, "Cob-Wallis." This was no bad pun, in a play of words.

Here I may be pardoned for digressing, to tell a Charleston anecdote connected with the surrender of Cornwallis. Count Rochambeau, it will be remembered, commanded the French forces who aided in the capture of Yorktown. A French barber's shop was the general resort of the proud officers of the English garrison, then occupying Charleston for the purpose of being shaved. The news of the capture of Yorktown had just been received, one of the officers was submitting his chin to be reaped by the handy Frenchman. He said to the barber, very contemptuously, "*I hear your great Rochambeau is a barber.*" "*Aha,*" said the knight of the razor, "*Rochambeau one barber! Bigar, me tink he shave Cornwallis damnation close!*" *It is needless to add, another Briton was defeated.*

After the war, Mr. Calmes married, and removed to the place before spoken of as bought by his father, and which had been by his will left to him, about 1782 or 1783. On this place he resided until 1806, when he purchased from Abel Insco the place near the town of Newberry. He removed to it for the purpose of educating his children at the Newberry Academy.

He was elected a member of the House of Representatives in 1804, and served his term, (two sessions); he declined to be a candidate for re-election, and spent the balance of his life (thirty years) in retirement. He had a large family, eight children, who lived to be men and women, of whom five now survive; the eldest of whom, Mrs. Nancy Harrington, is too well known to require more to be said of her than that as a wife, mother and friend, she has few equals. William Calmes died 8th January, 1836, in the seventy-fifth year of his age. He was about five feet nine or ten inches high; remarkable for the firm, compact figure of his person. He possessed singular vivacity and facetiousness—nothing delighted him more than to practice some innocent mischievous joke upon one of his friends. He bore with singular firmness the many trials of life to which he was subjected. While his heart was bursting with agony, he was seen *externally unmoved*. Like Col. Rutherford, he had the misfortune to lose, many years before his death, his wife—the excellent lady who had soothed his sorrows and moderated the whirlwind of his passions; and who was the mother of his many children. But, unlike him, he did not supply her place. He placed her remains in the burying ground, in full view of his evening and morning observation. There he sleeps, himself, surrounded by his children and grandchildren, and great-grandchildren. He was a Virginian, and possessed *the real old Virginian character, fearless and frank*. He loved his friends; he was ready to serve and do them good at all times. We cannot say he hated his enemies; we hope that what they called hatred, did not permanently abide in his heart. He, however, took great pleasure in making his enemies know and feel that he knew they were not his friends; and that between him and them *"there was no love lost."*

In all his public and private relations he did his duty as an officer and as a man. He liberally educated his children, and left them an ample patrimony to be shared among them. "He is gone, and the place which once knew him, shall know him no more, forever;" but he is known in his children and numerous descendants, and long may he be thus known—and may they, like our country, increase in honor, usefulness and glory, until a long line of virtuous and good posterity may be traced to him as its head and ancestor.

NO. 13.

Col. Philemon Waters, of whom I am about now to speak, was a native of Virginia, and I think he was raised in or near Winchester. The time of his birth cannot now be ascertained; he probably was about the same age as General Washington, who was born the 22nd February, 1732. His parents died, it is supposed, when he was very young, for he was an apprentice in Winchester, and was used hardly, from an anecdote which I have often heard. He was called by both master and mistress, until his stock of patience was completely exhausted; and he said to one of his associates, "It was Phil. *here* and Phil *there;* he wondered what they (his master and mistress) would do if the Devil had Phil." He had much of his early training in that rough and tumble school about Winchester, in which General Morgan and his early associates practiced fighting to such an extent as to give the village the name of Battle Town.

In 1754 he enlisted in the regiment raised by the State of Virginia to maintain her rights to the territory on the Ohio, then occupied by the French. This regiment was commanded by Col. Fry; his second in command, the Lieut.-Colonel, was George Washington, who in advance of the regiment, took post at the Great Meadows, with two companies; in one of them, it is believed was Philemon Waters. With these companies, Col. George Washington surprised and captured a party of French, who were on their way to surprise him. The commander, M. Jumonville, was killed. On the march of the residue of the regiment to join Lieut.-Col. Washington at the Great Meadows, Col. Fry died, and the command devolved on Lieut.-Col. Washington. He erected at the Great Meadows a stockade fort (afterwards called Fort Necessity) to secure the provisions and horses; and after leaving a sufficient guard to maintain the post, he pushed on with the balance of his command, less than 400 men, to attack and dislodge the French at Fort du Quesne, at the confluence of the Allegheny and Monongahela Rivers, (now Pittsburg). They were halted "at the westernmost foot of Laurel Hill," thirteen miles from the Great Meadows, by the intelligence of the friendly Indians, who informed them, in their figurative language, "that the enemy were rapidly advancing, *as numerous as the pigeons in the woods!*" A retreat was deemed necessary, and accordingly Col. Washington fell back to Fort Necessity, and commenced a ditch around it. Before it was completed, the enemy 1,500 strong, under the command of Monsieur De Villier, appeared and attacked the fort. The action was continued from ten in the morning until dark, when the Frenchman demanded a parley, and offered terms of capitulation. Those first offered were rejected, "but in the course of the night articles were signed by which the fort was surrendered, on condition that its garrison should be allowed the honors of war—should be permitted to retain their arms and baggage, and to march without molestation into the inhabitated parts of Virginia."

While this expedition was in progress, an incident in the life of Col. Waters occurred, which rests altogether in tradition, but which I have no doubt is true, from the source from which it is derived. It was stated to have occurred at Fort Necessity, and without looking to the historical account of the attack, and the surrender of that post, I supposed (as it was told to me,) that it had taken place during the siege. This version is given in Random Recollections of the Revolution, 4th vol. Southern Literary Journal, 97; but I am now satisfied there is some inaccuracy in this respect, as there was in fact no protracted siege. During the occupation of Fort Necessity, the sentinel had been night after night shot down at a particular post, Waters was detailed in his turn for that station; knowing its dangers, he loaded his musket with slugs or buckshot, and took his post, *"wide awake."* In the course of his turn, he heard some noise like the grunting of a hog, and observing by the moonlight, at the same time, the tall grass of the *prairie* shaking, as if some animal or person was moving therein, he put, to use his own expression, "three hails in one," fired and killed two Indians and three Frenchmen! They were on all fours, behind each other, stealthily approaching the sentinel, when his well directed fire defeated so fatally their purpose. On the surrender of the post, the French commander inquired for the sentinel, who had occupied the post, fired without hailing, and killed the two Indians and three Frenchmen, with a view of excepting him (as it was supposed) from the amnesty granted to the garrison. Washington, unwilling to expose his gallant young soldier, for *once* spoke falsely. He had fallen, he said, in the attack and defence of the post. Waters, in his after life, speaking of this incident, said, he stood behind his colonel when the question was made and the answer given, with his rifle well loaded, primed and cocked, and if, said he, "he had said Phil. Waters, he would never have spoken again."

He was one of the brave Virginians who fought in the disastrous battle of the Monongahela, where Braddock was defeated and slain. Of them Washington said, "The Virginia companies behaved like men and died like soldiers; for I believe out of three companies on the ground that day, scarce thirty men were left alive." He was present, at an earlier day, when the wagoner, Daniel Morgan, received five hundred lashes, under the sentence of a drum-head court martial. As this affair descended to the author of these sketches as a family tradition narrated by an eye witness, William O'Neall, it may not be amiss if it should, with a subsequent occurrence in the life of the undaunted wagoner, be here stated. Daniel Morgan and William O'Neall were wagoners from Winchester, Va., in Braddock's army. Morgan, in a frolic, took a twist of tobacco from an Indian; he complained to a young British officer, possibly the officer of the guard. He most haughtily ordered Morgan to give up the tobacco; in perfect Virginian recklessness, Morgan replied he "would give it up when he got ready." The officer struck him with the flat of his sword. No one ever struck the hero of *"Battle Town"* without being struck again, and accordingly he knocked the officer down. For this offence he was tried by a court martial, and sentenced to receive five hundred lashes—and he did receive it, without speaking or complaining. To those to whom he could speak, he swore he would, if ever opportunity offered, kill the officer who had subjected him to this degrading punishment. After Braddock's war, he and the officer met, mounted and armed, in the mountains of Virginia. Morgan said to him, he had long wished for the opportunity which was then presented. "I have sworn," said he, "to kill you, therefore fight for your life, or," drawing a pistol and presenting it, "I will

kill you like a dog." The officer declined the battle. Morgan
then said to him, "Get down on your knees and beg your
life." This he refused to do. Morgan returned his pistol to
the holster, remarking to him that "a life which was not
worth fighting for or begging for, *was not worth taking.*" He
rode on, and left his craven oppressor to his own contempla-
tions.

Whether Waters remained in the Virginia army till Washington's resignation in 1758, I do not know. He removed to
South Carolina before the Revolutionary war. At its commencement he lived in Newberry, near the ferry on Saluda
River, once well known as Waters', now Holly's. In that
time *which tried men*, and showed *how far professions were
supported by acts*, he took the part of Liberty and Independence. His sword, which was then drawn, returned not to its
scabbard until both were won and secured. He was in the
battle of Stono, on 26th of June, 1779; he was then a captain,
and on the retreat from the attack made on the British lines,
he observed an American field piece, which had been abandoned by its officers and men; he directed his men (some of
whom are remembered, to wit: John Adam Summer, Samuel
Lindsey, Thomas Lindsey, and James Lindsey,) to lay hold
of the drag ropes and carry it off; this was done, and the
gun saved. It seems from the records in the Comptroller's
office, that he was a captain in Thomas' regiment, Sumpter's
brigade State troops, to the end of the war in 1783. It seems,
too, he served in 1782 as a captain under Gen. Pickens. His
nephew, Philemon Waters, Jr., better known as Ferry Phil.,
was under his command at the battle of Eutaw, and after the
action was over, said to him, "Uncle do you call this *a battle,
or a scrimmage?*" I had supposed that in this action he was
a major; the tradition is, that he *then* commanded as such.
But it does not seem, from the public documents, he had any
such commission. In some of the partisan affairs with which
the country abounded after the fall of Charleston in 1780, he
was under the command of Col. Brandon. He captured a man
(a Tory) peculiarly obnoxious to the colonel. After this skirmish, when the prisoners were presented to the colonel, he, on
seeing Waters' prisoner, drew his sword, and was in the act
of rushing upon him to slay him. Waters threw himself

between them, and announced to his superior that the prisoner was under his protection, and *"should not be harmed."* The purpose of vengeance was not abandoned, and Capt. Waters was peremptorily ordered to stand out of the way. "Africa," said he to his servant, "bring me my rifle"; no sooner said than done. With his rifle in his hand, and an eye that never quailed, he said to the colonel, "Now strike the prisoner—the instant you do, I will shoot you dead." The blow was not struck: the prisoner was saved. He was an active, daring officer with a head to conceive and a hand to execute the most difficult enterprises. He was in most of the regular actions fought at the South, and in many a partisan affair. He often said he "never was in a pitched battle in which he was not defeated." "Eutaw," he said "was the nearest approach to a victory in such a battle in which he had ever participated; but," said he, in the boastful style pardonable in the veteran soldier, "I never fought a partisan affair, in which I was commandant, in which I was not victorious." After the battle of Eutaw, and after the British had been driven to the lines of Charleston, Waters erected a block house at his plantation at Waters' Ferry, Saluda, and encouraged the deluded tories to come in, lay down their arms, and become peaceable citizens. Many, very many, afterwards valuable citizens, were thus saved to the district and State.

After the war, he was for some time Collector of the Taxes, in a part of Ninety-Six District. He, as such, made his return to the Treasurer in Charleston, and paid over to him the money collected. Money then was in gold or silver, or indents; and traveling was performed on horseback, and always in some peril. In the country between Dorchester and Charleston this was particularly the case, from a gang of out-lying negroes, headed by a notorious fellow named Primus; they robbed all who passed the road by night, or who, like wagoners, were compelled to encamp within their accustomed walks. Waters passing with a considerable sum of public money in his saddle bags, was overtaken by night in this suspicious district. He was armed, having his trusty pistols in the holsters before him. Thinking about the possible danger, he involuntarily laid his hand upon a pistol, cocked, and drew it half out of the holster. As his horse passed a large pine tree, the bridle was seized, and a robber stood by his side; in one instant Waters' pistol was drawn and thrust into the side of the assailant; it fired, and, with an unearthly yell, he let go the bridle and fled. Waters put spurs to his horse, and galloped to the house where he intended to lodge, some two miles distant; there he obtained lights and assistance, and returned to the spot where he had been attacked; there they found a club and a large knife, and blood; following its tracts a short distance, a large powerful negro fellow was found shot through the body and already dead. It may not be improper for me here to say, that this gang of negro outlaws was at last driven from their fastnesses in the swamps by the Catawba Indians, who were hired by the planters to hunt them. Their leader, Primus, and perhaps others, were hanged.

Waters was an eminent surveyor—many of the grants in Newberry District were surveyed by him; he and William Caldwell located the courthouse square of Newberry District. He was a County Court Judge from 1785 to 1791. He was repeatedly a member of the Legislature. He was also a member of the convention which ratified the Constitution of the United States; he was opposed to it, being one of the *ultra Republican party* of that day; but fortunately his opposition was vain, and like his great countryman, Patrick Henry, he lived long enough under it to rejoice *at his defeat*, in this instance. He was colonel of a regiment of militia in the Fork, between Broad and Saluda Rivers, from the peace in 1783, until the reorganization of the militia in '94; he was not re elected; his opponent, John Adam Summer, was elected colonel of the 8th, now the 39th, regiment.

When General Washington, in 1791, made the tour of the Southern States, Colonel Waters met him at the Juniper, on his way from Augusta to Columbia. It was the meeting of brother soldiers, who, together, had faced many dangers and shared many difficulties. Both had been great shots with the rifle, and on a challenge from the General, their last meeting on earth was signalized by a trial of their skill off-hand, at a target one hundred yards distant, with the same unerring weapon. Who was conqueror in this trial of skill is not remembered.

Colonel Waters died between '96 and '99. He was taken sick at Newberry, and was carried in a litter by the way of O'Neall's (now Bobo's) mills on Bush River, to his then residence near the mouth of Bush River, now the property of Chancellor Johnstone. To the writer of this sketch, though then a mere child, the passage of Bush River through the ford by men bearing the litter, seems to be present, indistinct it is true, like an imperfectly remembered dream. Colonel Waters left four children—Philemon B. Waters, Wilks B. Waters, Rose, the wife of Colonel John Summers, and Mrs. Farrow, the wife of Wm. Farrow, of Spartanburg. One of the Colonel's grandchildren, John W. Summers, was a well-known citizen of Newberry, and ought to be gratefully remembered by all who prize the Greenville and Columbia Railroad, as a great public work, both for his energy and success as a contractor.

NO. 14.

The subject of this number is a soldier of the Revolution, alike remarkable for his ready wit, colloquial powers, and unflinching bravery; and yet the incidents of his life are buried in so much obscurity, that it is difficult to disinter even fragments; but it is a duty which I owe to the living and to the dead, to do as much justice to the memory of Dr. Jacob Roberts Brown as I can.

He was a native of Amherst County, Va. He entered the army of the United States at the beginning of the Revolution, in the Virginia line; he was a lieutenant, and was, at the close of the war, entitled to a large body of valuable land granted to him by the State of Virginia, and located in Warren County, State of Ohio, near Waynesville. This land, about 1799, he sold to Abijah O'Neall and Samuel Kelly, of this district, and who emigrated hence and took possession of their valuable purchase. One of the purchasers, Samuel Kelly, was still alive in 1850, and able to ride at the great age of eighty-seven, and possibly more. Of Dr. Brown's actual military service very little is certainly known; he bore his part from the commencement to the close. On the 11th of September, 1777, he was one of the Virginians who met the British regulars on the field of Brandywine, and of whom it was said they "behaved exceedingly well in some of the actions of this day, exhibiting a degree of order, firmness and resolution, and preserving such a countenance in extremely sharp service, as would not have discredited veterans."

An anecdote illustrative of this, may be here stated, as related by one of the actors: Towards the close of the day, when the American army was in full retreat, it was found that an attempt would be made by the British cavalry to cut off a part of the retreating columns. To prevent this it was necessary a pass should be gained and maintained; if this could be done, the enemy would be compelled to make a sweep of several miles before they could again strike at the retreat. A company of Virginians from Washington's immediate neighborhood volunteered for this perilous duty. They were, apparently, indeed a forlorn hope, and were so called; they were commanded by James O'Neall, who subsequently rose to be a major in the American army, and during the war, or at its close, threw the O from his name as an aristocratic distinction, and called himself afterwards James Neall; he settled and died at Wheeling, Virginia. Under his command was his youngest brother George, who imitated his example as to the name, and lived and died near Nicholasville, Jessamine County, Ky. From him the particulars herein related have been derived. It was well known if they (the forlorn hope) failed to reach the pass before the cavalry, they must be cut to pieces. They were young, athletic Virginians, accustomed to Indian warfare, with nerves strung for any service, and capable of a long and steady run. They therefore sprang forward to the race upon which depended their own lives and the safety of the army. They reached the ground and formed their hollow square, covering the pass, as the head of the British column of cavalry appeared in sight. A few moments' observation satisfied its commander—he was foiled. Wheeling his squadrons, he made the attempt to reach the retreating army through the longer route. The perilous duty was now only half performed; it remained to rejoin the army. Again the Virginian metal and bottom were to be tried, and again they succeeded; they rejoined in safety their regiment, under the command of Colonel Stevens, and aided in checking the pursuing enemy and covering the retreat. Next morning Washington reviewing his line, called for the forlorn hope; they presented arms, and were reported *as all present*. He lifted his hat, and with streaming eyes said, "God bless you, boys; I never expected to see you again!"

In the action of Brandywine, General LaFayette made the first offering of his blood in the cause of American freedom. When, in 1825, he visited South Carolina, and was met at Columbia by the Governor, his military family, and the militia of Fairfield, Chester, York, Laurens, Newberry, and Lexington, he was introduced to Colonel John G. Brown, and told that he was the son of Dr. Jacob Roberts Brown, a lieutenant in the Virginia line; and he instantly said, "I remember perfectly, that Dr. Brown, your father, assisted in binding up my wounds received in the battle of Brandywine." Lieutenant Brown was in the battle of Germantown, on the 4th of October, 1777. He was probably in Colonel Matthews' regiment, which penetrated to the centre of the town, and made a large number of prisoners; but, when the American army was forced to retire, they were surrounded and made prisoners. I do not know, nor is there any tradition, that Dr. Brown was taken prisoner; he was badly wounded in the action, and while prostrate from his wounds, a column of cavalry passed over him, the hoof of one of the horses struck him on the side, breaking one or more of his ribs. Of his revolutionary services, I know nothing.

Soon after the Revolution he came to South Carolina; indeed, it is possible he might have accompanied the American army to the South, and remained. He married Christian Neely, a rich young heiress, and settled in Newberry, near the Laurens line. From '89 to '99 he was one of the Judges of the County Court of Newberry. During most of that time, and perhaps for some years after, he was a member of the House of Representatives from Newberry. The late Edward Rutledge was a distinguished member of the House, during Dr. Brown's service. His habit in speaking was to lean against one of the columns; upon this, very much to Rutledge's amusement, Brown wrote, "It is not fair to shoot with a rest, when shooting off-hand is the fashion."

In that time intelligence did not travel by steam or electricity. The people generally had not even the opportunity of reading a newspaper once a month. For what was done in the Legislature, they had very much to depend on the verbal reports of the members. When Dr. Brown returned home from a session, his house was thronged by his neighbors of Laurens and Newberry, to *know what laws had been made*. The Doctor was fond of a joke, and one of his neighbors, a cynical man of the name of McGinn, was always ready to help out anything of the kind at anybody's expense, so that he did not get scathed. A neighbor, an Irishman, whom McGinn dubbed *"Cooney,"* was often the subject of their combined effort. On one occasion they represented him as returning from Dr. Brown's in great tribulation, and saying to his daughter, "Hoot, Matty, and what think ye—they ha'e taxed the mush pots; away, away, and make a wheen of the mushes, and stack it up, and put away the mush pots, so we will no ha'e them to be taxed." Again they represented the old gentleman as sitting on Sunday, in his own house, listening to the reading of his daughter Martha. She was reading the 15th chapter of Judges; she read the 4th and 5th verses: "And Samson went and caught three hundred foxes, and took fire brands and turned tail to tail, and put a fire brand between two tails. And when he had set the brands on fire, he let them go in the standing corn of the Philistines, and burn up both the shocks and also the standing corn, with the vineyards and olives." And just as she finished them, they represented her father as breaking in upon her and saying, "Hoot-toot, Matty, what na buke is that ye are reading?" "Father, said she, "It is the Bible." "Na, na, Matty; it is none of the Bible. The Bible is a gude booke—that is a lying booke. There is Dr. Brown, who has got as gude hounds as any Samson, and he never catched three hundred foxes; put it away, Matty, it is a lying buke." When this rather sacrilegious story was reported to the old gentleman, he very quietly remarked, "I reckon I ken the Scriptures as well as Dr. Brown, and I reckon I read them as much." This was a fair Rowland for an Oliver, and the Doctor did not soon again crack another joke on his neighbor.

Dr. Brown was an intelligent, useful man; he cared not for wealth; he improved, therefore, very little his wife's fine estate. His own princely estate in the rich military lands of Ohio he sold for a very inadequate sum. He took, perhaps, the poet's philosophical view of life:

> "Man wants but little here below,
> Nor wants that little long."

He certainly, in the most good-humored, easy way, enjoyed life. In the year 1805, he was in the act of mounting his horse to join in a hunting party; his hunter's horn was swung around his neck and resting upon the side injured at Germantown; his horse became restive, and he fell from his horse, deeply injuring the wounded side. He died in a few days, leaving his wife and four children, John G., Sarah, afterwards the wife of Henry Rees Hall, Esq., Willis, and Caroline Matilda, afterwards the wife of Dr. Anthony Foster Golding.

NO. 15.

In attempting to do justice to the memory of a gallant soldier, over whose body the rank grass has waved for more than sixty years, many difficulties have been encountered and overcome; and yet it is feared that a very poor measure of justice will be awarded.

Colonel David Glenn was a native of Ireland, and emigrated to the then British colonies about '73 or '74. He had been married a very short time, previous to his abandoning the green fields of his native land. I can very well appreciate the feelings of the gallant exile, forced by the unnumbered oppressions of British rule, to leave that beautiful gem of the ocean, described under the name of Scotia, by St. Donatus, while residing in Etruria, now Tuscany, in the seventh or eighth century:

"Far westward lies an Isle of ancient fame,
By nature blessed, and Scotia is her name,
Enrolled in books; exhaustless in her store
Of veiny silver and of goldon ore;
Her beautiful soil forever teems with wealth,
With gems her waters, and her air with health;
Her verdant fields with milk and honey flow;
Her wooly fleeces vie with virgin snow;
Her waving furrows float with bended corn,
And arms and arts her envied sons adorn;
No poison there infects, no scaly snake
Creeps through the grass or settles in the lake—
A nation worthy of its pious race,
In war triumphant, and unmatched in peace."

Colonel Glenn and his wife were among the last of the emigrants permitted to leave Ireland before the American Revolution. They landed in Savannah, Ga., and thence came to South Carolina and settled on Enoree, in Newberry District, at a place known as Glenn's Mills, now known as Brazleman's. Colonel Glenn, like all of the Irish Presbyterians, acknowledged "it was better to endure some evils than encounter the horrors of a revolutionary war"; but that yet, it was still better *"to endure all the protracted miseries of a revolutionary struggle, than to fail to enjoy liberty of person, property and conscience.*" Arriving in America when the dispute between the mother country and the colonies was waxing more and more fierce, he took the part of Liberty and Independence; and when, in '76, the United States declared themselves free, sovereign and independent, he made "no backward step," but grasped with a stronger hand and a more determined purpose, the naked sword of Independence. Like his noble countryman, General Montgomery, whose blood stained the ice-bound rocks of Quebec, he was ready to water with his the woods of his adopted Carolina.

Until the fall of Charleston (11th of May, 1780), the upper part of South Carolina scarcely knew the Revolutionary war, except in name. True, she had seen Colonel Richardson's gallant army in December, 1775, commonly called the Snow Camps; had heard the thunder of Moultrie's guns of deliverance, directed from the first Palmetto fort of liberty against the wooden walls of old England, and wept over a few of her slaughtered sons on the 26th June at Stono, on the 9th of October, 1779, at Savannah, yet, in the main, peace pervaded the country above tide-water. That horrible desolating war, which armed fathers against sons, sons against fathers, brother against brother, and neighbor against neighbor, had not yet commenced. After the fall of Charleston it began, and for nearly three years it swept with unmitigated fury over South Carolina, above the falls in the great rivers. At the close of the war, Ninety-Six District, which then covered all the tract of country lying above a line drawn from the Silver Bluff on the Savannah River N., 17° E., by the mouth of Rocky Creek on Saluda River, to Hughe's Ferry on Broad River, numbered, according to Ramsay's History of South Carolina, "fourteen hundred widows and orphans!"

According to the public records, it seems that Colonel Glenn, as a private soldier on horseback, did duty from 1st October to the 5th December, 1780. During this time, he must have been on duty with General Sumter, and must have participated with him in the glorious defeats of Major Wemy's at the Fish Dam on Broad River, on the 12th of November, and of Tarleton, at Blackstock's on Tyger, on the

20th of the same month. The tradition in his family is, that he bore his part in this last, but of the former they have no remembrance. Being, however, in his term of service, and in his immediate neighborhood, it is fair to conclude that he was one of the glorious militiamen who, rallied by the *Game Cock* of the revolution, after the disastrous defeats at Camden and Fishing Creek, were cheering their country with the hope of liberty, *even in her widowed weeds.* From the 25th of December, 1780, to the 4th May, 1781, one hundred and thirty days, he was on active duty as adjutant and commissary, under the command of Colonel James Giles and Colonel John Lindsey, then a captain. In this interesting period, was fought the battle of the Cowpens, on the 17th of January, 1781--in it Colonel Glenn participated, and was probably on duty as adjutant of Colonel James Giles' militia command. How or when Colonel Glenn and his companions were attached to General Morgan's little army, does not appear; it is probable, when Morgan reached Grindall Shoals, on Pacolet, and there encamped and sent off Colonel Washington, at the head of his own regiment and two hundred militia horse, to attack a body of Tories who were plundering the Whig inhabitants, that Colonel Glenn was a part of that command which routed them at Hammond's old store, (now Huntsville, Laurens District,) and a part of which, on the next day, under Cornet Simmons, captured William's Fort on Little River, where General Cunningham commanded. This is rendered probable by the tradition in Colonel Glenn's family, that on Green's retreat from the siege of Ninety-Six, Colonel Glenn accompanied Morgan, and thus was present at the battle of the Cowpens; but the battle of the Cowpens preceded the siege of Ninety-Six by several months, and Morgan never was in South Carolina, after the retreat from the Cowpens. The probability, therefore, is, that by confounding his services on the line towards Ninety-Six, under Colonel Washington and the retreat, as Tarleton's column placed its head upon the road leading through Newberry to Ninety-Six, to a junction with Morgan before the battle of the Cowpens, this tradition, erroneous in its main features, was created. It is, however, sufficient for us to know that at the Cowpens Colonel Glenn was present, and most likely as part of Wash-

1   M

ington's cavalry. For in that arm of service his first tour of duty (a private on horseback) had been performed. His family have preserved the remembrance that he was at the siege of Ninety-Six, commencing the 23d of May, and ending the 19th of June, 1781, although the public accounts do not notice any of his services as then rendered. The probability is, that his death, immediately after the close of the Revolution, prevented his accounts from being properly stated, that this is still rendered more probable, by the fact his family were never paid one cent for his variously revolutionary services! I hope they will be yet paid—for, notwithstanding the great lapse of time, in the language of Samuel Farrow, Esq., "time, or the Statute of Limitations, never ought to prevent the payment of the just claims of any revolutionary soldier."

It appears from the Comptroller General's accounts, that Col. Glenn, as the Lieutenant Colonel commanding the lower regiment in the Fork between Broad and Saluda Rivers, was on duty from the 20th of September, 1781, to the 1st of April, 1782; and from the 1st of May, 1782, to 1st of June, 1782. Here again is another oversight in stating the services of Colonel Glenn. He was in the battle of Eutaw on the 8th of September, 1781. There occurred an incident which he ever after lamented. In the pursuit of the British, when their lines gave way, and fled before the vigorous charge of the American troops, Glenn overtook a British soldier, and ordered him to the rear, as a prisoner. The man, frantic with terror, seized Glenn's horse by the bridle, and begged for his life; he was told he was a prisoner—he was safe; still he clung to the reins. He was ordered to let them go; he still held on. At this juncture, two of the British dragoons were seen approaching. Glenn had no other alternative than he or the prisoner should die; the latter fell beneath his sword, and thus freed, he was able to save himself.

Many incidents common to the partisan warfare of '81 and '82 occurred, which must be given without reference to date. Colonel Glenn was a stern, uncompromising Whig, who never took *protection*, and who exhibited unceasing hostility to the Tories, murderers, and horse-thieves, with which the country abounded. His life was, therefore, sought by them with unappeased avidity. On one occasion, Cunningham's mounted loyalists, as they were designated in the British service, surrounded Col. Glenn's house. A demand for entrance was made. Col, Glenn, not knowing why, or by whom it was made, sprang out of bed, and without dressing himself threw open the door. He was instantly seized by two of that ruthless band, whose previous or after service had obtained for them the unenviable distinction of the "Bloody Scout." On seizing him, they inquired for a man named McClusky, a friend of Colonel Glenn, who lodged with him that night. Not knowing still the party or their purpose, he informed them that McClusky was asleep in the upper part of his home. In a few moments a party had climbed to his place of rest, and stabbed him with their bayonets. He begged for his life, and that being unavailing, he cried murder, murder, at the top of his voice. This was more than Colonel Glenn could bear; he called for the officer in command, and demanded protection for his friend. The men who had hold of him (Colonel Glenn) ordered him "hold your tongue; your turn will be next." In an instant after, feeling that the grasp of his keepers had relaxed, he, undressed as he was, by a violent effort, jerked loose, and sprang through the crowd, and out at the door, and notwithstanding it was a clear moonlight night, he made his escape through his peach orchard. Several guns were fired, none took effect. In his race, he passed one of the party, who had retired for a few moments, and was in the corner of the fence, near to which the colonel passed; hearing the cry of shoot him, he snatched up his gun, which was lying by his side, and aimed it at the colonel; fortunately, it snapped; and before he could again prepare to shoot, Colonel Glenn had jumped the fence, and was sheltered by the trees of the wood!

At another time, excited to vengeance, bloody vengeance, by the death of a brother, Dick and Ned Turner, two of Cunningham's boldest and bloodiest braves, accompanied by Bill Elmore, and very probably others of their associates, made a descent upon the Whig settlement of the Long Lane, and captured two Whig lads, Robert and James Dugan, tied them and took them about a mile from home, where they left them under guard. The party went on to the houses of John

Ford and Jacob Anderson, and shot them both. They inquired for William Wilson (the uncle of Col. Wilson Nesbitt,) and Col. Glenn; fortunately, they were not at home, and thus escaped a vengeance which never knew to pity or to spare. Both were absent on the expedition to Eutaw. The party thus foiled as to two of their victims, returned to their prisoners, and hewed them to pieces. The next morning their poor mother, accompanied by Robt. Mars, found their bodies; one had his hand chopped off, the other a thumb and finger cut off; one of their heads was literally split open! The weeping mother, and sympathising friend, gathered those mangled remains, wrapped them up in sheets, and buried them without coffins! Horrible! horrible! is the exclamation of humanity; yet to such sad scenes must humanity come *in civil war!* It is the tradition, in Colonel Glenn's family, that Capt. William Cunningham commanded this party, and that his sword performed the shameful butchery to which I have just alluded. But I am sure it is a mistake. One who lived in those times, and who knew most of those who acted and suffered on that occasion, assured me that it was the sudden outbreak of two ferocious spirits, Ned and Dick Turner, raging like tigers to be slaked with blood! Cunningham's memory is loaded with a sufficient load of blood and vengeance, without adding to it the acts of others. *He was not present on that bloody night.*

The Long Lane settlement, consisting of Glenn, Casey, Wilson, the Dugans, Virgins, Murrays, Mars, McCrackens, Smith, Colonel John Lindsey, and others, was thoroughly Whig, and hence the inhabitants were often struck at privately, and in detail, by the Tories. *They never met them in a fair field and in broad day, without repenting their temerity.*

On one occasion, probably before the event just alluded to, a party of Tories from below stopped at old George Montgomery's, who then lived near where Col. Rutherford once lived, (lately called Bauskett's, now Wadlington's) and having previously heard that Col. Glenn had returned from a tour of duty, and was probably at home, inquired the way to Glenn's mills. Montgomery suspecting their object, directed them some rather roundabout way! As soon as they were out of sight, throwing a bushel of corn on his horse, to cover his real purpose, if he should fall in with the party, he went to Glenn's mill over the nearest route he could, and found the colonel in his mill; he had not more than time to warn him of the approach of his foes, and to give him time to plunge into the canebrake on Enoree, and conceal himself, before his house and mill were surrounded. *The bird was flown;* and all that vengeance could do, was to pour out execrations upon his name, and to call down impotent vengeance on his head

During the war, probably while acting as commissary for Capt. Lindsey's command, Col. Glenn and other Whigs made a tour beyond Bush River, through a notoriously disaffected settlement; on their return, they halted at Jacob Chandler's (known as Chandler's, now Senn's mills.) Col. Glenn was an expert swordsman; a Tory, or one who had taken protection, a man of the name of Steen or Skein, challenged him to a bout, at fencing. This is always a dangerous game with swords. But with swords, they passed through all the variations of attack and guard; striking, thrusting, parrying and guarding without harm. Glenn supposing the game over, was in the act of putting up his sword, when his cowardly opponent struck him a backhanded blow, on the jaw-bone, inflicting a deep wound, and knocking out one or two of his teeth. James McCart, (a brother Irishman,) on seeing the dastardly act, fell upon Steen or Skein, and took ample vengeance for the wound inflicted upon Glenn. In the meantime, Capt Lindsey (afterwards Col. Lindsey) sewed up Glenn's wound and otherwise dressed it, so as to secure it, and render the colonel as comfortable as possible. As soon as this was done he sought his assailant, and on finding him prostrate and bleeding from McCart's wounds, he sheathed his drawn sword, saying "it should never be said that it took two men to kill such a dastard." This piece of foul play, it was believed by Col. Glenn's friends, was the result of a premeditated scheme to cut him off.

Col. David Glenn, George Ruff and Esq. Leitner were the Representatives of Newberry in the first Legislature of South Carolina, which met in Charleston after the war. This was, I see on referring to the Public Laws, in March, '38, John Lloyd was President of the Senate, and Hugh Rutledge, Speaker of the House of Representatives.

One among the many losses sustained by Col. Glenn during

the Revolutionary war, was that of a valuable negro man, who was taken by the British to St. Augustine, East Florida. Thither, in 1784, Col. Glenn pursued him, in the hope that he would be restored to him; but he was disappointed; before his arrival, he was shipped to the West Indies, and was thus forever lost to his owner and family. Returning thence, he was for a part of the way exposed to a summer's sun, in the open boat. He reached Savannah in June, 1784, and there sicknened, and died in a few days. He left a widow and five young children, four sons and a daughter. His daughter became the wife of John Rogers, of Union, near Goshen Hill; she is no more; but her son, Gen. James Rogers, in all that is good, true, honest and firm, may well be hailed, as a worthy descendant of a Revolutionary soldier, "without fault and without fear." Three of his sons, David, Colonel John and Dr. George W. Glenn, still survive, and are entitled to all the love, veneration and respect which good and useful men may claim.

Col. Glenn was of ordinary height, stout, well proportioned and of a florid complexion. He had *an Irishman's heart*, he was generous and liberal, always ready to relieve the needy and distressed as far as his means extended. He was rather a taciturn man; but was prompt to act! An insult never passed without being resented!

"By reedy Euratos no braver e'er trod,
    When Greece against all Persia stood up in her pride,
And Pallas awoke in each bosom a God,
    Than when, at liberty's summons Glenn stood by her side

NO. 16.

Having indulged very much in attempting to rescue from oblivion the names of some of the worthy men of Newberry, I propose to-day to present one of the women of Newberry, over whose head near ninety-three years have fulfilled their course; and still she is here, one of the children of life.*

Elizabeth Gillam was born in Charlotte County, Va., about the 15th of October, 1757. Her parents, William Caldwell and Rebecca, his wife, were immigrants from Ireland. They first located themselves in Pennsylvania, thence the tide of emigration setting southwardly, carried them to Virginia, where they arrived about 1749; they settled on a very unclassically named creek; indeed, one the name of which I hope has long since been changed or lost in the lapse of time. Their residence, however, was on Louse Creek, Charlotte County, and *there* Elizabeth was born.

I am informed that the ancestors of Mr. Caldwell were of French origin; that they were Huguenots, who fled from France in 1685, at the revocation of the edict of Nantes; part settled in Scotland, another part in Ireland. William Caldwell, the father of Elizabeth Gillam, died in Virginia, leaving nine children—four sons and five daughters, John, William, James and David, Margaret, Martha, Eleanor, Elizabeth, Rebecca and Sarah. In 1770, the widow, Mrs. Rebecca Caldwell, and her numerous family, removed to and settled on Mill Creek, in Newberry District. This emigration was induced by her eldest son John, who was an active, enterprising man, and a distinguished surveyor. It is possible, as is suggested by a member of the family, that Patrick Calhoun,† had previously married Martha Caldwell, and had settled in Abbeville, and that to visit them, first induced John

---

*She died since this was written, ninety-six years old.

†From a document which I have seen in relation to the Philadelphia or American Land Company, I observe that the name of Patrick Calhoun was once written Patrick Colquohoun. He died in 1796.

Caldwell to leave Virginia. But I fear there is some mistake *here;* for none of the Calhoun's children of Patrick and Martha, with whom I have been acquainted, would be now (1850) eighty years old. The probability is, all the family came to South Carolina together, and that John Caldwell's previous exploration of the country led to their removal. It is a very remarkable fact, that this numerous family were reared to be men and women, and all lived to marry, and, with the exception of John, all had children. Of the sons, John, William and James, I shall have occasion to speak hereafter. David was a mere boy in the Revolution, and was so deaf as to be, in a great degree, incapacitated for the active duties of life. He, however, lived to be an old man, and had a numerous family. The daughters, Margaret married John Ritchie, Martha married Patrick Calhoun, (and was the mother of John C. Calhoun,) Eleanor married John Moore, Elizabeth married Robert Gillam, Rebecca married Josiah East, and Sarah married Dr. Martin. Their numerous descendants are scattered over South Carolina and the Southwest. They themselves, with the exception of Mrs. Gillam, in 1850, have passed away, and the place which once knew them shall know them no more forever!

Mrs. Gillam was a girl living with her mother during the Revolution, and had of course to submit to many of its privations, and to undergo many of its trials. In November, 1781, Cunningham's celebrated foray, known as the "bloody scout," took place. He and his men were, no doubt, led on to the horrible butcheries which they committed, by corresponding deeds of violence committed by some of the Whigs; and especially by the sufferings of the wives and children of the Tories, who, under Gov. Rutledge's orders, had been forced from their homes, and sent down to the British lines at Charleston. Cunningham, as I am now informed, crossed Saluda at Anderson's mills, now in the plantation owned by Cooper Boazeman. He then passed up the river by Daniel Dyson's, William Burgess', John Wallace and Robert Gillam's, to John Caldwell's, burning every house on the way, and plundering every thing which could be found. At Ensley's shop, he or his party, killed Oliver Towles and two others. Mrs. Gillam, *alone*, visited the shop soon after they left, to discover what consequences had followed from the report of the guns. She found the lifeless bodies of Towles and two others; one of the bodies, as in mockery, was regularly stretched, or laid out, on the vice-bench. She was the first of her family at the smoking ruins of her brother's house; his body was lying on the face in the yard! The widow was frantic with grief, walking around the smouldering ruins of their once happy home, and uttering such cries and lamentations as none but the bereaved widow can be justified in uttering. The account of this bloody transaction, as remembered by the surviving relatives of Major Caldwell, is that given by his widow. She saw the party before they arrived at the house, and persuaded her husband to make his escape. His reply was, that he had done them no harm, and he, therefore, had nothing to fear. The party halted at the gate, and hailed: Caldwell walked out, and when within a few paces, Cunningham drew a pistol and shot him dead! If this be correct, it constitutes a still heavier load of infamy to be placed upon the name of "bloody Bill Cunningham." But I confess that I think either Mrs. Caldwell was mistaken as to the person perpetrating the deed, or that in the lapse of years, some inaccuracy has crept into the recollection of it. The account taken from the lips of one who knew John Caldwell well, and who also had full opportunities of hearing the true version, and who certainly never failed to remember correctly, will be found at p. 42, 4th vol. Southern Literary Register. I extract it as follows:

"On his (Cunningham's) march to Edgehill's, Col. Hays' station, he passed the house of his old commander, John Caldwell. Two of his men, Hal Foster and Bill Elmore, were his videttes in advance. They found Major Caldwell walking in his garden, shot him down, and charged their horses in and out of the garden in fiend-like sport. When Cunningham arrived, he *affected* to deplore the bloody deed—he protested, with tears, he would as soon have seen his own father shot as Major Caldwell. Yet, in the next instant, his house, by his orders, was in flames, and his widow left with no other covering than the heavens, seated by the side of her murdered husband."

His account is confirmed by that given in Curwin's Memoirs, p. 644, in which it is said:

"On their way to Hays' station, some of the men, led on by one "Elmore," seizing the opportunity of Cunningham being at a considerable distance behind, proceeded to Capt. Caldwell's house, and finding him at home, they killed him and burned his house. When Cunningham came up, he regretted what his men had done; but it seems doubtful whether he could have restrained them, bearing as they did, such determined hatred towards their victim."

In the following incident Mrs. Gillam bore a part: In the years '81 or '82, (probably the latter,) a lad, James Creswell, afterwards Colonel Creswell, remarkable for his active hostility to the Tories, was at Mrs. Caldwell's, (Mrs. Gillam's mother.) A negro gave the alarm that Tories were approaching; in an instant the old lady directed her daughter Betsey (Mrs. Gillam) to hide herself, and Creswell to dress himself in clothes of her daughter, which she furnished. This being done, as the Tories were approaching the house, she ordered her own horse and that of her daughter Betsey's to be saddled, as she was compelled to visit Mrs. Neely. No sooner said than done; Sambo had the horses at the door. The old lady called Betsey—"come along," said she, "I am in a hurry." Out walked Creswell in Betsey's *toggery*, her bonnet slouched over his face covered his features; he and the old lady mounted in the presence of the Tories, and away they went to visit Mrs. Neely, while the Tories set about searching for Jimmy Creswell; but they searched in vain; they found the true Betsey, and then became aware that Creswell had escaped; they soothed themselves by sweeping pretty much all Mrs. Caldwell's household goods. One of them swore he thought Betsey took mighty long steps, as she went to her horse.

At the close of the Revolution, Elizabeth Caldwell married Robert Gillam, the son of a Revolutionary officer, and himself a gallant soldier of the same stormy period. The Revolution had stripped them of all their property. Robert Gillam's account of his commencement in the world, in his own words, is well worth preserving: "After I was married," said he, "my father gave me land for a settlement. I took my axe and went out into the woods about a mile from his residence to select a place for a house, leaving my wife to prepare my breakfast and bring it to me. I found a spring, and chose a place to set my house—cut down a tree for the first log, measured it, and began to think on the prospect before me. In my soliloquy, I said to myself: I am here without means, without help, and about to commence to provide for a family, without a thing to stand on. What shall I do? I have been so long in camp, I am not used to work. I think I had better quit the job, and *run away.* While thus musing, I saw my wife coming in search of me with my breakfast. When she came up we sat down together on the log, I to eat my breakfast and to talk, and she to look on and hear; I stated to her my plan for the house, but at the same time told her the prospect of living was bad; the difficulties great, and I could not see how I could get along and overcome them—and finally, that I did not know what to do. (The notion about running away, I kept to myself.) She, woman-like, listened to my doubts and fears; cheered me by pointing to others around us worse off than we were; and finally encouraged me to go on to work, and try to do the best I could. My meal (said Mr. Gillam,) was finished; I mounted the log, cut it off, and thought no more about running away." By honest, untiring industry, he and his wife overcame their early difficulties and obtained a competence. Mrs. Gillam was the mother of six children; three died in infancy.—Her oldest child, Sarah, married Philemon B. Waters, Sheriff of Newberry District; his early death in 1807, left her a young widow. She married a second husband, William T. Sheppard, by whom she had several children; both he and she are dead. Mrs. Gillam's two other children, sons, William and James, are alive. William lives at Pilot Mountain, N. C. Gen'l. James Gillam is a well known and highly respected citizen of Abbeville; with him his aged mother now lives, and of her he has most justly remarked, that "she and all the other members of the Caldwell family were Presbyterians, and hence she was strict in the instruction of her children. She strove to rear them up in the way in which they should go, so that when they should be old, they should not depart from it; and whatever pretensions I may have to a moral or religious character, I must mainly (under God) attribute it to her. I still remember many of her early maxims and pious trainings; and although I have often abused them and have wandered far from them, yet they have been indelibly impressed on my memory. Her own education was very limited—she enjoyed few advantages and facilities for her task, yet she did the best which she could, and for which I hope ever to be grateful."

She was baptized in infancy, by the Rev. Patrick Henry, uncle of Virginia's celebrated orator. She was long a member of Little River Church, near Belfast, Laurens; but when Aveleigh Church, near Newberry, was organized, she became a member of it. A year ago, I was permitted to see this venerable lady, then in her ninety-second year; she was then walking about, having lost the sight of one eye, and very much her memory; still her health was good, and I should not be surprised if she should attain her mother's great age of ninety-nine years. (In 1807 Mrs. Rebecca Caldwell died on Mill Creek, at the great age just mentioned.) Mrs. Gillam is under the middle size; she never could have been called beautiful, yet she had, and has yet, that kind, honest face which makes one always forget the absence of beauty. She possessed a strong, vigorous mind, untiring industry, cheerful, good humor and great love of social intercourse. She has long been a widow, and has borne a widow's lot with the same cheerful resignation to her mighty Master's will, with which she has passed through life. She is eminently pious. That her duties as a wife and mother were well fulfilled, needs no other proof than her husband's account of how she strengthened him to begin life, and her son's account of the rearing of her children. Of, and to her, may we not say, in the language of scripture, "many daughters have done virtuously, but thou excellest them all."

NO. 17.

I am about to speak of a gentleman, one of the earliest settlers of the district, a leading Whig, a well known man in the stormy period of the Revolution, John Caldwell; and yet, notwithstanding all this, it is with difficulty that a meagre account can be given of his life. His father and mother have already been spoken of in the life of his sister, Mrs. Gillam. Why, or when he came to this State, is not clear. My friend who kindly furnished me with some of the materials from which I small compile an account of his life and services, supposes that he came here to visit his sister Martha, the wife of Patrick Calhoun, who settled, as he supposes, on Long Cane, in 1756. In the debate of a law in the Legislature of the colony, to give a premium of so many shillings for a wolf's scalp, Patrick Calhoun is represented as saying he would much rather *"gie a poond for a lawyer's scalp."* He was the same who, in 1764, was called Captain Calhoun, and who, at the head of a company of rangers, was directed to escort the Palatines to their settlement called Londonderry.

Whatever was the motive of Mr. Caldwell in visiting South Carolina, it seems he was *here* certainly in 1769, and probably earlier. He was an eminent surveyor, and located much of the land in Newberry District. Some of the plats made by him bear the date of that year. He settled permanently on Mudlick, near Little River, as early as 1770, for deeds of that date to him speak of him as John Caldwell, of Little River. Before this time it seems he was married in Mecklenberg, N. C.

He was a member of the first Provincial Congress in South Carolina, which met at Charleston, 11th January, 1775. His colleagues for the district between Broad and Saluda Rivers where John Colcock, *Rowland Rugley, Esq.*, Jonathan Downes, Esq., Messrs. John Satterwhite, James Williams, John Williams, John McNees, Charles King and George Ross. It will be seen, on referring to Moultrie's Memoirs 1st volume 17, that at that day John Caldwell bore the title of major, and that he was the leading member from his district. This congress chose Charles Pinckney to be their president, and Peter Timothy their secretary. They approved the declaration, or bill of rights, and the association agreed on by the Continental Congress. They adopted resolutions sympathizing in the sufferings of the people of Massachusetts in consequence of their opposition to the action of the British Parliament, approving the resolutions of the Continental Congress, and returning thanks to their own members to that body, and also to the members of Congress in general. They recommended the use of *their own flour and other manufactures*, and that no action for debt should be commenced or prosecuted in the Court of Common Pleas, and that no seizure or sale under mortgage should be made without the consent of the committee of the district or parish where the defendant resided. They appointed committees to execute the Continental Association (which was pretty much for non-intercourse with Great Britain). The committee for the districts in the forks between Broad and Saluda were, *Col. Thomas Fletchall*, Major John Caldwell, Messrs. Charles King, John Williams, John Satterwhite, Jonathan Downes, James Williams, James Creswell, John McNees, *Robert Cunningham*, George Ross, Samuel Savage, John Thomas, *John Ford*, John Caldwell, John Gordon and John Prince. Those whose names are italicised in the Provincial Congress and the committee were afterwards Tories. The John Caldwell whose name appears towards the last of the committee was he who had been mentioned in No. 10, and who was killed at the head of a Revolutionary scout in the Dutch Fork, and I am very much inclined to think that the person called John Gordon in the list of the committee was Thomas Gordon, mentioned in No. 10.

In consequence of intercepted despatches from the British government to Governor Dunmore, of Virginia, Governor Martin, of North Carolina, Governor Campbell, of South Carolina, Governor Wright, of Georgia, and Governor Tonyne, of St. Augustine, by which it appeared to be the determination of the English government to coerce America, an intercepted letter of Governor Wright, of Georgia, requesting General Gage to send a detachment of His Majesty's forces from Boston to overawe the people of Georgia, and the battles of Lexington, the Provincial Congress was in April summoned to meet 1st of June, 1775. One hundred and seventy-two out of one hundred and eighty-four members met. An association drawn up by Henry Laurens was adopted, by which they pledged themselves "whenever our Continental or Provincial Congress shall decree it necessary, we will go forth and be ready to sacrifice our lives and fortunes to secure her (that is the United Provinces of America,) freedom and safety." Two regiments of foot in five days after the meeting were resolved to be raised, and on the seventh day a regiment of rangers (mounted riflemen) were also directed to be raised. In this last regiment, commanded by Col. Thomas, (who obtained the soubriquet of Danger Thomas,) John Caldwell was appointed a captain, and raised a company. The Provincial Congress appointed all the officers of their little army except the second lieutenant—these were given to the captains. The Provincial Congress appointed thirteen gentlemen, viz.: Cols. Henry Laurens, Charles Pinckney, the Hon. Judge Rawlins Lowndes, Thomas Furguson, Miles Brewton, Arthur Middleton, Thomas Heyward, Jun., Thomas Bee, John Huger, Esq., Col. James Parsons, the Hon. Judge William Henry Drayton, Benjamin Elliott, and William Williamson, Esq., as a council of safety. They were vested with the entire command of the army, with the power to contract debts, to stamp and issue money, to liquidate and pay all accounts, and to sign all commissions for the army. The following was the form of a commission:

"South Carolina.—In pursuance of the resolution of the Provincial Congress, we do certify that William Moultrie Esq., is colonel of the regiment in the Provincial service. Dated 17th day of June, 1775," and signed by all the council severally.

By the 17th July following, Col. Moultrie had recruited four hundred and seventy men for his regiment. This shows the spirit with which South Carolina went into the Revolution. I have no doubt the regiment of rangers was recruited with equal facility. Capt. Caldwell's company was soon filled. His own brother William, (William Cunningham, afterwards the Tory partisan, known as bloody Bill Cunningham, but then a highly influential and promising young man,) and many others of the most respectable young men of Saluda, Little River and Mudlick were Creek members. They were concerned in the capture of Fort Charlotte on the Savannah River, in Ninety-Six District, and were there stationed for some time as a check upon the Indians, from whom danger was apprehended. In the spring of '76 his company was ordered to Charleston. He arrived there, and was present at the repulse of the British fleet under Commodore Sir Peter Parker, by Col. Moultrie's Palmetto Fort on Sullivan's Island. This fort Gen. Charles Lee pronounced "a slaughter pen," and of which Captain Lanpereir, a brave and experienced seaman, said, in reply to Col. Moultrie's confident assertion that "we should beat them." "Sir," said he, "when those ships (pointing to the men-of-war,) come to lay alongside of your fort they will knock it down in half an hour." Moultrie's heroic Spartan reply ought to be written in letters of gold, on the glorious flag of liberty, which still floats on Sullivan's Island, and from a fort which bears his name: "*Then* we will lay behind the ruins and prevent their men from landing." The site of the old fort is now in the stream, and tradition is, that on the day when General Moultrie breathed his last, his old Palmetto Fort fell in ruins. The regiment of rangers was on the Island as early as the 8th of June. The regiment of rangers, and an eighteen-pounder, were stationed on the east end of the Island to prevent General Clinton from passing over from Long Island, where he had previously landed with a large body of men. No attempt was, however, made, and therefore the rangers had no other participation in the glories of the 28th June than that of holding in check Sir Henry Clinton and his veterans.

After the repulse of the 28th June, it is probable—indeed, I think it is certain—that Captain Caldwell's company of rangers returned to the upper country, and were in Williamson's expedition against the Cherokees, commencing 13th of September, for a part of his command were regulars, and none were so suitable as the hardy back-woodsman: accustomed to the use of the rifle on horseback or on foot. This expedition accomplished its purpose, and was disbanded in October, 1776. Whether Captain Caldwell was in any other service I do not certainly know. I presume he resigned his commission, and devoted himself to his own domestic affairs. In November,

1778, under the constitution of that year, Robert Cunningham was elected Senator, Major John Caldwell, Jacob Bowman, Jonathan Downes and Henry O'Neall Representatives from the Little River District. They all belonged to the moderate party, who were for conciliation, and were opposed to the French Alliance. The Senator, Robert Cunningham, and two of the Representatives, Jacob Bowman and Henry O'Neall were afterwards Tories. John Caldwell and Jonathan Downes remained Whigs.

After the fall of Charleston, in 1780, it is probable that Major Caldwell retired to North Carolina, but there seems to be no certainty about it. So, too, he may have returned with Greene to South Carolina, but his name does not appear in any of the accounts of this period. So distinguished a man as he was would hardly have been passed over in silence if he had been in active service.

In his company, as I have already remarked, he enlisted, among others, William Cunningham. In Curwin's Memoirs it is stated that he was promised the commission of a first lieutenant. This could not have been, as that commission had been filled when the officers of the regiment were appointed. The second lieutenants were to be appointed by the captains; and I have always understood, when the difficulty occurred which induced him to abandon the service, Captain Caldwell was about promoting him to the rank of lieutenant over his own brother William. It is stated in Curwin's Memoirs that when recruited he had stipulated not to be carried to the lower country, and that when, in the spring of '76, they were ordered below, he only agreed to go, on being allowed to resign as soon as he reached Charleston. That soon after reaching Charleston they were ordered to John's or James' Island; that Cunningham tendered his resignation, and claimed the fulfillment of the promises made to him; that at last he was prevailed on, to prevent a mutiny in the company, to cross; that the moment he was landed the captain put him in irons; that he was subsequently tried by a court-martial and acquitted, and then left the rangers. This may be correct for aught I certainly know, for I am aware the account comes from *too pure a source* to be, in any shape, willfully incorrect. I am sure, however, of one thing—if Cunningham had then

1   N

been a lieutenant his captain could not have put him in irons. The most which could have been done would have been that he would have been placed under arrest, and, in a very heinous case, put in charge of the adjutant or the regiment in the guard-house or under a guard. The account which I had received from one acquainted with Cunningham and Major Caldwell is given in "Random Recollections of the Revolution," 4 Southern Literary Register, 40—"some trivial offence prevented his (Cunningham's) promotion, and sent him before a court-martial, by which he was sentenced to be whipped, and he actually suffered this degrading punishment." For this cause he *very justly* deserted. While the British held the rule of the upper country he visited his former commander at the head of his company of mounted loyalists, or a part of them, sufficient to compel submission, and, as is stated in the Southern Literary Register, 41, "he found" Major Caldwell "on a summer's day, sitting in his own house, without shoes or stockings. He amused himself by stamping on his toes and kicking his shins, and concluded his visit by telling him this was ample satisfaction for the whipping he had received while under his command." In November, 1781, Major Caldwell was killed in his own yard, or garden, in the manner which was described in the memoirs of his sister, Mrs. Gillam.

As I have already stated, Major Caldwell was an eminent surveyor. He made many of the first surveys on Saluda, Little River, Bush River, and Mudlick and Mill Creeks. The country was then pretty much in the woods, and fare was generally pretty rough. Some idea may be formed of it by a supper made by Major Caldwell in one of his surveying trips, at the house of Barney Mounts, who was rather better provided with the means of living than some of his neighbors. The whole supper consisted of *mush and hog's lard.* During the progress of the Major's attack on the *mush,* his *host,* with kind and hospitable intent, was constantly exclaiming to his wife, "Bring a leetel more of the hock's putter to make the Major's mush go down slickery." The tradition is, that Major Caldwell was an active, energetic man, kind in all his purposes, and intelligent and useful. He was a Presbyterian, and having married in Mecklenburg, in addition to his own principles of liberty, it is likely he obtained with his wife, as her dowry, a full inoculation of that spirit of independence which gave birth to the celebrated Mecklenburg Declaration of Independence, and made Lord Cornwallis call the country around Charlotte, the "Hornet's Nest."

The memoir of John Caldwell was written and published a few days before the death of my mother, which took place, as appears by the subjoined notice, 4th October, 1850. A long interval occurred before I resumed the Annals.

DIED—At her residence, in the town of Newberry, on Friday, the 4th day of October instant, at 10 minutes after 10 A. M., Anne O'Neall, widow and relict of the late Hugh O'Neall, and mother of Judge O'Neall, in the 84th (eighty-fourth) year of her age.

She has left three children, Judge O'Neall, Abigail Caldwell, wife of John Caldwell, Esq., and Miss Sarah F. O'Neall. The latter lived with her mother, and the two had lived alone since 1834. The death of a mother is, under such circumstances, most distressing to a child. Mrs. O'Neall was born at the place where her son lives, (Springfield.) She has ever since lived in the district, and since 1814, in the town of Newberry. She was the youngest child of Samuel Kelly and his wife, Hannah Belton. There was no kinder mother—no more benevolent, unpretending woman. She was, until her last sickness, able to walk about and attend to her domestic business. She was a member of the Society of Friends.

Her children will always remember, with gratitude her early, pious and judicious training. Much of the commencement of their education depended upon her. Her last illness, protracted during more than six weeks, was borne by her with great fortitude. She was scarcely ever heard to utter a complaint. The evening before her death, she said to her son that "her time was to be short, and she wished it to be so." On his inquiring if "she thought the change would be for the better," she said, "she hoped so." In this pious confidence she was ready, and did meekly and quietly resign her life into the hands of her mighty Master. She is gone to that home "where the wicked cease from troubling, and where the weary are at rest." She is *there*, united to her husband, children, grandchildren, her parents, brothers and sisters, who have gone before her.

NO. 18.

"Far dearer the grave, or the prison,
　Illumined by one patriot name,
Than the trophies of all, who had risen
　On Liberty's ruins to fame !"

Since my pen wrote on the subject at the head of this article, years have sped, Revolution has threatened, blustered its day, and in its stead, peace has returned, and *liberty* is again, I hope, a *welcome visitor* in the *press room*, where I presume you preside. To the author it has been a period of sorrow, labor, and trial. As No. 17 went to press, the author's mother, endeared to him by a mother's watchful care, and more than an usual mother's instructions, was, in the fulness of time, gathered to her rest. Although she was, as he well knew, ripe for the harvest, he could not lay her honored head in the silent house, unwept with the tear of affection; and he cannot even now recur to it, without feeling that all things else might be got, but in the language of the poet, "minnie never anither."

"Hark ! she bids all her friends adieu !
　Some angel calls her to the spheres;
Our eyes the radiant saint pursue,
　Through liquid telescopes of tears.
Farewell, bright soul ! a short farewell
　Till we shall meet again above,
In the sweet groves where pleasures dwell,
　And trees of life bear fruits of love !"

The varied avocations of a bustling life have so occupied every moment, that in vain has the author looked for an opportunity to renew the labor of love, in chronicling whatever may be found to be to the interest, or glory of Newberry ! In the dark days of December, and, perhaps, while others enjoy the riot and misrule of Christmas, the author may beguile hours of idleness, by writing of the past.

But to the matter of to-day ! In No. 6 an imperfect account was given to John Boyce. Having now the means of enlarging it, from an authentic source, it is preferred to do so.

John Boyce was a native of Ireland, and belonged to that hardy, intelligent, active race of men in the north of Ireland called the Scotch Irish. He emigrated to the United States, then the British Provinces, in North America, in 1765. He was a pedler, and carried his pack from house to house until 1777, when he married Elizabeth Miller, daughter of David Miller, of Rutherford, North Carolina.

After this happy event, he ceased to be an itinerant merchant, and settled in Newberry District, about fifteen miles north of the town of Newberry; the section where he settled, resided and died, has been called Mollohon for many years.

The Revolutionary war before his settlement in Newberry, had reached the shores of this State. In June, '76, had been fought the glorious battle of Fort Moultrie. Along the whole line of our southern sea-board had been seen little, beyond the movement of the South Carolina troops to and from Savannah, Georgia. On the 15th of January, '78, happened that dreadful fire in Charleston, which laid in ashes a large part of the city from Queen street to the lower end of East Bay street, (Grenvill's Bastion) 232 houses of the value of £507,832, ($2,263,690,) were destroyed. This was supposed to be the work of the partisans of the British; parties of whom, from their shipping, were every night in the town. In the spring of this year, the Schophelites, so called from their leader Col. Scophel, a colonel of militia justly described by Moultrie as "an illiterate, stupid, noisy blockhead," and, he might have added, *rascal*, organized and moved across the Savannah River below Augusta, with a view to an union with the British troops in St. Augustine, who would, it was predicted, invade South Carolina. This called out all the military forces of the State. Alexander Boyce, a brother of John, obtained a commission as a Captain; in his company the subject of this article made his first essay in arms. At the siege of Savannah, Capt. Alexander Boyce on the unfortunate 9th of October, 1779, in the gallant attempt to carry the British line, fell at the head of his company.

John was the elder brother. He, after his brother's death, attached himself to the company of militia commanded by Captain (afterwards Colonel,) Thos. Dugan. General Levi Casey was the lieutenant, and most usually commanded that part of the company detailed for service out of the immediate neighborhood. Captain Dugan most usually commanded the scouts.

Mr. Boyce was in the battle of Blackstocks, King's Mountain, Cowpens and Eutaw. On his return to his family, after the battle of King's Mountain or Cowpens, (our informant is not certain which,) he had scarcely blessed the "gude wife and the bairns," and seated himself to taste their homely fare —a cup of milk and a piece of bread—until he was startled by the sound of approaching horses. He sprang to his cabin door, and saw a party of Tories, headed by the celebrated partisan, Wm. Cunningham, and a man of less note, but equally dreaded, McCombs, immediately before him. Four of the horses were already abreast of his door. His only safety was in flight. Death he knew was the result of captivity. Making a virtue of necessity, he threw his hat in the face of the horses before the door. This made them open right and left. He sprung through the opening, and ran to the woods, which were before him in about seventy-five yards. Before, however, he could reach the friendly cover, Cunningham was along side, and striking a furious blow, it took effect on his raised hand, as he avoided the charge, and cut off nearly three of his fingers. Before, however, the blow could be repeated, he was in the thick brush of a wood impenetrable to cavalry. From his cover he watched the retreat of his foes; then hurrying to his house his wounded hand was soon bound up, and he was in the saddle, on his way to his commander, Casey, and before night, with a party of fifteen, Casey was in pursuit, and on the Enoree River, near the mouth of Duncan's Creek, captured eleven or twelve of the party who had attempted the life of Mr. Boyce. Among them was McCombs. These were conveyed to the place where the Charleston road crosses the old Ninety-Six road, (now Whitmire's,) and there a "short shift," a strong rope and a stooping hickory applied speedy justice to them all. A common grave, at the root of the tree, is their resting place for all time.

On another occasion Mr. Boyce was captured, and tied in his own barn, while a bed-cord was sought for to hang him; his negro man (long afterwards known as Old Sandy,) being hid in the straw, and knowing the necessity of speedy relief, while his captors were absent on their fell purpose, arose to his rescue, and untying him, both made good their escape.

These are a few of the hair-breadth escapes which tried the men of that dark and bloody period, when home, sweet home, could not be enjoyed for a moment without danger, and when wife and children had to be left to the tender mercies of the bloody, plundering Tories.

John Boyce lived long after the war, and enjoyed the rich blessings of the *glorious liberty* for which he had periled so much. He lost his wife in '97, and died in April, 1806. He had seven children: Robert, John, David, Alexander, Ker, James, Andrew and Mary. All are no more, except Ker Boyce, the millionaire of Charleston.*

Mr. Boyce was a well informed, but not a well educated man. He had read much. He exercised a just and wholesome influence in the section where he lived.

He was a Presbyterian, and an elder in McClintock's Church, Gilder's Creek. In the grave yard, there, rest his remains. He was a merchant and distiller. He made and sold whiskey, and, strange to say, not one of his many sons ever drank to excess. This, no doubt, was to be attributed to the "let us worship God," heard night and morning at his family board.

---

*Since died.

NO. 19.

"Fling our sun-burst to the wind,
　　Studded o'er with names of glory,
Worth, and wit, and might, and mind,
　　Poet young and patriot hoary,
　　Long shall make it shine in story."

In undertaking to do justice to the name of a venerable
soldier, the difficulty of the task is greatly enhanced by the
poverty of the material in our possession. Could it have been
so that the author could have sat by his side, and heard the
narrative of the deeds of daring, the hair-breadth escapes,
and the trial and suffering of the dark and bloody period,
then, indeed, he could have sketched, as with a pen of fire,
and with life-like correctness held the portrait of the soldier
of other days to his fellow-men, and said this is Golding
Tinsley who fought through the whole perid of the Revolution, and tired not. But this opportunity was not offered;
and, from the short narrative which affection has preserved is
to be gathered the scattered materials, out of which the web
of his glorious story is to be woven.

Golding Tinsley was born in Virginia, Culpeper County,
about the year 1754; he emigrated to South Carolina about
the year 1771, and settled in Newberry District. At the commencement of the war of the Revolution, he, with his three
brothers, enlisted, as is believed, July, 1775, in Capt. John
Caldwell's company of rangers. If this be so, he was present
with the regiment of rangers, on the east end of Sullivan's
Island, where they were stationed on the day of the battle of
Fort Moultrie, to hold Sir Henry Clinton in check, and to
prevent his crossing from Long Island. This meritorious service received the thanks of Congress by resolution of the 20th
July, '76. The subsequent service of the rangers are so
obscure, that they cannot be spoken of with certainty. In
September, 1776, they were placed on the Continental establishment. Previous to this they had been employed in Williamson's expedition against the Cherokees. They, perhaps,

with the other South Carolina regulars, were employed in Georgia; a part of the regulars were placed as marines, in the little navy of the State, under the command of Captain Biddle, for a cruise to protect the commerce of the State. The expedition consumed about ten weeks. They fell in with the Yarmouth, a British sixty-four gun-ship, and in the engagement, the Randolph, Capt. Biddle's ship, blew up, and every soul perished; among them was a fine Carolina company of fifty men. To reduce the Schophelites, one hundred and fifty of the rangers were sent from Charleston, in April, '78, to Georgia; these, probably, were the upper countrymen, who were better calculated to meet such irregulars than any other troops. I presume the rangers were in the unfortunate expedition to East Florida, as I observed that Major Wise, one of the officers of the rangers, was in the council of war at Fort Tonyn, on the 11th July, 1778. At what time Golding Tinsley, and his brothers, terminated their services, in the regiment of rangers, cannot he ascertained.

Two of his brothers were killed by the Tories, on Fair Forest, near McBeth's Mills, Union District. He and James, his other surviving brother, rode ·out the storm of the Revolution. It seems that Golding and James were at the battle of Stono, on the 20th of June, '79, and in the fatal siege of Savannah, and the attempted escalade of the 9th of October. They, fortunately, escaped the calamitous surrender of Charleston, in May, 1780. After that event the Whigs scattered; some rendezvoused at Tuccasege Ford, on Catawba, under Col. Sumter. The probability is that the Tinsley's went with Col. James Williams to North Carolina, and returned with him, for on the 18th of August, they partook with him in the dangers and glory of the defeat of the British, under Col. Innis, at Musgrove's Mill.

In this affair Williams* "had about one hundred and fifty; Innis three hundred men." Musgrove's Mill, called in Mill's Atlas Gordon Mill, is in the northeast corner of Laurens District, on the Enoree River. The British forces occupied that position, south of the river, and in full command of a rocky,

---

*In Ramsay's History of Tenneesee Col. Shelby is said to have command in this battle. The statement will accompany the memoir of Col· James Williams.

bad ford. Williams' command was on the north side of the
river. His main body he drew up on a hill near a creek
which runs into Enoree, just below the Spartanburg line.
This portion was a half mile from Musgrove's Mill. It was
both protected and concealed by a wood. His little army was
drawn up in a semi-circle, and constituted a pretty ambuscade.
His arrangement was perfectly simple, and in partisan style.
With a few picked men he was to approach the river, show
himself to the enemy, fire upon them, induce them to cross
and pursue, while he held them in check; firing as he fell
back to the centre of his ambuscade, and thus bring them
entirely within his power. The scheme was fully and beautifully executed. Col. Innis eagerly pursued Williams' flying
sharp-shooters, and as he advanced, the extremities of Williams' semi-circle closed behind him. He was thus surrounded,
wounded, and most of his militia commanded were taken
prisoners. Innis, with his regular troops, escaped. Col. Clary,
who commanded a detatchment of loyalist militia in the action,
often related his own escape. His horse, he said, was seized
at the same moment by the opposite checks of his bridle-bit
by two of Williams' soldiers. He took advantage of the confusion of the melee with great presence of mind. He said to
his captors, "Damn you, don't you know your own officers?"
He was instantly released, and fled at full speed.

Johnson's Traditions of the Revolution, p. 519, informs us
that Col. Shelby, of North Carolina, and Col. Clarke, of
Georgia, united with Col. Williams in the affair of Musgrove's
Mill, and, as afterwards at King's Mountain, each commanded
his own men. The account there given is from Col. Samuel
Hammond's notes, who was then a captain, and present at
the action. It is a little more extended than that which is
here given. It is, however, substantially the same.

After this gallant achievement, a part of Williams' command, and other Whigs, took post at the Cedar Spring, in
Spartanburg District, called in Mills' Statistics "the Green
Spring, near Berwick's iron works," now Leitner's cotton
factory. There were either two partisan affairs at this place,
or there is an irreconcilable difference between Major Mc-
Junkin's statement, 2d Mag. 35, and that given in Mills' Statistics, 738, 739. In the former Mrs. Mary Thomas, the wife

of Col. John Thomas, is represented as riding from Ninety-Six in the day, and giving the alarm. In the latter, Mrs. Dillard is represented as reaching the camp before day, and and announcing the enemy's approach.

Col. Clarke, of Georgia, commanded the Americans, and is represented as advancing to that point, with a view of striking at a recruiting party of Ferguson's. This officer (Ferguson,) was on his way from Cornwallis' army, after Gates' defeat at Gum Swamp, near Camden, with a view of collecting the loyalists in the upper part of South Carolina, overawing the Whigs, and holding the mountaineers in check. Ferguson determined to surprise Clarke in his camp; he detached Dunlap with 200 picked mounted men to commence the battle. Fortunately their intention was disclosed in the conversation which they were carrying on, while Mrs. Dillard (the lady as I presume of the veteran Maj. Dillard, of Laurens,) prepared supper for them. As soon as the British were engaged in their supper, this gallant woman slipped out of the house, bridled a young horse and mounting, pushed him at full speed to the American camp, and was carried by one of the videttes to the Colonel, to whom she said "be in readiness to either fight or run; the enemy will be upon you immediately, and they are strong." The call to arms was instantly answered by the hardy woodsmen; they were ready, aye, ready; and when Dunlap's bugles sounded the charge, he was met by the unfaltering huzza of the Americans, as hand to hand they met and overwhelmed him. In fifteen or twenty minutes Dunlap was routed and flying; and when Ferguson reached the ground, he found his advance had been beaten, the prisoners taken had been removed, and Col. Clarke and his party, except two wounded men left on the ground, were beyond his power. In this glorious affair Golding and James Tinsley, bore a part. This occurred, probably, in September, 1780.

The two brothers were among those who joined Col. Williams before the battle of King's Mountain. The old song says:

> "Old Williams from Hillsborough came
> To him the South Carolinians flocked amain."

On the 7th of October they formed part of Col. Williams' advancing column, who poured the contents of their deadly rifles upon Ferguson's encircled hosts. They saw their gallant leader fall in the arms of victory; at the same instant the British commander, Ferguson, yielded up his proud spirit; and soon after the British lion at the feet of Campbell, the brave Virginian, who led to victory, and glory, the men of the mountains.

Soon after this great victory, the two Tinsley's attached themselves to Sumter, and were with him in the gallant and successful stand which he made on the 20th of November, 1780, at Blackstocks. In this well fought action, Sumter was wounded, and was borne by his faithful followers to some place of safety in North Carolina.

The Tinsleys were next found in Morgan's army. On the 17th of January, 1781, they formed part of his command, by whom the impetuous Tarleton was again repulsed. They remained in Morgan's army, and with it, when united with Greene, made the celebrated retreat to Virginia. Thence turning back with Greene they participated in Guilford's well fought field; on the 15th of March, 1781, and after the pursuit of Lord Cornwallis to Ramsay's Mill on Deep River, they accompanied the main army to South Carolina. Whether they were in the battle at Hobkirk's Hill, near Camden, is unknown; but it is most probable from their love of action, that they were.

The siege of Ninety-Six was another of the trials of the Revolution, in which the brothers took part. Gen. Greene on the 25th of May environed that post, which was defended with uncommon spirit by Col. Cruger. But he was reduced to the last extremities and must have soon surrendered, had not intelligence reached him that Lord Rawdon with two thousand men was near at hand. This intelligence, tradition informs us, was conveyed to Cruger by a lady. Rawdon wrote a letter and put it in the hands of a young lady, whose sweet-heart, a British officer, was in the garrison. She rode into the American lines talking to the officers and men until she reached a point opposite to the gate of the fort, when she wheeled her horse, and putting him to full speed, held the letter in full view of the garrison; the gate was thrown open, and she was soon in the arms of her admirer, and the letter in the possessiom of Cruger. Two alternatives were left to Greene to raise the siege, or to attempt the reduction of the fort, by assault. The latter on the 18th of June, 1781, was attempted, and failed. The retreat of Greene beyond Saluda followed.

The Tinsleys after this, for some cause, proceeded to Virginia; they were present at the surrender of Lord Cornwallis, at Yorktown, on the 19th of October, 1781. What part they bore in the siege is unknown; it is not, however, to be believed, that soldiers trained and inured to war, as they were, would stand idle, when arms and glory were before them.

They returned to South Carolina and were a part of Col. Hays command, when he surrendered to Capt. Wm. Cunningham, at Edgehill's, midway between Belfast and Milton, in November, 1781. This bloody catastrophe is susceptible of so many versions, and has been so often stated, that the author *here* mostly cites from Random Recollections of the Revolution, the following as the best within his reach: "Hays was a bold, inexperienced, incautious man." (This description, the author's subsequent means of information induces him to qualify; Hays had seen some service: he certainly was with Col. Williams at King's Mountain, and probably in most of his former services, as he is just before the action mentioned by Col. Williams, as part of his military family.) "His station was at Col. Edgehill's, in Laurens District, east of Little River and Simmon's Creek, on or near the old Charleston road from Rabun's Creek to Orangeburg. The dwelling house built of logs was his fort. He was told by William Caldwell to put himself in a position of defence; pointing to the smoke seen southeast, he said, "That is my brother's house, and I know Cunningham is in the neighborhood." Hays was at work in a blacksmith shop, making a cleat to hold a lady's netting, and hooted at Caldwell's suggestion, saying that "Cunningham had too much sense to come there." Caldwell said, "I will not stay here to be butchered," and mounted and fled at full speed. As he went out at one end of the old field he said he saw Cunningham come in at the other.

The surprise was complete and overwhelming. Hays, and his men almost without resistance were driven into the house, and Cunningham's pursuit was so close, that John Tinsley struck a full blow with his sword at Hays, as he entered the door. A few guns were fired from within and without. Two men were killed, supposed to have been slain by their own respective fires. Lockley Leonard was killed in the house, and one of Cunningham's men in the yard. A ramrod tipped with flax, saturated with tar was set on fire and shot out of a musket into the roof of the house. It was, in a moment, in a blaze. Hays and his party on a promise of good quarters (as it has always been said,) surrendered. Cunningham selected Hays and Maj. Daniel Williams, (a son of Col. Williams, who fell at King's Mountain,) as his victims. He was about hanging them on the pole of a fodder-stack, when he was accosted by a young son of Col. Williams, Joseph Williams, a lad of sixteen or seventeen years, who had from infancy known Cunningham. "Capt. Cunningham, how shall I go home and tell my mother that you have hanged brother Daniel?" "Cunningham instantly swore that he should not have that melancholy duty to perform. He hung him up with his brother and Hayes. The pole broke and with his sword he literally hewed them in pieces." Then the work of death went on, each member of the company had the right to kill or spare, as he pleased. Golding and James Tinsley, Maj. Wm. Dunlap, of Huntersville, Laurens, and John Cummins, commonly called King Cummins, were those who were spared in the savage slaughter. James and Golding Tinsley, the author supposed, were saved by their kinsman, John Tinsley, but in 1832, at Spartanburg, James Tinsley assured him this was not the case, and gave the name of another person who performed that meritorious deed. Who it was, has escaped the author's recollection.

This was the last of the bloody trials of the Revolution, which tried the courage and fortitude of Golding Tinsley. The British power was confined to the seaboard until the 14th of December, 1782, when they evacuated Charleston, and South Carolina was no more trodden by a hostile foot, from the seaboard to the mountains.

Golding Tinsley lived many years after the war in Newberry District. He thence removed to Spartanburg District, where he lived in honor and usefulness the balance of his days. He was for the last thirty years of his long and eventful life a member of the Methodist Episcopal Church, and this period was adorned by every Christian grace which showed itself in his conversation, in his precepts, and in his examples

He died near Cross Anchor, Spartanburg District, on the 11th of May, 1851, having attained to the great age of 96 or 97 years. He left two children, Isaac and Amelia, him surviving. The estimation in which he was held was evidenced by the immense concourse who followed his body to the grave. He was buried with the honors of war; not less than two thousand persons were present. In closing this account of that gallant soldier, well may we say, "Blessed are they who die in the Lord, and their works do follow them."

NO. 20.

"Day by day do thy great ones go down to the grave,
  But thy genius expires not, but soars like the moon,
When it rises pavilioned in light, from the wave,
  As glorious as though that moment 'twere born."

Maximilian Haynie, of whom we are to speak, to-day, came from Prince William County, Virginia, to Newberry, in '72 or '73. He was twice married. His first wife was a Miss Falkner, by whom he had two children, both daughters. The eldest married a Mr. Courtenay, remained in Virginia, and died without issue. The second married Burr Harris, and removed to this district, and after remaining here several years removed to Pendleton. Mr. Haynie's second wife was Elizabeth Buchanan. By her he had ten children. Eight of these were born after she was bed-ridden with rheumatism. Three of his children died when he was about setting out for South Carolina. This sad domestic event delayed his trip for a season.

By his brother-in-law, John Buchanan, he sent out two slaves (Edinborough and Beck,) to make a crop. In the fall of that year he and his family came to South Carolina. He settled on Second Creek. The mother of his first wife lived with him as long as she lived. She was a religious, and perhaps a superstitious old lady. At one period of her life she narrowly escaped shipwreck, and in the midst of her peril she prayed for deliverance, and vowed, if she was spared, that she would dedicate that day (Friday of every week,) to fasting and prayer. This she religiously observed. To be sure of a faithful remembrance, she stated to her son-in-law's second wife, when she came home, the obligation she had assumed, and requested her, if at any time she should be unmindful, that she would be pleased to remind her of it. On one occasion, only, was it necessary to remind her that it was Friday. She immediately retired to her room, knelt down, and returned thanks to God that she had been saved from violating her vow. What beautiful, truthful and child-like piety was here exhibited! What an excellent example is here set before our people, young and old! Few, very few, now follow it. Many vow, but few perform. This good woman hardly accompanied Mr. Haynie to South Carolina, for at his exodus from Virginia he must have been fifty-three years of age.

He was a carpenter by trade, and made many articles of domestic furniture, such as tables, bedsteads cupboards, &c., and exchanged them with the settlers around him for hogs, cattle, chickens and butter.

In the Revolution his age, and his afflicted wife, saved him from the peril and butchery which attended the partisan warfare of that dark period; but it did not save him or his family from plunder.

It seems a scamp, named Jim Buchanan, a distant relative, made himself acquainted with Mr. Haynie's affairs by continually lounging about his house, and reporting to the Tories whatever plunder he had, and which to them was desirable. On one occasion Mr. Haynie had sold a hogshead of tobacco in Charleston, and received nine guineas, which he brought home. This sum, equal to $40.50, he thought the Tories might find, and take away. To prevent discovery, and yet tell the truth, according to the letter, when questioned, he buried his gold, flattering himself he was safe, as he could now say "he had not a farthing upon the face of the earth." But the spy knew, and so did the Tories. They told him he had brought home nine guineas, and that he had buried it. "Tell," said they, "where it is, or we will torture you until it is produced." He knew that the same party, to force a disclosure, had sawed old Jacob Felker's leg to the bone. Fearing a similar fate, he told them where his treasure was They soon disinterred and pocketed *the shiners.*

Some of Mr. Haynie's daughters were grown, and with commendable skill and industry, laid their "hands to the spindle, and their hands held the distaff"; they made homespun for dresses for themselves which were the envy of all their neighbors. Two of the young ladies, Peggy and Nancy, had in the loom a web sufficient for their dresses. Loafing Jim was there occasionally admiring and praising it. He ascertained when the web was expected to be wove; his friends, the

1   O

Tories, attended accordingly, but found only one dress completed. This they cut out, and made off with it and all the made dresses on which they could lay their hands. In vain did the bed-ridden mother plead that they would spare to her children the covering which their hands had provided; but she asked for mercy from those who never knew the word The other dress was afterwards woven, and was of such fine texture, as my informant says, that "it was drawn through a finger ring." It is, or rather was in '52, in existence, in the possession of one of Mr. Haynie's old servants, cook Lucy, who lived with Dr. Wm. Hatton.

Mr. Haynie, in the latter part of his life, became a celebrated mathematician. His first attention to it probably arose from the necessity of educating his children at home. The mother, confined as she was to bed, instructed in reading, and even gave explanations in arithmetic to her son, John, but she could not use her hands to make figures, and hence her husband, at night, had that duty to perform. He and his son studied together, by fire-light, until the latter gave himself up to sleep; the former pursued his studies until his light gave out. He was more than sixty when he began his course of self-instruction. He mastered arithmetic and then turned his attention to astronomy. He produced some scientific work, which he patiently studied until he was able to work out the eclipses of the sun and moon, which he did to the 20th century. His grandson (Wm. H. Ruff, Esq.,) informed me that this work was carried by his son-in-law, Thomas Rutherford, to Georgia. Mr. Ruff remarks: "Several quires of paper, full of his astronomical calculations, were at my mother's when I was married, but they cannot now be found." This is deeply to be regretted, both on account of the information they might convey, and also for the proof which they would furnish of how much patient, toiling industry could accomplish. His studies were prosecuted without the aid of lamp, or candle and wick; the rich dry-heart pine, commonly called lightwood, gave the light to his eyes which enlightened his mind. One of his slaves, with that devotion which was not uncommon, before cotton became too much the God of this world, furnished the lightwood. At night, Beck would be seen approaching the door and talking to herself,

Very truly yours

John A. Chapman

"I wonder," said she, "if my master has had any lightwood to-night; depend upon it I must get him some, for I know right well he will want some, and I cannot sleep satisfied if I know my master wants any thing I can get for him." Her axe, a willing mind, and masculine power, soon cut and brought in the requisite supply. Little anecdotes like this are worth untold gold; they are the oasis, as our abolition neighbors would tell us, in the desert of slavery. But, in fact, they are the unchangeable evidences of the tie which binds together the master and the slave, the serf and the lord, the peasant and his landlord, the world all over. Society is like the wood with which God covers the earth; there are, and always will be, the great and the small, the high and the low, the fruit-bearing and the unproductive, the beautiful and the gnarled and rugged, the tree and the bush, the vine and the bramble—all know their places and their uses. So it is with men; the wise, the learned, the foolish, the ignorant, the industrious, the lazy, the rich, the poor, the free and the bond, all have their places; and it is useless for presumptuous men or women, to do more than to improve society; they cannot break up and recast it entirely.

Mr. Haynie's only son, John, was a young lad of fine mind; he trained him to be a mathematician and an astronomer, and though he was to be a crown of rejoicing to his old age. But in vain. Intoxicating drink, in a few years, pulled down and destroyed all which his father, and his father's God had done. *He died a drunkard!* What sad misfortunes are always produced by this accursed habit. But *here*, in this instance, let us stop, and meditate for an instant or two. Mr. Haynie had been sorely tried. His wife for many, very many years, had been confined to bed by rheumatism; for much of that time she was fed by her daughter, Mrs. Ruff, as an infant; in this sad condition, he had studied and made himself, like Dr. Franklin, in his old age, a celebrated man; he had led his son up the steep and slippery heights of science, and placed him on the summit; then came the serpent, intoxicating drink, encircling him with fold after fold, until at last he was crushed. Awful picture; yet, young friends of Newberry, John Haynie has many a parallel among you. Will you not pause; reflect; be warned, and abandon the fatal temper. Read what my informant says, "in 1811 or 1812," when his grandfather was ninety-two or ninety-three, John said he, "was *drinking* and *cross*," and therefore his aged sire abandoned his own home; and on foot, accompanied by one of his faithful servants, Edinborough, sought the friendly shelter of his kind son-in-law, John Ruff. Think of that rash young man. Father, teacher, friend, alike disregarded, and like old King Lear, turned out to feel that the ingratitude of a child is worse and harder to be borne than the howling, wintry tempest.

Maximilian Haynie died at the great age of ninety-three in the year 1812. His son survived him for a short time. His daughters, Mrs. Rutherford, Mrs. James Sheppard, Mrs. John Ruff, and Mrs. Robertson, have all followed him to the tomb; they all left families, of whom few remain among us; such as do, are not only respectable, but also highly useful men and women.

Mr. Haynie took no medicine, and like most of the old people of the Revolutionary war was scarcely ever sick. Out of his five slaves, whom he brought from Virginia, three attained to his great age. One still survives, at the age of eighty-seven and bids fair, says my informant, to reach ninety-three or one hundred.* Is Newberry a sickly district, when five out of six in one family, have gone beyond four score? Moderate exercise, little or no medicine, a cheerful happy temper, occupation of mind and body, a little attention to cleanliness about residences, to clearing in, not deadening timber, in planting, not to plant cotton about the dwellings, not to obstruct the running streams by felling timber in them, or suffering drift to remain therein, in drinking pure water, and in avoiding intoxicating drink, will produe health, strength, wisdom and length of days, *in Newberry* as well as under the mountains.

Imperfectly has the life of Maximilian Haynie been sketched; the materials were originally obtained to gratify the wish of a friend, who in the wilds of Matagorda, Texas, and in the evening of his life, wished to give an account of his native district, Fairfield, and who therewith desired to give some account of the "Astronomer Haynie," of Broad River. To him a copy has been long since sent. But the good old man belonged to Newberry, and to the benefit of his life, example and trials she was entitled.

---

*She died in 1858, ninety-three years old,

NO. 21.

"You're men! as such should know your right, and knowing should de-
    fend,
Who would be free, themselves must dare the tyrant's chain to rend;
O fruitless is the grief, that springs above a nation's fears—
One firm resolve of mighty man is worth a tide of tears."

Again we are about to turn back to the Revolutionary field,
and again are about to endeavor to add another name to the
worthies, who belong to Newberry.

We, to-day, propose to call up the name of William Caldwell from the sleep of thirty-nine years; and, as far as possible to give his life to the people.

He was born, in March, 1748, in the State of Pennsylvania,
in the next year the family removed to Virginia, where they
remained till they emigrated to South Carolina, about the year
1770; this is supposed to be correct, as it is compiled from
an account furnished by Gen. James Gillam, the son of Elizabeth Gillam, whose memoir has been heretofore published.

After his removal to this State, he spent two years at his
brother-in-law's, Patrick Calhoun, in Abbeville and then returned to Newberry, and with his brother learned surveying
theoretically and practically.

He joined in June, or July, 1775, his brother's company of
rangers; what was their period of service does not appear.
This regiment commanded by Col. Thompson was speedily
completed. Moultrie says a troop of rangers was sent to Fort
Charlotte, to dispossess the royal government, to take charge
of the guns, powder, and military stores, and to send down to
Charleston the two brass field-pieces, that were there, and to
endeavor to enlist the garrison. The troop of rangers sent on
this duty was Capt. Caldwell's.

How long, they there remained is unknown. The regiment
rendezvoused, at Charleston, before the attack of the 28th
June, on Sullivan's Island. They were posted, during the
battle, on the east end of Sullivan's Island to hold Sir Henry
Clinton in check, and to prevent him crossing over from Long's

Island. William Caldwell was present on that occasion. Whether he was then an office, is not certain; it seems to be certain, that the 2nd lieutenants were appointed by the captains. That Captain Caldwell intended William Cunningham for that office rests on very satisfactory tradition. After his desertion, it is believed, that the office was conferred on William Caldwell.

What were his services, afterwards, in this department of duty, are as uncertain as has been already stated, in the memoir of Golding Tinsley. It has been a traditionary statement, that he was part of the garrison of Fort Barrington on the Altamaha, left in '78 in the unfortunate expedition to East Florida, to protect the State of Georgia. That that post was subsequently reduced, and that he, Roger McKinnie and Captain Milton were delivered as hostages for the observance of the parole allowed to the officers, and, that for an alleged breach of it, he and his companions were immured in the castle of St. Augustine for more than a year.

From information, now in my possession from one connected with the family, it may be that there is some inaccuracy in the tradition. For it is there stated that he was a part of the South Carolina Militia, in the unfortunate affair of Brier Creek, Georgia. I see, on looking into the proceedings of the court of inquiry, held to ascertain, whether Gen. Ashe, the commandant of the American troops, was to blame for that disastrous surprise, that Col. James Williams of South Carolina, was a part of his command, and if so, it may be that William Caldwell was there and taken prisoner on the 4th of March, 1779. But I confess I doubt the correctness of this. For if *there* taken prisoner, I cannot perceive, why he should have been sent to St. Augustine, when the British garrison of Savannah was at hand. There is no doubt, he was confined in the castle of St. Augustine; and after a long imprisonment, reached home. My understanding always has been, that he, McKinnie, and Milton were discharged. Indeed, I have often heard related the anecdote, that McKinnie, on the day of his discharge, packed their crockery in a pot, and threw it down the stairs to alarm the sentinel on duty. It is stated in the memoir before me, that a lad of the name of Tinsley, who had accompanied him from home, but who was not confined, bribed the gaoler, and that the door was left ajar, and thus they made their escape, and traveled on foot home.

He and his companions were confined, in a room, or rooms, where they could only see the sun through a narrow aperture for a short time each day. Often have I heard one, who knew him well, say, that after his discharge and return home, he was as fair as the fairest lady he ever saw. Yet, in the narrative before me, he is represented as returning home in such a squalid condition, that neither his mother, sister, nor the young lady to whom he was engaged, and whom he subsequently married, knew him. If he was taken prisoner, at Briar Creek, he could not have reached home much sooner than the fall of Charleston, in May, 1780.

Be this as it may, it is very certain that he was not in any of the actions, which followed, until the battle of Cowpens, in January, 1781. Before that time he had been engaged in scouting, bearing expresses, and other duties. When Tarleton's command lay at Chandler's and Brooks', before he changed his route for Pacolet, and the pursuit, as he called it, of Morgan, Wm. Caldwell, Robert Gillam, and John Satterwhite were constantly in the neighborhood, observing the motions of the enemy. Shortly before his death, he pointed out the rock, on the right of the road to Belfast, and where the road to Mount Zion turns off, as that on which they fed their horses with shelled corn carried in their saddle-bags. When Tarleton turned the head of his column by the Tea-Table rock in Newberry District, in the direction of Morgan's camp, they pushed for the same point to report his movements. There they united themselves to the militia company to which they belonged, commanded by Capt. James Caldwell. The battle of Cowpens, on the 17th of January was fought, and won. In it William Caldwell bore a soldier's part. He returned with most of the militia, but probably after his brother James' wounds had been so healed, as to permit him to be moved, to their respective homes. He, however, was rarely allowed to stay any time at home. He was too well known to the loyalists to be not often sought. The time, to the close of the war, was mostly spent in the saddle, in the scouting parties of that time. How narrowly he escaped death at Hays'

Station has been narrated in the memoir of Golding Tinsley.

On another occasion, he narrowly escaped the vengeful sword of Cunningham. At Perkin's Ford, on Saluda, Cunningham and his party commenced his pursuit; by the time he reached the residence of William O'Neall, near O'Neall's, now Bobo's Mill, on Bush River, the bleeding flanks and panting sides of his mare told too truly that the fate of Cunningham's captives, a cruel death was at his heels. A fresh horse from the stable of the Quaker carried him beyond danger.

As the eldest brother, he inherited the fine real estate of his brother John, who was slain in Cunningham's bloody foray of November, 1781, and who died without issue. After the war he married Miss Williams, the daughter of Major John Williams, and settled on Mill Creek, at the place where his brother had lived.

He was a surveyor, and with Joseph Wright was appointed, in 1787, by the county court, to run the transverse lines of the district, to ascertain the central point for the location of the court house. It resulted, as stated in No. 1. In '89, he was one of the county court judges; and at March term, he with Colonel Waters, laid off the two acres now constituting the public square of Newberry, then presented by the proprietor, John Coate, for the public buildings. In 1804, he was elected Senator for Newberry District; in 1808, he was superseded by John McMorris.

He died in December, 1814; his wife soon followed him to the grave; in the summer or fall succeeding, his son, Williams, his executor, and a most promising young man, was borne to the same silent home. At his death, he flattered himself that his son, Wm. T. Caldwell, who had enlisted under Major George Butler, and who had been subsequently promoted to a lieutenancy, might still be alive. But that which was then rumor, is now certainty; he perished in the massacre at Fort Mims.

William Caldwell was the father of ten children, of whom five survived him, John, Williams, James, Patrick C., and Elizabeth, now the wife of F. B. Higgins, Esq. Of these, only one now remains, Elizabeth.

William Caldwell was about the size of his son, Patrick C. Caldwell, except that he was never fat; he was remarkable for his fine face, intelligent countenance, his perfect symmetry of form, and activity. He rode on horseback as long as he lived; he rode a good horse always, and rode well. I last remember seeing him 5th July, 1813. He then bore little the impress of years. It was *then* that he said, that he had heard people say Bill Cunningham was a coward; but, said he, they did not know him; no braver man ever walked the earth.

Mr. Caldwell was an eminently useful man. As a surveyor and magistrate, he rendered many public services. As a Senator, he faithfully discharged the duties of his office.

He was, I think, a member of the Presbyterian Church, Little River. He was a kind husband, father, and master; he was a good neighbor, and attached kinsman, and zealous friend. His death made a great void in the settlement where he had so long resided, and been so much respected.

NO. 22.

"Let your might be like the spirit of the tempest
Uprooting the pines of the hill.
And your vengeance as terrible
As the mountain torrent.
Sweeping over the valley of
The husbandman.

James Caldwell, of whom, to-day, I am about to write, was born on the day of the battle of Monongahela, Braddock's unfortunate defeat, 8th July, 1755.

He came with his mother to this State about 1770. He continued to reside with her, and bore no active part in the Revolution until 1780. After the siege of Charleston he commanded the company of militia in the neighborhood where he lived. On the 17th January, 1781, he commanded a company in the battle of the Cowpens. He was there under the command of General Pickens.

He was probably in the advance, as one of the Carolina riflemen, under the command of Major Hammond, afterwards Colonel Samuel Hammond, or he was formed, with the rest of Pickens' and Brandon's commands, on the left of the American line. In either position he was exposed to the charge of Tarleton's cavalry. Ramsay says, when the British attacked the second line, Tarleton "was cutting down the militia." It was in this part of the action, after the militia had delivered a most effective fire, within thirty or forty yards of the advancing British column, that Captain James Caldwell was cut down by a dragoon. His hands were severely mutilated in the attempt to protect his head. He had many sabre wounds in his head, and one blow took effect immediately below his right eye, on the cheek bone, leaving a scar and bump which disfigured his face as long as he lived. He was supposed to be dead, and after the action was sought for by his brother William among the slain. He was found still alive, and suffering more for water than his many wounds. This his brother brought to him in his hat. His wounds were bound up with strips torn from his brother's shirt, which was devoted to that purpose. He was then removed to a neighboring house, and after many weeks of suffering, recovered. He was thus incapacitated from active service.

Captain Caldwell, after the Revolution, bore a very prominent part in the execution of Matthew Love, at Ninety-Six. There is a statement of this affair given in Johnson's Traditions of the Revolution, which is very inaccurate. It seems to have been prepared by my friend Major Perry, of Greenville, who has there told the tale as .it was told to him. Love was tried at Ninety-Six in 1784, (while Benjamin Guerard was governor,) before Ædanus Burke, one of the associate judges, for sedition and murder, committed during the Revolutionary war.

It is worth while to pause *here* for a moment, and inquire, and answer, who was Judge Burke. Ramsay tells us he was an Irish gentleman, who, with the gallantry characteristic of his nation, came from the West Indies at the commencement of the Revolution as a volunteer to fight for American liberty. He was educated at St. Omers for the priesthood; he was a major in the American army; he was elected a judge of South Carolina in April, '78. He long filled with mercy and justice this highly responsible office. During his administration he perpetrated many an Irish bull for his own amusement and the people around him.

On the occasion to which we have just alluded he held the scales with an untrembling hand in the midst of the excited Whigs who thronged around the bar, demanding the blood of the Tory, Love. Burke held that the acts of which he stood charged were done *flagrante bello*, and that, therefore, he was protected by the treaty of peace, and that he must be acquitted, which was accordingly done.

Before he was discharged they (the Whigs,) determined he should not escape. Love was an Irishman. He was one of Cunningham's men in the *bloody scout*. He was, I presume, present at the massacre at Turner's Station. What part he bore in it has never been known. He was at Hays' defeat, and the bloody orgies there enacted. He was never charged with, there, killing any one. After the fatal massacre of *the ring*, in which every one placed in it, with the exception of Major William Dunlap and John Cummins (the two Tinsleys

were not in the ring,) were dispatched, Love passed over the
bloody ground, and plunged his sword into the reeking bodies,
to ascertain if life remained in any of them. For these
offences the Whigs, the relatives and friends of the slain,
determined he should die. The names of the party have descended to the present time. They are General William Butler, Captain James Caldwell, Colonel Zach S. Brooks, William
Brooks, John Satterwhite, Bartlett Satterwhite, Robert Gillam,
James Atwood Williams. Captain James Caldwell (not General Butler,) was placed at the head. The latter was too
prominent a man to be selected as the leader. Captain Caldwell, pistol in hand, marched into the court-house, took the
prisoner from the bar. He was taken to the door, and thrown
upon a horse, held by James Atwood Williams. He was
thence conducted to a stooping oak, at or near the spring,
and hanged. Judge Burke, amazed at the outrage, as it
began, ordered the sheriff to quell the riot. "It is more than
my life or yours is worth to attempt it," was the reply. The
Judge instantly adjourned the court, and called to his servant,
"Kit Kit, get the horses." They were soon got, and he left
the town, and paused not till he was under the friendly roof of
his countryman, Samuel Kelly, at Springfield. In his hurried
journey he dropped his razors. They were brought to him,
at Springfield, by Caleb Gilbert, whom the judge, in his racy
Irish, declared to be "an honest fellow."

He pursued his journey to Charleston, and probably reported
the matter strongly to Governor Guerard, who issued a proclamation for the apprehension of all concerned. After Burke
had time to cool and reflect, and was perhaps better informed
as to the motives of the actors, he wrote and published an
article excusing the rash act. This ended enquiry. The records
of the court at Ninety-Six, now in the clerk's office at Abbeville, contain a precise account of this transaction. It is to be
hoped some one will copy, and give the entry to the public,
as matter of history.

James Caldwell, at one period of his subsequent life, was
elected, and served one term as a member of the House of
Representatives. He never could be induced to be a candidate again. He had ascertained, he said, what few others
have discovered, or have been unwilling to acknowledge, that
"he was unfit for the place."

In 1807 (December,) he was elected sheriff of Newberry District by the Legislature. He entered on his duties in February, 1808, and served out his term of four years. Often has the writer, when a boy, seen him bearing the sword of justice, and wearing the cocked hat of authority, alongside of the venerable Judges Grimke, Bay, and others, and venerated the scarred veteran of the Revolution. His official term was not, I presume, of any great profit to him. The active duties were performed by James Farnandis and William Caldwell, (Long Bill, as he was familiarly called.)

He married, after the war, a Miss Forrest, by whom he had ten children, who survived him: six sons and four daughters. One of his sons and three of his daughters still survive. He died in 1813.

Before his death he united himself to the Presbyterian Church, Little River, and was a devout and exemplary member of it to his death.

Few men, in any country, were as deservedly popular as James Caldwell. Enemies he had none. Every body conceded that Uncle Jimmy Caldwell, as he was called, was like Bayard, without spot and without blemish.

As husband, father, master, neighbor and friend, he was all which those relations could demand.

A friend, Gen. McGowan, of Abbeville, noticing the fact that the records of Ninety-Six, at Abbeville, might furnish a more accurate account of the execution of Love, published in the Abbeville *Banner*, the result from examination, which I now append, with the short article preceding it, written for the *Sentinel*, and then published.

I have read with great interest the article from the Abbeville *Banner* of the 16th, signed "Abbeville."

I have no doubt his correctness of the traditions, which were embodied in the twenty-second number of Newberry Annals, Historical, &c., are correct. They were set out, as they often have been narrated to "Q.", by one whose memory he has seldom found at fault. His general accuracy in the matter of Love's execution, is shown by a fact stated in "Abbeville's" communication, by which it appears Love swore he was unable to pay the costs. It had been often stated to "Q." that Love swore he was unable to pay the costs, and

yet at the time when he saw death was inevitable, he drew
from his pocket a purse of guineas and handed it to his wife.
This was so strange a fact, and so much at war with the
present practice of the Court of Sessions, that "Q." hesitated
to state it. "Q.", as well as "Abbeville," regrets, and, probably, from the same feeling of nationality, that Love was an
Irishman : but the fact is indisputable. In Laurens, Newberry, and, he presumes, in Abbeville, many of the Irish were
Tories. They had received land on the King's bounty, as it
was called ; and hence, on a principle of gratitude, they were
loyalists.

If "Q's." conjecture is right as to the authorship of "Abbeville," he knows that the author has much of the same
means which "Q." has of preserving some memorials of the
Revolution ; and he hopes that the traditions which were
poured into the ears of "Abbeville," by a tongue too dear to
be forgotten, together with the rich gleanings which may be
gathered from the records of Ninety-Six, may be given to the
public.

MATTHEW LOVE.—In a late number of "Annals, Historical,
Biographical," &c., published in the Newberry *Sentinel*, over the
signature of "Q," understood to be written by a distinguished
member of the Judiciary, there appeared a very interesting
account of the circumstances connected with the execution of
Matthew Love, at Ninety-Six, soon after the Revolutionary
war. This account corrects, in several particulars, "the very
inaccurate statement" of this transaction, which has been
recently published in "Johnson's Traditions of the Revolution," and concludes with the remark that "the records of
court, at Ninety-Six, in the clerk's office at Abbeville, contains
a precise account of this transaction, and it is hoped some
one will copy, and give the entry to the public as a matter
of history."

The desire on our part, long entertained, to know the precise state of facts, in reference to the high-handed seizure and
execution of Love, by the patriots of the Revolution, has been
quickened into activity by this reference to the "records in
the clerk's office at Abbeville"; and, in order to obtain correct
information upon the subject, as well for our own gratification as for the benefit of all concerned, we have looked into
the record.

We find that the record contains no account whatever of
the tumultuous proceedings, which, we are informed by tradition, occurred after the discharge of Love by the court, but
it does contain a pretty good account of the judicial proceed-

dings against him. We suppose the clerk considered—and if so he considered rightly—that it was not his duty to place upon the records of the court any thing that occurred after the discharge of Love. The supplement was clearly *extrajudicial.* The proceeding at the *Post-Oak* was a matter for the records of history, but not the records of the court.

It seems that the distinguished author of the "Newberry Annals," notwithstanding his usual accuracy, has been misinformed in common with the whole community, in several important particulars, in reference to this remarkable transaction. It does not appear, from the record, "that Love was tried at Ninety-Six, between '85 and '87, while Gen. Moultrie was Governor, before Ædanus Burke, Esq., for horse-stealing, committed during the Revolutionary war." This has been the common opinion, but it is erroneous in several particulars.

There has been a slight mistake as to time. Matthew Love was before the court at Ninety-Six, (he was never tried at all, as we will presently see,) at the fall term of 1784. There is no records of any court held at Ninety-Six, after the Declaration of Independence, before spring, 1783. On the 26th April, of that year, the Hon. Thomas Haywood, Jr., seems to have held what, in the "Record of General Sessions," is termed the "Spring Assizes," for the first time, at Ninety-Six. The Journal of the proceedings of that term, commences as if it were the first court held there after the war, as we have no doubt it was. It begins in solemn phrase—"At a court of General Sessions, of the peace, held at Ninety-Six, for the District of Ninety-Six, the 26th day of April, 1783," &c. The preliminaries of peace between the United States and Great Britain, were signed on the 30th November, 1782, although the definitive treaty of peace and friendship—the *treaty of Paris*—was not formally signed until after this court was held, viz: on the 30th of September, 1783. On the 30th April, "the court was adjourned to the 26th of November next." The "November Assizes, 1783," was held by the Hon. Ædanus Burke, who, after a session of two days, adjourned "the court of the 26th of April, 1784." The "Spring Assizes, 1784," was held by the Hon. Henry Pendleton, who continued the court until Saturday, May 1st, when "the court adjourned to the 26th November next." The record of the ensuing fall term commences as follows:—"November 26th, 1784, the court met agreeable to adjournment; present the Hon. Ædanus Burke, Esq." This is the term which has been made famous by the execution of the Tory Love, in violation of the treaty of Paris, and in opposition to the law, and in contempt of the court and its officers. It commenced on the 26th November, and ended on *Tuesday, the 7th of December, 1784,* which last seems to have been the day of the discharge and execution.

Benjamin Guerard was Governor of the State at this time,

as appears from the following circumstance:—One Jesse Vann had been sentenced at a previous court to be hung for horse-stealing, but was pardoned by Gov. Guerard. The pardon was spread upon the records of the court at this term, and bears date 6th May, 1784. Benjamin Guerard was governor at the time Love was executed, but Gen. Moultrie succeeded him the year after, in 1785, and possibly may have "issued a proclamation for the apprehension of all concerned." As to this, however, we are uninformed by tradition or otherwise. If such a proclamation was ever issued, it would be a most interesting document, and it is hoped that some one will hunt it up and give it to the public.

It does not appear that Love was ever charged with the offence of horse-stealing, but the charge upon which he was committed was that of *"Sedition and Murder."* Nor does it appear that he was tried and acquitted. No indictment was ever given out against him upon any charge. The original documents have been examined, and no such indictment can be found among the records. Matthew Love's name first appeared, along with many others, in a report of the Sheriff, styled "A Return of Prisoners in Ninety-Six Gaol to November, 1784." Such a return seems to have been made to every court for the purpose of a general jail delivery. This return contained the names of the prisoners, when committed, by whom committed, and for what offence. By this return, it appears that Matthew Love was committed to the jail at Ninety-Six, October 3d, 1784, upon information lodged by one William Moore, for *"Sedition against the State."* The record shows that most of the prisoners named in the Sheriff's list were tried during the term, and nearly all of them convicted. It seems that Tuesday, the 7th day of December, was the last of the term, and *sentence day.* All the prisoners who had been tried and convicted were brought up and regularly sentenced. The sentences of *His Honor* are recorded at length in each case; and then a separate supplement order is made in two cases, one against two men by the name of Lochorn, and the other against Matthew Love, indicating clearly, as it seems to us, that they were in jail, but had not been tried. The Attorney General supposing, probably, that after the treaty of Paris, he could not convict them for offences of a political character, committed *"flagrante bello,"* had not given out indictments against them. The record stands *"verbatim et liberatim,"* as follows:

"Ordered that the following prisoners be brought up in Court:"

The State *vs.* Stephen Lochorn and Jacob Lochorn—Hue and Cry from Georgia. Ordered that they be discharged by proclamation. Sworn off as to fees.

The State *vs.* Matthew Love—Sedition and Murder. Ordered to be discharged. Sworn off as to fees.

"Ordered, that the treaty of peace between His Britannic Majesty and the United States of America, be recorded on the records of this court, which is as follows, to wit:—The whole treaty is here inserted at length, commencing the definitive treaty of peace and friendship, &c. Signed at Paris, the 3d of September, 1783," &c.

There is no mention upon the records of any disturbance whatever, or of the fate of Love. After the sentences were passed, and Lochorn and Love were discharged, it is stated that "the court adjourned to the 26th day of April next."

If we are not mistaken, we have seen somewhere the letter of Judge Burke, giving an account of what occurred after Love was discharged by the court. We would like to see it again. Who will have the kindness, also, to hunt up this paper, and give it to the public as matter of history?

The "Records of General Sessions," of old Ninety-Six, commencing in the spring of 1783, and ending in the fall of 1799, contain much rich and racy matter. They are a perfect mine for the antiquary and judicial historian. It seems that horse-stealing was the great offence of the time, and it was not checked until many, very many, had been hung for it. During the term at which Love was before the court, five persons, viz: James Mitchell, John Glover, Philip Campbell, James Irwin and William York, were tried, convicted, and sentenced to be hung on *Christmas day*, 1784. The first, named J. Mitchell, for "uttering counterfeit money," and all the others for "horse-stealing."

It is said that Matthew Love was an Irishman; we are really sorry to hear it, and hope that further inquiry will show that there is a mistake, also, in this particular. Love is reported to have been cruel, blood-thirsty and revengeful; these are not characteristics of an Irishman. The Irish were generally good Whigs, almost from necessity. They had left oppression in their own Emerald Isle, and therefore, knew the value of liberty. They had long known our enemies, the British, and entertained for them a hereditary hatred—a hatred arising out of long political oppression, and made more intense by difference of disposition, manners, race and religion. An Irishman could not be a bloody Tory, without doing violence to the generous, merciful impulses of his own nature, and all his political antecedents, associations and prejudices; in other words, without ceasing to be an Irishman. We sincerely hope it will turn out that Matthew Love was not an Irishman *by birth*—he certainly was not *by nature*. John Randolph once said he had yet to see that *"rara avis in terris,"* an Irish Tory.

1

NO. 23.

"Men exist in scorn of wrong ;
    Sons of the truth of things ;
True heart's, brothers, brave and strong,
    Fed from life's perennial springs.

"Self-devoted, self-denying,
For a world in sorrow lying,
Glorious is your God-like aim ;
Glorious be your deathless fame."

Father and son are now to be sketched; both belong to that glorious army of suffering, but conquering patriots, who held aloft the standard of liberty during the dark and gloomy period of the American Revolution.

Major Robert Gillam, (the father,) removed from Granville County, N. C., (where he was born) to Page's Creek, Newberry District, before the Revolution began. Before the war reached the interior of the State, he was major of militia, and in that rank went out against the Cherokees, under the command of General Williamson, called by the Indians the *cow driver*.

This service began, probably, before the 15th of July, '76; for on that day an engagement took place between the Indians and Tories, and a detachment from General Williamson's little army of five hundred men, commanded by the late Major Jonathan Downs, of Laurens. The Indians and Tories were defeated, and thirteen of their number being taken, were found to be white men, painted like Indians.

Just about that period, intelligence of the repulse of the British at Sullivan's Island, on the 28th of June, reached the back country. People of '54, think of the vast advantage you now enjoy over your ancestors of '76; twenty days brought them the news of victory and safety at Charleston—twenty-four hours now bring to you the most trifling events at the same place !

The glorious result of the battle at Fort Moultrie intimi-dated the Tories, and sent recruits, six hundred strong, to

Williamson's little host. With three hundred and fifty horsemen, Ramsay says he advanced to attack a party of Tories and Indians, who were encamped at Occnone Creek. He must have had with him also a party of infantry; for it seems he fell into an ambuscade, his horse was shot under him, and Salvadore, the proprietor of the Jew's land, Abbeville District, was killed and scalped by his side, and defeat seemed to be inevitable. At this critical moment, Leroy Hammond, who commanded a company, rallied twenty of his men, and directing them to reserve their fire, marched rapidly with them to the fence behind which the Indians and their allies were posted, fired upon them, and immediately jumped over and charged. The Indians fled from the approaching bayonet, and the fortune of the day was saved.

Williamson pursued his advantage; burned the town east of the Keowee; but his men could not be induced to pass the river until Captain Hammond volunteered, in place of the officer designated for that duty, crossed at their head, and destroyed all the houses and provisions which they could find.

Williamson returned to his main body and advanced with them to Eighteen Mile Creek, where he encamped 2nd August. As he advanced he sent out detachments to lay waste the Indian towns. This cruel, but perhaps necessary duty, was performed, and by the 15th the destruction of the lower towns was completed.

On the 13th of September, with an army of two thousand men, partly regulars and partly militia, Williamson marched into the country of the Cherokees; he again fell into an ambuscade. Ramsay says, in his History of South Carolina, vol. i. p. 281: "They (the army) entered a narrow valley, enclosed on each side by mountains. Twelve hundred Indians occupied these heights, and from them poured in a constant and well-directed fire. Detachments were ordered to file off and gain the eminences above the Indians, and turn their flanks. Others, whose guns were loaded, received orders from Lieut. Hampton (Henry Hampton) to advance, and after discharging, to fall down and load." Johnson, in his Traditions of the Revolution, calls him Captain Hampton, and says, "his orders were to his company to fire in platoons, and then fall to the ground to reload, while the rest advanced in their smoke. He thus led them to the charge, advancing in the smoke, then firing, and reloading on their backs. When he came near enough, he charged bayonet, and the enemy fled."

The army proceeded further without interruption, and on the 23d of September arrived in the valleys, and the sword and torch carried death and destruction to the poor, deceived Cherokees, and their habitations east of the Apalachian mountains. Williamson's army returned, and was disbanded by the 13th of October.

In this harassing, dangerous, and well-executed campaign, Major Gillam performed his part well and faithfully. Particular incidents attending it cannot now be obtained.

A circumstance which occurred during the Revolution shows what Major Gillam dared to do. He was on some business at Turner's, better known as Long's Bridge, on Little River. He was sitting on the fence cleaning his nails with a small pen knife; an athletic Tory, well armed, rode near to him, using daring and insolent expressions; Gillam sprang like a tiger at him, seized him by the breast, dragged him off his horse, and took him prisoner.

His age and a large family kept him from that active duty which devolved on younger men, after the fall of Charleston, in May, 1780. He, however, met with the usual share of suffering and loss which fell to the Whigs of that time. In Cunningham's bloody foray, October, 1781, his house and provisions were destroyed; he and his family, *generally*, had sought safety in a removal to Broad River. After the war, to wit, in 1785, he was appointed one of the justices of the county court for Newberry. In September, 1786, he entered upon the duties of Sheriff of the county. He served out faithfully his term of two years, and from that time to the close of his life, in 1795, he spent his days in the bosom of his family, in a peaceful retirement. He died at his original settlement on Page's Creek.

He is described by his grandson, General Gillam, as "tall and slim, erect in person, active and sprightly, having a clear head, discriminating mind, and remarkable for great goodness of heart and suavity of disposition"; but when aroused by injury, or impelled to act by duty, he was "violent, impetuous," and brave. Such was the father.

We turn now to the son, Robert Gillam, Jr. He was born in Granville County, North Carolina, 11th January, 1760. He removed with his father, being then a mere boy, to Page's Creek, Newberry District.

He was one of the expedition against the Cherokees in '76, under the command of his father; he was then a little more than sixteen. He was in the battle of Stono, 20th June, 1780; Musgrove's Mill, 18th August, 1780; Blackstock's, 20th November, 1780; and Cowpens, on the 17th January, 1781.

The battle of the Cowpens closed his active military services. He narrowly escaped, however, in October, 1781, the vengeance of Cunningham's bloody partisans.

After Green raised the siege of Ninety-Six, his father, with most of the family, had removed to Broad River, to escape the violence of the Tories. Mrs. Susan Finley, a widowed daughter of Major Gillam, occupied the place. Robert Gillam, Jr., had just finished hauling in the crop of corn, and had left for Broad River, when Cunningham's party reached the place, and applied the torch to the dwelling house, corn-crib, and out-houses generally. Mrs. Finley, knowing many of the party, begged one of them to save a bed for her, which he did, and put it in the smoke house, the only building left standing on the premises. The subject of this, memoir, ignorant of that which had taken place in his rear, was moving leisurely on his journey; when he arrived at Ben Collier's, on Mudlick, he, although a Tory, *loved his neighbor*, hailed Gillam, told him of Cunningham's movements: of the murder of John Caldwell, and pointed to the smoking ruins of his house, and bade him to fly for his life. He obeyed the friendly warning, and before the morning sun arose upon him, he was in safety.

After the war he married Elizabeth Caldwell. (Her memoir is given in No. 16.) After it was written, at the great age of ninety-five or ninety-six, she was gathered to her fathers. They had two sons and four daughters; of them, the sons, William and General James Gillam, alone remain. Robert Gillam was for many years a magistrate of the district; this office he filled with dignity and intelligence. In all other respects, his life was one of "retired happiness." His wife, children, and friends, with home, sweet home, were his enjoy-

ments. He died at his residence on Page's Creek, in Newberry. A recollection of his person, as seen from 1808 to
1813, shadows him forth as very much of the same size as
his son, William, perhaps a little stouter and more grey than
when I last saw him.

His son, General Gillam, says "he was a man of great
suavity and good nature; honest and upright in all his dealings." This short, but good character, he richly merited. No
man better deserved the name of an honest, good man. He
was, I presume, a member of the Presbyterian Church, Little
River.

Thus have been presented two soldiers of the old time citizens of Newberry. Seldom does it happen that the father
and son serve together in the glorious cause of liberty, and
are transmitted on the same page to posterity. But so it has
happened in the Gillam family, and to their memories Newberry points as two of the stars on her crown of glory.

NO. 24.

"Upward and onward. and who shall e'er pinion
  Our bold eagle's bright wing from the sun ?
Proudly unfurling o'er freedom's dominion,
  The star and stripe banner of thirty and one !

"Foes have assailed her, and seers of disaster
  Thundered of impotence, rupture and shame ;
Despots and *traitors* but speed her the faster,
  Upward and onward to glory and fame !"

The duty of to-day is to perform a promise to a much
respected friend, who still lives, but whose once active limbs
and tongue have been deprived of all their power. While we
mourn this sad chastisement of the mighty and everlasting
Ruler of the universe, it may be no unfitting tribute to him
who was once a citizen of Newberry, to write of those from
whom he derived his being.

Benjamin Eddins, the grandfather of Major William Eddins,
to whom allusion has just been made, was a native of Virginia, and migrated to South Carolina many years before the
Revolutionary war. He settled in Ninety-Six District, in the
vicinity of the village of Ninety-Six. By prudent industry,
he accumulated enough of this world's things to make himself
and family comfortable.

The assemblage of the Whigs and Tories in opposite camps
in '75—the treaty, or armistice, whereby it was agreed that
the Tories should be neutral—the subsequent seizure of
Robert Cunningham and others of their chiefs, and sending
them off to Charleston—the attempt to rescue the former by
his worthy brother Patrick, and his followers—their seizure of
the powder, sent by the committee of safety to the Cherokees
—the attempt by Colonel Williamson to force them to give it
up—the subsequent siege of him and his followers, at Ninety-
Six, and the treaty which disbanded both parties—the advance
of two thousand men into the interior, under the command of
Colonel Richardson, in December, '75, called *the snow camps*
—the final dispersion then, and for years afterwards, of the

Tories—the repulse of the British fleet in June, '76, at Fort Moultrie—the invasion of the State and approach to Charleston by General Provost, and the battle of Stono, in '79—were all of the war of the Revolution which South Carolina had seen, until Sir Henry Clinton environed and captured Charleston, in May, 1780. Up to that time, Charleston and the State had reaped a rich harvest of wealth from the Revolution. The port of Charleston was never blockaded, and hence trade flowed freely into it. Many of the merchants of Charleston realized fortunes. The interior, with the exception of a depreciated currency, and the high prices demanded for salt, iron, sugar, coffee, and tea, enjoyed abundance and ease.

When Charleston fell, well may it be said that South Carolina put on "the garment of heaviness." Everywhere misery, lamentations, and woe were to follow. The State was regarded by the British officers as a conquered, rebellious province. They posted garrisons at Orangeburg, Ninety-Six, and Camden. These, with intermediate stations and temporary posts beyond, were supposed to be enough to hold the people in subjection. They were required to come into the different stations and take protection. Some of the leading men of the upper country, or backwoods, as it was called, did so; General Williamson and Colonel Mayson were of that number. Many, such as Pickens, the Hammonds, Butlers, Williams, Glen, Casey, Dugan, Brannon, Waters, Lacy, Hill, McJunkin, the Thomases refused; and among them was found Benjamin Eddins.

In what particular service he was engaged is not known. He was captured in some partisan affair, and was confined at Ninety-Six, as a prisoner of war. While thus shut up, the Tories plundered his house, forced his wife to deliver up all his money and every valuable article, inflicted upon her person a serious wound, the mark of which she bore to her grave, and finally fired the dwelling and out-houses. In a few moments all were in ruins, and his family turned out houseless and penniless on the world. These trying circumstances did not move the Spartan man of liberty. He bore all, and would have borne more, if required for his country.

Colonel Cruger, the commandant of the garrison, desiring his services, as a pilot for his foraging parties, visited him, and offered him his liberty, liberal wages, a commission in the British army, and indemnity for his property which had been plundered and destroyed. All were rejected with scorn. Threats of punishment were then resorted to. To these he replied: "I am your prisoner; you may inflict any cruelty your imagination can invent, you may hitch a horse to each of my limbs, and tear my body into four pieces, or *you can* (baring his bosom,) *cut out my heart and drain it of its last drop of blood; but sir, my services belong to my country, and you can never command them!*"

This bold answer secured from Cruger a respect which perhaps nothing else could have obtained. He liberated him at once, without even a parole. He was soon after seen in the ranks of General Pickens' command, and served to the end of the war.

He was permitted to live long, and see his country mounting "upward and onward to glory and fame." He was one of the early emigrants to Alabama, and there died full of years and honor.

William Eddins, the son of Benjamin, and the father of Major William Eddins, deserves, in this connection a passing notice.

He was a boy in the Revolution, but, at the early age of sixteen, he entered the ranks of the few scattered defenders of his country. Not long after his service began, he was taken prisoner and, with other prisoners, started under a guard for Ninety-Six. His horse was taken from him and assigned to one of the guard. On their way his guard, who had possession of his horse, dismounted to take "a wee drap" of a dram, and placed his musket against a tree—young Eddins was allowed to halt with him—he drank and repeated, until the rest of the guard, who, with the prisoners, among whom was Eddins' father, had preceded them some distance. Young Eddins observing that his keeper had become careless, seized his musket, mounted his own horse and escaped. He returned home to inform his mother of his escape. He had the prudence to hide his gun in a hollow log. After night, and after the family had retired to bed, the Tories paid them a visit. William and his brother secreted themselves between the bed and the wall; but the prying rascals, who were engaged in the search, discovered the feet of the boys, and were in the act of dragging them out, when the mother said, "*do let the children alone.*" For a wonder, they desisted; and, after a short time. left the house. William, who was a most adventurous spirit, sprung up and declared he would have "*a shoot*" at them. His mother and brother used every dissuasive in their power, but in vain; he drew his gun from the log where it had been concealed, and as they passed around a swamp near the house, fired upon them; with what effect, was never known. If they pursued him, he made an easy escape.

In 1781, he formed a part of the force raised by General Pickens to chastise the Cherokees, for an incursion made by them, and a number of disguised white men, into the district of Ninety-Six.

Dr. Ramsay, in his history, tells us that Pickens penetrated the Indian country, and in fourteen days burned thirteen towns, killed upward of forty Indians, and captured many more. Not one of his party was killed, and only two wounded. He did not expend three pounds of ammunition, and yet only three Indians escaped after being seen. How such results could be obtained is at first a startling inquiry; but the solution is given by the Doctor, when he tells us that the troops, instead of firing, charged on horseback with drawn swords. The Indians never have been able to resist a charge of mounted men, or the bayonet.

It is told of William Eddins, that he was one of thirteen selected to burn an Indian town which had been reported as deserted. They advanced and crossed a river, which separated the Indian town from Pickens' command, and began the ascent of the hill on which it was situated. The wily Indians from their concealment poured a well-directed fire upon them. Two young men of the party who were in advance fell from their horses; the rest of the party retreated, and formed to resist the Indians until aid could come to them from Pickens. The horses of those who fell ran back to the river; the young men who had fallen were seen to rise to a sitting posture. Eddins proposed to attempt bringing them off. His captain, Maxwell, pointed out the danger of the attempt; the almost certain death which must attend it. Being, however, much pressed by Eddins, he consented. Eddins caught the horses, led them to the wounded men, helped them to mount, and brought them safely off. These, I presume, were the two men mentioned by Ramsay as wounded.

William Eddins remained with Pickens till the close of the war. He then entered upon life without money, or means of any kind. His first crop of tobacco he made without a horse; but persevering industry overcame all difficulties, and during his residence in Abbeville, Pendleton, and Edgefield, he realized a handsome fortune.

He early became the subject of converting grace; and was received into the communion of the Baptist Church. He soon felt it to be his duty to preach the gospel of "peace and good will towards men," to the people around him. He had been the soldier of his country—he was now the soldier of Immanuel—he had fought for civil and religious liberty—he was now to fight for that glorious liberty in Christ which makes a man *free* indeed. He was, until 1816, or 1817, an acceptable minister in South Carolina; about that time he removed to Tennessee, twenty-five miles north of Huntsville, Alabama, where he continued to exercise his holy calling, doing good on the right hand and on the left, and at the same time caring for his own household. He died on the 28th July, 1837, leaving a widow, a daughter and three sons.

His character may be drawn in a few words. He was faithful, true and good—he lived long, but he lived not in vain—he was an useful man, a Christian patriot, and an untiring servant of the Highest. He has gone to his rest, and has heard long since the welcome of his master, "Well done, good and faithful servant, enter thou into the joy of thy Lord."

NO. 25.

MEMOIRS OF COL. JAMES WILLIAMS.

"Servant of God, well done; well hast thou fought
The better fight who single has maintained—
Against revolted multitudes, the cause
Of truth, in word, mightier than they in arms;
And for the testimony of truth has borne
Universal reproach, far worse to bear
Than violence; for this was all thy care—
To stand approved in the sight of God, tho' worlds
Judged thee perverse; the easier conquest now
Remains thee, aided by this host of friends,
Back on thy foes more glorious to return,
Than scorned thou didst depart, and to subdue
By force, who reason for their law refuse.

[*Milton's Paradise Lost.*

Col. Williams was a native, it is believed, of North Carolina, probably of Granville County, from which place he migrated to South Carolina, in '73. He settled on Little River, Laurens District. His original settlement, (Mount Pleasant,) is in the possession of Drayton Nance, Esq., of Newberry, who married one of his granddaughters. He engaged in the mercantile business, as well as that of farming. The former he followed until the war of Independence compelled him to abandon it.

He early took part in the opposition to the measures of the British Government.* With Major John Caldwell, John Colcock, Rowland Rugely, Jonathan Downs, John Satterwhite, John Williams, John McNees, Charles King, and George Ross, he was elected from the district between Broad and Saluda Rivers, a member of the Provincial Congress, which assembled at Charleston, 11th January, 1775, and which, by the first article of the Constitution of '76, was declared to be the General Assembly.† He was appointed one of the committee for the execution of the American Association for the district

---

*1st Moul. Mem. 17.   †1st Stat. at Large, 130.

between Broad and Saluda Rivers.* In this section of the country, many persons from the beginning did not concur in the measures of resistance to the mother country. Two of the gentlemen named on the committee, Col. Thos. Fletchall and Gen. Robert Cunningham, were afterwards distinguished as leaders of the party called Tories. In the years '75, '76 and '77, the parties became more distinctly marked; but, with the exception of the capture of the powder, the affair of '76, and the Snow Camps, the interior of the State had seen very little of the war. The Declaration of Independence, and the treaty of amity with the French, gave great discontent to many who, in the beginning, had taken a deep interest in the opposition. In consequence of this, *it is said*, Major John Caldwell, who was then a captain in the regiment of rangers, resigned his commission, retired to his farm, and united with those who were for conciliation with the mother country. At the election of '78, under the constitution of that year, Col. Williams was a candidate for the Senate, from the Little River District.† He was defeated by Robert Cunningham, and the entire delegation of four members to the House of Representatives, was elected from the moderate party, or those who were in favor of conciliation. They were John Caldwell, Jacob Bowman, Jonathan Downs, and Henry O'Neall. All efforts at reconciliation were, however, soon abandoned, and the parties of Whig and Tory assumed irreconcilable grounds. The Senator, Robert Cunningham, and two of the Representatives, Jacob Bowman and Henry O'Neall, were decided Tories; the other two Representatives, John Caldwell and Jonathan Downs, were equally decided Whigs.

In the course of this election, or on some other occasion, when the people were called together, Williams was about addressing the people; before he began, he noticed that Robert Cunningham was standing at his elbow. He said to him, "you stand too near me." Cunningham coolly replied, without changing his position, "I stand very well where I am." A blow from Williams followed the reply; a fight ensued, in which Mrs. Williams, with a true woman's devotedness, took part with her husband, by seizing Cunningham by *his cue.*

---

*1st Moul. Mem. 45.   †1st Stat. at Large, 139

She was gently disengaged by a gentleman present, and the rencontre terminated in Cunningham's favor.

Col. Williams was appointed by the Governor and Council, elected by the people, colonel of the militia, and commanded on various occasions. From Gen. Williamson's order of the 19th of April, 1778, it appears that Col. Williams was then in command, and was called on to prepare men and means to carry aid to the Georgians, and also to protect this State. He went into actual service, as a colonel of the militia, in February, or April. 1779. (1st Moult. Memb., 309, 371.) A letter written to his wife, 3d June, '79, and another of his son, on the 12th of the same month, show that he had then been in service for some time. In his letter of the 3d to his wife, he speaks of "the probability of an action the other day." This refers to the attempt to bring on a general action near Stono, 1st June, 1779.* He commanded a detachment of militia, (probably a regiment,) in the battle of Stono, 20th June, 1779. It is believed he bore a part in the unfortunate siege of Savannah, for he was still in service on the 3d of September, '79, as appears by a letter of that date to his wife.

After the fall of Charleston, (12th of May, 1780,) it is supposed Col. Williams took refuge in North Carolina. On the 5th of July, 1780, he wrote to his wife from Sumter's Camp, "Catawba Old Nation." In that letter he tells her he left his brothers in North Carolina on the 27th of June, with his family, (who were, perhaps, his sons Daniel and Joseph, for they, it appears, accompanied him, and are spoken of in this same letter.) In this interesting letter, written obviously to encourage the friends of liberty in the neighborhood of his wife, as well as herself, he states the total of the American army then approaching Camden, under Gen. DeKalb, at seven thousand seven hundred men. He thus states the forces:— "Major General DeKalb, Generals Wayne and Smallwood, with the Maryland, New Jersey and Pennsylvania troops, to the amount of three thousand regulars—two thousand five hundred of Virginia militia, marched from Hillsboroufih, being in order to join General Caswell, with about two thousand regular light horse—on the whole, seven thousand seven hundred, that

---

*1st Moul. Mem. 468.

is now in motion, and will be at Camden in the course of six or seven days."

Here the sanguine patriot and hero was disappointed, for on the 25th of July, Gen. Gates found the army encamped on Deep River.* If Col. Williams be correct, the general gathering of the militia proceeded the arrival of Gates; whereas, most of the historical ascribe it to his great name and fame.

In this letter Col. Williams next proceeds to say, that "there are five thousand five hundred Virginia militia marching, that will be here shortly, (and two thousand North Carolina militia, under Gen. Rutherford, that are to march to Ninety-Six,) with some South Carolina militia, commanded by Col. Sumter, to the amount of five hundred, now in camp at this place, and in expectation of crossing the river to-day, with five hundred Mecklenburg militia. Over and above all this, there are four thousand North Carolina militia more to march, as soon as the harvest is over. On the whole, I expect to have day-about shortly, with the Tories, when they must give an account of their late conduct. I can assure you, my dear, there is a French fleet and army on our coast. On the whole, I think the state of things is very flattering at present."

He then narrates some of the events of the Revolution, which had just taken place. "I expect (says he) you have heard of Moore's defeat in the Forks of the Yadkin, by a detached party from Gen. Rutherford, under Capt. Falls, not exceeding three hundred and fifty, that defeated one thousand three hundred Tories, and took their baggage, with about five hundred horses and saddles and guns, and counted eighty-five on the field, *that they got dead?*† Since that, General Caswell has given the English a defeat at the Cheroys, (Cheraw,) and cut off the seventy-first regiment entirely."

As to this last item of intelligence, there must be some mistake; for, although it appears that at this time the Seventy-First Regiment was stationed at Cheraw, where they were joined by eight hundred loyalists, under the command of Col. Bryan,‡ yet we have in none of our histories any account of such a decisive action as that mentioned by Col. Williams; and at

---

*1st Otis' Botta, 206. †2nd Magnolia, (1843) p. 34. ‡12th Ramsay's Univ. His., 344. ‖ 25t hRam. Univ. Hist·, 418.

the battle of the Cowpens, in January, 1781, the first bat-
tallion of the Seventy-First Regiment surrendered.‖

In this letter Col. Williams further says: "I can assure
you and my friends, that the English have never been able
to make a stand in North Carolina yet; and they have slipped
their time *now*, for they are retreating to Charleston with all
rapidity." This is high and well deserved praise; for North
Carolina, although afterwards traversed by Cornwallis, yet
never was so far subjugated or reduced to the same straits
and sufferings as her sister, South Carolina.

For some reason Col. Williams did not participate with
Sumter in the affair of Huck's defeat, nor in the battle of
Hanging Rock. It is probable his anxiety for his family, and
the state of affairs in Ninety-Six, turned his attention to that
quarter, and that he was engaged in visiting his own fireside,
and gathering recruits. In the Magnolia of 1840, 2nd vol. p.
36, Major McJunkin states, that after the battle of Hanging
Rock, on the march towards Charlotte, Col. Williams joined
Sumter. It is probable that his force was not sufficiently
strong to cope with Col. Innis, and hence that he sought his
associate, Col. Sumter, and obtained from him the aid which
enabled him to turn back. He crossed Broad River at Smith's
Ford, on the evening of the 16th of August, and pressed his
march with the accustomed celerity of mounted militia men
of that time. On the 17th, they heard the disheartening intelligence of Gates' defeat at Gum Swamp, near Camden, and
Sumter's at Fishing Creek. Still Col. Williams and his brave
associates were not disposed to falter. Col. Innis and his
troops lay between many of them and their homes. At the
dawn of day, on the 18th of August, 1780, they were in the
vicinage of Innis' camp. Of this affair, Gen. Moultrie, in his
Memoirs, 2nd vol. 220, thus speaks: "On the 18th of February, 1780, he (Col. Williams,) attacked a large party of
British and Tories at Musgrove's Mills, on Enoree River,
under the command of Col. Innis, of the South Carolina Royalists, whom he defeated, and wounded Col. Innis." This
action, thus summarily disposed of by Moultrie, is dispatched
by Dr. Ramsay, in his History of South Carolina, (1st Ram.
So. Ca. 354,) in almost the same words, adding, however, that
"the whole of his (Col. Innis') party was obliged to retire."

This action deserves a fuller account. Williams had about one hundred and fifty, Innis three hundred men. Musgrove's Mills, called in Mills' Atlas, Gordon's Mills, is in the northeast corner of Laurens District, on Enoree River. The British forces occupied that position, south of the river, and in full command of a rocky, bad ford. Williams' command was on the north side of the river. His main body he drew up on a creek, which runs into Enoree, just below the Spartanburg District line. This position was a mile or two from Musgrove's Mill. It was both protected and concealed by a wood. His little army was drawn up in a semi-circle, and constituted a very pretty ambuscade. His arrangement was perfectly simple, and in partisan style. With a few picked men, he was to approach the river, show himself to the enemy, fire upon them, induce them to cross and pursue while he held them in check, firing as he fell back to the centre of his ambuscade, and thus bring them entirely within his power. The scheme was fully and beautifully executed. Col. Innis eagerly pursued Williams' flying sharp shooters, and as he advanced, the extremities of Williams' semi-circle closed behind him. He was surrounded, wounded and most of his militia command were taken prisoners. Innis, with his regular troops, escaped. Col. Clary, who commanded a detachment of loyalist militia in the action, often related his own escape. His horse, he said, was seized at the same moment by the opposite checks of his bridle bit, by two of Williams' soldiers. He took advantage of the confusion of the *melee* with great presence of mind. He said to his captors, "Damn you, don't you know your own officers?" He was instantly released, and fled at full speed.

After the battle at Musgrove's Mill, part of Williams' command took post at the Cedar Spring, Spartanburg District. With the residue of his prisoners he fell back (after visiting his family,) to Hillsborough, North Carolina. On the 8th of September, 1780, General Nash issued an order from Hillsborough to him, authorizing him to raise an hundred horsemen, and with them to proceed to such parts as he might judge proper. With the troops raised under this order he returned to South Carolina, and was joined by many South

1

Carolinians. For the old song, called the Battle of King's Mountain, says :

> "Old Williams from Hillsborough came :
> To him the South Carolinians flocked amain."

With this force he kept his eye constantly fixed on Colonel Ferguson's movements; for this partisan officer, recruiting and drilling the loyalists, had approached to the foot of the mountain. The hardy mountaineers of North Carolina and Virginia were in arms to prevent his crossing. Williams penetrated between him and the British posts in South Carolina, and was continually hovering around his camp. The mountaineers were collected under Campbell, Cleveland, Shelby and Sevier. According to my recollection of the contents of a letter from Colonel Williams to them, published some years ago, he stated that he had traced Ferguson to King's Mountain, and to prevent his escape to the country below, and junction with Cornwallis, he invited them to unite with him in pursuing and attacking him. They acceded to his request, and according to my recollection, appointed the Island Ford, on Broad River, as the place of rendezvous. Thence they marched to the Cowpens. But in the old song, called the Battle of King's Mountain, I see it is stated that the meeting of Williams with the other independent colonels was at the Cowpens. There they organized for the pursuit and battle by leaving all their inefficient men, and pursuing with nine hundred and ten men and their fleetest horses. They passed near the Limestone Springs, and crossed Broad River at the Cherokee Ford, and at the dawn of day, on the 7th of October, 1780, they were near Ferguson's encampment, on King's Mountain. The tradition is, that Col. Williams had, *at that time*, a brigadier general's commission from Governor Rutledge. This would have given him the command, as the officer highest in rank. If the fact were so, he nobly concealed it, and took his station as commandant of his own men, among the independent colonels who fought in that action. His command constituted one of the attacking columns by which Ferguson was successively and constantly assailed. When last seen, before he received his death wound, he was ascending the mountain. His charger had been shot through the mouth, and at every step was covering his rider with blood and foam.

When Colonel Williams was shot, he had turned to his command, and was cheering them onward. The ball, fired from the mountain heights above him, took effect just between his shoulders, and ranged downward though his body. He fell within a few feet of Colonel Ferguson. Colonel Williams was borne from the battle-field, lived throughout the succeeding night and died the next morning. He lies a mile or two from the field of his own and his companions' glory, without a stone to mark the spot where rests the body of "Old King's Mountain Jim," as he is familiarly spoken of to this day.

In the Orion of October, 1843, page 87, in the memoir of Major Thomas Young, is found an account of the circumstances attending Colonel Williams' death. In the main, they correspond with the traditionary account from which the preceding is compiled. Some additional circumstances may be gleaned from it, and therefore it is here given. Major Young says: "On the top of the mountain, in the thickest of the fight, I saw Colonel Williams fall; and a braver or a better man never died upon the field of battle. I had seen him but once before that day—it was in the beginning of the action— as he charged by me at full speed around the mountain. Towards the summit a ball struck his horse just below the jaw, when he commenced stamping as if he were in a nest of yellow jackets. Colonel Williams threw the reins over the animal's neck, sprang to the ground, and dashed onward. They carried him, says the Major, into a tent, sprinkled some water in his face, he revived, and his first words were, 'For God's sake, boys, don't give up the hill.' "

A letter from his sons, Daniel and Joseph, (who were present and in the action,) written to their mother from Col. Walker's, in North Carolina, dated 13th October, 1780, simply states that their father was wounded in the battle of King's Mountain, on the 7th instant, and died on the 8th, and was buried with the honors of war on the 9th.

An aged gentleman, who well knew Colonel Williams, but who was himself too young to take any part in the revolution, has furnished many of the particular facts contained in this memoir. He reported parts of the old song which is called the Battle of King's Mountain, which, as a revolutionary relic, imperfect though it may be, is yet worthy of preservation:

"Old Williams from Hillsborough came;
To him the South Corolinians flocked amain.
*   *   *   *   *   *
*   *   *   *   *   *
We marched to the Cowpens; Campbell was there,
Shelby, Cleveland, and Colonel Sevier;
Men of renown, sir, like lions so bold,
Like lions undaunted, ne'er to be controlled.
We set out on our march that very same night;
Sometimes we were wrong, sometimes we were right;
Our heart's being run in true liberty's mould,
We valued not hunger, wet, weary nor cold.
On the top of King's Mountain the old rogue we found,
And like brave heroes, his camp did surround;
Like lightning the flashes, like thunder the noise,
Our rifles struck the poor tories with sudden surprise.
Old Williams and twenty-five more,
When the battle was over, lay rolled in their gore;
With sorrow their bodies were interred in the clay,
Hoping to Heaven their souls took their way.
This being ended, we shouted amain,
Our voices was heard seven miles on the plain;
Liberty shall stand—the tories shall fall:
Here is the end of my song, so God bless you all!"

Those who have seen the late Col. James Williams, a son of him who fell at King's Mountain, will have a better notion of the personal appearance of the revolutionary chief than words can give. But to those who never saw the son, we must endeavor to convey some notion of the father. He was about five feet nine inches high, corpulent—of very dark complexion; his hair and eyes were black—his nose was uncommonly large, turned up and round at the end—his nostrils, when distended by passion or excitement, were so large as to give rise to the coarse jest, uttered by one of his militia men, as an excuse for his tardiness at a muster: "The boys (he said) had been out hunting, and had treed an opossum in the Colonel's nose, and hence he was not in attendance."

He left, at his death, five sons and three daughters— Daniel, Joseph, John, James, Washington, Elizabeth, Mary and Sarah. Of the sons, James and Washington only lived to be the fathers of families. The daughters married Major John Griffin, James Atwood Williams and James Tinsley.

Col. Williams is represented to have been a rough, rash man, but at the same time of remarkably good disposition. He was free in his intercourse with all. An example or two may give some notion of him in these respects.

At one time, with an old and favorite negro, he was engaged after night in clearing up his store-house. He was holding a torch; in one corner was a large pile of unbroken flax. As the negro was removing some stands, a large rat sprung by the Colonel; and as it plunged into the flax, he applied his torch to it, exclaiming, "I'll swinge you." In an instant the house was in a blaze, and in spite of all efforts was burned up. The Colonel patiently submitted to the rebuke of the negro, who cursed him "for all the d——d fools" he could think of.

At the battle of Musgrove Mills, he took as a prisoner a very diminuitive man of the name of Saul Hinson, who had been under the Colonel's command at the battle of Stono. Riding along the ranks after the battle, and examining the prisoners, he discovered Hinson, and very pleasantly said to him, "Ah, my little Sauly, have we caught you?" "Yes,'' replied the little man, "and no d——d great catch either!" Saul's repartee only caused a laugh, and neither that nor his false position subjected him to any thing beyond the restraint of a prisoner.

All who knew him concurred in ascribing to him great personal bravery, and from a review of his conduct at Musgrove's Mill, and in the events preceding the defeat of Ferguson, he is entitled to have it said that he exhibited great partisan skill. Of him, Gen. Moultrie says, in his memoir, he was a brave and active officer, and warm in the American cause. He raised a large body of men, and frequently attacked the British parties.* Ramsay says, in his History of South Carolina, "Col. Williams, of the district of Ninety-Six, in particular, was indefatigable in collecting and animating the friends of Congress in that settlement. With these he frequently harassed the conquerors." When he fell, at King's Mountain, the same accomplished historian, speaking of the result of the battle says: "The Americans lost comparatively few, but in that number was that distinguished officer, Col. Williams."†

---

* 2 Moul. Mem., 220.   † 1 Ram. So. Ca., 354.

His letters to his wife and son showed that he had a deep and sincere piety. In his letter to his wife of the 30th of September, 1779, he gives utterance to this feeling. He says, "Let us, with humble confidence, rely on *Him*, that is able to protect and defend us in all dangers, and through every difficulty; but, my dear, let us, with one heart, call on God for his mercy, and that his goodness may be continued to us, that we, under his blessing, may have topings of enjoying each other once more."

In his letter of the 5th of July, 1780, speaking of his anxiety touching his wife and children, and his uncertainty as to their situation, he says: "But I trust in God, that his guardian care has been around you for your protection. I have earnestly requested the favor of Heaven on you, which I hope has been the case."

In a rather apocryphal account of a visit to Col. Williams, during the revolution, by a missionary, the Rev. S. B. Balch, one fact is stated, about which I have no doubt, and that is, that the Colonel and his family accompanied him to the place of worship on Sunday, and that "the Colonel led the music with as much ease as he would have commanded his regiment in the day of battle."

Col. Williams was a Presbyterian, and, like all of that faith, his religion placed him on the side of freedom. He, and they, thought with John Knox, "that if they suffered the twins, *liberty and religion*, either to be infringed or taken from them, they had nothing left them whereby they might be called men." In the bloodiest trials, and darkest hours of the revotion, his faith upheld him, and enabled him to say with the Psalmist, "The Lord is my light and my salvation—whom shall I fear? The Lord is the strength of my life—of whom shall I be afraid?"

The preceding memoir of Col. James Williams was most carefully prepared from his letters, from the recollections of him by my father, who, when a boy, lived in his immediate vicinity, and knew him well, and from the histories of the country: Ramsay's South Carolina, Moultrie's Revolution in the Carolinas. Since its last publication, I have seen an account of the battle of Musgrove's Mill, which ascribes the command to Col. Shelby, and gives a different account of the action. As my object is truth, I append that account, together with a most admirable description of the battle of King's Mountain, from Ramsay's History of Tennessee.

[The following scraps of revolutionary history were found by Colonel Hardin, of Illinois, among the papers of his father, the late General Hardin. They were derived from conversations with Colonel Shelby, a prominent actor in the scenes which are related, who subsequently removed to Kentucky, and was there twice elected Governor. The papers were communicated to the American Review by Colonel Hardin.]

BATTLE OF MUSGROVE'S MILL.

In August, 1780, General John McDowell, of North Carolina, commanded about two thousand militia, who were stationed at Smith's ford, on Broad River, which was about fifteen miles below the Cherokee ford. Colonel Isaac Shelby, of North Carolina, commanded a regiment under General McDowell. The term of service for which the men had enlisted was just about expiring. It was ascertained that there were about seven hundred tories camped at Musgrove's Mill, on the Enoree River, a few miles distant from the camp of Major Ferguson. Col. Shelby conceived the plan of breaking up this camp and routing the tories. For this purpose, having obtained leave from General McDowell, he raised about seven hundred volunteers from the army, without regard to rank; very many field officers having volunteered, Col. Clark, of North Carolina, was made second in command.

To effect their design, it was necessary that the affair should be conducted with both secrecy and despatch. Accordingly, Shelby's force left General McDowell's camp on the 18th of August, a short time before dark. They traveled on through the woods until dark, and then fell into the road and proceeded on all night, passing within three or four miles of Ferguson's camp, and going beyond it to the tory camp at Musgrove's Mill. This post was forty miles from McDowell's camp.

Soon after daylight, when Shelby had arrived within half a a mile of the camp, a citizen was taken prisoner, from whom he learned that the night previous the Queen's American regiment, commanded by Colonel Emines, from New York, had reached the post at the mill, and that the enemy were then from twelve to thirteen hundred strong. Just as this information was received, the enemy's patrol fell in with the advanced corps of Shelby's force. The patrol was immediately fired on, and driven in with the loss of seven men. This gave the enemy the alarm. Although the tory force was so much larger than had been expected, neither Shelby nor his men thought of anything but meeting them. Ground was selected for an engagement, stretching at right angles across the road, about half a mile from the Enoree River. The army was formed, Shelby taking command of the right wing, and Colonel Clarke of the left. Colonel Williams, of South Carolina, was stationed in the road in the centre, though without a separate command.

Whilst the tory force was forming, Shelby and his men were not idle. Immediately after taking their places in line, and securing their horses, they commenced making breastworks of logs. In half an hour they had one breast high. So soon as this was completed, Shelby sent Capt. Inman, with a company of mounted men in advance, to make a false attack on the enemy. This feint was well executed. Inman and his men charged on the enemy, fired their pieces, and then, as directed, fled in apparent confusion. The enemy's centre, on whom the false attack had been made, seeing the flight of this force, immediately pressed forward in pursuit, in considerable disorder, shouting, "Huzza for King George." On approaching the breast-work, they were unexpectedly met with a deadly fire. The superiority of the enemy in numbers emboldened them to press forward their attack, notwithstanding the advantage which our troops possessed by the breast-work, After an hour's hard fighting, the left wing of the enemy. composed of the Queen's regiment, drove our right wing, under Shelby, from their breast-work. Our left wing, which was opposed by the tories, maintained its position. The battle was maintained some time longer, the right wing gradually giving way, whilst the left flank retained its connection with the centre at the breast-work. At this juncture, Col. Clarke sent his reserve, consisting of forty men, to Shelby's aid. Shelby thereupon rallied his men and ordered a charge, which was well seconded by officers and men, and the enemy were broken and fled in confusion. The rout now became complete along the whole line, and the enemy were pursued to the Enoree River, with great slaughter. Above two hundred of the enemy were killed, and two hundred prisoners were taken. On our side, Capt. Inman, who had conducted himself most gallantly, and thirty men, were killed.

The broken forces of the enemy having crossed the Enoree, it became necessary to follow up the pursuit on horseback. Shelby called back his forces, and mounted with the intention of pursuing the scattered tories, and then turning against Fort Ninety Six. While consulting with Col. Clarke, a messenger arrived from General McDowell, bringing a letter from Gov. Caswell to McDowell, informing him of Gates' disastrous defeat at Camden, on the 16th of August, and advising all officers commanding detachments to retreat, or they would be cut off.

Col. Shelby, perceiving the hazardous position in which he was placed by this unexpected calamity, with Cornwallis in front and Ferguson on his flank, immediately ordered a retreat. Taking his prisoners with him, he traveled all that day and the ensuing night, without rest, and continued their march the day succeeding, until an hour by sun, when they halted and fed their horses. Although they had thus been marching and fighting incessantly for forty-eight hours, the indomitable energy of their commander permitted his troops no rest, when there was danger of losing all by delay. Halting, therefore, no longer than was required to feed their horses, the line of march was resumed. It was well it was so; for the news of the defeat of the tories at Musgrove's Mill had reached Ferguson, who had despatched a strong detachment to intercept Shelby and release his prisoners. By making a hard forced march, this detachment reached the spot where Shelby and his men had fed their horses within thirty minutes after they had left it. But not knowing precisely how long Shelby had been gone, and the detachment being entirely exhausted, the pursuit was relinquished and Shelby reached the mountains in safety with his prisoners.

The time of service of the men having expired, and there being no opportunity of doing any immediate active duty by a partisan corps, when they reached the road which led to

Col. Shelby's residence, he and the men from his neighborhood returned home; the prisoners being left in charge of Colonel Clarke. After going some distance, Col. Clarke in like manner returned home, giving the prisoners in charge of Col. Williams, who conducted them to Hillsborough. At this place Col. Williams met with Gov. Rutledge, who, finding him in charge of the prisoners, supposed he had commanded the expedition in which they were taken, and as a reward for the gallant achievement gave him a brigadier general's commission. Without detracting from the merits of Col. Williams, who was a gallant officer, is it right to say that this is an example too frequent in military history, where the rewards of a bold achievement fall on the wrong shoulders?

Col. Shelby described the battle at Musgrove's Mill as the hardest and best fought action he ever was in. He attributed this to the great number of officers who were with him as volunteers. Considering the nature of the march and the disparity of numbers, the action at Musgrove's Mill must be considered as one of the most brilliant affairs fought by any partisan corps during the revolution.

BATTLE OF KING'S MOUNTAIN—SEQUEL TO NO. 25.

Gilbert Town is distinguished as the extreme point of British invasion in the direction of the home of the mountain men. To that place Ferguson, in the execution of his vain threat to invade and burn up their village, had advanced, and there erected His Majesty's standard, with the double purpose of securing the co-operation of the loyalists and of preventing the raising and concentration of the whigs.

At that place he received intelligence of the avalanche of indignant patriotism accumulating along the mountains, and ready to precipitate itself upon and overwhelm his army. From that place, enterprising as he was, he found it necessary to fall back and seek safety by a junction with the main army of Cornwallis, at Charlotte. Every movement of Ferguson, from the time he left his camp at Gilbert Town, indicated his apprehension of impending danger. He commanded the loyalist militia. He importuned them, he held out the language of promise or threatening, to stimulate their allegiance and their courage. He called in vain. A cloud was gathering upon the mountain, and his loyal militia knew that it portended a storm and a disastrous overthrow. Ferguson changed his language and appealed to them in the words of bitter reproach and contemptuous ridicule. On his retreat he issued a circular letter to the tory leaders, informing them of an "inundation of barbarians"—calls the patriotic riflemen "the dregs of mankind," and importunes his loyalists thus: "If you wish to live and bear the name of men, grasp your arms in a moment and run into camp. The backwoods men have crossed the mountains; McDowell, Hampton, Shelby and Cleveland are at their head, so that you know what you will have to depend upon. If you choose to be degraded for ever and ever by a set of mongrels, say so at once, and let your women turn their backs upon you and look out for real men to protect them."

Ferguson, after breaking up his camp at Gilbert Town, despatched Abram Collins and Peter Quinn to Lord Cornwallis, informing him of his critical situation and begging a reinforcement. After despatching his letter, Ferguson marched, on the 4th, over main Broad River to the Cowpens. On the 5th he continued his march to Tate's, since Dear's Ferry, where he again crossed and encamped about a mile above. On the 6th he marched about fourteen miles and formed his camp on an eminence, where he waited for the expected reinforcements of the loyalists in the neighborhood and of regulars from the royal army. The loyalty of the former quailed at the approach of the riflemen, and in this hour of need their assistance was withheld; they remained out of Ferguson's camp.

On Wednesday, the fourth of October, the riflemen advanced to Gilbert Town. But Ferguson had decamped, having permitted many of the loyalists to visit their families, under engagement to join him on the shortest notice. In the meantime he took a circuitous march through the neighborhoods in which the tories principally resided, to gain time and avoid the riflemen until his forces could be collected and join him. This retrograde movement betrayed his apprehensions and pointed out the necessity of a vigorous effort to overtake him.

Having gained a knowledge of his designs, the principal officers determined, in council, to pursue him with all possible despatch. Accordingly, two nights before the action, the officers were engaged all night in selecting the best men, the best horses and the best rifles, and at the dawn of day took Ferguson's trail and pursued him with nine hundred and ten* expert marksmen, while those on foot and with weak horses were ordered to follow on more leisurely.

On the pursuit the Americans passed near where several large parties of tories were collecting. At the Cowpens sixty men under Col. Hambright and Major Chronicle, of Tryon county, and Col. Williams, with the South Carolina troops, joined them. Here they were informed that a body of six hundred tories were assembled at Maj. Gibbs', four miles to their right, and would join Ferguson the next day. These they did not take time to molest. The riflemen from the mountains had turned out to catch Ferguson. He was their object; and for the last thirty-six hours of the pursuit they never alighted from their horses but once to refresh for an hour at the Cowpens, although the day of the battle was so extremely wet that the men could not keep their guns dry, by wrapping their sacks, blankets and hunting shirts around the locks, thus exposing their bodies in a heavy and incessant rain. The trail every hour became more fresh, and the Americans hurried on eagerly after the prey, which they determined should not escape their grasp. The advance met some unarmed men, who were fresh from Ferguson' camp; a short halt was made, and these men were closely examined. From them it was ascertained that the enemy was encamped three miles before them, and were to march next morning to Lord Cornwallis' headquarters; his position was accurately described, and the route to the camp minutely given. Col. Williams and some of his men were well acquainted with the shape of the ground and the approaches to it.

It was now after twelve o'clock: the rain had ceased, the clouds were passing off, the sun shone brightly, and nature

---

*I quote from the Shelby papers in my possession, and from which many of the details of this expedition have been derived. Haywood has extracted from them also.

seemed to smile upon the enterprise on hand. It was determined to march at once upon the camp, and decide the conflict without rest or refreshment. Each man was ordered to "tie up his overcoat and blanket, throw the priming out of his pan, pick his touch-hole, prime anew, examine his bullets, and see that everything was in readiness for battle." While this was being done the officers agreed upon the general plan of attack, which was to surround the eminence and make a simultaneous assault upon every part of the camp. The men were soon in their saddles and upon their march. When within a mile of the battle ground an express from Ferguson was arrested, on whom was found a despatch to Lord Cornwallis, urging him to send immediately reinforcements, and stating the number under his command, and that he was securely encamped upon a hill, which, in honor of His Majesty, he had named King's Mountain, and that if all the rebels out of h–ll should attack him they should not drive him from it. The contents of the despatch were, with the exception of the number of the enemy, communicated to the riflemen, the march was resumed, their pace quickened, and they rode in a gallop within view of the camp of Ferguson.

A closer examination of the ground and the position of the enemy demonstrated the feasibility of the plan of attack already concerted by the officers. More minute arrangements were immediately made and carried into execution. It was decided that the troops commanded by Winstone, McDowell, Sevier, Shelby and Campbell, being something more than half of the whole number of assailants, after tying their horses, should file to the right and pass the mountains nearly out of reach of the enemy's guns, and continue around it till they should meet the rest of the troops encircling the mountains on the other side and led by Hambright and Chronicle, and followed by Cleveland and Williams; after which each command was to face to the front, raise the Indian war whoop and advance upon the enemy. Accordingly the troops moved forward, and passing up a ravine between two rocky knolls came in full view of the enemy's camp above them and about one hundred poles in front. Here they dismounted, and having tied their horses left a small guard with them. The right wing or column was led by Winston and Sevier, the left by

Cleveland and Williams; the centre was composed by Campbell's men on the right and Shelby's on the left. In the order, each officer having formed his ranks led off at the same time to the position assigned him under pilots selected from Col. Williams' men, who were familiar with the ground.

On his march around the mountain the right column discovered that there were two gaps in the right at the enemy's left flank—one about twenty poles from it, the other fifty. It was decided to pass through the latter. About the time they entered it the enemy began to fire on them. The fire at first did not attract attention, until some of Shelby's men being wounded, that officer and McDowell determined to return the fire, and before they had crossed the ridge broke off towards the enemy through the gap nearest to his camp, and discharged their rifles with great effect. The rest of the column under Campbell ascended the mountain, and poured in a deadly fire upon the enemy posted upon its summit. The firing became so heavy as to attract the attention of Ferguson, who immediately brought up a part of the regulars from the other end of the line, and a brisk charge was made upon the American right by the British regulars and of the tories.

This charge pushed McDowell, Shelby and Campbell down the mountain. At this moment the column under Hambright, Chronicle, Cleveland and Williams had driven in the enemy's picquet at the other extremity of the encampment, and advancing up the mountain poured in a well-directed fire upon the enemy, protected here by their wagons and some slight defences, and commanded by Ferguson himself. Dupeister, his second in command, was immediately recalled, ordered into line on the ridge, and directed to make a charge with all the regulars upon the Americans at the end of the encampment. On his passage to the relief of Ferguson, Dupeister received a galling fire from the South Carolinians under Williams. The regulars soon rallied, made a desperate charge and drove the riflemen to the hill. Here Major Chronicle fell.

In the meantime, the recall of Dupeister from the charge at the other extremity of the mountain gave the appearance there of a retreat on the part of the enemy, and the men under Shelby, McDowell and Campbell having been disorganized, produced by the first charge, rallied to the pursuit. The cry was raised, "Huzza, boys, they are retreating! Come on." They advanced with great firmness up to the hill, almost to the lines of the encampment, and for some time maintained a deadly conflict with the riflemen. Ferguson, as before, decided to resort again to the bayonet. But the marksmen had so thinned the regulars the expedient was adopted of trimming the handles of the butcher knives, and adapting them in the muzzles of the tory rifles, and thus using them in the charge. With the number of his bayonets thus enlarged, Dupeister returned to his first position, and made another charge. It was short and feebly executed, and the regulars returned within their lines.

About this time the front of the two American columns had met, and the army of Ferguson was surrounded by the riflemen. Their firing became incessant and general in all quarters, but especially at the two ends of the enemy's line. Sevier pressed against the centre, and was charged upon by the regulars. The conflict here became stubborn, and drew to it much of the enemy's force. This enabled Shelby and Campbell to reach and hold the crest of the mountain.

On all sides, now, the fire was brisk and deadly, and the charges with the bayonet, though less vigorous, were frequent. In all cases where the enemy charged the Americans on one side of the hill, those on the other thought he was retreating, and advanced near the summit. But in all these movements the left of Ferguson's line was gradually receding, and the Americans were plying their rifles with terrible effect. Ferguson was still in the heat of the battle. With characteristic coolness and daring he ordered Captain Dupeister to reinforce a position about one hundred yards distant with his regulars; but before they reached it they were thinned too much by the American rifles to render any effectual support. He then ordered his cavalry to mount, with a view of making a desperate onset at their head. But these only presented a better mark for the rifle, and fell as fast as they could mount their horses. He rode from one end of the line to the other, encouraging his men to prolong the conflict. With desperate courage he passed from one exposed point to another of equal danger. He carried, in his wounded hand, a shrill sounding silver whistle, whose signal was universally known throughout the battle, and gave a kind of ubiquity to his movements.*

But the Americans having reached the top of the mountain were gradually compressing the enemy, and the line of Ferguson's encampment was sensibly contracted. A flag was raised by the tories in token of surrender. Ferguson rode up to it and pulled it down. A second flag was raised at the other end of the line. He rode there too, and cut it down with his sword. He was frequently admonished by Dupeister to surrender; but his proud spirit could not deign to give up to a raw and undisciplined militia. When the second flag was cut down, Dupeister renewed his admonition. To this he replied by declaring he would never surrender to such a damned set of banditti as the mountain men. These men, while they admired the unyielding spirit of Ferguson, had noticed, that whenever his voice or whistle was heard, the enemy was inspirited to another rally. They believed that while he survived, his desperate courage would not permit a surrender. He feel soon after, and immediately expired.

The forward movement of all the American columns brought them to a level with the enemy's guns, which heretofore in most instances had overshot their heads. The horizontal fire of the regulors was now considerably fatal; but the rapid advance of the riflemen soon surrounded both them and the tories, who, being crowded close together and cooped up into a narrow space by the surrounding pressure of the American troops, and fatally galled by their incessant fire, lost all hope from further resistance. Dupeister, who succeeded Ferguson in command, perceiving that further struggle was in vain, hoisted the white flag and claimed quarters. A general cessation of the American fire followed; but this cessation was not complete. Some of the young men did not understand the meaning of a white flag; others who did, knew that other flags had been raised before, and were quickly taken down. Shelby hallooed out to them to throw down their guns, as all would understand that as a surrender. This was immediately done. The arms were now lying in front of the prisoners, without any orders how to dispose of them. Col. Shelby

---

* Ferguson.

seeing the facility with which the enemy could resume their guns, exclaimed: "Great God! what can we do in this confusion?" We can order the prisoners from their arms," said Sawyers. "Yes," said Shelby, "that can be done." The prisoners were accordingly marched to another place, and there surrounded by a double guard.

The battle of King's Mountain lasted about an hour. The loss of the enemy was two hundred and twenty-five killed, one hundred and eighty wounded, seven hundred prisoners, fifteen hundred stand of arms, and a great many horses and wagons, loaded with supplies, and booty of every kind, taken by the plundering tories from the wealthy whigs.

General Bernard, an officer under Napoleon, and afterwards in the United States Engineer Service, on examining the battle ground of King's Mountain, said: "The Americans, by their victory in that engagement, erected a monument to to perpetuate the memory of the brave men who had fallen there; and the shape of the hill itself would be an eternal monument to the military genius and skill of Col. Ferguson, in selecting a position so well adapted for defence; and that no other plan of assault but that pursued by the mountain men could have succeeded against him."[*]

The loss of the Americans was thirty killed, and about twice that number wounded. On the former, was Colonel Williams, of South Carolina. He fell a victim to the true Palmetto spirit, an intemperate eagerness for battle. Towards the close of an engagement he espied Ferguson riding near the line, and dashed towards him with the gallant determination of a personal encounter. "I will kill Ferguson, or die in the attempt!" exclaimed Williams, and spurring his horse in the direction of the enemy, received a bullet as he crossed the line. He survived till he heard that his antagonist was killed and his camp surrendered; and amid the shouts of victory by his triumphant countrymen, said: "I die contented," and, with a smile upon his countenance, expired.

---

[*] The account of the battle of King's Mountain has been taken from the Shelby papers, the written statements of Gen. Graham and Lenoir, Mr. Foster's Essay, and manuscript narratives of several of the riflemen who participated in it. The official report has been seen for the first time by the writer, in "Wheeler's History of North Carolina," just out of press. It is given at page 243.

Major Chronicle, who with Colonel Hambright led the left wing, was, in passing round the end of the mountain, much exposed to the fire of the enemy above them, and little more than one hundred yards distant. He fell early in the engagement at the foot of the hill, near the junction of the two streams, while gallantly repulsing the British charge. A plain monument attests the grateful remembrance of his countrymen. It bears this inscription:

SACRED
TO THE MEMORY OF
MAJOR WILLIAM CHRONICLE,
CAPT. JOHN MATTOCKS,
WILLIAM ROBB,
AND
JOHN BOYD,

Who were killed at this place, on the seventh day of October, 1780, fighting in defence of America.

On the other side of the monument, facing the battle ground, is inscribed:

COL. FERGUSON,
An officer of his Britannic Majesty,
Was defeated and killed,
At this place,
On the 7th day of October,
1780.

Of Col. Campbell's regiment, Lieut. Edmondston, two others of the same name and family, and ten of their associates in arms, were killed. The names of the Virginia officers are Captains Dysart, Colville, Edmondston, Beattie and Graig; Lieutenants Edmondston, Brown; Ensign Robert Campbell, who killed the British Adjutant, McGinnis, at the head of a charging party. Capt. Robert Edmondston said to one of his men, John McCrosky, that he did not like his place, and broke forward to the hottest part of the battle, and there received the charge of Dupeister's regulars, discharged his rifle, clubbed his gun, knocked the musket out of the hands of one of the soldiers, and, seizing him by the neck, made him his prisoner and brought him to the foot of the hill. Returning again to the British line, he received a mortal wound in the breast. After the surrender, McCrosky went in search of his captain, and told him the battle was over and the tories were defeated. Edmondston nodded satisfaction and died.

Of the wounded in Col. Shelby's regiment was his brother, Moses Shelby, who, in a bold attempt to storm the enemy's camp, leaped upon one of the wagons out of which the breastwork was formed, and was wounded. Fagan and some others suffered in the same way. Col. Snodgrass, late of Sullivan county, belonged to Col. Shelby's regiment. His captains were Elliott, Maxwell and Webb, Lieut. Sway.

Of the regiment from Washington county, and commanded by Col. Sevier, the captains were his two brothers, Valentine Sevier, Robt. Sevier, Joel Gallahan, George Doherty, and Russell; Lieutenant Isaac Lane. Capt. Robert Sevier was wounded in the abdomen, and died the second or third day after, and was buried at Bright's.

Among the privates were four others of the Sevier family, viz: Abraham Sevier, Joseph Sevier, and two of Col. Sevier's sons, Joseph and James, the latter in his· xteenth year.

William Lenoir (since General Lenoir) was a captain under Winston. He was encouraging the men who had received Dupeister's second charge, to load well and make a bold push against their assailants, when he received a slight wound in his left arm, and another in his side, while a bullet passed through his hair, just below the tie, without touching the skin.

The victory of King's Mountain was complete. Not one of the enemy escaped during the battle; from its commencement they were surrounded and could not escape. The army encamped upon the battle ground the night of the seventh. They had more prisoners than whigs with whom to guard them. They were in the neighborhood of several parties of tories, and had reason to expect that Tarleton, or some reinforcements from Lord Cornwallis, would attempt either to pursue or intercept them. The next day was the Sabbath. Its dawn was solemnized by the burial of the dead. This mournful duty performed, the enemy's wagons were drawn by the men across their camp fires, and after they were consumed the return march was commenced.

Thus brilliantly terminated this hard fought battle. It

remains almost unnoticed, while *defeats*, in other sections, have been celebrated by anniversaries and monuments. Why, in these days of railroads and excursions, cannot the descendants of Shelby, Sevier, Campbell, McDowell and Williams, and the brave men who fought with them, assemble on the spot consecrated by so much valor and patriotism, and commemorate with appropriate ceremonies the glorious event on its next anniversary, the 7th of October?

In a memoir prepared by Col. Wm. Hill, late of York district, and by him placed in the hands of Gen. Sumter, he states that the battle at Musgrove's Mill was fought by men commanded by Wm. McDowell, Clarke and Shelby.

He also states what is stated in the account, purported to be taken from Col. Shelby, that really the great merit of the action was attributable to Shelby; but that Williams being in possession of the prisoners, and meeting Governor Rutledge at Hillsboro', who supposed that Williams was the hero of the battle, gave him the commission of a Brigadier General.

There is much in Col. Hill's memoir to detract from the merit of Col. Williams. He alleges that he, Col. Williams, desired to turn the independent Colonels from Ferguson and King's Mountain, and to direct them against Ninety-Six. This may be true: for he might have well concluded, with such a force, Ninety-Six would be carried as with a *coup de main*, and all that interesting country south of Broad River relieved from the presence of the enemy. Such an achievement would indeed have been worthy of the undertaking of one of the greatest commanders.

No doubt, however, that Campbell, Shelby, Lenoir, Cleveland, McDowell and Lacy were right in refusing to turn aside. They had the lion at bay, and his death, or capture, was of great consequence. Indeed, the battle of King's Mountain was the turning point of the revolution in the South.

Col. Williams, he affirms, had no command beyond his own small party, and that he was killed at the moment of surrender, and he says, "as was supposed by some of the Americans, as many of them had been heard to swear they would do it whenever they had an opportunity." This threat, he says, arose from Col. Williams' attempt to obtain command of the South Carolinians commanded by Lacy, under his commission as Brigadier General.

This is from an officer in command on that day, and yet, I think, there must be some mistake about it. There is everything in Col. Williams' life, letters, services and the tradition in relation to him, to make us believe that he was good and true.

NO. 26.

"Upward and onward, America, ever,
  Be thy bold Eagle's swift flight to the sun ;
Wither the arm ever lifted to sever
  Our golden link of the Thirty-and-One
Free as the breezes of heaven that fan her,
  Long as eternity, mortals await,
May the bright folds of the star-spangled banner
  Float at the stern of the old ship of State."

The duty now before me is to close this work, with the exception of addenda to some of the previous numbers, such as a biographical sketch of my early and late friend, Ker Boyce, Esq. This will, with those of Y. J. Harrington and John S. Carwile, Esqs., already published, take their places in No. 8.

To-day I propose to sketch, imperfectly, I know, and perhaps *too partially*, the life and times of Hugh O'Neall, one of Newberry's oldest and best citizens.

He was born on Mudlick, Laurens district, at the place, late the property of John Armstrong, deceased, on the 10th of June, 1767. He was the second son of William O'Neall and his wife, Mary Frost. They removed after the birth of their two first children, Abijah and Sarah, to South Carolina. The family remained in Laurens until after the birth of Henry, the third son, who, I think, was born in '77; indeed I think they did not remove to Newberry until 1779. The family consisted of six sons; Abijah, Hugh, William, John, Henry and Thomas, and one daughter, Sarah, all of whom lived to rear families. Abijah removed in '99 to Ohio, near Waynesville, Warren county. Sarah married Elisha Ford, and removed to Shelby county, Kentucky. William died on Bush river; his body rests in the graveyard of Friends, near Mendenhall's Mills. John, Henry and Thomas removed to Indiana. They have all been gathered to their rest, leaving families more or less numerous.

William O'Neall's father's name was Hugh; he was, I think, a midshipman in, or at any rate he belonged to, the English navy, and not liking his berth, while at anchor in the Delaware he jumped overboard, swam ashore, and landed near Wilmington, as well as I remember, at the little Swedish town of Christiana; this took place about 1730; here he lived many years, and married Annie Cox. On landing, to escape detection, he altered the spelling of his name, either from O'Neill or O'Neale to O'Neall; the latter is the tradition. His family consisted of William, James, Hugh, Henry, John, Thomas, a daughter, Mary, and a posthumous son, George. In his life time he removed to the Susquehanna, and there he died; his family thence removed to Winchester, Virginia; there William married his wife, Mary Frost; and there, as already mentioned, his two eldest children were born.

The family, with the exception of James and George, removed about 1766 to South Carolina. Thomas died at Parkins (now Crofts) on Saluda, and was the first person buried in that graveyard. Hugh married a Parkins, and settled and died at Milton, Laurens district. Henry married a Chambers, lived in Laurens, and there remained till the close of the revolution, when he removed to Florida, and settled the place at the mouth of St. Mary's river (where his grandson, the Hon. James T. O'Neill, now resides); he (Henry O'Neall) was killed in an attempt to seize an outlaw soon after his removal; he left a large family—James, Eber, Thomas, William, Henry, Asa, Hugh and Margaret; all are dead except Margaret, now Mrs. King, of Georgia; none had families except Eber, William and Margaret.

William O'Neall was a Friend; when he joined that body of religionists is not known; his wife also belonged to the same; his brother, Hugh, inclined the same way; so did his wife and the entire Parkins family. In the revolution neither of these brothers took any part, except to bury the dead, heal the wounded, and do good wherever they could. James and George belonged to the American army; the former was a Major in the Virginia line, the latter a common soldier. Both served the entire war, and at its close, ignorantly supposing that the O' in their names was some aristocratic distinction, instead of meaning, as it really does, the "son of," struck it off and wrote their names Neall. James settled at, or near, Wheeling, Virginia; George in Jessamine county, near Nicholassville, Kentucky: they both have been dead many years; each left families surviving them. I should be proud if their descendants would resume the O', which rightfully belongs to their name.

Henry and John, unfortunately, sided with the tories. Henry, it is said, after his determination was made, and he had accepted a Major's commission in the British army, passed into Virginia to see his brother James, and proposed, if they should ever meet in battle, that they would treat each other as brothers; but the stern republican would accept no such amnesty; "in peace, brethren; in war, enemies," was his reply. Fortunately, they never met in arms.

John married Grace Frost, the sister of his brother William's wife; he was a captain in the tory forces, and was killed in a skirmish with Colonel Roebuck, in Union district; he left two daughters, Sarah, and, I think, Rebecca; his widow married a well known citizen of Pendleton, Mr. Crosby. Mary married Frederick Jones. She had an only son, Marmaduke, who will be remembered as a resident of Laurens district, in the neighborhood of Milton.

Having thus stated his ancestral families, and his father's, I now propose to give a sketch of the life and times of Hugh O'Neall.

He went early to school, he learned rapidly: most of that which he learned was with a Virginian, Benj. Smith. In his school, in company with Major John Griffin, James C. Griffin, the Williams', Cresswells, Caldwells, he acquired the common elementary education, reading, writing and arithmetic. Reading, all his life, was his great delight; he began early and continued late. His memory was early developed and long retained; often in middle life, and even in old age, has he recited many passages in the tragedy called the Battle of the Boyne, which he had read when a boy among his uncle Henry's books. The poem called Sir James the Ross, was another read in the same way, which he often repeated. One of his early exercises was a riddle, propounded by his teacher, Mr. Smith, pretty much as follows, viz.:

> Beneath the heavens, a creature once did dwell,
> As sacred writers unto us do tell;
> He lived, he breathed in this lower world, it is true,
> But never sinned, nor any evil knew;
> He never shall be raised from the dead,
> Nor at the day of judgment show his head;

> He never shall in heaven dwell,
> Nor yet be doomed to feel the pains of hell—
> Yet in him, a soul there was, that must
> Be lost, or live above, among the just.

This he solved by giving Jonah in the whale's belly, and often repeated it in manhood, and age. Benj. Smith was one of the Virginia troops on service in '76, perhaps against the Cherokee Indians, under Christie, or in Gen. Lee's projected invasion of Florida, and was either left, as unable to travel on the return march, or discharged. From the description given of him, he was both a man of talents and education. His impress was to be seen on all his scholars.

In, I presume, the year '78 was the great May frost, which took place on the 4th, and utterly destroyed vegetation and the crops; a small crop of late wheat was saved by William O'Neall. In the same year was the total eclipse of the sun. The total darkness was so great that chickens went to roost. The upper part of South Carolina, as has been frequently and justly said, scarcely knew that there was war, until the siege of Charleston. The incursion of the Cherokees on the 30th of June, '76, drove the settlers nearest the frontiers from their homes. William O'Neall, with his family, fled from Mudlick to Benj. Pearson's, near Kelly's old store, now Springfield. Often has Hugh O'Neall pointed out the old field west of Dr. Wm. Harrington's attempted settlement, in Frost's old field, as being then in cultivation, and stated the fact, that he had swam in Pearson's Mill pond on Scott's creek, where Fernandes' pond lately was.

In 1780, when Charleston fell, William O'Neall and family lived at the place, about a mile west of Bobo's Mills, and on the southwest side of Bush river. He then owned the mill, known for thirty years as O'Neall's, now owned by Dr. J. E. Bobo, about one and a half miles below Mendenhall's. Hugh O'Neall, the subject of this memoir, was then thirteen years old; yet his services were so necessary to his father, that he either attended entirely to the mill, or was a constant assistant. In that way, although no actor in the revolution, yet he became fully informed of most of the events of that dark and bloody period. The mill was the most public place in that section of the country. Across Bush river, at that place, was the most common thoroughfare from the Congaree and Charleston to pass south beyond Saluda, and west to Little river and Ninety-Six. There, were often halted the scouts, sometimes the armies; there, too, were provisions seized, as want, or power dictated. There, as he often afterwards said, did he learn to hate the proud, overbearing character of the British officers. *There* he heard narrated the accounts of the many deeds of violence and blood with which the country was overspread. The various sketches of men and events heretofore given are in a greater, or less degree, dependent upon his wonderful memory for their accuracy.

To give a true sketch of the bloody partisan war from 1780 to 1783, would be a most Herculean task; much of it has been already done in the different biographical sketches and anecdotes already published. Blood and plunder were the watchwords of many of the different parties who swept over old Ninety-Six. "Each party," (as Gen. Moultrie, in his memoirs, vol. 2d, p. 301, appropriately says,) "oppressed the other as much as they possibly could, which raised their inveteracy to so great a height that they carried on the war with savage cruelty; although they had been friends, neighbors and brothers, they had no feelings for each other, and no principles of humanity left." At page 303 he says: "The conduct of these two parties, (whigs and tories,) was a disgrace to human nature, and it may, with safety, be said that they destroyed more property, shed more American blood, than the whole British army." The pictures thus given in a few words, are, unfortunately, too true, and ought to teach us to beware of the tendencies to civil war, which I sometimes fear are too much encouraged.

Having in the Random Recollections of the Revolution, published in 1838, given most of these atrocious scenes, as narrated by Hugh O'Neall, I shall not again repeat them. If ever these matters should see the light in book form, I shall take pleasure in revising and adding to them.

I may *here* mention an incident as occurring in the immediate vicinage of the quiet meeting house of Friends, on Bush river. One of the marauding parties had captured a man, whom they deemed worthy of death. Meeting with a young Quaker, Richard Thomson, between the meeting house and his father's, Tanner Joe Thomson, (as he was usually called,) they compelled the youth with a sword to slay the captive. How much of Richard Thomson's subsequent misfortunes, (for his life was one of misfortune,) are to be ascribed to this involuntary deed of blood, it is not for me to say. Though I can say, "I have been young, and now am old, yet *never saw I the man,*" *whose hands were stained with blood, who prospered, (or if prosperity attended him,) who went to his grave in peace.*

This single scene is enough to show, that fiends, not men, were too often engaged in the prosecution of the partisan war.

The desolation of the country was equal to what fancy may well depict, as an accompaniment of such a fiendlike scene as that which I have just related.

The march of the British army was marked by wasting and ruin. When Greene passed, with his ragged Americans, forbearance and pity for the people marked his course; plunder, cruelty and oppression, he sternly forbade. When a battalion of Tarlton's command, in his attempt to strike Morgan, as he supposed, in the neighborhood of Ninety-Six, (as is stated in a note to No. 5,) encamped at William O'Neall's, everything was seized and treated as if it all belonged to them, the fences were burned to make camp-fires, the cattle were butchered for beef, the officers billeted themselves on the unpretending Quaker family, without money and without price. When a part of Greene's army, on their retreat from Ninety-Six, passed the mill, everything needed was paid for, and perfect order prevailed.

The marauding scouts entered every dwelling, and carried off everything which suited them, bedding, clothes, provisions; often were families left without food or raiment; sometimes the houses were burned, and women and children turned out with no covering, save the forest and the heavens.

These scenes passed before the eyes of the youthful Quaker, Hugh O'Neall; his brave ancestral blood often boiled almost over at the wrongs and oppression which he witnessed, and to which he was called to submit. Yet the teachings of his parents, *peace, peace,* kept him quiet, and day after day he was seen at the mill, providing for his father's family and the neighborhood's necessities, as well as he could, until, at last, *peace, smiling peace,* and glorious liberty came to bless South Carolina with *law and order.*

Hugh O'Neall attended the mill, drove his father's wagon, or labored in the farm until his father's death in 1789. He and his elder brother Abijah were the executors of his father's will, and upon them devolved the care of a large real estate, their mother and a family of young boys. The elder brother, Abijah, being married, much of the burden devolved on Hugh. For three years he devoted himself untiringly to the discharge of his duties. Many of his adventures in wagoning between Newberry and Charleston, and in Charleston, would, if I had time or space, be interesting. I may state two: He and his brother Abijah were in Charleston when the old State House, now the Court House, corner of Broad and Meeting streets, and all that section of Charleston was burned. They had one or more wagons, and were employed to haul goods from the burning district to places of safety. Having made several successful trips, as Hugh was returning, and about to pass again into the circle of fire, his leader's bridle was seized by a policeman on duty, and he was told: The houses near you will be instantly blown up! He turned his team, quick as thought, in the crowded streets, and was soon in the wagon yard and safety. Neither the persuasions of his brother nor the tempting wages could again tempt him into such peril.

Roads, bridges and ferries were then, not as they are now, (though now bad enough.) Mud holes, crazy bridges, streams in flood, and badly managed ferries had to be encountered. He and his brother-in-law, Ford, were on their return from Charleston, with separate teams. Ford was in front. He struck the Four Hole swamp, covered with water. When he reached the bridge it was floating; he thought he could, however, pass it, and with the bold, adventurous spirit of a backwoodsman, well tried in the revolution, he made the attempt. The plank gave way under his horses, and into the stream they went. To cut them (except one) loose, and to swim them out was but a few minutes' work for him and his equally daring companion, Hugh. One horse, the old and favorite leader, was patiently lying across the sleepers of the bridge; to relieve him it was necessary to roll him over into the water. This was done by seizing his legs and literally turning him over. As he went, with one strong movement of his hind leg he threw Hugh twenty feet, into ten-feet water. This was, however, no serious matter, for he and the horse were soon on *terra firma.*

During this period, and for years after, tobacco rolling was a common mode of carrying tobacco from the upper country to Charleston. A tobacco hogshead was rimmed, so as to keep the bulge from the ground; a cross piece was made fast to each end; in them were inserted wooden gudgeons, which worked into a square frame, embracing within it the whole hogshead. To this were fixed single-trees and a tongue, and, thus prepared, the owner mounted on one of two horses geared to it, and leading the other, with his fodder and corn stowed between the frame and hogshead, moved on a free and independent roller to Charleston; and there leaving his hogshead, with his money for it, or a tobacco certificate, he returned, the sauciest mortal ever seen. Some rollers from Long Cane, Abbeville, and, therefore, called Long Canaans, met with an Edgefield man, (Clarke Spraggins,) and a companion, between Orangeburg and the Four Holes, attacked them first with words, and then were about to try blows. Numbers prevailed, and Spraggins, (though one of Butler's old soldiers,) and his companion had to fly. In his flight Spraggins sprang off his horse, picked up a lightwood knot, and knocked down senseless the foremost pursuer. The rest halted, and supposing their companion slain, desired to know who and whence was the slayer. Spraggins swore he was from "*killman,*" and was going to "*killmore.*"

In 1792 Hugh O'Neall married Anne Kelly, the third and youngest daughter of Samuel and Hannah Kelly, of Springfield, Newberry. He settled about a mile below the mill which, by his father's will, was devised to him. Subsequently he made an exchange with his brother, William, and fixed his residence in about two hundred yards of the mill, on a hill northeast of the same. From 1792 to 1800 he attended to his own mill, and by untiring industry created the means to rebuild it and to lay up a sum sufficient to embark in the mercantile business with Capt. Daniel Parkins. During this period was the great Yazoo freshet, in January, 1796, which has never been equalled or surpassed, unless the disastrous freshet of August, 1852, did so. Often has Hugh O'Neall described that freshet to the writer. In two respects it resembled the freshet of August, 1852: it was a freshet upon a freshet, and, like the latter, it spread ruin everywhere. Mills, dams and bridges went before it. Compte's bridge across Broad river, three miles above Columbia, just finished in apparently the most secure way, went. It is said the owner, a Frenchman, was upon the bridge, looking at the raging torrent, and impiously exclaimed: "Aha, God Almighty does tink we build bridges out of corn-stalks." Scarcely were the words uttered, until the cracking timbers gave notice that its end was at hand. With difficulty the owner reached the land. Hampton's bridges across the Savannah at Augusta and Saluda, were swept away. Fortunately, O'Neall's mill, which was just rebuilt, with its dam, escaped uninjured. Would that some certain memorial of that flood had been preserved. We would then compare it with that of '52, and thus learn a lesson of wisdom.

During this same period, or possibly in '93, certainly before April, he and Mercer Babb visited the quarry of Georgia burr millstones, in Burke county. He did not contract for a pair, but Mercer Babb bought, and started in his mills, now Mendenhall's, the first pair of burr stones ever run in the district. They were there used for many years, and when Dr. Mendenhall, in '27, started his merchant mills at the same place, the old Georgia burrs were refitted and again started, to manufacture flour.

Hugh O'Neall always affirmed that, with a good pair of Cloud's creek stones, he could make as good, if not better, flour than could be made with the best pair of burr stones.

On this trip he and his friend encountered a flood in the Savannah and Saluda rivers, then considered a great freshet, but not to compare with the subsequent one of '96.

In 1800 Hugh O'Neall embarked in the mercantile business, as the partner of Daniel Parkins, and most successfully pursued it until the death of the latter, October, 1802. It may be well *here* to pause and look over the statistics of the country at that time, (if I can use such a word in reference to the means and commerce of that period.) Cotton, in 1800, was beginning to be cultivated for market. In 1801 Hugh O'Neall started a water cotton-gin, made by William Barret. The plates for the saws were made at William Coate's shop. No machine ever ran with greater power or more success, although the first person, Joseph Wright, who attended to it had his hand torn all to pieces by the saws. Remittances were then made to Charleston in specie. Dollars were carefully packed in a box and put on board a wagon owned and driven by a careful, responsible man. The writer recollects aiding in counting, at Capt. Parkins', a large amount of silver, to be sent by Isaac Mills' wagon. Up to the year 1806 the upper country, and particularly Newberry, furnished flour, bacon, beef, cattle, butter, beeswax, skins, (raccoon, fox, rabbit, mink and muskrat,) for the Charleston market. In the same time boxes of screw-augers, invented and made by Benj. Evans, (at the place now owned by John G. Davenport,) and, after Evans' removal to Ohio, made by Joseph Smith and John Edmunson, were frequently sent. Cotton began to be sent by the load, in round bales, about the year 1801. After the Quakers left Bush river, (say after 1806,) very little flour, butter, beeswax or skins found their way to Charleston. I often recur to that period —when Newberry was covered with small farms, when each homestead furnished pretty much the means of food and raiment—and fancy that the people were then happier than they ever have been since.

A recollection of an incident in the beginning of 1802, I may, perhaps, be pardoned in repeating. A very large poplar tree lay at the mouth of the first branch, north of Hugh O'Neall's mills. Bush river was in flood; the water had entirely submerged the mill-dam. Hugh O'Neall, William Barret and Levi Hilburn concluded that, with a common batteau and a rope, after the tree was cut loose, they could tow it down to the sawmill of the latter, opposite to O'Neall's mill. Accordingly, they succeeded in getting the tree loose, and in towing it, until they neared the dam. Then the force of the water carried them beyond their point; the tree, batteau and all passed into an eddy below the sawmill. To get it above the sawmill was the object. Hilburn was persuaded to get out on the log, and with a pole force it along; the other two were to manage the batteau and tow. Having accomplished the most difficult part of the ascent, and reached a point where the water was deep, but comparatively still, the boatmen were continually calling out, "Pole, Levi; pole, Levi!" He, straining every muscle, made a mislick with his pole, and fell into water more than ten feet deep. Rising, he essayed to mount the log, but, it rolling under his hands, he received another ducking. At last he succeeded in mounting astride. Then again he was called on to "pole," but he swore one of his biggest oaths, (and anybody who ever heard Levi Hilburn swear must know it could hardly be excelled,) "that he would pole no more." Just then Barret, looking around at him, dripping, and with his usually large lips much swelled, said to Hugh O'Neall, "Did you ever see any one look so much like Tom Lindsey's Nero?" The name thus given adhered to him ever after. The poplar tree thus obtained was sawed into planks, and out of them were made the coffins for the two sons, the wife of, and Capt. Daniel Parkins himself, who died in the great epidemic of 1802, as detailed in No. 11.

In February, 1803, was the greatest snow ever seen in this State, unless it may be that that of 1851 equalled it.

In 1804 Hugh O'Neall, alone, began the mercantile business, and continued it until 1809. Until the close of 1806 it was manifest that he was doing an excellent business. But the two dread enemies of a mere merchant, universal credit and the use of intoxicating drink by the merchant and his customers, were sapping the foundation of prosperity, reason and happiness.

I may be permitted *here* to say, that then, for many years previous, and for the fourth of a century since, every merchant sold, with groceries and dry goods, intoxicating drink by the "small." Every one drank more or less; the morning bitters, the dinner dram, and the evening night cap were universal. Rum, (Jamaica, West India and New England,) was then almost entirely sold and drunk in stores. Whiskey belonged to the distilleries.

Often has the writer stood behind the counter until midnight, waiting on the maudlin talk and drinks of half pint customers. He hated the business *then*, and he pronounces it *now, not fit to be pursued by any decent man, or boy.* The use of intoxicating drink grew upon Hugh O'Neall, until, like Nebuchadnezzer, the judgment of God was upon him, and he was deprived of that which distinguishes a man from a brute, *his reason.* This sad result, however, was not the work of an instant; his habit of drink had made him negligent of his business and over-confident in cotton speculation. When the embargo of 1808 came upon the country he had in store with the Messrs. Bulow more than two hundred bales of cotton. He was largely their debtor, and he had authorized them to sell as they saw fit. Frequent attacks of mania *a-potu* foreshadowed the event. His son, a stripling of sixteen in 1809, ventured to ask him to abandon the cup. He made the attempt, but too late. Madness had already laid its iron hand upon him. He was a maniac. His cotton was sold at an immense sacrifice, his debtors were, many of them, insolvent, his creditors pressed their debts into judgments, his property was sold, and his wife and children turned out to shift for themselves.

Often has the writer seen his honored father caged like a wild beast; often has he seen him when it was dangerous for any one to approach him. For four years this was his unfortunate state.

Reader, stop and think! Has not the writer cause to hate the traffic in intoxicating drink? Ought he not to pursue it to its destruction? May not his case be yours? May not you suffer as he has done? Let me entreat you—let the truth teach you—let others' sorrows learn you wisdom.

In 1813, July, Hugh O'Neall was restored to his reason, and, like Nebuchadnezzer, he gave God all the glory! Not a shade was left upon his mind; his memory, wonderful as it was before his insanity, was just as perfect after his recovery. He became a Friend in reality, as he had been raised in profession. No humbler, better Christian ever stood before his Master.

He set himself most diligently about repairing the wreck of his fortune. He gathered up much that was apparently lost, and paid many of his creditors, *those* who most needed it. He made three trips to Ohio, Indiana, Kentucky and Tennessee. His descriptions of the countries which he visited, the people whom he saw, and especially his accounts of his visits to his relations, were most felicitous.

In 1815 he determined never to drink intoxicating drink, and to his death, in 1848, he faithfully maintained his resolution. In August, 1820, he became a member of his son's family, and there, *as a father*, he remained until his Father called him home.

He never desired or sought office. He was a Commissioner of Public Buildings from '99 for many years; he was a Commissioner of Free Schools from 1822 until he declined to serve longer.

In the unfortunate political schism, called Nullification, he was against it, and openly maintained the principles of the Union party. Like the venerable mother of Senator Butler, he could have said, as she did when secession was the prevailing sentiment of South Carolina, "I have seen two wars. and I never want to see another."

Hugh O'Neall's family consisted of one son, John Belton, four daughters, Abigail, (now Mrs. Caldwell,) Rebecca, who died in 1854, Hannah, who died in 1815, and Sarah Ford O'Neall.

Hugh O'Neall was not only gifted with a most superhuman memory, but he also possessed an excellent judgment and a clear and easy elocution. He was one of the kindest and most benevolent of men, and yet his sense of justice and right was such, he never, (after his recovery,) suffered his feelings to lead him astray.

In person, he was remarkable for a strong, vigorous, compact frame. He was five feet ten inches high; his head was a fine one; his hair receded on each side, leaving a high, intellectual forehead fully developed; his hair was thin, soft and silky, and perfectly black in his manhood; in age it was sprinkled with gray, still, however, leaving the black predominant. His eyes were blue, his nose long and Roman, his mouth was full and well formed. He died Wednesday, 18th October, 1848, about 2 P. M., having lived two months and eight days beyond eighty-one. He left surviving him his wife Anne, who on Friday, the 5th October, 1850, at ten minutes after 10 A. M., followed him to the silent house, having lived two months, wanting seven days, beyond eighty-three. His son and two daughters still remain.

Reader, my work is ended. The annals, historical, biographical and anecdotical, of Newberry, are closed. They have been to me both labor and pleasure. May they be the means of honor and good to my native district.

———

A dark December day recalls the past, and tempts the *soli-*

tary to give the remembrances which stir within him, to his younger countrymen.

In the progress of the war of 1812 everything became exceedingly high. When I use the word "high," I would not have you suppose that I use it in the sense of "tall," but in the meaning of "dear," or "costly."

Flour was a scarce article, selling readily at ten dollars to twelve dollars per barrel. The ladies at that time made *cakes* thin, and rather a holiday affair. Such a thing as using a whole barrel of flour in pound-cakes would have been regarded then as an astounding act of extravagance. I remember well, in 1816, hearing an old lady, who was seated at a table soon to be graced by a bridal party, as she was treated to a bit of pound-cake, say to the lady of the house, "It is mighty good, but mighty costly, though."

Near forty years of peace and prosperity have seen what was then a straggling village become a town, along whose western limbs daily speeds the iron horse, fed upon wood and fire, and drinking *naught but cold water*, bearing by his superhuman strength the trade and travel of our backwoods, and outstripping the wind in his flight from point to point, and have made us forget the use and wholesome economy of our ancestral homes.

As illustrative of the past, I recall an incident which occasioned much merriment when it occurred.

It will be remembered by those who know anything of the history of South Carolina, (though I confess there are few who can penetrate the dark veil of the lack of information which hangs over her history,) that General Joseph Alston was the Governor from December, 1812, to December, 1814, two dark years of the war.

In that time it frequently became necessary for orders to be borne to the militia. The *post*, now commonly called the mail, came then slowly dragging itself along on horseback. The great Western mail passed then once a week on horseback, under the riding of the late Mr. Waddell, of Greenville. The orders of the Commander-in-Chief could not be allowed thus tardily to travel. He sometimes sent *an aid*. The person who acted on the occasion to which I am about to allude was a Dominie Sampson sort of man, though not at all of his size, nor of his ungainly deportment. He was, or rather had been, however, a schoolmaster, private tutor—tutor *pro tempore* in college, and thus *his fitness* for private secretary and aid, or anything else in the shape of man of business for the Governor is shown.

General Samuel Mays, of Edgefield, then commanded the first brigade. For some cause (perhaps in the absence of the Major General, Butler,) he was waited upon by the gentleman whom I have described. The General was not at home when he called. His kind, excellent lady invited him to stay until he returned. In the mean time, (as the family dinner had passed,) a dinner was provided for the traveler. Flour had of course to be put in requisition for the Governor's aid, but, guided by the precious character of the article, the cook made the biscuits small, very small. Dinner was announced. The hungry guest was paying his respects to the real good Carolina dinner, over which the General's lady, with hospitable intent, presided. A little black boy waited; his was the duty to hand the biscuits. The famished aid devoured a biscuit at a mouthful, and called to the waiter: "Biscuit, boy !" The little negro could not bear such wholesale destruction of his mistress' good things, and addressed himself at once to her. "La, Misses," said he, "he has had six already; shall I give him another?"

THE LAST QUAKER MEETING.

The cold, gray sunshine of an October Sabbath morning, preceding the bright gorgeousness of the Indian summer, seemed appropriate to the invitation I received to accompany a dear lady friend to the last meeting which has been held by her sect at the Quaker church at Bush river, Newberry district, South Carolina. Two Friends, an aged lady and gentleman, had come from a distant land on a visit to the few who remained of their persuasion, and to look upon the graves of all who had so peacefully departed to the blessed home of rest. The venerable Hugh O'Neall, whose striking biography appeared last week in the local district newspaper, and his aged companion and youngest living daughter, were all who remained of that people who once, with the olive branch of peace and industry in their hands, made the rich lands of that section of the district smile with their examples of thrift and economy. As we rode gently along, I had ample leisure to reflect upon the many social mutations which have already swept over our land in her brief period of national infancy. We overtook the good old Father O'Neall a short distance from the church, mounted on his drab-colored pony, and looking like Old Mortality striving to defy time—that silently moving power which carries everything into nothing. Whosoever looked on that good man, in the over-ripe maturity of a virtuous old age, loved him. With a cheerful word and a heart-illumining smile for all, he was the practical example of purity and elevated virtue. Rest there, old fathers, in thy quiet graves. The roaring winds of this wintry storm disturb not thy slumbers to-night, for thou wast with peace, beloved by God and by man.

The plain Quaker carriage of the visiting friends stood before the churchyard, and they were walking in silent meditation amongst the carefully heaped-up mounds which pious devotion had preserved from common disorder and neglect. It was a picture which, since then, has dwelt with me, and one which I have often thought I would pen-paint, that others might receive the satisfaction which the touching spectacle afforded. I was a boy then—ambitious of the future—with the world spread out before me; and since, its trials, its disappointments, its vexing cares have beset my path. But that day, and its impressions, have dwelt in the chambers of memory— pure as a strain of music floating over distant waters. The gray old church, with its plain exterior, the singular garb of the pious Friends, the neatness of all the mounds—even those of nearly a hundred years—the bright colors of the dying leaves, already tinted by the autumnal frosts, were grouped into the picture, whilst the now mellow sunshine, reflected from the blue sky, draped it with beauty beyond the achievement of the pencil of art. The glory of that day's sunshine was God's smile upon the remnant of his children of peace. Silently, and one by one, as messengers from another land, they entered the church, and I felt at first that my presence might be an intrusion, where all was love and holiness; but the youngest, my lady friend, quietly bade me enter. We sat long and in meditation. Patience and meekness and long-serving and humility were thus silently taught to the hundreds who lay around in the peaceful slumbers of death; and the reflections which arose from the shrines of the past told the history of bygone years more eloquently than living words could have done. A cardinal red bird came and twittered among the delicate boughs of a red-fruited tree which grew over a grave, and its scarlet garb and shrill electric notes frequently, and for a long time repeated, were strangely contrasted with the quiet scene around.

Note after note he poured forth from his full-throated beak, whilst his swelling crest, and gay out-stretched wing, and voice of song, plainly told that he too was praising God in the bird recitative of nature's music. The aged mother arose, and the prose-voice of song in the mellow cadences, uttered in unison with the feelings of her heart, spoke of those who had passed away to light and peaceful glory in heaven. Whilst her words of love were poured out to the living and the dead, I fancied that one from another world, and from a long past age, was speaking. The old gentleman, with a clear, singing, mellow tone, then asked the empty seats and silent walls where those were who once peopled them. He bewailed the desolation in Israel, whose glory had departed, and whose land was peopled with strangers to the faith of their fathers. To me his words were as the lamentations of a second Jeremiah, saying: *"Our inheritance is turned to strangers, our house to aliens."* Again a brief silence: then the stillness is broken, and the voice of Hugh O'Neall, tremulous with emotion, tells the sad story of that faith by which he lived, and which, since then, made his dying bed a pathway of blessed ease, going home to God. The red mounds told the fates of many—over the blue mountains, beyond the broad Ohio—others had fixed their homes in the wilderness, nearer to the setting sun. He and his alone remained—here he had lived, and here he would lay down to rest in the grave. He said, still the seed of the faith was alive, for *"Thou, O Lord, remainest forever; thy throne from generation to generation. Turn thou us unto thee, O Lord, and we shall be turned; renew our days as of old."* I believe these words of eloquent lamentation from my aged friend were the last uttered in that silent house of God. Angels led out that little band of the true and faithful, and the sacred doors were closed forever. As we departed, the red-bird glanced through the tree-tops and chirped us a good-bye.

Death has since claimed all of those beloved Quakers save one, and may she long be spared to reflect the virtues of her heart in that social sphere in which she is a blessed and blessing visitant.

APPENDIX.

GREENVILLE AND COLUMBIA RAILROAD.

The damages sustained by this road from the late freshet, though very serious, are by no means as great as they were at first supposed to be. The principal injuries are below Alston. These have been carefully examined by competent agents of the company, and estimates have been made *at the price of new work*. None of the timbers have been washed away; it will only be necessary to replace them. The actual cost of the repairs will, therefore, fall below the estimates. An adequate force is now being organized, and the work of repair will be pushed forward to completion as rapidly as possible. From Alston to the terminus at Cokesbury, the injuries are comparatively trifling. We are assured by Captain W. H. Griffin, the able first assistant engineer, that this portion of the road will be in running order in a week or, at most, ten days. Over one hundred hands, under a well qualified supervisor, are engaged on this section. As soon as the repairs below Broad river are finished, which will be done in four or five weeks, the connection between the two sections will be established by means of boats across the river, until the bridge is rebuilt, so that travel and transportation will be but little retarded, notwithstanding the exaggerated reports put into active circulation in a certain quarter, and the bold, impotent attempt to depreciate the value of the company's stock by a sham sale.

COLUMBIA, September 4, 1852.

To the Stockholders of the Greenville and Columbia Rail Road Company:

The late freshet of the 28th, 29th and 30th ultimo, has produced a heavy loss to the company ; but that is comparatively nothing to the loss which the company, the community, and his family have suffered in the death of William Spencer Brown, chief engineer.

In attempting, on the 30th, to descend the river from Alston, in company with McCollum, Jefferson, and the son of Mr. McCollum, in a small batteau, it was overturned, and he, with Mr. McCollum's son, was drowned.

This sad event has caused me more suffering and sorrow than anything which has occurred. Mr. Brown was endeared to me by a long and intimate association, and felt to me more like a son than a mere subordinate officer. No purer man or better officer ever lived. No doubt, for wise, but inscrutable reasons, God has taken him to himself ! *It is our duty to submit !*

The loss to the company is a heavy one, but not to be compared with

what rumor has fixed. It is confidently believed that from thirty to
fifty thousand dollars will cover the entire damage. This is the opinion of an experienced mechanic.

The road from Crim's creek to Newberry, and thence to Little
river, is uninjured. This is a distance of thirty-five miles. A slight
injury to the trestle at Little river occurred. This will be remedied
in a day or two. The trestling along the valley of the Saluda is
thrown down. It can be restored in two weeks. The Saluda bridge
is very little injured. Thence to Barmore's, in Abbeville, thirty miles
is in running order. The road is uninjured thence to Anderson, and
to the north side of Saluda. Between Saluda and Greenville, three
culverts have been blown up; the loss may be four thousand dollars.

Beginning at Crim's creek, the serious injury commences. That
bridge and the trestle are overturned. The carpenter on the road
states that all the timber is there, and that he can replace everything
in two weeks. Four spans of the Broad river bridge are gone. One
pier is broke down to low water mark. The parts of the bridge carried off are entire in Bookman's and Rieves' plantation, about ten or
twelve miles below. They will be taken to pieces and brought back.
Little loss of timber, it is apprehended, will take place. Had not
Eichelberger's gin-house floated down against the bridge, it would
have withstood the flood. It is proposed to raise the bridge three feet
higher than at present. Raising and repairing it will hardly cost
$7,000, and may not cost $5,000. From Alston to and inclusive of
Smith's branch, within three miles of Columbia, the trestles are generally damaged, and in some places down. In some instances the
timber is washed away. The banks are generally uninjured. The
track is misplaced in some instances. The work of restoration commences to-day, under the energetic supervision of H. T. Peake, aided
by many experienced mechanics.

The road from Columbia to Alston was carefully examined by
Messrs. H. T. Peake and Z. Butler, and the following are their estimates of the sums necessary to repair the damages of the flood :

Smith's branch trestle and bank..................................$	2,000
Crane creek..	250
Trestle each side of Frost's mill	1,300
Slate Stone branch...	200
Through Bookter's	4,000
Frost's upper plantation..	1,450
From Frost's to Littleton...	6,000
Littleton to trestle below Alston..................................	1,000
Trestle at Alston	1,500
	$17,700

It is hoped that in six weeks we may be in full motion. It is intended to secure the track against all such accidents for the future,

though such a freshet will probably not occur again in the next half century. The Yazoo freshet occurred fifty-six years rgo.

The mails will leave Newberry, daily, on and after Wednesday, at half-past 9 A. M., and reach Hope Station at 11; thence they will be carried in stages by Mr. Epting to Columbia, at 6 P. M. The mails will leave Columbia, daily, on and after Thursday, at 6 A. M., and reach Hope Station at 3 P. M. They will leave instantly, and arrive at Newberry half-past 4 P. M.

JOHN BELTON O'NEALL,
President G. and C. Rail Road Co.

————

THE DISASTERS OF THE FRESHET.

ASHEVILLE, N. C., September 2.

We find the following account of the flood in the Asheville *News* of the 2d instant:

Never, in the memory of that wise individual, "the oldest inhabitant," were these mountains so deluged with water as they were last week. Friday of last week will long be remembered as the rainy day. From ten o'clock Thursday evening until some time Friday night, without one moment's cessation. As was anticipated, the streams were filled to overflowing. French Broad was higher on Saturday than it was in many years before—exceeding largely the great flood two years ago. Even the sweet Swannanoa got "high," and played some wild pranks—among other things carrying off the bridge at Mrs. Patton's, two miles from here. All the bridges, so far as heard from, are gone: the bridge at Captain Wiley Jones', Esquire Smith's, the one at Colonel Garmon's, Alexander's, Chunn's, Warm Springs, and all the smaller bridges in the country are either gone entire or greatly damaged. Mr. Smith, we are glad to see, is taking measures, with his usual promptness, to rebuild his bridge. The loss of this bridge will be a more serious inconvenience than any of the others, as it is on one of the most public roads in the country—the road leading to the western counties.

The crops in the bottoms along the rivers and creeks are considerably damaged. Many persons will be heavy sufferers. No idea can be had of the extent of the injury, as mail operations are entirely closed, not having had, up to the time of writing this article, (Tuesday morning,) a mail from any direction in four or five days. No doubt the mills and bridges in every direction have been swept away or greatly injured.

GREENVILLE, September 2.

There never was before, says the *Southern Patriot* of the 2d instant, since the settlement of the country, such a freshet as we had last week in Greenville district. The water courses were several feet higher than they were ever known to be before. All the bridges, and a great number of mills, have been swept away. The corn on the low grounds is destroyed, or most seriously injured. In several places the embankments of our rail road have been destroyed, and several of the culverts carried off, or entirely demolished. The cotton factory and paper mill of Mr. McBee, and the paper mill of the Greenville Manufacturing Company, have been greatly damaged. We have not heard from the other factories in our district. All communication has been cut off with the surrounding country by the loss of bridges, and the difficulty of fording 'he creeks and rivers. The Reedy Falls, in the village of Greenville, were quite an object of attraction on Saturday. They were Niagara in miniature, and our citizens and the visitors, men, women and children, turned out *en masse* to witness the grand spectacle presented by the raging and foaming waters dashing over the falls and down the precipice.

Every day the most distressing accounts are brought to us of the injury done by the late flood of rains. Lester and Kilgore's wool factory, saw-mill, blacksmith shops, are all carried off, their office turned upside down, and in the cotton factory everything covered with mud. Their loss is estimated at $2,000.

The factory of W. Bates & Co. very seriously injured. The factory of John Weaver, Esq., injured considerably. The Greenville Manufacturing Company have sustained several thousand dollars damage. The mills throughout the country have been swept away.

THE SOUTH CAROLINA RAIL ROAD.

We are indebted, says the *Carolinian*, to Mr. Bollin, the agent at this place, for the following letter from the energetic president of the South Carolina Rail Road Company. Mr. B. also informs us that the letter mails will reach here this morning, and the newspaper mails to-night. The telegraphic line, it is thought, will be in operation to Charleston to-day.

We regret to learn that it is true that a portion of the trestle work of the Camden Branch is swept away, and therefore it is uncertain when communication will be re-established on that line.

ROAD, September 2.

The damage at the Congaree is pretty bad, but we are making the most and best of it. But for the draw, we could soon fix up a temporary means of conveying goods over. That will throw us back. We will make that, and the whole bridge at Charleston, while the piles are driving, and not one hour or a single effort lost or left untried to get the work done in the least time possible; but a good deal of delay, with all we can do, must occur.

We will send passengers over on Monday. It would be unsafe to attempt it before. You will be particularly instructed before.

I have now a full view of all the damage everywhere, and my plans and arrangements are all made to remedy them.

There is nothing now but the work to be done, and that we will do. Yours,   H. W. CONNER.

We find the following information touching what is doing on the Hamburg end of the road in the Charleston *Standard* of Thursday:

The communication for passengers and mails with Augusta and beyond is now perfect. The trains from Hamburg arrived to-day, with the western mails, and a large number of passengers, at twenty-five minutes past one, being only thirty minutes behind the usual time.

The rail road at Hamburg will be repaired, and ready for the engines and cars by to-morrow night, which will run on to the depot there, after to-morrow, as usual.

It is expected, also, that by Monday next freight will be passed over to the Georgia Rail Road depot and to Augusta with promptitude and despatch.

HAMBURG, September 2.

We are indebted to the Hamburg *Republican* for an extra dated 2d instant, from which we make the following extracts:

On Saturday morning it was discovered that the river was rapidly rising, which continued throughout the day. At sunset it was out of its banks and still rising. At this time the water from below had backed up into town. Soon after nightfall the avalanche from above came rushing down upon us with such fearful rapidity that, within less than an hour the whole town was completely inundated, and the water rising at the rate of at least three feet to the hour. By ten o'clock the floors of stores, shops and residences were from two to seven feet under water.

The scene now presented beggars all description. The night was calm and clear, fortunately, and the moon shone equal to day. But for this fortunate circumstance the disastrous effects of the flood must have been much greater, and probably many lives lost. A number of small boats were immediately brought into requisition by the citizens, and those who manned them seemed to vie with each other in their zeal and activity to convey families in the more exposed part of the town ashore. The cries of women and children for help could be heard in all directions. Many persons, we learn, were taken from the roofs of their houses. No means of escape were left but through the medium of the boats, which were continually running and conveying persons ashore during the entire night, and throughout the day on Sunday. It was with great difficulty and danger that many were rescued from a watery grave. Only one life was lost, that of Mr. Thomas Rossiter, a worthy young man, in the employ of Mr. George Robinson.

About noon Sunday the water began slowly to recede, and by night had fallen some five or six inches, and by Monday morning about two feet, when it commenced running off very rapidly.

As soon as the opinion became prevalent that we should have an overflow, our merchants commenced to remove their stocks of goods to places of security. This was kept up so long as drays could run the streets. Such goods as were not removed were placed upon the counters, shelves, &c., as was supposed, entirely out of danger. Every one seemed to feel the utmost confidence in his entire security.

It is impossible to give the losses sustained by each of our citizens. Of all our business houses, Messrs. Richardson & McDonald, and Wright, Nichols & Co. alone escaped. In some instances the floors of the second stories were torn up, and goods raised from the first story after the water became six feet deep.

To give an idea to those familiar with the town, we will state, the only buildings that the water did not reach the first floor of, was the rail road (new) depot, Town Hall, Coleman's warehouse, Josiah Sibley's store, and the residences of J. W. Stokes and H. A. Kenrick. Depth of water at the Bank of Hamburg, about twenty inches; Hodges & Smith's store, seven and one-half feet; John Usher's store, six feet; B. S. Dunbar's store, six feet; Charles Hammond's store, (unoccupied,) eight feet.

A number of families suffered severely in the loss of furniture, bedding, &c., some being compelled to leave without an effort to secure anything. The water coming with such rapidity forced the doors and windows, and everything floated out. There is scarcely a citizen but what has lost out-houses, stables, garden fences, gardens, &c. We believe there were no dwellings or business houses washed away.

Our island and river planters suffer severely. Their entire corn crop is gone, and they are heavy losers in stock, fencing, &c.

From the *Constitutionalist and Republic* of Tuesday we copy the following further intelligence in relation to the late freshet at Augusta:

Yesterday exhibited a busy scene on Broad street. Turn your eyes what direction you would, it looked lively, and, as far as the eye could reach, the box pump handle, with from two to four sturdy pumpers, was seen busily employed. To-day all the cellars in the city will, no doubt, be relieved of water, and in another day the deposits will be removed. A number of cellars, we have no doubt, after the latter operation is gone through with, will be some foot or a half deeper than previous to the freshet.

Now that the waters have subsided, we can form a more accurate judgment of the injuries sustained by the freshet. It is nothing like as great as the loss sustained by the freshet of 1840. The city itself is the largest sufferer, and we have heard it estimated, by those who ought to know, that it will cost about $50,000 to repair damages. The streets are much cut up, but a large force has been engaged to put them in order, and when finished they will be in better condition than previous to the freshet, for the deposit by this freshet has been principally sand and gravel, while by former freshets it was mostly alluvial.

The loss of our merchants is comparatively trifling, as most of them had removed the principal part of their goods from their cellars, and but few stores were damaged above the first floor by water.

At the rail road freight depot the water was about five feet deep, but did not reach the floor. The depot was filled with goods, which escaped injury. At the passenger station the water was about twelve feet deep, but did not reach the second floor. The road is washed up about half a mile, but the embankments are safe, and the road can be put in good traveling order in a few days. At the old depot, which is now used as a private store-house, the water was about five feet deep on the floors.

The scene yesterday was distressing to behold. Look in what direction you would, you could see every one busily engaged in shoveling the mud from their stores; or washing such articles as were saved, not subject to damage by water.

THE BRIDGE.—Already has timber been engaged for the rebuilding of the lower bridge, and the services of a large force engaged, under a competent superintendent, for its reconstruction. A steam pile driver will be used, and as soon as the river falls sufficiently operations will be commenced. In the meantime transportation between the two roads will be kept up by means of flats and drays.

LAURENS, September 3.

We were congratulating ourselves last week on escaping from the August freshet, which, for two years past, did so much injury to the crops in this part of the country, but our paper had scarcely gone to press before the sky became darkened by black and lowering clouds, and the whole face of the earth covered with water. We have never seen such a rain. The earth was perfectly saturated with that which had fallen a few days previous, and as very little of it was absorbed, the creeks and rivers began instantly to rise, and at their maximum height they were far over the highest water mark that the "oldest inhabitant" can remember. In fact, we have heard of such astonishing rises in some of our streams that we find it difficult to give them implicit credit.

Of course, the injury has been immense. There were some twenty-eight or thirty bridges in the district, and we have heard of but one which is now standing, and that is a small one across Bush River, in Maj. Eigleberger's plantation, in the lower part of the district. On Enoree river, from Chick's Springs, in Greenville, to the limits of this district, great injury has been done the many fine merchant mills and saw-mills erected on this notable stream. We learn from a gentleman who came down the river from Chick Springs, under the hope of crossing at Woodruff's, that all the houses about Lester's Factory, in Greenville, except his cotton mill, are washed away. At Van Patterson's Shoals, the dam and race are injured. Fleming's mills are entirely washed away. Woodruff's are but slightly injured. Park's saw-mill dam, and a substantial wall for a merchant mill, on Durbin's creek, near Enoree, are washed away, and his race very much injured. We learn [also that all the mills below Woodruff's, except, perhaps, Yarborough's and Nesbit's, at the Mountain Shoals, are seriously injured, and many of them entirely gone.

Campbell's grist and saw-mills are both gone. Dr. Bobo's mills, formerly Musgrove's, are both gone. The saw-mill washed away during the freshet, and the grist-mill was so moved that when the waters subsided it fell and was crushed to pieces. Lewis Jones' mills —the finest, perhaps, on the river—together with a gin-house, are all washed away. In the mill, we learn, there were about 100 barrels of flour ready for market. His loss has been very serious.

On Duncan's creek, Pitt & Craig's (formerly Sheldon's) grist, saw-mill and woollen factory, are both gone. The same has happened to the mills and factory of Pitts & Duval.

On Little river, at Milton, we learn that the water was nearly over the saw-mill, and high up in the grist-mill; but, with the exception of some 40 barrels of flour, 120 bushels wheat, and 100 bushels corn, which were lost, the injury was but slight. The chain pump manufactory, however, of Robert Wilson, erected here, was entirely swept away.

On Raibun's creek, we learn that Rodgers' grist and saw-mills are both gone. Studdard's saw-mill gone, and his grist-mill moved from its foundation. Bolt's saw-mill gone. Crumbie's saw-mill and grist-mill both gone. The loss which Captain Crumbie has sustained is very serious. He had gone to great expense in their erection, and had just completed them. Mrs. Goodgion's and Joe Crews' saw-mill were both washed away, and Crews' grist-mill moved from its foundation. Garlington's and Culberton's gin-houses were washed away and their dams much injured.

On Reedy river, we learn that the saw-mill and gin-house at Tumbling Shoals, and the grist-mill and saw-mill at Boyd's, are all gone.

Many of the mills in the district we have not heard from, but presume that all on the larger streams are more or less injured.

The injury below us, we learn, is equally as serious. We have received but one mail below Newberry since Saturday last, in consequence of the loss of the fine bridge thrown across Broad river by the Greenville and Columbia Rail Road, and the washing away of a large portion of the embankment between that point and Columbia. We understand that the bridge was torn from its abutments by a large gin-house which came down against it from above. What other loss the company has sustained we have not heard.

We are gratified to learn that no damage has been done to the Laurens road, but in consequence of the injury below, its completion will be very much delayed for the want of iron.

The extent of the loss of the district, we are unable to compute, and from the number of mills washed away, (and no district can boast of finer ones); the large amount of grain and flour which was in them at the time of the disaster; the number of bridges gone, and the great damage done to the corn crop, it is almost incalculable.

No such calamity has ever before befallen the district, and we humbly trust that none will ever occur again.

MOBILE, August 27.

The *Tribune* of Friday morning says :

The storm which we mentioned in our last continued to rage yesterday until noon, when it began to subside. The wind blew all night and yesterday morning from the southeast. About midday it shifted farther south; then to the west, and finally set in from the north, or a point in that direction.

The flood began to decrease at noon, and towards night it fell back as far as front street, leaving a deposit of mud, boards and wood, and the debris of timber everywhere in the low streets.

It is imposible to give at the present time any accurate idea of the extent of this great flood, or the damage which it produced.

On St. Francis street, in the north part of the city, the waters came up to the office of St. John, Powers & Co., where we saw a large steamboat barge moored. Further up, it reached St. Joseph street, to a depth sufficient to float a boat. The railroad depot was completely surrounded by water, and the railroad for a distance of two miles, the only part examined, was covered to a depth of one or two feet.

On Dauphin street the water came up as far as this printing office. On Conti street it reached about the same height. On Government street, near the lower part of the market-house, a small steamboat might have plied. In the southern part of the city the flood was still greater. At Spanish alley the houses almost floated, and men were called thither to rescue the inmates from drowning.

Apprehensions are entertained that the foundations of some of the stores, particularly those in the course of erection, are so much injured as to require reconstruction; but this, we presume, is imaginary. The chief general injury is in the destruction of the wharves, and it is feared that unless extraordinary efforts are made to clear the streets, sickness will inevitably follow. The first object should be to effect this purpose. The floors of the submerged stores should also be immediately raised, and drained and lined. With such precautions as these, we think there will be no danger.

At Choctaw Point Light House a sad result of the storm occurred. The tenement which was occupied by the keeper, Mrs. Philbert, being undermined by the flood, gave way, and Mrs. Philbert, her son-in-law, William E. Coglin, and his wife, with their two children, and Oscar Philbert, were forced to seek shelter as best they could. They attempted to save themselves by a rude raft; but Mrs. Philbert and her two grandchildren, after being driven about by the wind, and by the water, were washed from their frail bark and drowned. Mr. Coglin and his wife were rescued. Mr. Philbert and a negro are missing. Both, doubtless, were drowned. The body of Mrs. Philbert was found terribly mutilated, and has been interred to-day. The bodies of the children have not been recovered.

Near Government street the bodies of a woman and child were found. They were the family of a gardener, commonly called Dutch Charley, who cultivated the marsh opposite the city. It seems that when the flood came their house was carried away. The husband and father, by means of a log and imperfect raft, attempted to put his wife and child on a peach tree, but they were carried away by the water, and drowned before he could reach them.

The houses on the island, and elsewhere opposite the city, were chiefly destroyed. One house was carried up the river, and but for the timely arrival of the steamboat Heroine, on its way to the city from Bladon Springs, and the humane exertions of Captain H. Johnson, the inmates would, doubtless,. have found a grave in the angry flood. Capt. J. rescued them all, five in number—one a mother with an infant only three months old. They had been exposed some twenty hours without food or shelter, and were nearly dead. They were taken on board the Heroine, and treated with extreme kindness; so that within a brief time they were completely restored. Several cattle were found at the distance of ten miles above the city, whither they had been driven from the island opposite the city.

The *Advertiser* of Sunday contains the following :

We learn by the captain of a fishing smack, who came up to the city last evening, that five smacks with their crews were lost between Dog river and Dauphin Island, during the late gale. The number of lives lost with them is supposed to be from fifteen to twenty.

Taking it altogether, this has been the highest and most disastrous flood ever known to Mobile, and, doubtless, the destruction here is not greater than that on the coast. On the lower part of the eastern shore the land lies low, and there, we fear, there have been much distress and loss among the residents.

GEORGETOWN, September 1.

The Winyah *Observer*, speaking of the late freshet, says :

The mighty rush of water must soon be upon our planters of the Santee.

The news reached this place by the steamer from Charleston, on Monday, and we understand that the planters high up on the Santee commenced at once to harvest their crops, with the view of saving as much as possible before the water came down upon them. The rice crop on that river is all of it nearly ready for the hook, and the damage will be most grievous to such planters as reside within the range of this lamentable freshet. There is also quite a rise in Pee Dee, but the extent of it we do not know.

The Evening News learns from a reliable source that the rise in the river at Cheraw was only fifteen feet, and it passed rapidly off. Consequently, there is no danger to our Pee Dee friends.

MARIETTA, GA., August 31.

The Marietta *Advocate* says:

The incessant and heavy rains of last Thursday and Friday have done great damage. Bottom lands have been to a great extent overflowed, and the standing crops of corn, &c., have been greatly injured, if not ruined. We hear of bridges and mill-dams destroyed on almost all the water courses in this section. The Rome Rail Road is so much injured as to prevent the running of the cars on yesterday.

ATLANTA, August 31.

The Atlanta *Intelligencer* has the following notice of it:

We had the most violent storm of wind and rain on last Thursday night, and Friday, and part of Friday night, that we have witnessed for years. The rain fell in torrents. The creeks and rivers have all overflown their banks, and vast destruction to the corn and cotton crops must be the unavoidable result. The mills are nearly all carried away in this section of country. We fearfully anticipate the report of the destruction of large amounts of property, besides the ruin of the maturing crops.

MONTGOMERY, ALA., August 31.

The Montgomery *Advertiser and Gazette* says:

The Alabama is "booming," though about on a stand. The prospect is, that we shall have a good river for the balance of the season. So those living South who have been spending their leisure time at the North, will meet with no hindrance here on their return trip. Plenty of boats will be in readiness for their transportation.

The Tallapoosa River is very high. The stage from this city to Wetumpka has not crossed for three or four days, and our up-country people are cut off from communication with us. We presume the stage will be able to go to Wetumpka to-day.

MEMPHIS, TENN., August 30.

A telegraphic dispatch, dated at Memphis, says:

The recent rain storms have destroyed property to the amount of $20,000 in this vicinity. In the adjacent counties the corn and cotton crops are washed out of the ground.

UNION, September 3.

The *Journal* says:

It is painful to think, even, upon the sweeping destruction. Not less than ten thousand acres of bottom land, in this district, have been submerged. The loss is incalculable, but may be safely put down at three hundred thousand dollars. Every bridge in the district, we believe, with perhaps one exception, has been swept away, while almost every saw-mill, and several very valuable flour mills, have met with a similar fate. Thousands of bushels of wheat and hundreds of barrels of flour have been swept off in the wreck. Yet, with all our losses, we have abundant reason to be thankful. The uplands give promise of an abundance, and although cakes may not be as plenty as blackberries, we trust that old Union may have enough, and some to spare.

SPARTANBURG, September 2.

Any attempt at description would be vain. Suffice it to say, that this has been the greatest and most destructive flood with which this section of the country has ever been visited. Lawson's Fork river was ten feet higher than ever known before; and we presume this was the case with the rivers and creeks generally. Thus, it may be seen at once that the loss of property and produce must necessarily be greater than on any former occasion. Any attempt to estimate the value of property lost would be fruitless; but we feel warranted in saying, from the reports coming in from the country, that the loss to our district amounts to more than one hundred thousand dollars. Some intelligent gentlemen, however, estimate the loss at a much higher sum.

PICKENS, August 28.

The last Pickens *Courier* says :

For a week past we have had a flood of rain almost without cessation. On yesterday the rain fell in torrents, which continued with great violence for the space of eighteen hours, causing much destruction to the growing corn in and about this place, and we fear in the adjoining districts.

The rivers and creeks in this vicinity rose, on the 27th, to an unprecedented height, flooding the lowlands, and sweeping away everything which might impede their progress.

As far as our knowledge, it is the general impression that not less than one-third of the corn crops will be destroyed. We hope, however, that this may be an ever-estimate of what will be really destroyed. Keowee river is this morning twenty feet above low-water mark.

WILLIAM SPENCER BROWN,

CHIEF ENGINEER GREENVILLE AND COLUMBIA RAIL ROAD.

It is with feelings which can scarcely be restrained, after the lapse of a month, that a friend undertakes to speak of him whose name heads this article, as one "who was, and is not!" Alas, how brief is time, and how uncertain are all its issues ! He who is now in the silent chambers of the dead, for years has been the valued friend and administrative officer of him who now writes, and who, by many years, was his senior, and who, according to the course of nature, ought to have preceded him to the tomb. But God sees not as man. The younger has been taken from the trials and troubles of life; the elder has been left to encounter many of them single-handed, where the services of the younger would have been invaluable. But God gave, and God has taken away; blessed be His name forever and ever !

William Spencer Brown was the son of Major General Jacob Brown, Commander-in-Chief of the Army of the United States, and of his wife, Pamela. He was every way worthy of such an illustrious parentage. He was born at Brownville, in the State of New York, 27th May, 1815. He graduated at West Point in 1835. He received a second lieutenant's commission in the army in the same year, but never joined his regiment. He resigned in 1836, and became assistant engineer on the enlargement of the Erie canal. In 1836 and 1837 he was employed on the Norristown and Valley Rail Road. In 1837 he was married to Elizabeth D. Barnes, the daughter of Judge Joseph Barnes, of Philadelphia. This accomplished lady accompanied him, immediately after marriage, to the South, and encountered cheerfully all the privations of an engineer's life in an almost Indian country. No two people were ever more devoted to each other. Often has the writer had the opportunity to see the perfect happiness which pervaded the family circle when the husband and father, the idolized "Willie," was present. This, alas, is no more to be seen! Still the lovely, mourning widow has much to live for in rearing up the interesting little ones, the pledges of their loves and the living monuments of their worthy father.

In 1837 he was appointed assistant engineer on the Western and Atlantic Railroad, Georgia. He held this place to 1843. It seems, too, that in this time he became chief engineer on the Memphis Branch Rail Road, and so continued from 1840 to 1847; and in the same time, beginning in 1846, he had charge of the Coosa and Tennessee Rail Road.

The writer of this tribute to his memory has often heard him say he drove the first stake where Atlanta now is, and that he laid out and named "Gadsden," on the Mississippi river. In his services, in Georgia, he made the acquaintance of, and served under, General Brisbane. *Here* began a friendship, pure and worthy, which was only terminated by his death.

In June, 1847, Mr. Brown, without the personal acquaintance of either the president or any of the directors, was elected second assistant engineer of the Greenville and Columbia Rail Road, with the small salary of $1,000. He made the acquaintance of the president in Augusta, Georgia, shortly after, and in his company visited Columbia, and determined to accept the appointment. It was, on this occasion, that he gave the memorable reply to an inquiry of the president whether a road could be constructed from Columbia to Greenville: "Give an engineer money and he can go any where."

It seems that, in this year, Mr. Brown was elected Professor of History and Ethics in the State Military Academy, but declined to accept. At what precise time this was the writer does not know, for he was never aware of the fact until very recently.

Under that excellent, clear-headed, prudent officer, John McRae, chief engineer, in July, 1847, he organized the Brigade of Engineers

—consisting of himself, his class-mate Wm. Henry Griffin, J. Y. Mills and George Walker—who ran the experimental line of the Greenville and Columbia Rail Road, directly from Columbia to Greenville, one hundred and ten miles, in about forty days. On the termination of this survey he became first assistant engineer, with a salary of $1,750.

Subsequent consideration (after the survey of a line from Newberry through Abbeville District to Anderson and Greenville, made by that able engineer and worthy gentleman, Major Horace Bliss,) induced the company to locate their road, in November, from Columbia, for twenty-six miles on the eastern side of the Broad River to Alston; thence across the river, and up the valley of Priester's fork of Crim's creek to Newberry; thence to the Saluda valley, following it to the mouth of Wilson's creek; thence across Saluda, and crossing Wilson's creek twice, and Ninety-Six creek once, to the Saluda ridge, and pursued it to Belton; it then turned to Anderson, and thence over a rough country, and again crossing Saluda to Greenville. This location was highly displeasing to many of the stockholders.

Laurens, whose subscription was conditional that the road should be located within one mile of her town, was of course thrown out. The stockholders of Greenville District declared themselves unwilling to pay up their stock. The President, too, who felt that his word (which had been given in the presence and by the authority of the directors, that if the subscription of Laurens amounted to $140,000 the road should be located by that town,) was disregarded, and, indeed, repudiated, by the action of the stockholders, declared his purpose to resign. After reflection, and the belief that his resignation would be fatal to the enterprise, induced him to retain his post, and press the work.

Mr. Brown located the road on the east bank of Broad River in the winter of 1847 and '48, and it was put under contract. The company devolved upon him, as a commissioner, the duty of obtaining relinquishments of the right of way from Columbia to Saluda, and increased his salary to $2,000. This very delicate duty he performed admirably well. Few men possessed the same facility of persuading people to do what he desired, which he did.

In 1848 the line to Anderson was located, and grading contracts offered to stockholders, who were entitled, under the charter, to work out half their stock. These contracts were generally accepted, and the work was begun with great activity.

In December, 1848, the Legislature generously subscribed one-half of the bonds of the South Carolina Rail Road to the State, amounting to more than $250,000.

In February, 1849, Mr. McRae, to accept the post of chief engineer on the South Carolina Rail Road, resigned his place as chief engineer on the Greenville and Columbia Rail Road, and Mr. Brown was instantly advanced to his place, with a salary of $2,500.

By the advice of Mr. Brown, in the spring of 1849, a contract was made with the South Carolina Rail Road to take, at $45 per ton, delivered in Columbia, in payment of their bonds at par, so much of their flange iron as would stand his inspection. It resulted, in 1851 and '52, in the Company receiving a little over thirty miles. Many persons have been disposed to censure Mr. Brown for this. But unquestionably he was right; the bonds could not then have been sold for more than $90 in the hundred; the iron, so far as received, is good, and capable of many years service. In the summer of that year a contract was made with Col. Gadsden for the purchase and delivery in Charleston of about sixty miles of iron (chunk bar), the bonds of the South Carolina Rail Road to be received in payment at $90. In the summer of that year negotiations were opened with the recussant stockholders of Greenville, which led to a reconnoisance by Mr. Brown from Greenville to Belton. He pronounced the route practicable; a survey was ordered, and, a very favorable report being made, the stockholders were assembled at Abbeville to consider the propriety of changing the location made in 1847; and after a protracted discussion, and on securing to Anderson the road from Belton to Anderson, the location from Anderson to Greenville was abandoned, and that from Belton to Greenville adopted. Thereupon the stockholders of Greenville (with a large accession of stock from Buncombe and Henderson, and an increase by one of the stockholders of Greenville, Vardry McBee, of his stock to $50,000,) assented to the compromise; and at Greenville, in November, the terms of payment were arranged. At the meeting at Abbeville a branch from Cokesbury to Abbeville was established, and additional stock for the same received.

In September, 1849, the track began to be laid down to Columbia; and during the session of the Legislature of that year the engine Abbeville ran up a few miles on the road, very much to the gratification of the members and the judges. In December, 1849, the Legislature again very generously subscribed $75,000 in the South Carolina Rail Road stock—$25,000 to be paid on the grading being completed to Abbeville, and $50,000 on the same being done to Greenville.

The year 1850 began with the most favorable auspices; everything promised a rapid completion of the road. But the spring rains of that year retarded the work most materially, *especially the bridge* across Broad River. In June or July the track was finished to the river. Previous to this the undertaker of the stone work had been dismissed, and Mr. Brown took upon himself the arduous duty of having this work done. He succeeded; but in July many of Mr. Denmead's hands engaged on the wooden superstructure were struck down with sickness and fled from the work. *Here*, again, Mr. Brown's unconquerable energy was put in requisition. He, with the assistance of Mr. H. T. Peake, the superintendent of the road, and of Mr. Fry, of Columbia, took the whole construction on himself. He hired hands, and by passing all down every evening to Columbia secured their health. The work progressed uninterruptedly till the 24th of August, when the memorable freshet of that year occurred. Three spans of the bridge were up, and the scaffolding for them and a fourth span were standing. The freshet swept away the scaffolding, but left the bridge and road uninjured. Mr. Brown, on that occasion, showed the fearless intrepidity which, at last, probably, consigned him to a watery grave. On Sunday and Monday, when the freshet was at its height, he ascended the road, and when, as he afterwards said to the writer of this memoir, "it looked like running right up Broad river, there being almost as much water apparently to the right as to the left of the road."

From the abatement of the freshet to the 14th of October, when the bridge was finished and crossed, Mr. Brown might have been seen, day after day, standing on the flats and scaffolding in Broad river, urging on the work. Often did the writer, anxious as Mr. Brown about the work, caution him against the exposure and risk to which he was subjecting himself. In his usual, quiet way he said he was willing to encounter it, though he thought by sleeping every night in Columbia he would be safe, and so it turned out.

In 1850 he became the consulting engineer of the Laurens Rail Road Company, and put that road under way.

The Greenville and Columbia Rail Road reached Newberry in March, 1851. Previous to this time a contract was made for a supply of the T iron, which began to be laid down at Little River, Newberry. The work was pressed with unceasing ardor—but the country from Newberry to Ninety-Six, in Abbeville, was one presenting great difficulties. Bush River, Beaverdam creek, Saluda River, Wilson's and Ninety-Six creeks, all had to be crossed; so, too, the Saluda Valley, for miles, had to be ascended! To some of the stockholders living in Abbeville and Anderson the road seemed to move entirely too slow. The July meeting, 1851, of the stockholders at Newberry exhibited some discontent, and strange to say, the mover of the discontent had not finished his own grading contract at the nearest point to Newberry, where the road was delayed.

In 1851 Mr. Brown became the consulting engineer of the King's Mountain Rail Road, and gave it its successful beginning, which has now carried it through. In the latter part of the year he ceased to be the consulting engineer of both it and the Laurens Rail Road—neither longer needing his important services.

In March, 1852, the road reached Ninety-Six. Between this point and Greenwood, ten miles, a delay of more than two months was encountered, from the fact that the iron could not be forwarded by the South Carolina Rail Road. The first week in July the road reached Greenwood, and Cokesbury by the 1st of August, and Barmore's in the next two weeks, having in six weeks made a distance of fourteen miles. The timber superstructure is upon the road to Saluda on the main line, and the Greenville extension. No doubt was entertained that by the first of October the road would be completed to Belton, and to Anderson by the first of December. But God thought proper, no doubt, for wise purposes, to defeat all these expectations.

On Tuesday, 24th of August, Mr. Brown left Columbia for a brief visit over the road, intending to return on Friday. To accommodate his friends of Laurens, he was induced on Thursday to visit that town to locate their depot. The rain of Thursday night and Friday detained him until Saturday morning, when, in company with Col. Irby, president of the Laurens Rail Road, on horseback he swam Little river at the upper ford, near the town, and reached the head of the Laurens Rail Road; thence he came to Helena, where he stopped the Greenville and Columbia passenger train; from which place his anxiety carried him as far up the Greenville and Columbia Rail Road as he could go; he made his way to Chappell's and saw the great flood in Saluda; he dined with his friend, Dr. Moon, on Sunday, and on that evening in a telegraph car, himself and A. C. Garlington, Esq., descended the road from Little river to Helena. On Monday morning, the 30th of August, he left in the train for Columbia; it was obliged to stop, on account of the injuries done to the road, before it reached Crim's creek; he ordered it back to Helena, telling the conductor that he would find some way of getting to Columbia.

He got on the Broad River bridge, opposite Alston, and there he saw Broad River in a flood never surpassed and only approached by the Yazoo freshet of '96. There he saw Alston in ruins, and four spans of Broad river bridge swept away. There he met his friend, Col. A. G. Summer, and stated to him his plans for restoring the road and bridge; and on expressing his anxiety to reach Columbia, Col. Summer offered him his pony, which he had concluded to accept, but seeing Mr. McCollum on the other side of the river, he said: "There is McCollum, and he is fixing a boat to come over." In a brief time McCollum, his son and Jefferson committed themselves, in a large batteau, to the angry waters, and, ascending three-fourths of a mile above the bridge, they struck across, apparently intending to strike Hampton's Island, but the force of the current carried them to the point of it, and thence shooting through between the piers of the bridge they landed below. On conferring with McCollum, and fearing that the Columbia bridge was gone, and understanding from McCollum that he had bought the batteau, he (Brown) determined on crossing and finding his way in it by water to Columbia.

This rash conclusion Colonel Summer combated, in every way he could, but in vain; he then endeavored to prevail with them to leave McCollum's little son with him, telling them, as a prudent man, that "they were men, and if they chose to peril their lives, it was their own act, but that they had no right to jeopardize the life of the child." The child's anxiety to go, and the father's belief in his son's power of swimming, prevailed over this prudent counsel. They crossed the river safely. Mr. Brown borrowed the money and paid for the batteau. His double purpose was to examine the injury to the road, and to reach his family. They decended near the line of the railroad for nearly four miles; then Mr. Brown, observing that it was very laborious to row in the still water, and that McCollum's hands were blistered, proposed to throw the batteau into the current and float to Columbia. To this McCollum says he objected, as he did not know the river. Mr. Brown replied that there was no danger till they came near to Columbia. The batteau was thrown into the channel. In less than a mile, McCollum states that he saw the danger ahead, and therefore took the steerage paddle from his little boy. In a few moments they ran into a cross current in Freshley's falls. The batteau went under the water, overturned, and the party rose, Jefferson clinging to the bottom of the boat, Brown, McCollum and his son swimming. Jefferson maintained himself until the batteau, several miles below, struck against a tree, which he climbed, and was thence taken off next day. Mr. McCollum soon saw that his son could not keep pace with him; he, therefore, waited until he got him up alongside, told him to lay his hand on his shoulder, and swim all that he could to lighten him. This was done, and they and Brown, swimming near each other, swam, McCollum states, at least two miles, when a floating limb carried him and his son down. On rising, he found his child was gone, and could nowhere be found. Brown he saw swimming near him, and said to him, "Colonel, I hope we shall get out yet!" Some reply was made; what it was he could not hear. He struck out for the land, reached it, and was saved. Brown, after swimming still further down the river, below Littleton, was seen to rise and sink, by a man and his wife, who knew him not, but described part of his dress, so as to identify him. His body, after being three weeks in the sand, and under water, was found in a short distance of the place described, where he was seen to sink.

Thus, in his 38th year, perished William Spencer Brown. He has left a widow and five interesting children, with the prospect of another soon to be added. His mother still survives. Sad upon her widowed ear fell the intelligence of the death of her son, who hurdied far from her and the home of his nativity.

In the providence of God he was permitted to visit her, and his relations generally, last June.

William Spencer Brown was about six feet high, of a rather slender frame, but capable of great endurance. His features were regular, and he more resembled his mother than his father.

He was a man of great energy and indomitable perseverance. He was quick in his perception of any matter; he was prompt in execution. If he had a fault (and who is without them?) he was too impetuous.

He was quick to resent an insult, but equally quick to forgive. He was a warm, generous, devoted friend and relative.

As a son, husband and father, none who ever saw him in the presence of his mother, and at home, could doubt that he was all which such relationships could demand.

He was a moral man. Never heard the writer of this sketch an oath from his lips; never was he intoxicated; indeed, ardent spirits he never touched. His life, to the eye of his friend, whose memory clings to him with a tenacity never to be broken, seemed to be without fault.

Much, he would have thought, was in store to crown him with honor and usefulness ; but it was not so ordered. He was cut down in a moment, and in the waste of waters, without an arm to help, a voice to say God have mercy, or an eye to drop a tear. His body sank to rise no more until the general resurrection, and his spirit fled away to the bosom of his Father and God.

THE GREENVILLE AND COLUMBIA RAIL ROAD.

The junior editor (as the representative of a large portion of the Greenville stock,) had the pleasure of attending the convention of the stockholders of this road, which met at Newberry on Wednesday last. A pleasant day's drive took us to Donaldsville, thirty-eight miles, being the present head of the road. On next morning, in company with near two hundred passengers, we passed rapidly over our railroad, and arrived at Newberry just as the convention was ready for assembling. The meeting was organized in a large room of the hotel lately kept by Mr. Bierfield, but being found too small, there being near two hundred stockholders present, it was adjourned to the Newberry theatre, to hear the address of the President, setting forth the present condition of the affairs of the road and the propriety of calling on the stockholders for an assessment on their stock. He spoke for more than two hours, showing, in a clear, candid and eloquent manner, the history of the road, its disasters, the progress of repair and construction, and its future prospects. We cannot describe its affairs better than by giving a synopsis of his speech. He gave a history of the road, its original organization, the location, the difficulties arising out of it, and took occasion, *with great emphasis,* to say to them that they *knew* if there was a fault in the location that he was not responsible for it; that the present route of the road was forced upon him, and as soon as it was fixed he had thrown himself into the work with all the zeal and energy which he possessed.

He stated that the stock subscribed to build the road by the State and individuals did not exceed $1,231,120 ; that of that there was still remaining unpaid, or unaccounted for, the sum of $175,755.48; that a large proportion of this sum was covered, probably, by certificates of work not yet brought in, and which would, *pro tanto,* diminish the apparent debt of the company; that the cost of the road, when finis bed, would be $2,040,219.60; that this covered everything—stocking the road, workshops, repairs, &c.; and it would still be the cheapest road ever built within his knowledge, the cost being $12,501 per mile, $1,499 per mile less than the Charlotte and South Carolina Rail Road.

He gave a rapid description of the road for one hundred and five miles completed, pointing the attention to the immense work done, not less than eight bridges being built, and a rolling, rich country penetrated. Had it not been for the great August freshet, said he, we would now have been at Anderson! That freshet injured and swept down more than thirty miles of the road. The work of repair has been more tedious than was anticipated. But, said he, it is impossible for men *to labor against disease or to resist the elements.*

The work in the Saluda valley, comparatively slight when compared with that in the Broad River, was done within the time expected, by the self-sacrificing contractors, Messrs. Singleton & Hair, Messrs. Pennington & Burns, and Messrs. Miller, Henry & Miller, under Feaster and La-Salle, as directed by the energetic chief engineer, Mr. Griffin.

In the Broad River valley, Mr. Peake, the superintendent, aided by Mr. Chamberlaine, Butler, Duncan, Feaster, Pennington and Burns, have, in a succession of the worst weather, and amid disease, repaired and put in beautiful operation twenty-six miles of road; building, in the mean time, a beautiful and substantial bridge across Cedar creek. So, too, Mr. Owens, under Mr. Peake's direction, restored the trestle near Crim's creek. All these great works of repair have been done in less than four months, two of which, September and the latter part of November, and all December, have been storm and rain, with rare glimpses of sunshine. Notwithstanding, *these faithful, devoted men* have worked *on* and *on,* until all is finished except the Broad River bridge. That has been delayed going up, until the road could be finished; first, on account of the difficulty of transporting stone seven miles by wagon to rebuild the piers; and, second, to bring back the spans of the bridge, washed twelve miles down the river. Two spans, it is hoped, will be brought back this week, and in the next six weeks, he said, he had great hopes all might be repaired, and the engine pass continuously from Columbia to Donald's and *above!* For the present, ample arrangements were made and making to pass travelers and freight across Broad river. The repairs had been, and would be completed at, probably, $6,000 beyond the estimate submitted to the public.

He stated that there was an actual necessity now for $416,980.20. To meet this, independent of our outstanding stock, which will be considered equal to the contractors' demand and the finishing of the road, we have, said he, $157,978 in present available means; and by the sale of the bonds it might be possible to reduce this further ($182,-000,) leaving only about $77,000 to be provided for. But, said he, we have contracts for iron and rolling stock to more than $100,000 which must soon be met.

It is hoped Congress may put the duties, say $35,565.21, on time, and allow them to be paid in mail service, and thus relieve the company from paying out that much cash.

So, too, he hoped, he said, the Bank of the State might take the company's bond on time, and give up $73,000 of hypothecated securities, which could be turned into money, and thus further relieve the company. Still it was necessary there should be an assessment to provide means and to put the company above the suspicion of interested men, who are constantly endeavoring to affect its credit. An assessment of one-fifth—$4 per share—to be called for in installments of $1 per share every sixty days, making an aggregate of $246,188, was necessary. This sum, he hoped, would carry the road through all difficulties. The Treasurer, he recommended, should be directed to issue certificates for each installment, as paid, to be refunded out of the income, with 7 per cent. interest.

He said that there was iron on hand, or coming in, to finish the whole road; that it was the opinion of the chief engineer that the whole road could be finished in four months, and certainly before next July. This opinion, he said, he thought was correct. The wooden superstructure was down on the Abbeville Branch, with the exception of three miles; that it was down to, or nearly to, Anderson; that it was also down on the road to Saluda, within fourteen miles of Greenville.

He said the iron was promised to be forwarded rapidly from Charleston, and would be as rapidly put forward by this road. Everything assured him, he said, that success, speedy success, was before him. We have been chastened sorely, but, said he, God does not punish always. He recommended that there should be a change, as soon as practicable, of the location of the road at Frost's, Bookter's, Chambers', Cedar creek and Turnipseed's. This being done, the road is out of all danger from water. He said, *now* he believed the road was perfectly safe. The entire road would now challenge comparison with any road in the State for its construction. He said to the stockholders, "You have this morning passed over the whole of it—*am I not right?*"

He said, in conclusion, that he hoped he might be permitted to say that no desire of power had caused him to linger at the head of this great work. He never was satisfied, he said, to leave a work unfinished, and he never was willing to abandon a ship in danger of stranding, *nor to repudiate, when he could, by faith or loss, avoid it!* The wreck, said he, has been cleared, and the past is before you; and if, like Columbus' men, you will hold on and toil on a little longer, we will reach the long expected and desired land.

At the close of his address the convention adjourned to meet in the Baptist church at half-past 6 o'clock P. M. In the interim of the meeting the effect of the president's address was visible upon every countenance, for whereas the stockholders had met in the morning under circumstances of doubt and gloom, and in some few instances even of disaffection to the administration of the affairs of the company, own; all was confidence and cheerfulness, and a willingness to pay the assessments, and thus secure the benefits of their previous outlay. There was also manifested, with scarcely an exception, a feeling that the interests of the company were safe in the hands of the president, and that no misfortune which had yet befallen it could equal that which it would sustain were he to withdraw from the administration of its affairs. It was evident that the storm was past, and sunshine and prosperity awaited us in the future.

At the appointed hour the convention met in the Baptist Church, and without discussion the resolution for assessing the stock of the company 20 per cent. was passed almost unanimously. It was also resolved that the assessments should be called in by four instalments of $1 per share each, after notice on each instalment of 60 days, and that the treasurer should issue receipts for each payment, binding the company to refund the amount, with 7 per cent. interest from the date of payment, out of the first income of the road. This makes the assessments amount to nothing more than a loan of money by the stockholders to the company, at legal interest, returnable at an early day—an arrangement that must give satisfaction to every stockholder who truly desires the success of the road.

It was also resolved, as soon as practicable, to change the location of the road at all the exposed points between Alston and Columbia, and surveys for this purpose will shortly be made. But this arrangement, as well as every other, except the completion of the road, is to be delayed until the repayment of the assessments has been effected.

After some little discussion in regard to a rumored abuse of the free ticket system on the road, which was properly placed in the hands of the directors, the convention adjourned; and the next morning the members sped swiftly and pleasantly to their respective homes. Hard after the passenger train up, followed the regular freight train, the first time of its running under the new arrangement. Freight, as well as iron for the road, is now brought up regularly, and the road is already regaining the heavy business which it did before the freshet in August.

We were delighted to hear that our excellent friend, Col. Irby, Lieutenant-Governor of the State and president of the Laurens Rail Road Company, (who was present at the convention,) subscribed $1,000 of stock of the company, as a pledge of his confidence in the enterprise and a token of his interest in the prosperity of the road.

SENTENCE OF MOTLEY AND BLACKLEDGE.

Thomas Motley ads. The State—Murder of a Slave.—Whitner, Judge. Motion for new trial dismissed.

William Blackledge ads. The State—Murder of Slave.—Whitner, Judge. Motion in arrest of judgment and for a new trial dismissed.

His Honor, Judge O'Neall, pronounced on the prisoners the following eloquent, impressive and affecting sentence, worthy, in its general character, and especially honorable sensitiveness to true Southern character and sacred regard for the right of humanity, to take its place by the side of that of Judge Wilde, many years ago, in the case of Slater, when the murder of a slave was punishable only with a pecuniary mulct:

Thomas Motley—William Blackledge.—Two months have passed away since you stood before me, in the midst of the community where the awful tragedy, of which you have been convicted, was performed. I hope this time has been profitable to you, and that in the midnight watchings of your solitary cells you have turned back with shame and sorrow to the awful cruelties of which you were guilty on the 5th of July last.

Notwithstanding the enormity of your offence, you have no reason to complain that justice has been harshly administered. On the circuit and *here* you have had the aid of zealous, untiring counsel— every thing which man could do to turn away the sword of justice has been done; but in vain. Guilt, such as yours, cannot escape the sanctions of even earthly tribunals.

My duty now is to pass between you and the State, and announce the law's awful doom! Before I do so, usage and propriety demand that I should endeavor to turn your thoughts to the *certain results* before you. Death here, a shameful death, awaits you! I hope it may be that you may escape the everlasting death of the soul.

It may be profitable to you to recall the horrid deeds, which you jointly and severally committed, in the death of the poor, begging, unoffending slave. I will not repeat the disgusting details of the outrages committed; the public are already fully informed, and your own hearts, in every pulsation, repeat them to you. I may be permitted, however, to say to you, and to the people around you, and to the world, that hitherto South Carolina had never witnessed such atrocities; indeed, they exceed all that we are told of savage barbarity. For the Indian, the moment his captive ceases to be a true warrior (in the sense of which he understands it) and pleads for mercy, no longer extends his sufferings—death, speedy death, follows. But you, for a night and part of the succeeding day, rioted in the sufferings and terrors of the poor negro, and at length your ferocious dogs, set on by you, throttled and killed him, as they would a wild beast. Can't you hear his awful death cry, "Oh, Lord!" If you cannot hear it, the Lord of Hosts heard and answered it. He demanded then, and *now*, from you, the fearful account of blood!

You have met with the fearful consequences of the infamous business in which you were engaged—*hunting runaways with dogs*, equally fierce and ferocious as the Spanish bloodhounds. With one of you (Motley) there could have been no excuse. Your father, young man, is a man of wealth, reaped and gathered together by a life of toil and privation; that the son of such a man should be found more than a hundred miles from home, following a pack of dogs, in the chase of negro slaves, through the swamps of the lower country, under a summer's sun, shows either a love of cruelty, or of money, which is not easily satisfied. To the other prisoner, Blackledge, it may be that poverty and former devotion to this sad business might have presented some excuses.

The Scriptures, young men, with which, I fear, you have not been familiar, declare, as the law of God, "Thou shalt not kill." This divine statute, proclaimed to God's own prophet, amid the lightning and thunder of Sinai, was predicated of the law, previously given to Noah, after one race of men had perished. "Whoso sheddeth man's blood, by man shall his blood be shed: for in the image of God made he man." In conformity to these divine commands, is the law of the State under which you have been condemned. No longer is the blood of the slave to be paid for with money; no longer is the brutal murderer of the negro to go free! "Life for life" is demanded, and you, poor, guilty creatures, have the forfeit to pay! A long experience as a lawyer and a Judge, makes it my duty to say to you, and to the people all around you, *never have I known the guilty murderer to go free!* If judgment does not overtake him in the hall of justice, still the avenger of blood is in his pursuit: still the eye, which never slumbers nor sleeps, is upon him, until in some unexpected moment the command goes forth, "Cut him down," and the "place which knew him once shall know him no more forever." Since your trial, one of the witnesses, much censured for participation, in some sort, in your guilty deeds, has been suddenly cut off from life.

I say to you young men, "You must die." Do not trust in hopes of executive clemency. It seems to me, however much the governor's heart may bleed to say "no" to your application, he will have to say it. Prepare yourselves, therefore, as reasonable, thinking, accountable men, for your fate. Search the Scriptures—obtain repentance by a godly sorrow for sin. Struggle night and day for pardon. Remember, Christ the Saviour came to save sinners, the chief of sinners. Learn that you are such, and he will then declare to you that, "though your sins be as scarlet, they shall be white as snow; though they be red like crimson, they shall be as wool."

The sentence of the law is, that you be taken to the place whence you last came, thence to the jail of Colleton District; that you be closely and securely confined until Friday, the third day of March next, on which day, between the hours of ten in the forenoon and two in the afternoon, you and each of you will be taken, by the Sheriff of Colleton District, to the place of public execution, and there be hanged by the neck till your bodies be dead, and may God have mercy on your soul.

———

TRIBUTE TO THE MEMORY OF EX-GOVERNOR JOHNSON.

A meeting of the bar was held in the chamber of the Equity Court of Appeals, at half past 9 o'clock A. M., yesterday, to pay a tribute of respect and regard to the memory of the late ex-Governor Johnson.

On motion of J. L. Petigru, Esq., Isaac W. Hayne, Esq., Attorney General, was called to the chair, and Thomas J. Gantt, Esq., (Clerk of the Court of Appeals and the Court of Errors, on the nomination of the deceased,) was appointed Secretary.

The Chairman stated the object of the meeting in a few appropriate remarks.

The Hon. Mitchell King then rose, and introduced the following preamble and resolution :

The State of South Carolina is again called to mourn the death of one of her most distinguished citizens. On the 7th day of this month, at his residence at Limestone Springs, the venerable and venerated David Johnson paid the debt of nature, and his ashes repose in Union District, near the place where he first saw the light. The sympathies and affection of the community gather around his tomb. Every man feels that he has lost an enlightened friend. But the Judiciary, of whom he was long the presiding officer—who were so long associated with him in their high duties, and who were bound to him by the strongest ties of mutual kindness and confidence—and the bar, who sustained before him the toils of their laborious and anxious profession, have the deepest cause of sorrow.

We shall leave to the biographer the duty of commemorating the domestic and private virtues of our departed friend; and well, in them, will he deserve a faithful chronicler, for no kinder and more generous man, according to the full measure of his ability, ever lived. In every relation of life he strove to perform his duty. His heart overflowed with the best feelings, and was governed and guarded by his enlightened intellect. To speak of him as a lawyer and a judge is the special privilege of the bar ; and if the voice of friendship mingle in our commemoration, it is because we cannot well separate our love for him as a friend, from our admiration of him as a jurist.

David Johnson was indeed one of nature's noblemen. He was no less remarkable for his presence than for his virtues. His frame was large, well proportioned and athletic ; his countenance grave, thoughtful and benevolent; his whole bearing and deportment conciliated esteem and commanded respect; his form was a fitting abode for his masculine and powerful intellect.

He studied law under the direction of the learned and upright Abraham Nott. After some years' successful practice at the bar, he was in 1815 raised to the bench, and from that time until in 1846 the spontaneous voice of the people, expressed by the votes of every member of both branches of our Legislature, called him to the gubernatorial chair, he continued as a Judge at law, a Judge of the Court of Appeals, or as a Chancellor in Equity, to perform his judicial functions in the highest tribunals of the State. To the execution of these functions he brought a mind well stored with legal lore—unwearied industry—invincible patience and perseverance—great natural abilities and stainless integrity. No man was freer from prejudice—none firmer in his opinions, or maintained them with more urbanity and consideration for the opinions of others. Truth was his object, and he never, against his convictions, or to show his intellectual strength, contended merely for victory. The most inexperienced member of the bar, in addressing him, was sure of an encouraging hearing and a fair, impartial consideration of his arguments, while he enforced the rules and maintained the decorum and dignity of the court. His manner was so mild, and his firmness so gentle, that the most sensitive feelings were not wounded—the most irritable could not take offence. The examination of witnesses before him was always conducted with a due regard to the cause of truth and justice. The modest, the diffident, and the candid were protected—the reluctant, or equivocating, subjected to the full rigor of a searching scrutiny. Nothing could exceed the impartiality with which, as a Judge at law, he laid the evidence in a cause before a jury, or the candor with which, as a Chancellor, he determined on it for himself. In all ordinary business of the court he was prompt and decisive. In cases of complexity or difficulty, he was patient and slow in coming to his conclusions, but when they were once formed he adhered to them with great firmness. This, however, was the firmness of a clear and self-relying mind, devoted to the right; and, in any matter that he had adjudicated, brought again on appeal before him, no Judge ever lent a more willing ear to the arguments urged against his own opinion, and if, on full reconsideration, he was satisfied he had been in error, no man was ever more magnanimous in acknowledging that error, and in giving his reasons for changing his opinion, and agreeing to the reversal of his previous judgment. He was seldom wrong, but he claimed no patent of infallibility, and was not only willing, but glad to correct a mistake. When, after tasking all the energies of his mind, he remained satisfied that he was right, no power on earth could have induced him to let go his integrity. He was tried, well tried, in times of the deepest excitement, when many of his nearest and dearest friends, who held opinions different from his own, and with whom he might have been happy to agree, pressed their views earnestly and zealously upon him, he had formed his opinion on the clearest dictates of his own conscience, and to these dictates he unostentatiously and inflexibly adhered. He knew that, before his country, when excitement had passed away, and finally before his God, he must be tried on the truth and purity of his own correctness; and he has reaped his reward. The respect of the good and the wise clustered around him. His country spontaneously crowned him with her highest honors; and when advancing age caused him to withdraw from public life, followed him to his retreat with her cordial well-done and best wishes.

He has been taken from us, and has gone to receive the recompense of all his labors. We shall no more, in this world, see that manly form, or listen to the accents of that paternal voice. But though dead he still speaketh in his high example—in his recorded judgments—in his wisdom; embalmed in the records of our courts. As lawyers or as judges, let us strive to imitate him in all his noble qualities—let us strive to guard from every profane touch the hallowed flame that burns on the altar of justice, and to transmit the sacred principles to which he devoted himself, unimpaired to our latest posterity.

Resolved, That the bar of South Carolina, attendant on the Court of Errors, and on the Courts of Appeal, now in session, deeply deplore the death of the Honorable David Johnson. While he remained with us he was an honor and an ornament to the profession. We looked to him and to the dignities which he had achieved and worn so nobly, as the just reward of indefatigable industry, high talents and unsullied integrity. We pointed to him as an encouragement to the studious advocate, and as a model of judicial excellence. We admired and loved him while he lived, we mourn for him now he is dead; we will cherish and revere his memory.

2. That we very respectfully tender our sincere condolence to the bereaved members of his family, and beg leave to assure them of our sincere sympathy.

3. That these proceedings be presented to the Judges of the Court of Errors, with the request that the same be entered on their records.

The preamble and the resolutions were seconded by James L. Petigru, Esq., with the remark that, although the eulogy they embodied was high, the consciences of all present would testify that it was well deserved.

The preamble and resolutions were then unanimously adopted.

At the opening of the Court of Errors, composed of all the Law and Equity Judges, at 10 o'clock A. M., the Attorney-General, in conformity with the third resolution, after a few touching remarks, presented the preamble and resolutions to the Court.

On receiving the preamble and resolutions, the Hon. John B. O'Neall, President of the Court of Errors, as the organ of the Court, responded as follows:

Gentlemen:—The intelligence of the death of the great and good man of whom you have just spoken, has been to me, as well as to the other members of the court, no ordinary cause of grief. From me, as his friend and associate of many years, it may well be expected that I should testify of his great, his excelling worth. Before I do, may I be permitted to say, that to me, personally, David Johnson was more than a friend; had it not been for the difference of many years in our ages and services, I should have called him brother, with even more than a brother's love. I am sure I felt for him all that love, respect and reverence that I did for my own father. When I presented myself in May, 1814, to the Constitutional Court for examination as a student of law, he was the solicitor appointed on the course of examination. From that time our friendship has been continued and unbroken. It is, therefore, with almost filial feelings I stand up to answer you, and to say of him, that full of years and glory, he has "finished his course." In his seventy-second year, or having completed it by a few months, "like the ripe grain," he has been gathered into the garner of his Master.

His life, *as we all know*, was one eminent for usefulness. He was a native of Virginia. In Spartanburg District, South Carolina, where he resided after his removal from Virginia, lie the remains of his father, Christopher Johnson, a Baptist preacher. His education was as good as an academy then furnished, but he mainly made himself the plain but forcible writer for which he was so remarkable. Looking at his portly person, his capacious head, his beautiful handwriting, and his clear and forcible written opinions, I have often said to myself how much, in many respects, he is like George Washington.

He studied law with Judge Nott, then a lawyer, living in Union District, for four years, the period of study then prescribed for a law student not a graduate of a college; he read and reread the scanty legal libraries then in possession of even the most eminent. He has told me that a portion of his preparation was the reading carefully of the whole of Bacon's Abridgement.

He was admitted to the bar in, I presume, 1805, or 1806. He was for several years the Ordinary of Union District, and resigned it to qualify himself to receive a fee of $100 to settle, as the lawyer of the administrator of the estate of John McCall, deceased.

He was returned to the Legislature in 1812; and in the same session elected Solicitor of the Middle Circuit, in the place of David R. Evans, Esq., who had long filled the office, and who then resigned.

He was then little known; his practice was not extensive. The case of Tucker and Stevens, 4 Eq. Rep., 532, he has told me was the only bill in equity which he ever filed.

In December, 1815, at the age of thirty-three, he and Richard Gantt were elected Judges of the Law Court over the late Benj. C. Yancey and Robert Starke, Esqs.

By labor, continuous and untiring, he made himself one of the most accomplished Circuit Judges before whom I ever practiced. His opinions in the Constitutional Court were prepared with wonderful care, often written over three times. They thus became models of judicial arguments.

He was one of the majority who declared at this place the Act of December, 1816, requiring the Judges to clear the dockets, unconstitutional, because it was passed with the amendment of the Constitution. No decision ever created such an excitement. An extra session of the Legislature in April, 1817, was convened to remedy the matter, and another law was passed to the same effect by it. Judge Johnson's mild and temperate opinion saved him from a loss of popularity. His eminent friend and legal instructor, Judge Nott, received the largest measure of the displeasure of the Legislature. For, in the succeeding December, when the Judges resigned to be re-elected.

under the increased salary, Judge Nott was elected by a very slim majority, while his young associate and former pupil was almost unanimously chosen.

In 1824, he, with Judges Nott and Colcock, was placed on the Appeal Bench, and performed its herculean labors until that Court was abolished in 1835. Having, with the late Judge Harper, gone upon that bench, in the places of Judges Nott and Colcock, in 1830, I may be permitted to say, as the only survivor, that the terms of '30, '31, '32, '33, '34 and '35 demanded and received labor, attention and care far beyond anything which I have since experienced. In them, Judge Johnson performed a full part of the work, and as the President of the Court was, as everywhere, fully equal to his duty. In December, 1835, he was placed, as I well know, much against his wish, on the Equity or Chancery Bench. He distrusted himself from his early want of training for that department of judicial labor, yet he performed the duties of a Chancellor admirably well. No Chancellor with whom I have been acquainted, better sustained himself, or more dignified or adorned his office.

In 1846 he was elected and assumed the duties of Governor and Commander-in-Chief of the State; he desired this office as the crowning reward of his labors! It was unanimously conferred upon him. Its many worrying duties he calmly and patiently performed. He was emphatically a civil magistrate; he had no military tact, yet he organized the brave Palmetto Regiment, with almost paternal care—accompanied them to the border of the State, and standing on the Augusta bridge, with streaming eyes, bade them farewell! He welcomed Shields and Quitman as the leaders in battle of the sons of South Carolina, on their journey through this State, and made them feel that South Carolina and her Chief Magistrate were worthy of their homage. He saw return the wasted but gallant remnant of those with whom he had parted as the hope of the State, and gave them a father's welcome.

Since 1848 he has been in retirement, and has suffered more from disease and accident than has fallen to the lot of most men. All these he bore with that noble, uncomplaining, patient fortitude, for which he was always so remarkable. But successive attacks of disease and injuries bowed his giant frame and subdued his iron will, and on Sunday, the 7th of January, he quietly, and in the full hope of peace—everlasting peace—passed from earth. His remains, on Monday, the 8th of January, were, in the grave yard at Unionville, placed by the side of his wife, in the presence of his numerous and devoted friends and children, and earth received and covered all that was mortal of David Johnson.

Gone, forever gone, from us of earth, is the pure patriot, the just judge, the loved friend and the man *who had not an enemy!* Take him all in all, we may well say of him, South Carolina will vainly seek his equal. He is the last of the judges of law and equity who were on the bench when I came upon it in 1823. All, all, are in the presence of the King of kings. His mind was eminently judicial. His charges to the juries were plain, clear and short. He went upon the bench with the notion that the jury was to decide all questions of fact; but he soon learned that he must share with them the responsibility, and he never afterwards hesitated to place his opinion, both of the law and also of the facts, plainly before them.

His opinions on the Constitutional Court, the Court of Appeals and the Court of Appeals in Equity, will speak for themselves, and whoever reads them carefully will say that they will compare most favorably with those of the most eminent Judges of our great and growing country.

He was slow, and even reluctant, to begin a course of laborious reasoning; but, when aroused, he overthrew all opposing obstacles, and most clearly reached his conclusions.

He had no pride of opinion, no passion to gratify, no prejudice to turn him aside. Truth and justice were alike his objects. He freely surrendered his opinions whenever error was presented to his mind. If he had a fault, it was that he yielded his opinions too readily.

His very nature was kindness and benevolence; he never wilfully injured a human being. As a friend, he was sincere and unchanging. As a husband and father, no man was more kind and just. His letters to me, after the burning, in a house, of twenty of his negro children, was a most touchingly eloquent expression of a master's grief for the poor little ones thus destroyed.

As citizen, officer and neighbor, he fulfilled every duty and met every expectation. Wherever he lived, wherever he was known or seen, he was loved. In his grave, he will be remembered; and you, brethren, as you run your eyes over his recorded labors, will drop many a tear upon the pages, and rise from them to reverence and perpetuate, *in your hearts*, the memory of the great and good David Johnson.

Your motion is granted. The clerk will spread your preamble and resolutions on the records of the Court of Errors, and furnish copies to the children of the deceased, and also for publication, and for the State Reporter.

The court will adjourn until to-morrow at 10 o'clock, so that, in silent sadness, we may reflect upon the death of our friend and brother.

In further testimonial of respect to the deceased, the court then adjourned until 10 o'clock, A. M. this day.

BEAUFORT, So. CA., }
17th January, 1855. }

My Dear Sir:

I this moment closed your noble and eloquent reply to the resolutions of the bar of Charleston on the death of the late venerable David Johnson. Your remarks seem to have come so direct, warm and glowing from your heart that I trust you will excuse me for saying that they have found their way direct to mine; and I cannot refrain from addressing you a line expressing the sympathy I feel in every word that you have so feelingly and so eloquently said upon the solemn occasion referred to. As a younger member of the bar, I feel that one to whom we have been accustomed to look up to and regard as one of the fathers of the law has been called away from us forever. I never had the honor nor *pleasure* to practice before the late Chancellor Johnson, nor even to make a motion before him; but I knew him as well as the differences of our ages and the distance of our residences would allow, and he impressed me with a degree of respect and regard that I delight to acknowledge. Just before I was admitted to the bar I chanced to spend a month or more in the same house with the venerated deceased, and was permitted to enjoy such delightful intercourse with him that I feel it has been of advantage to me ever since. He was so kind and fatherly in his manner towards me, he was so full of information on most subjects, and so willing to impart it to me, that he completely carried my affections along with him when we parted, and from that time to this he has held them. Whenever we met afterwards I felt his kindness, and learned more and more to appreciate his many substantial virtues.

I trust, my dear sir, you will excuse me for the liberty I have taken in expressing my private feelings to you, as I have done; but from "the fullness of the heart the mouth speaketh," and I only wish I had it in my power to throw upon his grave a chaplet worthy of the virtues, the learning, the gooodness, the public and private worth of David Johnson.

With considerations of the highest respect for you personally, permit me to subscribe myself,

Very respectfully and sincerely yours,

JOS. DAN'L POPE.

His Honor Judge O'Neall, Charleston.

THE

Annals of Newberry,

HISTORICAL, BIOGRAPHICAL AND ANECDOTICAL;

ALSO

RELIGIOUS, MEDICAL AND LITERARY:

PART SECOND,

BY

JOHN A. CHAPMAN, A. M.

I.

THE FRIENDS AND THEIR MIGRATION TO OHIO.

The readers of the Annals of Newberry will be glad to find, I think, the following supplementary chapter to Judge O'Neall's work, contributed by Mr. David Jones, of Ohio, a relative of Lambert J. Jones, Esq., of Newberry. The chapter is strictly supplementary and not a continuation in time of the former work:

"I have read one very interesting narrative or history of Newberry District written, as I have been informed, by the late John Belton O'Neall, a resident of said district, from birth until death, embracing a period of more than sixty years, during a long portion of which he held the office of Supreme Judge of the State. Having learned that another history of said district is in preparation by Mr. John A. Chapman, I will furnish, at his request, some account of the most prominent families who left there near the beginning of this century, and contributed to the peopling of three counties, namely, Miami, Warren and Clinton, in the State of Ohio.

"I feel interested in the task because my parents and maternal grandparents came from there, bringing those grand traits of the pioneer, namely, industry, enterprise, fortitude and indomitable courage. I know that the present inhabitants of Newberry District will not feel dishonored when they learn something of what has been wrought by her emigrant citizens and their descendants.

"In O'Neall's history we are told in part of the Friends, or Quakers, who resided in the district, the exodus of whom and others between the years 1800 and 1810, reflexively decimated the district. He says, also, that they held a large quarterly meeting on Bush River, where he had often seen more than five hundred Friends assembled.

"There must have been some great moving cause or causes that induced such an exit in so short a period. O'Neall ascribes it to their repugnance to the 'peculiar institution' of the South, together with frightful predictions of war and carnage made by an itinerant minister of this church, named Zachary Dicks. During the year 1803 this minister made a visit to Wrightsborough monthly meeting, in Georgia, an integral part of Bush River quarterly meeting. He there told the Friends of a terrific internecine war not far in the future, during which many men like those in the Apocalypse would flee to the mountains and call on those mountains to hide them. With reference to the time of fulfilment, he said the child was then born that would see it; thus intimating the time, not as immediate, but not very far off. He also advised them to leave there, which they did. Forty-eight years after came the predicted war. I heard this account more than forty years ago from a man who was at the meeting. From Wrightsborough, Z. Dicks went to Bush River meeting, held in a well made house erected only five years before with the full calculation of a long continued occupancy. I give his first words there as related by a dear aunt of mine who was present, and was just blooming into womanhood: 'O, Bush River! Bush River! How hath thy beauty faded away, and gloomy darkness eclipsed thy day!' Going into particulars, he depicted the silence and loneliness that would attend that house after its abandonment by those who had erected it; that herbage would ere long grow in its now well beaten paths. I did not understand that he advised removal here as at Wrightsborough, but only foretold it. Indeed, it did not suffer during the war like the other place, for I have learned no hostile troops came near it.

"Friend Dicks must have been at this time rather elderly, for I am informed that not long before the Revolution he had been at Guilford, North Carolina, and foretold that war. Pointing to the walls of the meeting house he said its floors and walls would be stained with human blood. This was literally fulfilled, for, after the bloody battle of Guilford, the Friends carried the wounded soldiers, both British and American, into the house and performed for them the part of the good Samaritan; the stains of whose blood, though faded, were on its walls many years afterwards. To those who are skeptical as to Z. Dicks' prophetical attainments, I will only say that he was at least a 'good guesser.' Whatever effect his (Dicks) visit may have had in causing the Friends' removal, other causes co-operated. Those living east of the Alleghanies had looked upon them as a barrier against savage invasion, and also as one against removing to an unexplored and unknown savage wilderness. Such had been the view until the arrival of the time thus described by the poet, when,

> " 'Boone had with bold adventurous tread,
>   Beyond the mountain barriers prest;
> And saw a richer landscape spread
>   In the broad valley of the West.
> Fiction had lent her magic hand
> To paint that second Fairy land;
> For it was drawn a clime as fair
>   As youthful fancy's brightest dream;
>   And all who heard might justly deem
> Another Eden blooming there.'

"Allowing much for exaggeration, the description was still tempting enough, with the first-named cause, to produce the exodus which began soon after Dicks' visit. I must remark, however, that this exodus was far from being confined to the Friends. The Barretts, Elmores, Halls, Dennys, Campbells, Laytons and others, who removed during that period, were not members of the Friends' Church, and many of them were not of any. The first removal, as well as I can find, took place some months after Dicks' visit there. This was John Jay, the only Jay mentioned in the Annals, though with him came seven sons and three daughters. They came to Miami County, I think, during the autumn of 1803. They found Friends from Guilford, North Carolina, who had come the year before, and as all belonged to the same yearly meeting, namely, Guilford, North Carolina, the matter of removal seems to have been well understood between them. The same may be said of Wrightsborough Friends in Georgia, for they came in great numbers, leaving the parent meeting in the same condition as that of Bush River.

"I will now give an account of some of the most prominent persons who came from Newberry and settled in the three counties previously mentioned. Many of those emigrants being unknown or forgotten by the author of the Annals of Newberry, are not mentioned by him, and we need not wonder, for he was a boy at the time of their emigration. The traits of some, however, are given with almost surprising accuracy; and could he have known their subsequent lives it would no doubt have given him much satisfaction, and would have been a supplement to the Annals.

"The first I'll mention is Thomas Pearson, 'Little Old Tommy,' who lived to the greatest age of any who came from Newberry, besides being the oldest emigrant to his township and, as near as I can learn, county. Born in 1728, he was older than the Father of his Country, a fact which seemed to attach additional importance to him. In early life he lived in Philadelphia, following the trade of saddler and harness-maker. Years before, and during the Revolution, he and his family resided in Newberry District and had their full share of its honors. Once, when a captive, his enemies required his service in saddlery and harness work, regardless of his lack of tools. He answered them by saying that 'Neither wise men nor fools can work without tools,' the piquancy of which caused them to laugh and excuse him. He appears to have occupied the first seat in the 'Common Meetings' of Friends. A granddaughter of his told me that once during the solemn quiet of a meeting a partially insane woman came in with fruit in her apron and going up to him said, 'Here, Mr. Pearson, I'll give you the apples if you will preach to-day.' Being a harmless person they got rid of her in a quiet way; but whether or not they regarded her interruption as a rebuke upon their silent worship I was not informed. I think it was in 1805 or 1806, that Father Pearson left Newberry with a numerous retinue of children, grandchildren and one great-grandchild. Coming directly to Miami County they pitched their tents in proximity to the Jays and Jenkinses, who had preceded them. It was not many years before his many descendants were settled comfortably around him and he saw teeming fields, in place of dark, tangled forests. His wife died, and, though in advanced age, he took another. A few years more and his walk became tremulous, his eyes grew dim, and his hearing blunted. The writer saw him in 1820, when he had Old Dodson's Three Warnings:—'he was lame, and deaf, and blind.' He could walk only with

support on both sides, could hear only by loud speaking
in his ear, both day and night were alike to him. In this
lamentable condition we may well suppose time hung heavy
on his hands. Upon asking what time it was, if answered
ten o'clock, he would say and repeat, 'Ten o'clock, ten
o'clock,' striving, but in vain, to impress it upon his mem
ory, for it would not be long before he repeated the question. The author, child as he was, pitied him whose lamp
of life, so nearly gone out, seemed to be leaving him rather
impatient. At this time the great human butcher, but now a
captive of Europe, whose

> " 'Evil deeds were writ in gore,
>   Nor written thus in vain;
>   Whose triumphs told of fame no more,
>   Or deepened every stain;'

was languishing like Prometheus upon his sea-girt rock, say
ing sorrowfully to his followers: 'I once dictated to four or
five secretaries at once; I was then Napoleon; I am now no
longer anything; my senses, my faculties, forsake me; I no
longer live, I only exist.' How much the weight of blood
upon his soul distressed Napoleon, we cannot know; but we
do know he had his sight and hearing, which old Thomas
Pearson had not. In natural ability they bear no comparison,
neither did they in ambition. The first died in the calmness
and quiet of Christian resignation; the second a few months
after with his spirit deliriously engaged in the strife of battle
and the rage of tempests around him.

"A short time after the above-described sight of Old Thomas,
the author heard a grandson of his announce his death and
burial, which elicited but little remark, seeming to be acqui-
esced in because of his relief from his lamentable condition.
Of some of his relatives I will write hereafter, but will now
take up the names seriatim of persons, of whom I know something, mentioned in the Annals of Newberry, on pages 31, 32
and 33,* who emigrated to Ohio.

"David Jenkins and family came to Miami County, Ohio,
in 1805. He had married Martha Evans a few years after
the Revolution and brought several children with him. He
made a good selection of land which he cultivated to advan-

---

* Part I., 28, 29 and 30.

tage. He built a hewed log house of good size, which is considered the oldest one in his (Monroe) Township. He reared two sons and four daughters, not one of whom, I think, was born in Ohio. They all did well except one son, who became intemperate. A very quiet and unassuming little man, he performed his part well and died in good old age about the year 1842.

"Benjamin Pearson, a relative of Old Thomas', emigrated about the same time as David Jenkins, being nearly his age. He was the father of seven sons and two daughters, but few of whom were born in Ohio. They all married to good advantage; all prospered and lived to good age, but none of them are now living.

"Of William Pearson but very little is now known, and his descendants do not appear to have belonged to the Friends.

"Robert Evans, at least one of that name, went with his family to Tennessee. His brother Joseph, not mentioned in the Annals, came with his family to this county. Being of an enterprising turn, he purchased land on the west fork of Stillwater River, located a village, West Milton, there in 1807. This site was a good selection, being seventy-five feet above low water mark; in proximity to several perennial springs that poured over precipices nearly, or quite, fifty feet perpendicular, affording ample power for the propulsion of machinery. Evans built, I think, the second mill on Stillwater, the first being by Frederick Yount, from North Carolina. The scenery here was grand and almost inspiring. The towering, umbrageous forests; the magnificent cascades; the slopes and grassy banks of Stillwater, might make it seem to the imaginative beholder as the place where the queen Violenta led her *fairy troupes* in their mazy moonlight dances. On the first sale of lots the buyers were few and the prices low. Two boys rode two steers to the sale, which would have seemed singular at Newberry. Evans started the first store and postoffice on the place and continued them until after the war of 1812, when he went to Cincinnati to engage in greater business. About 1828 he returned to Milton; opened a store which he continued a number of years, dying of abdominal dropsy in 1837; having, a number of years before, lost his right among Friends. Father Evans' four daughters and son were, as near as I can learn, born on Bush River. They were well educated and highly accomplished, but, like their father, left the Friends. The eldest daughter was such an admirer of Paradise Lost that, 'tis said, it induced her father to name his village after its illustrious author. Evans was a man of more than ordinary ability, who, it was said, could see as far into a trade as any man. He was a full-handed man in Cincinnati, but the shrinkage of currency and of values after the war of 1812, so reduced him as to cause his return to Milton. His family was for years what might be called 'Quaker Aristocrats,' when disowned. He possessed much courage, decision and fortitude. Whilst sitting at his bedside one night during his last sickness, at his request I read a newspaper article on the machinery propelling powers of animal magnetism. When done he said, 'Young people will live to see wonderful things in mechanical and physical science, which I have not seen.' A prediction fully realized. Not one of his descendants now lives in this county, but a grandson is a millionaire in St. Louis, Missouri.

"John, Joseph and William Wright, next mentioned in the Annals, settled and died, I think, (except John, who died in Newberry,) in Clinton County, Ohio, in Indiana and Illinois. Two other brothers not mentioned, namely, Thomas and Isaac Wright, came West also, where, in 1834, the author saw Isaac, his great uncle. He was then a little, old, dingy man and said to be intemperate.

"James Brooks must have died in early times, but two sons who came with him, Nimrod and John, were practical farmers, both rearing many children and living to good age.

"Joseph Thompson came with a number of children, some of whom were married, and settled in the region called Ludlow's Creek, a tributary of the Stillwater. He did not, however, live long at his new home, but his children did. One of his sons was a preacher, though never recommended, awhile among the Friends, and next among the New Lights, or Christian Church. But few of them belong now to the Friends.

"James Patty must have been the father of James, David and Charles Patty, who came also from Newberry, as did three married sisters. The author well knew the last three

Pattys, but not the first; so he must have died not many years after arriving. James Patty had a large portion of '*suaviter in modo,*' and perhaps much '*fortiter in re.*' Such were his pleasantness and equanimity that

> "'Along the cool, sequestered vale of life
> He kept the noiseless tenor of his way.'

"His marriage with Anna Brown at Bush River not long before their removal is said to have been partly caused by the jocular recommendation of some, or one of the young folks. James was not acquainted with her, but had seen her at church and noticed that she limped a little in her walk. After hearing her fitness for him described he answered with characteristic gravity: 'Who is this Anna Brown? Is she the girl that when she walks goes *one pound ten?*' After marriage he found that she would '*Storm like March, but not weep like April.*' It seemed through their whole marital life that he was as proper a mate for her as Socrates was for Xantippe. On one occasion I heard of when she and her husband went to a magistrate's office to sign a deed of land conveyance; she was asked in private by the magistrate, as the law required, if she did this signing under her own will, or under fear of her husband. 'No,' said she, almost indignant, 'I ain't afraid of Jimps.' 'That's one time,' said Squire T., laughing, 'that I know she told the truth.'

"She, however, like others had good qualities. She brought him four sons and five daughters, only two of whom are now living. The sons were of more than ordinary ability, and three of them followed professions, all showing that they had not received bad maternal training. One anecdote of James Patty is similar to that of John Wright told in the Annals. For many years he rode a mule to West Branch. whose hybrid neighings or brayings often broke upon the stillness of the meeting. Forgetting the mule once he walked home and when told of it was taken aback; but whether he said 'Dads me, Anna!' or 'O pshaw!' I am not informed. In conclusion, his whole life was economical, quiet and peaceful. He died in 1833 and his widow about the year 1846.

"Gabriel McCoole, with his five sons and two daughters, came here, I think, in 1806. His wife dying some years after, he spent his last days among his children and grandchildren. He was a highly conscientious and good old man, but his sons partook far more of the ways of the world. One of them, Thomas, who was married to a daughter of old 'Tanner Thompson,' [see Annals] in Newberry District, had a hankering as well as an aptitude for office. He served for many years as Squire, in what was called the 'Creek Nation,' composed mainly of Newberry people and their descendants. If he did not exhibit the wisdom and legal acumen of a Hale he tried to the dignity of a Mansfield. Many of the suits which he decided were unique in their character; two of which I will briefly relate. One F. Jones, not a Newberry but Georgia Jones, the laziest man 'in all creation,' had rented a small farm to W. Friend, reserving a small house in which he lived, and a favorite apple tree. Their residences were near together and for a time things went well. After awhile Jones, who, though too lazy to work, was not too lazy to get mad, became offended at something, and as Friend's geese had eaten a few of his reserved apples lying under the tree, he sought satisfaction by suing him, Friend, for damages. Spectators, as well as witnesses, attended the trial, which, being managed by the parties, was rather devoid of declarations, replications and argued technicalities, resting entirely upon its proved merits. When the one-sided and almost infinitesimal testimony was ended, Squire McCoole put on his dignity and slowly patting the floor with his foot to keep time, thus gave his decision: 'I hardly know how to apply law to this case, so I will just strike at *Justas*. I decide that W. Friend pay F. Jones six and one-fourth cents damage, and each party pay his own costs.' The guffaws of the spectators can be better imagined than described. The defendant was well pleased. He, having made little or no cost, had little or none to pay, while the plaintiff had several dollars. He, the plaintiff, was the only one there that could see nothing to laugh at. Could any one have decided that case better than did old Squire McCoole?

"The other case was between a German and a Tennessean. It was hard to tell which of them was most tricky. Lawyers managed the case, and, of course, there was much wordy warring. One of them being more prolix than pointed, the magistrate's patience gave out and he stopped him short with,

2   A

'Well, Samuel, I guess you've spoke about long enough; I guess I'll have to give judgment against you.' 'Why,' said Samuel in much affected surprise, 'haven't I proved thus and so?' 'Yes,' answered the Squire, 'you've proved it, but I don't believe your witnesses.' The discomfited attorney felt about small enough to crawl into an auger hole. Squire McCoole's decisions were believed to be generally correct and were but seldom reversed through a long official course. His chirography was almost unreadable and may have resembled Senator Choate's, whose writing was said to look like the marks made by a spider, after crawling out of an inkstand.

"Squire McCoole reached good old age and died in Iowa but a few years ago. I may mention that Gabriel, his father, died on Stillwater not far from the year 1828. None of his other sons merit being mentioned.

"John Coate is next mentioned in the Annals, but I think 'John' is a mistake. Marmaduke Coate, with six sons, came here among the earlier emigrants. His sons, Moses, Henry and Samuel, having married at Newberry. His other sons, John, James and Jesse, married here. They all became prosperous farmers, reared numerous families, some dying at advanced age; all dying in membership with Friends. Henry Coate became a most useful and efficient blacksmith, making sickles for many years, supplying that desideratum to the farmers of Stillwater Valley. He amassed a handsome estate and left it to his children. Old Marmaduke, the father, did not live many years after coming here; so, little is known about him, but of his numerous descendants it may be said: They are an honor to Miami County and do no discredit to Newberry District.

"Big Isaac Hollingsworth comes next, who is so graphically, though briefly, described on pages 32 and 33* of the Annals. He possessed great physical strength and unbounded courage During the Revolution when a British officer approached his corn crib he was forbidden entrance. The officer drew his sword and threatened. Big Isaac went to him, took the sword from him, saying: 'Thus far shalt thou go, but no farther.' The officer succumbed. Once, when he was about starting to meeting, a poor Irishman accosted him desiring employment.

---

* Part I., 29, 30.

Isaac having nothing else for him to do set him to moving a pile of stones. On returning from meeting and finding the job done he had him to move the stones back. After which he paid him. While on the road to Ohio he was one day sitting upon a log while his horses were eating. A man came along and asked him where he was moving. 'I am not moving,' said Isaac, 'I am sitting still.' 'Well, where are you bound then?' 'I am not bound at all,' said he, 'I am a free man.' The discomfited man passed on. When reprimanded by his daughter for his uncourteous answers he naively answered that he did not know that it was any of that man's business where he was going. Five daughters and three sons, six of whom were married, accompanied him, making quite a company. All of them, except two daughters and with husbands, settled near him in Miami County. There amongst wolves, deer and other wild animals, they built their rude cabins in the

" 'Dark, mephitic tangled woods.'

"Those woods or forests they began to level; to build cabins for shelter and clear the lands for cultivation. Log rollings, which I need not describe, became common. The practice of wearing suspenders, vulgarly called gallowes, was then coming into vogue among the young men. Big Isaac looked upon this innovation as savoring of pride, and as he possessed '*fortiter in re*' without '*suaviter in modo*,' when he met the young men at log rollings or stable raisings, with suspenders unprotected by coat or jacket, he would, when opportunity offered, thrust his forefinger under one of them and giving a jerk the button had to fly. It was useless for the boys to get angry on such occasions, so their plan was to watch and avoid him. Yet with all his exterior rudeness he had a good and tender heart; more internal than external piety. This I have learned from his children. He used to say that his crops never grew better than when Susie, his wife, (mentioned on pages 33 and 34* of the Annals) was away from home preaching. By which it seems he gave her all necessary assistance. He died of pleurisy in 1809, aged about 61; and though having enjoyed but three years residence, the opening in the forest, the buildings and fences long remained as the work of his hands.

---

* Part I., 31, 32.

"His second son Joel merits a place in Newberry history. Born in that district in 1778 he married there and came to Ohio with two children. Possessing the size, strength and courage of his father, he had more suaviter in his deportment, making himself agreeable to every one. Of his five stalwart sons, none were quite equal to him, and the man was not known who could break him down at the handspike. The forest soon showed his power and industry, for it melted away, succeeded by teeming fields of grain and grass. Being of an adventurous spirit he made frequent voyages to New Orleans on flat-bottomed boats loaded with pork and flour, for himself and neighbors. These enterprises were attended with much hardship and danger, yet Joel appeared to delight in them. During the year 1830 he, with his wife, returned on a visit to Newberry and hunted up their friends and relatives yet living. Boating and clearing having measurably ceased, Joel's rather restless spirit induced him to move again and settle in the Indiana forests. There he cleared another farm and lived until near his 80th year, when one day being engaged in butchering and rendering lard, he fell upon the floor and died, perhaps of heart disease. I believe he is the only Newberry man emigrant that met with instantaneous death. His elder brother William and younger brother John had left Ohio long before he did and the deaths of the three occurred within three months of each other, the news of which was received by their only surviving sister all in one day.

"Of Isaac Hollingsworth's daughters, namely, Rachel, Ruth, Keziah, Sarah and Susanna, the four first were married at Bush River, and the last, Susanna, in Ohio. She married Elisha Jones, a twin brother of Elijah Jones mentioned on page 115 of the Annals. As Elisha moved to Ohio in 1805, Susanna the following year, and they married soon after, it looks as if they might have made the marital agreement in Newberry District. They settled on land joining their father's, and being young, courageous and industrious, a farm was opened and plenty was smiling around them. Nearly eleven years of married life had passed and they had become the parents of five children, when a terrible event occurred, which no human prescien could discern, nor human power avert. They each had a saddle which hung together against the wall.

One night they awoke and saw a bright spot on Susanna's saddle. They first thought a hunter was passing with a torch ; but the bright spot did not move and a visit to the window disclosed no torch. What could this mean? they wondered. Not long afterwards, about 10 o'clock in the morning, a small cloud was passing southeastward. Its ominous rumblings were heard while passing and it went over the house. Susanna had stepped to the open door with something in her hand, when a tremendous peal was heard, not only there, but far over the country, and she fell lifeless on the floor.

> " 'The fiery bolt from upper air,
>   Attendant of the rain,
>   Which oft assumes the Ash to tear
>   And Oak to rive in twain;—
>   Descending from its lofty height,
>   To kill instead of save,
>   With speed of thought and matchless might,
>   Had hurled her to the grave.'

"This occurred in 1817, not far from the time of her brother-in-law, Elijah Jones' death. On the 66th anniversary of Susanna's funeral, two surviving children, too young to have retained her image, went to her grave to drop their tears there and etch anew the moss-grown inscription on her tombstone. I may further add that she was the youngest daughter of Susanna Hollingsworth mentioned in the Annals, and that I, the author, am her youngest child. Further, I may mention the remarkable fact that the brother, Joel, and the sister, Susanna, met instantaneous deaths. Newberry, I believe, furnishes no more such examples.

"Before Isaac Hollingsworth's family is dismissed I must give a short after-biography of his wife, my most revered maternal grandmother. Left a widow, as before stated, in 1809, at the age of 54, she lived among her children the remainder of her life. She made religious visits after her husband's death, one of which was, I think, to Newberry, others to the East. Possessing an excellent memory and having long experience, she was an excellent conversationalist. With great interest have I heard her tell the fearful tales of the Revolution in Newberry District; of Hal Foster, the desperate Tory and criminal, who, refusing to heed the warning her father had given, was shot through the head after peace was made. Her piety, equanimity and kindliness, particularly towards her grandchildren, were such that they loved her with the most ardent affection, believing that no grandmother could be better. One Sunday evening in July, 1830, she went on horseback from her daughter's residence to that of her son-in-law, his wife being dead. On the way she said to her accompanying young grandson : 'I am going to thy father's just to die.' This was said with as much calmness of feeling as though she had said I am going there to live. The next day she was taken ill. To her son Joel who visited her she said 'I am going, but not as speedily as I could wish.' Death came to her as a friend. Near the close of the week she died and was buried on the following Sunday. Her sister, Charity Cook, mentioned in the Annals, traveled extensively in the ministry. She once crossed the Atlantic, visiting the Friends' churches in England and Ireland. In the last country she had an interview with the Irish giant, Patrick O'Brien, who respectfully received her testimony. She died in 1820, but the particulars thereof are unknown. Another sister, Kirial Hanks, not mentioned in the Annals, a widow, came here with three sons and two daughters. Her second son, James, became a school teacher and most efficient surveyor. Her eldest daughter, Mary, possessed more than ordinary ability; was useful in the church, but was the only one of the children not disowned.

"Judge O'Neall appears to have forgotten Big Isaac Hollingsworth's brothers, namely, James, George and Nathan, who went also to Ohio; the two first bringing families. Their descendants were strong, hardy and adventurous, spreading themselves over portions of Ohio, Indiana and Iowa. Of all the Newberry emigrants none were equal to the Hollingsworths in physical strength and none excelled them in courage. Being of peaceable natures they sought no quarrels, and being of superior prowess, quarrels were not sought with them. I do not know of any criminal record that has the name of a Hollingsworth upon its pages; which is honorable to them, though many are not now members of the Friends' Church.

"William O'Neall, whose name in the Annals follows that of Isaac Hollingsworth, was a Quaker minister somewhat advanced in years when he left Newberry. He seems to have dropped the O' from his name, for, in Ohio, he and his decendants have Neall as their surname. Two sons, James and Mahlon, came with him and James became a preacher at an early age, living and dying a very humble and pious man. William was employed to teach some of the earliest schools; but really was better qualified to preach the gospel than to teach the sciences, as the following anecdote will show: A young full grown man took a sum in long division to him which he had worked out, desiring to know if it was done correctly. After examining it the teacher handed it back, saying with serious candor : 'Well, Jonathan, it looks very pretty, but I really don't know whether it is done right or not.' His school government was not, like that of Richard Clegg, of Newberry, sustained by the birch, but by pleasantness and kindness, by which he generally succeeded. It indeed took a hard-featured boy to violate the rules of so old and good a teacher. Once, however, they trespassed so far upon his forbearance that he told them 'if they did not behave he would bring Granny tomorrow.' This seems to have had the desired effect, for one of the offenders said many years afterwards, 'I thought if Granny had to come and see my misbehavior I'd quit right off.' This good old man, it was said, was once accosted by a presumptuous skeptic who said: 'Mr. Neall, I am an unbeliever in the Bible, but can deliver as good a discourse as you, and if you do not believe me just listen and I'll convince you.' The old man assenting, he took his place and spoke his piece. Asking what he thought of it, the answer was: 'What thee has said is good enough, but it has come through a very dirty channel.' He died at an advanced age more than sixty years ago.

"In following the Annals I mention only those with whom I've had personal or second-hand knowledge, and whose life here was worthy of a brief notice.

"Samuel, David and William Miles, relatives, were worthy, industrious and prosperous farmers, who lived to good age, leaving behind them a numerous and enterprising posterity, many of whom are living in other and newer States.

"Samuel Brown was a rather elderly man when he left Newberry. He was a man of more than ordinary ability, but rather too much governed by strong impulses that sometimes caused him trouble. He left, when removing, a son, Joshua, who departing from Quaker habits and teachings, went to Charleston and became quite rich by privateering during the last war with England. Being elated with riches, he treated his venerable father, who in after years returned to Newberry and then went to see him, with such coldness and neglect that it greatly wounded the old man's heart. Returning to Ohio, he was said to have spoken condemnatorily of the manner by which his son had obtained his wealth ; uttering the trite but rather vulgar expression 'that what comes in over the devil's back generally goes out under his belly.' In after life this was fulfilled, the sheriff selling even his bed to pay his creditors. He brought another son, Samuel, to Ohio, who also caused more sorrow than joy to him. He was the father of Anna Brown, mentioned before as the wife of James Patty. He died in 1827 at an advanced age.

"William Mills lived and died a plain farmer in Warren County, Ohio. Charles Mills, not mentioned in the Annals, was educated at Newberry by John B. Mtichell and Richard Clegg. Coming to Ohio, he made school teaching the principal business of his life for a period of forty years. He was a good penman or scribe, and was remarkable for his success in school government, causing his scholars to both respect and fear him. Some of his scholars were children of parents who had gone with him to the Newberry schools, and who always showed willingness to employ him in teaching. In his latter days he used to speak with pleasure of the positions his many pupils occupied in different communities. He died in Indiana some twenty years ago, remembered with the kindest regards by his few living scholars, whose hair is now whitened by age.

"James, John, Benjamin and Samuel Coppock emigrated from Newberry, with many more of that name, and settled in Miami County. Many of them did not retain their Society rights, but were nevertheless good citizens. Moses, son of James, was a very solid and useful member of the Friends' church, dying at an advanced age a few years ago.

"Abel and James Insco were brothers. Abel was son-in-law of Thomas Pearson mentioned near the first of these memoirs. He was remarkable for stuttering, and doubtlessly caused many a laugh at Newberry, as he afterwards did in Ohio. I've heard it told that while living at Newberry he was at a corn-shucking where a man who had been caught stealing a turkey kicked his dog. Not liking it, he said to the man, 'I don't even allow thee to say, tut, tut, tut-turkey to my dog.' I was told that at another corn-shucking, or husking, a man who had offended him accused him of having given him a blow and threatened prosecution. To this Abel replied whenever accused : 'Sh sh-sh-show the wound.' The men who were carrying away the shucks in the dark were much amused, and as no one saw him strike and he wouldn't own it, the matter had to drop. Abel more than fifty years ago died childless, and James' children being all girls the name Insco is now possessed only by his grandson, Insco Yount, and which being his first name, will at his death become extinct.

"The Annals mention Jesse Spray, which may be a mistake. I well knew old Samuel Spray, who lived in another county. He was a minister who lived in the time of the Revolution, and one whom I have heard preach. His daughter Dinah, who was born in the South, was rather eminent as a minister, and often traveled as such. Both father and daughter have for many years been dead.

"Samuel Teague was not originally a Quaker. He was reared near Black Jack, in Newberry District. Being a lad during the Revolution, he had escaped conscription by the Whigs, but was exposed to the cruelties of Tories. One day they were seen approaching the house, when a puncheon was lifted and he was hidden under the floor. The Tories came in and by their terrible demonstrations so frightened his sick father that he rose from his bed and ran across the adjoining lot. The Tories shot him down, hacked him over with their swords and so stripped the house of everything in the clothing line that Samuel had to take the shirt from his back to bury his father in. Truly, these were the times that tried men's souls. Samuel Teague, to avenge the murder of his father, to serve his country, or both, afterwards enlisted in the service of the patriots, but to what extent I have never learned ; but presumably until the end of the war. He married and lived at Newberry until the exodus, when with a considerable family he came to this (Miami) county. He purchased and cleared land successfully and became an efficient and useful citizen. He joined the Friends, I think, some time before leaving Newberry. He

was a Quaker in the strictest sense of the word, hardly toler-
ating singing. One day as he was husking corn under his
crib-shed, assisted by two Newberry boys named John Turner
and Elisha McCook, he was asked if McCook, who was a good
singer, might not give them a song. Consenting rather reluc-
tantly, McCook did his best, acquitting himself well. When
finished and asked if that was not good singing, he replied,
'Perhaps it was if there is such a thing as good singing.' It
was said he could have obtained a pension in his latter days,
but he would not apply for one. He was very useful in his
church, lived to advanced age, leaving a numerous train of
descendants, his children all keeping their rights in the church,
though none of them are now living.

"Three Pemberton brothers, namely, Isaiah, Robert and John,
came from Newberry to Miami County, perhaps being sons of
George, mentioned in the Annals. They opened farms and
reared families some of whom yet live. John in after life went
into a state of 'melancholia.' Concluding he was useless to the
world and had better leave it, he sent for James Hall, a once
Newberry neighbor, but not a Quaker, and asked him if he did
not think that he (John) had better commit suicide. Hall,
who, though illiterate, had common sense, encouraged him in
the project. Well, how had it better be done? Would not
drowning in Ludlow Creek, which was near, be the best way
of accomplishing it? 'Yes,' replied Hall, 'and I'll go down
with you and if necessary help you do it.' Having arrived at
the creek, Pemberton stood hesitating upon the bank, when Hall
shoved him in. He would not drown, however, but came out
with a good wetting and, what was better, an entire cure of his
suicidal desires. He lived many years afterwards, but in a state
of semi-dementia, an object of pity to those who saw him.

"The Inmans, several in number, settled near the above
named creek and were plain, unpretentious farmers.

"James Steddam must have settled in Warren County, and
must have died long ago. His two sons, John and Samuel,
not mentioned in the Annals, settled there and became two of
the most prosperous farmers in the county. They lived to good
age and left behind them numerous and worthy posterity.
John Crumpton, or properly Campton, and Isaac Cook appear
to have settled in the adjoining county of Clinton, and, like

the others, were industrious, prosperous and efficient church members.

"John Jay merits special mention, the removal of whom and family was more loss to Newberry than that of any other. He was married during the Revolution, and his seven sons and three daughters were born and, in part, married there. Courage, industry, enterprise and thrift were characteristics of the entire family. He and his sons were remarkable for rearing and training horses. No other seven brothers drove as many fair horse teams as they; could crack their whips as loud and haul as heavy loads. In those early days grain, flour, pork and merchandise were transported on wagons and often long trips had to be made. Their names were Jesse, Samuel, Walt D. (always called Denny), Thomas, John, William and James. All lived to advanced age except Thomas, who died soon after the birth of his fourth child. Five of them lived on lands adjoining and reared such families that they long had the name of the 'Jay Settlement,' a name that carried with it the idea of industry, enterprise, success and independent fortune, coupled with such honesty, probity and morality as made them a blessing to the country. John, the father, died in their midst in or about 1828, having lived to see his good example followed by both his sons and daughters, all retaining their rights in church and some being pre-eminent in it. Walter Denny, the third son, was a most remarkable man. One who knew phrenology said he had a head much like that of Napoleon Bonaparte, and in many traits he resembled him. In planning and carrying on difficult enterprises he showed large combination and concentration, qualities essential for a general. He also showed indomitable courage with prudence, hardly knowing what fear of men was. These, together with great activity and push, which made him succeed in his enterprises, would have made him a formidable leader of armies had he turned his mind that way. Indeed, he was past middle life before, as he himself said, he had been completely changed from a state of nature to one of grace. A part of his sons attained to eminence in the college and pulpit. He was the first man that refused to furnish whiskey at his log-rollings, having seen evil grow out of it. And when some of his invited neighbors told him that they would not help him without it, he replied, 'They might stay away, for he and his horses would try to do the rolling without them.' So they had to succumb.

"In the year 1850, after an absence of forty-seven years from Newberry, he, together with this writer, returned to it. He sought out the few of his old acquaintance living. Amongst these was Judge O'Neall, who, though a number of years his junior, had gone to the same school taught by John B. Mitchell and Richard Clegg. They had a long, pleasant talk over the scenes of their early days and other matters, during which Denny asked the Judge this question : 'Does thee remember when thee and my brother Sam spent nearly all an afternoon in trying to divide twelve by four, and then didn't get it done?' The Judge, who was then quite a boy, and who, like brother Sam, was a tyro in figures, did not remember it. O'Neall, like many others when divested of official robes, exhibited that vein of humor and facetiousness to his old schoolmates which runs through much of his writings. He told of two tom-cats that fought over the mouth of a poorly covered dry-well and both fell into it. The owner of the well descended to help them out; but the belligerent felines not only resented his proffered help, but ran repeatedly up its sides, falling back upon his neck and shoulders, scratching him severely. He quickly got out of the well, but how the cats escaped I did not learn. Another story he told, which, if comical, was almost tragical. A warlike family of many years back, perhaps the Jess Dorvis one, of which I've heard my father tell, often had family battles, the father leading one side, the mother on the other and the children dividing. One day, after a set-to in which, as usual, they were only bruised and blood-stained, the chivalrous husband proposed that they finish after the manner of 'the honorable code.' 'You take this gun,' said he, 'and I'll take that; you get behind this post; I will get behind that yonder, and we will shoot whenever one of us can see enough of the other.' The wife agreed; they took their places, and when she peeped around the post her husband fired and she fell. He and the boys promptly dug a grave, but when they went to take her to it they found she had risen and gone into the house. To ease their disappointment the father said, 'Never mind, boys; I'll fetch her sure next time.' She was wounded near the eye, but not fatally. The Judge told this with such an air of *nonchalance* that even old Quaker Denny was almost amused by it. Denny, while at Newberry, also made visits to his old church sisters, the widows Hawkins and Pugh, the latter being seventy-five years old and eleven years his senior. These, with Nancy O'Neall, whom he also visited, were the only survivors who attended Bush River meetings when he did. He and myself were guests of L. J. Jones the most of the time when at Newberry; and perhaps L. J. Jones and his lady may remember how, to show his activity, he would skip upon their porch floor, letting himself clear down on one foot with the other thrust out; then, rising half way up, would reverse them and sink upon the other, continuing the exercise until he had set them all to laughing. This feat I have never seen performed by any other one. In Ohio those who saw it called it the Quaker dance. He could take a wagon whip, throw himself on his back, or spring astride of the ridge-pole of his wagon, and crack it round his head, following the tune of 'Yankee Doodle.' We may well suppose his horses knew what the cracking of his whip meant. It was said that he could come nearer hitting all four of them at once than any other teamster, and his team never failed to pull its best when he required it. Though his business brought him often in the company of rude and immoral men, his candor and courage preserved him from imposition. Once when a bullying fellow threatened to whip him he replied, it is said, 'Well, if thee will whip me thee must, but I'll keep the mosquitoes from thee while thee's at it.' That was enough; the man let him alone. He had been a most incessant laborer, and it might almost have been said of him, as the poet said of Charles XII. of Sweden :

> "'A frame of ádamant, a soul of fire ;
> No dangers fright him and no labors tire.'

Not the fire of unhallowed ambition and war, but the baptismal fire of the Prince of Peace. Highly conscientious, he never swerved from walking in the path of apparent duty; he never departed from plain apparel or language; and whatever enterprise of a public nature received his sanction also received his support. His vigor at the time of his Newberry visit, though he was sixty four years old, was such that, though he walked all day, ascending and descending the mountains, he was not weary. He had given up labor shortly before that time and after his return to Ohio lived at his ease, often visiting other meetings until his death, which happened near 1870. Though he had more of Luther's firmness than Melancthon's mildness, he was well fitted to accomplish what he did during a life of over eighty years. That he had faults, is true; and who has not? But they were nearly hidden by his virtues, and I feel warranted in saying that I would have trusted his word, his honesty, probity and reliability as far as those of any man I ever knew. I admire him as a man the like of whom I never saw before and will never see again; not seeking

> " The boast of heraldry, and the pomp of power,'
> *　　*　　*　　*　　*　　*
> But 'down the sequestered vale of private life
> Pursuing the noiseless tenor of his way.'

Such was Walter Denny Jay, an honor to Newberry, his native county, and to Miami, his adopted one. Well might we inscribe upon his tombstone :

> " 'Requiescat in pace !'

"Thomas and Isaac Hasket left Newberry during or about 1806. They were carpenters, as Hugh O'Neall informed me, and built the Bush River meeting-house in 1798. Thomas, of whom I knew but little, went to Indiana, but Isaac to Ohio. He was born in 1778, married at Newberry, and took his wife, Rebecca Evans, and their first child to Miami County on horseback. He was a large and strong man, but very modest and diffident. One anecdote of him shows that, though a serious young man, he could be jocular. One morning while at mill, perhaps Hugh O'Neall's, he was standing by an out-door fire, when David Jones, uncle to L. J. Jones, and myself, came also to the fire. In crossing the mill-pond he had fallen into it and was dripping wet. Wishing to be funny and make the best of it, he said to Isaac, 'Mr. Hasket, you see, I'm a Baptist; but I suppose you're a Quaker.' 'Yes,' said Isaac, 'I believe in going to the fire this cool morning, but thee believes in going into the water.' Friend Hasket, young and sturdy, went to work with his axe, felled the forest, and soon had fields in cultivation. He helped to build the West Branch Quarterly meeting-house in 1808, just twenty years after building the one at Bush River. The West Branch house, built of brick, by the Newberry Friends mainly, still stands, having been lately renovated, while the parent one, I learn much to my regret, has been demolished. Friend Hasket prospered. and reared five stalwart sons, none of whom ever thought of being broken down at a handspike lift. He was a very worthy and upright man, respected by all who knew him. He died in 1848.

"Thomas Pearson, following Hasket, has already been written about. The two Enoch Pearsons next mentioned were born in 1760 and 1761. One was the son of Thomas, the other was his nephew. They brought, or came with, many children, not one of whom is living. Three other Enochs came, which, with one born here, made six. They were designated thus: Preacher Enoch, Blacksmith Enoch, Lame Enoch, Pony Enoch, Nuck Enoch and Teent Enoch. All are now dead. Preacher Enoch was a man of high standing, both at Newberry and West Branch. He was a son of Thomas. He visited as minister once, if not more, North Carolina yearly meeting and the remnant of Bush River Friends. He traveled much. His sons, Robert, Thomas and Isaac, were worthy and useful men. He died in 1850, and the Blacksmith in 1860.

"Of the Thomases who emigrated, several are not mentioned. They were Abel, Isaac, John, William and Nehemiah. They came with considerable families and formed a settlement for a while called Thomastown. They were plain, modest, clever and moderately successful farmers, which about comprises their history. The same may be said of the Duncans, who came here with them, who died in early times, not leaving many children.

"The elder David Jenkins, next mentioned, was the man to whom my father, Elisha Jones, an orphan nine years old, was apprenticed in 1795. Baal Butler, a Quaker of some note, was the guardian who bound him until his eighteenth year.

"Barclay Benham and another Friend with two initials, B. D., in his name, seem to have escaped the author of the Annals. Their descendants are in Indiana, Clinton County and elsewhere, so I know but little about them. It was said that David found a joint-snake at Newberry which, on being switched, flew to pieces, afterwards becoming united. The present inhabitants ought to know if such an incredible thing ever happens there.* David removed to Ohio with Elisha Jones in 1805, who, though out of his apprenticeship, had continued with him and learned the chairmaker's trade. Settling with his family near the Great Miami, he cleared a farm, where he died nearly forty years afterwards. David Jenkins, Jr., went to Ohio a young man full of expectation and promise. He became school teacher and magistrate, holding the last position, I believe, until his death. He twice at least returned to Newberry, the last time during the winter of 1839. His long continuance in office made him about as good a judge of law as the Troy attorney, and his decisions were seldom reversed. He was so useful in his township that the people could hardly do without him. His death occurred many years ago, but at what time I have not learned.

"Two Wallace Joneses, father and son, emigrated from Newberry about the year 1806. The son was born in 1773, but the time of the father's birth I cannot learn. The most that need be said of him is, that he reared a family and died in 1823. Wallace, Jr., possessed much skill and courage. Not born a Friend, he was in early life not governed by their principles, and so at times violated one command of the Decalogue. One night when at a neighbor's where he should not have been, the wronged husband unexpectedly came upon him. While the man was jerking down his gun the guilty one rushed into the yard, hurrying across it. The man fired, but, it being dark, missed him. Wallace, fearing nothing but the loaded gun, now empty, turned round and coolly said : 'You are a d——d poor marksman when you can't hit a man ten steps off.' It is not reported that he stayed till the gun was reloaded, nor that he went there afterwards. He became a military officer, and continued such until he emigrated, when he took his uniform with him. His four sons and two daughters were nearly all, if not quite, born in the district, which some of them remembered. Being a carpenter and mechanic in wood, his services were sought after and he did well at his

---

* NOTE.—The compiler of these Annals when he was a boy often heard such stories told of the joint-snake, but the stories were never true. The joint-snake, poor fellow, is like other snakes. If he is ever broken up into two or more pieces, he never becomes whole again.

trade. His wife, the daughter of James Patty, was a mild, forbearing Quaker, and her influence, together with that of her neighbors, caused him to become seriously concerned for himself, and he at length applied to the Friends for membership among them. They, according to custom, appointed a committee to visit, learn the sincerity of his heart, and report accordingly. During their conference they asked him what he had done with his uniform. Forgetting himself, he answered, in his old strain, 'I've sold it to Sam Edwards (his Newberry nephew), and I reckon he thinks he'll play h—l with it.' Whether the committee smiled or frowned at this expression I am not informed; but they reported favorably. He was accepted as a member, becoming a very consistent and useful one. His brusqueness and comicality, however, never entirely left him. Once, after reading at West Branch church a marriage certificate which was to be signed only by the groom and bride, he forgot to read the one to be afterwards signed by the witnesses. Discovering his mistake, he exclaimed: 'I'll be whipped if I haint forgot the last of it !'' and then read it amidst the tittering of the large congregation. After sitting down with the married couple, together with a large number of guests, to a sumptuous repast, and thinking there was useless delay in giving the signal to 'fall to,' he exclaimed: 'I wish somebody would tell us to go to eatin', for I am tired of settin' idle so long.' This provoked another titter, but every one knew what allowance to make for Uncle Wallace. We went back to his native Newberry, I think, in 1836, but found only few of his old neighbors and acquaintances living. Returning to Ohio, he lived until, I think, 1854, when he peacefully passed away, having, notwithstanding a few peculiarities, lived a very correct, useful and conscientious life. His second son, John, born in 1798, became when young a minister of some note and traveled in other lands. During 1831 he returned with an approving mission to Newberry, where at Bush River meeting-house (where he had gone when quite a child) he preached to a large congregation of willing listeners. Judge O'Neall, who remembered him of old, I learned, attended his meeting, and after its close invited him to his house. Seeing John's timid hesitancy, the Judge became earnest and told him he would almost consider it an 'open affront' if he did not go home with him.

2   B

This expression caused compliance, and no doubt the visit was mutually satisfactory. John traveled considerably in the ministry after that trip, removing to Missouri long afterwards, where a few years ago he died. A grandson of his elder brother, Philemon, is an active surveyor and lawyer, being now prosecuting attorney of Miami County.

"I must not omit to write of Samuel Reagan, called Blacksmith Sammy by way of distinction from younger ones of that name. He came here, I think, in 1806, with five sons and one daughter. Four sons were born in this county, in all nine, who grew up to respectability and married here. Only three and his daughter Rachel, who married Isaac Pearson of Newberry, retained their rights among the Friends. Samuel bought and settled on good land, having a large spring, on which he cleared a large farm and raised an abundance of fruits, particularly cherries. He was a most skillful and useful mechanic in both iron and wood, not ceasing work until compelled by age. Regular in attendance at meeting, he was almost as regular in nodding, if not sleeping, when there, attributable, perhaps, to his almost ceaseless activity. The time of his death I know not, though it happened many years ago.

"Tanner Thompson, the leather man, I think came here and died a great many years ago. I knew several of his sons, but their lives do not warrant particular notice.

"I have given a short biography of those of whom I had personal knowledge, mentioned on pages 31 and 32 of the Annals, besides some not mentioned there. On page 33 first comes the name of Joseph Furnas. Perhaps he was the father of Robert and Thomas W. Furnas, whom I well knew and who emigrated from Newberry with a considerable number of children. The old man must have died not long after his emigration. He must have had other sons whom I never knew, for there is a long list of Furnases, all related. A granddaughter, Sarah, traveled in Egypt, Palestine, and about all the countries of note in the old and new worlds. A short time ago she published at West Milton her 'Ten Years' Travel,' as interesting a work of its kind as I have ever read. Robert Furnas lived in Warren County, dying there many years ago a plain old Quaker; while his brother Thomas W. lost his right, became a politician, and was several times sheriff of Miami County.

He had a wonerfully active son, perhaps the most fleet-footed man in the country. His son Robert, I have heard, went to California* and became its governor.

"John Furnas, born at Newberry in 1798, became wealthy, reared a numerous family, did much public business, besides going to the Legislature. A man of irreproachable life, and member of the Christian Church, he was in the fullness of his years not very long ago gathered in the garner of the great hereafter as a shock of corn fully ripe. The few Furnases of whom I have written may serve as specimens of the race; a race of whom the present inhabitants of Newberry need never feel ashamed. The Kellys and Kirks, I think, settled in other counties, and little is known about them.

"Samuel Gauntt never came here. James Brooks I think I mentioned before. Of the O'Nealls I have seen John and Henry many years ago living among my Newberry relatives in Green County, Indiana.· John was a plain old Quaker professor, but Henry seemed to be more of a politician than churchman. Thomas taught school in Miami County nearly seventy years ago. His wife, the daughter of old Thomas Pearson heretofore mentioned, died about that time, which caused the breaking up of his family. When and where he died I know not.

"Of the women who emigrated to Ohio mentioned in the Annals on pages 33 and 34 I have already written. One sister of Charity Cook and Susannah Hollingsworth, named Kesiah and not mentioned, deserves to be. She was born in 1763 and married a man named Hanks. After becoming the mother of three sons and two daughters her husband died leaving to her the support of their minor children. She brought them to Ohio with her relatives, among whom they were divided until maturity. The eldest daughter, Mary, became a woman of uncommon sense and ability. Coming to the wilderness at the age of fourteen she soon accustomed herself to all its conditions, making the best of whatever happened to her. While living with her uncle, Big Isaac Hollingsworth, she learned the art of making corn mush, which I think needs no describing. It was said that when her uncle found a lump of dry meal in his mush encrusted in a covering of dough, he would take it in his spoon and dash it across

* Nebraska, instead of California.—[J. A. C.]

the table at her, which, if it hit her on the face, was not pleasant. Remonstrance she knew was useless, as the old man was immovable in his way of thinking and doing. So her only remedy was to stir the mush better in the future. In after life she was a very useful member in the female part of the Friends Church, who, as my readers may not know, had a department to themselves. She died in Iowa a few years ago. Her brother, James, was born in 1796, and was about ten years old at the time of their removal. He had uncommon mental ability, easily became a scholar and school teacher. He learned trigonometry and became one of the most efficient surveyors in Miami County. Liking the employment he followed it until age rendered its abandonment necessary. His conversation was always moral, instructive and entertaining. He possessed the philosophy of contentment and was satisfied with the realization of Agar's prayer, 'Give me neither poverty nor riches,' etc. If he had possessed the energy and push of some of the Newberry emigrants he would have made his mark in the world. But these he had not, and made what the world calls a failure; but perhaps stands as high in the estimation of his Maker as though he had filled great earthly positions. He died several years ago in Iowa. His brothers and other sister need no particular notice.

"There were many Halls and Pennys went from Newberry; also Barrets, Elmores, Laytons, Campbells and others, of whom some were very worthy, but need not further notice.

"The school teachers who taught the Ohio emigrants must next be noticed. They were Richard Clegg, John B. Mitchell and James Howe. I have often heard my father speak of going to Richard Clegg's school in Newberry District· From his description and that of others I infer that he in part answered the description given of one in Goldsmith's Deserted Village:

> "'A man severe he was and stern to view.
>
>   *   *   *   *   *   *
>
> Well had the boding tremblers learned to trace
> The day's disasters in his morning face.'

An Englishman with native domineering spirit, to which intemperance was added, one could hardly have expected him to be much different from what he was. The previous history of this man is given in a book called The Permanent Documents, pages 128, 129 and 130. It is the seventh chapter of the 'Drunkard's Looking Glass' written by Judge O'Neall, who kindly gave me the volume when at his home. He, Richard Clegg, reached Ohio, I think, not far from 1819, though I've no certain account. He resumed his old practice of school teaching and continued it till age compelled its abandonment. One remarkable thing is, that he taught in Ohio some of the children whose parents he had taught in South Carolina. Not one remembers him with reverence. Stern and irritable they feared but loved him not. It is said that he once when old fell asleep in his chair when a coal of fire was laid upon his head. When wakened by its burning not a scholar would tell who did it and Poor Richard had to bear it. It does not appear that he drank much liquor here, perhaps because hard to get, or perhaps because forbidden by his employers. He died in poverty more than fifty years ago, and his silly wife, Creese or Creesy, went to the poor house where in blindness she died. Richard is represented as having married this silly woman while he was silly from the effects of liquor, and however much he regretted it he could not undo it when sober. Their children partook somewhat of their mother's silliness and their father's improvidence, though not of his intemperance, and never amounted to much. Such are some of the fruits of intemperance. Richard has wealthy and respectable relatives in Dayton who avoided the rock on which he split.

"John B. Mitchell also taught many of the Newberry people who came to Ohio. I remember in my youth seeing a long well written manuscript, which my father told me was written by Mitchell for him. It was called the 'Advantages and the Disadvantages of the Married State.' I did not learn that Mitchell was its author. It was an Allegory, the scenes of which were laid in ancient days, old Babylon being mentioned in it. His concluding advice, beginning with 'From thy old friend John B. Mitchell,' showed him to be a man of fine thoughts and profound religious convictions, which, with his learning, made him a proper instructor for young people.

"It appears that James Howe taught a school or two here as far back as 1808 or 1809. I have seen a birth record, of my parents married here in 1806 and their eldest child born here in 1807, of incomparable beauty of penmanship. I was told this writing was done by James Howe, and as the next birth of 1809 was not his writing it would seem that he soon returned to Newberry where he died.

"In closing these brief memoirs of the emigrants from Newberry, far the most of whom I knew personally, besides a great many more not mentioned, I must say with sorrow that but one of those early emigrants is living. This one is Benjamin Pearson, born in 1805 and brought here in 1808. He is bowed with age, and only remembers crossing the Ohio on the way here. Those heroic adventurers left the balmy South, the land of the chestnut, the cedar and the pine; crossed the Alleghanies and entered the 'dark mephitic, tangled woods' of the far-off Northwest, whose giant oak, towering hickory, majestic walnut, spreading beech and lofty poplar, &c., frowned upon them and seemed to forbid their ingress. But with heads to plan and hands to execute, the forests disappeared, the wild beasts fled, waving fields of grain arose, dwelling houses, churches, villages and towns were built, all by the courage, industry, skill and labor of the brave people of the South. Should the question be asked, what county or district in the United States has furnished the most men, women and children to people the great Northwest? the answer must come from all the knowing ones that to Newberry District, South Carolina, belongs this great honor.

"DAVID JONES.

"WEST MILTON, OHIO, August, 1889."

I well remember the John B. Mitchell mentioned by Mr. Jones in the foregoing. He moved into Edgefield County, where he lived to be quite an old man. He was a Methodist and a local preacher, and I used to see him at Zoar church at love feasts and class meetings, for in my boyhood the class meeting was a regular institution of the church, and should be yet, I think. The last time I remember to have seen Mr. Mitchell was at a Baptist camp meeting at Mount Enon, where he preached and related some remarkable experiences he had then recently had. In a dream or a vision he thought he had passed into the other world, where he saw many of his old friends and neighbors; some in the good world and some in the other, and some in neither, but midway between the two, seemingly hesitating as to which they should at last gravitate.

This camp meeting was held some time between 1835 and 1840, but in what year I do not remember. But I very well remember seeing a young man, who had been at school at Mount Enon with me in 1835 and 1836, but was then in the South Carolina College, parade the camp ground, dressed in old style, with knee-breeches, silk stockings, with buckles in his shoes and ribbons and buckles at his knees, and coat and vest of the antique Revolutionary cut. His father was a staid, well-to-do farmer who lived near by, a member of the church, and you can well imagine how supremely disgusted he was at the exhibition.

Mr. Mitchell died not a great while afterwards, probably in that same year. He was then very feeble, both in mind and body. After a long and useful life he quietly fell asleep. His remains lie buried, I think, but I am not sure, at Zoar church. He has descendants, great-great-grandchildren, now living in that neighborhood, in Edgefield, and others in Georgia, mostly Methodists.

In regard to the O'Neall family I am able to give the following additional information which I learn from a letter received from G. T. O'Neall, of Waynesville, Ohio, written October 2, 1889.

Henry O'Neall, a native of Newberry, was the father of fourteen children, twelve of whom lived to rear families. One of his daughters, Rhoda, married Lewis Chapman, youngest son of Rev. Giles Chapman, and was living in Missouri in the year 1884, in her 82nd year. Elizabeth married John Bays, and was living in Warren County, Illinois, in her 72nd year; and Rebecca, who married Jno. T. B——, was living at the same time near Newberry, Indiana, in her 64th year. These are all the children of Henry O'Neall who were living at the above date.

The Hon. John H. O'Neall is the son of Henry Miles O'Neall, and the grandson of Henry, and was born near Newberry, S. C. He and his sisters were left orphans at an early age, and he became the ward of Judge John Belton O'Neall. About 1846 his grandfather Henry removed both him and his sisters to Southern Indiana, Davis County, where he has since remained. He is a lawyer and politician of prominence, was a member of the last Congress, and was, I think, re-elected last fall.

II.

According to promise given to some friends it devolves upon me to continue the Annals of Newberry from the time Judge O'Neall closed his labors down to the present.

His work was begun in 1850 and takes up the story from the earliest settlement of the county and records the principal events occurring down to the year 1858, or thereabouts, closing his labors with that year. He also traces the career of many families in the county, telling whence they came, &c. He closes with sad forebodings for the future, disapproving as he did entirely, the agitation then going on looking to secession and the dissolution of the Union. He had always been a consistent Union man and had suffered obloquy and reproach for his staunch adherence to his principles. He lived to see his country divided into two great sections arrayed in deadly conflict against each other, and to know that many very dear to him had gone to their eternal rest, slain upon the battle field. He lived long enough to know that the South was beaten and would soon be at the mercy of the stronger section. But he was spared so far as to be kept from witnessing the humiliation and the trampling under foot of his beloved State by men who cared naught for her save to drain her of all her resources. Had he lived, it may be that he could have been of use in helping his people in their time of trial. But he was taken away, perhaps in mercy to him.

It is with great diffidence that the present writer undertakes the task to which he has pledged himself, and he is conscious that the work cannot be otherwise than very imperfectly done. To gather up the loose material for history that lies scattered about and weave it into a connected whole, fair to the sight and memory, requires, I fear, a greater degree of patient industry than is his. But his word is given and with him this labor is a labor of love.

JOHN BELTON O'NEALL.

Perhaps I cannot better begin this work than with a sketch of John Belton O'Neall. Possibly no truer narrative of his life could be found than one prepared by himself and published in 1859 in his "Bench and Bar of South Carolina." I quote from it:

"He is the son of Hugh O'Neall and Anne Kelly, his wife, both of whom were members of the Society of Friends, on Bush River, Newberry District, South Carolina, and consequently he was, by his birth-right, a member. The society there has, for nearly half a century, been, from the diminution of its members, incapable of transacting business; and he is, therefore, still one of them, although he knows perfectly well, from his habits, pursuits and mode of life, that he has forfeited his right to be called *"a Friend";* yet, he confesses to a great partiality for Friends, when *indeed and in truth they are such.*

"His ancestry on both sides were Irish, his paternal greatgrandfather belonging to the ancient house of O'Neall of Shane's Castle, Antrim, Ireland. His maternal grandfather, Samuel Kelly, was of King's County, and his grandmother, Hannah Belton, was of Queen's County, Ireland; so that he may rank as a full-blooded Irish-American.

"He was born on Wednesday, 10th of April, 1793, about half a mile below Bobo's Mills, on Bush River. At his earliest recollection his father removed to the mills, and *there* his boyhood was spent.

"He began to go to school when he was five years old. A young man, the son of a friend of his father's, boarded at his house and went to 'Master Howe,' (as the teacher, James Howe, was familiarly called,) about one mile and a half distant. He took the child-like pupil with him, day by day, carrying him across the branches on his back. The first shock of death which he ever experienced, was in the decease of this young gentleman, Capt. Abraham Parkins, in October, 1802. He (young O'Neall) learned rapidly, but his subsequent life satisfies him that he went to school at least two years too soon. His nerves were unstrung by an attack of what was then called nervous fever, when he was about three years old, and which had the effect to render his hand so unsteady as to make him incapable of writing a good hand, although taught by the best teachers of penmanship with whom he was acquainted.

"The other children of his father were girls. They were all remarkable for talents. His eldest sister, Abigail, went to school with him, and learned more rapidly than he did. She is still alive, and is the widow of John Caldwell, Esq. His two next sisters, Rebecca and Hannah, have long been tenants of the 'silent house.' His youngest sister, Sarah Ford O'Neall, is still alive, and is a member of the Society of Friends.

"In 1804, a library society was organized at Newberry, of which his father was a member. The books were selected and bought in the city of Boston, by Elijah Hammond, the father of Senator Hammond. This afforded to young O'Neall the opportunity of reading, a taste for which he had acquired by Mr. Howe having permitted him to read, under his direction, his books, of which he had a pretty good selection. He recollects to this day with what avidity he read the first book placed in his hands—the 'Pilgrim's Progress.'

"He continued to go to English schools, with slight interruptions, until 1808. Occasionally he was employed as a clerk in his father's store, where he learned to abhor the liquor traffic. At the schools to which he went for the first thirteen years of his school life, he learned to spell and read well, and to write an indifferent hand, and came to understand arithmetic perfectly.

"He acquired great facility in memorizing promptly whatever was put in his hands. He committed to memory, in an hour, the 9th chapter of II. Kings. In May, 1808, he became a pupil of the Newberry Academy, then under the care of the Rev. John Foster. He pushed his young pupil forward much too rapidly. By January he had him reading Virgil, without at all understanding it as he should have done. In January, 1809, Charles Strong, of the class of 1808, South Carolina College, became the preceptor in that year and the next. Young O'Neall became a thorough Latin scholar, and was sufficiently instructed in Greek and all the branches of English to prepare him for the Junior Class of the South Carolina College. During this time he acquired the habit of extemporaneous speaking, by practicing to speak every night, after he had got his lesson for the next day, before his uncle and grandmother, with whom he boarded at Springfield.

"In the year 1810, his father was deprived of his reason,

and this kept him home from school for several months, to endeavor to close up satisfactorily his deranged mercantile affairs. But all was in vain. Bankruptcy came down upon him, and his creditors nearly crushed every hope by suing him in his unfortunate, insane condition, and forcing his property to a sale at an immense sacrifice. Thus his family were turned out of doors, and had it not been for the kindness of his father's bachelor brother, must have been left without even a shelter for their heads.

"In February, 1811, young O'Neall was allowed to enter the Junior Class of the South Carolina College. In December, 1812, he graduated with the second honor of that institution. His diploma bears date 7th December, 1812, and is signed by Jonathan Maxcy, S. T. D., Præses.; Thos. Park, Ling. Prof.; B. R. Montgomery, D. D., Mor. Phil. and Log. Prof.; Georgius Blackburn, A. M., Matt. and Astron. Prof.; and by Henry Middleton, Governor and President of the Board, and twenty two Trustees, only one of whom, John J. Chappell, is alive.

"The expenses of his collegiate education were paid in part by himself, and the balance out of his father's dilapidated estate by one of his committee-men, and which was not allowed in his accounts. His father (in 1813) recovered his reason, and, in gathering up the wrecks of his fortune, succeeded in being able to reimburse Mr. Caldwell such sums as he had expended on his son's education.

"In 1813, for about six months, O'Neall taught in the Newberry Academy. At the end of that time he devoted himself to the study of the law, in the office of John Caldwell, Esq. At that time Anderson Crenshaw, Esq., afterwards Judge Crenshaw, of Alabama, lived in the village; he gave O'Neall free access to his library, and imparted to him much valuable instruction.

"A debating society then existed at Newberry, to which the young men and many of the middle aged belonged. A meeting was held every Saturday, and subjects debated with much energy. O'Neall then improved his habit of extemporaneous speaking very much.

"In August, 1813, O'Neall performed, at the muster of a demi-brigade, in Frost's old field, his first military duty, as a

member of the artillery company under the command of Capt.
McCreless; the militia, under the orders of the Governor, were
classified. The company to which he belonged was placed in
the first class. That class was called into the State's service
in March, 1814, and marched for Camp Alston, four miles
below Pocotaligo, in Beaufort District, where there was about
as much necessity for troops as there would be, in time of
war, at Chalk Hill, near Columbia.

"The first class was mustered into service under the command of Col. Starling Tucker, at Newberry, on the 1st, 2nd
and 3d days of March, by Maj. Thomas Wright, Brigade
Major of the then 2nd, now 10th, Brigade of Militia, and on
the 4th commenced their march for Camp Alston. O'Neall
was appointed Judge Advocate for the command, but was
allowed to remain as part of the artillery company. The line
of march was by the way of Lee's Ferry, Bord's, in Lexington,
Pine Log, on Edisto, the White Pond, in Barnwell, Barnwell
Court House, Buford's Bridge, across the Saltkehatchie, thence
across many swamps to Pocotaligo and Camp Alston. The
campaign was inglorious, and closed about the 1st of April. . . .

"A few weeks after his return home (in May, 1814,) he was
admitted to the practice of law and equity. . . . He immediately entered into partnership with John Caldwell, Esq.,
(who was Cashier of the Branch Bank of the State at Columbia, and had removed to Columbia). He opened his office at
Newberry, and from the commencement was honored with a
large and lucrative practice.

"In October of that year a volunteer company of artillery
(in the place of that in which he had served at Camp Alston
and which had been disbanded) was raised at Newberry, and
he was elected Captain. To this point in his life he always
refers as conferring more pleasure and pride than any other.

"His first equity speech was made at Laurens, before Chancellor DeSaussure, at the June Term of 1814, for Washington
Equity District. The Chancellor's approving smile was of
great benefit to him *then*, and so was his friendship ever after.
His first law speech was made at Union Court House, in October, 1814, in a malicious prosecution case; notice of which
was made in the sketch of James McKibben. When the case
was going on, Judge Crenshaw, then a practicing lawyer, said

to the defendant, James Duncan, son of Alexander Duncan,
'You had better employ me; the young man who is about to
speak against you is not known to you.' 'Never mind,' was
the old man's reply; 'Cousin Josey (meaning Colonel Joseph
Gist) will fix them.' But the old gentleman learned, in the
sequel, by a verdict of two hundred dollars, that 'the race was
not always to the swift, nor the battle to the strong.' His
first law speech at Laurens was, in November, 1814, in defence
of a poor fellow, for stealing a sheep, who was acquitted.
These were voluntary speeches, and led the way to reputation
and future employment. Young lawyers mistake much their
duty to themselves in declining opportunities to speak without
fee or reward. His early success at the Bar he always attributed more to the favor of the people, and the encouraging
helping hand extended to him by the Bench and Bar, than
any intrinsic merits which he possessed. For he knows *now*
that his legal acquirements *then* were very slender.

"In October, 1815, he had the misfortune to be visited with
an attack of fever ; he, however, kept pace with the business
of his office, in the midst of successive and daily intermittent
attacks. At Court, by the blessing of God, he was able to
maintain his usual stand at the Bar.

"At the October election of 1816, he was returned third, out
of four members of the House of Representatives, from Newberry District. This gave him the opportunity of being more
generally known, and probably furthered his views of ad-
vancement ; but if he had the privilege to live his life over,
he would not seek such a position so early in life. On the 2d
December, 1816, the degree of Master of Arts was conferred
on him by the South Carolina College. On the 7th of August,
in 1817, he was elected from the rank of Captain to that of
Colonel of the Eighth and Thirty-ninth Regiments of Militia.
He was enthusiastically fond of the military, and soon raised
his regiment to a proud position as militia. The whole regiment were devotedly attached to their Colonel. Like many other
young men, his vanity was played upon by professed friends,
and he was presumptuous enough to offer for Major-General
against his commander and friend, Brigadier-General Tucker.
That he was defeated was exactly what he deserved. The officers of his own regiment evinced their fidelity by giving him

an unanimous vote. This consoled their young Colonel in his defeat, and has ever since been gratefully referred to.

"In the December Session of the General Assembly of that year he voted for the increase of the Judges' salaries. The consequence was, that at the elections of 1818 and 1820 he was left at home. This period of rest from political pursuits, he thinks, was of immense advantage to him; it made him a much better lawyer and increased his reputation and business.

"In 1816 he was appointed by Governor Pickens one of his Aids, with the rank of Lieutenant-Colonel. This appointment he resigned, in consequence of his election as Colonel. In December, 1817, he was elected a Trustee of his Alma Mater, the South Carolina College, and he has filled that office ever since, with the exception of a year, from December, 1821, to December, 1822. Thus, for forty years, he has sedulously watched over the interests of that great institution.

"On the 25th of June, 1818, he was married to Helen, eldest daughter of Captain Sampson Pope and Sarah Strother, his wife, of Edgefield. For forty-one years they have together toiled through life, enjoying much of happiness, and, in the death of all their children, drinking the cup of sorrow to its dregs.

"In June, 1820, his grandmother, Hannah Kelly, died. By her will she devised to him 'Springfield.' Thither, in August of that year, he removed, and there he has resided ever since, adding to it many adjoining farms and the mills on Bush River, just above the forty-fifth line, railroad crossing.

"In 1822 he was returned second to the House of Representatives in the General Assembly of South Carolina, and by successive biennial elections he was returned in 1824 and 1826. In 1824 and 1826 he was elected Speaker of the House of Representatives, without opposition. During the four years in which he held that great office there was only a single appeal from his decisions, and in that his decision was sustained. No Reading Clerk existed at his first term. The consequence was that he read all bills, reports and resolutions. He had a wonderful facility in this respect. His voice was clear, his enunciation distinct; he read with great ease and rapidity any writing presented to him. His quick and ready eye, and a prompt understanding of the scope of the writer, constituted the whole secret of his art of reading. Being able to make out a word going before and another after an obscure writing, enabled him to read the sentence.

* * * * * * *

"In February, 1823, he was elected Brigadier-General of the Tenth Brigade, Fifth Division, of the South Carolina Militia, and on the 20th of August, 1825, he was elected and commissioned Major-General of the Fifth Division. In that and the previous election for Brigadier-General the officers of the Thirty-ninth Regiment gave him an unanimous vote. In his election as Major-General he succeeded in rising over the head of a friend and relative—a much older officer and a most worthy man—Brigadier-General Dawkins, of Union. His commission as Major-General is signed by his much-valued friend, Governor Manning, and is therefore carefully preserved.

"In 1827 the appropriation of ten thousand dollars, for the relief of Mr. Randolph, was made. The Speaker was known to be favorable to the measure, though he did not vote. In 1828 the people of Newberry, who have always been remarkable for seizing upon matters of money appropriated as objections to their members, did that which no other district could have been persuaded to do—refused to return the Speaker—and, of consequence, lost the honor of having that officer as one of their representatives.

"On the 20th of December, 1828, John Belton O'Neall was elected and commissioned as an Associate Judge. He immediately accepted the great trust; qualified, and entered on its duties. He rode the Southern, Western and Middle Circuits, and commenced, in the fall of 1830, the Eastern, now the Northern Circuit; but, at Chesterfield, he was taken dangerously sick. As soon as he could ride, his friend, Dr. Smith, insisted on his accompanying him to his residence, at Society Hill, which he did; this kind attention was rapidly restoring him, when intelligence reached him that two of his children were dead, and a third at the point of death. He returned rapidly home, and in a few days saw his eldest daughter die, a lovely child of ten years of age. He did not resume his circuit; his friend, Judge Johnson, of the Court of Appeals, held the Courts from Marion to the close.

"On the first day of December, 1830, Judge O'Neall was

elected a Judge of the Court of Appeals, and entered immediately upon its duties. With Johnson and Harper, he encountered and performed the labors of the Court of Appeals—herculean as they were—until December, 1835. The extent of them may be judged from a reference to 2 Bailey, 1 and 2 Hill, Bailey's Equity, 3 Rich., 1 and 2 Hill's Chancery Reports, Richardson's Equity Cases.

"The decision, The State *ex parte* McCrady *vs.* Hunt, 2 Hill, so displeased the dominant party that the Court of Appeals, which had done more to give symmetry to the law than had ever been known before, was abolished, and Johnson and Harper assigned to Equity and O'Neall to the Law. He has ever since then given most of his attention and labors to the Courts. The fact is, he has neglected his own affairs, and much injured his own estate, to serve the people. In May, 1850, on the death of Judge Richardson, he became President of the Court of Law Appeals and of the Court of Errors. His recorded labors from December, 1835, are to be seen in 3 Hill, Dudley, Rice, 1 and 2 McMullen, Cheves, 1 and 2 Speer, 1st, 2nd, 3d, 4th, 5th, 6th, 7th, 8th, 9th, 10th and 11th Richardson, and 1st, 2nd, 3d, 4th and 5th Strobhart.

"In 1846, the degree of LL. D. was conferred on him at Columbia College, District of Columbia, and was repeated a few years since at Wake Forest, North Carolina.

"In May, 1847, he was elected President of the Greenville and Columbia Railroad. Aided by an unfaltering devotion, he succeeded in carrying the enterprise successfully forward to Anderson, and within eighteen miles of Greenville; when, in May, 1853, he surrendered the work to other hands. Afterwards, the work had to be carried forward by the individual credit of the president and his friend and endorser, Colonel Simeon Fair. At different times, himself and all the directors were bound for more than one hundred thousand dollars. When the great freshet of 1852 broke down more than thirty miles of the road, and Wm. Spencer Brown, the talented and energetic chief engineer, was drowned, there devolved upon the president a work requiring sleepless vigilance and determined energy. That he was enabled to overcome all obstacles is cause of devout gratitude to God, which he has always acknowledged.

"On 31st December, 1832, to save a friend, he abandoned the use of spirituous liquors, and in June following gave up the use of tobacco. To these two causes he ascribes his health and ability to perform more labor than most men at his time of life can accomplish. He joined, soon after, the Head's Spring Temperance Society, Newberry District, where his membership now is, and of which he is president. He became a teetotaller; and, in December, 1841, he was appointed President of the State Temperance Society, which office he still holds. In 1849, he joined the Sons of Temperance, Butler Division, No. 16, at Newberry. He was elected G. W. P. of the Grand Division of South Carolina, October, 1850; and in June, 1852, at the city of Richmond, Virginia, he was elected and installed M. W. P. of the Sons of Temperance, of North America. He attended, in 1853 and 1854, the annual meetings at Chicago, Illinois, and St. John's, New Brunswick. Then he surrendered his office to his successor, Samuel L. Telby, of St. John's.

"In the spring of 1834, the Judge and his wife lost, by the scarlet fever, two of their lovely little girls.

"In 1837, he was elected President of the Newberry Baptist Bible Society. To this office he has annually been elected; much good has been accomplished by this society under his direction. He is now the President of the Bible Board of the Baptist State Convention—of which body (the Baptist State Convention) he was elected president in July, 1858, and again in 1859.

"He was elected President of the Newberry District Agricultural Society in 1839, and has been annually elected ever since. The good accomplished by that society is known by the fact that Newberry has reclaimed her wasted fields and made more and better improvements in agriculture than any other district in the State. The society has, once or twice, been on the verge of dissolution; but the people of Newberry know too well its importance to permit it to perish.

"On the 5th of August, 1857, the crowning sorrow of their lives occurred to the Judge and his wife. Then, their excellent daughter, Sarah Strother Harrington, the wife of Dr. Harrington, their only surviving child, was taken from them by death. They are consoled by the fact that she was a

2   C

Christian, and that she has left seven representatives, (four daughters and three sons,) whom may God spare to comfort and assist their grandparents, and to become good and useful women and men.*

"Judge O'Neall has written and labored much for his fellow-men. He has always believed where he could contribute even a mite to knowledge, education, temperance, religion and agriculture, it was his duty to make the effort. . . . . He is sensible that he has worked hard and endeavored to do good. If he has succeeded, *then* every wish of his heart will be gratified; and, he will only add, may he be succeeded by others more, much more, useful than he has been."

In 1859 the Legislature again established the Separate Court of Appeals, to consist of a Chief Justice and two Associate Justices. Judge O'Neall was elected Chief Justice at the same session of the Legislature, which position he held to the time of his death.

The Temperance cause never had a more faithful and persistent advocate, and the work that he did is now bearing fruit.

As stated by him, his parents were of the Society or Church of the Friends, but after the great exodus from Newberry in the early part of this century, in consequence of the preaching and prophecies of Zachary Dicks and the consequent ruin of the church, he, with some others of the family, united with the Baptist Church, in which communion he remained until death, a faithful and consistent member.

I have heard many public speakers, at the bar, in the pulpit, and on the stump, but I am sure that the greatest *natural* orator I ever heard was Judge O'Neall. His manner was so animated and earnest, his voice so full and strong, and his words came so readily and with so much energy, that he gave great interest to whatever subject he might be speaking on.

---

* Helen H. married Dr. S. Pope and is now living in Newberry; Moriat H. married Capt. J. W. Gary and died several years ago; Hattie H. married Col. T. J. Lipscomb and is living in Columbia, S. C.; Hugh O'Neall is living in Texas; Young John was a promising lawyer at Newberry and died several years ago; John Belton O'Neall is a physician and is living in Mississippi; Sallie H. married Charles Kier and is also living in Mississippi.

Even though his position might be untenable, and he might be engaged in the advocacy of an erroneous cause, yet his very earnestness and eloquence would oftimes make his hearers feel that he was right. William C. Preston, McDuffie, Clay, Calhoun, Webster, all these great orators of a past generation, I never heard; but I feel sure that O'Neall would not have been insignificant even among these giants and great men.

He died December 27th, 1863, at his home at Springfield, near Newberry.

Closing his Annals amid the mutterings and thunderings of the storm soon to burst upon the country, O'Neall says nothing of the Kansas trouble, nor of the great excitement here at the time, nor of those persons who left Newberry for the purpose of helping to make Kansas a slave State. Contrary to the wish and advice of some of the wisest and most thoughtful Southern men, the Missouri Compromise had been repealed. They thought that repeal full of danger, as it would tend to precipitate and intensify a conflict between the sections and parties, each one doing its utmost to fill the Territory with settlers pro and anti slavery, according to its proclivities, as by that repeal the Territory was equally open to all, previous to that time slavery having been prohibited.

The people of Newberry, in common with all the people of the State, anxious to make Kansas a slave State, held public meetings and raised funds to send settlers to the Territory for that purpose. Among those who went from the District of Newberry I call to mind Milton Fair, a younger brother of Col. Simeon Fair, Stanmore B. Chappell and E. J. Goggans. Fair never returned, but died in Kansas. Jerry Goggans was a graceful and easy letter writer, and I remember reading with much pleasure some letters written by him descriptive of scenes and incidents in Kansas, and published in our Newberry papers at the time. He is now living in Edgefield County, but is scarcely as lively and jolly as he was thirty years ago. Stanmore Chappell also moved to Edgefield after the war, but he is no longer living.

There were others also who went to Kansas at or about the same time, John Holly and family, from Holly's Ferry, on Saluda River, who settled on a place purchased by E. J. Goggans, remaining there some time, but finally moving to Missouri, where his children and grandchildren still live. Thomas DeWalt, who was then a young lawyer, or student of law at Newberry, afterwards went to Texas. James Mangum, son of John Mangum, killed in the war of Secession. His name appears upon the monument in the Square, below the Court House. Simeon Harris, brother of James Y. Harris, married and settled in Kansas, and is still living. J. Milton Wilson, who was a merchant and died at Newberry in 18—, was also one; and John B. Harrington, also known as French Harrington, cast in his lot with the Kansas emigrants, his mother, who was then at Newberry, following him in about a year. John B. Harrington and his mother afterwards returned to Newberry, but nothing is now known of them.

The agitation grew more and more intense. The blood of the people of the whole South—whatever it may have been North —was at fever heat. The struggle for the possession of Kansas and the invasion of Virginia by John Brown were the beginnings of the great civil war between the States, as these events took place only a few years before the secession of South Carolina. On the election of Abraham Lincoln, the candidate of the Free Soil party in 1860, as President of the United States, South Carolina withdrew from the Union. Other Southern States soon followed her example. Then came four years of bloody and disastrous war, the result of which was the conquest of the seceding States and the reconstruction of the Union.

It is not my purpose at this time to give a history of that war; but Newberry was a great sufferer, not only in material wealth, but in the sacrifice of the lives of many of her best and bravest men, who died in what we all thought a noble and heroic cause. Every day we still meet in the streets of Newberry maimed and crippled men, some with only one leg, some with one arm, some with one eye, and others halting and lame who have all their limbs, victims, uncomplaining, of that sad and disastrous war. My pen will trace lovingly the names of these, and of others equally true and patriotic, whose lives have gone to make up the Annals of Newberry.

In 1859 John Brown made his celebrated raid into Virginia. He was captured and hanged, which was a strictly legal proceeding, as he had violated not only the laws of the State and of the United States in trying to incite servile insurrection, but the laws of the United States in taking possession by force of arms of the arsenal at Harper's Ferry. But his hanging was a great mistake, as I thought and said at the time, as his death only added fuel to the flame of hatred that was already burning in the Northern heart against the South.

In 1860 the Democratic party still had a considerable majority in the Union, and might have elected the President for the next term. But with a strange fatuity—madness, the ancients would have termed it, sent upon them by the gods for their destruction—instead of concentrating their strength upon one set of candidates, with a folly unsurpassed in the history of the party, they had three: Stephen A. Douglas for the Presidency, with Herschel V. Johnson for the Vice-Presidency; John C. Breckenridge for the Presidency, with Gen. Joseph Lane for the Vice Presidency; and John Bell for the Presidency, with Edward Everett for the Vice-Presidency. The consequence was that the Free Soil party elected their candidate without a majority of the popular vote, either by the States or of the people. Soon after the result was known, a sovereign convention of the people of South Carolina was called, and by that convention an Ordinance of Secession was unanimously passed on the 20th day of December, 1860. The act of the Legislature calling the convention was ratified on the 13th day of November, and the delegates from the several election districts of the State assembied in the Baptist church, in the town of Columbia, at 12 o'clock on the 17th day of December, 1860. Of that convention D. F. Jamison, of Barnwell, was elected President. The delegates from Newberry were: John P. Kinard, Robert Moorman, Joseph Caldwell and Simeon Fair. Of these delegates not one is living at this date, February, 1892. It is perhaps worthy of note that at the election of delegates to this convention the majority of those entitled to suffrage in the District of Newberry did not vote. Nor was the Ordinance of Secession passed by the convention referred back to the people for their approval. It seems to have been a foregone conclusion with the people of this State that upon the dominance of the Free Soil party and the election of a Republican President the Union was virtually dissolved, inasmuch as there would be no longer any safety for their institutions and property in the Union.

Here follows the Ordinance of Secession, which I take from a copy of the Journal of the Convention, printed by R. W. Gibbs, State Printer in 1862, now lying before me :

AN ORDINANCE

To dissolve the Union between the State of South Carolina and other States united with her under the compact entitled "The Constitution of the United States of America."

We the People of the State of South Carolina, in Convention assembled, do declare and ordain, and it is hereby declared and ordained,

That the Ordinance adopted by us in Convention, on the twenty-third day of May, in the year of our Lord one thousand seven hundred and eighty-eight, whereby the Constitution of the United States of America was ratified, and also all Acts, and parts of Acts, of the General Assembly of this State, ratifying amendments to the said Constitution, are hereby repealed; and that the Union now subsisting between South Carolina and other States, under the name of the United States of America, is hereby dissolved.

Such was the brief, though plain, direct and positive Ordinance by which the momentous act of Secession was consummated. There was not a single dissenting voice. When the Ordinance was engrossed the members from Newberry, with all the other members of the Convention, affixed their signatures.

The young people of this time, when everything is so calm and quiet, and when all the excitement attending the Presidential election and others is a mere ripple upon the surface of the political sea, and is a subject of mirth rather than of apprehension, are little able to realize the intense feeling of anxiety that prevailed for years before Secession was an accomplished fact, and filled the minds of many persons with an awful sense of some impending and dreadful evil. As an instance, it is well to give here a brief notice of a public meeting held at Beth Eden on the 31st of October, 1860, of which Dr. Glenn was President and John P. Kinard Secretary. The object of the meeting was explained by the president, which was to form an association for the purpose of assisting our fellow-citizens throughout the State, and of giving additional security to the county against the incendiary attempts of the Abolitionists. He referred to the present state of affairs; the designs of the Black Republican party—their threats—and showed the necessity of union among all classes and parties of men at the

South. The necessity of vigilance, caution and prudence. Suitable resolutions were passed, all looking to the preservation of quiet and good order. The following named gentlemen were elected officers of the Association : Dr. George W. Glenn, President; James Caldwell, P. W. Gilliam, Jos. Y. Hunter, James Spence, H. H. Folk, Vice-Presidents; John P. Kinard, Secretary.

It is well, I think, to insert here, before proceeding further, a brief sketch of those worthy and good men and good citizens, signers of the Ordinance of Secession, all of whom have passed away—Simeon Fair, Robert Moorman, Joseph Caldwell and John P. Kinard. I knew them all personally, and they were all good men and true. Two of them were near neighbors for a number of years before their exit from this life—Simeon Fair and Robert Moorman.

Simeon Fair was the son of William Fair, and was born in Newberry County, five or six miles southeast of the Court House, in or near a section of country known as the "Stoney Hills," on the 17th day of November, 1801. He was a descendant of the Scotch-Irish, his father being of one of the families that came from Ireland about the year 1770. Colonel Fair was married on the 23d of December, 1840, to Miss Mary Butler Pearson, of Newberry. She was an excellent woman, loved for her many good traits of character, and died on 31st December, 1867.

He read law and was admitted to practice in the year 1824. When quite a young man he was elected Colonel of the Thirty-ninth Regiment of Militia. In 1840–1841 he was a member of the Legislature, but failed to be returned at the next election on account of having supported a certain measure in the House which, though right and good in itself, yet did not please the people at the time. One of the Circuit Judges, Judge Gauntt, had become unable and incompetent to perform properly the duties incumbent upon him, on account of age and infirmity. As he could not be impeached it was thought good to make it worth his while to resign. Accordingly an act was passed giving him a year's salary extra after resignation. Mr. Thomas H. Pope, who was a Representative from Newberry at the time, also voted for the measure, and he, too, was defeated at the next ensuing election. Colonel Fair was afterwards re-elected.

During the Seminole war in Florida, when men were called for from this State to serve for three months, he volunteered and was elected Lieutenant in the company in which he had enlisted. This was in 1836. When James J. Caldwell, father of J. F. J. Caldwell, Esq., author of a History of McGowan's Brigade—by the way, a very excellent book—was made one of the Equity Judges, for the Courts of Law and Equity were at that time separate and distinct, Colonel Fair was appointed Solicitor in his place, which position he held continuously from 1846 up to and during the war of Secession. He was again made Solicitor in 1866, but our State government was then overthrown by act of Congress. Reconstruction and Radical rule followed, and Colonel Fair was, of course, displaced. He continued the practice of law at Newberry until his death. He died 15th July, 1873.

I knew him well for many years. He had as few faults as most men—fewer than many. He was a good man, sociable in disposition, genial, kind and pleasant. Generous and forbearing to young and inexperienced practitioners at law, he was not anxious to take advantage of their want of skill in pleading.

His descendants are living here amongst us. One of them, John S., is a lawyer and has been Town Clerk for a number of years, and still (1892) holds the position. The other sons, William Y. and James I., are farmers. His daughter married Col. W. Drayton Rutherford, a gallant officer, Colonel of the Third Regiment S. C. V., who was killed at the battle of Strasburg, 13th October, 1864, leaving one daughter whom I, an old man, may be permitted to say that I love for her many good qualities and her courtesy to the aged. Ah, Katie, may you be happy with the man of your choice. Mrs. Rutherford is now the wife of Y. J. Pope, Esq., who was a brave and good soldier and officer during the war; lost an eye in the service, and is now Associate Justice of the Supreme Court of the State, having been elected in December, 1891.

Colonel Robert Moorman was a native of Union County. His education was limited, as he was not a graduate of any college. But being a man of strong good sense, pleasant manners, genial and sympathetic disposition, he became a successful farmer and merchant, and was at one time one of the most popular men in the county. During and after the war, until the close of his life, I knew him intimately and well, as his home was then at Newberry, and I found him to be a man of strict integrity of character, a devoted Christian, zealous in every good word and work and entirely free from Pharisaical bigotry and exclusiveness. Some years ago, a few years before his death, at the meetings of our Prayer Circle, which was an occasion for devotional exercises, frequently the tears might be seen rolling down his cheeks when moved by feelings of adoration and of love. At such times it was good to be with him. Being very social in his disposition and nature, in his youth he was fond of the dance, and he has told me that of an evening, after the business of the day was over, he would gladly ride a dozen miles in order to engage with young people in the dance, or other social amusements of the time. The same social disposition after his conversion made him love the house of God and the fellowship of religious people.

He represented Newberry District in the Lower House three terms, two terms in the Senate—except one session—having resigned on account of ill health. Afterwards he was elected again and served four years. He was an ardent States Rights man, and when the dark days of trial came he was ready, and pledged all that he had in defence of what he thought was right. Without hesitation, without scruple, he signed the Ordinance of Secession with as firm and high a heart as the men of 1776 signed the Declaration of Independence.

He was twice married. Three children are still living: Thomas S., son of his first wife, practicing law at Columbia, and also Librarian of the Supreme Court; was Second Lieutenant Third Regiment S. C. V. during the war, serving with honor and doing his duty faithfully; and Robert, son of the second wife, and his sister, Mrs. Simkins, wife of Lewis W. Simkins, Esq., of Laurens C. H. There were other children, Elizabeth, known to me as Bettie, a lovely, frank-hearted girl whom I knew from her childhood. She became the wife of Captain Clark Wardlaw, and died too soon for those who loved her. She left one child, which did not long survive her. Captain Wardlaw has also passed away. Nancy (Nannie) died unmarried.

I have never known a man for whom I had a warmer feeling or a more devoted attachment than I had for Colonel Robert

Moorman. He was warm-hearted and deeply religious, and I always found him a true man and a firm friend. The following lines, being the conclusion of a poem entitled "The Walk," and descriptive of a three days' pedestrian tour into the country and back, fitly express the feelings I had for him :

THE DAY AFTER.

I miss one friend who lately passed away
From earth's dark clouds to heaven's eternal day;
He was a man whose heart was free from guile,
Who sought in life his God's approving smile;
The poor, the weak, the sorrowful, distressed,
On him with confidence could lean and rest.
As man, as father, neighbor, husband, friend,
In him the virtues all did sweetly blend.
No more this side the grave I'll see his face,
But if there be a heavenly dwelling place
Where good men go, I hope to meet him there,
And breathe with him that pure celestial air,
Where death comes not, the weary are at rest,
Nor throes of pain disturb the peaceful breast.
Yes, Moorman, yes, in that immortal land,
I'll meet thee, know thee, clasp thy true right hand.

Joseph Caldwell died June 25th, 1888. His was a long and useful life, being about eighty years of age at the time of his death. He was a man of strong natural good sense, and though he was always a farmer, never having made law a study, yet I have heard it remarked of him by one who knew him well, that he was about as good a judge of law as any lawyer at Newberry. His sound judgment was relied upon in 1860 as of one into whose hands the interests of the State being committed, they would receive no detriment. As we have seen, he signed without hesitation the Ordinance of Secession. Children and grandchildren were about him in his declining years to cheer him at the close of a long and worthy life.

John P. Kinard, one of the signers of the Ordinance of Secession, had the honor of representing his native county in the Legislature, in the House and also in the Senate; he has also been Sheriff of the County. He lost his wife, a devoted and good wife, November 1, 1882, aged sixty-three years. He was then left alone, the sole survivor of five sisters and four brothers. He died suddenly at the residence of Mr. H. O. Henson, at Kinards, September 3, 1890, aged about eighty years,

CHANCELLOR JOB JOHNSTONE.

and was buried at Beth Eden Lutheran Church graveyard. One grandson, son of Dr. W. M. Kinard, is a student in Newberry College.

These four, Simeon Fair, Robert Moorman, Joseph Caldwell, and John P. Kinard, having been thought worthy to represent the District of Newberry in the Secession Convention, have acquired a conspicuous and eternal position in the history of the District of Newberry and the State. As a fitting conclusion to this chapter, it is well to give a brief sketch of two eminent citizens of Newberry, not actors in the civil war, who have passed away: Chancellor Job Johnstone and General H. H. Kinard.

Chancellor Job Johnstone was born June 6, 1793, and was the son of John Johnstone,* who came to Newberry in 1806, already a married man and the father of several children. It is thus seen that Job Johnstone was not a native of Newberry, being about thirteen years of age when his father moved here. He was born in Fairfield, near Winn's Bridge. Judge O'Neall in his Annals says that John Johnstone was poor when he started in life, but that by persevering industry and energy he became quite wealthy, and was able to educate his children liberally and to provide for them handsomely.

Job Johnstone, after graduating in the South Carolina College in December, 1810 (being the youngest graduate who, up to that time, had received a diploma), in 1811 entered the law office of John Hooker, at York, where he remained one year. The next year he was in the office of Mr. Clark, of Winnsboro. Without completing his studies in the law, he quit and went home, where he spent about two years, devoting his time to general reading. In 1814 he concluded to take up the study of medicine, and began under the direction of Dr. Davis, an eminent physician in Columbia. He took a course of lectures in New York, and in 1817, having graduated, he returned to Newberry and

---

* John Johnstone and four of his brothers (whose ancestors were Scottish) emigrated from Derry, Ireland, two of them previous to, and the others just after, the Revolutionary war. They spelled their names always with the *t*, but most of them dropped the final *e*. One of them wrote his name Johnstown. Chancellor Johnstone formerly wrote his name without the final *e*, and nearly all his equity decrees are so signed, but in later life he replaced the final *e* and spelled his name as it was originally written by his Scottish ancestors —E. H. A.

practiced for but a short time, and in the fall of 1817 he renewed the study of law in the office of Judge O'Neall at Newberry, and was admitted to practice in the winter of 1818, and entered into partnership with Judge O'Neall. Why he discontinued the practice of medicine, I am not able to say. I have heard several whimsical reasons given to account for it, but I am not disposed to credit any, as he was a man of too good sense and judgment to be moved by a mere whim. Doubtless he deeply felt the insufficiency of medicine to remove disease, and consequently his own helplessness in the presence of sickness and suffering. The successful practitioner, or the one who would be successful, must have no doubt whatever of his own skill and knowledge and of the virtue and efficiency of his medicine.

He was a successful lawyer, and never entered the arena of politics. In 1826 he was elected Clerk of the Senate of South Carolina, which position he held until he was elected Chancellor, on the 3d of November, 1830. In 1836 he was made an Equity Judge, and in 1859, when the Separate Court of Appeals was established, he was elected Associate Justice of this Court, which position he held until death.

In 1860 he was very doubtful of the expediency of Secession, as he had always been opposed to every movement, Co-operation,* for instance, the tendency of which was towards the

---

* This is probably a mistake. My information from the members of his family is that he was thoroughly States Rights. He believed that the States were sovereign and that the Union of the States was a Union of Sovereignties, with only the powers and authorities, and no more, that were delegated by these Sovereignties to the Federal Government, and that his allegiance was due to the State.

He was a Co-operationist in 1852 and with Judge A. P. Butler, at a meeting of citizens at Silver Street at that time, carried the people against separate State action.

He was a Nullifier in 1832, and being a member of the Convention, framed the Ordinance of Nullification.

He was in favor of the Confederacy, and, just a day or two before his death, had issued an address to the people calling for private contributions for the purpose of getting up a Confederate Navy—the scheme for which he had advised with Secretary Mallory.

He was a Commissioner to the first General Assembly of the Southern Presbyterian Church which met in Augusta, Ga., in 1861.

These are evidences of his full and entire sympathy with the South and of his true and loyal devotion to the South and her cause.—E. H. A.

dissolution or loosening the bonds of the Union between the States. Nullification he did not regard in that light, as that was simply open resistance to a law which the State deemed unconstitutional; and the trouble in that case might be, or might have been, amicably settled by compromise, or by an appeal to the courts. But Secession was a declaration of Independence, a complete severance of all ties of duty or obligation to the Union; and the trouble, in that case, could only be settled by an appeal to arms, coercing the seceding State or States, so making a forced Union instead of a free one; or by letting them go, and so permitting the Union to dissolve and return, by disintegration, into its elementary and chaotic condition. Both courses, to the wise philosopher and statesman, were full of grave and appalling dangers. With his clear and far-seeing mind, he shrank from the prospect. He thought that the Government at Washington would not permit any State to leave the Union in peace. Indeed, he felt that it *could not*. He was not one of those sanguine souls willing to drink all the blood that might be shed during the war that would follow Secession. But after the State seceded, after the die was cast and the Southern Confederacy formed, he was as true to the cause of the South as any citizen in the State. It was as a judge of law, and in his profound knowledge of that science, that he was pre-eminent. He never formed an opinion or came to any conclusion hastily; but patiently investigated every question and weighed every difficulty that might present itself. He wanted the *truth* in every cause, and having the sense of justice woven into every fibre of his being, his supreme desire was that every decision rendered by him should be clear, decisive and right. He was a just Judge, and being just in all his private dealings with his fellow men, he wanted justice from all. But he was not hard. I have had money transactions with him ; I have worked for him ; and I always found him gentle and true and kind. He was a gentleman, modest and unassuming in his manners, making all, even the unlettered, feel at ease in his company. He was twice married, having sons and daughters by both unions. Paul I remember as one of the gentlest of men. And notwithstanding his long-continued ill health (he died early), he was overflowing with a genial and kindly humor. Silas was for a number of years Commissioner in Equity. He is now Master. George is a lawyer and a successful practitioner, has recently represented his county in the Legislature, and is now a Member of Congress, having been elected in 1890. J. Malcolm was elected to the Legislature in 1888. He and Allen are both farmers, and good ones.

Chancellor Johnstone died April 8th, 1862, long before the conclusion of the great civil war. He saw dark days ahead, and was not sanguine, as he never had been, of the success of the South.

Gen. H. H. Kinard was certainly for many years one of the most influential men of Newberry County. He was born in the Dutch Fork of Newberry on 29th March, 1806. When Judge O'Neall was writing his Annals Gen. Kinard was serving his second term as Sheriff. Thus being placed alongside of Mr. John S. Carwile as worthy, in the judgment of the people, of being twice Sheriff of Newberry. He was afterwards elected for the third term. For twelve years he filled the responsible office of Sheriff, a greater number of years than any other person has ever held the office in Newberry.

Gen. Kinard was twice married. Only three children, a son and two daughters, survive him. There are, however, several grandchildren. He left a widow who became in due time the wife of my long time friend, Dr. O. B. Mayer. His eldest daughter married first, Col. W. B. D'Oyley. Being left a widow she married Rev. J. W. Humbert of the Methodist Church. Mrs. Humbert is the Secretary of the "Woman's Missionary Society" of the Methodist Church of this State. A sketch of the history of this Society will be given elsewhere. His youngest daughter is happily married to Rev. A. Coke Smith D. D., of the Methodist Conference of South Carolina. His grand-daughter, Alice, who is also the grand-daughter of my old friend, Dr. P. B. Ruff, married Mr. E. H. Aull, of Newberry. Of her father, Capt. J. M. Kinard, who was killed during the war, I shall have more to say at the proper time. His grandson, John M. Kinard, is Clerk of the Court by appointment and by election (1888). His son Henry is now living in Newberry. His other grandson, brother to John M., is a graduate of the Citadel Academy and was a Professor or teacher in that Institution, but is now a student of Johns Hopkins University, Baltimore. Gen. Kinard had one son whom I never knew, who was said to have been a young man of great promise. He died in Paris while attending a course of medical lectures in that city in the year 1856 or 1857. I write from memory. His remains were brought home and buried here.

Gen. Kinard was a native of Newberry County, born in the Dutch Fork. Having been elected Sheriff he removed to the County Seat about the year 1840 where he passed the remainder of his life. He lived some years after the war, dying on the 17th of June, 1869.

III.

As part of the Annals of Newberry, as well as the Annals of the whole State, I think it well to insert here the address of D. F. Jamison, President of the Secession Convention. When called to the chair Mr. Jamison said:

"*Gentlemen:* We have met here under circumstances more solemn than any of us have ever been placed in before. No one, it seems to me, is duly impressed with the magnitude of the work before him, who does not, at the same time, feel that he is about to enter upon the gravest and most solemn act which has fallen to the lot of this generation to accomplish. It is no less than our fixed determination to throw off a government to which we have been accustomed, and to provide new safeguards for our future security. If any thing has been decided by the elections which sent us here, it is, that South Carolina must dissolve her connection with the Confederacy as speedily as possible.

"In the progress of this movement we have two great dangers to fear—overtures from without, and precipitation within. I trust that the door is now forever closed to all further connection with our Northern confederates; for what guarantees more strictly guarded, or under higher sanctions, than the present written compact between us? And did that sacred instrument protect us from the jealousy and aggressions of the North, commenced forty years ago, which resulted in the Missouri Compromise? Did the Constitution protect us from the cupidity of the Northern people, who, for thirty-five years, have imposed the burden of supporting the General Government chiefly on the industry of the South? Did it save us from Abolition petitions, designed to annoy and insult us, in the very halls of our Federal Congress? Did it enable us to obtain a single foot of the soil acquired in the war with Mexico, where the South furnished three-fourths of the money, two-thirds of the men, and four-fifths of the graves? Did it oppose any obstacle to the erection of California into a free-soil State without any previous territorial existence, without any defined boundaries, or any census of her population? Did it throw any protection around the Southern settlers of Kansas, when the soil of that territory was invaded by the emissaries of Emigrant Aid Societies. in a crusade preached from Northern pulpits, when churchmen and women contributed Sharp's rifles and Colt's revolvers, to swell the butchery of Southern men? And has not that Constitution been trodden under foot by almost every Northern State, in their ordinances nullifying all laws made for the recovery of fugitive slaves, by which untold millions of property have been lost to the South?

"Let us be no longer duped by paper securities. Written constitutions are worthless, unless they are written, at the same time, in the hearts, and

Robert Moorman.

John P. Kinard.

Simeon Fair.

Joseph Caldwell.

SIGNERS OF THE ORDINANCE OF SECESSION.

founded on the interests of a people; and as there is no common bond of sympathy or interest between the North and the South, all efforts to preserve this union will not only be fruitless, but fatal to the less numerous section. The other danger to which I referred, may arise from too great impatience on the part of our people to precipitate the issue, in not waiting until they can strike with the authority of law.

"At the moment of inaugurating a great movement like the present, I trust that we will go forward, and not be diverted from our purpose by influences from without. In the outset of this movement I can offer you no better motto than Danton's at the commencement of the French Revolution: 'To dare! and again to dare! and without end to dare!'"

This was on the 17th of December, 1860. Three days thereafter, December 20th, the Ordinance of Secession was passed by the Convention without a dissenting voice.

Secession was an accomplished fact; the long talked of dissolution of the Union had taken place.

South Carolina having seceded, six other Southern States soon followed her example and passed similar Ordinances, viz: Mississippi, on the 9th of January, 1861; Florida, on the 10th; Alabama, on the 11th; Georgia, on the 19th; Louisiana, on the 26th; and Texas, on the 1st of February. These States met by delegations at Montgomery, Alabama, on the fourth of February, 1861, and immediately formed a Provisional Government for one year, with Jefferson Davis as President and Alexander H. Stephens as Vice-President, for that time. The Constitution of the new Union was almost identical with that of the United States, but the name of the new Union was that of the Confederate States of America. Commissioners were immediately sent to Washington for the purpose, if it were possible, of making a peaceful and amicable adjustment of all matters pertaining to the common property and public debt. These Commissioners, Mr. Buchanan, whose term of office as President had not yet expired, refused to receive in any public capacity. In the meantime the seceded States had, before this, taken possession of all Federal forts and arsenals within their limits respectively, except Fort Sumter, near Charleston; Fort Pickens, of Pensacola, and The Keys on the Southern Coast of Florida, and had granted jurisdiction over them to the Confederate States. Mr. Buchanan's term of office being about to expire, he made no efforts to adjust the existing difficulties and none to coerce the seceded States.

2   D

On the 4th of March, 1861, Mr. Lincoln was inaugurated President of the United States, and the Confederate States Commissioners, who were still at Washington, made every effort possible to bring about a peaceful settlement of troubles between the sections, so that a parting might be effected on friendly terms. Evasive replies were always made to all overtures. In the meantime preparations for war were made, but not very energetically made, on both sides. It was very desirable that the evacuation of Fort Sumter should be brought about without a resort to force. Efforts to this end were made by the Confederate Government and by the authorities of South Carolina; but in vain. All efforts to this end having failed, and it being well known that the Government at Washington was intending to re-enforce Fort Sumter as speedily as possible, all talk and promises to the contrary notwithstanding, Gen. Beauregard, who was then in command at Charleston with about six thousand Confederate troops, was ordered to open fire upon the Fort. Firing commenced at half-past four on the morning of April 12th, 1861. After a bombardment of thirty-two hours the Fort surrendered. On the Sunday morning following the writer of this was at the depot at Newberry waiting for the train to come in. A great crowd was present waiting to hear the news. There was no telegraph here in those days. As the train rolled in at eleven o'clock Major J. M. Baxter, standing on the platform of the passenger car, waved his hat and with a strong, sonorous voice cried out: "Fort Sumter is ours." With eyes moist with tears I then hastened to church.

THE FIRST VOLUNTEER FROM NEWBERRY.

In the Newberry *News*, Volume III., a Friend thus writes of the First Volunteer from Newberry:

"South Carolina had seceded. A call was made for men to support her action and defend her against the horde of fanatics that every thinking man knew must needs come. This call reached Newberry. Immediately one says, 'Enroll my name for the war or until death.' A brother who has since gone to that bourne whence no traveler returns, said, 'I'll go with you,' but the first, with his usual far-seeing eye and generous heart, turned upon him with womanly love and prophetic vision. 'No, you shall not; your health, family, business connections, all say no. But I'm in for the war, though I know at its close we will be a poverty stricken people, the niggers will be free, and grass will grow in now pub lic, frequented highways.'

"By the energy of a few noble men soon a company was reported for duty. And *a gallant one it was;* its deeds alone would give to any State *a glorious history.* It was assigned to Col. Gregg's Regiment, First South Carolina Volunteers. This first volunteer patiently bore the monotonous life on Morris Island, the marches and labors incident to camp life in Virginia, with its advances and retreats, until came the hard fought battle of Cold Harbor. By this time he had become the pride of the company, the confidential counselor and friend to all. Standing erect, above ix feet high, weighing 180 pounds, a model man in physique, old army officers would remark that he was a born soldier. With sword drawn, pressing the enemy in his very trenches, he was struck by a ball between the second and third ribs, which passed entirely through his body, leaving his shoulder blade shattered. Over 100 pieces of bone were afterwards taken, from time to time, from the wound. He was laid with the dying and the dead, all believing that death in a few hours at furthest would relieve him of his sufferings; but he said 'not yet,' and alone by superiority of will he lived, though in continual pain, with no use of his left arm, until paralysis set in on his left side and gradually continued to increase till a collapse of the bronchial tubes closed the sufferings of his life.

"Thus ended the life of Capt. Basil Manly Blease on the 2nd of January, 1877, in his fifty-first year, having been born at Edgefield Court House on the 11th day of December, 1826."

To the foregoing notice of Captain Blease the compiler of these Annals feels constrained to add: I was frequently with him when he was lying at home with his shoulder shattered, helpless and suffering. And I always found him as patient and uncomplaining, it seemed to me, as it was possible for any one to be suffering so greatly. He was far more patient than I was myself, when afterwards I passed through a similar experience, as I lay in hospital for ten weeks, suffering from a gunshot wound through my right leg. The smaller bone was broken and torn to pieces by the ball. I had no patience; the pain was too acute. But Captain Blease murmured as little as it was possible for man to do.

Again I was with him when he came to die. When he felt his last hour approaching he sent for me—I had visited him frequently before during his illness—and he asked me to read the Scriptures and to pray with him. I did so, and it seemed to me that he was at peace, such peace as only those know, or can know, whose hopes are stayed on the eternal God. And so he died.

The company thus formed in Newberry, the first company, became part of the First South Carolina Regiment of Volunteers, which Regiment, says Lieutenant J. F. J. Caldwell in his history of McGowan's Brigade, was of various origin; some of them being volunteer militia companies of long standing; some of them being raised by officers commissioned by Governor Pickens for that purpose. It formed part of the six thousand men under Beauregard at the reduction of Fort Sumter. And thus Newberry was represented by brave and gallant men at the very beginning of the war, even as she was at the close. In another place will be found the roll of this company with the list of casualties during the war.

There is now lying before me the roll of Company B, Third Regiment South Carolina Volunteers. The whole number of names on the roll is 141. Number living May 1st, 1888, is 41. Some few in this company were not from Newberry, but as they were assigned to a Newberry company, I record their names here with the others of the company.

COMPANY "B." THIRD REGIMENT.

Here follows the list in full: Samuel N. Davidson, Captain; Thomas W. Gary, Captain; Thompson Connor, Captain; William P. Hunter, Lieutenant; Thomas J. Lipscomb, Lieutenant; Milton P. Buzhardt, Lieutenant; Charles S. Davenport, Lieutenant; Samuel W. Pullig, Lieutenant; Martin B. Summer, 1st Sergeant; James R. C. Reeder, 1st Sergeant; R. Drayton Maffett, 2nd Sergeant; J. Frank Clark, 4th Sergeant; Leland M. Speers, 1st Sergeant; J. Anderson Copeland, 3d Sergeant; Warren G. Peterson, 4th Sergeant; Andrew J. Livingston, 4th Sergeant; Elijah P. Bradley, 2nd Sergeant; Andrew K. Tribble, 2nd Sergeant; Thomas M. Davis, 1st Corporal; John D. Smith, 2nd Corporal; John C. Gary, 3d Corporal; Julius Dean, 4th; Dennis Lark, 5th; Joseph H. Chalmers, 6th; M. Frank Anderson, 2nd; William W. Wallace, 6th; Andrew S. Speers, 6th; Henry S. Perkins, 3d; Benjamin W. Gibson, 4th; Robert Workman, 6th; Pickens J. Stevens, 6th; Middleton Suber, 1st.

Privates—Elijah A. Brooks, Kay Burton, J. Calvin Butler, William Bishop, John Bishop, A. W. Bailey (Spartanburg), David

Brown (Spartanburg), John A. Brown (Spartanburg), Ephraim A.
Butler, I. Newton Butler, Bluford R. Butler, Daniel M. Butler,
Isaac P. Cannon, Lewis F. Crooks, John A. B. Crooks, Ebenezer
P. Chalmers, Daniel F. Craddock, Theodore Craddock, Joseph G.
Chupp, John Cole, John B. Campbell, Jesse P. Cleland, Gilbert
E. Clark, Robert Cannon, David L. Clamp, James B. Chappell,
Harrison Davenport, Ephraim W. Davenport, W. Philip Daven-
port, John Dalrymple, Asa P. Davis, Daniel P. Davis, Joshua T.
Davis, James H. Dumas, J. C. Davenport, John S. Floyd, John
N. Floyd, J. Wistar Gary, Martin H. Gary, Charles M. Gary,
Jesse Gary, Sanders B. Griffin, William B. Griffin, William
Ac. Grimes, Thomas A. Grimes, Merideth Gibson, William W.
Gibson, James W. Golding, John Galloway, Thomas J. Gra-
ham, Robert P. Green, John F. Golding, David Harp, Green
T. Hopkins, William C. Harmon, Hugh T. Harmon, John S. B.
Jones, William Johnson (Spartanburg), W. Ross Johnson, Wil-
liam A. James, William H. King, Walter J. Keller, James M.
Lark, Jesse E. Lyles, Henry Livingstone, Emanuel Livingston,
Euclydus C. Longshore, Andrew J. Longshore, James W. Mc-
Kittrick, J. Henry Middleton, Jeff L. Moates, Florida Moates,
Daniel B. Montgomery, R. N. McElhenny, John M. Neel,
Thomas M. Neel, James M. Pitts, William Pitts, Joseph Pitts,
David Pitts, A. Newton Pitts, Elam Richey, Alfred M. Reeder,
Jr., Samuel J. Robinson (Spartanburg), William W. Reid, Wil-
liam Reeder, John S. Spruel, William F. Spruel, John P. Stewart,
David R. Senn, Richard S. Satterwhite, Graves R. Scurry, G.
Pinckney Stirling, G. Wash. Sadler, George A. Suber, Andrew
Suber, Calvin Thrift, George W. Thrift, R. W. Templeton, War-
ren W. Willingham, John A. Workman, James M. Workman,
Perry Workman, J. Christopher Whitman, George F. White,
George F. Wells, Wilson W. Waldrop, Barnett Williams, Har-
rison Workman.

Of these Lieutenant W. P. Hunter and Privates Robert Work-
man and William W. Gibson were killed at the battle of the
Wilderness; Lieutenant M. P. Buzhardt at Gettysburg, Pa.;
Lieutenant C. S. Davenport and Private Jesse Gary at Sharps-
burg, Md.; Privates E. A. Butler, Daniel P. Davis, Andrew J.
Longshore and Samuel J. Robinson at Fredericksburg, Va.;
Privates Lewis T. Crooks at Chickamauga; John Galloway at
Knoxville, Tenn.; John S. Spruel at Savage Station. Total, 13
killed during the war.

The following died of wounds received in battle, viz.: 1st Sergeant James R. C. Reeder, 3d Sergeant J. Anderson Copeland, Privates Ephraim W. Davenport, Gibson Merideth, J. Henry Middleton, Chickamauga; died at same place. James M. Pitts, Savage Station; died at Winchester, Va. William Pitts, Savage Station; died at Manchester, Va. William Spruel, Savage Station; died at same place. George A. Suber, Fredericksburg; died at Richmond, Va. Warren W. Willingham, not known where wounded; died at Columbia, S. C. Total, 10.

The following died during the war from hardships and diseases incident thereto: Captain S. N. Davidson, Petersburg, Va.; 1st Sergeant Martin B. Summer, Gettysburg, Pa.; 4th Sergeant J. Frank Clark (at home), Laurens, S. C.; 1st Corporal Thomas M. Davis, at Manassas, Va.; 3rd Corporal John C. Gary (at home), Newberry, S. C.; Private W. Frank Anderson, at Richmond; Private Middleton Suber, at Culpeper, Va.; Private William F. Bishop (at home), Newberry; Isaac P. Cannon and Theodore Craddock, at Richmond; Joseph G. Chupp, John Cole, place of death unknown. [It is probable that these two were special friends and comrades and that they died at some humble house, tended by kind hands, together, as they could have wished.] Jesse P. Cleland died at his home in Newberry; E. Gilbert Clark, Richmond; William B. Griffin, Charlottesville, Va.; James W. Golding, New Market, Tenn.; David Harp, Culpeper; William H. King, at his home in Newberry; James W. Lark, Manassas Junction; Jesse E. Lyles, Richmond; Henry Livingston, Staunton, Va.; Jeff. L. Moates, Winchester; Alfred M. Reeder, Jr., at home, Newberry; Andrew Suber, Calvin Thrift, Culpeper. Total, 25.

It is thus seen that in a company of 141 men the total number of deaths occurring during the war was 48, 10 of whom were killed in battle and 13 mortally wounded; and 25 died of diseases and hardships incident to the war.

Many of those who survived were wounded in battle, some quite severely and some as many as four or five times. Thompson Connor was wounded four times, Savage Station, Strasburg, Gettysburg, Averysboro; L. M. Speers five times, Savage Station, Fredericksburg, Chickamauga, Wilderness, Strasburg; Warren G. Peterson four times, Savage Station, Fredericksburg, Chickamauga, Wilderness, and being disabled was retired from service; Andrew J. Livingston twice, Savage Station and Wilderness, leg amputated; John Drayton Smith twice, Gettysburg and Wilderness. His arm was amputated and he was discharged. He is now well and hearty, and long may he live to do the State good service. Daniel M. Butler was wounded once, at Chancellorsville; Philip W. Dalrymple. twice, at Savage Station and Knoxville; John Dalrymple, once, Knoxville; Asa P. Davis, twice, Wilderness and Savage Station; Joshua T. Davis, once, Fredericksburg; Martin H. Gary, once, Knoxville; Euclydus C. Longshore, twice, Fredericksburg and Knoxville; James W. McKittrick, twice, Fredericksburg and Wilderness; Joseph Pitts, G. W. Sadler, G. W. Thrift, once each, Savage Station. Total, 16 wounded who lived through the war. The others escaped unhurt. Some few were discharged, and some were transferred to other commands.

The favors of fortune seem to be very unequally distributed. I remember talking with some soldiers after the war, who told me that they never lost a day from duty during the whole time, either from wounds or sickness; while some, whenever they went into battle, were almost sure to be hit.

In *The Century* for May, 1888, there is a very interesting paper on the "Chances of Being Hit in Battle," and the statistics therein given agree very nearly with the casualties of the company whose fortunes we have been considering. This company at Marie's Heights had thirty-six men under fire during, or nearly, the whole day. The next morning there were only four able to answer to roll call. The other thirty-two were not all killed nor mortally wounded, but were broken down and weary almost to death, so as to be temporarily disabled.

COMPANY "E," THIRD REGIMENT.

The roll of Company E, Third Regiment, with the list of killed and wounded, here follows: James D. Nance, Captain; John K. G. Nance, Captain; Robert H. Wright, Captain; Edward S. Bailey, 1st Lieutenant; John S. Hair, 2nd Lieutenant; B. S. James, 3d Lieutenant; D. Julius Hentz, 3d Lieutenant; Richard H. Haltiwanger, 2nd; Pickens B. Langford, 3d; Robert L. Wier (Laurens), 3d; Thomas S. Moorman, 1st, 2nd;

James N. Martin, 3d; Joseph E. Cofield, 2nd, 3d; Young J. Pope, 1st Sergeant; Calhoun F. Boyd, 1st Sergeant; W. Drayton Rutherford, 2nd; Thomas H. Lake, 1st; John S. Ruff, 1st; Thomas M. Paysinger, 2nd Corporal; William H. Thompson, 2nd Corporal; Samuel R. Chapman, 2d Sergeant; Andrew J. Kilgore, 3d; Beauford S. Buzhardt, 4th; H. Bachman Reid, 4th; William Hood, 4th Sergeant; Thaddeus S. Duncan, 4th; Drayton W. Ramage, Corporal; Richard A. Leavell, Corporal; Thomas G. Sloan, Corporal; John Blats, Corporal; John R. Harris, Corporal.

Privates—John K. Anderson, Jasper N. Abrams, Calvin B. Adams, Samuel L. Atchison, R. W .Adkins, Henry M. Assman (Lexington), Haman Brantley, Henry C. Bernhard (Lexington), William H. Blats, John F. Bell (Laurens), Jerome D. Bruce, William W. Boazman, Ed. Boazman, Grant Boazman, A. W. Bramlett (Laurens), David C. Boozer, Erskine P. Boozer, William Pitts Boyd, Charlie H. Bridges, Thomas C. Brown, Jeff. E. Brown, James Blackburn (Laurens), William A. Bailey (left the service 1862), J. Calvin Butler, Archie B. Canedy, M. Pinckney Cline, J. Edward Caldwell, A. B. Collins, George Clamp, James S. Cameron, J. Presley Cameron, Samuel D. Cromer, Joseph H. Davis, John Davis, James Davis, S. S. Derrick, John G. Duckett, John P. Duckett, Joseph Duckett, Thomas Duckett, William Y. Fair, Robert Fair, George A. Fair, Michael Foot (procured a substitute in 1862), I. Newton Gary, Leonidas K. Glasgow, C. A. Graham, Henry Gallman, Monroe M. Harris, John R. Harris, Patrick H. Hargrove, Samuel J. Hiller, George E. Hiller, William Hatton, —. Hodge (received from cavalry in exchange for J. W. Miller in 1864), John A. Johnson, William Johnson (Georgia, received as a substitute for William Sultzbacher in 1863), I. J. Kelly, George Koon, George Kerney (received as a substitute for M. Foot in 1862), J. Middleton Kibler, James Lindsay, B. H. Lovelace, Thomas M. Lake, Enoch G. Lake, William Lee (Laurens), William K. Lindsay (substituted for James Davis in 1863 and was killed at Chickamauga same year), Lawrence R. Marshall, John B. Mayes, Samuel T. McCoy, Samuel J. McCaughrin, William J. McMillan (Chester), William W. Miller, John W. Miller, John W. Mathis, Thomas Marshall, William Metts (Laurens), McDuffie Metts, W. Glenn Metts, Samuel W. Murtishaw, E.

F. Neil (Laurens), Alfred E. Nance, William F. Norris (discharged in 1861 before entering service), J. Wirick Odell, Simeon Pratt, Simeon Price, Bert H. Pope, William Henry Pope, Thomas H. Pope, Harrington Pope, John M. Reid, William W. Reid, William W. Ruff, Thomas W. Sligh, Benjamin W. Schumpert (Georgia), O. L. Schumpert, Frank A. Sawyer, J. Ebenezer P. Sloan, John W. Wright, J. W. Wilson, B. Frank Summers, William Thompson, Hugh Renwick, Reuben F. Ruff, Thomas P. Marshall, J. A. Tribble (Laurens), Caleb Wilson.

J. H. Ruff lived through the war; J. M. H. Ruff, promoted to Assistant Surgeon; Peter Rodelsperger, discharged in 1861 at expiration of term; Jacob Rice served through; John W. Riser served through; Wallace W. Riser, wounded at Chancellorsville, Gettysburg and Cedar Creek, lived through the war; George C. Riser served through; Moorman Ruff served through; George Sligh, discharged in 1861, physical disability; William C. Sligh, wounded at Fredericksburg, served through; Hillary W. Suber, wounded at Fredericksburg, served through; G. Benjamin Suber, transferred to 5th Cavalry in 1862; Frank A. Souter, wounded at Sharpsburg, disabled and discharged; William Sultzbacher, substituted by William Johnson in 1862; D. V. Scurry enlisted for State service only; William T. Tarrant, promoted to Lieutenant, assigned to another company, in 1865; J. Owens Turnipseed served through the war; Daniel B. Wheeler, wounded at Savage Station, disabled and discharged in 1862; Mike H. Witt, transferred to cavalry in 1862, served through; Thomas R. Wilson, transferred to Company C, Third Regiment, 1861; Samuel J. Wood, discharged at Manassas in 1861; Henry S. Wingard, wounded at Knoxville, discharged from Union prison at surrender, 1865; Silas Wedeman served through; W. Pleasant Willingham served through; Thomas W. Weir (Laurens), served through; A. J. Willingham, served through; Julius Zobel, wounded at Knoxville, leg amputated, discharged from Union prison at close of war; Jesse D. Hornsby served through; James Y. Harris served through.

The following is a list of those killed in battle : Richard Henry Haltiwanger, 2nd Lieutenant, Gettysburg; Pinckney P. Langford, 3d Lieutenant, Gettysburg; Bluford S. Buzhardt, Sergeant, Savage Station; John R. Harris, Corporal, Sharpsburg; Richard A. Leavell, Corporal, Knoxville; Privates: L.

Pinckney Glymph, Knoxville; W. Calvin Butler, Gettysburg; Erskine S. Boozer, Strasburg; George Clamp, Cold Harbor; John C. Davis, Chancellorsville; William Hatton, James River; George W. Koon, Chickamauga; Jasper Kelly, Cedar Creek; William R. Lindsay, Chickamauga; Samuel McCoy, Sharpsburg; W. J. McMillan, Fredericksburg; John B. Mayes, Chickamauga; William Henry Pope, Averysborough, N. C.; William W. Reid, Chancellorsville; William W. Ruff, Petersburg; Thomas W. Sligh, Gettysburg; Benjamin W. Schumpert (son of Amos K. Schumpert, of Georgia, who went from Newberry; was a student in Newberry College when the war began, volunteered, joined the Quitman Rifles, and was killed in battle at Chickamauga in 1863); Frank A. Sawyer, Knoxville; J. Ebenezer P. Sloan, Knoxville; John W. Wright, Sharpsburg; W. W. Wilson, Strasburg. Total, 26.

The following died from wounds received in battle: H. Bachman Reid, Corporal, died at Richmond, wounded at Savage Station; Thomas G. Sloan, Corporal, died at Newberry, wounded at Chickamauga; David C. Boozer, died at Lynchburg, wounded at Second Wilderness, 1864; William H. Johnson, died in Georgia, wounded at Chickamauga; B. Frank Summers, died at Richmond, wounded at ———; William Thompson, died near Richmond from wounds received in a skirmish near that city. Total, 6.

The following died of disease during the war: Robert L. Weir, near Centreville, Va., 1861; Thomas Lake, 1st Sergeant, Fairfax, Va.; Thomas G. Harris, Corporal, Winchester, 1862; Drayton W. Ramage, Corporal, Chancellorsville, 1862; Jasper N. Abrams, Private, Charlottesville, Va., 1861; —. Atkins, 1861; Henry C. Buzhardt (Lexington, S. C.), Richmond, 1861; George C. Derrick (S. S.) Culpeper, 1861; George A. Fair, Culpeper or Staunton, Va., 1861; Robert P. Fair, Newberry or Columbia, S. C., 1861; John A. Johnson, Newberry or Charlottesville, 1861; William Lee (Laurens), Union prison; Thomas P. Marshall, Chattanooga, 1863; Simeon Price, Staunton, 1864; Bert Pope, Newberry, 1862; John Reid, Richmond, 1862; Hugh Renwick, Richmond; Reuben F. Ruff, Culpeper; J. A. Tribble (Laurens), Camp Johnson, S. C.; Caleb Wilson, Richmond. Total, 20.

We thus find that in this company of 167 men, 26 were killed in battle, 6 mortally wounded, and 20 died from sickness and hardships incident to camp life; total, 52. Making the loss of Company E a little greater than that of Company B.

Captain James D. Nance, first Captain of this company, was also killed during the war, but his death occurred while he was Colonel of the regiment, having been elected to that office in 1862, on the reorganization of the regiment after the expiration of the first year's term of service.

No man, perhaps, was ever more endeared to his personal friends than Colonel James D. Nance. I have heard some of them speak of him often as the Chevalier Bayard of Newberry, a man without fear and without reproach. No higher praise can be given to a soldier than this. He was a strict disciplinarian, and could allow no breach of military duty. But as an officer, whether as Captain or Colonel, he never forgot nor neglected to see to the comfort and welfare of his men.

He was quite a young man at the time of his death, not yet twenty-seven years old, having been born October 10th, 1837, and killed in the battle of the Wilderness, May 6th, 1864.

General Johnston's army, of which I was at that time not *magna pars*, but a very small unit in the 19th S. C. V., had just crossed the Etowah River on the retreat from Dalton towards Atlanta, and had stopped to rest for the afternoon and night, when I received a letter from home informing me of the death of Colonel Nance; that he had been killed in the battle of the Wilderness. The information made me very sad, not only on account of the loss to the country, but the loss was also personal, for he was a young man for whom I entertained a warm feeling of friendship. This was about the middle of May. Not many days thereafter we fought the battle of New Hope Church, or Pumpkin Vine Creek, as it was called by the other side, in which we inflicted heavy loss upon the Federals with very little detriment to ourselves. I remember as well, as though it were only yesterday, the appearance of the road, the scenery around, and the church as we approached it. The day was lovely, warm but not hot, the road was firm and good, of a white or grayish soil. When distant about a hundred, or perhaps two hundred yards of the church and just before we halted, I said to my comrades near: "Boys, this would be a mighty pretty place for a fight." Little did I know that we would be fighting so soon. Very soon the line was halted, marched off into the edge of the woods on our right, and in a short time the two armies, or portions thereof, were hotly engaged. One of my comrades, who was near me at that time, J. D. Smith Livingston, is now living just outside the corporate limits of the town of New-berry; and one whom I am now glad to call friend, but whom at that time I had never seen, as he was a Georgia boy, George McWhirter, was also in that fight, and now lives at Newberry. Not many days thereafter, on the night of Sunday, the 29th of May, I received a wound which disabled me, sent me to the rear, and rendered me unfit for active service the balance of the war. And even now, more than twenty-five years after the wound was received, it still pains me.

General Howard in his article in the *Century Magazine* descriptive of the campaign from Dalton to Atlanta, says that it rained almost incessantly during the month of May, 1864. In this he is mistaken. It was not May, but June. The month of May was very pleasant, with scarcely any rain—no heavy rains except one, which fell in the early part of the night of the 8th, or 9th, I think the 9th, and that was one of the greatest downpours it was ever my fortune, or misfor-tune, to be exposed to. From that time to the end of the month I felt only one slight shower. I was placed in hospital on the 31st of May, at Atlanta. Soon after, a rainy spell set in and all through June it rained almost continually, so that the wells dug for the benefit of the hospital became filled with water, as the nurses told me.

Others of my comrades, who were in the fight at New Hope Church, were killed at Atlanta, and some not killed whom I have never seen since. One brother, Thomas E. Chapman, was mortally wounded, but lived to get home. W. S. Peterson, captain of my company and a native of Newberry, was killed. J. D. S. Livingston, a Newberrian *now*, was severely wounded; James M. Abney, his brother-in-law, was wounded. Jacob Crouch, the father of P. N. Crouch, a former landlord of the Newberry Hotel, was killed. There was one other Newberrian besides myself, a member of Captain Peterson's Company, 19th S. C. V., whose name should be inserted in these Annals— William Gentry, who died in camp at Lightwood Knot Springs, near Columbia, S. C. John C. Wheeler, brother of D. B.

Wheeler, born in Newberry, color bearer of the Regiment, brave as the bravest, was killed at Atlanta.

In Colonel Johnson Hagood's command there was only one from Newberry, Randall Johnstone, son of my old friend Silas Johnstone, Esq. Only four, if my information be correct, in the Fourteenth Regiment: Christian H. Suber, Esq., Quartermaster with rank of Captain, promoted to Brigade Quartermaster with rank of Major, (Major Suber died at his home in Newberry, 12th March, 1890, in his 62nd year); Robert L. McCaughrin succeeded Major Suber as Quartermaster in 1862, with the rank of Captain. He is now a good citizen of the town and President of the Newberry National Bank and of the Newberry Cotton Mills; Albert Boyce, who was killed at the battle of Gaines' Mill; and Henry McCullough—died since the war.

The following were members of the Macbeth Artillery and were all still living May, 1888: R. S. Davidson, J. D. Davidson, John Henderson, L. H. Sims, J. D. Epps, Willie Morris and James Morris, to which names I have been told I must add the following: J. P. Sims, who was wounded, and James Redpath—died since the war.

Roll of Company "G," Thirteenth Regiment, S. C. V.

William Lester, Captain, promoted to Lieutenant-Colonel, died 1886; J. B. Fellers, 1st Lieutenant; John F. Banks, 2nd Lieutenant; J. H. Cannon, 3d Lieutenant; J. M. Wheeler, 1st Sergeant; J. D. A. Kibler, 2nd Sergeant; J. L. Fellers, 3d Sergeant; W. C. Hussey, 4th Sergeant; A. P. Dominick, 5th Sergeant; H. M. Singley, 1st Corporal; B. A. Boozer, 2nd Corporal, died from wounds July 3d, 1863, at Gettysburg, Pa.; M. M. Pitts, 3d Corporal, dead; A. H. Wheeler, 4th Corporal.

Privates—W.. C. Aull, died from wounds in 1863; J. M. Aull, Geo. B. Aull; G. S. Bobb, died 15th April, 1862, from wounds; J. F. Bobb, died 14th May, 1862; J. R. Y. Brown, died 3d September, 1862, from wounds; J. B. Boland, died August 1st, 1862; S. N. Baird, Carwile Baird; W. A. Bedenbaugh, died July 8th, 1863; L. S. Bowers; Newton Boozer, dead; Henry Boozer, died in 1890; R. C. Boozer, died since the war; J. M. Bowers, died in 1884; J. S. Bowers, died at Petersburg, Va.,

from wounds; W. F. B. Bobb, killed 29th August, 1862, at
Second Manassas; J. H. Counts; P. W. Counts, died 1864—
smallpox; J. A. Counts, died July 7th, 1863; P. B. Cook,
killed 29th August, 1863, at Second Manassas; S. A. Connelly,
J. C. Counts; William Chapman, died January 19th, 1863;
P. C. Cook, killed 29th August, 1863, at Second Manassas;
J. T. P. Crosson; Carwile Clamp, dead; W. P. Counts, died
5th July, 1862, from wounds; William Connelly; Ed. Cox,
died 1864; J. W. Dennis, killed in battle; M. V. Dalton, died
July 1st, 1862; A. B. C. Dominick, killed at Manassas Junction; W. T. Dennis, D. L. Dennis; J. M. Duncan, died De-
cember 20th, 1862; Mord. Duncan, dead; D. T. Dominick, J.
H. Dominick, Henry Daniels, A. Y. Enlow, Nathan Enlow;
John Elmore, dead; W. L. Fellers, died September 1st, 1862;
W. W. Griffith; J. C. Griffith, died 28th May, 1862; Geo. P.
Griffith; H. F. Holloway, died in 1887; H. C. Hartman, died
during the war; Geo. E. Hawkins; L. P. Hawkins, killed in
retreat from Petersburg, Va.; Joseph Hiller; Jacob Hawkins, died
in 1892; Wm. Jennings, J. F. Kibler, M. D. Kinard, S. J. Kinard,
T. D. Kinard, Andrew Kinard, J. A. C. Koon; B. King, died
since the war; J. A. Kinard, died since the war; M. L. Kinard,
J. P. Kinard, Washington Lever, Charles Lester; George Liv-
ingston, died in hospital; N. Livingston, dead; Leander Long,
S. Lagrone, John A. Long, M. M. Long, M. L. Long, Frank
Moss, B. H. Miller, G. S. Moore; John McCullough, killed at
Bloody Bend; J. H. McCullough, died since the war; J. D.
Morris, died during the war; Wm. C. McNinch, killed 1st
July, 1863, at Gettysburg; B. B. Moore, killed at Gettysburg,
July 1st, 1863; Ferdinand Morris, died since the war; Joab
Mathis, killed at Gettysburg July 1st, 1863; Ben Mathis, died
July 13th, 1863; D. L. Moore, A. H. Miller, A. A. Nates; G. H.
Nates, dead; Wm. Nobles, dead; Joseph Nobles, J. N. Parrot,
J. E. Quattlebaum, Jefferson Quattlebaum; S. P. Quattlebaum,
killed August 29th, 1862, at Second Manassas; J. A. Rikard,
killed at Gettysburg; A. J. Rankin, H. C. Rankin; D. F. Reid,
died 25th December, 1861; T. W. Reid, died during the war;
John Rikard, dead; J. M. Rikard, killed at Spottsylvania;
Levi Rikard, died during the war; W. M. Stockman, died July
6th, 1862; J. H. Stockman, killed in battle; J. O. Shealy, killed
at Deep Bottom; Wm. H. Shealy, killed in battle; J. E. Smith,

died during the war; J. W. Smith, died in 1861; D. C. Singley, died September 18th, 1863, from wounds; F. P. Shealy, John Shealy; E. K. Schumpert, died since the war; J. J. Summers, dead; D. H. Taylor, J. M. Taylor; Drayton Taylor, died July 25th, 1862; S. P. Taylor, John F. Taylor; J. H. Wise, died September 30th, 1861; L. E. Wise; O. Simeon Werts, James Wood; Charles Wilson, died in Federal prison; D. M. Ward, Jefferson Wicker, James M. Werts.

Officers, 13; privates, 127—total officers and men, 140. Killed in battle, 16; mortally wounded, 7; died from sickness, 24—total deaths during the war, 47. Died since the war, 21—grand total, 68. Still surviving, 71.

Company G, known as the DeKalb Guards, was organized at Prosperity on the 17th of August, 1861, and was mustered into the service on the 4th of September, by Captain Black, C. S. Army, having arrived at Camp Johnson on the 26th of August. It numbered, when received into service, seventy privates and thirteen commissioned and non-commissioned officers, making a total of eighty three. It afterwards, from time to time, received accessions, so as to make the whole number enrolled one hundred and twelve. Left Lightwood Knot Spring on the 3d of November and arrived at Charleston the same day at 11 o'clock P. M. On the 7th were moved to North Edisto Island; on the 13th by steamer Marion to White Point, where they lay one night, and took up line of march next morning for Adams Run, on the Savannah Railroad, at which place they stayed two nights and one day, and then moved to Coosawhatchie Station, where they joined the regiment on the 16th, the regiment having been separated at Camp Evans, Charleston, S. C. On the 13th December, 1861, left Coosawhatchie for Pocotaligo, which place they left on the 19th for Combahee Ferry. At Camp Pemberton the DeKalb Guards and the Newberry Rifles were detached from the regiment and encamped near Far Bluff, on the Combahee River, 26th December, 1861, and named their camp "Newberry." Pickets go to Far Bluff and Field's Point. The DeKalb Guards left Camp Newberry on the 11th of January, 1862, and on the 21st arrived at the headquarters of the regiment at Camp Pemberton. Here the company was sent to guard the Charleston and Savannah Railroad from Salkehatchie to Ashepoo Ferry. They were relieved about the first of February, and on the 6th left Camp Pemberton and camped on the Far Bluff road, six miles from Green Pond Station.

Captain Lester's record of the movements of his company ends here. There are a few notes and memoranda of trials and punishments of some non-commissioned officers and soldiers for misconduct, and notes of promotions of others, and memoranda of the deaths of some. At what time his company and the regiment were ordered to Virginia, he does not say, but it was early in 1862. Mr. Caldwell, in his "History of Gregg's (McGowan's) Brigade," which was composed of three regiments —Twelfth, Thirteenth and Fourteenth—says that it was ordered to Virginia in April, 1862. As this company formed part of the Thirteenth Regiment, which was part of McGowan's Brigade, you will find its history traced until the close of the war in Mr. Caldwell's history of that brigade, which, I must be permitted to say here, is a valuable and well written work.

William Lester, Captain of Company G, 13th S. C. V.— raised to the rank of Colonel before the close of the war—was a man of more than ordinary merit. He was the son of Allen Lester and was born in Newberry County. When the war broke out he was peacefully pursuing his business as a farmer, but, like a true citizen, he soon offered his services to his country, which he served with honor and fidelity until the close of the contest. Some of his comrades have told me that on the field of battle and in times of the greatest danger he was as calm, cool and collected as it was possible for a man to be, or as he himself might have been when at home entertaining a welcome guest. He lived for some years after the war, and when his work was ended here he passed peacefully and hopefully into that other world where, we hope, there are no wars.

COMPANY "G," SECOND REGIMENT, STATE TROOPS.

Other company rolls should precede the one I give now, but as I have not received them yet I proceed to give the names of officers and men of Company G, Second Regiment of State Troops, who were sent to the coast near Pocotaligo, S. C., in 1863: George H. Chapman, Captain; John R. Spearman, George Shealy and William R. Lane, Lieutenants. The other officers, sergeants and other non-commissioned, I do not now remember, except Frederick Cromer, Orderly Sergeant; Privates: William Chapman, John A. Chapman, Archibald Chapman, R. L. Bradley, Robert Pratt, Matthias Miller, John Miller, Jacob Kibler, James Sloan, William Caldwell, William Caldwell, W. W. Waldrop, Drayton Waldrop, James Mangum, Martin Bickley, Simeon Bickley, Sampson Bickley, C. C. Teague, Allen Nichols, Yates Myers, George Mayer, Drayton Cureton, Jesse Dennis, James Hunter, John Mathis, Allen Hawkins, Jacob Hawkins, John Boozer, David Boozer, Daniel Amick, Henry Amick, Levi Amick, George Counts, John Counts, Saunders Cummalander, Middleton Cummalander, A. W. Bundrick, —. Weed, Joel Wise, John Epting, —. Epting, Levi Sheppard, John R. Bangle, James Cromer, Matthias Wicker, Jefferson Wicker, Anderson Wicker, Dempson King, John Wedeman, —. Haltiwanger, John McCullough, Lewis Perkins, William Summers, —. Kibler, John Riser, Washington Lorick, Stanmore B. Langford, James Stillwell, M. Aaron Dominick, George Rikard, Stanmore Black, Christian H. Enlow, Noah Enlow, Jacob Werts, Henry A. Bailey, —. Balentine, Wm. D. Frick, J. W. B. Lever, John Livingston, John R. Lake, C. H. Kingsmore, James F. Harrington. Total, 77 rank and file.

Some few were from Lexington; but I will let their names remain, as nearly all were from Newberry.

These troops were called out for six months, and during the latter part of their service they were stationed in the swamp region not far from old Pocotaligo, where a fatal kind of sickness attacked them and carried off four or five of their number. I have since learned that it was meningitis. Several died in the tent on the opposite side of the street in front of the one occupied by the mess of which I was a member. There was one remarkable fact in regard to this sickness which, I think, is worthy of note. The lines of tents ran from north to south, and the tent occupied by myself and mess was on the western side of the street, facing the east. In our tent we had no sickness whatever, and there was very little, if any, all along the line on the western side—no deaths. Whatever may have been the cause of the different states of health on the different sides of the street, I know not; but such is the truth of the case. The western side was nearly or entirely exempt

2   E

from sickness, while the eastern had many cases, some of which did, indeed, recover. One lingered at home for several months and then died; one died on the train on his way home. The greater number died in a few days from the first attack, and one in less than twenty-four hours, having lost consciousness almost immediately.

Some few of this company were discharged soon after their arrival at McPhersonville, as being unfit and unable to undergo the hardships of camp life and to discharge their duties as soldiers. One of these was my old friend, William Frick, a good man and true, who was incurably lame, having been a cripple ever since he was fourteen years of age. Some were detailed for light duty, at home or elsewhere. So that I lost sight of them for the remainder of the war.

John Mathis died in camp in less than twenty four hours after he was taken sick; Drayton Cureton on the way home; John Boozer at home, after lingering several months. There were, I think. some other deaths in camp, but my memory fails me here. R. L. Bradley and Stanmore Langford died in service after we were discharged from Pocotaligo. James Hunter also died during the war.

Jacob Kibler, after several months, procured a substitute; and so the name of Willis Philips must be recorded here as a member of Captain Chapman's company, Second Regiment State Troops.

This regiment was disbanded and discharged at the expiration of the term of service, and those who were liable to duty, after a few weeks' furlough, sought other commands. This writer cast his lot with Company G, commanded by Captain W. S. Peterson (at the time, however, under command of Captain Chatham), Nineteenth Regiment S. C. Volunteers; Gabriel Manigault, Brigadier-General; —. Shaw, Lieutenant-Colonel, commanding the regiment.

It was delightful to pass from the swampy, submerged country where we had been camped near Pocotaligo, to the region of breezy hills and snow-tipped mountains, near Dalton, Ga. While in winter quarters there, near the close of winter, in March, I think, there came a fall of snow one night, and when we were called out to roll-call in the morning we found several inches of snow on the ground. About nine o'clock a regular battle began between two different brigades, or divisions, of the army, lasting several hours. This writer was on the losing side, was beaten and taken prisoner. However, I fell into kind hands and was well treated. That was my last snow battle, at this writing—March 7th, 1892—just twenty-eight years ago.

Captain W. S. Peterson was a native of Newberry County, and was born near Saluda, on an old road, long disused, I think, running from Higgins' Ferry down the river by William Wilson's plantation, Mrs. Peterson's and others, to New Chapel. He grew to manhood in the county; taught school several years at or near the Dead Fall; married, in Edgefield, a sister of this historian; after marriage carried on mercantile business at Dead Fall (name now obsolete); finally bought land in Edgefield and moved to that county, where he was living, engaged in farming, when the war broke out. On the organization of the company he was elected captain, which position he held until Hood's disastrous battles at Atlanta, in one of which he was killed, shot through the head while charging, sword in hand, at the head of his company. He was a brave man and true, and as he was a native of this county I felt bound to record his name and this brief sketch in these Annals.

His brother, John T. Peterson, was Ordinary or Probate Judge of the county for several years, after the war. His knowledge of the laws pertaining to the duties of his office was good and his decisions were seldom, if ever, reversed. He died at his home on the 19th of June, 1889. He had good literary taste and judging from some stories and sketches of his that I have read in print and in manuscript, I feel sure that, under propitious circumstances, he might have attained to some distinction in the world of letters.

I hope the reader will pardon me for a brief recital here of some merely personal reminiscences, especially as they are connected with descendants of Newberry people.

While in winter quarters near Dalton, Ga., I met and became acquainted with Lieutenant Stephen P. Chapman, of the 24th Alabama Regiment, a grandson of my father's brother, Elijah Chapman, who had married Miss Elizabeth Martin, of Edgefield, and had moved to Clark County, Alabama, while still a young man. Lieutenant Chapman was taken prisoner near Dalton, while in command of picket line, was carried to

Johnson's Island prison, where he remained a captive for ten months. He survived the war and at this date is still living in Alabama. While lying in hospital at Forsyth, Ga., another relative named Fluker, a grandson of my father's brother, Joseph Chapman, came to see me and made himself known to me. He was on furlough for a short time, having been wounded, I think. I do not know whether he was a relative of Mr. Pink. Fluker, whose experience as a hotel keeper was so disastrous, as related by Mr. Richard Malcolm Johnstone, of Georgia, but I think not, as he appeared to be a young man of very excellent sense and not at all puffed up with overweening self-conceit. At the same period of time, another near kinsman, a cousin, Rev. Henry O'Neall Chapman, son of my father's brother Lewis, and grandson of Henry O'Neall, one of the old Quakers of Bush River, was chaplain of a regiment in Sherman's army. He passed through Georgia and South Carolina, and through the lower part of Newberry County in which he was born, with that army in its triumphant progress. Ours was truly a fratricidal war.

While giving these personal reminiscences I may be permitted to mention that after the expiration of my furlough for sixty days when I reported to hospital in Columbia in October 1864, I there met, and my wound was xamined and probed by, Dr. Todd, a brother-in-law of President Lincoln, then in the Confederate service. He afterwards became a citizen of this State and was called to see a patient at Newberry, or in Newberry County, some time during the year 1888.

There are many descendants of Newberrians in Clarke County and in other parts of Alabama, in Georgia, Texas, Mississippi, and indeed all over the West to the golden shores of California; but their fortunes I do not know and only a few of their names. I can mention the names of Pugh and Coates and Summers, all familiar to the people of Newberry. Sidney Pugh in March, 1889, took his degree in medicine at the Medical College in New Orleans.

I did have hopes that some one acquainted with them would write for these Annals the fortunes of some, at least, of the many families that went to the great Southwest from Newberry in the olden time, as did Mr. David Jones of those who emigrated to Ohio. I had such hopes but I fear they will bear no fruit. I can say, however, that Robert Furnas, a descendant of Joseph Furnas, a Quaker of Bush River, so favorably mentioned by Judge O'Neall in his Annals, was, in 1874, Governor of Nebraska.

ROLL OF COMPANY "B," FIRST REGIMENT, S. C. V.

Whitfield Walker, Captain, age 40; volunteered January 5, 1861; resigned March 27, 1862. Captain Walker left the service in Virginia and entered as colonel of a regiment in the West. E. Knotts, 1st Lieutenant, age 25; volunteered January 5, 1861; discharged July 14, 1861; afterwards killed in battle. R. B. Ligon, 2nd Lieutenant, age 25; volunteered January 5, 1861; discharged July 14, 1861. S. B. Chappell, 3d Lieutenant, age 27; volunteered January 5, 1861; resigned February, 1861. —. Douglas, 1st Sergeant, age 27; volunteered January 5, 1861; discharged July 14, 1861. Calvin S. Taylor, 2nd Sergeant, age 22; volunteered August 27, 1861; discharged May, 1862; promoted to 1st Sergeant; died from disease. M. Bowers, 2nd Sergeant, age 35; volunteered January 5, 1861; discharged July 14, 1861. P. Cromer, 4th Sergeant, age 22; volunteered January 5, 1861; discharged July 14, 1861. B. M. Blease, 4th Sergeant; age 40; volunteered January 5, 1861; resigned August, 1863; first volunteer from Newberry; promoted to 3d, 2nd, 1st Lieutenant and Captain; severely wounded at Cold Harbor, which disabled him and compelled his resignation. James H. Boyd, Corporal, age 23; volunteered August 27, 1861; discharged December, 1862; promoted to corporal and to sergeant. W. W. Boazman, Corporal, age 24; volunteered January 5, 1861; discharged July 14, 1861. D. P. Goggans, Corporal, age 24; volunteered January 5, 1861; discharged by surrender of Army, April 10, 1865; promoted to 3d and 2nd Sergeant, 1st Lieutenant and Captain; disabled in battle March 31, 1865, by loss of leg. B. S. Higgins, Corporal; age 23, volunteered January 5, 1861; killed in the charge at Cold Harbor, June 29th, 1862. James C. Hill, Corporal, age 23; volunteered August 27, 1861; discharged by surrender April 10, 1865; promoted to sergeant. E. C. McCoy, Corporal, age 24; volunteered August 27, 1861;

retired August, 1864; lost a leg in battle at Second Manassas. P. B. Watts, Corporal, age 24; volunteered January 5, 1861; discharged July 14, 1861; afterwards killed in battle. H. Williams, Corporal, age 27; volunteered January 5, 1861; discharged July 14, 1861.

Privates—Joseph Abrams, age 20; volunteered January 5, 1861; discharged by surrender April 10, 1865; promoted to corporal and to sergeant. Thomas Abrams, age 21; volunteered January 5, 1861; discharged July 14, 1861. W. J. S. Abrams, age 40; volunteered September 21, 1864; discharged at surrender April 10, 1865. J. H. Adair, age 40; volunteered December 24, 1863; discharged at surrender April 10, 1865. P. B. Aldridge, age 18; volunteered. January 5, 1861; discharged July 14, 1861. Love Anderson, age 45; entered service October 27, 1864; killed at Petersburg, Va., April 2, 1865. Moses Barker, age 18; entered service July 2, 1863; discharged at surrender. William Bean, age 20; volunteered January 5, 1861; discharged July 14, 1861. James W. Beard, age 19; volunteered January 5, 1861; discharged September 15, 1864—wounded and disabled. John Blats, age 22; volunteered January 5, 1861; discharged July 14, 1861; S. Boozer, age 23; volunteered January 5, 1861; discharged July 14, 1861. —. Boulger, age 45; volunteered January 5, 1861; discharged July 14, 1861. D. C. Boyd, age 20; volunteered August 27, 1861; killed at Gettysburg, Pa., July 3, 1863. Pinckney Boyd, age 21; volunteered January 5, 1861; discharged July 14, 1861. Pitts Boyd, age 19; volunteered January 5, 1861; discharged July 14, 1861. E. P. Boazman, age 20; volunteered January 5, 1861; discharged July 14, 1861. R. S. Bradley, age 40; entered service January, 1864; discharged at surrender. David I. Brown, age 45; volunteered August 27, 1861; discharged at surrender. Good soldier: served in Mexican war. Wm. Burnam, age 18; volunteered January 5, 1861; died July, 1861. J. F. J. Caldwell, age 23; volunteered May, 1862; discharged at surrender; promoted to 2nd and 1st Lieutenant; several times severely wounded in battle. Spencer Caldwell, age 24; entered service August 27, 1861; discharged at surrender. Jacob Campbell, age 20; entered service August 27, 1861; discharged at surrender. John Carr, age 22; volunteered January 5, 1861; discharged July 14, 1861. William Henry Carter, age 23; volunteered January 5, 1861; discharged July 14, 1861. Joseph A. Chalmers, age 24; volunteered August 27, 1861. Good soldier—killed at Cold Harbor, June 29, 1862. Daniel Gibbs Chambers, age 18; volunteered January 5, 1861; killed at Gettysburg, Pa., July 1, 1863. M. Aleck Chambers, age 24; volunteered January 5, 1861; supposed to have died in prison, July, 1863. H. Clamp, age 17; volunteered January 5, 1861; died of disease December, 1861. William Clamp, age 25; volunteered January 5, 1861; discharged by exchange April, 1863. Newton F. Corley, age 23; joined March 5, 1864; discharged at surrender. W. C. Counts, age 20; volunteered January 5, 1861; deserted October, 1862. James Cromer, age 22; volunteered January 5, 1861; discharged July 14, 1861. J. D. Cromer, age 18; volunteered August 27, 1861; died November, 1862. John Caldwell, age 18; volunteered January 5, 1861; died of disease August, 1862. Thomas Davenport, age 18; volunteered August 27, 1861; discharged at surrender. —. Deal, age 22; volunteered February, 1861; discharged July 14, 1861. Daniel Dendy, age 24; George Denson, age 40; James Denson, age 21, and Augustus Dickert, age 20, all volunteered January 5, 1861, and were discharged at the same time, July 14, 1861. Peter Duckett, age 35; entered service October 27, 1864; discharged January 31, 1865. J. C. Evans, age 40; volunteered January 5, 1861; served through the war; surrendered at close. Thomas Odell, age 25; volunteered July 27, 1861; surrendered at close. John L. Parrish, age 40; entered service March 15, 1864; surrendered at close. B. Perry, age 18; volunteered July 27, 1861; surrendered at close. John Perry, age 25; volunteered July 27, 1861; surrendered at close. Burton Pope, age 17; volunteered January, 1862; died of disease August, 1862. Sampson Pope, age 25; volunteered January 5, 1861; promoted to 3d and 1st Lieutenant, then Captain; afterwards resigned, July 12, 1862, and was transferred to the medical department, where he did good and able service. James Plumer, age 22; volunteered August 27, 1861; promoted to corporal and to sergeant; died of wounds at Gettysburg, Pa., July 3, 1863. William Pulley, age 21; volunteered January 5, 1861; discharged July 14, 1861. P. R. Ramage, age 21; volunteered July 27, 1861; died of disease December, 1862, very suddenly, at Fredericksburg, Va. Hayne

D. Reid, age 25; volunteered January 5, 1861; discharged November, 1862. Hiram Reid, age 23; volunteered July 27, 1861; killed at Cold Harbor, Va., June 29, 1862. William Rice, age 20; volunteered January 5, 1861; surrendered at close. John W. Riser, age 21; W. W. Riser, age 19, William Ridlehuber, age 18; volunteered January 5, 1861; discharged July 14, 1861. Warren F. Robertson, aged 40; volunteered July 27, 1861; promoted to hospital steward—did good service in medical department. George Rollinson, age 27; volunteered July 27, 1862; died of disease July, 1862. R. L. Ruff, age 25; volunteered January 5, 1861; surrendered at close. John Ruff, age 18; volunteered August, 1861; promoted to corporal; killed May 12, 1864, at Spottsylvania C. H., Va. Brave youth, says Captain Goggans. H. W. Ridlehuber, age 19; volunteered January 5, 1861; promoted to 3d, 2nd and 1st Sergeant. Brave soldier—killed at Wilderness May 5, 1864. James Roebuck, age 30; volunteered August 27, 1861; promoted to corporal. Good soldier—killed at Second Manassas. Samuel W. Sample, age 25; entered January 4, 1864; surrendered at close. Wade Sanders, age 40; volunteered July 27, 1864; surrendered at close. William Sanders, age 23; volunteered January 5, 1861; discharged July 14, 1865. F. Satterwhite, age 40; volunteered May, 1862; died of disease 1862. James S. Sims, age 21; volunteered August 27, 1861; wounded several times; promoted to corporal; died of disease August, 1864—good soldier. H. Snell, age 16; volunteered April, 1862; surrendered at close. John Stewart, age 40; entered February 1, 1864; surrendered at close. Edward Stephens, age 22; volunteered January 5, 1861; killed at Cold Harbor, June 29, 1862. Thomas Stirling, age 17; volunteered January 21, 1864; died of disease January, 1865. —. Stripling, age 45; volunteered January 5, 1861; discharged July 14, 1861. Served in Mexican war. Enoch Suber, age 45; volunteered July 27, 1861; died of disease December, 1862. Samuel Suber, age 25; volunteered July 27, 1861; surrendered at close. D. P. Summer, age 19; volunteered August 27, 1861; surrendered at close. Henry Summer, age 45; volunteered January 5, 1861; discharged July 14, 1864. H. C. Summers, age 21; volunteered July 27, 1861; surrendered at close. Larkin J. Summer, age 17; volunteered October 19, 1863;

surrendered at close. Harmon Taylor, age 23; volunteered July 27, 1861; supposedto have been killed at Wilderness, May 5, 1864. Griffin Thomas, age 18; volunteered July 27, 1861, with Sharp Shooters—good soldier—killed July 27, 1864. T. Thornton, age 30; volunteered July 27, 1861; died from wounds received at Cold Harbor, June 29, 1862. Drury Todd, age 25; volunteered July 27, 1861; surrendered at close. William Vance, age 21; volunteered January 5, 1861; discharged July 14, 1861. M. A. Voght, age 19, volunteered August 27, 1861 —brave and intelligent youth—killed at Chancellorsville May 23, 1863. —. Wesson, age 35; volunteered February, 1861; discharged July 14, 1861. James C. Wilson, age 23; volunteered July 27, 1861; surrendered at close. James R. Wilson, age 48; volunteered July 27, 1861; promoted to corporal and to sergeant; surrendered at close. A. F. Workman, age 42; entered January 12, 1864; died of disease July, 1864. W. D. Workman, age 40; entered December 25, 1863; surrendered at close. Drury Wright, age 20; volunteered January 5, 1861; surrendered at close. Daniel Young, age 21; volunteered July 27, 1861; transferred to the Artillery, for special reasons, March, 1863. George Farbairn, age 25; volunteered January 5, 1861; discharged July 14, 1861. D. S. Felder, age 16; volunteered August 27, 1861; promoted to corporal and to sergeant—brave and noble youth—killed at Jericho Ford, Va., May 23, 1864. E. Ford, age 20; volunteered January 5, 1861, discharged July 14, 1861. Eli Franklin, age 25; volunteered January 5, 1861; surrendered at close. George Franklin, age 23; volunteered January 5, 1861; discharged July 14, 1861. William Franklin, age 27; volunteered January, 1862; surrendered at close. W. R. Franklin, age 30; volunteered January 5, 1861; died of disease November, 1862. —. Gallaspie, age 22; volunteered January 5, 1861; discharged July 14, 1861. George Garmany, age 24; volunteered August 27, 1861; discharged January, 1862. John L. Glasgow, age 40; entered January 5, 1864; discharged March, 1864. William Tandy Goggans, age 22; volunteered August 27, 1861—good soldier—killed at 2nd Manassas, August 29, 1862. John F. Golding, age 40; volunteered August 27, 1861; exchanged August, 1864— good soldier, faithful in battle. Washington Golding, age 25; volunteered August 27, 1861; died of disease 1862. B. W.

Goodman, age 22; volunteered January 5, 1861; discharged July 14, 1861. John Harris, age 23; volunteered January 5, 1861; discharged July 14, 1861. C. M. Harris, age 40; volunteered July 27, 1861; surrendered at close. John W. Hill, age 24; volunteered January 5, 1861; discharged July 14, 1861. John Hood, age 20; volunteered January 5, 1861; promoted to 3d, 2nd and 1st Sergeant; surrendered at close. R. S. Howard, age 24; volunteered August 27, 1861; promoted to 3d and 1st Lieutenant; disabled by wound at Wilderness; retired March, 1865. N. S. Hood, age 16; entered February 29, 1864; surrendered at close. R. W. Hill, age 24; volunteered January 5, 1861; discharged July 14, 1861. ——. Humphrey, age 40; volunteered August 27, 1861; discharged 1862. James Hunter, age 16; volunteered August 27, 1861— brave boy—killed at Chancellorsville May 3, 1863. J. K. Hunter, age 22; volunteered August 27, 1861; promoted to corporal; surrendered at close. P. S. Hunter, age 24; volunteered January 5, 1861; died of wounds received at Cold Harbor August 1, 1862. William Hunter, age 18; volunteered August 27, 1861; promoted to corporal and 2nd Sergeant; surrendered at close. David F. Hutchison, age 40; entered October 27, 1864; surrendered at close. George Hutchison, age 22; volunteered January 5, 1861; discharged July 14, 1861. James Hutchison, age 20; volunteered July 27, 1861; surrendered at close. Williams Hyler, age 23; volunteered May, 1862; deserted June, 1863. Frank Enlow, age 25; volunteered January 5, 1861; discharged July 14, 1861. Daniel Johnson, age 40; volunteered July 27, 1861; surrendered at close. ——. Johnson, age 25; volunteered February, 1861; discharged July 14, 1861. John Johnson, age 40; volunteered June, 1864; surrendered at close. William Kelly, age 35; volunteered July 27, 1861; surrendered at close. George D. Lathrop, age 16; volunteered February, 1862; surrendered at close. James A. Lathrop, age 20; volunteered January 5, 1861; surrendered at close. W. H. Lathrop, age 18; volunteered August 27, 1861; surrendered at close. R. S. Leek, age 18; volunteered August 27, 1861; died of disease at Danville, Va., December, 1862. W. Y. Leek, age 22; volunteered August 27, 1861; died of disease at Suffolk, Va.—body sent home November, 1861. Albert Leister, age 30; volunteered January

5, 1861; died suddenly of disease on Morris Island April, 1861. B. Leitzsey, age 20; volunteered August 27, 1861; promoted to corporal and to sergeant; surrendered at close. H. Little, age 25; volunteered January 5, 1861; discharged July 14, 1861. James Livert, age 24; volunteered January 5, 1861; discharged July 14, 1861. Samuel Livingston, age 23; volunteered July 27, 1861; died of disease 1862. William Lowry, age 40; volunteered January 5, 1861; died of wounds received at Second Manassas September, 1862. Burrell Lyles, age 18, volunteered August 27, 1861; surrendered at close. Erskine Lyles, age 20; volunteered January 5, 1861; promoted to sergeant and 3d, 2nd and 1st Lieutenant and Captain; died of wounds received at Second Manassas August 29, 1862. F. H. Lyles, age 20; volunteered January 5, 1861; killed at Fredericksburg, December 13, 1862. James Lane, age 16; volunteered August 27, 1861; killed at Chancellorsville. A. P. McCarty, age 25; volunteered August 27, 1861; promoted to corporal; killed at Chancellorsville. —. McCoe, age 22; volunteered February, 1861; discharged July 14, 1861 —an Irishman—I know nothing of his history. David McCullough, age 25; volunteered July 27, 1861; surrendered at close. Jas. McDavid, age 20; volunteered January 5, 1861; discharged July 14, 1861. David McGowan, age 27; volunteered July 27, 1861; discharged November, 1861. J. C. McLemore, age 25; volunteered January 5, 1861; promoted to sergeant, to 2nd and 1st Lieutenant and to Captain; died of wounds received at Second Manassas September, 1862. —. Merchant, age 30; volunteered July 27, 1861; discharged July 14, 1861—(an error here in the roll). William Milligan, age 23; volunteered July 27, 1861; surrendered at close. Daniel Montgomery, age 25; volunteered July 27, 1861; died of disease in 1862. Thomas Montgomery, age 18; volunteered February, 1862; discharged January, 1863. Thomas Motes, age 24; volunteered July 27, 1861; died of disease November, 1862. John Nesley, age 40; volunteered July 27, 1861; surrendered at close.

The whole number of men who saw service in this company from its formation January 5, 1861, to the close of the war was one hundred and seventy-one. Of that number there were killed thirty-one; died of disease and hardship twenty-four; desertions two. There were sixty-four discharged and one transferred. I suppose that some of those discharged afterwards joined other commands, as a number of discharges took place at the end of the six months' service, but how many I am not now able to say. The number of *officers* and *men wounded*, besides those killed, was forty. Total number of *wounds received* by the company was one hundred and twenty.

This company, known as the Rhett Guards, was the first from Newberry, formed January 5, 1861, and was received into the *State* service January 14, 1861, for six months. At the expiration of that term of service it was reorganized and received into the Confederate service August 27, 1861, to serve during the war. Served first in Gregg's Brigade, afterwards McGowan's; in A. P. Hill's and Wilcox's Divisions; Jackson's and A. P. Hill's Corps.

Raised and organized by Whit. Walker, who was the first captain. Killed, 31; died, 24; total loss by death, 55.

Roll of Company "F," Twentieth Regiment, S. C. V.

John M. Kinard, Captain, age 31; killed at Strasburg, October 13, 1864. Wm. M. Kinard, promoted to captain; died since war. Hillary J. Sligh, 2nd Lieutenant; resigned 1862. Edward R. Kingsmore, 2nd Lieutenant; died since the war. Will S. Cannon, wounded at Fort Sumter, promoted from sergeant to 3d Lieutenant; died since the war. S. W. Reid, wounded at Petersburg; promoted from 2nd Sergeant to 1st. Baylis W. Buzhardt, 3d Sergeant; died since the war. Jasper N. Epting, 4th Sergeant; discharged. F. D. Graham, 5th Sergeant. W. O. Goree, 1st Corporal; wounded at Deep Bottom; promoted to 5th Sergeant. C. M. Richie, 2d Corporal. Jesse C. Dickert, 3d Corporal; discharged at Sullivan's Island. Frank D. Rikard, 4th Corporal.

Privates—Zeb P. Abrams, wounded at Bentonville and discharged. Simeon S. Abrams, wounded at Cedar Creek. Daniels Abrams, discharged at Cold Harbor. Mike Baker; I suppose he came out all right. B. Barrett, discharged at Sullivan's Island. Henry J. Brooks, killed at Petersburg. Jim

Boozer. Manning R. Brown, wounded at Petersburg. Spencer P. Baird, discharged at Richmond. O. Hope Buzhardt. Jeff Buzhardt, died of disease at Sullivan's Island, 1862. Walter F. Buzhardt, died in some Union prison. Wash. Bowles. Henry Boozer, died of disease at home in 1862. William Buzhardt, died of yellow fever in Charleston, 1864. Sam. C. Barre. Joe P. Bedenbaugh. F. N. Cady. C. Wash. Calmes. Edd. Campbell. George Cannon, killed at Strasburg. Dave N. Chapman. John C. Counts, wounded and discharged at Cedar Creek. Adam Counts, wounded at Cedar Creek. John R. Counts. Jacob L. Cromer. A. B. Collins, killed at Petersburg. Henry Chapman, killed at Strasburg. Enoch Cromer. R. Press Cromer. John Crooks, discharged at Sullivan's Island. John F. Denson. George Denson. William T. Dickert, discharged at Richmond. Sam. H. Dunwoody, murdered since the war while acting as guard at the Newberry depot. John D. Davis, wounded at Cold Harbor. S. F. Dominick. John Duckett, killed at Cedar Creek. Warren Dickert, died of disease in hospital. William T. Epps. Micajah · Epps. William A. Eddy. Ham. H. Folk, discharged at Mount Pleasant. Wood H. Farrow, discharged at Mount Pleasant. William H. Glenn, killed at Petersburg. John D. Glenn. J. Belton Glymph, wounded at Petersburg. R. P. Greer. Wm. Glenn, wounded at Strasburg (from Laurens County). I. N. Gary, discharged at Richmond. David Glenn, from Laurens County. Jeff Gauntt, died of disease at Petersburg. Henry O. Henson. G. Andrew Hough. John I. Houseal. D. Julius Hentz, wounded at Battery Wagener. George Hawkins, wounded at Battery Wagener. Sullivan Herbert, discharged at Sullivan's Island. J. E. Jones. Lewis James. Adam Kibler. J. M. Kissick. Walter F. Koon. D. W. T. Kibler, discharged at Sullivan's Island. Minor Kinard, killed at Petersburg. John E. Lane, wounded at Petersburg. James C. Livingston, died of disease at Sullivan's Island. Robert J. Livingston, died of disease at Sullivan's Island. Ham Livingston. James Lindsay, died of disease at Richmond. Martin Cline. Archie McGill. H. Spence McCullough. William McCullough. J. Frank Miller. Joe T. Miller, died of wounds at Cold Harbor. David J. Muller. William Montgomery. Joe P. Moody, from Charleston. Jacob Nates. John E. Norris. Andrew Nichols. Andrew Rikard·

J. Wesley Rhodes. Thomas J. Rook. Arthur J. Ropp, killed at Fort Sumter. A. J. Rembly. Sam. J. Rook. James W. Rook. William Reeder. James M. Sanders. Wade H. Setzler. John P. Sloan. J. M. Stone. Henry Stone. David F. Suber. John C. Stewart. Monroe Sligh, died of disease at Charleston. Spencer F. Stewart, killed at Strasburg. Mid. Spence, wounded at Strasburg; discharged at Richmond. Edd Thomas. John Thrift. W. Dickens Watts, killed at Strasburg. J. David Wedeman. Silas Wedeman. J. Frank Wheeler. Robt. H. Williams. W. P. Wilcox, died of disease at Richmond. Lang. Wicker. Drayton Wicker. David R. Wicker, discharged at Richmond. Thomas V. Wicker. Belton Wicker. Pleas. W. Willingham. James S. Wilson, killed at Strasburg. John C. Wilson. M. John Wright, wounded at Bentonville; discharged at Richmond. Custer Wilson, wounded at Bentonville. Gilliam Wilson, died of disease at Charleston.

Whole number of men, officers included, 132. Killed, 12. Died of disease, 11. Died of wounds, 1. Total, 24. Whole number of wounds received besides the killed and mortally wounded, 17.

Some few were from Laurens County—very few. So I let their names stand. As their services during the war were rendered in a company from Newberry, it is but right and proper that they should be counted Newberry soldiers. I follow this rule in all cases where the number of men from this county is largely in the majority.

Roll of Company "D," Thirteenth Regiment, S. C. V.

Isaac F. Hunt, Captain, age 32; promoted to Colonel of regiment in 1863. Philander W. Cromer, age 26; Captain; promoted from 3d Lieutenant, 1863; killed at Gettysburg. James Y. McFall, age 26; Captain; promoted to 2d Lieutenant 1862; to Captain July 2, 1863; wounded at Ox Hall, Va.; Spottsylvania, Va.; served to close of war. Emanuel S. Coppock, age 31; 1st Lieutenant; resigned. Thomas F. Hunter, age 28; 1st Lieutenant; elected in 1863; killed at Chancellorsville. Henry L. Fuller, age 27; 2nd Lieutenant; elected in 1863; killed at Chancellorsville. William J. Lake, age 28; 1st Lieutenant; resigned. Andrew M. Bowers, age 39; 1st Lieutenant; wounded at Gettysburg; promoted from the ranks to 1st Lieutenant July 1, 1863. John H. Ruff, age 26; 1st Lieutenant; elected at Bunker Hill, Va. Joseph W. Hill, age 23; wounded at Deep Bottom; elected from corporal to 2nd Lieutenant at Bunker Hill; served through war—as did John H. Ruff and A. M. Bowers. William D. Goggans, age 23; killed at 2nd Manassas; appointed Adjutant in 1862, from 1st Sergeant. Pettis W. Gilliam, age 30; 1st Sergeant; discharged. James R. Campbell, age 18; 1st Sergeant; died at Richmond of wounds received at Cherokee Ford, Va. Jefferson A. Sligh, age 25; 2nd Sergeant; discharged. John W. Caldwell, age 22; 4th Sergeant; killed at 2nd Manassas. Lemuel H. M. Boozer, age 24; 1st Sergeant; discharged. Robert H. Land, age 25; Commissary Sergeant; served through war. Thomas M. Chapman, age 35; 5th Sergeant; served through war; also through Mexican war. John R. Wicker, age 22; 1st Corporal; wounded at Deep Bottom; served through war. J. Marion Boyd, age 25; 2nd Corporal; discharged. J. Glenn Rikard, age 23; 3d Corporal; Appomattox.* Andrew J. McCollum, age 24; 4th Corporal; killed at Chancellorsville. Travis P. Boyd, age 23; 3d Corporal; wounded at Wilderness; Appomattox.

Privates—Newton F. Butler, age 22, Appomattox. David P. Buzhardt, age 21, wounded at Chancellorsville; Appomattox. S. Dugan Boyd, age 18, Appomattox. James A. Boyd, age 25, wounded at Fredericksburg; killed at Gettysburg. William A. Barre, age 23, wounded at Ox Hill; Appomattox. John J. Barre, age 18, Appomattox. Samuel P. Boozer, age 29, discharged. James Boozer, age 18, Appomattox. A. W. Bramlett, age 26. G. Henry Cromer, age 24, killed at Spottsylvania. J. Preston Cromer, age 19, killed at Spottsylvania. Andrew Conwell, age 18, Appomattox. C. Calvin Clamp, age 22, killed at 2nd Manassas. Spencer J. Caldwell, age 18, killed at Petersburg. William Clamp, age 26. Henry Cóates, age 18, died of disease at Richmond. Drayton N. Coates, age 21, Appomattox. Edward H. Christian, age 35, Appomattox. Moses M. Coppock, age 35, wounded at Spottsylvania; Appomattox. John C. Duncan, age 21, died of disease at Ashland, Va. Wilson W. Davenport, age 35, Appomattox. Warren P. Ellisor, age 21, killed

---

* By "Appomattox" in this Roll the reader will understand the place of final surrender of Lee's Army.

at Gettysburg. W. Frank Enlow, age 25, killed at Chancellorsville. Edward B. Ferguson, age 28, discharged. Thomas F. Greneker, age 35, discharged. John W. Glasgow, age 20, died of disease at Lebanon, Va. William J. Hunter, age 25, killed at Spottsylvania. Elijah Hipp, age 30, died of disease on South Carolina coast. Asbury Hipp, age 23, died of disease on the South Carolina coast. John Halfacre, age 21, killed at Manassas. Fred Halfacre, age 18, died of disease on South Carolina coast. John W. P. Harmon, age 24, killed at Manassas. William H. D. Harmon, age 18, killed at Manassas. Walter W. Houseal, age 44, discharged. James A. Henry, age 37, Appomattox. William Higgins, age 30, from New York City; Appomattox. Henry M. Johnson, age 22, died of disease at Richmond. Jesse M. Johnson, age 25. Marcus J. Jenkins, age 32, Appomattox. D. Walter Kinard, age 23, wounded at Petersburg. John B. Kinard, age 27, wounded at Gettysburg. Walter J. Kinard, age 23, killed at Gettysburg. John P. Kinard, age 22, wounded at Gettysburg; Appomattox. Walter J. Kelly, age 21, killed at Chancellorsville. Jasper Kelly, age 21, killed at Chancellorsville. John B. Lake, age 22, killed at Spottsylvania. John W. Livingston, age 19, died of disease at Richmond. George Larsen, age 35, discharged. William R. Lane, age 21, killed at the Wilderness. Robert Y. H. McCracken, age 25, killed at Gettysburg. John McMorris, age 22, died of disease at Ashland. John McCarley, age 32, Appomattox. Frank S. Murgott, age 19. Benjamin P. Neel, age 28, wounded at the Wilderness; Appomattox. Robert H. Norman, age 23, discharged. William H. Pitts, age 22, killed at Cold Harbor. James Pitts, age 21, wounded at Gettysburg. George L. Pitts, age 27, Appomattox. Charles G. Plunkett, age 23, Appomattox. Drayton S. Plunkett, age 21, died of disease at Richmond. Drayton S. Paysinger, age 19, died of disease at Richmond. John P. Rikard, age 21, killed at Manassas. John J. Ruff, age 22, killed at Cold Harbor. David A. Ruff, age 22, Appomattox. Walter M. Rikard, age 29, killed at Fredericksburg. Andrew C. Rikard, age 23, killed at Manassas. Marcus S. Shell, age 32, Appomattox. James P. Senn, age 16, died of disease at Fort Delaware. David B. Sligh, age —, died of disease on the South Carolina coast. Robert D. Suber, age 19, killed at Cold Harbor. George M. Senn, age 22, wounded at Spottsylvania; Appomattox. John D. Senn, age 24, wounded at the Wilderness; Appomattox. Ketchum M. Senn, age 19, killed at Petersburg. John P. Sims, age 25, died of disease at Richmond. Thomas F. Senn, age 22, Appomattox. Jesse Sparks, age 32, died of disease at Fredericksburg. John D. Suber, age 23, wounded at Petersburg; Appomattox. David Sims, age 23, died of disease at Richmond. Jesse Spears, age 19, killed at Cold Harbor. Frank M. Setzler, age 23, Appomattox. Spencer F. Smith, age 35, discharged. George D. Smith, age 38, discharged. Bluford M. Summer, age 23, died of disease at Fort Delaware. John S. Toland, age 38. Williams Welch, age 20, Appomattox. Spencer G. Welch, age 24, Appomattox. Daniel M. E. Wicker, age 25, died of wounds received at Manassas. James B. Wilson, age 18, killed at Ox Hill. William H. B. Werts, age 19, killed at Chancellorsville. Hiram Wicker, age 35, Appomattox. Thomas J. Wh'tman, age 19, killed at Chancellorsville. D. Jeff Wicker, age 40, Appomattox. Zebulon B. White, age 35, Appomattox.

Whole number, rank and file, enlisted, 117; and unless I have made an error in summing up, the total loss of Company D, Thirteenth Regiment, during the war was 49 : Killed in battle, 34. Mortally wounded, 2. Died of disease, 13. Total, 49. Wounds received not mortal, 13.

Roll of Company "M," Mounted Rifles, Twentieth Regiment, S. C. V.

The following names of men from Newberry I find on the roll of Company M, Mounted Rifles, commanded by Captain E. S. Keitt, 20th Regiment, S. C. V.:

F. D. Graham, Sergeant; volunteered December 24, 1861. C. M. Richie, Corporal, December 24, 1861. J. E. Dickert, Corporal, December 24, 1861.

Privates—A. C. Black, September 7, 1861. A. M. Berley, September 15, 1863. J. C. S. Brown, October 25, 1863. A. F. Cromer, February 4, 1863. J. N. Epting, December 24, 1861. S. G. Gallman, September 7, 1863. J. A. Hipp, January 2, 1863. P. Halfacre, September 7, 1863. W. H. Knight, December 1, 1862. A. Kibler, March 25, 1862. J. O. Koon, October 25, 1863. T. M. Neel, March 6, 1863. J. W. Stone, March 26, 1862. J. A. Summer, September 7, 1863. J. N. Thompson; September 7, 1863. J. A. Welch, February 10, 1863. M. D. Werts, February 10, 1863. M. A. Renwick. Rogers Renwick. Curtis Attwood. Total, 23 men.

This list is taken from the muster and pay roll of the company (the original) from the 31st day of October, 1863, to the 31st day of December, 1863, and I find no record or report of wounds or casualties happening to the men.

Roll of Company "G," Holcombe Legion, S. C. V.

Joel B. Heller, Captain—resigned; living. J. E. Brennan, Captain—promoted from 1st Lieutenant; dead. B. B. McCreery, Captain, resigned—promoted from 3d Lieutenant; living in New York. John Williams, Captain—from private elected 3d Lieutenant and promoted to Captain; died since the war. William Hatton, First Lieutenant—from 1st Sergeant elected to 1st Lieutenant; killed at Second Manassas. Nathan Hipp, 1st Lieutenant—from private elected 1st Lieutenant—discharged from Union prison at surrender; living. John Chaplin, 2nd Lieutenant—elected at the organization of the company; died at home. Wm. Suber, M. D., 2nd Lieutenant —elected from corporal: dead. J. J. Reeder, 2nd Lieutenant —elected from private—wounded at Petersburg; died in Union prison unknown. James Wilson, 1st Sergeant—promoted from private; killed at Petersburg. Wesley Koon, 1st Sergeant— promoted from private—discharged at Point Lookout; living. Frank Lominick, 1st Sergeant—promoted from private; killed at Second Manassas. John M. Glymph, 2nd Sergeant—promoted from private; discharged at Point Lookout.* Drayton Pitts, 3d Sergeant, killed at Petersburg. Henry Hendrix, 4th Sergeant, mortally wounded at Second Manassas. W. W. Waldrop, 4th Sergeant, discharged at Point Lookout; living. J. M. Suber, 1st Corporal, mortally wounded at Second Manassas. Drayton Suber, 1st Corporal, lost near Gordonville. C. S. Cleland, 2nd Corporal, discharged at Point Lookout;

----

* Point Lookout was a Union prison.

living. M. W. Longshore, 2nd Corporal, discharged at Point Lookout; living. W. Pinckney Johnson, 3d Corporal, wounded at Petersburg; discharged at Point Lookout; living. Pinckney Hendrix, 4th Corporal, mortally wounded at Petersburg. Madison McClung, 5th Corporal, wounded at Suponey Church; discharged at Point Lookout.

Privates—Hampton Abrams, dead. James Abrams, wounded at Suponey Church; discharged at Point Lookout. Jas. Ashford, Fairfield, wounded at Second Manassas; discharged at Point Lookout. Richard Anderson, Abbeville, discharged at Point Lookout. Thomas H. Alewine. Thomas H. Adams, wounded at Rappahannock, Kinston, Suponey Church and Petersburg; discharged from prison in New York. Melvin Adams, discharged at Point Lookout. David Blair, killed at Goldsboro. George Beam, Fairfield, transferred to 17th S. C. Regiment. John Boozer, discharged at Point Lookout. John Barksdale, Laurens, discharged at Point Lookout. Martin Butler. J. H. P. Cromer, wounded at Second Manassas; disabled and discharged. James C. Clary, discharged at Point Lookout. Samuel Cohen, wounded at Suponey Church; discharged at Point Lookout; living in New Jersey. George S. Cannon, discharged at Point Lookout. Franklin H. Cromer, died at Adams Run, June 30, 1862. Stephen Cromer, killed at Second Manassas. Ivy Cromer, discharged from prison in New York. Robert Cromer, discharged at Point Lookout; dead. Franklin Cromer, discharged at Point Lookout. William Chapman, killed at Petersburg. George Cromer, discharged at Point Lookout; dead. Whitfield Cromer, killed at Petersburg. Frederick J. Cromer, discharged at Point Lookout; dead. Drayton S. Chandler; living in Greenville County. Marion Dickert, discharged disabled. E. P. Davis, discharged disabled. John Davenport, discharged at Point Lookout. Jacob W. Felker, wounded at Suponey Church; discharged at Point Lookout. Adam F. Felker, discharged at Petersburg. Thomas Felkman, discharged at Point Lookout. D. B. Glymph, Abbeville. John Gibson, Abbeville, discharged at Point Lookout. Jefferson Gregory, Union, discharged; over age. Newt. F. Gilliam, killed at Kinston. A. Y. W. Glymph, discharged on detached service. J. H. Hayes, discharged at Point Lookout; dead. Elijah Hipp, mortally wounded at Second Manassas. George Harvey, wounded at Second Manassas; disabled and discharged. Wm. Hoyle, Fairfield, died of disease in service. Thomas D. Hogg, killed at Second Manassas. John N. Hendrix, killed at Second Manassas. John H. Harmon, discharged at Point Lookout. Simeon Johnson, wounded at Petersburg and discharged from hospital. Wm. P. Jackson, Union. Wm. Kersey. Ivy Ropp, died of disease, not known where. M. W. Longshore, killed at Petersburg. Levi F. Longshore, discharged at Petersburg. Madison Longshore, discharged at Point Lookout. Young Longshore, discharged at Point Lookout. Jacob Lietzsey, died in prison at Point Lookout. John Reeder, discharged at Point Lookout. Hilliary Mangum, discharged at Point Lookout. James Morris, died of disease at home. Robert McClung, died, place and time unknown. J. J. McAfee, Kentucky, transferred to Kentucky Cavalry. Abner Reeder, wounded at Suponey Church. John Oxner, discharged at Point Lookout; dead. Uriah Oxner, wounded at Suponey Church; discharged at home. Isaac Roebuck, died at home on furlough. John Pitts, discharged at Point Lookout. Jonathan Pitts, discharged at Point Lookout. Joe Pitts, discharged at Point Lookout. William Rutherford, discharged at Point Lookout. E. W. Reese, discharged at Petersburg. John Thomas Suber, discharged disabled. David F. Suber, discharged at Point Lookout. Edward Stokes. Thomas Stokes, dead. Jacob Smith, discharged over age. Richard S. Satterwhite, discharged at Point Lookout. Simpson Sligh, discharged at Point Lookout. James Singley, killed at Petersburg. William Senn, wounded at Petersburg. James Turner, Union, died of disease at Adam's Run. Press Thompson, died of disease in hospital at Richmond. Arnold Thomasson, lost near Gordonsville, Va. Samuel Wicker, wounded at Second Manassas and Kinston; discharged at Point Lookout. B. F. Williams, Greenville, killed in battle, time and place not known. Walker Willingham, wounded at Second Manassas; discharged at Point Lookout.

Total rank and file, 105 men. Of that number, were killed in battle, 13; mortally wounded, 2; died of sickness, 8; total loss by death, 23. The reader will also perceive that several were rendered unfit for service by being severely wounded and were in consequence discharged.

Roll of Company "H," Third Regiment, S. C. V.

I give only the names of the men from Newberry, as the company was made up mainly from Lexington, with four from Edgefield. The company was first commanded by Drury Nunnamaker, who resigned at the reorganization, April 13, 1862. He died since the war. John P. Summer was elected Captain. Killed at Fredericksburg. George S. Swygert succeeded Summer. Was wounded at Malvern Hill, Fredericksburg and Chickamauga, disabled, and resigned. D. A. Dickert then became Captain. He had been wounded at Savage Station, Fredericksburg and the Wilderness, and was wounded at Knoxville after his promotion. The two first named were from Lexington. Wistar C. Swindler, Newberry, over age; discharged. Simeon Wheeler, Newberry, Color-Sergeant; wounded at Knoxville; leg amputated; discharged. Levi C. Kempson, Newberry, 5th Sergeant; killed at the Wilderness. Wesley W. Werts, 4th Corporal, died of disease at Charlottesville, Va.

Privates from Newberry—Melvin Adams, over age, discharged; re-enlisted in Company G, Holcombe Legion, on the roll of which his name appears. Lemuel L. Boozer, wounded —. Frank B. Boozer, wounded at Strasburg. Daniel T. Boozer, discharged for disability. Littleton Bedenbaugh, wounded at Greensboro, N. C. Samuel J. Cook, killed at Chickamauga. J. G. Dawkins, transferred to Company H, Thirteenth S. C. V. Henry M. Dominick, wounded —. Belton Enlow, killed at Sharpsburg. Eli Frost, killed at Savage Station. John N. Feagle. Silas Hartman, killed at Fredericksburg. George Hiller, wounded; transferred to Company E, Third S. C. V. Jacob J. Kinard, wounded at Chickamauga; leg amputated. George W. Koon, transferred to Company E, Third S. C. V., and afterwards killed. D. S. Long, died in Union prison at Point Lookout. D. P. Long. G. Adam Long, died since war. Enoch J. Lake, transferred to Company E, Third S. C. V. Thomas M. Lake, transferred to Company E, Third S. C. V., died since war. Jacob Livingston Sol Livingston, wounded —. George Lester, wounded at Maryland Heights; leg amputated. A. B. Miller, wounded at Sharpsburg. John W. Monts, wounded at Maryland Heights. Lee Rikard, killed at Sharpsburg. Robert E. Riser, deserted. Wade H. Setzler, transferred. Lewis Spillers, killed at Chickamauga. Andrew Suber, died of disease in hospital. Press Thompson, transferred to Company G, Holcombe Legion. Andrew Werts, wounded —. Luther B. Wheeler, killed at Maryland Heights.

Whole number, rank and file, 36. Of whom were killed, 8. Died of disease, 3. Wounded and not killed, 8. Total casualties, 19.

I take pleasure in giving here a brief sketch of the history of this company from the time of enlistment in the Confederate service, at Lightwood Knot Springs, June 2, 1861. The company enlisted for twelve months, with 73 men, and was then assigned, by lot, its position, "H," left color company. The whole enlistment was then furloughed until the 17th. On the 25th, Company H embarked for Virginia, and took position on the outer post at Fairfax C. H. About the 15th of May, 1862, the first year's service having expired, the company re-enlisted for the war. The company at this time numbered 82 men, but was recruited from time to time until, at the close of the war, the roll showed 147 names. Of this number 21 were killed, 24 died in service, 5 had legs amputated (all living), 1 had arm amputated, 3 deserted, 2 missing (supposed dead), 33 were wounded and still living, 8 have since died, 8 were discharged, 3 officers resigned, 2 officers were killed, 19 privates were transferred to other companies.

The first member of the company killed was L. F. Russell, at Savage Station, June 29, 1862. Fletch was a merry boy, and the pet of the company. He was killed instantly. We wrapped him in his blanket and buried him on the battle-field. "Let me kiss him for his mother." The last man killed was B. F. Chapman, at the Wilderness, May 5, 1864. W. W. Hipp was the first man who died in the company, at Bull Run, July, 1861.

Of the original enlistment of 73 men only two returned home, after going through the whole war, without wounds or scars from the missiles of death. William Monts had five sons in the company. One was killed, three died in service, and one (J. W.) was desperately wounded.

One of those who returned home without a wound or scar was H. H. Chapman, who was always with his company and in every battle from the beginning to the end of the war.

The foregoing facts are gathered from the statement written

by U. B. Whites, dated Newberry, S. C., July 15, 1884. Mr. Whites was from Lexington at the beginning of the war, and Lieutenant of this company, but has long been a citizen of Newberry County.

It appears that the losses of this company were very unusually heavy. One out of every 7 of the whole number of 147 was killed outright in battle, and something over 1 out of every 7 died in service; thus making the total loss very nearly 1 out of every 3. The deaths in Company B, First Regiment, known as the Rhett Guards, were very nearly in the same proportion, but the loss was not quite as great as in this company.

Roll of Company "C," Third Regiment, S. C. V.

R. Clayton Maffett, Captain, promoted to Lieutenant-Colonel; captured and died in Fort Delaware. Chesley W. Herbert, Captain—promoted from 1st Lieutenant—wounded at Gettysburg and the Wilderness; killed after the war. Daniel S. Maffett, 1st Lieutenant—promoted from 2nd Lieutenant—killed in battle at Knoxville. John C. Wilson, 1st Lieutenant—promoted from 1st Sergeant—wounded at Savage Station. Joseph Culbreath, 2nd Lieutenant, promoted from the ranks. J. L. Speake, Laurens, 3d Lieutenant, resigned. Spencer J. Piester, 3d Lieutenant, killed at Fredericksburg, December 13, 1862. Amos A. Kibler, 1st Sergeant, promoted from 2nd Sergeant. Thomas J. Maffett, 2nd Sergeant, promoted from 4th Sergeant. E. Pinckney Cromer, 3d Sergeant, promoted from ranks. Thomas R. Wilson, 4th Sergeant, wounded at Savage Station, Chickamauga and North Anna; dead. G. Frederick Long, 3d Sergeant—promoted from 1st Corporal—wounded at Knoxville. John B. Fellers, 5th Sergeant, promoted from 3d Corporal. M. H. Young, 1st Corporal, promoted from ranks. David W. Boozer, 2nd Corporal, died of disease at Fairfax C. H., 1861. John S. Bowers, 4th Corporal, transferred. Jacob B. Fulmer, 2nd Corporal—promoted from the ranks—wounded at Gettysburg; dead. George Sites, 4th Corporal, promoted from the ranks. James W. Kelly, 5th Corporal, killed at Savage Station. Samuel S. Paysinger, 5th Corporal—promoted from the ranks—wounded at Wilderness.

Privates—William H. Adams, transferred to Cavalry, 1862. Joseph Allbritton, killed at Wilderness May 6, 1864. James

C. Banks, transferred.   Henry Baird.   Henry Baughn, Lexington, detailed as scout; dead.   Fletcher Bouknight, transferred. Thomas S. Blair, wounded at Wilderness.   James P. Blair. Samuel D. Boland, transferred.   James M. Boland, transferred. Cornelius P. Boozer, wounded at Knoxville—lost an arm; is now Rev. C. P. Boozer, member of Legislature from Edgefield County.   D. Simeon Boozer, transferred to Cavalry, 1862.   I. Herbert Boulware, lost an arm at Wilderness.   George M. Boyd, discharged in 1862.   Henry D. Cannon.   John T. Calmes.   Washington Calmes, dead.   Joseph D. Carmichael, discharged in 1862.   Walter F. Counts, transferred to Cavalry in 1862, dead.   A. Barron Cromer, wounded at Chickamauga, H. S. Newton Crosson, wounded at Chancellorsville.   David A. Crosson, wounded at Wilderness, dead.   Jacob Crouch. dead.   Wade W. Crouch, Edgefield.   William Davenport, killed at Chickamauga September 20, 1863.   James M. Davenport, died of disease in hospital.   John Davis, transferred and afterwards killed at Chancellorsville.   J. W. Duncan, transferred, D. W. S. Dominick, transferred.   John A. Elmore, transferred, dead.   Nathan Enlow, transferred, dead.   Gideon Ferguson, transferred.   J. Pressley Fellers, killed at Chickamauga.   S. Hamilton Fellers, lost an arm at Wilderness.   Henry S. Folk, died in hospital of wounds.   Eli Frost, killed at Chickamauga. D. Frederick Gallman, color bearer, killed (supposed) at Sharpsburg, September 17, 1862.   Henry G. Gallman, killed at Sharpsburg.   Jefferson J. Gallman, lost an arm at Savage Station. James M. George, killed in Georgia.   Nelson B. George.   Lewis O. G. George.   George W. Griffith, killed at Gettysburg.   J. Henry Gruber.   Levi Gruber.   Thomas Grimes, transferred. Albert Guise, transferred, dead.   James B. Hair, discharged. J. Melvin Hartman, wounded at Gettysburg and Wilderness. Pierce M. Hawkins.   J. Miles Hawkins.   E. Pressley Hawkins, discharged.   John E. Hendrix, wounded at Bean's Station; killed at North Anna.   James W. Herbert, wounded at Wilderness.   Carwile Hussa.   David N. Halfacre.   Andrew Huff, transferred.   J. Harrison Kelley, died of disease in hospital.   Y. Simpson Kelly, killed at Fredericksburg December 13, 1862.   William J. Kelly, transferred.   Levi Kinard, killed at Savage Station June, 1862.   Levi Kibler.   J. Middleton Kibler, dead.   J. Hamilton Kibler, wounded at Chick-

amauga. R. Calvin Kibler. George G. Lane. Walter R.
Lane, discharged. Allen Lester, discharged. Alfred Lester,
died of disease in hospital. Charles Lester, discharged.
Michael J. Long, died of disease in hospital. Andrew J.
Long. Latimer W. Long, wounded at Wilderness, dead.
J. Marshall Livingstone, killed at Knoxville. Peter T. Mc-
Graw. Benjamin F. McGraw, dead. Langdon C. McCracken,
dead. John McCracken, killed at Cold Harbor. John Mc-
Nealus, deserted at Gettysburg.. R. J. Mansell, transferred.
R. Drayton Maffett, killed at Chickamauga, September 20, 1863.
Allen Martin, killed at Wilderness May 6, 1864. Francis Moon,
wounded at Wilderness. Stanmore Morris, wounded at Gettys-
burg, dead. J. C. Nates, transferred. J. Belton Neil. J. Calvin
Neil. J. Spencer Neil, killed at Chickamauga. John G. Nel-
son. Henry M. Paysinger, killed at Gettysburg. Thomas M.
Paysinger, wounded at Gettysburg and Cold Harbor; promoted
to Captain of Scouts; dead. W. P. Pugh. Hawkins Pugh.
Joseph E. Quattlebaum, transferred. D. Belton Quattlebaum,
transferred. Andrew J. Rankin, transferred. George W.
Rankin, transferred. J. Saunders Rawl, killed at Wilderness.
Jamess B. Reagin, transferred to Cavalry in 1862. Henry
W. Reagin, killed at Bentonville. John W. Reagin. Newton
Reid, dead. S. Pressley Reid, died of disease in hospital.
David Richardson, transferred. J. W. Rikard, transferred.
J. A. Rikard, transferred. L. C. Rikard, transferred. Noah
A. Sease, wounded at Gettysburg. G. Luke Sease. John R.
Sheppard, transferred. Jesse E. Sigman, scout, supposed to
have been killed by a prisoner. Samuel Spence, supposed to
have been killed by a prisoner. John D. Spence, lost a leg
at Cedar Creek, October 19, 1864. J. Wesley Sligh, wounded
at Wilderness. David P. Sligh, wounded at Malvern Hill,
July, 1862, and died in hospital at Richmond. Thomas
J. Stillwell, wounded at Wilderness. J. Quincey A. Stockman,
J. Matt. Stribling, discharged. John C. Stockman, killed at
Malvern Hill. Whitfield Stuart, transferred. Charles T.
Stuart, wounded at Wilderness. Robert J. Sulton, died of
disease in hospital. T. Jefferson Thompson, killed at Wilder-
ness. Joseph D. Whites, killed at Wilderness. G. J. Whites,
discharged. Michael Werts, discharged. Andrew J. Werts,
Edgefield, dead. John A. Werts, dead. J. William Wilson,

transferred; killed in battle at Strasburg. Hayne Williamson.

Whole number of men belonging to the company from the beginning to the end of the war, rank and file, 150; killed in battle, 25; scouts killed by prisoners, 2; died of wounds in hospital, 2; died of disease in hospital, 7; died in Fort Delaware, (Colonel Maffett, prisoner,) 1; total number of deaths, 37; wounds received not mortal, 31.

It would appear from this summing up that this company enjoyed good physical health—wounds healed readily and the number of deaths from disease not large.

COMPANY "G," SECOND REGIMENT CAVALRY, S. C. V.

I give of this company the names only of those officers and men who went from Newberry County.

Thomas J. Lipscomb, Captain, discharged at Chester, S. C.; Colonel of the regiment at the close of the war. J. Wistar Gary, Captain, discharged at Chester. John N. Floyd, 1st Corporal, discharged at Chester.

Privates—Edward P. Boazman, discharged at Chester. Grant S. Boazman, wounded at Gettysburg; discharged at Chester. Wash. M. Boazman, discharged from Union prison. William W. Boazman, discharged from Union prison. Simeon D. Boozer, discharged from Union prison. Elijah A. Brooks, discharged from Union prison. Kay Burton, discharged from Union prison. M. P. Cline, died in Union prison. W. F. Counts, discharged from Union prison. Thomas J. Davenport, discharged from Union prison. Harrison Davenport, discharged from Union prison. James H. Davenport, discharged from Union prison. William M. Feltman, discharged at Chester. Dorsey L. Gary, discharged at Chester. W. H. Hancock, discharged at Chester. Pat. H. Hargrove, discharged at Chester. Benson M. Jones, discharged at Chester. Dennis Lark, discharged at Chester. W. W. Miller, discharged at Chester. A. Newton Pitts, discharged at Chester. John D. Pitts, discharged at Chester. James B. Reagin, discharged at Chester. John S. Ruff, discharged at Chester. G. Benjamin Suber, discharged at Chester. William W. Wallace, discharged at Chester. James M. Workman, discharged at Chester.

Total officers, 3; privates, 26; total, 29. One was wounded at Gettysburg; 10 were captured, 1 of whom died in prison; 9 were discharged from prison at close of war.

COMPANY "H," HOLCOMBE LEGION.

Only the names of officers and men from Newberry County are given.

James M. Maffett, Captain, died of disease at Lockhart, Miss., in 1864. He had just been elected sheriff, and was on his way home to assume the duties of the office. Jacob Warner, killed near Petersburg; promoted from 1st Lieutenant to Captain. Henry S. Boozer, discharged at Johnson's Island; promoted from 2nd to 1st Lieutenant and to Captain. John S. Hair, 1st Lieutenant, resigned in 1862. Bennett J. Kinard, 2nd Lieutenant, killed at 2nd Manassas. Langdon C. Kibler, promoted to 3d Lieutenant, resigned in 1863. George C. Maffett, 1st Lieutenant, wounded at Kinston, N. C.; promoted to 3d, 2nd and 1st Lieutenant. Joseph D. Carmichael, Sergeant, wounded at Boonsboro, Md.; discharged at Point Lookout. W. Simpson Harmon, Sergeant, died in prison at Point Lookout. George M. Singley, Sergeant, killed at Hatcher's Run. Jacob A. Bowers, Sergeant, killed near Petersburg. J. Belton Werts, promoted Ordnance Sergeant, discharged at Appomattox. E. Pressley Hawkins, Corporal, wounded at Boonsboro; discharged at Point Lookout. John L. Hunter, Corporal, wounded at 2nd Manassas; discharged at Point Lookout. J. Smiley Bowers, Corporal, wounded at Boonsboro and at Kingston; died at Point Lookout. John L. Derrick, Corporal, discharged at Point Lookout.

Privates—Stanmore S. Boozer, died of disease, at home. R. Calvin Boozer, surrendered at Appomattox. Frederick A. Boozer, wounded at Second Manassas and Kinston; discharged at Point Lookout. Jacob W. Boozer, wounded at Kinston; died of disease, at home. Asbury Bedenbaugh. George A. Bedenbaugh, wounded at Jackson, Miss.; discharged at Point Lookout. William J. Bedenbaugh, wounded near Petersburg; discharged at Point Lookout. Francis Bobb, wounded at Second Manassas; discharged at Point Lookout. Hamilton B. Buzhardt, discharged at Point Lookout. James M. Boland, discharged at Point Lookout. John Bowers, wounded at Hatcher's Run; fate unknown. James C. Banks, discharged at Point Lookout. Tranmore F. Black, discharged on South Carolina coast. J. Harrison Cannon, wounded near Petersburg.

H. Wesley Dominick, wounded at Jackson, Miss., and Saponey Church, Va.; discharged at Point Lookout. Aaron M. Dominick, discharged at Fortress Monroe. B. Lindsay Dominick, discharged at Point Lookout. George A. Dominick, wounded at Rappahanock; died at Culpeper. Henry F. Dominick, died of disease at Stoney Creek, Va. Orlando A. Dickert, discharged on South Carolina coast. John A. Enlow, discharged at Point Lookout. Charles Force, wounded near Petersburg. S. Christian Gruber, wounded at Saponey Church. George P. Griffith, transferred to Company G, Thirteenth Regiment. Henry Griffith, died of disease, at home. E. Lambert Hendrix, wounded at Hatcher's Run; discharged at Point Lookout. Robert T. C. Hunter, wounded at Saponey Church and Second Manassas. Samuel A. Hunter, discharged at Point Lookout. Drayton P. Hawkins, discharged at Point Lookout. Thomas T. C. Hunter, discharged at Point Lookout. J. Martin Hartman, wounded at Kinston, died at Goldsboro, N. C. James M. King, died of disease on South Carolina coast. William H. Long, discharged on South Carolina coast. William K. Lindsay, discharged at Wilmington, N. C.; over age. M. Luther Kinard, wounded at 2nd Manassas; transferred to Thirteenth Regiment. James C. Moore, discharged at Point Lookout. Robert S. Moore, discharged in camp. Frederick R. Moore, killed at 2nd Manassas. George H. Morris, discharged at Point Lookout. Thomas B. Morris, discharged at Point Lookout. Chauncey H. Morris, wounded at Sharpsburg; died at Point Lookout. George Mayer, discharged at Appomattox. Hance C. Moseley, discharged at Wilmington; under age. Florida Moats, wounded at Sharpsburg, discharged at Wilmington; under age. John Matthews, discharged at Appomattox. J. Lamar Maffett, died at Point Lookout. Nicholas S. Merchant, discharged at Point Lookout. Jacob Perkins, discharged at Appomattox. Lewis A. Perkins, wounded near Petersburg; discharged at Appomattox. Elihu Perkins, wounded at Saponey Church; died of disease at Petersburg. J. Belton Quattlebaum, died of disease, at home. Samuel L. Rook, wounded at 2nd Manassas; discharged at Wilmington; over age. Wiley Rikard, died of disease at Richmond. George W. Rikard, wounded at 2nd Manassas. Levi Rikard, discharged at Appomattox. George W. Rankin, died of disease at Point Lookout. H. Middleton Singley, discharged at Point Lookout. Franklin Shealy, transferred to Thirteenth Regiment. Samuel C. Sheppard, discharged at Point Lookout. John N. Sligh, wounded at Sharpsburg; killed at Fort Steadman, Va. J. Belton C. Stockman, died of disease at Wilmington. Bluford Waits, discharged at Point Lookout. Drayton Waits, wounded at Kinston; died at Point. Lookout. Samuel Waits, discharged in camp. D. Hilliard Werts. H. Middleton Werts, died in prison at Point Lookout. Henry Werts, discharged at Appomattox. James Wood, discharged at Appomattox. John A. Wise, wounded at 2nd Manassas; died at Warrenton, Va. John C. Wise, killed near Petersburg.

Total rank and file from Newberry. 86. If I have made no error in summing up, I find: Killed in battle, officers and men, 6; died of wounds (some in prison), 7; died of disease (some in prison), 11. Total, 24. Wounds not mortal, 21. Captured and discharged from Union prisons at the close of the war, 18.

COMPANY "C," HOLCOMBE LEGION.

This company was mustered into service December 3, 1861. Names only of those from Newberry County are given, except that of the second captain.

John R. Spearman, Captain, resigned and was succeeded by J. Wash. Williams, Laurens. Levi Slawson, 1st Lieutenant. Silas Walker, 1st Lieutenant, from 2nd. Ebenezer P. Chalmers, 2nd Lieutenant, wounded at Cold Harbor. Chesley D Spearman, 3d Lieutenant, discharged at Adam's Run with measles. James L. Blackburn, 3d Lieutenant. James W. Spearman, 1st Sergeant. Richard W. Hill, Orderly Sergeant. Wilson W. Waldrop, 2nd Sergeant. Robert R. Hill, 2nd Sergeant. G. Calvin Ridlehuber, 3d Sergeant. Daniel Dandy, killed at Ridgeley's Shoals, Va. William L. Chalmers, 4th Sergeant. John F. Watkins, 4th Sergeant. Graves W. L. Spearman, 4th Sergeant. Calvin Satterwhite, 5th Sergeant. Jas. R. Payne, died of disease at Adam's Run, S. C., May 6, 1862. Henry D. Boozer, 1st Corporal. Frank G. Spearman, 2nd Corporal, discharged to Arsenal (Citadel) Academy. John A.

Workman, 2nd Corporal. Lewis G. Ferguson, 3d Corporal. Samuel W. Spearman, 3d Corporal. Charles C. Teague, 4th Corporal. William G. Glenn, 4th Corporal.

Privates—Thomas H. Adams. Aaron D. Burton, wounded at Cold Harbor. John P. Buzhardt. Henry D. Boozer. John C. Chalmers, died of disease in Virginia. William Y. Cradock. Wm. L. Davis. Jno. M. Davenport, died of disease in Virginia. James A. Davis, wounded at Cold Harbor. Thomas J. Denson, discharged, over age. Richard J. Dean. James J. Denson. Napoleon B. Davenport. Thomas Floyd. David Garrett, died of measles at Adam's Run, March 9, 1862. William G. Glenn, wounded at Cold Harbor. Elijah M. Lake, wounded by shell at Adam's Run, February 8, 1862; died. Samuel W. Spearman. James K. P. Spearman, died of measles at Adam's Run. John F. Spearman, died of disease at home February 10, 1862. Jacob Smith. John M. Pennington. Henry Willen, died of disease in Virginia. Seth Williams. William R. Spearman, discharged to Arsenal Academy. Harry P. Wadlington. John C. Whitman. R. G. Gilliam. William Boozer. W. A. Clark. R. C. Davis. J. C. Davis. R. Julius Dean. Thomas Hatton. G. W. Johnson. Miller Johnson. Abe Johnson. Wash. Johnson. Warren H. Jones. George P. Lake, died of measles at Adam's Run. William Dean. G. Pope Mangum. John W. Miller. Wash Monroe, wounded at Drill Ground, Va. Drayton Pitts. John W. Satterwhite. Thomas P. Slider. E. P. Stillwell. J. Davis Taylor, wounded at Darbytown, Va.

I find the following remarks written upon this roll: "Volunteered for 12 months for local defence, but resigned when the company was mustered in for the war after the conscript law was passed; and J. Wash Williams was elected captain of the company. Good many of the members of the company were over the conscript age, but were not released till they were carried to Virginia, and, notwithstanding they had volunteered for local defence, they were carried against their wishes. The matter was reported to the War Department and they were ordered discharged. JOHN R. SPEARMAN."

Of the 72 from Newberry, died of disease, 8; killed in battle, 1; wounded, not mortally, 7; discharged over age and disabled, 4.

COMPANY "H," THIRTEENTH REGIMENT, S. C. V.

Only the names of officers and men from Newberry County are given.

Philip A. Eichelberger, Captain. William L. Leitzsey, age 20, 3d Captain, wounded at Gettysburg, Manassas and Spottsylvania, killed at Deep Bottom, Va. George A. Hutchison, age 22, 2nd and 1st Lieutenant, promoted from Orderly Sergeant, discharged at Orange C. H., Va. David Leitzsey, age 24, 2nd Lieutenant, promoted from the ranks in Virginia in 1863, killed at Gettysburg. John W. Chapman, age 24, 1st Sergeant, died of disease on South Carolina coast. David J. Wedeman, age 26, died of disease on South Carolina coast. William F. Ridlehuber, age 21, 4th Corporal, promoted from the ranks, killed at Gettysburg.

Privates—Jacob J. Busby, age 16, killed at Deep Bottom. John W. Cromer, age 18, died of disease at Camp Johnson. John P. Dickert, age 18, died of disease at Camp Johnson. A. Osman Eargle, age 22, killed at Manassas. Jacob Epting, age 45. J. Felix Hutchison, age 22. Augustus Kibler, age 26, transferred from Co. G, 13th S. C. Regiment, in Virginia March, 1863, and furnished a substitute. William Koon, age 23, wounded at Chancellorsville. D. Luther Koon, age 18, wounded at Gettysburg. Miles S. Singley, age 22, missing at Gettysburg; supposed to have been killed. E. Harrison Wedeman, age 21, died of disease at Richmond. John A. Elmore, age 30, captured near James River, 1864.

Total from Newberry, officers and men, 18. Of these there were killed in battle, 6; (Captain Leitzsey had been wounded three times before he was killed,) died of disease, 4; total number of deaths, 10; wounds not mortal, 2; discharged, 1.

I find on the monument below the Court House the names of four hundred and sixty-eight men (468) who perished during the war, killed in battle, mortally wounded and died of disease. The rolls furnished me, from which I have carefully copied, give the names of only three hundred and eighty-three (383) short by eighty-five names (85.) But the rolls I have give about fifty names (50) of the dead which I do not find on the monument. However, I may have made some errors, though I have tried to be very careful. I give here the names on the monument which I did not find in the rolls: J. J. Hatton, T. W. Henderson, W. C. Hunter, W. Huskey, T. A. Johnson, J. L. Johnson, John Johnson, J. J. Johnson, M. Johnson, H. Jones, W. H. Kelley, L. C. Kinard, W. W. Koon, A. H. Koon, D. A. Koon, W. Lake, W. F. Lake, W. J. Lake, J. D. Lake, E. M. Lake, W. A. Lake, S. Langford, Wm. Lee, G. Livingston, M. Livingston, H. Long, J. H. McCullough, —. McCain, D. B. McClung, W. P. McClung, H. A. Milligan, J. D. Norris, W. W. Monts, F. Monts, T. D. Nance, J. C. Nates, R. L. Neel, W. F. Nobles, R. M. Norman, E. O'Dell, D. Oxner, J. A. S. Oxner, B. F. Paysinger, J. Peas, E. Perkins, E. A. Pitts, W. Reid, J. J. Reeder, Jr., A. W. Reeder, Jr., B. Richards, W. L. Ridlehuber, L. F. Russell, G. W. Rankin, J. L. Schumpert, G. Senn, J. Sharp, F. Sheely, J. M. Sheely, W. H. Sheely, E. Sheely, S. M. Sheely, Lieutenant-Colonel J. C. Simkins, David Sims, Davis Sims, Albert Smith, C. Snelgrove, J. Sparks, R. S. Speers, W. F. Spruel, R. Sulton, J. J. Summers, J. Thomas, —. Tribble, C. C. Turner, D. Waldrop, A. S. Werts, T. S. Whitmire, J. B. Whitmire, F. Wilson, H. Wilson, T. B. Wilson, D. M. E. Wicker, J. Glenn, F. J. Glymph, C. H. Morris, J. Long, Captain W. P. Cromer, T. H. Lyles, J. M. Kinard, D. S. Maffett, J. S. Piester, J. S. Chapline, W. M. Hatton, C. M. Singley, J. A. Bowers, J. F. Clark, A. H. Young, L. Sheely, J. C. Cary, J. D. Sheely, T. A. Maffett, R. Moore, R. A. Abrams, D. Adams, L. Anderson, F. D. Ballentine, H. C. Bernhardt, T. Berry, J. C. Bishop, N. Boozer, J. Boozer, E. P. Boozer, H. Boozer, R. L. Bradley, W. G. Butler, A. B. Cannon, J. P. Cannon, B. F. Chapman, H. Z. Chapman, D. B. Chambers, D. C. Chambers, J. C. Chapline, N. A. Clark, C. C. Clamp, D. Cleland, E. Cox, A. S. Conwell, H. Coate, S. Crout, J. W. Cannady, J. S. Dennis, J. Dennis, J. W. Dorroh, W. P. Dorroh, W. B. D'Oyley, J. Duckett, H. M. Epting, G. Feagle, C. C. Felder, J. Fellers, H. S. Folk, C. H. Gasaway, J. Galogly, M. Gibson, —. Gillespie, D. M. Gordon, W. S. Golding, S. P. Hawkins, H. C. Hartman, H. T. Harmon, J. H. Hardy, F. D. Hatton. Total, 152, who died during the war and whose names do not appear on the rolls of the lists of killed and wounded. But the rolls call for about fifty dead whose names do not appear on the monument.

I regret these discrepancies. I wanted no name to perish

A VOLUNTEER OF '61.

[Copied from Life.]

unrecorded, and in this matter I have done my best. If any names appear more than once, better so than not at all.

I find that Newberry County had in regular service during the war about fourteen hundred and fifty (1450) men, and that very nearly one-third of them died in service—killed, mortally wounded and of disease.

Add to the above the ninety-five in the following roll, and you will have fifteen hundred and forty (1540) names, and I do not think this is quite all.

ROLL OF COMPANY "A."

It is my good fortune to find at last a roll of Co. A, being that of a company of boys or young men about eighteen, who went into service as volunteers in the early part of the year, about April, 1864, and continued until the close of the war, April, 1865. Eighteen of these, whose names I have marked with the letter t, were transferred to Col. E. S. Keitt's mounted men and served under him. I had given up all hope of being able to find these names, but happily I have before me the original roll. No casualties given.

W. H. Holman, Captain. Thomas W. Thompson, 1st Lieutenant. H. C. Moseley, 2nd Lieutenant. Legare Gary, 3d Lieutenant. C. M. Williams, 1st Sergeant. A. M. Wyse, 2nd Sergeant, t. D. M. Ward, 3d Sergeant. Geo. Haltiwanger, 4th Sergeant. Adolphus Maffett, 5th Sergeant. J. A. Werts, 3d Corporal. J. G. Martin, 2nd Corporal. N. B. Wheeler, 3d Corporal, t. Fred Cureton, 4th Corporal, t.

Privates—J. H. Aull, t; C. B. Abrams, J. Albritton, J. W. Boozer; T. P. Boozer, t; C. Butler, Y. M. Bedenbaugh, F. S. Bedenbaugh, B. C. H. Bedenbaugh, O. M. Buzhardt, P. S. Brooks; C. Bookman, t; H. P. Coats, R. J. Campbell, J. L. Connelly, C. F. Chandler; J. W. Cromer, t; S. D. Caughman, t; Henry Colter, John A. Counts, A. C. Chapman, J. Caldwell, H. H. Chambers, T. W. Davis, C. H. Derrick, J. L. Dominick, Henry Dominick, Drayton D. Dansby, Samuel Duckett, C. P. Dickert, M. Dickert, David DeWalt, M. Epting, H. H. Epting, P. M. Ellisor, G. M. Ellisor; J. W. Fulmer, t; M. A. Fellers, J. H. Fellers, H. T Fellers, J. N. Feagle, C. Felder, W. C. Gallman, E. C. Harrington, Tom Hair; T. M.

2   G

Hentz, t; J. J. Hipp, t; Y. J. Hutchison; W. J. P. Kinard, t;
J. D. Lake, M. C. Lake, J. D. Lietzsey, R. Y. Leavell, J. D.
Moore; J. A. Mitchell, t; T. McCullough, G. F. Monts, W. N.
Miller; J. F. Oxner, t; W. P. Pugh, E. H. Pugh, W. D.
Riser, W. F. Suber, J. B. Suber, J. P. Spearman, James
Schumpert; W. W. Summer, t; J. M. Stevens, Robert Stewart,
W. B. Spearman; F. M. Trotter, t; S. S. Taylor, J. R. Vaughan;
J. W. Watson, t; E. P. Whitman, t; J. L. Williams, W. S.
Wilson, G. P. Werts; J. L. Werts, t; J. W. Werts, J. W.
Wicker, A. C. Welch. Total, 95 officers and privates. Seven
died of yellow fever on South Carolina coast, two of whom
were J. H. Fellers and Adolphus Maffett.

BATTALION OF STATE CADETS.

The following were members of the Battalion of State
Cadets commanded by Major White:

Jas. S. Spearman, Jno. R. Spearman, George Johnstone,
Thomas T. Moore, Frank G. Spearman, Thomas A. Johnson,
John F. Spearman, Wm. R. Spearman.

Of these Wm. R. Spearman died not long after the war;
Thomas A. Johnson died in the Confederate service on the
23d of March, 1865, a little over 19 years of age, having
been born on the 5th of February, 1846. The others, I think,
are still living.

COMPANY "K," FIFTH REGIMENT, S. C. CAVALRY.

The following from Newberry were members of Co. K, 5th
Regiment, S. C. Cavalry:

M. M. Buford; F. S. Boozer, killed at Tresillian; D. B.
Boozer, dead; Wm. Boozer, dead; Robert Goree, gone West;
J. C. Hargrove; Dr. Wm. Suber. dead.

M. M. Buford, as escort for Col. Rawlins Lowndes, of
Charleston, S. C., was with the officer who carried the last
dispatches from the Confederate authorities when General
Joseph E. Johnston surrendered.

Doubtless there are errors in the foregoing lists of names of
men who saw service in the Confederate Army during the War
of Secession. Doubtless there are errors in the statement of

casualties, and in other respects. There are probably some names not given which should have been inserted. There are some on the monument not found on the rolls in the Adjutant-General's office, and some not on the monument which should be there. The compiler of this record has faithfully copied from the rolls which were furnished him. He would have entered upon a career of endless inquiry had he undertaken to interview each living soldier and officer of the Confederacy from Newberry. In many cases he did inquire and receive information from private sources which it was impossible to obtain from the public records.

The reader who has any spark of charity in his composition ought to be, and must be, pleased to find that the errors in the lists are so few. Nothing can please one who has no charity for others.

The compiler must here be permitted to thank Mr. Elbert H. Aull, who, as the book is passing through the press, has put himself to a great deal of trouble and inconvenience to eliminate from the rolls and the statement of casualties all errors possible to be eliminated.

Addendum by E. H. Aull.

In addition to the rolls and records already given, more information has been obtained as to the part Newberry had in the War of Secession. As has been stated by the compiler, every precaution has been taken to be accurate in this part of these Annals. As those who can give information from personal experience and knowledge are fast passing away, and the rolls are sometimes unsatisfactory, it has been difficult to obtain accurate data. If this history is not preserved now, it will soon be so that the facts cannot be obtained. It is the purpose of this book to be accurate and full, though it is realized that that purpose will not be attained completely in either particular. With that in view, however, I have decided, with the permission and assent of the compiler, to make the following addition to this part of the book.

A careful examination of the rolls printed will show that the compiler is not entirely correct in his statement of discrepancies between the names on the rolls and those on the Confederate monument; but as it was not observed until portions had gone through the press, and as it was the purpose to err rather on the side of repetition than omission, it was thought best not to undertake to change that.

A good number of Newberry men were in companies not from Newberry, and it is difficult to locate all of them, but in talking of the matter and asking questions, as the book was going through the press, the facts given herewith have been learned.

From Captain W. D. Hardy the following names and data of men who were from Newberry as members of the Fifth S. C. Infantry, J. T. Douglass, Captain, were obtained:

J. H. Hardy, T. W. Henderson, James A. Oxner, Thomas Wilson, Jenkins H. Smith, Walker Glymph, J. McD. Kinard, D. B. Kinard, George Kinard, Calvin Kinard, S. J. Long, B. H. Maybin, Emanuel Sligh, David Gross. Of these the following were either killed or died of wounds or disease during the war: J. H. Hardy, T. W. Henderson, James A. Oxner, Thomas Wilson, Calvin Kinard. The following have died since the war: D. B. Kinard, George Kinard, S. J. Long, B. H. Maybin, Emanuel Sligh, D. Gross.

The company and regiment of Thomas Roebuck not known; killed or died during the war.

In the Fifth S. C. Cavalry was Berry Richards; killed in battle about the close of the war.

In Captain Frost's cavalry company were W. B. Oxner, Dr. James A. Cofield and John A. Henderson—all from Newberry.

In DePass' artillery company were J. L. Lyles, J. D. Sharp, Preston Sharp and James Nance.

The name of Mr. W. D. Hardy does not appear on the rolls printed, as he was in a Spartanburg company. He entered the service on April 13, 1861, in the Fifth S. C. Infantry. At the reorganization, in April, 1862, he was appointed Sergeant-Major. After the battles around Richmond in the summer of 1862 he was appointed Adjutant of the Fifth Regiment, in which capacity he served until General Lee surrendered at Appomattox C. H.

In the early part of 1861 Col. J. C. S. Brown organized a company composed altogether of Newberry men, and he was elected Captain. After having his company thoroughly drilled he was ordered to Columbia, where they went into camp. It was one of the smaller companies, and in the formation of the regiment there were two companies more than were needed, and it, with a Laurens company, had to be left out. Captain Brown transferred his men to other companies and resigned. After remaining at home for some time, Captain Brown joined Captain Keitt's company as a private and served through the war.

John N. Bass, who is now a citizen of Newberry, was a member of Company A, State Guards, a Laurens company, and lost a leg at Deep Bottom.

I. A. Blanton, now a Newberry man, enlisted March, 1862, in Barnwell in Company D, Third S. C. Cavalry, and served through the war.

Joseph Brown was a member of Company F, Tenth Regiment, S. C. V. He lived in Horry County, but enlisted in a Marion company in 1861. He was captured at Missionary Ridge, November, 1863; confined in Rock Island prison; was taken sick and released just before the close of the war.

Charles B. Buist, for thirty years a citizen of Newberry, should also have a place among the Confederate veterans from this county. He lost a leg at the battle of Secessionville, and came to Newberry soon after, where he resided until his death, March 25, 1892.

M. A. Carlisle entered in a company of South Carolina College Cadets in April, 1861; afterwards, in 1862, enlisted in Company E, Palmetto Battalion, Light Artillery, E. B. White, Colonel, and served as ordinance officer of the battalion, which was stationed at and around Charleston.

Dr. R. C. Carlisle entered the Confederate army just after his graduation in medicine in 1861, as assistant surgeon in the Seventh Regiment, and was promoted to Surgeon and served through the war. He entered the service from Union County, but has long been a citizen of Newberry.

William A. Fallaw was a member of Boykin Rangers and afterwards in the Second S. C. Cavalry. He enlisted from Lexington County in 1861, served through the war and has been a resident of Newberry since its close.

William J. Lake, after resigning from Company D, Thirteenth Regiment, S. C. V., joined Company C, 23d S. C. V., and was afterwards elected Lieutenant in Company B, 22nd S. C. V., where he served until he was wounded at Petersburg, July, 1864, disabled and retired.

Isaac K. Lake, a Newberry man, was a member of a Lexing company and afterwards joined Company C, Twenty-third Regiment, S. C. V., and was killed at Petersburg, July, 1864.

James N. Lipscomb went to Virginia with the first command from South Carolina, on the staff of Gen. M. L. Bonham, as Lieutenant-Colonel. When the Second S. C. Cavalry was formed he was appointed Quartermaster of the regiment by Col. M. C. Butler, with the rank of Captain. Upon Colonel Butler's promotion to Brigadier-General he made Captain Lipscomb his Adjutant-General with the rank of Captain, and he served with General Butler after he was made Major-General.

N. B. Mazyck was Captain of Company E, Twenty-fifth Regiment, S. C. V., Colonel C. H. Simonton, commander. He served through the war and came to Newberry from Charleston in 1869.

Dr. James McIntosh, now a citizen of Newberry, joined Company F, Eighth Regiment, S. C. V., upon its going into service, and was soon made Assistant-Surgeon in the S. C. State Troops. He resigned this position upon the Eighth Regiment being ordered to Virginia, rejoined his old company, and served in the field until November, 1861, when he was appointed Assistant-Surgeon, C. S. A., and ordered to the hospital at Charlottesville, Va., where he remained in the service to the close of the war.

Andrew J. McCaughrin was in the Calhoun Guards, Hagood's command, when he first went into the service, at the battle of Secessionville. He was afterwards in the Quartermasters' department. He was living in Charleston when the war broke out.

R. Simpson Moore, of Newberry, was a member of Company A, Tenth Georgia Battalion, Captain Frederick, and died of disease in the South Carolina Hospital at Petersburg, Va., May 16, 1863.

G. S. Noland, now a citizen of Newberry, enlisted in Company B, (from Union County), Eighteenth Regiment, S. C. V. He was wounded at Petersburg, July 30, 1864, and served through the war.

Augustus P. Pifer was living in Newberry when the war broke out, but when Virginia, his native State, seceded he returned home and entered the service in 1861. He was a member of General Lee's personal staff and the Captain of Lee's body guard, known as Lee's Scouts, Guards and Couriers. He was wounded in the foot and slightly in the head by a shell at Gettysburg. He remained with General Lee until his final surrender. After the war he returned to Newberry, where he has since resided.

Joseph S. Reid, who was a citizen of Mississippi when the war broke out, a native of Newberry, and now a citizen, organized the first company that went from Winston County, Miss., and was elected Captain. It was Company G, Twentieth Regiment. He was afterwards Major, and also Lieutenant-Colonel.

George A. Riser was a member of Captain King's company, Rhett's Regiment of Regulars, and was killed at Bentonville, N. C.

Dr. Peter Robertson, now a citizen of Newberry, was a member of Hart's Battery, Hampton's Cavalry Division, enlisting in 1864. He served until the surrender of Johnston's army.

E. A. Scott, a native of Ireland, and a citizen of Newberry for twenty-five years, was living in Alabama when the war began. He enlisted in the Second Regiment, Alabama Volunteers and afterwards served in the Forty-Second Regiment, Alabama Volunteers, which formed a portion of the army under General Bragg.

J. C. Simkins was Captain of Company B, First Regiment; promoted to Lieutenant-Colonel, and afterwards killed at Battery Wagener.

Alexander Singleton was a member of Company G, Tenth Regiment, S. C. V., and was discharged on account of ill health.

John F. Speck, now a citizen of Newberry, enlisted in 1861 for six months in Company K, First North Carolina Regiment. He then returned to his home at Lincolnton, organized Company E, Fifty-second Regiment, N. C. V., was elected Captain of the company, and served until he lost a leg at Fredericksburg, December, 1862, when he retired.

Thomas F. Tarrant, now a citizen of Newberry, was a member of Company A, Thirteenth Regiment.

In Company D, Holcombe Legion, Troop C, Seventh Cavalry, I. G. McKissick, Captain, were the following from Newberry: H. C. Kenner, 2nd Lieutenant, promoted from ranks. Privates—James L. Atchison, Joab Dean, James Herron, John Odell, T. J. Eison.

Morgan Gordon, Wesley Canady and Nathan R. Mars, from the Mollohon section, were in Captain Jones' company, Laurens, afterwards Capt. J. S. Johnson's company. Gordon was killed at Maryland Heights. Canady was killed at Gettysburg, Pa. Mars was wounded at Chickamauga, February 20, 1863. W. H. Husky, killed—not known where. Robert Abrams, died at Charlottesville, Va. Mitchel Suber. David Graham. John Oxner. Hib Cannon.

COMPANY "C," NINTH REGIMENT, STATE TROOPS.

There seems to be no roll in the archives in Columbia of Company C, Ninth Regiment of State Troops. From other sources I have obtained the names given herewith of those who were members from Newberry. They entered the service in the fall of 1862 and were stationed on the South Carolina coast for State defense: Jas. H. Williams, Colonel. Benj. Mathis, Captain. Reuben Davidson, 1st Lieutenant. Joseph Duckett, 2nd Lieutenant. G. B. Boozer, 3d Lieutenant. Privates—A. G. Maybin, John Satterwhite, Milton Spence, Levi Williams, Archie Sloan, James Adams, L. J. Jones, Melvin Adams, Pettus Gilliam, John Lyles, John C. Boozer, T. N. Boozer, Thomas Murtishaw, Hardy Suber, A. W. T. Simmons, W. Y. Fair. In the fall of 1863 Thomas Crooks was Captain and Thomas Alewine 1st Sergeant, and the following were added to the company: T. B. Chalmers, J. H. Gordon, David Murphy, Geo. A. Sligh, Jesse Senn, Johnson Pitts, Ed. Campbell, Mitchell Suber, Alf. Reeder.

These names are given from memory and may not be entirely correct nor full, but it was thought best to record them here.

ROLL OF COMPANY "H," FOURTH REGIMENT OF STATE TROOPS.

This company was called out towards the close of the war, in 1864 or 1865. J. W. Ferguson, of Laurens, Colonel commanding; John R. Spearman, Lieutenant-Colonel. All hope had been given up of getting these names, as the roll had long been lost, and there is no record of them in the archives of the State in Columbia. It was the purpose of the compiler from the beginning of this work to give the name of every one who saw service in any capacity in the War of Secession, and it will be a source of life-long regret to know that any one has been left out. This roll is prepared from the memory of those who could now be seen. It was composed of boys from fourteen to seventeen and those who were over sixty. They spent most of their time on the coast: Roscius F. Atwood, Captain. Pettus W. Gilliam, 1st Lieutenant. William Boyd, 2nd Lieutenant; promoted to Captain. G. B. Boozer, 3d Lieutenant. J. M. Johnstone, 3d Lieutenant. E. C. Jones, 1st Sergeant. Privates—B. F. Goggans, Clarky Houston, J. Singleton Ring, Fred Hendrix, John McCollum, James L. Henderson, Thomas B. Aughtry, R. B. Holman, Jr., John W. Smith, Calvin Caldwell, John C. Sligh, — Bobo, Richard Sondley, Gilliam Fulmer, William I. Harp, W. H. Wallace, (Laurens, but now a citizen of Newberry) G. W. Oxner, David DeWalt, James Glenn.

Men under John F. Sims, Captain: Wm. E. Gibson, Jonathan G. Martin (now in Texas), Andrew Willingham.

COMPANY "I," FIFTEENTH REGIMENT, S. C. V.

From the roll of Company I, Fifteenth Regiment, S. C. V., J. A. Derrick, Captain, procured for me by Mr. J. N. Feagle from Mr. W. C. Sheely, I find the following names of Newberrians: Walter W. Monts, 3d Lieutenant, wounded at Gettysburg, July 2, 1863, and died July 10, from amputation of leg. G. Mike Monts. William C. Sheely. George M. Sheely, wounded at Boonsboro, Md. J. Wilson Long. George Feagle, died in prison at Point Lookout, August 13, 1864. Walter W. Koon, wounded at Gettysburg, July 2, 1863, and died from wounds same month. A. Hamilton Koon,* wounded at Deep Bottom, Va., July 27, 1864, and died at home, August 18, 1864. Melvin Sheely died at home of disease. The other names on this roll were of men from Lexington.

---

* The name is now spelled Kohn. His son, Arthur H. Kohn, is a merchant at Prosperity.

SCHULTZ'S BATTERY.

The following belonged to Schultz's Battery, and spent most of the time on the South Carolina coast. None of the members from Newberry were killed or died during the war: Calvin Meetze, Levi Monts, Levi W. Bowers, Jacob Sheely, Drayton I. Sheely, B. Frank Sheely, M. S. Boland, G. Mike Bowers, J. K. Chapman, Noah L. Chapman, Junius E. Chapman, B. Frank Dawkins, James Sheppard, Hughey Turner, John C. Hill, Adam Long, John Hutchison, Adam George, J. Mid. Wheeler, George Hipp, William A. Hipp, Warren P. Cannon, Hayne Reid, Nathan Williamson, James A. Riser, Adam W. Monts, George Meetze, Drayton I. Long.

COMPANY "D," THIRD S. C. BATTALION.

The following Newberry men were in Company D, Third S. C. Battalion, (G. M. Gunnels, Captain—a Laurens company): Hosea M. Barger, enlisted in 1861 and served through the war. John B. Chambers, enlisted at same time; wounded at Spottsylvania C. H. and served through the war. W. F. Kelly, wounded at Boonsboro, Md., September 14, 1862. John L. Speake. George T. Speake. John Bishop. William Bishop, died of disease at home while on furlough. John Peas, wounded and captured and never heard of afterwards —supposed to have died. F. M. Harmon. Robert Speers. Silas Bishop, died of disease at Bunker's Hill in 1863. H. C. Jones, died of disease at Danville, Va., in 1863. W. P. Jones, color bearer, wounded at Frazier's Farm.

ROLL OF COMPANY "E," SEVENTH CAVALRY, S. C. V.

A roll of Company C, Holcombe Legion, is given at page 429. This roll was made when the company first went into the war in 1861. After the reorganization, in fall of 1863, the name of the company was changed and was known as Company E, Seventh S. C. Cavalry, commanded by Col. A. C. Haskell. I give herewith the names of the company as they appear on the roll. Some of them were from other counties, but as they were near the line and some have become citizens of Newberry I let it go in in full. In May, 1864, Captain Williams retired and the company was commanded by Lieutenant Walker, (as it had been some time before Capt. Williams' retirement) who was made Captain just before the close of the war:

J. Wash. Williams, Laurens, Captain, age 33; retired May, 1864. Silas Walker, 1st Lieutenant, age 34; wounded at Cold Harbor, June, 1864; in command of troops for some time. E. P. Chalmers, 2nd Lieutenant; wounded at Cold Harbor, June, 1864. J. L. Blackburn, 3d Lieutenant, age 24. R. Watts. Hill, Laurens, 1st Sergeant, age 24. R. R. Hill, Laurens, 2nd Sergeant, age 29; wounded at Savage Station in 1863. Daniel Dendy, 3d Sergeant, age 25; in prison in 1864; wounded at Riddle's Shop; captured. J. A. Workman, Laurens, 4th Sergeant, age 25; wounded at Williamsburg. C. A. Satterwhite, 5th Sergeant, age 24. John Watkins, 1st Corporal, age 26. H. D. Boozer, 2nd Corporal, age 24. W. G. Glenn, 3d Corporal, age 32; wounded at Cold Harbor. Samuel Leaman, Laurens, 4th Corporal, age 34.

Privates—J. H. Adams, age 25. W. H. Adams, age 22. Jno. W. Arnold, Laurens, age 32; killed at Williamsburg in 1863 on scouting duty. William Boozer, age 35. John Buzhardt, age 36. J. F. Boyd, Laurens, age 33. W. D. Boyd, Laurens, age 19. W. H. Boyd, Laurens, age 18. H. W. Boyd, Laurens, age 20. W. W. Boyd, Laurens, age 40. A. D. Burton, age 19; wounded at Cold Harbor. W. B. Bell, Laurens, age 17. W. P. Burkhalter, Edgefield, age 21; died of disease at home in 1864. N. M. Burkhalter, Edgefield, age 19. W. H. Clark, Laurens, age 18, died of disease at home in 1863. A. J. Coleman, Edgefield, age 30. A. P. Coleman, Edgefield, age 26; wounded at Deep Bottom. W. H. Coleman, Laurens, age 19. W. Y. Craddock, age 19. G. L. Crisp, Laurens, age 37. R. C. Davis, Laurens, age 21. J. C. Davis, Laurens, age 28. W. S. Davis, age 33. J. A. Davis, age 21; wounded at Cold Harbor. J. M. Davenport, age 27; died of disease at Columbia in 1864 on the way home. Samuel Davenport, age 21. L. E. Ferguson, Edgefield, age 26; wounded at Adam's Run, 1862. J. H. Finley, Laurens, age 20. H. G. Finley, Laurens, age 19. J. B. Floyd, age 36; wounded at Darbytown in 1863. J. R.

Fox, Edgefield, age 19; died of disease at home. Tillman Fuller, Laurens, age 40. S. B. Griffin, Laurens, age 21. B. F. Griffin, age 20. W. F. Golding, Edgefield, age 24; wounded at or near Barnville while scouting. W. S. Golding, Edgefield, age 22. W. P. Garrett, Laurens, age 29; wounded at James' Gate while scouting. Jasper Gibbs, Union, age 40. J. C. Gregory, Union, age 30; died of disease at Appomattox in 1865. B. A. Gregory, Laurens, age 38. N. B. Goodman, Laurens, age 26. H. D. Huntington, age 35; wounded at Williamsburg in 1863 while scouting. Thomas Hill, Laurens, age 27; captured at Darbytown in October, 1863; died in Union prison. J. A. Hill, Laurens, age 23. J. T. Hill, Laurens, age 22. S. L. Hill, Laurens, age 28. F. G. Holloway, Edgefield, age 27. Thos. J. Hatton, age 28. Daniel Jones, Laurens, age 40. W. H. Jones, age 24. Absalom Johnson, Laurens, age 55. A. M. Johnson, Laurens, age 26. T. J. Little, Laurens, age 22. S. W. Lowe, Laurens, age 19; captured at Petersburg. William Leaman, Laurens, age 30. Augustus Mason, Laurens, age 37. J. P. Mangum, age 18. G. H. Monroe, Laurens, age 20. D. A. Monroe, Laurens, age 25. W. M. Milam, Laurens, age 35; wounded at White Oak Swamp and captured; died in Union prison. William W. Milam, Laurens, age 30; wounded at Riddle Shops. J. C. Miller, Laurens, age 30. John Miller, age 22. J. W. Nichols, Laurens, age 18. B. F. Payne, Edgefield, age 26. J. W. Payne, Edgefield, age 21. W. B. Pulley, Edgefield, age 22. D. S. Pitts, Laurens, age 45; captured August 27, 1863. D. Proctor, Edgefield, age 21; killed at Cold Harbor, June, 1864. John M. Proctor, Edgefield, age 23. G. C. Ridlehuber, age 28. Sumter Rodgers, Laurens, age 30. John Satterwhite, age 45. B. G. Smith, ley, W. C. Beck, J. C. Belcher, W. E. Black, E. P. Boazman, G. S. Boazman, William Boazman, W. W. Boazman, J. M. Boazman, D. S. Boozer, S. M. Bowen, C. E. Bowen, R. F. Bradley, W. Brisbane, E. A. Brooks, T. J. Brough, J. A. Brownlee, M. C. Bullock, T. E. Burton, J. Butler, G. W. Calhoun, J. A. Calhoun, William P. Cline, R. H. Cochrane, D. Cohen, W. T. Counts, J. C. Cowan, J. B. Cowan, W. C. Curry, H. Davenport, T. J. Davenport, J. H. Davenport, M. L. Deal, J. A. Devlin, W. D. Devlin, N. O. Drennan, W. M. Feltman, J. M. Fin-

Edgefield, age 23. W. S. Smith, Edgefield, age 28. G. S. Smith, Edgefield, age 21. R. F. Spearman, Laurens, age 30; wounded at Cold Harbor. E. G. Stillwell, age 46. Fred Scurry, Edgefield, age 30. J. L. Schumpert, age 18; died of disease at Coffin's Farm in 1864. Samuel Schumpert, age 18. J. D. M. Shaw, Laurens, age 19. J. D. Taylor, age 28. T. S. Teague, Laurens, age 30. M. P. Tribble, Laurens, age 22. A. K. Tribble, age 40; wounded at Farmville. J. W. Tribble, Laurens, age 17. C. John Tribble, Laurens, age 20; killed at Tylersville on picket. R. G. Trunnal, Laurens, age 18. Charles C. Teague, discharged in May, 1861; over 45. John Wilson, age 28; died of disease at home on sick furlough. Seth Williams, age 30. R. G. Williams, age 24. C. J. Workman, Laurens, age 22. Aaron Wells, Laurens, age 40. W. J. Wells, Laurens, age 20. John Workman, Laurens.

Rank and file, 107 men; from Newberry, 34; Laurens, 52; Edgefield, 8; Union, 3. Killed, 3—one in battle; one scouting; one on picket. Died of wounds, 2; of disease in prison, 6. Total deaths, 12. Wounds not mortal, 16.

J. C. Tribble and C. W. Tribble were members of Com. C, Holcombe Legion. The former was killed at New Kent C. H. in August, 1863. The latter died of disease in the Manchester hospital in January, 1863.

MUSTER ROLL OF COMPANY "G," SECOND REGIMENT, S. C. CAVALRY.

At the suggestion of Captain J. W. Gary, who has a complete roll of Company G, Second Regiment, S. C. Cavalry, from October 31, 1864, to December 31, 1864, I insert it here, although the Newberry names already appear, and many of the company were from other counties:

T. J. Lipscomb, Colonel and first Captain. J. W. Gary, Captain. J. F. Hodges, 1st Lieutenant. T. J. Hearst, 2nd Lieutenant. A. W. Teague, Brevet 2nd Lieutenant. W. A. McClintock, 1st Sergeant. J. E. Bradley, 2nd Sergeant. H. D. Bedon, 3d Sergeant. M. J. Young, 4th Sergeant. J. W. Cowan, 5th Sergeant. J. N. Floyd, 1st Corporal. R. M. Seawright, 2nd Corporal. J. L. Blackesly, 3d Corporal. W. A. Limbecker, 4th Corporal.

Privates—J. A. Adams, S. Z. Ashley, J. H. Austin, B. H. Beas-

ley, T. G. Gaillard, D. L. Gary, V. Griffin, J. T. Griffin, R.
H. Haddon, W. H. Hancock, P. H. Hargrove, S. Holloway, A.
G. Irby, B. M. Jones, J. M. Jordan, W. A. Kay, W. P. Kil-
lingsworth, H. C. King, W. D. King, D. Lake, A. B. C. Lind-
say, M. B. Lipscomb, T. J. Lipscomb, H. S. Long, G. W. Lor-
ick, J. E. Lyon, M. L. Martin, A. J. McAdams, R. O. Mc-
Adams, W. N. McAdams, W. H. McCaw, E. P. McClintock,
W. W. Miller, J. A. Morene, W. B. Morgan, W. B. Morrow,
J. A. Morrow, J. P. Morrow, W. L. Mosely, B. B. Neel, F. M.
Nelson, J. B. Oneal, W. H. Henderson, S. A. Henderson, G.
E. L. Palmer, A. N. Pitts, J. D. Pitts, T. J. W. Pratt, F. V.
Pruit, F. E. Randell, J. B. Reagin, J. S. Ruff, J. R. Seals, J.
B. Seawright, W. C. Scott, G. M. Sibert, J. H. Sibert, J. H.
Simpson, S. Smith, T. N. Smith, G. M. Smith, J. E. Stone,
G. B. Suber, G. Taylor, M. M. Teague, P. A. Tribble, J. S.
Turner, W. L. Turner, W. I. Turney, A. J. Waddell, J. A.
Wakefield, W. W. Wallace, J. B. Watts, J. Q. Wilbur, J. L.
Wilson, J. S. Wilson, W. W. Wilson, A. E. Woodham, J. M.
Workman.   Total Privates, 116; Commissioned officers, 4;
Non-commissioned officers, 9.   Rank and file, 127.

Benjamin F. Clark, Jasper G. Clark, W. S. Jennings, M. H.
Witt, detached as musicians and buglers at headquarter line.

The roll of Co. E, 3d Regiment, as published (p. 391), gives
only a partial list of the casualties. The data was obtained
from the roll. Why only a part of the casualties was given,
I do not know. I am glad to be able to give this additional
history, obtained from C. F. Boyd, W. H. Blats, B. H. Lovelace and W. W. Riser, members of the company, who now
reside in Newberry. It is only from memory, but I feel sure
it is accurate, and no doubt covers the case fully. I regret
that it did not appear along with the roll. Y. J. Pope was
promoted to Adjutant of the Regiment at the reorganization,
April, 1862; lost an eye at Cedar Creek, October 19, 1864.
C. F. Boyd was shot through the lungs at Cedar Creek. W.
D. Rutherford was made Adjutant soon after the company
entered the service, and at the reorganization in 1862 was
elected Major, and afterwards promoted to Colonel. He was
killed at the battle of Strasburg, October 13, 1864. Thomas

S. Moorman was wounded at the Wilderness. William H. Thompson was the first member of the company killed in battle, and is the same man mentioned as William Thompson in the roll of privates. William Hood was wounded at —. The name of John K. Anderson, in the printed roll, should be John K. Andrews. Calvin B. Adams, mentioned in the roll, should be Colvin B. Adams; wounded at Gettysburg. Samuel L. Atchison was wounded at Gettysburg. R. W. Adkins died of disease at —. William H. Blats was wounded at Cedar Creek, October 19, 1864, and at Spottsylvania, May, 1864. William Pitts Boyd, mentioned in the roll, should be Minor P. Boyd; wounded in a skirmish around Richmond in 1862. Charlie S. Bridges, in the roll, should be Charlie S. Burgess. Thomas C. Brown was promoted to Assistant-Surgeon of the Third Regiment, and did good service. Jeff. E. Brown was detailed as a courier to General Longstreet. S. S. Derrick. in the published roll, should be George C. Derrick. John G. Duckett was wounded at Fredericksburg. Michael Foot was wounded at Savage Station. Leonidas K. Glasgow lost an arm at 2nd Wilderness, May, 1864. Samuel J. Hiller lost a leg at Cedar Creek, October 19, 1864. James Lindsay was killed at Cedar Creek. B. H. Lovelace was shot through the face at Chickamauga, September 20, 1863. Thomas M. Lake was wounded in the battles around Richmond. Lawrence R. Marshall lost an arm at 2nd Wilderness, May, 1864. Samuel J. McCaughrin was wounded at Chickamauga. J. W. Mathis, in the roll, should be John M. Mathis; wounded at —. There was only one Thomas Marshall in the company, and his name was Thomas P. Marshall. He died of disease in Tennessee in 1863. J. Wirick Odell was wounded at Bentonville, N. C. Osborne L. Schumpert was wounded at Cedar Creek, October 19, 1864, while acting as Orderly to the Colonel of the regiment. George C. Riser was wounded at Cedar Creek; taken prisoner, and exchanged at Richmond just before the surrender.

Lieutenant John F. Banks, of Company G, Thirteenth S. C. Regiment (p. 388), was promoted to Captain. Jacob B. Fellers lost an arm in battle at Second Manassas and resigned. J. H. Cannon, 3d Lieutenant, resigned in 1861. J. M. Wheeler was promoted to 1st Lieutenant, wounded at Sharpsburg—disabled and resigned. Wm. Jennings lost an arm. G. S. Lobb in the roll should be G. Luther Bobb. The name of David Duncan should be added to this roll.

John P. Stewart, on the roll of Company B, Third Regiment, (p. 388) was wounded at Knoxville, Tenn., and died of disease at Rock Island, Ill., in 1864.

To the roll of Co. H, 3d S. C. Regiment (p. 421), should be added the names of Jacob J. Hipp, W. Anderson Werts, Charles P. Dickert, the latter being from Lexington at the time of enlistment, but long a citizen of Newberry. William Monts had six sons in the war, five of whom were in this company. The four who were killed in battle or died during the war were: Frank, James, Thomas and Nelson. John W. is already mentioned. The sixth is Jacob, still living. Henry M. Long, a member of this company, died in service from measles. Adam I. Hipp, who was a sergeant of the company, was wounded at Maryland Heights. B. Fletcher Dickert, a brother of Captain D. A. Dickert, also a member of Co. H, was killed in battle at Chickamauga. J. J. Gallman, wounded at Gettysburg. S. H. Folk, died in service. Dr. J. O. Dickert, originally from Lexington, but after the war a citizen and physician near Chappells for many years and until his death. George Long, died in service. M. Livingston, died in service. Thomas Metts, wounded. Robert I. Stoudemire, from Lexington at beginning of war, but for many years a citizen of Newberry.

R. S. Bradley, Company B, First Regiment (p. 406), should be Pinckney Bradley. James Lane (p. 411) should be James Love.

S. Dugan Boyd, printed in the roll of Company D, (p. 414) Thirteenth S. C. Regiment, should be Dugan L. Boyd. To this roll should be added the names of Thomas Gordon, J. A. Rikard and G. A. Setzler. Dr. Spencer G. Welch, a member of this company, was detailed as assistant surgeon

The name of Robert Cannon in the roll of Company B, Third Regiment (p. 389), should be Robert Connor. On the same roll Robert P. Green should be Robert P. Greer.

Frank S. Murzott, printed in the roll of Company D, (p. 416) Thirteenth Regiment, S. C. V., should be Frank S. Margart.

I regret the necessity of having to make this addendum, but it seemed impossible to get the data before the preceding pages were printed, and, rather than have the facts lost, they have been inserted in this irregular way. I feel that there are yet names and facts we ought to have; but the printing has been delayed and the rolls re-examined and every effort made to get all the facts, and if there are still errors we feel that we have done the best we could, and no name nor important fact has been intentionally omitted. It is hoped the reader will appreciate the effort that has been made.

THE FURNAS FAMILY.

In addition to what Mr. David Jones, of Ohio, has related of this family, I have learned that Joseph Furnas, one of the old Quakers of Bush River, mentioned by Judge O'Neall in his Annals, never moved to Ohio; that he died either in Charleston or Newberry; that the family first located at Charleston when they came to South Carolina. From Charleston they moved to Newberry. Joseph Furnas left four sons, Robert, Thomas W., William and John. Sarah, the great traveler, mentioned by Mr. Jones, married Dr. Wells, who was also a traveler of note.

Thomas W. was, a number of terms, member of the Ohio Legislature, and also several terms Sheriff of Miama County in that State. His active son, William, was the father of Robert W. Furnas, Governor of Nebraska in 1874, in which State he has resided for thirty-six years, from the beginning of Territorial government. During this period he has held many important State and national offices. He was Colonel and General in the War of Secession, and came very nearly being a member of President Harrison's cabinet as Secretary of Agriculture. At this time, 1892, he is Secretary of the State Board of Agriculture. His son John resided for a time in California; and this fact led Mr. Jones into his error.

O'NEALL—BURNING OF COLUMBIA.

While writing of the far off descendants of Newberrians I feel moved to introduce here an extract from a letter written by Hugh O'Neall, of Bellevue, Nebraska, dated December 7, 1890. He says: **H**

"You spoke of a man 'doing right while in the army. Obedience to orders makes a good soldier.' I did many things under orders that I considered wrong, but never anything voluntarily that I thought was wrong. One thing that I witnessed I always condemned, and always shall—that was the burning of Columbia. That town was surrendered to the brigade I belonged to. We marched into town about eleven o'clock, February 17, 1865, and my regiment stacked arms in the market-house; and by four or five o'clock, it seems to me, there were not twenty sober men in the brigade. The drug stores were burst open and whiskey carried out by the bucket-full, and men got drunk before they knew what they were doing; and I consider the burning the work of a drunken mob, and surely was not sanctioned by Logan or Sherman, or any other reasonable man. I know I was sober, for I never drank of intoxicating liquors in my life, and think I saw things as they were as near as any man that was there. Although history is silent on a great many points, they are as fresh in my mind as when I witnessed them. As I stood there that night and witnessed these things, I could but think, if God was a just God, these things would surely come home to the parties that upheld these things.

"It may not come in my life time, but I surely think it will come. I think it will come in the shape of labor against capital, and will not be confined to any particular section, but the East willl suffer the worst."

This writer has always thought that General Sherman should never have denied that he burned Columbia. He ought to have owned it and justified the act. The purpose of the war was to crush the "rebellion," and the more effectual the means taken, the better. The burning of Columbia was an act of vandalism no greater than the laying waste of the country through which his army passed. It was an act of vandalism no greater than the issuing of the Emancipation Proclamation by President Lincoln, January 1, 1863. War is no children's pastime; and it is a fact that the outposts of hell are planted all along in this world. It is a terrible fact that every human bosom is the battle-ground between the firmly planted pickets and hosts of hell and the angelic and heavenly bodies.

And what are *you* going to do about it?

REFLECTIONS.

In writing the Annals of Newberry it has not been any part of my purpose to write a history of the War between the States. I have sought only to make a record of the names of all from Newberry who were engaged in that great conflict. In this I hope I have very nearly succeeded. On the 9th of April, 1865, General Lee surrendered the remnant of his army—just four years after the war began.

THE WAR WITH MEXICO.

As part of the military history of Newberry I give here the roll of Co. L, No. 11, being the names of the volunteers in the war with Mexico, with the casualties of the company during that war:

J. H. Williams, Captain, age 30, Newberry; entered service January 20, 1847. C. P. Pope, 1st Lieutenant, age 27, Edgefield; entered service January 20, 1847. J. W. Stewart, 2nd Lieutenant, age 21, Newberry; furloughed by General Scott. E. F. Williams, 3d Lieutenant, age 35; in charge of sick at Puebla. J. C. C. Enlow, 1st Sergeant, age 28; died at Vera Cruz, May 4, 1847. James Denson, 2nd Sergeant, age 30; killed at Churubusco, August 20, 1847. H. P. Pratt, 3d Sergeant, age 21; sick at Puebla, August 8; died October 26, 1847. T. B. Thomson, 4th Sergeant, age 32; discharged August 7, 1847, at Vera Cruz. J. Culbreath, 1st Corporal, age 27, Edgefield; 1st Sergeant, August 20, 1847. John A. Spears, 2nd Corporal, age 35, Laurens; 2nd Sergeant, August 20, 1847. W. P. Feltman, 3d Corporal, age 24; resigned 3d Corporal, August 20, 1847. John Watts, 4th Corporal, age 26; 3d Corporal, August 20; died at Mexico, October 12, 1847. Julius Harris, musician; died July 15, 1847, at Puebla.

Privates—Anderson, Wm., age 19; sick at Vera Cruz, April 18; died May 30. Armstrong, C. W., age 20; sick at Jalapa, May 7; died at Pereta. Abney, G. H., age 19; wounded severely at Churubusco. Anderson, Thomas, age 20; transferred to Co. D., P. R., S. C. V., April 8. Bundrick, Abner, age 24; died at Vera Cruz, May 17, 1847. Brook, John B., age 27. Brown, W. T., age 22. Bone, Geo., age 28; sick at

Puebla, August 8; died September 23. Burton, Ferdinand, age 20, Edgefield. Brown, D. J., age 20. Chapman, Thos., age 19. Culkin, Wm., age 28; died at Jalapa, June 5, 1847. Clopton, Mastin, age 19. Clanton, J. H. Carwile, R. C., age 19; died at Jalapa. Callohum, Thos., age 20; left sick at Penal, May 14. Cole, David, age 25; died at Pereta. Clodfelter, L. H., age 30; died at Tacubaya, September 15, from wound received at Chepultepec. Dun, John, age 22; sick at Puebla, August 8; died August 20. Downing, J. W., age 22; sick at Puebla, August 8; died August 23. Ennis, Aldrich, age 19; died at Vera Cruz, May 30, 1847. Feagle, Adam, age 19; wounded severely at Chepultepec, September 13. Ford, Thomas, age 23; died at Jalapa, May 18, 1847. Gushman, Geo., age 36, Hamburg, Holland; died at Pereta, July 11. Gary, V. R., age 23; wounded severely at Churubusco. Griffin, L. D., age 26; died at Pereta, June 16. Graham, John, age 35; wounded severely at Chepultepec. Hilburn, Hugh, age 40; died at Pereta, June 30, 1847. Hollis, Livingston, age 34; sick in hospital. Hutchinson, Wm., age 22; died at Vera Cruz, May 1, 1847. Hogg, Thomas, age 20. Hair, Mathias, age 19; died at Puebla, August 3. Hilburn, Wm., age 19; died at Pereta, June 30. Higgins, J. C., age 21; wounded severely at Chepultepec. Howard, John, age 32; died at Mexico, August 8. Holt, Joseph, age 35; died at Jalapa, June 4, 1847. Jackson, J. P., age 19; left at Puebla, June 4, 1847. Kerr, A. J., age 20; sick at Puebla, August 8, 1847; died. Lane, J. J., age 21; died at Jalapa, June 7. Lindsay, Thos., age 20; left sick at Puebla, August 8. Little, Allen, age 20, Edgefield; wounded at Garieta; died October 25. Lyles, R. B., age 21, Fairfield; wounded severely at Garieta. Morris, Ferdinand, age 35; left sick at Puebla, August 8. McGill, Samuel, age 24; left sick May 12; died May 13. Mathis, Ben J., age 19. McFarlane, John. McClelland, Fergus, age 34; left sick at Vera Cruz, April 18. McClelland, Wm., age 25; died at Vera Cruz, June 29. Meek, Wm., age 24; died at Puebla. Nance, F. S., age 19; promoted 3d Sergeant, August 20. Nance, Rutherford, age 26; appointed 4th Sergeant, August 20. Nates, Jesse, age 38; died at Puebla, August 31. O'Neall, J. Belton; killed. O'Neall, McBelton, age 21, Union; wounded at Churubusco. Presnell, Jacob, age

27. Pitts, Zadoc, age 28. Pitts, John, age 26; discharged by General Act of Congress. Pope, V. B., age 32; appointed Corporal, August 20, 1847. O'Neall, Wm., age 30; left sick at Puebla, August 8. Riser, D. M., age 26. Spense, James, age 36; died at Puebla, June 12. Summers, Wm., age 41; died at Puebla, July 5. Summers, H. H., age 25. Summers, J. P., age 28; died at Puebla, July 28. Smith, M. D., age 32. Sheppard, Wm., age 18; wounded severely at Churubusco. Suber, Hiram, age 27; wounded slightly at Garieta. Stanal, L. B., age 40; died at Jalapa, May 18. Sheely, John S., Edgefield; Corporal, August 20; killed at Chepultepec. Warner, Jacob, age 21. Warner, Henry, age 19. Warner, G. W., age 20; sick at Pereta. Watson, H. W., age 28; left sick at Pinal, May 14; not heard of since. Wood, Charles, age 23; wounded at Churubusco; died in Mexico from his wounds, September 23. Weathersbee, Owen, age 26; left sick at Puebla, August 8. Waldrop, W. R., age 22; wounded at Churubusco. Thomas, M. M., age 23. Tencle, James J., age 25. McFarland, John, age 26, from Boston, Mass. Mustered into service April 30, at Jalapa, by Captain Dent.

I am not at all sure that all the names in this roll are spelled correctly. I had two lists before me and they did not entirely correspond one with the other. The reader will perceive that but few were killed in battle, but that the loss from death by disease was considerable.

Giles Chapman, an elder brother of the writer, in the 2nd Indiana Regiment, was killed at the battle of Buena Vista, with two others, while endeavoring to remove a wounded comrade from the field, choosing to die with him rather than desert him. Pierced with ten wounds without a stain of blood on his shirt.

DR. JACOB H. KING AND NICHOLAS SUMMER, ESQ.

The following incident of the Florida war in the lives of Dr. Jacob H. King and Nicholas Summer has been kindly contributed by Dr. O. B. Mayer, Sr.:

"In 1840–41, I and Dr. Jacob H. King practiced medicine in copartnership, in the Dutch Fork. In our rides together he narrated to me some of his adventures in the Florida war.

He and Nicholas Summer, of the Newberry Bar, were officers
in the same company, if I am not mistaken. A grave difficulty was still pending between them; and it had been prevented from ending in a hostile meeting only by the inter-
ference of friends. The incident now to be narrated, and
which I give as nearly as possible in the Doctor's words, is
an instance of true nobleness of heart that well deserves
preservation.

" 'It was our first battle with the Indians,' said the Doctor.
'I was mounted upon a fleet horse and was riding at full
speed towards the hammock into which the enemy had fled,
and from which was issuing their war whoops in the most
infernal shrieks and yells imaginable. The cracks of their
rifles could scarcely be distinguished one from another; and
the pine needles, cut from the pine tops by the Indians aiming
too high, were falling like a shower of rain. I heard the
voice of Nicholas Summer, between whom and myself there
had for a long time been no friendly feeling. He had just
received a serious wound and had fallen from his horse. The
words he shouted were these: 'Don't let them scalp me.' I
rode up to him and found him screwing a bayonet to his
musket, with a view of selling his life dearly. A feeling came
over me which made me insensible to danger, and I placed
myself and horse before him to screen him from further hurt.
It was surely at the risk of my own life, for the bullets were
whizzing fearfully around me. Just then the Richland company came past us and charged the hammock, driving the
Indians out of hearing. I dismounted and placed Summer
in as comfortable a position as was possible, and enjoyed a
luxury of feeling I had never before experienced, when, during
the mutual pressure of our hands, he said to me: 'I can never
forget your kindness to me.' My great regret is that I never
saw him again; for, as you know, he died of his wound some
months afterwards at Tampa Bay.'   O. B. M., Sr."

IV.

WAR TIMES IN NEWBERRY.

THE CLOSING DAYS OF THE SOUTHERN CONFEDERACY.

The following is from an occasional correspondent of the *News and Courier:*

BIRMINGHAM, ALA., February 9, 18—.

Judge O'Neall, in his "Annals of Newberry," quotes Colonel Robert Rutherford, one of the early settlers, as saying that "South Carolina was the garden spot of the world, and Newberry was the garden spot of that garden spot." That was certainly an enthusiastic expression, but it may be said, perhaps truly, that Newberry is the prettiest farming district in the State, the lands being beautifully undulating over almost the entire boundary.

My present purpose is to call up some recollections of Newberry during the closing days of the war, now nearly twenty years ago. After the burning of Columbia, in February, 1865, Newberry became something of a military post and station on the line running across from Chester to Abbeville, S. C., and Washington, Ga. All couriers between the two armies reported at the Newberry office, which was in charge of the writer, who was compelled, from the necessities of the times, to assume a kind of military governorship of the place. A company of sixty veteran Georgians, commanded by a lieutenant, on their way to Johnston's army, were willingly pressed into service, besides a number of home guards and others, aggregating in all about one hundred men. With this force to back him, the commanding officer undertook to defend Newberry against Kilpatrick's bummers, that hung upon the skirts of Sherman's passing columns. Regular pickets were posted at Hunt's Cross Roads, two miles from town, and scouts were sent out day and night to watch the enemy. One of these scouts, a photographic artist, was captured at Pomaria Station, on the Greenville and Columbia Railroad. With an eye to the beautiful in nature, he had ridden up the hill to view the enemy from afar, but he never rode down again. He was carried over into Chester, and after a few days was released and returned to the bosom of his profession at Newberry, a sadder but wiser man.

One morning the scouts brought in four of the house-burners and robbers, who were at once ordered to Chester, but the guards returned next day and reported the prisoners "lost." On another occasion a prisoner was "lost" near Frog Level, but was found next day suspended from the limb of a tree. Mr. Henry Summer, who lived in the Fork, told me a thrilling story of how these vandals came to his house, placed a rope around his neck, and forced him to give up his money. Mr. Summer was a man of fine reading, and a learned lawyer, and often kindly called upon me. It was a treat to hear him talk. During those times of vigilance and anxiety, one morning at four o'clock a note was received from General B. F. Cheatham, who had reached Frog Level with troops from the Army of Tennessee. He was trying to join General Johnston, in North Carolina, and requested me to send a scout to a certain ford on Broad River, and report at once. Which was done. General Cheatham was at and around Newberry about a week, and his manœuvring there is matter of history. General Stewart was there at the same time, and remained at my office a number of days. He had just been appointed Lieutenant-General, but too late, as the war was nearly over. A number of prominent Generals were passing through Newberry about this time, without commands, and were going, they knew not where. Vice-President Stephens passed through, *en route* to his home in Georgia. Being asked at the depot what he thought of the prospect, he replied : "Well, we will hold on till the breechings break." The first straggling soldier who brought the news of Lee's surrender was discredited and questioned sharply by Y. J. Pope. He replied : "Well, gentlemen, it won't be long before you will see lots of them that will tell you the same." They came.

But the most grateful recollection in the time of my duties at Newberry was that in which I had the honor of transferring and forwarding Mrs. President Davis and party and the Confederate gold. Lieutenant Harker reported at my office on Sunday morning at six o'clock, and said he was in charge of Mrs. Davis and the government specie, with a guard of sixty marines then entering the town. He requested transportation, and a suitable special car was at once ordered from the Helena shops. During the few hours that Mrs. Davis was in waiting she remained at a small government office on the railroad platform, and declined all hospitalities from the good citizens who sought to do her honor. While standing on the platform a courier dashed up and handed her a note from the flying President. She and her sister, Miss Howell, were quite pleasant to those around them, and at times even cheerful. Miss Howell, on being playfully asked to remain, laughingly replied that she "wanted to go with the money."

At two o'clock all were on board, and the last and best part of the Confederacy rolled out for Abbeville and Washington, Ga. Not long after—but you know the rest.

During an administration of fourteen months in Newberry John P. Kinard, George DeWalt and Dr. Harrington were my advisers, and we held many a secret council of state—I mean, of war. Mr. DeWalt often dissented from the opinion of the council, but was a safe counsellor, guide and friend. Dr. Harrington was the courtly and refined gentleman, and Major Kinard the genial, affable and sagacious man of the people. Take them all in all, I shall not see their like again. Dr. Mayer and Silas Johnstone were my companions in chess, friendship and joy. Dr. Mayer was a believer in ghosts, and told me he could show a troop of them any time at a place six miles from Newberry. But I never went to see them. During those days Mr. Lambert J. Jones and Burr J. Ramage were regular practitioners in the Conscript Court. Sometimes some of their clients paid their fees in provisions. When Mr. Ramage had received a good, large country-cured ham from down about Frog Level, he pressed his case very hard, and often with success ; for meat hath its victories as well as war.

Many other pleasant reminiscences of Newberry abide with me, and fonder names cluster near my heart, but are to be mentioned *"nevermore."* *Good-bye.*

The foregoing was written by Captain F. N. Walker, of Spartanburg, who, having been disabled by a wound, was stationed at Newberry as enrolling officer, in performance of the duties of which office he remained, as he states, about fourteen months at that place.

"By the way," says 'Gilderoy,' in the *Southern Christian Advocate*, "I will never forget a thing that occurred in Newberry as we came home after the surrender. The soldiers raided the government stores in that town, and in every other town as we came on home. At Newberry they rolled some barrels of molasses into the streets and knocked in the heads, and each man as he passed by dipped in his canteen and filled it with 'treacle,' as they call it in England. We had with us a low, squatty, duck-legged Jew, a jolly good fellow, not more than five feet high, if that tall. Levi was exceedingly anxious to fill his canteen, but the molasses had gotten down so low he could not reach it over the chime of the barrel, and his taller Gentile friends were too busy helping themselves to wait on him, so he jumped with his stomach on the chime of the barrel and reached down and began to fill his canteen. Some wicked Gentile just behind, with a keen eye for fun, took Levi by the off hind leg and set him square on his head in the barrel, where the molasses was a foot and a half or too feet deep. Some kind friends pulled him out and laid him on a plank to dry. I do not think I would be putting it too strong to say he was the sweetest looking Jew I ever saw. Levi was 'as mad as an old wet hen,' as the old saying goes."

THE WOMEN OF NEWBERRY DURING THE WAR.

That the women of Newberry did their duty, and their whole duty, during the war, it is almost needless to say.

Boxes of goods, consisting of clothing, shoes, and occasionally a little coffee and home-made delicacies—the best possible that could be obtained—were forwarded by every opportunity to the men in camp during winter quarters, and at all times, through soldiers returning to their commands. Ginger bread, or simply cakes, sweetened with sorghum, was very nice. But sorghum rum, of which there was some made—but not by the women—was not nice. There was a good deal of corn whiskey and peach brandy, which were much better than sorghum rum. By the way, the last drink of whiskey I ever bought in a grog shop I bought from a woman at a bar in Columbia when once on my return home from the army on furlough. I do not say it was the last whiskey I have ever drunk, but the last dram I ever took at a bar. But I do not think the women of Newberry ever helped to make the sorghum rum, corn whiskey or peach brandy.

Before I joined the army, which I cannot say was altogether voluntary, though I went as a volunteer, I saw the women of Newberry doing all they could and exerting themselves daily to forward supplies of whatever might be needed to their loved ones in the army. And when the sick and wounded and disabled began to pass through Newberry to their homes elsewhere, there were always at the depot some ladies to meet them, to wait upon them and to supply their wants as far as possible This was the rule at every station on the road, not only at Newberry, but everywhere and every day. I remember one good lady who made it her daily business for a long time to feed the returning soldiers, especially if disabled, on the road between Columbia and Branchville. Her home was at Orangeburg, and being at that time quite wealthy, she felt it no hardship nor any loss to spend in this way. On my return home, disabled and still suffering from my wound, when the train stopped at Orangeburg she stepped on board with a basket on her arm. I had scarcely had anything to eat since I left Macon, and being convalescent I was quite hungry. I smiled and bowed to her and she came to me at once. She opened her basket and gave me to eat as long as I wanted. This good woman, Mrs. Rowe, lived about twenty years longer, dying in the year 1883 or 1884, loved and honored by all who knew her. I never saw her afterwards, but I hope to meet her and thank her in heaven. She did what she could.

On the night of the 12th of August, 1864, I lodged at the Wayside Hospital in Columbia, S. C. At Silver Street, in Newberry County, the ladies had a most bountiful dinner for the sick and wounded soldiers going home, a supply of which they brought me to my seat, as I was not able to get out without help, and I ate until I was ashamed.

The ladies of the town of Newberry not only furnished clothing and other supplies for the men in the army and fed the passing soldiers, but they also, in the year 1864, I think it was, established a house of rest and repose for the wounded and weary who were compelled to stop awhile on the way. They also converted the Court House into a hospital for the sick. Where all the women were trying to do their best, and did it, I hesitate to write any names. But I have heard mentioned in this connection Mrs. Higgins, Mrs. P. B. Ruff, Mrs. Lambert J. Jones and Mrs. J. J. Brantley; and from their well known active benevolence of character, I can very readily believe that they would be foremost in every good word and work.

The compiler of these Annals knows very little of what took place at Newberry from the summer of 1863 to the close of the war, and, indeed, until the first of 1866, as he was a soldier at the front and did not return to Newberry until some months after the close of the war. But he remembers well, before he went into service, how active, how nobly active, all the women of Newberry were in relieving the necessities and sufferings of the soldiers.

In this connection it may be well to revert to old times. and relate one or two incidents that occurred in Newberry County in our Revolutionary struggle, illustrating the heroic courage and strength of women under trying circumstances. Judge O'Neall gives these incidents in his "Random Recollections of Revolutionary Characters and Incidents," published in the *Southern Literary Journal*, 1838, pages 104 and 105, but he did not insert them in his Annals.

James Gauntt, who was long a worthy citizen of Newberry, and who died on the 21st day of January, 1890, at the advanced age of 89 years, was a grandson of the Israel Gauntt mentioned in the narrative. The daughter, Hannah, was the grandmother of Joseph Mooney, who once owned and occupied the brick house that stood, and was destroyed by the fire of 1866, on a part of the ground now covered by the Crotwell Building. I quote from "The Women of the American Revolution," by Mrs. E. F. Ellet, vol. 2, p. 298:

"A man named Hubbs, who had served with the bloody tory and renegade Cunningham in South Carolina, was an 'out-lier' during the war. At one time he proposed, with two confederates, to rob an old man of Quaker habits—Israel Gauntt—who was reputed to be in the possession of money. The three rode up one evening to the house and asked lodging, which was refused. Hubbs rode to the kitchen door, in which Mrs. Gauntt was standing, and asked for water. He sprang in while she turned to get the water, and as she handed it to him she saw his arms. Her husband, informed of this, secured the doors. Hubbs presented his pistol at him; but his deadly purpose was frustrated by the old man's daughter, Hannah. She threw up the weapon, and, being of masuline proportions and strength, grappled with and threw him on the floor, where she held him, though wounded by his spurs—in spite of his desperate struggles—till he was disabled by her father's blows. Gauntt was wounded through the window by Hubbs' companions, and another ball grazed his heroic daughter just above the eye; but both escaped without further injury. Hannah afterwards married a man named Mooney. The gentleman (Judge O'Neall) who relates the foregoing incident has often seen her, and describes her as one of the kindest and most benevolent of women. She died about the age of fifty, and her grandson, a worthy and excellent man, is now living in the village of Newberry.

"The same company of marauders, with Moultrie, another of Cunningham's gang, visited Andrew Lee's house, at Lee's Ferry, Saluda River, for the purpose of plunder. Moultrie succeeded in effecting an entrance into the house. Lee seized and held him, and they fell together on a bed; when he called to his wife, Mary, to strike him on the head with an axe. Her first blow, in her agitation, fell on her husband's hand; but she repeated it, and stunned Moultrie, who fell on the floor insensible. Lee, with his negroes and dogs, then drove away the other robbers, and on his return secured Moultrie, who was afterwards hanged in Ninety-Six."

In the next Section I will relate the story of Emily Geiger, the brave Newberry girl of the Revolution.

V.

THE STORY OF EMILY GEIGER.

When General Greene retreated from Ninety-Six after his unsuccessful assault upon that place in June, 1781, he crossed the Saluda River and passed through the upper part of what is now Newberry County, pursued by Lord Rawdon until he crossed the Enoree. Before his rear-guard had left the south side of this river the van of Lord Rawdon's army appeared in pursuit. But his lordship hesitated to make an attack upon General Greene's cavalry, which was commanded by Colonels Lee and Washington. And while he paused at this place, Greene moved on towards Broad River, near which he halted and encamped, in the fork of Enoree and Broad Rivers, in Newberry County. About two miles from where he had camped with his weary and disheartened troops stood the residence of a well-to-do farmer named John Geiger, an ardent patriot, but an invalid and unable to serve his country in arms. His daughter Emily, about 18 years of age, was as ardent a patriot as himself, and was often heard to say: "Oh! that I were a man, that I could fight for my country," whenever she heard of any American reverses, or of any outrages committed by the British or tories.

On the third day of General Greene's encampment at this place a neighbor of Geiger's dropped in to see him.

"What news?" asked Geiger.

"Lord Rawdon has determined to abandon the Fort at Ninety-Six."

"Are you certain?"

"Yes. General Greene received the intelligence this morning. Rawdon has sent word to Colonel Stuart to move with his regiment from Charleston to Friday's Ferry, on the Congaree, where he intends to join him as soon as possible. Cruger is left at Ninety-Six with orders to move at once with his tory recruits and their property and take a route that will put the Edisto between him and the American forces. Moving down south of the Edisto to Orangeburg, he will, from that place, make a junction with Rawdon at Friday's Ferry."

"Then they will divide their forces?"

"Yes."

"Greene will then attack Cruger?"

"No," replied the neighbor, "Greene proposes to pursue Rawdon and strike a more effective blow."

"Why did he not fight him at the Saluda?"

"General Sumter was not with him."

"Nor is he now."

"No," said the neighbor, "and I fear that he will not join him as he so desires, as he can find no one willing to become a bearer of despatches to Sumter. All the country between here and Sumter is full of tories, elated by our defeat at Ninety-Six, who would certainly murder any man who undertakes the journey."

"Oh! that I were able," said the old man; "I would risk it. But these feeble limbs refuse to bear me on the journey."

"You would commit an act of folly," said the neighbor.

"No," replied the farmer, "but one of true devotion to my country."

Emily Geiger heard all that passed between her father and the neighbor, and she murmured to herself, as she had so often done before: "Oh! that I were a man." But she was only a girl, and what could a girl do when brave men shrank from such an undertaking. "If I were only a man!" she murmured, again and again, long after the neighbor had departed.

In the meantime, General Greene had been informed by Colonel Lee of the proposed abandonment of Ninety-Six, and he was now preparing to strike Lord Rawdon a decisive blow while the British forces were divided. But it was necessary, in order to make sure of victory, that Sumter should be informed of his designs and that they should unite their forces. But so far he had found no messenger. The service was too dangerous.

On the morning of the day in which he proposed to begin his movements, General Greene sat in his tent lost in deep thought. Since taking the command of the Southern army, the odds against him had been fearful and the difficulties appalling. But still he had gained and the enemy was weaker than at first. And now, if he could strike one more good blow, he felt that he could destroy him. But the force with him was too weak and Sumter was far away—over a hundred miles. If he could effect a junction with him before Lord Rawdon reached Friday's Ferry on the Congaree, he had hopes of success. But the messenger was wanting. While deeply pondering these things an officer entered and said:

"A young country girl is before the tent and wishes to speak with you."

"Tell her to come in," replied the General.

The officer withdrew, and in a short time returned in company with a young girl, who was dressed in a closely fitting riding habit, carrying a small whip in her hand. She curtsied respectfully as she entered. The General rose and returned her salutation.

"I have been told, General," she said, while a deep blush suffused her face, "that you are in want of a bearer of despatches to General Sumter."

"I am," replied the General, "but I have found no one yet bold enough to undertake the mission."

"Send me," said Emily, while a brave light shone brightly in her eyes.

"Send you!" exclaimed the General. "You! Oh, no, child; I could not do that. It is a journey from which brave men hold back."

"I am not a brave man," said Emily; "I am only a woman, but I will go."

Pausing awhile, General Greene then said: "Will you go on this journey alone?"

"Give me a fleet horse and I will bear your message safely."

"Alone?"

"Yes, alone."

"What is your name?" then inquired the General.

"Emily Geiger."

"Is your father living?"

"Yes."

"Have you his consent?"

"He knows nothing of my intention. But he loves his country, and were it not for sickness he would now be in arms with you; but he is not able. His head and heart both must approve my act, though his heart might fail him were I to ask his consent. Do not hesitate, General. Heaven has sent you a messenger, and you must accept the service when so much is at stake."

"Noble girl!" said the General. "You shall go. And may God speed you and protect you on your journey!"

"He will," murmured the brave girl in a low voice.

The General then ordered a swift, well-trained and gentle horse to be saddled immediately, while he wrote a despatch to General Sumter. After writing it he read it over to her until she had completely memorized it, so that should she be compelled to destroy it she would still be able to communicate it verbally. He then gave her minute directions in regard to her journey, and how she should act if so unfortunate as to fall into the hands of the enemy.

"And now, my good girl," he said with deep emotion, "I commit to your care this important message. Everything depends on its delivery. Here is money for your journey."

But she refused his purse, saying that she had enough for her wants and his necessities were greater than hers.

Just at this time the officer re-entered the tent and said that the horse was ready.

"And so am I," said Emily, as she stepped out into the open air.

A whisper of what was going on had already circulated all through the camp, and many officers and men had gathered before the tent to see the brave girl as she came out to start upon her perilous journey. She showed no fear as she placed her foot upon the hand of an officer and sprang into the saddle. Her face was very calm; her eyes were slightly raised, and her whole bearing was as that of one who knew no fear—not reckless, but fearless.

General Greene stood near, and when she was firmly seated and had grasped the bridle reins, he extended his hand and taking one of hers he said, while he held it tightly:

"God speed you on your journey, and may heaven and your country reward you."

Then, impelled by sudden emotion, he pressed the fair hand to his lips, and turning sought the seclusion of his tent.

As he did so the officer, who, until now, had continued to hold the bridle, let go his hold, and Emily, touching the reins, spoke to the horse and he instantly darted away, bearing the fair young courier from the camp rapidly in a south-westerly direction. No wild shout of admiration went up from officers or men. But tears fell silently from the eyes of many, who were deeply touched by the heroic act of the brave girl.

About five miles from General Greene's camp lived one of the most active and bitter tories in all South Carolina. His name was Loire or Lowry. Two of his sons were in the British army at Ninety-Six (by the way, the British army at Ninety-Six was composed altogether of tories, 300 from New York and 200 from South Carolina; the Colonel commanding, Cruger, was a New Yorker;), and he, himself, had fought against the Americans at Camden. Since Greene had camped in the neighborhood, this man had had his spies continually in the vicinity to pick up whatever information might be of use to the British.

About four hours after Emily's departure on her mission, one of these spies rode up to Lowry's house.

"What news?" he asked, knowing from the man's face that he had something to tell.

"The rebel Greene has found a messenger to carry a despatch to Sumter?"

"Are you sure?"

"Yes, and she has been gone some four or five hours."

"She, you say?"

"Yes, she; that girl of Geiger's went to the camp this morning and volunteered her services."

"The devil she did!"

And the man swore by all the gods of the infernal regions that she should never reach the camp of Sumter.

"But she has the swiftest horse in Greene's camp," said the man, "and unless she is pursued right away she will soon be out of reach."

"Take Vulcan," said Lowry," and if you kill him you must catch the huzzy between this and Morgan's Range."

"She has nearly five hours the start," said the man.

"But you must make two miles to her one."

2   I

"Even then she will be ahead of the Range before I can get there."

"In that case you must start Bill Mink after her with a fresh horse."

With these instructions and a hastily written letter to Mink, the man started in pursuit. He was mounted on a large strong horse, who bore his rider swiftly away.

In the meantime, Emily, who was no stranger to the way she had to go, having already been over the route more than once, struck boldly into the dense forest through which she had to go. Her way was only a bridle path; but wide, open roads were rare in those days in that part of the country. Borne up by intense enthusiasm for the success of her enterprise, she felt no fear. Nothing of special moment happened to her during her first day's journey. In passing Morgan's Range, which she did about four o'clock in the afternoon, she swept around it in a wide circle, as she knew that some of the worst tories in the whole country lived in that neighborhood. She was successful in passing the place unobserved, and again entered the road upon which her direct course lay. She was aiming to cross the Saluda at Kennerly's Ferry, not far above its junction with the Broad, then cross the Congaree at Friday's Ferry, just below the junction of the two rivers, and then as direct as possible to Sumter on the Wateree. Her horse by this time was very weary, but bore up at the word of his rider as if he understood the importance of her mission. As day declined and the shadows of evening began to grow more and more dense, the house at which she expected to stop for the night was still many miles distant. And she, fearing that she might become lost in the darkness, thought it better to stop at the first farm house she might come across. As soon as she saw one she rode up to the door, when she was met by a man who accosted her kindly, and asked her where she was from and how far she was going.

"I did hope," said Emily, "to reach Elwood's to-night. How far is it?"

"Over ten miles," said the man, "and the road bad and lonely. You'd better get down and stay with us all night."

"If you will let me," she said, "I will be very glad."

She then dismounted, and while the man led her horse to the stable his wife invited her into the house.

"Have you come far?" she asked, as she untied Emily's bonnet and looked earnestly into her face.

Emily did not know the people she was with, whether friends or foes, and she gave a brief, evasive answer.

"Your horse looked very tired; you must have ridden a long distance."

"I rode fast," said Emily, "and still I have failed to reach the place I started for this morning."

"It is hardly safe for a young girl like you to take such a long journey alone in these times."

"I am not afraid," said Emily; "no one will hurt me."

"I am not so certain of that, child; it is only a day or two since Greene was in full retreat, and it may be that some of his ragamuffins are about, whom it would not be safe to meet."

As the woman said this a chill passed over Emily, for she knew from her words and manner that she was not a friend to the whig cause. She made no reply.

"What is your name?" said the woman.

Emily, hoping that the woman knew nothing about her father, replied at once: "Geiger."

"Not John Geiger's daughter!" exclaimed the woman.

"Yes," said Emily with a smile.

Just at this time the woman's husband came in. "Would you believe it," she said, turning to her husband, "that this is the daughter of John Geiger, of whom we have so often heard?"

"Well," he said "if she were the daughter of my worst enemy she should have food and shelter to-night. No wonder your horse is tired," he said to Emily, "if you have ridden from home to-day. And no doubt you are hungry; so, wife, let us have supper."

No other pointed questions were asked during the meal, and after supper as Emily was very tired she asked to be shown to her room for the night. She felt that her position was very precarious. Her father was known as an active whig, and she was in the house of a tory who might suspect he mission and prevent its successful conclusion. After retiring she mused a long time as to what was best for her to do in case her host should try to detain her. But after awhile overwearied nature could bear no more and she sank into a deep sleep. In about two hours she woke with a start from hearing the sound of a horse's feet dashing rapidly up to the house. As the horse was reined up and halted before the door, a voice called out in a familiar way to the farmer who had just opened it:

"Hallo, Preston, have you seen anything of a stray young girl in these parts?"

"Bill Mink," replied the farmer, "what in the world brings you here at this time of night?"

"A fool's errand, maybe, but I received a message from Lowry about an hour ago, that Geiger's daughter had gone with a despatch from Greene to Sumter; that she had been gone some hours, and that I must overhaul her at the risk of everything."

"It isn't possible!" exclaimed Preston's wife.

"It is, though; and it strikes me that she must be a confounded clever girl."

"It strikes me so too," said Preston. "But I rather think you will be on a fool's errand, sure enough, if you go any further to-night."

"What! have you seen anything of the jade?" asked Mink.

"Perhaps I have," said Preston in a lower tone.

"Oh, ho!" said Mink, "so I am on the right track: she is here."

"I did not say so," said Preston.

"No matter; all right," said Mink, and he hitched his horse and went in like an old acquaintance.

The weather being very warm the window of Emily's room was open and she had heard every word that passed. And for a long time after they went into the house she heard the murmur of voices. Then some one went out and the horse was led round to the stable; so that it was clearly the intention of Bill Mink to stay all night and make the capture in the morning. The brave girl could now think of nothing but the possibility of making her escape. She lay quiet for an hour or more until all had retired to rest and everything was still in the house, and she could hear nothing except the loud breathing of the men in their sleep. Rising from her bed and dressing herself in haste she looked out through the window and saw the rising moon shining feebly through the trees. While thus looking forth and doubting whether she should venture into the silent night, a large watch-dog came up, and, placing his great head upon the window sill, looked into her face. She patted his head and the dog wagged his tail as though much pleased. She hesitated no longer but jumped from the window, and, the dog going with her, she went quietly to the stable. At the stable it was some time before she could find her own horse, saddle and bridle. At length she succeeded, and bridling and saddling her horse she led him from the stable. She made a wide circuit around the house so as to gain the road at some distance away. The dog had gone with her all this time, as if he was guarding her—and I do not doubt that he was—but when she mounted and rode away he stood still and watched her until she was out of sight and then returned to the house.

The danger thus happily escaped made Emily almost forget the solitude of her situation. The joy she felt left scarcely any room for fear. Ere day broke she reached the house of that friend where she had intended to pass the night. To him she told the nature of her journey and of the narrow escape she had just made. A meal was quickly prepared, a fresh and strong horse was provided, and before the sun rose she was sweeping away on her journey. A letter from this friend to another twenty miles further on procured her another horse.

More than two-thirds of the distance she had to go was safely passed before the sun set on the evening of the second day of her journey, and she was riding along pondering as to where she should pass the night. She had crossed the Saluda and was on her way to Friday's Ferry on the Congaree. Very soon the question as to where she should stop for the night was settled for her without any will of her own. Suddenly three men in the British uniform came into view directly in front of her. To turn back would be of no use, so she rode on, trying to be brave. On coming up to her the soldiers spoke to her in a rude and familiar manner. She did not reply, but tried to pass on, when one of them caught hold of the horse's bridle. Escape, being hopeless, Emily replied to their questions as best she could.

Not satisfied with her answers, they told her she must go before Lord Rawdon (whose camp was only about a mile distant), as it was clear that she was a rebel, and probably a spy.

When before his lordship, she was asked where she was from, where she was going, and what was the object of her journey. She would not tell a direct falsehood, and her answers, being evasive, created strong suspicions in Lord Rawdon's mind against her.

"We'll find a way to get at the truth," he at length exclaimed, impatiently. "Take her over to my quarters at the farm-house, and see that she don't escape you."

The officer to whom this command was given removed Emily under guard to a house near by, and locked her up in one of the upper rooms.

As soon as she was left alone she took the despatch from her pocket and was about to throw it out through the window, but she immediately thought that would not do. Hide it she could not, as she felt sure that the room would be searched, and herself also. Delay she could not. So she immediately tore off a piece and ate it. Another and another piece followed. But before she could dispose of the whole of it in this way the door was opened and a woman entered. Turning quietly her back to the woman, she put the balance in her mouth, and, covering her face with her hands, as if she were weeping bitterly, she remained in that position until it was all gone. Then turning to the woman, who had several times spoken to her, she asked by whose authority she was shut up in that room.

"By the authority of Lord Rawdon," replied the woman.

"I think he might find work more befitting his noble lordship," said Emily, "than locking up poor girls who are peaceably traveling the highway."

"You'd better not be saucy," said the woman; "your tongue may get you into trouble. You are suspected of bearing a message from Greene to Sumter, and it is my business to search you, to see if I can find it."

"You must think General Greene poorly off for men"—

"No matter what I think, Miss Pert. You are suspected, and I must search you."

"You can do so," said Emily; "but I think you might be better employed."

The search was made, but brought nothing to light that could implicate Emily as being a messenger of the rebel general. The search being over, the woman went out, leaving Emily alone in the darkness, where she remained for nearly half an hour undisturbed. She then heard steps approaching. The door was unlocked and opened, and a soldier appeared, and just behind him a woman holding a light.

"Lord Rawdon wishes to see you," said the man.

Emily followed in silence. She was conducted to a room below, where she found Lord Rawdon and several other officers at a table. After several questions, in answering which she succeeded in allaying his suspicions, he said to her:

"As it is now night, you do not think of proceeding on your journey?"

After a moment's reflection, Emily said: "If your Lordship do not object, I would like to go back a little distance. I have friends living on the road not far from camp."

"How far?"

"About six miles from here."

"Very well; you shall go back, and I will send an escort with you for your protection."

She thanked him for the offer of the escort.

Her object in going back was to stop at the house of a friend there, and when she resumed her journey she purposed making a wide sweep around the camp, and then, beyond it, strike the direct road to meet General Sumter on the Wateree. The danger most dreaded now was the man Mink, whom she had happily escaped, but who, she felt certain, was not far from Rawdon's camp.

In about an hour she found herself safely housed at the home of her father's friend. Fortunately, the escort had left her before she met any of the family. About a half hour after her arrival a member of the family came in and said that just a short while before he had passed Mink, who was riding at full speed towards Rawdon's encampment.

"Then, I must go at once," said Emily, starting to her feet. "If I remain here the balance of the night I cannot hope to reach Sumter with General Greene's despatch; for in less than an hour, if I stay, I shall be arrested and carried to Rawdon's camp. Let me go, and I will trust heaven for my safety."

After a hurried talk it was decided that she should go on, but not alone. A fresh horse and a guide were provided, and in a few minutes they were galloping in a direction away from the British camp. A few miles brought them to a road which struck off towards the point on the Wateree that she was desirous to reach. Of this road Emily had not known. But her guide was familiar with the country and able to conduct her by a safer and shorter route. All night they rode as rapidly as the road and the darkness rendered safe, and at daybreak they were far from Lord Rawdon's neighborhood. As the sun rose, after giving her accurate and minute directions as to the way she was still to go, the guide left her to pursue her journey alone. Without stopping to rest herself or her horse, she pressed on, though it grew hot and hotter as the sun rose towards the zenith. Faint, weary, worn out, and almost sick with hunger and excitement, she was urging on her tired horse, when, about three o'clock in the afternoon, in passing out from a thick wood, she came suddenly upon a file of soldiers, whose uniform she knew to be that of friends.

"Where will I find General Sumter?" was her first eager inquiry.

"He is camped about a mile from here."

"Take me to him quickly. I have a message from General Greene."

The excitement by which Emily had been so long sustained now died out, and before she came into the presence of Sumter she was so weak that she could not sit up in the saddle without support. She rallied when brought before him, and, sustained by rising enthusiasm, delivered, clearly and succinctly, her message to the astonished officer. In an hour General Sumter was on the march to reach the place of junction mentioned in General Greene's despatch.

Two weeks passed before Emily got back to her father, who had been informed, soon after her departure, of what she had done. Of his fears during her absence, I need not speak. But who can imagine the emotions of love, pride and happiness that almost stifled him as he pressed her to his heart once more?

After the war Emily Geiger was married to a planter in the neighborhood named Threwits. Whether she was more than once married, I do not know. She lived to a good old age and died at Granby. She left children; but of her descendants at this time I know nothing—not even whether there are any now living. But I hope there are some, and that they are brave, heroic and true, as ever Emily Geiger was.

VI.

NEWBERRY COUNTY.

ITS CLIMATE, SOIL, SOCIETIES, SCHOOLS, ETC.

The writer has passed about thirty years of his life in the *county* and *town* of Newberry, and during all that period he has enjoyed almost uninterrupted good health. Our doctors tell us, and they so report through the Board of Health, that the town of Newberry is healthier than most, and that the death rate is less than in most other cities in the United States. And the death rate of the county, notwithstanding the prevalence of malarial diseases, I have no doubt is as low as that of the town. It is not uncommon to meet with old people hale, hearty and active, seventy, eighty, ninety, and even more, years of age. I have no doubt that as many aged people can be found in this county as in any other in the State, even in those which are usually regarded as more salubrious. And surely long life is good evidence of the healthfulness of any country.

The soil is good, and well adapted to the production of all the cereals and grasses, and of that great crop, cotton. No better lands are to be found in the State, or perhaps anywhere else, than on Saluda, Little River, Beaver Dam, Bush River, Enoree River, Heller's Creek, and other streams flowing into the Broad and Saluda Rivers. The whole county is well watered, streams intersecting it in every part, giving moisture and fertility to the soil. The county has no mineral wealth, except its granite, which is found in great abundance and of superior quality. From the quarry a few miles north of the town many tons have been shipped to Augusta, Georgia, for the erection of certain public buildings. I saw one block on a wagon, which, I was told, weighed about five thousand pounds. Trap rocks show themselves in various places, especially southward of the town, the decomposition of which always produces soils of the best quality. It is true, though, that there are some poor lands in the county—it would be strange were there not—but the natural poverty of the soil in such places is more than made up for by the intelligence, industry and general thriftiness of the people who live in those sections. The Stoney Battery section is rocky and rough, but those who cultivate those rough hills reap from them abundant harvests and are as properous as any people in the county.

The climate is mild and genial, the thermometer very seldom indicating a degree of heat above 98 in the shade, and as seldom as low as ten degrees above zero; though I have seen it below zero twice since 1870. I have had the same thermometer for forty years, and once, on the 3d of August, 1864, the mercury went up to 102 degrees, the highest I have ever seen it. The greatest fall I have ever known was forty degrees in twenty-four hours. Violent winds and storms are very rare. Upon the whole, taking the county of Newberry with all its advantages of soil, climate and salubrity of air, I consider that it will compare favorably with any part of the world.

The people are generally God-fearing and religious, the Lutheran Church being the strongest in the county. About thirty schools for white children are kept going for as many as eight months of the year, and also a number of colored schools, although the Free School funds are enough to run them only three and a half or four months. In the town of Newberry the College, the Graded Schools, and other and smaller schools for white children, are kept open the full scholastic period, nine months in the year—all well supported and in a flourishing condition. The Hoge School for colored children has been made a part of the Graded School system, and is well equipped with teachers and is kept open the full scholastic year. The town is growing more rapidly continually as it grows older. Skilled workmen find constant employment in erecting new dwelling houses for the rapidly increasing population. As a rule, the churches are well attended, and there is as little desecration of the Sabbath as in any town of its size in the United States.

Prosperity is also quite a flourishing town, about eight miles below Newberry, on the Greenville and Columbia Railroad. The population is about one thousand—perhaps not quite so many—with a large High School, with over one hundred pupils in attendance. This school is for children and youth of both sexes. There are four churches in the town, Lutheran, Methodist, Baptist and Associate Reformed, the latter one of the oldest churches in the county, originally a mile below the town, and from which it takes the name Prosperity. A new edifice for this Church was erected within the town and dedicated in 1890. I believe the Lutherans predominate here, as indeed they do in the county at large, but with quite a respectable sprinkling of other churches and denominations—and also of sinners for all to work upon.

Helena was originally entirely a railroad town, but after the removal of the workshops it wholly changed its character. There is no longer the clang of machinery nor the noisy hum and stir of workmen moving about, nor the smoke rising from the tall chimneys of the shops. But still it is a very thrifty though quiet town, with good schools, both white and colored. There are two houses of worship. The one for the whites is known as the Union Church; is open to Christians of all denominations, and divine services are frequently held, though I believe there is no organized church in the house, the professing Christians there all holding their membership at Newberry. The Sunday school, which is also "Union," is well attended every Sabbath afternoon. The Church for colored people is Methodist, and also has its Sunday school.

While on the subject of schools in the county and town of Newberry, it may not be amiss to state that by an Act of the Legislature, passed December 17, 1807, the trustees of Newberry Academy were authorized to raise a sum of money, not exceeding three thousand dollars nett, by lottery.

By the same Act a religious congregation of Beaufort was authorized to raise, in the same manner, as much as thirty-eight hundred dollars. This congregation is styled in the Act an "Independent Religious Congregation," so it does not appear with what denomination of Christians it was connected—I suppose with none. William Smith was President of the Senate, and Joseph Alston Speaker of the House of Representatives when these Acts were passed.

And again on the 13th of December, 1817, just ten years after the passage of the first, another Act was passed by the Legislature, empowering the trustees of Newberry Academy to raise the sum of five thousand dollars nett, by lottery, for the benefit of the school. James B. Pringle, President of the Senate; Thos. Bennett, Speaker of the House.

The names of the trustees are inserted in both Acts, but it is not necessary to give them here.

These facts are given to show the great change that has taken place in the feelings of the people since that day. *Then* lotteries were not regarded as immoral or wrong; *now* they are looked upon as mere gambling institutions, wrong altogether in their tendencies and results. The trustees of the academy at those dates were the most prominent and influential men of Newberry, some of whom in after years became distinguished public men. The State of Georgia disposed of part of its public domain—lands acquired from the Cherokee Indians (among the best in the State)—in a similar manner, by lottery for educational purposes, by authority of the Legislature. This fact Mr. Stephens would not permit me to insert in his School History of the United States, thinking it best that such things should be permitted to drop out of history and be forgotten. I think otherwise. History is said to be Philosopy teaching by example, and if we suppress and ignore the facts and examples, looking only at results, the lesson is not, and cannot be, learned properly. If our ancestors and forerunners here did wrong we should know wherein, so that we and succeeding generations may be able to avoid similar errors and mistakes in life.

The origin of the name of the County of Newberry is unknown. Judge O'Neall was unable to trace it and gives a fanciful story to account for it. Mills in his Statistics is entirely silent, though he gives the origin of the names of some counties. Ramsay in his history of South Carolina says nothing on this point. All these historians leave us in the dark, so that now we can only conjecture. There is a city in England bearing the name of Newbury, near which Cromwell defeated the Royalists during the civil wars of his time, but there is no place in that country with the same form of spelling that we use. There are several Post towns in the United States, five I think, with the spelling as we have it. And there is a family now living in this State, if I mistake not, bearing the name of Newberry, but we have never had one in this county, as far as I have been able to learn. Nor is there any tradition that would lead us to suppose that our town and county were called after a man or family bearing that name.

In the Act of March 12, 1785, dividing the State into

smaller districts, those before in use having been found
entirely too large, in the part relating to this county we
find these words: "One other county beginning at the
Island Ford on Saluda River, thence along the old road
to Odell's Ford on Enoree River, thence down Enoree to
Anderson's Ford, thence along the road to Hill's Ford on
Tyger River, thence down Broad River to a point theron
eight miles below the district line, thence to the mouth of
Bear Creek, thence up Saluda to the beginning, and known
by the name of New*bury*." I quote from the Public Laws
of South Carolina, published in 1790. Five days after the
passage of the above Act, that is to say, on the 17th of
March, 1785, in the Act establishing County Courts in the
various new counties of the State, the name is spelled as
we have it now, New*berry*. The same change occurs in the
spelling of the word Shrewsbury. In the Act of March 12,
1785, the word is spelt with a u, and in that of March
17, five days later, it is Shrewsberry. In all Acts relating
to our town and county since 1785 the word Newberry is
spelled just as we spell it now.

Judge O'Neall in his Annals says that the present form
of spelling it is the correct one. But from all the information I can gather, and I have tried to investigate the
subject carefully and thoroughly, it was once almost, if not
quite, a matter of indifference which form was used. The
town in England, near which one of Cromwell's victories
was gained, is now spelled Newbury, but I see that Evelyn
in his Diary spells it Newberry. It seems to be almost a
matter of indifference with him whether he uses an e or
a u, for I see that he spells Cornbury with an e, Corn-
bery. And so with other words of a similar form. In an
old history which I have just been looking through, Win-
terbotham's America, when the word Newberry first occurs
it is spelt with a u, and then two or three pages further
on it changes to the present form. The same change occurs
in Ramsay's. Is not "bury" the same as "burg" or "burgh?"
It is according to Webster, and is old English or Anglo-
Saxon. This being the case it is very clear that Newbury
is the proper form and that "berry" is a corruption and
counterfeit. But it is the form established by custom and
by law and must so remain.

And now a few facts in regard to the early history of our town, which I think I have not stated before, nor do I remember that they were mentioned in the first part of this work.

The first County Court ever held here was held in a barn which was afterwards moved to the place now owned (1892) by Mr. R. H. Wright, where it still stands. And the hotel for the entertainment of the Judge and lawyers, and other gentlemen attending court, was a country tavern, or house of entertainment for the travelling public, situated about a mile and a half from where the Court House now stands, on the road leading to Lorick's, Young's, Huiett's, Bouknight's, now Herbert's Ferry on the Saluda, and near a strong, bold spring which gushes out of the earth at the foot of the hill on the right of the road as you go south. Who kept the hotel at that time I have never learned, and what jolly times the guests had, there is no one to relate. The house disappeared long ago; the landlord and his guests are all dead, but the spring is there yet. The naiad that guards it may be able to tell something.

THE MASSACRE AT HAYES' STATION.

Near the close of the year, in October, 1781, while the American army was near Charlestown, and there were very few, if any, Whigs embodied and in arms in the upper part of the State, a band of Tories, actuated seemingly by a desire to take one last and ferocious taste of revenge, carried fire and sword into the Whig settlements of Ninety-Six district. They were led by Major William Cunningham, known always as Bloody Bill. His watchwords on this expedition seemed to be plunder, burn and murder. In the dead of night, in the hours of sleep and apparent security, they entered the solitary farm houses and sacrificed to their revenge the heads of families and all obnoxious persons. Their cruelties compelled parties to arm and band together in self-defence. A Captain William Turner, in the upper part of what is now Newberry County, with twenty men acting thus in self-defence, took position in a thick-walled house and defended themselves until their ammunition was very nearly expended, when they surrendered upon the solemn assurance of Cunningham that they should be treated as prisoners of war. But after the surrender the whole party were immediately put to death. The same band of Tories soon afterwards burned the house of John Caldwell and killed him. His brother William, the father of John Caldwell the great lawyer of Newberry, and of the Hon. P. C. Caldwell, fortunately escaped, and endeavored to bear the news of the approach of Cunningham to Colonel Joseph Hayes, but was unable to reach the station in time. The attack was made; the house in which Colonel Hayes and his company had taken shelter was set on fire, and they were compelled to surrender. But they did not surrender until they had received the solemn assurance of Cunningham that they should be treated in all respects as prisoners of war. Colonel Hayes and Captain Daniel Williams were instantly hanged. But the pole breaking, Major William Cunningham cut them to pieces with his own sword. Then turning upon the others, he continued to hack and hew and kill until he was exhausted and his arm could scarcely raise the sword. He then told his men to kill whomsoever they chose; which they did. Only two had fallen in action, and fourteen were deliberately cut to pieces after the surrender. The following are their names and rank: Colonel Joseph Hayes, Captain Daniel Williams, Lieutenant Christopher Hardy, Lieutenant John Niel, Clement Hancock, Joseph Williams, Joseph Irby, Sr., Joseph Irby, Jr., John Milven, James Ferris, John Cook, Greaf Irby, Benjamin Goodman, Yancy Saxon.

Hayes' Station is in Laurens County, but I thought it well to insert this account in these Annals, as some patriotic Newberrians were sufferers there. Some years ago a monument was erected at the place of the massacre, with the names of the slaughtered engraved thereon. The monument still stands, though I have been told that the iron railing around it has been somewhat mutilated, whether by a bolt of lightning or by some vandal, is not known. If any damage has been done by any means to the monument or to the railing, it should be repaired and the monument made perfect, as at first.

VII.

OLD TIMES IN NEWBERRY.

THE DUTCH FORK SECTION, AS SEEN THROUGH THE EYES OF
MAJOR J. P. KINARD.

"The great German pioneers of Dutch Fork, in the lower
part of Newberry, between Saluda River and Enoree River
up Broad River, from 1800 up to 1833, were two leading
Germans, Henry Ruff and Capt. Martin Kinard. These
two Germans were looked up to and obeyed by the balance
of Germans in Dutch Fork. I will attempt to name the
German families living about that date: Koon, Folk, Set-
zler, Suber, Eichelberger, Epting, Wicker, Ridelhoover, Lake,
Glymph, Wood, Ruff, Dickert, Swittenberg, Counts, Gallman,
Summer, Hipp, Kinard, Eigners, Heller, Adams, Lane, Cromer,
Meares, Aull, Berley, Riser, Chapman, Kibler, King, Bundrick,
Rikard, Rutherford, Meetze, Alewine, Hentz, Goree, Crooks,
Henderson, Cannon, Sligh, Eargle, Turnipseed, Bishop, Huey,
Wadlington, Hatton, Caldwell, Brown, Darby, Ashford, Lyles,
Miller, Eppes, Boyd, Davidson, Martin, Werts, Graham. I
would say from names mentioned there were at least two
hundred families—for instance: Subers, Kinards, Koons and
Cromers were very many.

"Never were more honest and just people on the face of
th's earth than Germans in those days. I do not suppose
one of those good Germans is living to-day.

"William Rutherford was the first man to own a cotton gin
in the Dutch Fork. When cotton planting was first introduced in the Dutch Fork, after the land was prepared, the
seed—the old green seed—was planted by heel and toe, the
father leading, mother next; then children and negroes, if
any, following. Had very few negroes in those days, but what
there were were treated like white children. The seed were
put in little baskets hung on the left arm; the planter then
made a dent on the bed with his heel, dropped five or six

2   J

seed in the dent and covered with his toes—distance apart measured by the foot. The Dutch were superstitious, the seeds *had* to be covered with the toes or they would not come up.

"Everybody wore home-made clothing in those days. The girls had draw-strings in their dresses around the waist—had no bustles like the present day.

"After the cotton was made and opened it was gathered in the following manner: Of mornings after a heavy dew, or after a shower of rain, the open bolls were picked off the stalks, taken into the house and put on a pile; and then of nights all would gather round the pile of bolls and pick out the cotton by light of tallow candles, picking off all trash. It would take three or four to make one bale of three hundred pounds—would join together and take to Billy Rutherford's to be ginned. Then in the fall four or five neighbors would join teams of five fine bay horses—no mules —-take six or eight bales of cotton and go to Charleston and sell for twenty-five or thirty cents per pound; the father with the oldest son going along with enough provisions prepared at home by good women to last them during the trip, with the best of bread baked in Dutch ovens. They camped out at night, sleeping with their feet to the fire, with only the sheltering branches of a tree above them, in fair weather, with the stars glimmering through. It took about sixteen days to make the trip, hauling goods back for merchants in the county, getting from two to three dollars per hundred for hauling. O, what happy and industrious people in those days!—raised everything to live on—nobody owed any money —always had plenty of money, but did not take much to do. But most of the Germans soon got rich and began to buy African negroes that were shipped here from Africa. About thirty thousand were annually brought South up to 1812, by way of New York, in vessels.

"The people in Dutch Fork had no doctors in those happy days. All diseases were cured by our Dutch doctors by *using* for man and beast. Dutch ladies would cure children by *using* —all being done in German. Faith was so great and good all would get well. The midwives were the only doctors to ladies. Aunt Polly Wicker went far and near. If people of the present day had such faith as Germans had in our Saviour there would be much better times. Germans never needed Doctors in Medicine; all lived up to time in those days what was allotted for man to live. Had no railroads—no fast traveling. Members to Legislature or to Congress had to go by private conveyance or by stage.

"In addition to those names of German families already given there were also the following: Houseal, Stoudemire, Hope, Swygert, Wessinger, Wilson,, Busby, Lorick, Eleazer, Dominick, Shealey, Griffith, Bobb, Neel, Perkins, Cureton, Moore, Maffett, Bowers, Fulmer, Bedenbaugh, Wise, Hair, Leaphart, Reid, Cappleman, Henry, Fellers, Hartman, Singley, Wedeman, Baker."

The compiler of these Annals is bound to think that his old friend is mistaken as to the nationality of some of the family names mentioned in the foregoing. Some of them were certainly Irish, or Scotch, or Scotch-Irish; and one, Griffith, was neither German, Dutch, Irish nor Scotch, but Welsh. However, their nationality is not a matter of the first importance, as they were all kin in having the same honest and industrious habits.

I may add here that, from information received since the above was written, it is probable that Martin Riser was the first one who owned and used a cotton gin near Pomaria, in Newberry County.

We add here all the data given by Major Kinard: William M. Kinard, his only son, died 3d of April, 1877, aged 35 years. At the commencement of the war he had just graduated in medicine, but volunteered and was elected 1st Lieutenant in Company F, 20th Regiment, S. C. V., of which J. M. Kinard was Captain. After Captain Kinard's death, he having been killed in the valley of Virginia, Wm. M. Kinard was elected Captain and served in that capacity until the close of the war.

––––––

OLD TIMES AS SEEN THROUGH THE EYES OF DR. P. B. RUFF.

"There was a log house built twelve miles from the Court House on the public road leading to Henderson's Ferry on Enoree River. It was built especially for the Rev. Jacob

King to preach in. It was called Malone's Meeting House. It was built about eighteen hundred and four or five, and was the only house of worship in that section of the county. The country was thickly settled, entirely by white people. There were very few slaves and they belonged to a few men. Mr. King had a large congregation whenever he preached; and, as there was no other place of worship to go to, a great many would go from ten to twelve miles to Malone's Meeting House to hear preaching. A very large majority of the women had to walk to the meeting house, and when they were ready to start they would tie up their shoes and stockings in a large striped cotton handkerchief and go barefoot until they got within a hundred yards or so of the meeting house. Then they would stop and sit down in a fence corner and put on their stockings and shoes, and so, having completed their toilet, would go on into the house, take their seats with the congregation and give due heed to the preaching of the Word. After the service was over and the congregation dismissed, these women would wait until those on horseback would get out of sight; they would then pull off their shoes and stockings, tie them up in the handkerchiefs and walk home barefoot.

"The women in those days had nothing to wear to meeting but the homespun clothes they made with their own hands. The bonnets worn were what are now known as sun-bonnets.

"After awhile a great many of them grew tired of the sunbonnets to wear to meeting and tried to make an improvement. They spun thread, coarse and slack-twisted, and when they had a sufficient quantity they put it in a loom and wove it. After taking it out of the loom they carded one side so as to raise a fur or nap like that on a fur or silk hat. Some dyed the cloth so as to have colored bonnets; others preferred them white. When they cut out the cloth for the bonnet, they cut it to fit the head like a cap. The front of the bonnet extended six or eight inches beyond the face, so that you could not see the face of the woman unless you were in front of her.

"There was in those days no black leather, nor blacking and brushes to be had, so they had to wear nice yellow shoes made of leather of the natural color from the tan vat or trough. Their shoes were made to come up just high enough to cover the ankle. The married men who rode horseback to meeting would take their wives up behind them and the babies in front. When there were not horses enough for the young women to ride single, one would take the saddle and one ride behind her. Women who had babies would take them to meeting and whenever they began to fret or cry they would nurse them in the meeting house, and if that did not quiet them they would spank them well, if the children were old enough to profit by the infliction. When the mother would get home from church she would spread a quilt upon the floor for the babe, and it had to kick and cry until she got through with preparing dinner, as she had the dinner to cook herself and no one to take care of the child. Children did not receive the attention that they do now; the mother had to work and the child had to lie on the pallet and kick and roll and squall until its mother had time to nurse it. Everybody had to work, both men and women, in the field. Young women would plough and hoe with the men and boys, barefooted and sun-bonnets on, and gloves made of homespun, with the one finger of the glove for the thumb. I believe they called them mittens. Generally one of the women had to lay down her hoe about eleven o'clock to get dinner for herself and the other workers in the field. When dinner was ready she would blow the horn for them; they would then come in, feed the horses and get their dinner about twelve o'clock. About two o'clock they would return to the fields to work, and the cook would take her hoe again and work with the others until nearly sunset, then go to the house and get supper. Whenever she went to the house to get dinner or supper and found there was not wood enough already cut for the purpose, she did not need to call some one to cut it for her, but took the axe and cut it herself. The young women were strong, active and healthy. To see them whilst at work in the field you would call them very pretty young women; and some were called beautiful, with such rosy cheeks and coral lips. Notwithstanding they worked in the field in the hot sun with sun-bonnets on and mittens on their hands, they were as pretty as the women of later date. No doubt they were as lovely in the eyes of the young men of that day as the girls now are in our eyes, although they could not dress in muslin, silk, nor even in calico, nor in anything but homespun dresses made with their own deft fingers and industrious hands. They had no bustles nor bangs, not even a ribbon to tie around their hair to keep it in place, but a plain cotton cord or string. But if you could have seen them at preaching, dressed so neat and nice in their pretty homespun dresses and new-fashioned fur bonnets of their own make, you would scarcely have believed that they ever worked in the field, not being the least sunburnt, neither face nor hands. But they rejoiced when they heard that there was calico in the stores of Y. J. Harrington and William Pinchback, just arrived from Baltimore. The price was eighty seven and a half cents per yard, and it was nothing like as handsome as the eight and ten cents calico here in the stores now. About the time the goods arrived from Baltimore there was a small dry-goods and *millinery* store started, which caused more rejoicing, for they could not only get a calico dress but a nice straw bonnet trimmed with pretty ribbon. What a change! A nice calico dress and new shoes, and a nice straw bonnet trimmed very prettily, to take the place of the homespun dress and yellow shoes and homemade fur bonnets. If ever a young woman was proud of her dress it must have been at that time. It was not very long before the meeting house was full of calico dresses and nice straw bonnets. It was a great surprise to the young men; they said the women looked so pretty they hardly knew them. But they all fell in love and got married in those days just as they do now.

"When a man wanted his wheat cut he would let his neighbors know what day he wanted them to help him, and as soon as the day arrived they came with reap-hook in hand ready for work. His wife would have two quilts hanging in frames to be quilted the same day. When as many of the young women as could find room would sit around the quilt and ply their needles, the other young women would go out into the fields and bind the wheat after the reapers. They cut the wheat with reap-hooks or sickles; scythes and cradles had not yet been heard of. The quilters would always banter the reapers for a race, saying that they intended to beat them. It put a little more energy into the reapers and they would not stop long to rest under the shade tree where they kept a pail of water and a bottle of whiskey. When the work was finished the reapers came to the house with the young women, making preparations for a dance after they got their dinner. Dinner was generally late, but it was good, for they had everything on hand to make it good—turkeys, chickens, milk, butter, eggs, etc., and good cooks—for all the girls knew how to cook. As soon as dinner was over they commenced the dance and kept it up until twelve o'clock generally. Then they would all leave for home, satisfied and contented with the day's work. When a man wanted help to do anything that he could not do himself, if he would just let his neighbors know it he would soon get plenty of help.

"That part or section of the county that lay up and down Broad River, from Enoree River to Lexington County, was called the Dutch Fork. It was settled almost entirely by Germans. They were honest, truthful and reliable, and had great confidence in the honesty and integrity of each other. Their confidence was so great that they would lend their neighbors money and take no note for it. I will give one case as an instance of this neighborly trust: John Ruff lost two farm horses in the month of February, and he was compelled to buy two more to fill their places to enable him to carry on his farm. There was a drove of horses for sale in the neighborhood at the time, and he selected two horses that suited him for the farm, but not having the money to pay for them he sent word to a neighbor that he wanted to see him on a little business. The neighbor soon came and John Ruff said to him that he needed two horses to fill the places of the two he had lost, but he did not have the money to pay for them. His neighbor told him he could let him have the two hundred dollars, which was the price of the horses, and that he would go home and get the money and bring it to him right off. In a short time he brought the money. John Ruff paid for the horses and wrote a note for the two hundred dollars after asking when he would want the money. On being told 'next Christmas day in the morning,' he made it payable on that day. John Ruff handed his neighbor the note, but he would not take it; he said, 'you can keep the note better than I can, and then you will know when to pay it. I will go to your house on Christmas day in the morning

for the money and take an eggnog and breakfast with you.'
When he came Christmas, John Ruff counted interest on the
note at seven per cent.; but he would not have any interest,
only the two hundred dollars. This is not the only case of
the kind, such was the general kindness and good feeling
that they had for each other.

"The Dutch Fork people were very fond of dancing—there
was no other kind of dances but reel dances. What a great
time they would have at weddings! As soon as the bride and
groom were married, which was generally about twelve o'clock,
then the young folks would walk for the cake hanging up in
the house, nearly as large as a grindstone, with a gold finger
ring in its centre. Each young man would take a partner to
walk for the cake, there being generally about a dozen couples.
In walking for the cake they would walk around the house,
and the man who started in front had a walking stick in his
hand, and when he would get around the house to the place
where he started from he would give it to the man next behind him, and he to the next when they again came round,
and so on until they heard the firing of a gun, when he, in
whose hands the stick then happened to be, won the cake.
About the firing of the gun, be it known that a man had
been sent off with a gun charged with powder only, clear out
of sight, with orders not to shoot in less than half an hour.
After the firing of the gun, the young lady, the partner of
the winner, cut the cake and gave the gold ring to the bride.
By this time dinner was ready. A long table was set in the
yard loaded with everything that could be had to make a
good dinner. As soon as dinner was over they commenced
dancing, and kept it up frequently for two or three days.
They danced the old-fashioned reels. Not only the young
women and the young men danced, but the married women
and married men also took part in the amusement. It was
only the old women who could dance a jig. Two straws were
crossed on the floor; the fiddler would begin to play a lively,
quick tune; the old woman would pull up her dress high
enough to keep it from moving the straws, then dance the jig
over and between the straws for several minutes without
moving a straw. It was very amusing and really wonderful
to see how light and nimble, and how fast they could use
their feet."

PERSONAL REMINISCENCES OF DR. P. B. RUFF—WRITTEN BY
HIMSELF.

"I studied medicine with Dr. Burr Johnstone in 1828 and
1829. In November, 1829, I was making preparations to go
to Charleston to attend the medical lectures. I had to borrow
the money, and I asked a man in the county who was lending
money and shaving notes if he would lend me three hundred
dollars. He said he would if I would give him good security.
James Fernandis said he would sign the note as surety. The
man said he could not give the money then, but would pay
it to Fernandis in a couple of weeks, and he could send it to
me by Thomas Pratt, as he was going to Charleston to buy
goods. I could not wait for the money, and as some wagons
were about to start to Charleston I put the few clothes I had
in a pair of saddle-bags and went with them. When I got
to Charleston I stopped at the American Hotel, kept by Lu-
prey Chisholm, with six dollars in my pocket. In about two
weeks I heard that Thomas Pratt was at Miot's Hotel, and I
went to see him to receive the promised money from him,
but he told me that the man who had promised it was unable
to lend it. I thus found myself in a rather unpleasant fix, at
the Charleston Hotel with only six dollars. What was I to
do? It is true that lectures had not yet commenced, but I
had not money enough to return home by the stage. However, there was a former schoolmate by the name of Lewis N.
Shelton, who was doing a heavy wholesale business near the
wharf, and I went to see him and told him what a tight place
I was in. He asked me to take a seat, and he then went to
his desk, wrote a check on the Charleston Bank for five hundred dollars and gave it to me. I said it was more money
than I wanted—please write a check for three hundred dollars, as I wanted to make as little do as I could. He said
to me: 'If it is not enough come and let me know and you
shall have as much as you need.' I went to the bank,
handed in the check, received the money and started for the
hotel. As I passed up King Street I looked into Seigler's
music store and saw so many nice fiddles hanging that I
thought I must have one. I began to price them, and some
I found worth twenty, some thirty and some forty dollars.

After awhile I saw one lying down on a shelf, very much faded and looking as though it had been used and had seen considerable service. I inquired the price of that one and he said he would take ten dollars for it. I then asked his son if he would put strings on it, fix the sound board and let me have a bow to try it. He fixed it up for me and I took it into the back end of the store to give it a trial. After trying it I gladly gave the ten dollars for it and a new bow. I found it better and that I could play much better on it than on the one at home. Taking my fiddle I hurried to the hotel, went up into my room and commenced playing. As soon as Chisholm heard it he ran up to my room, which was right over his, and began to dance by himself. He danced a good long time, seeming to enjoy it very much, and when he stopped he asked me if I had engaged boarding. When I told him I had not, but would look for a boarding-house in the morning, he said I must not engage board but go round and see what the boarding-house keepers would charge me. When I returned and told him that I could get board for three dollars per week, he said he would board me for the same if I would play for him whenever he wanted to have a stag dance. I said that I would play for him anytime soon after supper. He generally had dances twice a week, sometimes oftener; and whenever he wished to dance he would ask some students into my room and tell them to choose partners enough for the reel. I believe the students were as fond of the dance as he was. He was so pleased with my performance that he told me he had a barrel of Newark cider in his bar-room and to go in and take a glass of it free of charge whenever I felt like it. He was a noble, kind-hearted man, and the students were very much pleased with him—he was so jolly and lively.

"When I was about twelve years old I had what is called white swelling just above the knee. I was confined to my bed on my back for four months—June, July, August and September. I suffered a great deal, not only with the disease, but also from the heat. I could not move my body nor lie on either side. My mother kept the swelling poulticed all the time, yet the inflammation was so great that it was exceedingly painful to the touch. William Rutherford came to see me one day and brought a thumb lancet with him. He had the poultices all taken off, and I thought he only wanted to look at and examine the rising. But before I was aware, or could say him nay, he ran the blade of the lancet plumb up to the handle into the abscess. You better believe it hurt some, but nevertheless the lancing relieved me very much as it let off a great deal of pus which had collected in the rising. After the operation he made a *tent* of flax and covered it with tallow and pushed it into the opening made by the lancet as far as it would go. The *tents* had to be used and renewed three times a day. In two or three weeks' time I could use crutches, but the leg was flexed so much that I could not put the foot within twelve inches of the ground. Mother was afraid that I would be a cripple for life. One day I asked her to let me go out where the men were at work clearing up a new ground. She said she was afraid they would cut a tree down upon me, but I told her I would keep out of the way. When I came to the new ground I sat down on a log near a pile of brush, and presently some one called to me to take care as a large pine tree was coming towards me. I sprang up and ran about twenty yards, fainted and fell. One of the men saw me fall, ran to me and put me on his back and carried me home. When mother saw him coming with me on his back, she, very much frightened, came running to see if I had been crippled by a falling tree. As soon as she came near I stretched out my leg and said: 'I can go without crutches now.' Had it not been for that fright and running from that falling tree, I might have been a cripple to this day going upon crutches.

"When I was about seven or eight years old I went every Saturday to Major Hog's store for the Charleston newspaper. There was scarcely a man in the neighborhood who took the paper, and every Sunday morning after breakfast a dozen or more men would come to hear it read; and frequently the women would come with them to hear the news. Everything in the paper from the first column to the last, advertisements and all, had to be read. The people of these days who have a constant surfeit of news can little imagine how hungry our neighbors became.

"I transcribe here two cases of hypochondria, which, I think, have never been recorded in any medical work, though doubt-less similar cases have been:

"Some years ago there was an old lady living a few miles out of town who was confined to her bed the greater part of the time, complaining very much of her stomach and having no appetite for food. She sent for Dr. Waldo, and when he came to see her she told him that one hot day, while on the way to visit a sick neighbor, and being very thirsty, she stopped at a spring by the roadside to drink. She had no cup nor gourd with which to dip up the water, and so she kneeled down upon her knees to drink from the spring. While drinking a spring lizard ran down her throat into her stomach, and she had never felt well since. Indeed, she says, 'I can feel the lizard moving about in my stomach now.' Doctor Waldo told her that he had no medicine with him to relieve her of the lizard, but that he would visit her again in a day or two, and that he thought he could get the animal away with very little trouble. Soon after he went home he started a negro boy off on a hunt for a spring lizard, telling him to bring it to him alive immediately after he caught it. The boy caught a lizard and brought it to him as ordered, and he went immediately to see the old lady. Keeping the lizard concealed he administered an emetic, and as soon as the medicine began to operate quite freely he slyly slipped it into the vessel into which the patient was discharging the contents of her stomach. As soon as she had a little respite from the exercise which the medicine gave her she saw the lizard swimming about in the vessel. 'There, Doctor,' she says, 'don't you see the spring lizard I told you about? Now I will get well." That ended the case, and she was soon as well as ever.

"The other case is equally as strange, perhaps stranger, but the cure was not altogether so sudden. The patient in this case was of the stronger sex, though, in his own imaginings at the time, composed of rather brittle material.

"One night he retired to rest as usual but did not get up for several days, and when his wife inquired of him if he was sick he replied that he did not feel sick, and then when she insisted that he should get up and walk about his reply was that if he attempted to walk his legs would break all to pieces, as they were just as brittle as glass. His wife became very uneasy, fearing that he might be going crazy, so she sent for the doctor, and when the doctor came he was very nearly, or quite, as nonplussed as the wife was and did not know what to do, as he could discover no physical ailment. He had another physician sent for, and the neighbors, hearing that another doctor had been called in, collected in considerable numbers at his house to hear what the consulting physician would say about the case. After a very careful examination he declared that he could detect no physical disease, that his legs were certainly not glass, and that if there was any disease at all it was of the mind, which might be, and perhaps was, in a more glassy condition than his legs. The doctor then inquired if there was a gig to be had anywhere in the neighborhood, and when told that there was one he ordered it sent for. When it came it was driven close up to the steps of the house and the doctor told the men present to take the sick man out of bed, wrap him up carefully, put him into the gig and give him a ride of half a mile. When they brought him back and helped him to bed he said to the man who had driven the gig: 'If you had kept me out five minutes longer I would have been a dead man.' However, the doctor told them to give him a ride the next day of one mile, and the next day after a ride of two miles; and when the sick man heard, that on the next day after that, they were to ride three miles, he said he would get into the gig himself without help. After they returned he did not go to bed, having become convinced that his legs had not been converted into glass. The cure was complete, and I never heard that he was ever similarly afflicted afterwards.

"Whilst Doctor Joseph Warren Waldo lived at Newberry he took a trip up North, and while there he bought a bell for the market. On the night after the arrival of the bell at Newberry he procured a keg of wine and placed it at some convenient point; he then made two negro men get a handspike, swing the bell to it and carry it thus suspended on their shoulders. He employed another to ring the bell. In this way they marched around the village (it was not called a town then). Everybody turned out, and when they made the round they would stop at the keg of wine and all take a

drink. Then they would start again, and when they made
the round they would stop and take another drink. And so
they kept up the serenade until after midnight, and when
they quit they were all full of wine and the keg was empty."

FROM THE RECOLLECTIONS OF DR. P. B. RUFF, WRITTEN IN THE
SUMMER OF 1888.

"I am now on a visit for a few days in my old schoolboy
neighhorhood, looking around to see if I can find one man
whom I knew when going to school here. They are all gone
to their eternal home. I felt very sad to meet no one who
seemed to know anything, or very little, about Doctor Reuben
Flanagan, once the most prominent and intelligent man in
this section of the county. He had very smart children. His
son, James Flanagan, who taught the school, was well educated
and a fine scholar. His daughter, who married Henry Gray,
was a very intellectual woman, and *her* three sons, Reuben,
Henry and John, were all men of superior ability. Reuben
was eminent as a physician, and Henry was considered to be
one of the best lawyers in Mississippi, a State·that has always
had lawyers of talent equal to any in the profession elsewhere.
And now it seems that Dr. Flanagan and his children are all
forgotten. The lawyer, Henry Gray, mentioned here, was a
Confederate Major-General during the war between the States.
Whilst I was going to school here I often visited Dr. Flanagan to hear him talk. It was quite a treat to me, as he was
so interesting. The father of his son-in-law, Henry Gray, was
Major Frederick Gray, who married Dr. Geddings' mother.
He educated his step-son, Eli Geddings, who became one of
the most eminent physicians and surgeons in the State. Dr.
Geddings was quite a boy when his mother married. He lived
with his step-father, at the Gum Spring, a few miles from
Newberry C. H., until he finished his medical education. I
believe he was the first graduate from the Medical College at
Charleston, S. C. After he graduated he commenced the
practice of medicine at White Hall, in Abbeville County. He
practiced only two years at that place and then went to
Charleston and went into copartnership with Dr. Holbrook.
Reuben Gray and myself were private pupils in medicine

under Dr. Geddings. He was very kind and did a great deal for me without charge. He was a kind and good-hearted man. On one occasion whilst Reuben Gray and myself were undergoing an examination by Dr. Geddings, there stepped into the office the Rev. Jacob King, a Baptist preacher from Newberry whom Dr. Geddings had known during all the time he had lived with his step-father, Gray. They had lived not more than three miles apart. Mr. King was dressed, when he came into the office, in ordinary homespun and his hat was nearly worn out. Dr. Geddings rose up from his chair and shook hands with him heartily for several minutes. He stopped the examination and took Mr. King to his boarding-house, which he made his home for three or four days. He also took him to a ready-made clothing store, and gave him a fine suit of black broadcloth, a nice hat, a good pair of shoes, and also some money; but how much of the latter I do not know.

"I do not think that such a man as Dr. Flanagan should be entirely forgotten or his name buried in oblivion."

—

"Mr. Neddy Finch, as he was called, was the founder of Mount Bethel Academy. He boarded many of the students. His house was called the preachers' home, and the first Methodist Conference was held in his house. One of his daughters married Doctor Adams, and after his death she married Doctor Atwood. Another daughter married Mr. Foster. His son, Doctor Finch, went to Columbia to witness the inauguration of Drayton for Governor and Major Frederick Nance for Lieutenant-Governor. Dr. Finch was riding in a sulky, and soon after he started for home his horse became frightened in Butcher Town and ran away. The Doctor attempted to jump out, but his foot got caught between the shaft and footboard, and being firmly held in this position he was dashed against the ground and killed."

—

ANECDOTE OF JONATHAN DAVENPORT AND THE LIMBLESS WOMAN.

"Some years ago, but the year not remembered, a man brought a woman to Newberry—a well-developed body she had, but was entirely limbless. She talked well and was quite intelligent. She came from Buncombe County, North Carolina. The people here sympathized very greatly and gave her a good deal of money. I happened to be in the room in the hotel where she was staying when Jonathan Davenport came in to see her. He walked right up to her and began to talk to her, and soon the tears began to pour out of his eyes. He placed a ten dollar bill on her breast, bade her good-bye, and left her with the tears running down his face.

"This woman was carried about in a chair made expressly for her. She appeared to have plenty of life, and she would talk and laugh with the women. She said her appetite was good and that she rested well at night. If she had not been limbless I think she would have weighed as much as a hundred and forty pounds."

—

JOHN YOUNG AND THE GHOST.

"The young men in the town hearing that the dam at Mendenhall's Mill had broken down and that it would be a good time to seine the ford, procured a one-horse wagon, took the seine, their dinner and a good supply of whiskey, as it was supposed to be absolutely necessary to drink pretty freely while they were in the water.

"It happened that John Young, one of the men who dragged the seine, drank too much and had to stop somewhere on the road and take a nap of sleep in order to get sober enough to go home. He went into the Quaker Meeting House as the most convenient place, lay down on a bench, soon fell asleep and slept until about two hours in the night. When he awoke he heard a very mournful groaning under the floor beneath him. It frightened him very much, as he thought it must be a ghost, there being a large graveyard near by and the place having the reputation of being sometimes haunted by mysterious beings. He hunted for his hat, and as soon as he found it he started for home and ran as fast as he could until he came to the village, the distance being about four miles. He told several persons that it was a ghost that had disturbed him. However, the explanation of the matter soon came. The same day a man by the name of Dickerd had been in the village and had managed to take rather more than was good for him. He started for home about dark in

O. B. Mayer.

P. B. Ruff.

David Jones.

John T. Peterson.

CONTRIBUTORS TO "THE ANNALS."

the evening. He had to pass the Quaker Meeting House on his way, and by the time he got to that point he was so far gone that he was not able to go any further, and lying down he crawled under the house, as it happened, right under the position occupied by John Young, who was on a bench in the house. It thus appears that Dickerd, all unconsciously, played ghost."

THE FIRST CHURCH IN NEWBERRY VILLAGE.

"There was no church in the village of Newberry until the year 1832. It seems that the people were satisfied and con tented to continue without a church and to travel the broad road to misery and torment until Preacher Hodges, a Baptist preacher, commenced a protracted meeting in the old Academy Grove, in the year 1830 or 1831. He was assisted by Worthington, Childs, and a preacher from Fairfield, whose name I have forgotten, and Preacher Presley, who lived in the village. It was a great meeting, with a large congregation all the time for two or three weeks. After the meeting had continued a few days it seemed that a great change came over the people very suddenly. By the grace of God they left the broad rod and were ready now to walk in the narrow way that leadstoa happiness in the upper and better world. Fifty or more porfessed to be converted and joined the church, the most of them the Baptist Church. They were ready and willing now to build a house of worship. That of the Baptists was built in the year 1832, the Methodists in the following year. If God had not sent Preacher Hodges here to wake up the people, when would a church have been built? The old men and their wives were the first to join—they joined the Baptist Church. Previous to this time there were about four or five in the village who were professors of religion and members of some church. The only churches accessible, that is the nearest, were those at Head Spring, Cannon's Creek and Prosperity."

THE CRATING CLUB.

"The exact date of the existence of this club I do not now remember, but it was formed by Alexander Bartholomew, commonly called Big Andy, a very large and powerful man physi-

2   K

cally. The club consisted of five or six members. In time of court, as on saleday in the evening, after freely imbibing mean whiskey all day, probably some of Sterritt's, some men would be sure to become quarrelsome and want to fight. As soon as the fun would begin Big Andy would 'Hello Crate!' as loud as he could bawl; he would be answered by several of the club in different directions. Then there would be a great stir in hunting horses, and if any one of the rowdy and turbulent ones remained he was sure to go under the crate. This club did a great deal of good. It stopped many men from fighting, and made many go home to their families before they got too drunk. It was no use to resist; Andy could handle any of them as easily as he could a child. Out in the country, not far away, there lived a man named Dick Ayres, a desperate fellow, and when he came to town he would, by his violence in throwing rocks and brickbats at everybody passing along the streets, make the merchants close their doors, until Mr. Carwile would call for Big Andy to take Dick Ayres to jail. Dick would try to resist, but Andy would take him by the seat of his pants with one hand, and with the other applied to the back of the neck would throw him over his shoulder, walk to the jail and put him in, where he was kept until he became perfectly sober. Dick was fond of fighting and he would very often try to get up a row by pushing men about and cursing them, and most men were afraid of him, as he was very large, weighing as much as one hundred and eighty pounds. But his frolics always ended in his being put in jail, as Big Andy was too much for him, and whenever his boisterousness became entirely unbearable Mr. Carwile, who was then Sheriff, would call for Big Andy, and Dick's fun resulted in his being locked up in jail."

EARLY COTTON.

"Silas Wood, who once had a store where Frederick Glymph now (1888) lives, gave a barbecue on the fourth day of July. A great many people attended, one of whom was William Rutherford, who showed the crowd of men a vest he was then wearing made from cotton grown that same year. He opened the immature bolls with the fingers, pulled the cotton out and put it in the sun to dry. It was then finger-picked, carded and spun, and woven and made into the vest."

A SURGICAL OPERATION.

"There once lived in Newberry County a large man by the name of John Haney, son of Maximilian Haney, who was a little too fond of whiskey. He had a large wen on his back, and he was very much troubled about it, as it continued to grow and enlarge to such an extent as to produce a deformity in his form, especially his back. On one occasion, going to a store not far off, he, as was his usual custom, soon became pretty well intoxicated and got into a quarrel with one of the men who were present in the store at the time. The quarrel resulted in a fist fight, and during the struggle his opponent pushed him back against the wall and against a nail which had been driven into the wall for the purpose of hanging articles upon. Fortunately there was nothing on the nail at the time. He was pushed back with great force, and the wen upon his back struck right against the head of the nail, which penetrated the wen and tore it entirely out. He had on neither coat nor vest, and as the wound bled freely, soon saturating the shirt, the spectators present accused his opponent with stabbing him. But after removing his shirt they saw that the wen was torn out, which caused the bleeding. He had been unwilling to submit to an operation, and he was so glad that the wen was removed that he made friends with his adversary and treated him for performing the cure."

—

A WIFE SWAP—A FISHY TRANSACTION.

"A man named Fish went one day with his wife to Major Hog's store to do some trading. After awhile another man by the name of Durret and his wife came to the store, and whilst the women were trading the men were drinking whiskey. The women in the meantime drank rum, of that kind known as nigger rum, which they liked better than whiskey on account of its sweet taste. By the time they were through trading, both the men and their wives began to feel pretty happy, and the men agreed to swap wives, if the wives were willing. One said she was willing to be swapped; and the other said she was willing, but she required a bottle of rum extra. So the trade was concluded and all parties went home satisfied and happy."

GRAHAM'S ESCAPE FROM JAIL.

"A man named Graham once stole a negro, at that time a capital offence, from Joseph Caldwell, but he was soon caught and lodged in jail. A crazy negro man by the name of Rob, belonging to Patrick Caldwell, had been in jail some time for safe keeping before Graham was put in. After Graham had been in jail awhile Rob asked him one day why he did not get out. His reply was that he did not know how. Rob then told him that when Coates comes in with his supper he must have both hands full of sand and stand behind the door, watch his chance and, after Coates had opened the door and entered the room, just as he turns round to close it, to throw the sand into his eyes. Graham did so; Coates dropped the candle and supper to get the sand out of his eyes, and Graham passed around him and made his escape. Rob was so glad that he had got out and made his escape that he yelled as loud as he could for Graham to go it! and kept it up until quite a crowd of men collected at the jail to see what was the matter. After his escape Graham went to a little island in Broad River, where he was soon discovered, and Mr. Joseph Caldwell sent a negro man to the island to bring him out. He was taken back to jail; tried at the next term of court; plead guilty, and sentenced by the Judge to be hanged on a certain day. When the day came a great many people went to see him hung. H. H. Kinard, the Sheriff, took him to the gallows; put the cap on him. The spectators looking to see him swing in a few minutes, to their great surprise his pardon, or rather commutation of sentence, was read by the Sheriff while he was under the gallows with the cap on. Then the cap and robe were removed and the Sheriff gave him a very severe whipping and told him he had to leave the State. After it was all over and Graham was discharged, men came galloping into town cursing, and swearing that they had ridden twenty miles to see him hung and the Sheriff would not hang him. No sympathy for the poor, unfortunate man, but anger at their disappointment."

—

JESSE GILDER.

"This unfortunate man, who was badly bewitched, lived a mile beyond Bush River on the public road leading to

Longshore's Store. He lived alone, was never married, and did all his own work, cooking, washing, etc. He was almost always complaining of being ridden so much by the witches that he got very little sleep. He was advised to marry; to get a good wife; that she would be company and a comfort to him, and the witches would not ride him any more. He said he could not support a wife; that he had made a trial of it to see if he could support one. When he helped himself at breakfast and dinner he had another plate by him for the wife, and whatever he put in his own plate he put the same quantity and quality for the wife. After he was through eating he said there was too much on the wife's plate—it would be too expensive to support her. So he gave it up and moved to Edgefield to get away from the witches. But in this he did not succeed."

[The compiler of these Annals knew Jesse Gilder well in Edgefield, and he complained of being frequently and terribly witch-haunted. He finally molded a silver bullet and shot it into the picture, or effigy, of her whom he supposed to be the witch, and he flattered himself that he had killed her, as she did not live a great while longer.]

—

An Alarm of Insurrection.

"One evening in the year 18—, I cannot now recall the exact date, a man named Thompson, who lived about four miles from the Court House, came into the village and told the people that there were five hundred negro men collected together, just above where Jalapa now stands, for the purpose of burning the village and killing everybody in it. There was great excitement; the women went into the hotel and into the Court House to be guarded. Every man in the village who had a gun was making all the haste he could for a fight. Sentinels were stationed all around the village. But as the negroes did not make their appearance as soon as they were expected, Bert Harrington, taking a companion with him, went up the Laurens road some distance above the place where they were said to be collected, but not finding any, the county being entirely quiet, they returned. Their report of the true state of affairs removed all anxiety from the minds of the people."

ALMOST A FIGHT.

"On the corner of Mollohon Row, where Summer Brothers now (1889) have a store, was once a long wooden building with a piazza in front. Robert Stewart kept store on the corner where Flynn's now is. [Now Jamieson's.] The Monday night of Court a large crowd of people from the country stayed all night, some with Cheshire in the Pinchbeck Hotel, and some at Robert McCullough's Hotel. After supper, when there was a large crowd collected in the long piazza of the hotel, some mischievous boys quietly tied a rope extending from one piazza to the other, suspending it about one foot above the ground. They then went down near where Ed. Scott's now is and made a loud noise and uproar as if there was a tremendous fight going on. About fifteen or twenty men, anxious to see the fight, ran as fast as they could to get there before it ended. The rope piled them all, and suddenly the noise ceased and all was still. And as suddenly it flashed through the minds of all the fallen that they had been made the victims of a practical joke and there was no fight."

I close here Sketches and Recollections of the Olden Times in Newberry as seen through the eyes of my good old friend, Dr. P. B. Ruff, and proceed to give a chapter from another very important section of our county. The writer of this sketch, if I have been rightly informed, is Mr. R. H. Wright, for many years engaged in mercantile business on Mollohon Row. It was written July, 1886.

REMINISCENCES OF MOLLOHON.

"This name designates a large section of country lying in the northeastern part of Newberry County. The origin of the name is not positively known. There is a tradition that it sprang from a family of that name who once lived somewhere on the head waters of Hunting Fork anterior to the Revolutionary War. The name was not always popular as now. There was a time when to call a man a Mollohonian was as sure to provoke a fight as if a would-be bully, at a general muster, should lay a chip on his shoulder and dare any one to knock it off.

"Mollohon was a bad character, a stench in the nostrils of his neighbors. He kept a little tavern, a rendezvous for the idle and vicious of that section of country. At certain seasons he ran a distillery, and at such times the neighbors, after a week's work, would be drawn hither to enjoy socially a swig of beer. It also attracted the neighbors' pigs, and while they innocently went, like their owners, for simply a swig of slop, they were sure to leave with their ears and tails so manipulated as to correspond with the Mollohon mark, viz.: a smooth crop of both ears and a very short tail. These, with other disreputable habits which are not necessary minutely to describe, rendered the old man, with his three sons, Tom, Dick and Shadrack, quite obnoxious in that vicinity. Nor did the old woman and the daughters, Betsy Jane and Dorothy Ann, receive more sympathy from the neighboring females; for they all declared at the same time that 'old Patsy Mollohon and her gals' were the meanest things they ever did see. But, perhaps, there should be some allowance made for the existence of the last sentiment, for it is said that Dorothy Ann was a very pretty girl; that she managed to wear the nobbiest hat and the nicest stockings of any girl thereabout, and, notwithstanding the cloud resting upon the family, the boys of the neighborhood, or at least the best looking ones, asserted that Dorothy Ann was all right. But when the women set their heads together something must be done, and so old Mollohon had to leave, lock, stock and barrel, including Dorothy Ann.

"But the name of Mollohon did not leave with them. It began to be applied to first one and then another in jest, afterwards to the community; and thus it spread until we have the popular 'Mollohon' of the present.

"Mollohon has long been noted for her schools of learning. The first classical school founded in the State, outside of Charleston, was within her present borders. Old Mount Bethel Academy, once situated on the east of the Columbia road, on lands now belonging to Dr. Thomas C. Brown, was at the time of which we write a flourishing institution of learning. It was established and conducted under the patronage of the Methodist Episcopal Church, and for a number of years, until removed to a more eligible and central locality, dispensed, under the tutorship of Rev. Mr. Dougherty, Elisha Hammond and Josiah P. Smith, as high a grade of learning as was to be found anywhere in the State. It will be remembered that the name applied to this sect of Christians, 'Methodists,' like Mollohon, first originated in derision, and for a long time no one could be induced to ally himself with this sect, unless he was truly concerned to flee from the wrath to come. It is also somewhat strange that this sect, at one time so universally ridiculed, especially under the charge of illiteracy, should be the first pioneers to establish a classical school of high grade in the State and draw its patronage from the first families of the same. Since that time Mollohon has not been slow to manifest her high appreciation of education by securing the services of able teachers. The fruits of the services of James Flanigan at Mollohon Academy, between the years 1820 and 1830, have not ceased to be felt, not only in Mollohon, but throughout the State. Our worthy townsman, Dr. P. B. Ruff, whose life and services as a physician have been a benediction to the town of Newberry for more than half a century, received his academic instruction at this institution, and has no cause to be ashamed to point to it as his *alma mater*. Later the same institution was presided over by Rev. Clough S. Beard, a ripe scholar and an apt teacher, as many now living can testify. Several boys from this town were his pupils; among them was R. B. H., who is still a resident of this county."

—

Revolutionary Incidents.

"During the period of the Revolutionary War this section was sorely afflicted by opposite political sentiments, from which sprang the bitterest strife. Neighbor was arrayed against neighbor, until the excess into which they were led by this antagonism was truly shocking to every sentiment of humanity. Perhaps it is well that no one has attempted to write her history, and that time has faded out the many thrilling traditions that once circulated in this section. Oft have I, when a small boy, sat at the feet of a favorite kinswoman and listened to her stories of these troublous times, as they were told to her by those who experienced in person the horrors which they described.

"At this period, on the road tending southeast from Mrs.

Cromer's to what is known as the Dulin place, on land now owned by M. A. Carlisle, Esq., a few hundred yards south of the crossing of Gilder's Creek, there lived Major Thomas Dugan—the *debris* from the old chimneys may yet be seen on the bluff—and his wife Margaret. They had nine sons and one daughter—Robert, ——, John, James, William, Hiram, Thomas, Park and George and Margaret. Major Dugan was a staunch whig, and took an active part in the service of the colonies. He was early appointed to the rank of Major, and is supposed to have served with General Sumter. Only two of his sons, Capt. Robert Dugan and a younger brother, ——, were old enough to take an active part in the war. They were also active whigs, and did good service, taking part in all the work of that stirring period. This rendered the Dugan family particularly obnoxious to the tory element of Mollohon and of Laurens and the Saluda country and subjected them to special and repeated insults and plunder. But the crown ing tragedy was thus described:

"On one occasion Captain Dugan and his brother were on a sly visit to their mother, expecting to spend the night with her and on the early morn to hie away to their commands. The hour of midnight had passed and all was quiet. They had made similar visits before without molestation and were thus beguiled into careless watching. About the hour of 2 A. M., when both the young men were indulging a few short hours in sleep, and only a faithful mother kept watch lest some harm should befall her two boys, her anxiety was aroused by hearing a slight but not unusual noise in the yard. Going to an opening in the wall, she peered out into the darkness; but all was quiet. Again stilling her fears by reasoning that she was probably mistaken, that it might be only her anxious solicitude exciting her to undue forebodings, she again re- sumed her quiet vigils. Not many minutes had elapsed before she heard at the back door a gentle but unmistakable rap, immediately followed by a like signal at all the other open- ings of the house. After this a vigorous knocking at the front door suddenly aroused her worst fears. Entrance was de- manded by a dozen or more boisterous voices. There was no mistaking the situation or the purpose of her untimely vis- itors. Her presence of mind did not forsake her, but speedily mustering her stock of expedients she thrust one of her boys into the opening of the chimney; the other, perhaps more rash, threw himself from the upper window, hoping to elude his pursuers by rapid flight under cover of the darkness; but an unlucky alighting shivered a bone of his leg, which left him in the hands of his bitter foes. The heart-rending sequel then begins. The room is suddenly filled by a band of tories, some of whom are recognized as neighbors, young men not older than their captives, boys whom that kind matron had nursed in infancy and waited upon their childish whims. With savage taunts, threats and insults, they toyed with the sensibilities of that fond mother until they were satiated with their own orgies. To carry out their hellish threats and to make sure that no torture would pass unseen, they fired a small house in the yard, and while it crackled and shot its ruddy glare athwart the yard, in the presence of that mother, they proceeded to hang their victims to the limbs of an oak hard by, under the shades of which they had often played in childhood while she watched them with fond delight. Is this not enough? Wait and hear the final sequel. Before the eyes of that mother, with their broadswords, they hewed the limbs and quivering flesh from the bodies of their suspended victims, and when their ingenuity could invent no greater torture, skulked away through the darkness, leaving the mother amid the wailings of her little ones to bear her burden of anguish while they would gloat over their deeds of valor. God nerves his servants to bear the yoke that he permits to rest upon them. After a brief spell, employed in quieting her tortured mind and bringing herself to the full realization of her sad surroundings, she began to collect with her own hands the mangled remains of her murdered boys. Somewhere on the hillside near the scene of this revolting tragedy she buried the pride of her heart. The precise spot is not known, but no doubt good angels are keeping their vigils over their dust.

"This is a tradition of Mollohon, tamely related, it is true, and wanting in minuteness, but embodying as fully as is now remembered, after more than forty years, the facts of the story as they were told to the writer. It may be a satisfaction to some who may read this story to be assured by another tradition that several of the actors in the foregoing tragedy were subsequently executed on the gallows at the cross-roads near the present residence of Mrs. Henry Whitmire, and thus received in part a just penalty for this and other crimes committed.

"In the possession of Mrs. Elizabeth Dugan, the widow of Wm. Dugan, whose brothers were the victims in the foregoing tragedy, was a dagger of fine steel nicely finished, with ebony heft and silver bands, upon one of which was engraved the initials of Captain Dugan. This weapon had been presented, it was understood, by General Sumter in token of his appreciation of valuable services rendered. Strange to say, these associations seem not to have imparted any special value to this relic; but it was prized only as a convenient instrument for opening bee gums, topping hedges, and the like. Its accustomed place was on a nail near the clock. On one occasion while on a visit, not seeing the familiar blade that had so often started my youthful imaginings, I said, 'Aunt Betsy, what has become of the bowie knife?' She remarked, 'Bless your soul, child, I had Jimmie Toland to make me two as good butcher knives of it as you ever saw.' Thus perished a relic I had imagined could not have been bought; but long familiarity and a fading away from the mind of the associations imparting almost its sole value, and having great confidence in the skill of Jimmie Toland to impart the proper shape and temper that a butcher knife should have, the good old soul was beguiled into subjugating sentiment to utility.

"But she still had another relic from the same source, viz., a knife and fork of peculiar shape and finish, once the property of Captain Dugan, captured by him from a British officer of dragoon. This I hoped to save from the fate of the other, but on searching for the same only the fork could be found, driven in the wall and serving to hold hanks of cotton yarn as they came from the reel. This she kindly presented to me. Seeing my disappointment at the use to which she had turned the dagger, she assured me that if she had known that I prized them she would have been more pleased to have given them to me than to have the butcher knives, notwithstanding Jimmie Toland had fashioned them in his best style.

"Many other traditions of like tenor were once current in Mollohon, but are not sufficiently remembered by this writer to warrant the attempt to reproduce them. He will, however, be pardoned for introducing a character who once lived and claimed Mollohon as his home, inasmuch as this character gave to his mind its first and last ideal of a perfect hero:

"Charles Charity was a negro; an old man when I first knew him, which was more than fifty years ago. I saw him as he visited my father (his guardian). He had been freed by the General Government, and for several years before his death received a pension on account of service rendered as a private soldier in the Revolutionary war. Of these services there can be no doubt, as his identity has been satisfactorily traced. His appearance to a child of four or five years was simply awe-inspiring. Of medium height, spare build, straight and erect, but beginning to totter, his motion quick and nervous, his voice short and husky, his complexion black, his head covered by a mass of semi-kinky hair as white as wool, his eyes fierce and glistening set in their deep ebony sockets —all combined to make up a figure never to be forgotten. True to the peculiarities of his race, he delighted in magnifying his exploits, his deeds of daring and hairbreadth escapes, on occasions of general muster. When the patriotism of the country was expected to exhibit itself, then Charles Charity was a central figure, honored by the undivided attention of the uninitiated 'melish.' But the proudest thought of Charles Charity's life was that he had once belonged to a gentleman and was therefore no ordinary free negro. How he came to be an enlisted soldier is not definitely known, but from his own account it is believed that he was in the beginning of the war the body servant of a young officer serving under General Sumter; that by the vicissitudes of war said officer was cut off, and that Charles, being enamored by the excitement of war, asked to be enrolled as a soldier, which request was granted; and thus his name stands to this day among the honored defenders of our common country. Some time after the war Charles married a slave woman, the property of John Hatton, who lived on Patterson's Creek in Mollohon, and there he died and was buried; and though his name is inscribed on our Nation's archives as one of her noble defenders, his dust sleeps on the banks of Patterson's Creek in Mollohon without a tablet to mark his last resting place."

Sketches by John T. Peterson.

The following sketches, facts and items of local history are from the pen of the late John T. Peterson, Esq., so long and so favorably known as a man and citizen and as a public officer:

Shady Grove.

"The old Methodist Church called Shady Grove stood a little over a hundred yards from the road now leading from Newberry to Island Ford by way of Mount Zion Church and the long bridge and only a little distance from Dr. J. M. Thompson's residence. It was, I think, in its prime about the year 1820. But soon after this, or about this time, it began to wane, though it was continued as a church and had regular preaching until 1835 or 1836, when it was amalgamated with the church at Kadesh, which stood on the side of the Belfast road, close to the present residence of Dr. Thomas W. Boozer, and formed the church now known as Trinity.

"Shady Grove, I believe, was the fruit of the labors of the Rev. Mr. Russell, who, in some of the first years of the present century, did so much towards giving the Methodist denomination a foothold in that section. A great many, it may well be supposed, joined the church through excitement, and some because it seemed to be the fashion at the time. So it is not to be wondered at that in a few years the calm, which is sure to follow a storm, came on and Shady Grove began to lose ground.

"I remember to have heard it told on a man by the name of Scott that at the time of one of the greatest religious excitements at Shady Grove he lost his grip by accident. It seems that a protracted effort was being made and mourners were crowding the altar every day. Mr. Scott, who lived near by, was very much interested, so he and all his family attended church every day. On his return home one evening he found that his old sow had broken into his potato patch and ruined it, whereupon he flew into a great rage and exclaimed: 'D——n the old sow! I wish she was in h–ll and the preacher tied to her tail.'

"Besides this there were other drawbacks. Quite a number of her most zealous and influential members moved West.

The whole complexion of the neighborhood was changed, and judging from the following story I would suppose that the morals of the community fell off somewhat:

"After Shady Grove was considerably on the wane, a local preacher had an appointment to preach there on a certain Sunday, and after he had finished his discourse he took occasion to compliment the congregation on their good behavior. He said their behavior had been very good. 'In fact,' said he, 'remarkably good for the people of this place.' From this I would infer that the general demeanor of the congregations which attended Shady Grove did not, as a general thing, stand very high.

"The old church, however, continued to struggle until about the time before mentioned, when, finding the church at Kadesh in about the same condition, it was concluded to unite the two, and so the church at Trinity was formed. This church was built about half way between the two and has ever since continued to prosper. There was, however, occasional preaching at Shady Grove for several years after this; and even after it had been entirely ignored by the denomination the old veteran, Daniel Stewart, who had been one of the founders, and for many years an official member, continued to hold prayer meetings at the old church. His congregations, however, gradually fell off in members until the writer was the only person who attended. He did so, not so much with the expectation of being benefited by the prayers and exhortations, as from respect to his old friend.

"There was quite an extensive burying ground near the church, and for a long time after the church had been discontinued persons, whose forefathers and other relatives slept in the old graveyard, continued to bury their loved ones there. But at length it was given up and is now but a mass of briars and bushes. The last person buried there was the old man Daniel Stewart, and he was buried in the spot selected by himself many years before.

"But after the church had begun to wane there was a considerable interest kept up in the old place by large and flourishing schools. We all know that in neighborhoods where the people are generally poor there is sure to be a large number of children. The late Daniel Goggans, when quite a young man and just starting out in life, taught there for some time and his schools were always large and flourishing. He was a most excellent teacher and a firm believer in the old saying that a bird that can sing and won't sing should be made to sing. So when occasion required he did not fail to use the rod freely.

"I presume it would now be difficult for any person to locate the exact spot where the old church stood; and it will not be many years until a person happening upon the graveyard will wonder how it was that any people would choose such a place for a burying ground."

—

OLD KADESH.

"The old Methodist Church called Kadesh was on the road leading from Newberry C. H. to Belfast, six miles from Newberry, and very near to where the present residence of Dr. Thomas W. Boozer now stands. I am inclined to think that at one time the membership at Kadesh was pretty large, but for some cause or other it gradually dwindled away until it was finally joined with old Shady Grove to make Trinity. For many years before and several years after its final abandonment as a church it was used as a school house, and several pedagogues with whom I was acquainted once swayed the birch within its walls. Col. James L. Gilder once taught there. His school was large and flourishing, and among his pupils at one time was my old and staunch friend, W. D. Reagin, who was then nearly a grown man. During the year he had a difficulty with some of the other boys, and it turned out that he was given the choice of leaving the school or taking a whipping. Being anxious to get an education he decided at once to take the whipping, and accordingly did so. The trustees of the school, however, heard of the difficulty and took the matter in hand. They had a meeting and investigated the affair and decided that although he had taken the whipping he should leave the school. He then began attending the school at old Shady Grove taught by the late Daniel Goggans.

"I remember to have heard an anecdote told as having happened in Colonel Gilder's school, which I will relate for the benefit of other teachers who may sometimes happen to meet up with similar cases. The Colonel was examining a class, and among other things asked if they could tell in what zone we lived. The pupils to whom the question was put hesitated so long that it was repeated, when a little girl who was sitting at some distance spoke up and said: 'I know, I know.' 'Well,' said the Colonel, 'if you know, tell us.' Said she: 'We live in South Carolina, Newberry District.' 'Yes,' said the Colonel, 'you are correct, and if you belonged to the class you should go head.'

"William Owens lived and kept a store just on the top of the hill about one hundred yards from D. Boozer's present residence and down the road in the direction of Newberry. In those days it was a rare thing to find a storekeeper who did not keep among his stock in trade a pretty liberal quantity of something to keep the spirits up. Mr. Owens being in Rome of course did as Rome does, and so Owens' store became famous as a place for fun and frolic. Mr. Owens died young, leaving, for that day and time, a pretty fair property. Fergus McClellan married the widow, with whom he lived a good many years, and after her death he removed to Alabama.

"Andrew McConnell lived about one mile further up the Belfast road, near Kadesh, at the place now owned by his nephew, Andrew J. Longshore. He was descended from Irish parents and, I think, was born on the Green Isle, but brought to this country by his parents when a child. After the death of his father the support and maintenance of the family devolved on him and his mother, but she was a host within herself. I suppose there is still quite a number of the old persons living in that section of country who remember Mary McConnell and the anecdotes that used to be told of her shrewdness at a bargain and of her untiring industry and perseverance. I have always understood that they began keeping a little jug tavern in a room of the dwelling house, and, as they prospered, gradually increased it to a store. He continued to merchandise up to the time of his death and left quite a handsome property.

"Andrew J. Longshore's mother was McConnell's sister. He has lived at the old place for the last forty years, and has exhibited, in a marked degree, those characteristics of industry and perseverance possessed by his grandmother and his uncle Andrew McConnell.

[This very excellent man and neighbor, and good citizen, died on Monday, March 28, 1892, at about the age of 75 years. He died of paralysis at his old home, where he had lived so long, in Township No. 6.]

"An old lady by the name of Reese was one of the nearest neighbors to Kadesh. She owned and lived upon the plantation now owned by our County Treasurer, M. H. Gary. Her residence, however, was some two or three hundred yards from where his dwelling now stands. Mrs. Reese, besides carrying on a farm, was also a cake baker, and for many years might always be seen at public places with her little Jersey wagon loaded with cakes—and beer of her own make, which sparkled like champagne, and I have no doubt was much better—drawn by a horse as fat as a butter ball. Everybody knew that anything made by Mrs. Reese was sure to be as nice as nice could be, so she never failed to have her full share of custom. She was one of the last of the generation of old time women, always amiable, kind and obliging, and whom to know was an honor to any person. She stuck to the old spinning wheel, flax wheel and loom as long as she lived. One of her descendants now lives in the town of Newberry, and her herculean efforts to support, rear and educate her two sons mark her as one who deserves a place among the grandest women of the land.

"Robert Cleland lived within less than a mile of Kadesh, at the same place where his elderly maiden daughter, Nancy Cleland, now resides. He had a good farm which he cultivated nicely and profitably, making all his supplies at home and generally having some to sell. He was a blacksmith by trade and worked at it for a good many years after his age and easy circumstances would have admonished most men that it was time to give up work and take their ease. Notwithstanding he lived so near the Methodist Church of Kadesh he was a member of the Baptist Church, and, I think, one of the most attentive attendants upon the services of the church that I have ever known. During the summer there were generally protracted meetings held at the various Baptist churches and he was sure to attend every day if within reach. The

2   L

only drawback was that when he became still he was almost sure to go to sleep; so it happened that he seldom heard the sermon. Few better men ever lived in the neighborhood of old Kadesh.

"John Cleland, a brother of Robert's, lived about a mile up the Kadesh road from McConnell's, on the place where Clarke Mingo now lives. He once removed to Newton County, Ga., but came back in a few years, bought his old place back and there remained until his death. I suppose he came to the same conclusion that my friend, Charles Scott, once did. Said he: 'I never want to go to h–ll or to Georgia.' John Cleland was the father of my true and tried friend, Charles S. Cleland, who now lives in the nighborhood of Bush River Church, and if all men were as honest and honorable as he was, there would be less need for civil service reform. His word was as good as his bond, and neither ever failed.

"George Boozer, the father of Dr. Thomas W. Boozer, George B., Samuel P. and Henry D. Boozer, lived just on the west side of Beaver Dam Creek and not much more than half a mile from Kadesh. He and his family were Presbyterians and he took no stock in Kadesh, except in its schools, where, I believe, most of his sons and daughters obtained the rudiments of their education.

"Henry Cromer lived for some years within about a mile of Kadesh. He was one of the pillars of the church at that place and an official member. He frequently prayed and exhorted in meeting, and, though a very quiet and somewhat bashful man, he generally got on the high horse on these occasions, and as he began to warm up he was sure to begin to rub his ear with his hand, and the warmer he got the harder he rubbed, so by the time he concluded his ear was as red as if it had been painted. He afterwards removed to Franklin County, Ga., where he spent the remainder of his life. His son, George Cromer, was also a member of Kadesh and also removed to Georgia at about the same time his father did. They settled in the same neighborhood, where, while the old man continued to make a good living, George accumulated a handsome property. From information which I have received I suppose that George Cromer did as much, if not more, towards the building up of Methodism in his neighborhood as any other man. He was very zealous and had a stentorian voice which he did not spare when occasion required. In proof of which it is said that he was often heard to pray at a distance of three miles, and some say more. He died some time since, but some of his children and grandchildren still live near his old home.

"The writer has heard the names of a number of other persons who once lived in the neighborhood of Kadesh, but who either died or moved away before he ever knew much about them. He remembers to have seen some of the Plunkits, Murdocks and McClungs, who, at one time, lived near Kadesh, and of whom he never heard a disparaging word spoken.

"There was a graveyard at Kadesh of considerable extent, but which has been long since utterly neglected and is now all overgrown with trees and briars; and, as in those days there were but few graves marked by anything more than a plank, or, at best, a rough rock, it would now be difficult for any of those who have loved ones there to find the place where they rest. Col. James L. Gilder, several years before his death, had a house built over and around the graves of some of his own family, and room left therein for his own remains, which were there deposited after his death. With this exception there are very few, if any, graves in the burying ground which could be identified by any person now living. So old Kadesh has passed away; as all other things now on earth of a like transitory nature must also pass."

—

Old New Chapel.

"When the writer first knew the New Chapel Methodist Church it stood about a half mile southwest of where it now stands. This was about the year 1820. The membership of the church had dwindled away, and I am not sure if there were not several years in which there was not a member on the roll.

"Like most other meeting houses, as they were then called, it was also used for a school house, and the writer has quite a vivid recollection of the red stripes he used to wear on his legs received at Old New Chapel. Immediately around where the meeting house then stood there was a dense thicket of black jack bushes and briars. There were but few small patches of cultivated land for quite a distance in any direction. There was also a burying ground of considerable extent near the house; but even then it was all overgrown with black jack and briars. I remember to have seen more than one burying there, but of whom I cannot now say. It was a very old meeting house and showed signs of several settlements near it, so that I presume the skeletons lately exhumed (as I have heard) by Daniel Stewart, must have been of persons who had been buried at, or near, old New Chapel, and who have long since ceased to be remembered by the present generation. The neighborhood was quite populous at the time of which I am speaking. There were the Rileys, the Lashleys, the Knights, the Wyatts, the Curls and several others, who now, so far as I know, have no representatives in South Carolina; certainly not in Newberry County.

"As I have before stated, the membership of New Chapel had dwindled down, until, I suppose, it would have been difficult to raise a corporal's guard. But the circuit preachers still kept it on their list of appointments, hoping, I presume, that something would turn up, and they had their reward. About the years 1831 to 1833 that old veteran, David Derrick, was appointed to the Newberry Circuit, and made a long pull, a strong pull and a pull all together to raise up old New Chapel, and he succeeded. The late Isaac Herbert and his most exemplary wife were among the first of his converts, and from that time forward New Chapel continued to flourish.

"Isaac Herbert was the son of Walter Herbert, who was the first man that I ever heard called Esquire. He was a large, portly, dignified looking man, and when in after years I saw a little weasel of a looking man called Esquire, I felt perfectly astounded, and this feeling sticks to me yet. Thus going to show that first impressions are hard to eradicate.

"Walter Herbert had been raised among the Quakers, though I don't think he ever joined their society. He was a plain, substantial, common sense man, and represented Newberry County in the State Legislature more than once. He lived to a good old age, and, I believe, allied himself with a total abstinence society and joined the Methodist Church at New Chapel some years before his death. No better or more useful man in his sphere ever lived or died in the neighborhood of New Chapel.

"His son Isaac was his successor as a Magistrate, and also, for a time, as a Representative, and had the best interests of his fellow-men at heart. Some thought him a little precise and hidebound in his notions; but to the writer, who was surely wild enough in those days, he was a firm, unwavering friend.

"An Irishman by the name of Nelson once lived near where the church now stands. His oldest son, Thomas, whom he always persisted in calling wee Tammy, afterwards became famous as a manager and overseer. He carried R. R. Nance's hands to Alabama and remained in charge of his plantation there for several years, and I think Mr. Nance retained him in his employ for a length of time after his removal to that country. He was a genial, jovial man and used to tell innumerable anecdotes on his father. The old man was a strict Methodist and of course held family prayers every night. Some of the older people will remember how much sport they used to have in their childish days, when a bat would come into the house of a night, by closing doors and attacking it with brooms and sticks. One night Mr. Nelson was at prayer and wee Tammy was on his knees enjoying as such boys always do, when happening to look up he saw a bat. In a moment all else was forgotten, and springing to his feet he exclaimed, 'D—n the bat!' The next moment he was again on his knees as devout as ever. But his hasty repentance did not save his hide, for the next morning the old man interviewed him for about the space of half an hour.

"When the writer first knew Old New Chapel, David Dominick lived but a few hundred yards from where the church now stands, but left the country before it was built. Adam Monts then lived at the Dominick place for a number of years, but he, too, went West with the exodus from the neighborhood of Isaac Arnold, Wilks and Joseph Conwill, John Jenkins, Daniel S. Black and others.

"Jeremiah Morgan once lived on the place now owned by Dr. D. S. Cannon on Saluda, then called the old Clary place. He attached himself to the church at Old New Chapel and became an official member, though after a few years he left the Methodist and attached himself to the Baptist Church, and, I think, preached occasionally. His son, Jesse Morgan, is now living in Mississippi and is a Lutheran minister in fine standing. The writer had the pleasure of hearing him preach some three years ago and was much pleased with the effort.

"About the year 1832 or 1833 a new church was built on the ground where it now stands, and the old house was abandoned and has become a thing of the past. And I doubt if there are a half dozen persons now living in the neighborhood who could point out the spot where it once stood, or even remembers that it ever was."

COATE'S MEETING HOUSE.

"Coate's Meeting House was on the public road leading from Newberry C. H. to Long's Bridge on Little River, by way of Deadfall, and between Deadfall and the bridge about two hundred yards from where Mr. G. Henry Werts now lives. It was built of large hewn logs and had been originally built by the Quakers on the place now owned by James B. Clary, and was called White Lick. Shortly after the exodus of the Quakers in the early part of the present century it was occupied for a time by the Methodists, as I judge from an anecdote which I remember to have heard when a small boy.

"An itinerant preacher by the name of Russell had the Newberry Circuit in charge. He was a great revivalist, and I suppose did more to build up the Methodist denomination and give it a firm foothold in the county than any man has done, before or since. Houses of worship were very scarce, and he, therefore, was in the habit of preaching at any neighbor's house who would let him do so, either day or night. One night he was having quite a stormy meeting at a neighbor's house and at the close of the services opened the door of the church for the reception of members. A man by the name of Arthur Barrett had been quietly sleeping through the whole sermon, but when the call for joiners was made the rush and noise were so great that he awoke, and, seeing quite a number going up and giving their hands, he did likewise, and then quietly went back and resumed his nap. When it was all over the preacher took out his book and began reading the names of those who had joined and calling upon them to state at what church they wished their names enrolled. When Brother Barrett's name was called, some person went and waked him up, when the preacher said: 'Brother Barrett, where do you wish to have your membership recorded?' Said he, 'At White Lick, I imagine.'

"Doctor Clements was a cabinet-maker and had a shop at Esquire Henry Coate's. Among other things he made was a musical instrument called a dulcimer, upon which he also played with much skill. Some time after Mr. Barrett had joined the church he called on Mr. Clements and asked him to play a tune for him. To the Doctor's query, 'What tune will you have?' he replied, 'A spiritual tune, by all means.' The Doctor then struck up 'Leather Breeches,' and looking around saw his auditor sitting as if in a trance, with the tears rolling down his cheeks, and when he had finished Barrett remarked: 'That was delicious,' at the same time wiping his eyes.

"Some Esquire, perhaps Esquire Coate, once appointed him a constable and directed him to serve a summons in a case of debt on one of the neighbors, remarking that he wished it served immediately. Barrett mounted his horse and started as if life and death depended on his speed. At a sudden turn in the road he met a woman on foot and called to her, 'Get out of the way, for I am on urgent business.' She was too slow, however, and he ran over her.

"The meeting house at White Lick, having fallen into disuse, was purchased or procured in some way by the people of the Deadfall settlement and rebuilt at the place, before mentioned, on land belonging to Esquire Henry Coate; hence the name of Coate's Meeting House. It was free to all denominations and was also used as a school house for many years. The writer remembers the names of quite a number of pedagogues who once swayed the birch within its walls, and looks back with wonder at the number of exercises that fell to his share.

"At the number of teachers who, at one time or another, taught in Coate's Meeting House, we will mention only three. Capt. Ross Bird was a man rather past middle age, a good scholar and most excellent teacher. He was a stranger in the neighborhood, and if the writer ever heard where he came from it has escaped his mind. He was a large, portly man an very fond of his cups. He almost invariably spent Saturday at a place where something to drink was to be had, and it was not always the case that he was able to keep his reckoning on his way home. On one of these occasions he was found by a neighbor who took him to his house and put him to bed. Sometime during the night he awoke and had lost, not only his surroundings, but even his own identity. Said he, 'Where am I? Who am I? I can't remember who I am. O!' said he, 'I believe this is Captain, Major, General Ross Bird.'

"A man by the name of Evans once taught at Coate's Meeting House for a short time, and I now have the impression that he was a most excellent teacher. I think he was an entire stranger in the country. He was quite a large man and rode a very small pony. He seemed to be a monomaniac on the subject of grammar. He boarded around among the scholars and made it a point to deliver a lecture on grammar every night, and in this way got the nick-name of Big Syntax, and his pony that of Little Syntax. He was, moreover, a great lady's man and attempted to court every woman with whom he came in contact. On the 14th of February, however, he received a valentine which broke up the school. Valentines in those days were not, as now, neatly printed and perfumed, and a person wishing to send one had to make and write it. The verses contained in the one which he received were as follows:

> " 'You hog, you dog, you dirty swine!
> I drew you for my valentine;
> I drew you from amongst a dozen,
> Because I thought you was the old sow's cousin.'

That straw broke the camel's back. The school was given up and I never heard of Mr. Evans afterwards.

"A. R. Able was the last of the Mohegans. He taught at Coate's Meeting House for quite a number of years and always had from forty to sixty pupils. He was a good teacher and a firm believer with Solomon as to the use of the rod. If a pupil was too lazy or too stupid to learn in the ordinary way he never hesitated to maul it into him. The writer can remember dancing many a hornpipe on the floor of Coate's Meeting House while Absalom R. Able made the music. He thought it mighty hard and perfectly unnecessary at the time, but of late years he has come to the conclusion that perhaps it was but bread cast upon the waters.

"But Coate's Meeting House has long been a thing of the past. No sign now remains to mark the spot where it once stood. And we can now call to mind scarcely a dozen of the urchins who used to dance to the music with us who have not yet passed over the river."

—

Cox's Fishing Place.

"Sixty years ago when the writer was a small boy he remembers to have heard old persons say that at the first settling of the country, and for many years afterwards, Saluda River was as clear as a mountain stream. Shad in large numbers annually visited its waters, and fishing places were established at intervals all along its course.

"Cox's Fishing Place was on the Newberry side, some two miles below what is now known as Kinard's Ferry. This ferry was then owned by Francis Higgins, and was known far and wide as Higgins' Ferry. Francis Higgins was, I think, an Irishman by birth, who, by persevering industry and rigid economy, accumulated a competence, gave all his children a good education, lived to a good old age and left behind him a large fund of anecdotes.

"Mr. Higgins was the father of our late much esteemed fellow-citizen, F. B. Higgins, of the town of Newberry. He was also survived by a younger son, Mark, and by two daughters, Ann and Mary. Mark lived for many years on the old homestead, but, a few years before the late war between the States, he caught the Western fever and removed to Mississippi, where he died a few years ago. Ann married a man by the name of Etheredge. They went West and I never heard of them afterwards. Mary married Dr. Rudolph. They also went West.

"A short distance below the ferry sixty years ago lived Mrs. Elizabeth Webber. She had been the widow of Cox, after whom the fishing place was named. The writer remembers her three sons—James, Cornelius and William Cox—who had all attained to man's estate when they removed to Georgia about the year 1824. Her last husband, Webber, was killed at the Deadfall by a man named Banister, who, I think, made his escape and was not heard of afterwards.

"A short distance below Mrs. Webber's and nearly opposite

Cox's Fishing Place (on the Edgefield side of Saluda) lived the Turners, William and David. Their father was a brother to the celebrated Ned Turner, and, I believe, the only one, of a large family of brothers, who did not take part in the Revolutionary struggle. This subjected him to the suspicions of both parties, and between the two he had a pretty hard time. He died before the recollection of the writer; but his wife, who was a Spraggins, survived him for a number of years. She kept a great many geese, and fed them from the corn crib every evening. The writer remembers to have seen her, many and many a time, catch two old ganders who were fighting over their food and bump their heads together to make them quit. He remembers her death as well as if it had been yesterday.

"She left four children, two sons and two daughters; William and David, who both died childless; and Elizabeth, who married William Burgess, and also died without issue; and Polly, who married David Peterson. Polly left seven children, four sons and three daughters, all of whom are now dead with the exception of a daughter, Matilda Stephens, of Attala County, Mississippi, and a son, John T. Peterson, with whom, I suppose, most of the grown people in Newberry County are acquainted.

"A little lower down lived Hugh Gregg, an Irishman by descent and a blacksmith by trade. He was a genial, whole-souled man, worked diligently at his trade until about the year 1830, when, having acquired a tolerable competency, he removed to what was then Pendleton District. The writer spent two nights with him some years ago at his home, in what is now Anderson County and near the Savannah River, talking over old times, scenes and persons. He has since passed away, but the recollection of the two nights spent with the old friend, who was middle-aged when he was an infant, will not pass from the mind of the writer until he, too, shall have been numbered with the dead.

"Just across the Saluda, and not more than five or six hundred yards from Cox's Fishing Place, lived William Stewart, whose wife was a Spraggins and, I think, a sister of old Mrs. Turner, spoken of above. William Stewart died before the recollection of the writer, but his wife, who survived him some years, is remembered. It was at their house that the shooting of Ned Turner by the Towleses took place in, I suppose, 1813 or 1814. During the Revolution most of the Turners were tories, and the Towleses, who were also a large family and lived in the same neighborhood, were whigs, and it seems that during the struggle a most bitter feud had sprung up between the two families and that considerable blood had been shed on both sides. I remember to have heard it said that one of the Towleses, being sick with smallpox, was concealed by his friends somewhere in the swamps of Saluda or Little River. The Turners, however, hunted him down with the perseverance of a sleuth hound, and that, helpless as he was when found, he was shot by Ned Turner. About the close of the Revolution Ned Turner made his escape to Florida, which then belonged to Spain; but about the time mentioned above he came to his old home on a visit. He was very cautious and used all the means in his power to keep clear of the Towleses; but they soon heard that he was in the country and at once set about hunting him up. They found him at William Stewart's on a Sunday night and shot him. It seems that he was sitting in the door at the time and had no warning of the danger until they were within a few feet of him, when they fired and he fell forward on his face in the yard. Not doubting for a moment but that their purpose was accomplished they then rode away. Turner, however, was entirely unharmed and as soon as the party was out of sight he arose, and, getting the ball out of his cravat, declared that he could have made a better shot with so good a ball. He left the country that night and never visited it again, though he lived many years after and took part in the rebellion of Florida against Spain; was captured and imprisoned in the Castle of St. Augustine, where he remained for more than seven years and was only released after the purchase of Florida by the United States.

"It seems that the habit was for the neighbors to form themselves into companies or squads of four or five and each squad had one day in the week to fish during the shad season. In this way all the neighbors living near enough could take part in the fishing and enjoy its advantages. Connected with one of these squads was Thomas Rainey, an Irishman by birth, and of him it was told that on one occasion he was in the canoe to which the seine was attached when making a haul, and that as they approached the shore the canoe sank. Rainey saw the danger and called out in great alarm: 'The cunue is sunkin and I can't swam.' In fact he did come very near drowning, but was rescued by some person on the shore. John Tinsley, who lived not far from Rainey, was also an Irishman, and the two were great friends. Charleston at that time was the only market where the people of this section disposed of the tobacco and what little cotton they raised, and to that place the two brother Irishmen sometimes went together. In one of their trips as they neared the low country they heard that there had been a good deal of stealing from wagons lately. So they agreed that one of them should stay awake each night and watch. Accordingly when bed time came, Tinsley inquired: 'Well, Tam, which will you do the night, sleep or herd?' Rainey said he would sleep tonight, herd to-morrow night. The next night the same question was asked and the same answer given. So it turned out that one did all the watching and the other all the sleeping.

"Thomas Rainey once joined the Methodist Church and became an exhorter, and, I believe, preached sometimes. But in his old age, after the loss of his wife, he fell from grace and became too much addicted to strong drink. He left three sons, William, John and Thomas. William married a Miss Wright and removed to the State of Tennessee. John went to Pendleton District and I do not know if he ever married. Thomas married Sally Sheppard, a sister to the late Washington Floyd's first wife, and removed to Chambers County, Ala.

"John Tinsley died before the recollection of the writer, but he has a distinct recollection of his widow, Margaret Tinsley, and when a small boy often heard an anecdote told of her that I think is mentioned in some of Judge O'Neall's writings. Having heard old Dr. Moon, the father of the late Dr. Peter Moon, preach a sermon on the Day of Judgment she questioned him on the subject. 'You tell me, Doctor,' said she, 'that everybody will be there on that day?' 'Yes.' 'Will that lying Vines Dailey be there?' 'Yes.' 'And that big bullying Bill Turner?' 'Yes.' 'And that big fighting Billy McGlamery?' 'Yes.' 'Then it is sure to be a great day of rioting. Doctor, give in my excuse; I will be there the day after.' Her two sons, Arthur and Jonathan, commonly called Jock, both left this country when I was very small and I never heard of them afterwards.

"But Cox's Fishing Place has passed away, and I do not suppose there is a person now living who could point out the spot where it once was. From the tilling of the lands all along the river its waters have become muddy and scarcely fit for the production of fish, other than the cat and eel. Dams have been erected across the stream at various places, so as to entirely obstruct the passage of fish, and we would now almost as soon expect to find a shark or whale in the Saluda as a shad."

HEAD'S TAVERN.

"When the writer can first recollect, the place where Noah Martin now lives, on the road leading from Newberry Court House to Kinard's Ferry, was known as Head's Tavern. The old house stood just where the road leading from Jesse Senn's shop to Mendenhall's Mill crosses the Kinard's Ferry road, and on the right of the latter road as you go from Newberry towards the ferry. How the place came by the name I do not know, but I have always supposed that, in those days, when all travelers went either on horseback or on foot, and most persons living on public highways took in travelers, a man by the name of Head lived at the place, took in travelers and kept a tavern.

"When the writer first knew the place there was nothing about it but the name to lead one to suppose there had ever been a tavern there. I remember several persons who lived there at different times, one of whom was Samuel Hogg, who carried on the business of a wagon maker and general Jack-of-all-trades. But I will say here that, unlike the ordinary Jack-of-all-trades, he did his work well and in a workman-like manner. He afterwards removed to Georgia and was killed by a falling tree.

"Powell Cooper, who was the coroner of the county from my earliest recollection up to his death, lived about two or three hundred yards up the road towards Senn's, from Head's Tavern, and on the hill upon which W. D. Reagin now lives, though not at the same spot. Some years after Mr. Reagin came into possession of the place he built a short distance higher up and on the opposite side of the road. Mr. Cooper was much respected by his neighbors, and I think Newberry has never had a better coroner. He was a plain, unassuming farmer, and utterly opposed to fashion and show. It was related that on one occasion when some gentlemen visitors had ordered their shoes to be blacked, he called another servant and said: 'Here, take my shoes and black them with fat.'

"His only daughter, who was in fact his only child, married Henry G. Sibley, who some years afterwards moved to Texas.

"Henry Cooper lived on the Kinard's Ferry road and only a short half mile from Head's Tavern in the direction of Newberry. W. D. Reagin now owns the place, or perhaps has sold it or given it to one of his sons. Henry Cooper's widow married John Edmundson, of whom I will speak further on.

"James S. Gilliam lived on the left of the Kinard's Ferry road and nearly opposite Henry Cooper's. I do not know who first settled his place, but it must have been done in the olden time when everybody built on a branch or stream of water so as to be close to a spring. Mr. Gilliam was a plain, unostentatious gentleman and always spoke his mind without reserve. He lived to be very old and always stuck to the old time hospitality of setting out his bottle when a friend called; and in doing so he never failed to take the first drink, to show, as he said, that it was not poison. If he called on a friend he adhered to the same rule—the host must drink first or he would not drink at all. His aged widow still survives and resides with her brother, our old faithful public servant, E. P. Lake.

"Down the road towards Mendenhall's Mill lived James McCann. His house was in a flat near the spring and surrounded on three sides by hills, which ran down near the house. It had been built, however, by some former owner, I think a Captain Barrett. McCann was an Irishman and much given to making mistakes. On one occasion when loading his rifle the ball stuck fast, which he and his son John attempted to remove. Finding all other means to fail they attempted to melt it out. John was holding the breech of the gun in the fire while the old man stood by looking on. At length an explosion took place and the ball entered the old man's thigh and knocked him down. John caught him in his arms exclaiming: 'Father, father, are you dead?' 'No,' said he, 'John, but I believe I am speechless.'

"Some years after the death of his first wife, McCann married the widow Ann Davenport, who then lived at the place where John W. Reeder now lives near Silver Street. After they became engaged the old man was highly elated, and often said: 'Here's James McCann, the best of man, who's going to wed the widow Ann.' But the marriage did not prove propitious. In a short time they separated for good, and he removed to Holmes County, Miss., where he died. Mrs. Davenport at the time of her marriage had a lad, of seventeen or eighteen years of age, living with her, by the name of Levi Rodgers. During McCann's stay he and Rodgers had a falling out, and McCann went for him with the intention of giving him a whipping. Rodgers, however, caught up a rock and taking the old fellow square, in the forehead knocked him down. A kind of cross indictment followed and both were convicted; McCann for an assault, and Rodgers for assault and battery. McCann was sentenced to jail for one week and Rodgers for two. While in jail together they buried the hatchet and became great friends. When McCann's time was out and he was about to leave they hugged and kissed and cried. Said McCann, 'Lev, it nearly kills me to leave you here. If I was allowed to do so, my boy, I would carry you out on my back.'

"Who first built on the spot where my friend Noah Martin now lives I have forgotten. But I remember that Capt. James Moore once lived there and after him Henry S. Dickert. The place finally took the name of Dickertsville, and I suppose there are persons still living who will remember it by that name. After a time it was purchased by Patrick O'Farrell, who for a number of years carried on the mercantile business there with success. He had a sign painted over his store door which read: 'P. O. Farrell.' A stranger was passing on one occasion and seeing the sign he stopped and attempted to read it. After spelling it over several times he made it out to read: 'Poor old fellow.' 'Well,' said he, 'I suppose I must patronize the old fellow,' so he went in and called for a drink.

"Mr. O'Farrell was an Irishman and as unsophisticated as a child. It was told of him that on one occasion, while riding out a short distance from home, he became lost and had no idea where he was. But seeing some cows which he thought looked very much like his own he began to ride around them and halloo as if he was driving them. They at once started for home, which was not more than three hundred yards distant, and so soon led him to where he could see the house. His place was for many years the muster ground of what was known as the Dickertsville Beat Company, and on muster days we generally had a high old time. On one of these occasions two men were sitting in the fence corner behind the store playing cards for a dollar a game. Mr. O'Farrell walked out and saw them. Said he: 'Boys, quit that; this sort of thing does nobody any good. Henry,' said he, addressing one of them by name, 'you know that if you win the other man loses, so in the end there is nothing made to the community.'

"On one occasion it was known that two of the neighbors, Bowen and Prewitt, had had a falling out and that Bowen had proposed to fight it out, but Prewitt demurred. So on the next muster day a crowd of the boys gathered around Prewitt and insisted on him to fight it out, informing him that if they saw Bowen was getting the better of him they would part them at once. So a ring was formed, and for a few moments I don't think I ever saw the fur fly in better style. Very soon, however, Bowen got the upper hand and Prewitt squealed. Just then old Mr. John Edmundson, who had been standing in the piazza looking on all the while, exclaimed: 'Part them, men! Part them, men! Now,' said he, 'you have egged on this thing for your own amusement, and now look at that young man's face! It is a drotted shame, and every one of you ought to be taken out and given fifty lashes.' The writer happened to be standing by one of the men who had been foremost in getting up the fight. Said he: 'I will give him ten dollars to hush.' Said another: 'I noticed that he never interfered till the fight was over.' Mr. Reagin happened to be near and he said: 'Yes, Uncle John, it is a shame and I am very sorry that it happened.' 'Yes,' said he, 'you drotted scoundrel, I expect you are very sorry; I believe you was the very rascal that got it up.'

"Mr. Edmundson owned and lived upon the plantation now owned by N. B. Davenport, and when the writer first knew him he had accumulated quite a handsome property. When a boy I think he had been apprenticed to Robert Evans, who was said to have been the inventor of the screw anger. I remember when Edmundson's augers had a reputation over all other makers; though, having accumulated a competency, he had given up work, but occasionally made a few augers for friends as a special favor. I expect a few augers might still be found in the possession of some of the older men in the county with the brand of Edmundson upon them. His last wife, which, I think, was his third, was the widow of Henry Cooper, and shortly after this last marriage he removed to Giles County, Tenn., where he died some years afterwards. In 1856 the writer passed through that country and called on his widow, who was then a most genial and clever lady. His son, Isaac Edmundson, bought the Powell Cooper place at the sale of his estate, and lived upon it for a few years, but finally sold it, with most of his stock, and some of his negroes, to W. D. Reagin. He then removed to Tennessee, and settled for a time near his father, but afterwards went to Texas, where, I think, he died.

"When Mr. Reagin made the purchase almost everybody prophesied that he could never pay. In fact I think there is not one man in a thousand that could have done so. But he fought the situation like a hero and conquered in the end, and for a good many years has been looked upon as one of the most prosperous farmers in our county.

"Head's Tavern is now a thing of the past, and I do not suppose there are a great many persons now living who remember that there ever was such a place."

—

GOGGANS' OLD STORE.

"James Goggans, the first occupant of Goggans' Old Store,

2   M

and from whom it took its name, was, I believe, related to all the Gogganses in Newberry County. He was a brother of old Mrs. Mangum, who was the mother of the late Rev. Daniel Mangum, who did more to build up the Baptist Church in the upper part of Newberry County than any other man has ever done. The old store was on the road leading from Newberry to Laurens by way of Belfast and Milton, about three or four hundred yards above where the late Washington Floyd used to live. The writer has now in his possession the deed of conveyance given by James Goggans and Ezekiah Eastland to Stephen Herndon on the 22nd day of March, 1809, and signed by their wives, Cassandra Goggans and Elizabeth Eastland, relinquishing their right of dower, on the 4th of April, 1809; also a deed from James Goggans to Stephen Herndon, 21st of March, 1809, with relinquishment of dower by his wife, Cassandra Goggans, on 4th of April following. One or the other of these deeds, I suppose, conveyed the site of the old store.

"The writer has the impression that James Goggans then lived for a time in Georgia; from there he went to Perry County, Ala., and finally settled in Coosa County, where his two sons, William and Dr. James P. Goggans, and several of his daughters still reside.

"Abram Belton merchandised for a time at the old store after the removal of Goggans, after which, I think, it was unoccupied for several years; then Cary Pitts came into possession and carried on the mercantile business for several years. But it finally passed into the hands of Washington Floyd, and is now the property of his grandson Lou W. Floyd.

"When the writer can first remember, the muster ground of the Western Battalion of the 38th Regiment, the post office called Belmont, and the election precinct for what is now called Floyd's, or No. 6 Township, was at or near the old store and remained there for a long time. But as the place fell into disuse as a place of business, all these passed to McConnell's, two miles nearer to Newberry Court House, where A. J. Longshore now resides and still carries on the mercantile business. Since the war the post office at Belmont has been discontinued and mustering has played out, so there remains only the election precinct.

"At one time the neighborhood around Goggans' Old Store was very populous. There were the Clelands, Butlers, Floyds, Andersons, Gogganses, Wallaces, Manns, Jarrases, Sterlings and more Pittses than a man could count in half an hour. And besides these there was quite a number of families whose names I have now forgotten. But now all is different, and white families are few and far between.

"Capt. John Floyd, who lived near the old store, was the ancestor of all the Floyds. He had been a soldier in the Revolution and was at the battle of Stono, where he commanded as lieutenant, and he used to boast that he alone ran a large number of the British, and when urged to tell how he managed to accomplish such a feat he said that he ran and they ran after him. On one occasion his son Washington was very sick and making a good deal of complaint, sometimes calling out, 'Lord, help me!' At length the old man said to him: 'Come, Washington, my son, if you have to die, die like a man; and if you want help, call on some of the people you are acquainted with; don't call on strangers.'

"I have said before that James Goggans was related to all the Gogganses, and I think he was in some way also related to the Eastlands; for I have heard it said of him that he used to tell one of his sons, who was inclined to play a great many mischievous pranks, that he was at a loss to tell which he took after most, 'Honest Bill' Goggans or Joseph Eastland.

"Bailey Goggans, son of 'Honest Bill,' lived and died in the same neighborhood; and we can say with truth that no man was ever more universally respected by his neighbors. A family of his grandchildren are still living in the neighborhood of the old homestead, and I have no hesitation in saying that they are the peer of any family in the country.

"When Goggans' Old Store was in its prime it was, I suppose, one of the most public places in the county; but a stranger, to see the place now, could scarcely realize that it once had so much life and activity; for of all the people who once used to rendezvous at the old store for the purpose of fun and frolic, there is not one left to tell the tale."

THE MURDER OF DAVID WATERS.

"David Waters lived on the road from Higgins' (now Kinard's) Ferry to Newberry Court House, about one mile from Deadfall, on the place where the widow of Edward Stephens now lives. He was a thoroughgoing, energetic man, and at the time of his death was, I suppose, the wealthiest man in that section of the county. He was murdered on the night of the 25th of February, 1819, as he was returning from a cotton gin where he was having his cotton prepared for market. The murder was committed on the side of the road between where Mr. G. Henry Werts now lives and Mr. Jeff Waldrop's, and very near the residence of the latter. The writer was then only about five years old, but he remembers as if it was but yesterday hearing the messenger, who came after his father that night, tell that David Waters had been killed. The messenger was James Wadsworth, a free negro who lived in the same section for many years afterwards, and may still be remembered by a few old people yet living.

"For a man to be found murdered at this day and time seems to attract but little attention; but at that time it must have been very different, for by daylight next morning I suppose every grown man within five miles of the place was on the ground, and each man constituted himself a committee of one to discover the murderer. The inquisition which was held on the next day, 26th February, 1819, by Powel Cooper, coroner, with David Thomas foreman of the jury, failed, however, to get any clue to the perpetrator; but it was not many days before the whole thing was brought to light. It was ascertained that he was killed by one of his own negroes, named Jerry, and that two others, Will and Jim, were accessories before the fact. The negro man, Jerry, was hung and his body burned a few yards from where the murder was committed. Will and Jim were terribly whipped and then cropped and branded. The wagoner, a negro man named Ned, was also given one hundred lashes. But I have always thought that in his case the punishment was wrong. It seems that Waters and his wagoner, Ned, left the gin at the same time about dark. Waters rode on ahead and when Ned saw him lying in the road he turned out into the woods and drove round him. His explanation was, that some time previous to that he had found a man lying in the road drunk one night, and that he had taken him up and laid him to one side and then drove on; and that when he told his master, Waters, of the circumstance he gave him a severe reproof, and told him never to touch nor go near any person whom he might see lying in the road after dark. This story has always looked reasonable to me, and so I have been impressed with the idea that his punishment was not justly inflicted. At the sale of the property of the estate of Waters, Ned was purchased by a Mr. Morgan, and was killed some years afterward by Mark Morgan, one of his young masters. It appears that they were engaged in building a chimney, as was then quite common, with sticks and clay, when some dispute arose and Morgan struck him with one of the sticks and killed him.

"One of the negroes, Will, who was implicated in the murder, was bought by Daniel Clary, the father of Col. M. W. Clary, now of Edgefield, who lived at the place on Saluda River where Cannon's Ferry now is. Will lived to be rather an old man, and died with dropsy after a long illness and much suffering. The other negro who was implicated in the murder was purchased by Mr. John Taylor, who then owned and lived on the place now owned by Col. John R. Leavell on Bush River. I do not know what became of him, but I recollect that it was said to have been through his agency that a circumstance happened which distressed the family very much and made quite a scandal in the neighborhood.

"David Waters' wife was a 'Miss Elleson, by whom he left four children, William, David M., Daniel and Elizabeth. The widow married Edward Stephens and died some years afterwards with consumption. William Waters was killed by a kick from a horse, and David died a few years afterwards. David M. Waters will be remembered, I suppose, by a good many of the people of the county. He removed to Tennessee about the year 1844 or 1845, and was there killed in a row some twelve or fifteen years afterwards.

"Elizabeth Waters married James M. Davenport and after

his death, which happened in about 1848, she married J. D. Heuston, with whom she is still living in Brunswick, Ga."

SALUDA OLD TOWN.

"It is only a matter of conjecture with the writer how the place came by the name; but he has the impression that there was once an old Indian town there, and being one of the oldest towns on the banks of the Saluda River it was accordingly called Saluda Old Town.

"Judge O'Neall, in his Annals of Newberry, makes mention of the fact that there was once an old Indian trail leading from the settlement at Old Town on the Saluda, by way of Long's Bridge on Little River, the point where the C. & G. R. R. crosses that stream, Silver Street and Senn's Mill, to another settlement which they had on Enoree. The writer remembers that part of the old trail from Little River to Senn's Mill as being for many years the dividing line between the 38th and 39th Regiments of South Carolina Militia; persons living on the southeast side went to Lever's and those on the northwest side to Teague's old field to regimental muster.

"When the writer first knew Old Town it was the property of Robert Dunlap and was even then very much on the wane. Old people, however, used to say that at one time it was quite a noted place. The old Charleston road, by which the people for many miles around carried their produce to Charleston, crossed the Saluda at Old Town, which was the only crossing place, with the exception of Island Ford, for many miles. This road, after crossing the river, ran down the Edgefield side, and nearly parallel with the river for a good many miles, having first, about a mile beyond the river, joined or united with another old road leading up Saluda from the lower country, and known as the old Charleston and Ninety-Six Road. It crossed the road now known as the Higgins' Ferry Road, or Kinard's, just at the old brickyard beyond where A. P. Coleman, commonly called Dandy, now lives. A Major Moore lived on the road a short distance below Old Town. I suppose it was on the place now owned by General Hagood, or the Bonham place, where he carried on quite a large mercantile business.

"As ferries began to be established along the Saluda, thus opening up newer and better roads, Old Town began to decline, and I think before it passed out of the hands of Mr. Dunlap the ferry had been discontinued, and in a few years if a stranger had been told that Old Town had once been a considerable thoroughfare he would have been forced to believe that the speaker was trying to hoax him.

"Old Town remained in obscurity for some time, but in the year 1852, after the G. & C. R. R. passed there, a depot was built at the place and a ferry across Saluda was re-established. But it did not succeed well as a place of business. It did not grow and flourish as a town, although a mineral spring, giving forth water of highly cura-tive powers, was discovered in the immediate neighborhood, and a fine hotel was built for the accommodation of visitors. The spring dried up, the hotel failed and was sold, and bought by Col. M. W. Clary and removed by him to his Southern Saratoga, down in Edgefield near Cannon's Ferry, where it was soon afterwards destroyed by fire.

"At present Saluda Old Town is a station with a depot on the G. & C. R. R. There are also some stores at the place, if I mistake not, where some business is done. Just across the river on the Edgefield side is General Hagood's Grass Farm, which is well worth a visit. It is a pleasant sight to ride through it when the grass is just ready for the mower.

"At Saluda Old Town there was once undoubtedly a large Indian town, as many Indian arrow heads, pieces of pottery and other relics are found, or used to be found, in the neighborhood."

In addition to the foregoing I may add that it was en-acted by Hon. Wm. Bull, Lieutenant-Governor and Commander-in Chief in and over His Majesty's Province of South Caro-lina, by and with the advice and consent of His Majesty's Council and the Commons House of Assembly of the said Province, and assented to on the 7th of April, 1770, that a public ferry be established over Saluda River at the place called Saluda Old Town, at the lands of Charles Carson on the south side of the river, to the opposite shore at the lands of William Turner; and that the said ferry shall be vested in Charles Carson, his heirs, etc., for fourteen years. And for any unreasonable delay in putting passengers across the ferry, Carson, his heirs, assigns, etc., shall forfeit and pay ten pounds currency, if the delay is as much as one hour; and if it exceeds one hour, five pounds for every additional hour after the first—to be recovered before a justice of the peace in *Colleton* County if sued for within ten days after the offence.

We thus see that Saluda Old Town is one of the oldest ferries across Saluda River in this section, and that even then, when the ferry was first established in 1770, it bore the same name it has now. In truth it was an old Indian town when the whites came and took possession, and so they called it. The road crossing Saluda Old Town passed out southwards through the country, crossing the old Charleston and Ninety-Six road about a mile from the river. We learn also that what is now Edgefield, or that part of Edgefield, was then part of Colleton County, and Newberry was in Craven County. It may be that the boundaries of these counties were not very well defined.

—

POSTSCRIPT TO COX'S FISHING PLACE.

The manner of Turner's escape from the Towles attacking party who went to kill him, as related to the writer by persons who were living in that neighborhood at the time the affair occurred, was as follows: When Turner was fired upon he fell in the yard as though he were dead. One of the party then approached him with a loaded pistol in his hand and was about to shoot him through the head when the others objected, saying that it was useless and barbarous to shoot a dead man. They then rode off. The Stewarts, Turner's friends, to conceal the fact that he was alive, and to facilitate his escape, procured a coffin next day, dug a grave and went through the form of burial. The Towleses never learned of his essape until after it was too late to pursue him.

HAMMOND'S OLD STORE, OR STONEY BATTER.

In a letter to William Henry Drayton, bearing date September 12th, 1775, published in Gibbes' Documentary History of the American Revolution, we find the following mention of Hammond's Old Store: "HONORED SIR—The Association paper was delivered the 7th instant, at James Ford's, as you desired. There was but a small gathering—the chief of the whole were liberty boys. They put fourteen members up, but did not close the poll, while the 26th of this month which is appointed, will be at Hammond's Old Store on Bush River," etc. In Johnston's "Traditions and Reminiscences of the American Revolution," Hammond's Old Store is mentioned as being near Ninety-Six. These expressions are used, and there is nothing more definite by means of which its location can now be identified.

There was a battle, or skirmish, at Hammond's Store fought by Colonel Washington, in which he defeated and dispersed a body of tories, who fled to Colonel Cunningham, who was then posted at Williams' Fort, about thirty miles distant, on Mudlick Creek, and he, apprehensive of the approach of an overwhelming force, hastened to Ninety-Six.

Putting these references together, with that found in the history of the Cunninghams in *Curwen's Journal*, I conclude that Hammond's Old Store, so called as far back as 1775, was situated at the place which has long been known as Stoney Batter. Stoney Batter thus becomes a place of interest in the history of Newberry County, as the birthplace of Governor James H. Hammond, son of Elisha Hammond, one of the greatest teachers at Mount Bethel Academy, and as one of the battle-grounds of our Revolutionary struggle.

I have in my possession a piece of writing bearing date May 6th, 1815, and written and signed by "E. Hammond," Principal of Mount Bethel School.

Judging from the name, Stoney Batter was evidently so called from its peculiar surroundings. It is situated on a stony eminence on the Holly's Ferry Road, about two and a half miles from the town of Prosperity, in former times called Frog Level. The stones which lie on the surface in very great numbers are of the species commonly known as flint rocks.

It was here that Governor James H. Hammond was born and reared; and here he received his primary education. He was a graduate of the South Carolina College, prepared for admission under his father at the celebrated school at Mount Bethel.

After the removal of the Hammonds, Dr. Francis Hatton came to Stoney Batter; for awhile living there and practicing medicine. His practice not being as lucrative as he desired, he moved West and was succeeded by Dr. James Kilgore. Dr. Kilgore became very popular and had a large practice, enjoying the entire confidence of the people, which he deserved and held as long as he lived. Not long after he came to Stoney Batter he and Col. John Hair, who was a man of some means, formed a partnership and engaged in the mercantile business. A prominent feature of "the store" was the "grocery," or "grogery," attached; and in connection with this was established a distillery on a branch near by. Dr. Kilgore, at that time thinking that the distillation of peaches into brandy would be a lucrative business, planted about twenty acres in peaches. About the time the trees began to bear he was converted and joined the Methodist Church. He then destroyed his distillery and cut down his fruit trees, which he had planted and nurtured for a purpose which his awakened conscience no longer approved. He became a local preacher in the Methodist Church. I do not think he was ever on the circuit. He married a daughter of Col. John Summers. He settled near Ebenezer Church, where he reared a large and respectable family, some of whom, daughters only, (May, 1892), still survive. Andrew J. Kilgore, a son of his, a man much loved, has only recently died at the home near Ebenezer, where he was born. Dr. Kilgore died some years before his wife. Her I knew well, and I think her face was one of the most chastened, sweetest and most angelic I ever saw.

It is said that the mercantile firm of Kilgore & Hair was not a decided success. Kilgore sold his interest to Fred Boozer, and Hair & Boozer became the successors to Kilgore & Hair; and they lost their entire stock of goods and groceries by an incendiary fire. After their misfortune John Cannon opened a store at the Battery without the grocery feature.

About this time Frog Level began to outrival the "Batter" and it began to lose its former prestige. Business, however, continued there in a small way until 1872, when "Bill" Davis (who was said to be a Red River man), who was running an illicit distillery in an excavation under his house, conveying the smoke from the furnace in flues to the chimney, was routed by revenue officers, and "Stoney Batter," except in name and traditions, passed into oblivion.

Seventy-five years ago Stoney Batter was noted for its game of "long bullets," shooting matches, fisticuffs, etc. For the edification of the present and succeeding generations it is necessary to explain. Long bullets was an innocent muscular pastime, and was engaged in by two or any greater number of persons at one time. The "bullets" were small cannon balls of twelve or twenty-four pounds weight, and were thrown on a level surface with all the muscular force of the arm of the man throwing. This writer has often seen this game played, but he never had sufficient muscular power to be a successful player. He was the winner who threw and rolled the ball farthest.

Shooting matches were of frequent occurrence and were greatly enjoyed by nearly everybody in that day. A beef was provided; a valuation was placed upon it, and then the "shootists" proceeded to make up the amount at, say seven-pence, $12\frac{1}{2}$ cents, per "shoot." The beef was usually divided into eight choices. The shooting at that day was usually done at a distance of sixty yards, and with old time sporting or squirrel rifles. The man whose ball struck nearest the centre of the target was entitled to first choice, and so on. Some of these old men, by frequent practice, attained a wonderful degree of accuracy with the rifle; so great was it that nothing but a centre shot would get beef. Of course the companionable half pint was always on hand and not unfrequently at such times was the precursor if not the instigator of a fisticuff. Neither knives nor pistols were used or known in fisticuffs. After a fight, which usually continued until one of the parties cried out "enough," it was customary for the combatants to get the half pint and make friends.

It is a remarkable fact that in these "long bullet" games, shooting matches, and even fisticuffs, no foul play was ever permitted; and woe to the fellow who would attempt such a thing. Everything was conducted on a high plane of honesty and integrity.

These old games and amusements, which once made Stoney Batter famous, have passed into obscurity, and now churches, school houses, Sunday-schools, factories, etc., have taken their places; and the country, which was then sparsely settled, is now almost a continuous village.

But young folks and college boys have their games and athletic sports yet, and I hope always will have them.

—

THE HAMMOND FAMILY.

Wishing to be sure of certain facts, I wrote to Harry Hammond, Esq., of Beech Island, and in reply to mine I received the following letter, which I hope the readers of the Annals will find of interest:

BEECH ISLAND, S. C.,
18th May, 1892.

John A. Chapman, Newberry, S. C.:

DEAR SIR: Replying to your letter of the 16th, let me say my grandfather, Elisha Hammond, descended from William Hammond of London, (whose son Benjamin immigrated to Sandwish, Mass., in 1634); was born at New Bedford, Mass., 10th October, 1774; graduated at Dartmouth, in Daniel Webster's class; came to South Carolina in 1802; taught in South Carolina College in 1803; married in 1806. My father was born in Newberry County in 1807. I once passed a place called Stoney Batter and an old gentleman, in whose company I was, pointed to the spot where the house had stood in which my grandfather lived, and said he had seen my father, a boy of six years, riding on an ox there. I think it quite likely my grandfather kept store there, for he tried a great many occupations in his time, and I remember my father's saying that he recollected seeing several teams unloading goods at his home in Newberry, which had been hauled all the way from Philadelphia, where they had carried cotton to market.

But this store could have had no connection with the Hammond's Old Store of 1775. My grandfather was the first of his family to come to Carolina, and was followed some years later by his brother, Dr. Ebenezer Hammond.

*   *   *   *   *   *   *   *   *

You are right in saying my father was James H. Hammond.

Very truly yours,

HARRY HAMMOND.

FROG LEVEL.

The following was contributed by Mr. U. B. Whites:

"Name uncouth—name seemingly without meaning. It is impossible to trace the name or its meaning to any satisfactory origin. There is a tradition, however, which says that the place received the name of Frog Level long before there was any settlement made at the place. As late as 1830 there was a pond of water where the Prosperity ginnery now stands, near the depot on the C., N. & L. R. R. This pond was infested with innumerable frogs, the surrounding surface being quite level. The legend says that an old man became intoxicated, and lay down at the edge of this pond and went to sleep. He awoke, and, still being stupefied by whisksy, the frogs were croaking, and in this dazed condition he imagined the frogs were crying out 'frog level!' frog level!' and he repeated it, and from this incident the pond or place was called Frog Level, which name as a place and a postoffice it retained until the year 1873, when, by a petition of a majority of its citizens, the Legislature changed the name to Prosperity.

"The first building erected at Frog Level was built by Capt. Matthew Hall, about 1830. He built a small dwelling and a little log store I2x16 feet. In this first store the half pints and pints were the principal articles of merchandise. Major Graham built the next house, and used a part of the lumber which was in Captain Hall's house. This dwelling is still standing, a monument to the olden times, and is occupied by William A. Moseley.

"Soon after Captain Hall built his store, David Kibler opened a store near his house, on the site where A. M. Wyse now has a beautiful residence. About this time Charles Stewart, a school teacher, came to Frog Level and taught school successfully. Unfortunately the poor fellow was addicted to strong drink and soon fell a victim to its influence. Samuel Moore, William Bridges, Henckle, Mower, Wicker, L. C. Kibler and others followed in the mercantile business.

"Like Stoney Batter, Frog Level was noted for its games of 'long bullets' and shooting matches in its early days. As a place for whiskey drinking it had always occupied a position in the front rank, from the time Captain Hall built the first store, about 1830, until in the year 1881, when, at the request of a large majority of its citizens, the Legislature passed a bill prohibiting the sale of all alcoholic liquors in any shape or form whatever.

"On the night of July 5th, 1873, the entire business portion of the town, except one store—that of H. S. Boozer & Co.— was destroyed by fire. On account of some disagreement of the property holders, concerning the laying off of certain streets, the town was not rebuilt on the old site. 'New Town' sprung up near by, which consisted of eight or ten stores. This state of affairs lasted nearly ten years, when the merchants began to rebuild substantial business houses on the old site; and now there are six large brick stores and a number of wooden ones on the old site.

"Prosperity, as its name indicates, is a prosperous and growing town, with a good, staunch, Christian citizenship. There are situated here four churches—Lutheran, Associate Reformed Presbyterian, Methodist and Baptist—with two Methodist and one Baptist Church for the colored people. There are also two steam ginneries, one fruit and vegetable canning factory, one flouring and grist mill, one high school, two blacksmith and wheelright shops and one brick manufacturing company; also one investment and improvement company and one bank. These things have taken the place of 'long bullets,' shooting matches and bar-rooms."

CHAPPELLS AND UPPER NEWBERRY.

About the year 1756 the Chappells came into the upper part of Newberry and settled on the north side of Saluda, while the Culbreaths, who came with them, or about the same time, crossed the river and settled on the south side. It is said that the Chappells were also Scotch, or of Scotch descent; but from the name I would rather suppose them to be French.

In my younger days I was well acquainted with Mr. John Chappell, grandfather of John Henry and John W., who have both made their homes at Newberry for a number of years. Mr. Chappell owned the ferry on Saluda known as Chappell's Ferry. I think it has been Chappell's Ferry ever since it was

established as a ferry by any name. Mr. Chappell carried on
mercantile business for many years and made money, and
became quite wealthy. The ferry itself was worth considerable
in those days. Hamburg was a great place of trade, and
Chappell's Ferry was on one of the great leading highways
from Laurens and the up country to that cotton market, which
was for a great many years one of the best in the State.

Old Mr. John Chappell had one brother only, and he was
killed by Cunningham in his celebrated raid of 1781; and
the ferry was kept during the Revolutionary war by John
Chappell's mother, she herself acting as ferryman.

Efforts have been made to make Chappell's Depot, on the
G. & C. R. R., a place of business, but with only moderate
success. There are some stores there and considerable business
is done. On the 19th of February, 1884, the great cyclone
or tornado struck it and swept the whole concern away.
Some persons were killed and others very seriously injured.
Mr. Wash Boazman was very badly broken up and it was
many weeks before he was able to walk at all; and at this
time, 1892, though eight years have passed since the storm,
he is still unable to walk without the assistance of a crutch.

Leaving the river and passing out from Chappells a few
miles brings us to the place once owned and occupied by Mr.
Foster Wells, one of the old settled places before the days of
the Revolution. Further on we come to Vaughanville, where
lived, when this writer first knew the place, Drury Vaughan,
who was then an old gentleman and was quite wealthy.
From him my old friend and schoolmate, Drury V. Scurry,
got his name—Drury Vaughan Scurry. He died several
years ago, and his son-in-law, Mr. Joseph G. Jenkins, now
lives at the old homestead, and in addition to his farm
conducts a mercantile business. Spring Grove Meeting
House was not far away and above Vaughanville, but that, I
believe, is in Laurens County. It was through this country
that General Greene, in his retreat from Ninety-Six, passed,
crossing at the Island Ford. It was at Williams' Fort on
Mudlick that Cunningham was stationed, and from which he
hastily decamped when he heard of the defeat and rout of
the tories at Stoney Batter by Colonel Washington. All that
upper part of Newberry adjoining Laurens was near the home

of the Cunninghams and Williamses—one taking the tory and
the other the whig side. Not far from the upper Newberry
line was Hayes' Station, the scene of Bloody Bill's most bloody
triumphs. Since those old bloody days no hostile foot has
ever tramped upon Mudlick, or Little River, or any other of
the streams that flow downwards to the sea, giving fertility
to the soil. Though no hostile armies have ever marched
through there, yet, in the late unpleasantness from 1861 to
1865, many gallant men turned out from that section of
country and gave their lives for the Confederate cause.
Their names are all recorded elsewhere in this book and
need not be repeated here.

I used to know an old gentleman, and a very worthy man
he was, who lived near the Laurens line, named Ephraim
Andrews. I had the pleasure of passing one night at his
house many years ago when I was young. He was then old,
or seemed so to me, had married a second wife and had several children, merry little fellows, running and playing about
whom he threatened dreadfully, but whom he never hit,
though he had a switch in his hand the whole time. He was
a good man and they were good boys and understood each
other.

Moon's Meeting House, mentioned in the notice of Rev.
William Harmon, is not far, or was not far, from Chappells.
When this writer first knew that country that house was
standing and was used as a place of worship. In fact I
think I once attended divine service in that house. By the
way, writing of Moon's Meeting House makes me think of it.
It is said that a house—a dwelling house—not far away is
haunted, and has been haunted, by something uncanny for a
great many years; whether ghosts or spirits of the departed,
or what, this deponent saith not. I have heard of other
houses in the same fix. In fact I went to see and investigate
a house in Edgefield County once, but I made nothing by it,
though the ghost was about.

John Hopkins Williams and the Rudds lived not far from
Chappells and were all men of wealth. Indeed all the upper
part of the county from the Saluda to the Rich Hill place,
lately owned by Mr. F. H. Dominick, was once in the early
days of the county and until the war of Secession one of the

fairest, richest and loveliest parts of the county, or of the State, or of the world.

Chappell's Ferry is now owned by Mr. William R. Smith, son of an old acquaintance and schoolmate of this historian, at the celebrated school at Mount Enon in Edgefield County. It was Mr. Smith's mother who was there, not his father. I knew his father also, but after his marriage. Miss Cornelia Boazman, now Mrs. Irwin, was a lovely and intelligent girl, amiable and good; and was born and reared near Chappell's Ferry. Her brother, John B. Boazman, it has been told to me, was one of the best men in Newberry County. Their mother was a Scurry.

I have recently been informed, and the information is authentic, that Mr. Smith, the owner of Chappell's Ferry, has given it with all its rights and hereditaments as his contribution towards the erection of a free bridge at Chappells over the river.

In the neighborhood of Chappells once lived Mr. William Watkins, John Watkins, Dr. J. O. Dickert and Andrew Lee Lark, all good and true men. Mr. George T. Reid, merchant at the Depot, now owns a great deal of land in that section —several thousand acres—amongst others land once owned by Mr. Lark and that of Capt. James N. Lipscomb.

Like the changes in a dream we come and go. We lie down to sleep, but the work goes on forever, forever, forever, forever.

WHITMIRES.

Continuing our route along the Laurens and Newberry line, we come after awhile to the new and flourishing town of Whitmires, which takes its name from the old and respectable family of Whitmires, which was amongst the earliest settlers of that part of the county; that is to say, one hundred and twenty-five to a hundred and fifty years ago. Whitmires is on the Georgia, Carolina and Northern Road, and is a flourishing business place with eight or ten stores (the first store was opened by Spearman & Tidmarsh, November, 1890), a school and divine service twice each month. As yet there is no church building, but I am assured that there soon will be.

2   N

In August, 1890, the Georgia, Carolina and Northern Railroad was completed through this section, thus giving it connection with the great world North and South and West. The town is about central between Newberry, Clinton and Union, being about eighteen miles from each.

About six miles from Whitmires, in the direction towards Newberry, lives the Hon. John W. Scott, on the same lands which his grandfather settled when he came from Ireland about one hundred years ago. How many of us can say that we live upon and own the lands upon which our fathers settled when they came to Carolina from the old world, or across the country from the colonies of Virginia and Pennsylvania?

During the unpleasantness of from 1860 to 1865, Whitmires, and the neighborhood, was not backward in duty and in furnishing the full quota of men required in the country's defence. Their names are all recorded elsewhere in this book. And it would give this writer great pleasure to make note of any special acts of heroism or daring performed by any one. But when every Confederate soldier, from the very fact of his being a Confederate soldier, was expected to be without fear, it becomes very difficult to find one who was the bravest of the brave.

The country above Beth Eden is broken and rolling, but the soil is fertile and productive, and there is no reason why the inhabitants of that part of the county should not be prosperous and happy, as, indeed, I am well assured that the most of them are. How is it possible for people to be otherwise who are blessed with a genial climate and fertile soil, and who are God-fearing and religious?

The town was incorporated in 1891, and the sale of intoxicants as beverages was prohibited by the Act of Incorporation. The first City Council was composed of John P. Fant, Mayor; Aldermen: H. E. Todd, Dr. R. R. Jeter, Charles Tidmarsh and B. F. Morrow. The first election was held in January, 1892.

MAYBINTON.

By reference to the first part of this work—pages 150-5 it will be seen that this place, one of considerable importance in the county for many years, derived its name from Colonel Benjamin Maybin, son of William Maybin, who settled there soon after the year 1771. Col. Benjamin Maybin was born in 1775. William Maybin, the settler of 1771, left three sons, Robert, Jesse and Benjamin—the Col. Benjamin from whom Maybinton derives its name. Jesse, the father of A. G. Maybin, served on the staff of General Jackson at the battle of New Orleans.

Maybinton for many years was a lovely little village, where refined and intelligent people made their homes, and which was surrounded by a fruitful and well cultivated country. Being the centre of a rich and flourishing section, with good schools, and somewhat remote from the County Seat, it became the Capital to the surrounding country, and often public meetings were held there to take into consideration important affairs, such as pertained to the State at large. P. C. Caldwell received his nomination for Congress by a convention held there in 1840.

The writer did not know Col. Benjamin Maybin, so enthusiastically mentioned and written of by Judge O'Neall; but for many years he knew and honored A. G. Maybin—son of Jesse and grandson of Colonel Benjamin—commonly known as "Bert," as a man of sterling integrity and worth. Bert Maybin was born and reared at Maybinton, where he lived until after the war of Secession, when he moved to Newberry and engaged in mercantile business with Col. Robert Moorman until the death of Colonel Moorman caused a cessation of the business. At the time of Mr. Maybin's death, and for some time before, he was engaged in superintending and conducting a Dairy Farm at Newberry, now owned and managed by Silas J. Mc-Caughrin.

The situation of Maybinton was one well adapted to make it a place of great local importance—on Broad River between the Enoree and Tyger. By way of Broad River, which was navigable for flat boats, the inhabitants could send, and did send, large quantities of cotton and other produce to the markets below. I have seen such boats on the bosom of Broad River. A flat boat loaded with cotton moving down the river would be a rare and novel sight now, with a train of rail cars speeding up or down on the north bank.

Since O'Neall wrote his Annals, and especially since the war, great changes have taken place at Maybinton, as in other parts of the county. The parts of the county which were richest, when the old system of labor was destroyed, suffered most. Maybinton section did not entirely escape, though there is still a considerable degree of prosperity, and the people are slowly but surely recuperating. There, as well as everywhere else, we find that there is life in the old land yet. Maybinton is near the birthplace and early home of the celebrated Emily Geiger.

POMARIA.

Continuing our circuit review of the county I conclude with a brief sketch of Pomaria and of its people. The Pomaria Postoffice in the Southeastern part of the county was established about the year 1840. The name was given by Mr. William Summer, the founder and proprietor of the Pomaria Nurseries, which were so long and so favorably known throughout the country. Mr. Summer, if I mistake not, was the first Postmaster. About the year 1850 the Postoffice was moved to where the present town of Pomaria now is on the completion of the Greenville and Columbia Railroad to that point. William Summer was Postmaster and Thomas W. Holloway (who is, in 1892, P. M.) Assistant.

J. A. Folk & Sons did a large business as merchants at Pomaria until the year 1855, when they were succeeded by Thomas W. Holloway and his brother-in-law, H. H. Folk, who continued until Secession and the war.

After the war Thomas W. Holloway and Hayne D. Reid formed a copartnership and carried on a large and lucrative business, until the murder of Reid and the burning of the house with the body of the murdered man in it by the assassin, Thompson, on the 24th of December, 1875. Thompson confessed the crime and was hanged. The burning of the house and the goods in it entailed a heavy loss upon the firm.

The next mercantile house established at this place was that of D. A. Dickert and David Hipp. They were succeeded by D. Hipp & Co. E. R. Hipp, now (1892) of Columbia, represented the company. Upon the dissolution of this firm Mr.

Wm. T. Hatton took the place of E. R. Hipp, and the firm name, D. Hipp & Co., still stands.

A store house was built by Thomas W. Holloway and his son, J. B. O'Neall Holloway, in 1878, and they carried on the mercantile business together until the fall of 1889, when the stock of goods on hand was sold to E. R. Hipp, son-in-law of the senior member of the firm. The junior member, having married in Orangeburg, moved to that county, near Fort Motte, and engaged in farming.

Mr. Hipp continued the business until the 14th of January, 1891, when the store was burned with a large stock of goods, entailing a heavy loss on Mr. Hipp.

J. William Stone in 1889 built a store house in the town and was carrying on business there, when his house and goods were burned at the same time.

Among the earliest settlers of Pomaria and the neighborhood was the family of Summer. John Adam Summer—I think is the name—came across the country from Pennsylvania. The country traveled by him was then almost an unbroken wilderness peopled by several different tribes of Indians. Wherever he went, whatever tribe or family of natives he met with, he always received the heartiest and warmest welcome. And when he reached his destination, the natives there were waiting for him, extended him a friendly greeting and made him feel at home. Rumors of kindness he had shown to some Indians in Pennsylvania preceded him, and runners were sent on ahead to tell the tale and to give notice of his coming.

John Summer was the father of John, Nicholas, Henry, Adam, William, Thomas and Miss Catharine P. These are all gone, except Miss Catharine. John and Nicholas I never knew. Nicholas was killed in the Seminole war in Florida; John went down there to bring the body home and he took sick and died in Florida without being able to accomplish his mission. Elsewhere in this book an interesting anecdote is related of Dr. King and Nicholas Summer. Henry was a lawyer at Newberry whom everybody knew and respected. Towards the close of the war of Secession, Kilpatrick raiders burnt his home in the lower part of the county, with his valuable library, and hung him up by the neck to the limb of a tree in the effort to make him tell where he had his money concealed, of which they imagined he had an immense amount. He had none concealed and they at length released him. Adam was a man of great and versatile genius. He left one child, who lives in Florida. William never married, but might be called the father of Pomaria and the Pomaria Nurseries. Henry Summer left three children, only two of whom were alive in 1892, his son John Adam, and daughter Catherine, who is happily married to Rev. J. F. Kiser, a Lutheran minister. John Adam owns the homestead of his grandfather, John Summer. The other daughter of Henry Summer, Mary, married Dr. J. K. Chapman. At her death she left three children, one daughter and two sons. Thomas Summer, the youngest brother of Henry Summer, I knew for awhile in his youth. He died early. He was a student, I think, in some German university.

The late John A. Folk owned the land upon which the town of Pomaria was built. He died in 1855, leaving three sons and two daughters, J. D. A., Dr. H. M., H. H., Martha, the wife of Thomas W. Holloway, and Eustatia, half-sister of the above, who was married to John David Wedeman, who died leaving two sons.

Solomon Suber, who resided where Dr. J. A. Berly afterwards lived, left four children, John W., who moved to Florida after the war, where he has since died; Major Christian H. Suber, also now deceased, a lawyer at Newberry, who was so long and so favorably known socially, not only in his native county, but also throughout this State, and I may justly add, the United States, at least in many others besides his own. Christian Suber was a man of more than ordinary ability; of mild and amiable deportment and averse to strife. He gave by will three thousand dollars for benevolent purposes—two thousand dollars to Newberry College and one thousand for the purpose of assisting in rebuilding the Lutheran Church at Newberry. He had two sisters; Ann C., who was married to the late Walter F. Ruff—they both died before the war, leaving no children. The other sister, Lavinia C., was first married to George Ruff, who died before the war, leaving one son, John S.; since the war she has become the wife of George Burder Boozer and they make their home in the town of Newberry.

John Folk, the original of the family of that name, resided a short distance from the site of the town on Tanner's Hill, known to wagoners prior to 1850 as Folk's Hill. It has been said that when wagoners left home with wagons loaded with cotton or tobacco for market in Charleston if they succeeded in getting up Folk's Hill they would have no more trouble. Mr. Folk left two children by his first marriage, John A. and a daughter who became the wife of David Cannon and the mother of John A. Cannon. By a second marriage there were five children who grew to maturity: John Wesley, David and Levi E.—daughters Elizabeth Graham and Eve Busby, mother of Prof. D. B. and Rev. L. E. Busby, one a teacher of youth and the other a Lutheran minister.

Dr. John A. Berly, who owned and lived and died at the Solomon Suber place, as already mentioned, left two sons, John Eusebius and W. W. Berly. John Eusebius died unmarried. He was a young man honored and respected by all who knew him; of great ability, and preached the gospel with great power and effect. Those who knew him from his infancy speak of him as having been blameless in all respects. After his graduation from Newberry College in June, 1879, he read medicine and practiced for awhile, a year or two, after taking his degree, when he became deeply impressed with the feeling that it was his duty to devote himself and his life to preaching the gospel. He accordingly prepared himself for that work, studied in the Theological Seminary in Philadelphia and graduated with distinction. He was called to the ninth pastorate of the Lutheran Synod in the Fork, in which charge he continued until his death on the 19th of July, 1890.

W. W. Berly is the owner of the old homestead and is giving his undivided attention to the fine farm which he inherited.

Dr. John A. Berly, the father of these young men, was a kind and obliging neighbor. He was assiduous in the practice of his profession for more than forty years. No man was more charitable, kind and attentive, going at all hours, and often to a great distance, to give relief to suffering humanity, when he knew that he would receive no pecuniary recompense for his labor. He was always ready and willing to assist with his means all benevolent and charitable objects. His place it will be difficult to fill. He never used tobacco, nor alcoholic drinks, because he knew from the study of physiology and from observation the evil effects resulting from their use.

Christian Suber was another of the old landmarks and resided within a half-mile of the site of the present town of Pomaria, long before the Railroad was built. He was engaged in the mercantile business and farming. Mr. Suber accumulated a fortune; he grew rich and earned and secured the reward due to his wonderful energy and perseverance. His wife was Caroline Counts, daughter of Jacob Counts. Three sons and one daughter survived him, viz.: John D., George Benedict, J. Benson and Isabella Eleazer, who was first married to Philander Cromer, who was killed in battle during the war of Secession. Rebecca, the eldest of the children, married James A. Welch, and by this union two sons and two daughters survive. One of these is Professor C. W. Welch, who has filled various professional chairs and has recently been elected Professor of Physics in Clemson College.

Thomas W. Holloway is still living as I compile these Annals. In the building of the Greenville and Columbia Railroad he was appointed Agent at Hope Station, Pomaria, Prosperity and Newberry, successively, as the Road advanced. While Agent at Newberry he was elected Cashier of the Bank of Newberry, which position he held until 1855, when he resigned and removed to Pomaria and engaged in the mercantile business. He was the Secretary of the State Grange of the Patrons of Husbandry for many years. He was also connected with the State Agricultural and Mechanical Society from 1857 to the breaking out of the war. The Society was reorganized after the war and he occupied the first position of the Society under the late D. Wyatt Aiken. In 1875 Col. Aiken declined re-election to the position of Secretary and Mr. Holloway was elected. He has been re-elected each succeeding year to the present, 1892.

—

POSTSCRIPT.

The compiler of these Annals first saw Henry Summer just after his admission to the Bar, when he was about to start to Alabama to hunt a new home in a new region and practice his profession there. He and my father went to Alabama together, riding on horseback. Chambers County, Ala., had just been thrown open to settlers, the Indian titles to the lands having been extinguished, and the Indians themselves having nearly all been, removed further Westward.

My father had a mild attack of Western fever, went to Alabama, entered some Government land, which he afterwards sold without ever having moved to it. On the outset of the trip, according to previous arrangement, Mr. Summer came to my father's house, remained all night with him and they set out next day together on a horseback journey of several hundred miles. Mr. Summer found a suitable location at Talladega, Ala., where he remained until the death of his brother Nicholas (who was a lawyer at Newberry) in the Seminole war, when he returned to Newberry; his brother Nicholas having left him a valuable Law Library on that condition.

I have often heard my father tell one anecdote of their trip through Georgia. It was during the days of Nullification and the high tariff, when political excitement ran high, as I believe it always does in this country. One night their landlady, who was a woman of very decided opinions, and very decided in her manner of expressing them, caused my father to remark to her: "Madam, I perceive that you and your husband differ in your politics." "Yes, indeed," she said, "we differ in our politics and a good many other 'tics' besides."

SMOKEY TOWN.

The origin of this name is lost in the mists of antiquity, but the place itself is well known and lies in the Southern part of Stoney Batter Township and was originally settled by the Bankses, Snelgroves, Kinards and Mannings.

"Seventy years ago," says Esquire P. W. Counts, "Smokey Town was the worst place in Newberry District. John Kinard had a whiskey distillery which was a constant rendezvous for bacchanalian rowdyism. This lawlessness has been inherited in a few families and has come down to the present generation. It is only a few years since Smokey Town has been freed entirely from the curse of the midnight brawler and marauder.

"The Longs, Koons, Pughs, Garrets, Boozers, and many others, who compose a good, sturdy, staunch and quiet citizenry, reside in that section now. Instead of the 'still house,' those good people have Bethel Church, Baptist; Mount Olivet, Lutheran; and O'Neall Academy, named in honor of Judge O'Neall.

"Instead of repairing to the still house on Sunday the people go to their respective places of worship. Prayer meetings and songs of praise have killed off and stilled forever the sounds of midnight revelry and debauchery. Midnight is no longer rendered hideous by the yells and shouts of drunkenness; but the stars rise and set undisturbed by the songs of Bacchus. Smokey Town is no longer smoky. The name and place remain, but the smoke has departed."

Our old friend, Squire P. W. Counts, in a quiet, dreamy mood continued his reminiscences. It is pleasant at times to meet with one of these old patriarchs and listen to his talks of times and people long since become historical, or, perhaps, only occasionally mentioned by the faint and feeble voice of tradition. It makes one feel as though he were sitting and listening to the gossip of tradition on the shores of old romance:

"From a point at Calk's Ferry Road, about three miles South of Prosperity, where Fred Stockman now lives, begins the Ridge Road. This road leads by the Elmore place, and on to and beyond Schumpert's Mills. It was once known and recognized as the 'dead line' between the Dutch and Irish settlers. It was considered a high crime and misdemeanor for an Irishman or Dutchman to cross this dead line. South of this line lived the Dominicks, Boozers, Fellows (now Fellers), Bedenbaughs (formerly Peterbocks), Schumperts, Countses, Harmons and others, who composed the Dutch settlement. North of this line were the Youngs, Browns, McQueers, Hawkinses, Thompsons, Lindseys, Carmichaels, Capt. Matthew Hall and others, who composed the Irish settlement.

"A few examples will illustrate the strong feeling that existed, and how important they felt it was that each party should keep on its own side of the line: On one occasion one of the McQueers, Charlie Thompson and Nathan Young, of the Irish party, each bought a tract of land which lay South of the line in the Dutch settlement. As soon as they realized what they had done they sold out as speedily as possible and returned to their Irish brethren.

"Capt. Matthew Hall, a gay young Irishman, was casting about for a partner for life with some means, not less than a thousand dollars. Miss Polly Schumpert, a noble daughter of a Dutch sire, filled his bill, and by stealth he ventured across the dead line, secured his coveted prize and carried her away to live amongst the Irish. A wail of horror and indignation arose among those good Germans because 'Hall had cum und sthole avay dere Dudtch Bolly.'

"The climax of indignation was reached when George Dominick took vengeance upon the Irish by crossing the line and stealing away Miss Sallie Hunter and making her his Irish-Dutch wife. From this marriage we have to-day a large number of auburn-haired Dominicks, who are most excellent citizens.

"After the excitement and feeling caused by these raids had subsided it was found that the force of the dead line was materially weakened, and a better feeling between the Irish and Dutch began to prevail. They married and intermarried, and exchanged business relations with each other, until now as a result of these marriages we have a Dutch-Irish and an Irish-Dutch citizenry, which, for honesty of purpose, hardihood, thrift, economy and perseverance, has no superior, if equal, anywhere.

"The dead line is where it was seventy-five years ago, but *that* name is no longer applied to it; *now* it is only known by the appropriate name of the Ridge Road."

The Squire sat still, and, musing awhile, looked as though he saw many things yet in the past. After a little he raised his head and looking at us with his kindly eyes, said: "Yes, I could tell you much more; but is not this enough for Smokey Town? The people are now industrious, thrifty and happy, and I feel that God's blessing is on them."

VIII.

THE PHYSICIANS OF THE COUNTY.

"The physicians of Newberry village," says Judge O'Neall in his Annals, "deserve a more thorough knowledge to portray their skill and character than I possess. Of the living, Drs. Thompson, Ruff, Long, Harrington, Caldwell, Pratt and James, I may not speak; they must speak for themselves in their lives and conversations. But of the dead, Drs. Waldo, Adams, Shell, Dobson, and the absent, Drs. Johnstone, Mendenhall and Benjamin Waldo, I may venture to speak." Soon after this was written, and before it was printed, Dr. Mendenhall died—Tuesday evening, the 2nd of November, 1852.

Following the example of Judge O'Neall, I propose to write briefly of the physicians of Newberry, relying upon notes and memoranda given me by one of themselves, who has long and deservedly filled a high place in the minds and the affections of the profession and of the people.

Drs. Thompson, Long, Harrington, Caldwell, Pratt and Ruff are all gone. Of Dr. Long's descendants, if there are any, I know nothing. One son of Dr. Thompson read medicine, and after having practiced his profession for many years at Silver Street, in Newberry County, removed to Florida, where he is now living. One son, Willie, married, and died after a few years' married life, leaving one child, a fine, intelligent boy. Drs. Pratt and James were, for some years, in partnership in the drug business before the war. After the war Dr. Pratt continued the business alone. He was a cripple, and his infirmities grew upon him so that for a long time before his death he was unable to walk. Caldwell and James both left Newberry. James went to Walhalla and Caldwell to Greenville. A notice of Dr. Harrington will be found elsewhere.

Dr. P. B. Ruff was born on a Christmas eve, 1801, while his father's friends and neighbors, as was the custom in those days, were firing Christmas guns around, about and under the house. God sent him as a Christmas gift to his father and mother. The hope that his long and useful life would round the century and that he would pass away and rise to a better world on a Christmas eve was almost realized, in that he reached his ninetieth year, dying December 28th, 1890.

Drs. Caldwell and James, mentioned above, started the first drug store that was ever opened at Newberry.

Dr. Meredith Moon and his son, Dr. Peter Moon, are both mentioned in O'Neall's Annals, but to what is there stated my friend, Dr. O. B. Mayer, Sr., adds the following: "Dr. Meredith Moon came to this country from Scotland about the year 1790. He was looked upon as a man of high education. His field of practice was extremely large, extending as far as sixty miles from his home, which was in the neighborhood of Chappell's Ferry. He became a Methodist preacher and practiced medicine, and when he had time made appointments to preach. It is recollected by many yet living how his language was tinged with the Scotch brogue. He lived to be a very old man."

Dr. Peter Moon was the son of Dr. Meredith Moon. His education was good. It is not remembered where he graduated in medicine. He practiced his profession only a few years, when he married and turned his attention to planting, at which occupation he succeeded admirably, becoming a very wealthy man. He died very suddenly at the age of eighty-two years.

Dr. William Moon was a younger brother of Dr. Peter Moon. He did not live long enough to achieve much reputation as a physician.

To the notice of the elder Dr. Waldo, Dr. Mayer adds the following: "Dr. Joseph Waldo came to Newberry County in the year 1799, and practiced medicine in the upper part of what was known as the Dutch Fork. After remaining several years in that part of the county practicing his profession he went to Charleston, S. C., where he remained a few years, and then came to Newberry village, about the year 1810, and bought the house known for a long time as the Graham house, now (1892) in the possession of Mr. J. F. Todd and in which he resides. Dr. Waldo was regarded as the ablest physician in Newberry as long as he remained there. He was a man of violent temper, very opinionated, and, being possessed of powerful muscular strength, he not infrequently employed it to bring his patients, especially the negroes, into obedience to his prescriptions. He *sometimes*, *not* frequently, indulged in drinking sprees, during which, it is well known, he would attend no patient, obstinately refusing all calls until he became sober. After practicing medicine in Newberry village he bought a farm in Edgefield County, just across Saluda River, and married Mrs. Smith, a widow lady of that neighborhood. Two children were the fruit of this marriage, Benjamin and Sarah (Judge O'Neall says Elizabeth). In the year 1829 he went to Connecticut, but after the death of his wife he returned to Newberry, and, having remained a short time, took his children to his native place at the North, where he died.

"Contemporaneous and in copartnership with Dr. Waldo was Dr. Thomas Shell—Big Tom. He was a very large man, hence his familiar nickname of Big Tom. He was a very worthy man and largely gained the confidence of the people. As is the case with all fat men, he was a famous humorist. His only fault, a common one in those days, was a too ungovernable fondness for drinking.

"Drs. James Shell and Thomas Shell—Little Tom—were relatives of Dr. Thomas Shell, Big Tom. They located in Newberry village about the year 1820, but they never gained much hold upon the esteem of the people. They moved Westward, and, swallowed up in the Great West, little is known in regard to them."

"Dr. Burr Johnstone," says Dr. Mayer, "came to Newberry village from Fairfield County about the year 1813. He was first cousin of the late Chancellor Job Johnstone. After practicing medicine a short time in Newberry he married a Miss Foote, in Fairfield. An epidemic of typhoid pneumonia prevailed in Newberry and adjoining counties (districts), and Dr. Johnstone was brought into a very large and laborious practice, in which he gained the warm affections of the people everywhere for his kind-heartedness, his self-sacrificing attention to the sick, and his philosophic consideration of disease. He at once took his stand against the use of the lancet in the management of the terrible scourge that afflicted the country. While his brother physicians, under the leadership of the obstinate Waldo, thrust the lancet into the arms of every patient affected with the typhoid pneumonia, Johnstone, often with tears in his eyes, opposed the practice as altogether unreasonable. As it may be well supposed in this enlightened age, a better success followed the withdrawal of the lancet.

"Dr. Johnstone sold his possessions in Newberry in 1841, and moved to Tuskegee, Alabama. He lost his eyesight not long after his removal. He died in 1851."

Soon after his marriage in 1818 he bought from Mr. Y. J. Harrington his plantation, on which there was a new house which Mr. Harrington had just built for his own use but had not moved into. It stood where now stands the large brick house owned and occupied by Judge Y. J. Pope. The house was a moderate-sized two-story building, and some years after it came into the possession of Colonel Simeon Fair, he, wishing to build a larger and more commodious structure, moved it some three or four hundred yards out onto the street, raised it off the ground and built a story of brick underneath, so that the house is now a three-story building. Dr. Johnstone lived in it almost continuously until the year 1841, when he removed to Alabama. The house is now owned and occupied by J. W. Chapman and family. The upper, or wooden, part of the building is seventy-one years old; the lower brick story is about half that age.

Dr. John Foote Johnstone, a son of Dr. Burr Johnstone, was born at Newberry, S. C., May 10th, 1821. In the way of education he received all the advantages that Newberry then afforded, and his education was completed at the celebrated school of Dr. Waddell at Willington, Abbeville County. After a short illness he died on the evening of the 6th of June, 1892. He graduated from the South Carolina Medical College in 1848, and went to Montgomery, Ala., in 1849, to begin his life work. At that place he lived and labored for forty-three years, and passed away at the ripe age of 71 years.

"The father of Dr. John Long was Bartly (Bartholomew) Long, who lived about four miles below Prosperity. Dr. Long was a man of limited education, but by dint of hard study managed to become well informed in the profession of medicine. He obtained the confidence of the citizens of Newberry and for several years, from 1840 to 1860, enjoyed a large patronage. He went West a short time before the late war, and it is not known at this time whether or not he is still living.

"Dr. Benjamin Waldo was the son of Dr. Joseph Waldo. He was regarded by the people of Newberry as a very accomplished physician. He practiced his profession in the town of Newberry about nine years, from 1838 to 1847. He married Miss Lipscomb, of Edgefield, and after serving Newberry District one year in the Legislature he moved to Florida before his term expired. His health became very much impaired after his removal to Florida. He died at St. Augustine in the year 1880.

"Dr. Daniel Dobson came to Newberry as a school teacher from Alabama, where he had been engaged in the same occupation. He soon satisfied the people that he was a man of uncommon talents and attainments. While teaching school in 1843 he began reading medicine under the instruction of Dr. Benjamin Waldo. He began the practice of medicine about the year 1845; was engaged in it for two or three years, and went to Mexico for the purpose of bringing back the body of Lieutenant John Stewart, where he contracted the malignant diarrhea prevailing there, and died, not long after his return to Newberry, much lamented.

"Dr. —. Norris came from Union County somewhere about the year 1843–4. He left this part of the country, and has never since been heard of.

Dr. H. H. Toland was the son of John Toland, living about nine miles northwest from the town of Newberry. He attended lectures in Lexington, Kentucky. His ambition to distinguish himself in surgery was stimulated by the operations of Dudley for stone. Dr. Toland, as soon as he graduated, commenced the practice of his profession at Reeder's, nine miles north of Newberry C. H., and while in practice there performed the operation of lithotomy twice. After this he was advised and encouraged to go to the city of Paris, in France, where he remained a year, the year 1832, when the cholera was raging so fearfully in that city. He escaped the disease, and upon returning to this country selected the town of Newberry for the field of his labors; but he did not remain there long ere he removed to Columbia, S. C. There he entered into copartnership with Dr. Thomas H. Wells, and the history of his life after this belongs to that city. He finally removed to California, where he died some years ago (1885 or 1886). Success attended him there also."

The compiler of these Annals once saw Dr. Toland perform a not very difficult, but a very neat and delicate surgical operation. A negro child, a little girl belonging to my father, had a soft, spongy, fungus growth on the inside of her upper eyelid, completely covering the eye and turning the lid back. Our local physician, Dr. J. C. Ready, who, by the way, was unfit to perform the simplest surgical operation on account of unsteadiness of nerve, was unable to do anything in the case. Dr. Toland was sent for. After looking at the case he placed the child on her back, raised the eyelid with his left hand as far as he could, and, with a pair of fine, sharp scissors in his right, clipped the growth off at one snip and the work was done. One tiny jet of blood from a very small artery followed and that was all. The growth never returned.

"The general education of Dr. Jacob H. King was imperfect. He never graduated in a medical college, but was examined, after reading the usual course, by a committee of physicians, who readily gave him a license to practice medicine. He began to practice medicine in the town of Newberry in the year 1828, but was unfortunate. Some friends then gave him a new outfit and sent him to the Dutch Fork. His second field of labor was near Pomaria, where he gained the confidence of the people to a remarkable degree. He married while in that neighborhood a daughter of Henry Ruff, whose house of entertainment was so long and so favorably known many years ago. He removed to Newberry Court House about the year 1840, where he was elected to the Legislature and there delivered a most touching speech in regard to the drougth of 1845. It is impossible to follow him in his wanderings and callings. He finally drifted to Alabama where he died some years before the commencement of the war."

"Dr. Samuel Fair was the son of Mr. William Fair, a very worthy farmer living between Prosperity and the town of Newberry. He received the best education that could be obtained in those times at the country schools, working on the farm through the spring and summer and going to school after the crop was laid by. He read medicine with Dr. Burr Johnstone. He practiced his profession in the town of Newberry and surrounding country from 1830 to 1842, when he went to Europe. After his return he formed a copartnership

2 O

with Dr. Thomas H. Wells, of Columbia, to which city he removed, and where he suddenly died a short time after the war."

"Dr. Samuel Myrick graduated in Charleston in the year 1842 or 1843, practiced in the southeastern part of Newberry County, and died at the house of his brother-in-law, Dr. Thomas W. Thompson, in the town of Newberry, in the year 1849."

"Dr. Robert Campbell was the son of Dr. Campbell, of Laurens County. He practiced the profession of medicine in the upper part of Newberry County, between the years 1840 and 1846, and removed to Cross Hill, in Laurens County, where he died not very long ago. He will live long in the remembrance of the people for his kindheartedness and his steady moral and religious character."

"Dr. Williamson practiced medicine for several years in the neighborhood of Ashford's Ferry on Broad River, beginning about the year 1830. He left that part of the country and moved to the vicinity of Chappell's Depot. It is not remembered when he died."

"Dr. Watkins came to Newberry County about 1842 and located himself at the house of Mr. John Glymph, near Ashford's Ferry on Broad River. It is believed that he came from Camden. He was a young man of considerable address, but he did not remain long enough where he was located to establish a fair reputation in his profession. It is not remembered where he went from Mr. Glymph's. About, or near, the close of the war in 1865, he made his appearance with his wife, at the town of Newberry, as a refugee. They were both in broken down health. He left Newberry in 1866, returning to his former home. He has since died."

Drs. Ferguson, Worthington and Pitts all lived and practiced medicine, but at different periods of time, at or near the Dead Fall. Dr. Ferguson I remember as a rather good looking man but pale. He died young, leaving a son, John W. Ferguson, who became a successful lawyer at Laurens Court House. When the writer of this was quite a boy Dr. Ferguson was called to my father's family to see some one who was sick, and the thought occurred to me that doctors, whose business it was to cure the sick, should never die themselves. That idea was soon dissipated by a larger observation of events and of the world.

Dr. Benjamin Worthington I knew from my boyhood. He was a good man and a good physician. But he had one great weakness which detracted from his usefulness and success in life. Upright in all his dealings he had the respect and kindly regard of all who knew him. He was married but left no children.

Dr. Wylie K. D. Lindsey was also a practicing physician of Newberry, but I am entirely without data as to his career. except that for a time he practiced in partnership with Dr. Toland.

I must say the same of many others, good and worthy men, successful in their day and time, working faithfully and well and dying regretted by their friends and neighbors. In this connection I must mention Whipple, Stevenson, Hancock, Conwell, Lyles, Atwood, Finch, Todd, Chalmers, Hatton, Fant, Wicker, McKellar, Mayberry, Evans, Hodges, Eichelberger. Spearman, Herbert, Hall, Kilgore.

Dr. Elijah Gates I never knew, but from others I have learned that he was a man of fine attainments, a genius and a poet. He practiced medicine in the middle and lower part of the county, sometimes also appearing before the public as a Baptist preacher. He is said to have been a graceful and eloquent orator and I can well believe it.

Judge O'Neall in his Annals makes honorable mention of Drs. Finch and Todd and tells of Dr. Finch's tragic death. Drs. Hatton, Fant, Wicker, McKellar, Hodges, Eichelberger. Spearman, Herbert, Hall, Kilgore, were well known to most of the citizens of the town of Newberry. Dr. Hodges was the son of the Rev. N. W. Hodges, the great Baptist preacher, so useful and influential in his day. Dr. Hodges practiced medicine only about ten years and died in the prime of life a few years before the war.

Dr. Hatton, once quite well off, was ruined by the war and died in reduced circumstances. Dr. Fant was a druggist at Newberry for several years previous to his death. He was a sterling friend and an honest man. Eichelberger moved to Florida. Spearman practiced his profession in the neighborhood above Little River. Herbert, a son of old Squire Walter

Herbert, moved to Alabama long ago. I never saw him. Hall, son of my old friend Matthew Hall, died young, leaving a widow. Kilgore, the patriarch of Ebenezer Church, married a daughter of Col. John Summers, who bore him a fine household of children, sons and daughters, who married and did well, bearing always an honorable name. Mrs. Kilgore, the doctor's widow, was a sufferer from ill health for many years previous to her death. Her ill health did not make her peevish and fretful but seemed to have a refining and purifying influence, as her face was certainly one of the most saintly I ever saw. I have observed in other cases that suffering when patiently borne always refines and elevates the sufferer to a height of Christian excellence, perhaps not possible of attainment in any other way.

One whose name I may not mention here, for it is sacred, lived in almost continual pain for more than a year before she died, but murmured not; thinking always, even to the last, of the comfort of those about her. She was made perfect through suffering; and at last, when the hour of departure came, she passed away as calmly and quietly as a little child falling asleep listening to cradle melodies. Surely such a departure is almost enough to make one in love with death. And there are others I know now whose faces grow brighter as they approach the end. As if they caught the light from the sun rising on the other side.

That Dr. Elijah Gates, mentioned above, was a man of fine poetical genius is evidenced by a poem of his which I reproduce here. This is his only work that has been preserved, and this was never committed to writing by himself. It was composed and memorized and recited by the author to several friends, who were so much pleased with it, that they made copies from his recitation. The copy from which I copy was written, I think, by William Summer, Esq., of Pomaria, who knew the author well.

The poem is called

THE DOGWOOD—AN ODE TO HYMEN.

I saw the Oak, the forest's pride,
And the young Dogwood at his side,
Blooming like an Eastern bride.
How much she loved she never told,
For virgin young is not so bold;
But though her heart not yet she breathes

In words, she decks herself in wreathes
Of whitest flowers all gay and fair,
And spreads her sweetness to the air.
The Oak, the storms could never move,
Whose rugged arms had boxed with Jove,
Felt all the mighty power of love.

Next by her stood the cherry tree
And softly whispered "Marry me!"
"Marry thee," she blushed and said,
"I'll wed the Oak or never wed."
The cherry tree in haste replied:
"Too haughty then to be my bride!
Full often hast thou ta'en the cherry
From me and said "How sweet the berry!"
"As often hast thou kissed the flower
Of Dogwood washed by morning shower:
But shouldst thou wed my sylphy form,
Thou couldst not shelter from the storm,
Nor shade me when the burning sun
Pours down his rays meridian.
And when the axeman comes along,
Jovial with his morning song,
And lays this mighty forest low,
The cherry tree will make a show
In a toilette or bureau,
To be admired by girls and boys,
And hold their trinkets and their toys.
But the firm Oak a keel shall be
To some tall ship that rides the sea,
And ploughs the billows swift as wind,
And leaves a gulf of light behind,
Bearing the spirits of the brave
To send proud tyrants to their grave.
And sooner than thou shouldst unclasp
The sacred zone, I'd bind the asp
Both to my arm and to my heart,
And bid my virgin soul depart
To join the vestals who have given
Their spirits white as swans to heaven."
'Twas said; and quick a listening breeze
Came rustling through the leafy trees,
And softly kissed the Dogwood flower;
Loitering awhile around her bower;
Then into thinnest mits it spread,
And rose in vapor round the head
Of the tall Oak, and told the tale
Of her the monarch loved so well.
Iu sighs the Oak prefers his prayer
To Him, who rules Earth, Sea and Air:
"Almighty Jove! my passion crown,
And send propitious omens down!"
Thrice Jove thunders on the night.
And fills the heavens with dazzling light;
And next a silver shower he sheds,
And sets the bow above their heads;
Sure omens that immortal Jove
Will bless the happy pair in love.
The cedar bowed to them and said:
"This is the man and this the maid;
When hearts unite as well as hands
Great Jove approves the holy bands,
Crowning with bliss the wedded life;
And Love hath joined you, man and wife."

Incense arose from plant and flower,
Just washed by the refreshing shower,

And woods and winds, and waters round,
Poured forth their soft assenting sound;
And Orpheus did sing and play
To wild Nature's minstrelsey;
"How Hymen's rites were first from Jove,
And every thing below, above,
Was conquered by the power of Love."
Jove heard the soft subduing strain,
And hung his head and heard again:
And quick he laid his thunders by
And tuned the spheres to harmony.
Music can soothe the savage breast,
Or lay the thundering god to rest;
The sun that rode behind the cloud
Far in the West, shook off his shroud,
And stood to hear the Poet sing
The origin of every thing,
From the ivy on the wall
To Lebanon's cedars tall;
From the glow-worms spark at night
To his own transcendent light;
And from the smallest drop of rain
To the deep and rolling main.
But as the minstrel swept his lyre,
Every note ascending higher,
He kindled with celestial fire,
And rose from earth to things above,
And sang the UNCREATED LOVE,
That, brooding on the vast abyss,
Made pregnant all with life and bliss:
"The smallest insects o'er the earth
Owe to this Love their wondrous birth;
The purple myriads on the plum
Bask in its smiles and feast at home;
They first enjoy their short repast,
And man receives the plum at last,
That he may have as well as they,
His luscious fruit and festal day.
The spark that warms the mother's breast,
Whilst she sings her babe to rest,
And makes her press it to her heart,
And the streams of life impart,
Is not of earth but from above,
The Fount of Uncreated Love.
Man's love is partial to his friends,
And that too oft for selfish ends;
The Uncreated knows no bound,
Whate'r has life it circles round;
Hears the young ravens when they cry
For food, and sends a quick supply;
And in compassion moves to bless
The widow and the fatherless;
But most displays its sovereign power
To bless man in life's latest hour;
For when his glass of time is run,
Nor he expects another sun,
It sends him hope to cheer his gloom
And gild his passage to the tomb;
Nay, more, it bears him through the night
Of Death to upper worlds of light,

Where the weary pilgrims rest
From their labors and are blest;
Nor these alone, but Cherubim
Drink of this Love, and Sera•him."

The Poet ceased and echo still
Gave back the song from every hill,
Repeated by the babbling rill;
And as it floated on the breeze
The stones replied and bending trees;
From caverns deep and rocks around
To mountain tops rolled up the sound,
Then died away from mortal ears
And joined the music of the spheres,
And echoed through the realms above
In loudest pæans "God is Love."
The sun shook from his golden locks
Light that all other beauty mocks,
And smiling on the wedded pair
Sprinkled with gems their leafy hair;
Then quick he bade his charioteer
Down the Western steeps to steer,
And to hold the middle track,
Nor give the flowing rein too slack;
For though his steeds well knew the way
They bolted on a certain day,

When Phæton rashly took the reins
And lashed them o'er the azure plains.
The sun no sooner orders told,
Than quick on burning wheels he rolled,
And seemed a sea of liquid gold;
Still enlarging as he flew,
And deepening to a richer hue,
Until he reached the horizon,
Where his daily course was run,
And there his parting glories shed
And sank to sleep on Thetis' bed.

No candles now that smoke the wall,
Nor lamps that stench the lovers' hall;
The moon and all the stars appear
Hung o'er their heads a chandelier.
No golden goblets grace the board,
Such as are by fools adored,
And no such viands mar the feast
As turn immortal man a beast.
In leafy cups they drink the dew,
And quick their leafy cups renew,
And drink and revel all the night,
And quaff the dew till morning light.
For Hymen's rites were first from Jove;
And every thing below, above,
Is conquered by the power of Love.

I hope my readers will not complain of the foregoing as being too long. To me the lines seem very beautiful, and I feel that they ought to be preserved in a permanent form and handed down to posterity as worthy a place in the Annals of Newberry.

Not many years after the death of Dr. Worthington, or perhaps before, Dr. Pitts began the practice of medicine in the neighborhood of the Dead Fall, living just above. He, too, died young, passing away in the very prime of life.

Dr. Rutherford was a son of William Rutherford and grandson of Colonel Robert Rutherford, a memoir of whom is given by Judge O'Neall. He was a man of wealth, a successful farmer and planter, and, notwithstanding the disastrous results of the war, left a handsome property at his death. He died not long after the war. He was the father of Colonel William Drayton Rutherford of the Third S. C. Regiment.

I may be permitted to mention here that when Col. Robert Rutherford came to this county from North Carolina there came with him a widowed sister, Mrs. Boulware, who had some sons who were well grown young men. Mrs. Boulware, with her sons, did not stop and settle in Newberry, but passed across Saluda into Edgefield. A grandson, Humphrey Boulware, was for some years Sheriff of Edgefield District. Some of the family returned to Newberry or Laurens, and their descendants are still living in those counties. Judge O'Neall says that Colonel Rutherford made no profession of religion. In fact, the family were Episcopalians. Mrs. Boulware after her removal to Edgefield united with the Baptists, lived and died in that communion, and was buried at Red Bank Church, in Edgefield County.

Dr. O. B. Mayer, Sr., one of the best citizens that Newberry ever had; one of the most useful and unselfish men that ever lived in the county, left this world for a better on Thursday afternoon, July 16th, 1891, at half-past two o'clock. It is impossible for me to write of him as I should, or as he deserved. For many years he was an intimate friend and associate, and the very sight of his kind, genial and benevolent face kindled good and pure thoughts in my mind and caused my own face to glow with a better light.

Dr. Mayer was born near Pomaria on February 24th, 1818, and spent the days of his boyhood at his birthplace, to which he so often referred in his writings with filial devotion. He attended school at Lexington (after receiving the primary education at home), where he prepared himself for the South Carolina College, from which he graduated in 1837. After his graduation he read medicine and received the degree of M. D. from the Charleston Medical College. After practicing a few years in the Dutch Fork he went to Europe and attended some of the best European and German universities. He left Pomaria on the 25th of April, 1844. He spent three years in Europe (they were not idly spent), dividing his time between the universities of Edinburgh, Paris and Heidelberg. He returned to Pomaria in April, 1847. After two years' practice at that place he removed to Newberry, where he lived, honored and useful, for nearly forty-five years.

Dr. Mayer was married three times, first in 1839. His first wife was Miss Mary Davis, of Fairfield, but who at the time was living in Mississippi. She died in less than a year after the marriage. His second wife was Miss Carrie DeWalt, of Newberry, whom he married in 1851. She died in 1861, leaving one son and four daughters to a father's care. Later he married Mrs. Louisa Kinard, who survives him.

Dr. Mayer attained eminence in his profession, and was also distinguished as a writer. He contributed largely to the periodical press in early life, and continued to contribute occasionally to almost within a week of his death. His last work of this character was the revisal of the Dutch Fork Sketches for The Herald and News; and on the day before he was taken with his fatal sickness he finished these sketches. He left incomplete a work on which he was bestowing great pains and labor, entitled "Malladoce, the Britain; His Wanderings from Druidism to Christianity." This fragment has been published since his death in book form. Other stories and sketches fully equal, I think, to those which have been printed, remain in manuscript. His best printed stories are, perhaps, "The Voice, the Hand and the Silhouette," and "The Music Girl of the Rue de la Harpe." These appeared in Russell's Magazine, then published in Charleston, 1857. In "The Voice, the Hand and the Silhouette" he predicted the invention of the telephone.

Dr. Mayer was a skillful surgeon, and performed during his practice many difficult operations. He retired from active practice several years before his death.

Dr. Mayer did not seek the applause of men, or he could have obtained a world-wide distinction in his profession, and also in literature, in which he took great delight. He did not seek wealth, or he might have grown rich, as his practice was extensive. He lived to be of use. He was pure-hearted, honest, overflowing with generosity and kindness.

Dr. Mayer was a thorough English scholar, and spoke and wrote the German language. He was also a good French, Latin and Greek scholar and a good musician, and translated many German hymns into English and arranged appropriate music for them.

He was Professor of Physiology and Hygiene for many years in Newberry College, before its removal to Walhalla, in 1868, and after its return to Newberry.

Dr. Mayer was a truly religious man—one of the most faithful and devoted students of the Bible I have ever known; a firm believer in it as the Word of God, making it the rule of his life. He was a consistent member of the Lutheran Church, but not a bigot—an humble, pious, devoted Christian. His faith was childlike, taking God at His word, and relying upon His promises undoubtingly.

How can I write more of him than that I knew and loved him?

Four children survive him, Dr. O. B. Mayer, Jr., Mrs. Martin, of Laurens; Mrs. Connor, of Cokesbury, and Mrs. J. T. Mayes, of Newberry. Miss Alice Mayer died in December, 1884.

Dr. James A. Cofield was born in Union County, S. C., on the 25th of May, 1844, and died at Newberry, S. C., on the 3d of November, 1888, of aneurism of the innominate artery. After serving through the war as a brave and dutiful soldier, he studied medicine, and graduated at the South Carolina Medical College in 1874. For some years he practiced medicine very successfully in and around Maybinton. In 1884 he moved to Newberry, S. C., where he was actively engaged in the practice of his profession when he died. He was a pleasant, kind hearted man, and much loved by those who knew him.

Dr. David A. Cannon was a native of Newberry County, in which his life was spent. He died April 18th, 1890, leaving a widow, his second wife, who brought him one child. His first wife, who bore him several children, was the daughter of Isaac Herbert, Esq., and her sons and daughters are all grown, one daughter being the wife of Rev. M. M. Brabham, of the M. E. Church, South.

Dr. James A. Renwick, a descendant of the old Scotch Covenanters, than whom the world never produced a braver or more liberty-loving race, after a not very long but useful career as a physician and a man, died on the 13th of March, 1865. He was a brother of Col. John S. Renwick, and, like him, a consistent member of the Church of his fathers.

In the death of Dr. John K. Gary, says the Newberry *Herald* of April 7th, 1880, Newberry has lost one of her best citizens. He was born near where he lived and died. During his whole life of seventy-two years no blemish ever rested upon his name. Prompt to respond to the calls of duty; as a physician he was skillful, kind and successful. He waited upon the poor and humble with the same kindness and assiduity as upon the wealthy and refined. But physicians are usually the most benevolent of men. Seeing so much suffering they grow tender in feeling. Dr. Gary died in harness, laboring to the last to relieve others. While suffering

great pain from the disease which caused his own death, he
continued to visit his patients until Friday, the 26th, when he
made his last. On Saturday he was in Newberry, suffering
great pain, returned home, took to his bed and died Tuesday,
30th. His death occurred March 30th, 1880. He was buried
next day at Bush River Baptist Church, of which he had
long been a member. He left sons and daughters—Martin H., J. Wistar; D'Orsay L., dead; Rebecca, wife of John
Watts, of Laurens.

As a physician I knew nothing of Dr. Thomas B. Kennerly,
though I have no doubt that he was a good one, as he was a
man of good judgment and great intelligence and a most
genial and pleasant companion. He died on the 31st of
October, 1884, after two months' illness, of typhoid malaria,
in the 64th year of his age, and was buried at King's Creek
Church Cemetery on Saturday following. Dr. Kennerly was a
native of Lexington County, but had been living in Newberry
for a number of years. He left a large family to mourn
their loss. Two children, one son, James L., one daughter,
Lilla R., now, 1892, make their home at Newberry. The
daughter is the wife of Alan Johnstone, Esq. Edward lives
on the old homestead, as also does one daughter, Amelia K.
Samuel is in Texas making his home there.

Dr. Beaufort T. Yarbrough once practiced in Newberry
County. He was a native of Edgefield, born on Big Creek.
He was a man of fine intelligence and amiable nature. He
died 16th of April, 1880, at the house of his sister, Mrs.
Culbreath, mother of James Y. Culbreath, Esq., in Edgefield
County, near where he was born.

Drs. John A. and J. Eusebius Berly have both been mentioned
already in our notice of Pomaria; but as they were both
practicing physicians, we feel that they ought to occupy a
place in the group.

Dr. John A. Berly was truly a good man, and his death
was a loss to the community. He died on Sunday, 16th of
December, 1888, aged about 65 years. The date of his birth
I am not able to give.

John Eusebius, son of Dr. John A. Berly, died unmarried.
After leaving college he read and took his degree in medicine, but feeling it his duty to preach the gospel he prepared

himself for the ministry and was engaged in that work at the time of his death, July 19th, 1890.

Dr. David E. Ewart was the son of Mr. David Ewart, for many years a merchant in Columbia, and who conferred honor upon the calling. Dr. Ewart was born in Columbia, S. C., on April 9th, 1830; graduated from the Charleston Medical College March 15, 1851; went to Paris in 1853 to perfect his studies, and remained in that city until near the close of the year 1854. He married Miss Laura E. Graham, of Newberry, and was practicing medicine in that town when the War of Secession broke out. He was appointed Surgeon of the Third South Carolina Regiment, which position he held for some time, but finally resigned and was appointed Assistant Surgeon Confederate States Navy. He died of yellow fever on board the gunboat Chicora in the harbor of Charleston, S. C., September, 1864.

Dr. Thomas C. Brown was one of the most solid and useful citizens of Newberry County. He graduated at Erskine College, and having just completed a full course in medicine, he served in the Medical Department of the Confederate States of America with Dr. Ewart. After the close of the war he devoted himself with success to his large farming interest. In 1880 he was elected Senator from this county by a very flattering vote. The leading members of the Senate who survive him speak in the highest terms of his efficiency in that honorable position.

He had an attack of paralysis about five years before his death, but was not disqualified for the active duties of life. Dr. Brown was a ruling elder in the Mount Bethel Presbyterian Church. He died in the prime of life, on Friday, the 26th of June, 1891, and was buried at King's Creek Church on Saturday, a very large number of friends attending. Rev. E. P. McClintock, a college mate, and Rev. E. C. McClure, his pastor, conducted the funeral services.

Dr. Higgins, son of F. B. Higgins, Esq., lived and practiced medicine near Chappells in the upper part of the county. His success as a practitioner was good, and his good sense and judgment as a doctor were much esteemed and relied upon.

Of other physicians who have passed away I must mention Law, McCants, Chapman, S. Godfrey Kibler (died in 1865),

Lester, Sheppard, Weir, Enlow, Pearson, Payne, Hill, Sims. Speake, Vanlew, Douglas, Patton, Walker, Holmes, Parr, Bobo,

And I feel that I ought not to close this record of the physicians of Newberry without some notice of Dr. Geddings of Charleston, not mentioned, I think, in the first part of this work. Although his life was mainly passed in Charleston and the greater part of his life-work was there, yet he was a native of Newberry County, and Newberry has the right to enroll him in the list of her illustrious sons. Dr. Geddings was born near Chappell's Ferry, in the upper part of the county, of poor and obscure parentage; lived in early boyhood near the Gum Spring, a few miles from the village of Newberry, his mother having been driven by adverse circumstances to leave her home near Chappells. He was seen, adopted and educated by Maj. Fred. Gray, who lived long enough to know that his *protege* was a great man and one of the ablest surgeons of the world.

Dr. Calmes, toward the latter part of his life, and long after he had quit the practice of medicine, I used to meet often in the law office of my friend Henry Summer, where we held frequent discourse of Providence, fixed Fate, Free Will and kindred subjects. The science of Evolution had not been discovered in those days, or if it had been discovered, it had not begun to agitate the thinking world as it does now, or doubtless we would learnedly have held forth on that also. Dr. Calmes was a man of extensive reading and liberal education. I never knew him in his best days, but in the latter part of his life I found his conversation entertaining and stimulating. He was the son of William Calmes of Revolutionary fame, so honorably mentioned in the first part of this work.

Dr. George W. Garmany served the Confederacy, entered the ranks as private, was promoted to surgeon of the 62nd North Carolina Regiment, Colonel Love commanding; died December 20, 1890.

The other medical officers, surgeons and physicians from Newberry County who were in the Confederate service I also give here: Sampson Pope, surgeon 22nd Georgia Regiment and senior surgeon Sorrel's Georgia Brigade; now living at Newberry and practicing his profession.

R. C. Carlisle, surgeon 7th South Carolina Infantry; now living and practicing medicine in Newberry County.

James McIntosh, assistant surgeon C. S. A.; now living and practicing in Newberry, S. C.

Spencer G. Welch, assistant surgeon 13th South Carolina Infantry; living at Helena, near Newberry; not in practice.

Of those physicians who have passed away I have not yet mentioned Blackburn, Gilder, Jeter, Irby, White, Dickert, Jenkins, Bond. Of these doctors I know nothing, save the names as given to me, except Gilder, and by Gilder I mean Col. James K. Gilder, who, though not holding a diploma from any medical college, was as truly worthy of the title of Doctor as any physician who ever practiced medicine in the county. He made disease a study and he also made a study of the remedies for the various forms of disease. And besides, he was a man of great intelligence and uprightness of character. He kept a drugstore at his home in the upper part of the county, where he sold a great many medicines. He was a disciple of the Botanic system and never administered minerals in his practice.

IX.

BIOGRAPHICAL.

Thomas Bauskett.

Thomas Bauskett was the son of John Bauskett, of Orange County, N. C., and married a daughter of John O. Daniel, of the same county and State. He came to Newberry County about the year 1780. He served one term in the Legislature. After his wife's death he remained a widower for forty years, thus affording a rare instance of faithful and devoted attachment. He died leaving two children, John Bauskett and Ann.

John Bauskett became an eminent lawyer, well known to the people of Newberry, and, indeed, to the people of the whole State. Ann became the wife of James Wadlington.

The remains of Major Thomas Bauskett lie buried at the Baptist Church, in Newberry County, known as Bauskett's Church.

—

Thomas Wadlington.

Thomas Wadlington, Sr., was one of the original settlers of Newberry County. He came from Frederick County, Virginia, in 1767 and settled on Enoree River and was a large landed proprietor. He brought with him four sons, William, Thomas, James and Edward, and one daughter, Ann, who married Benjamin Hampton.

William was an officer in the Continental Army. He left a son, James Wadlington, who was Lieutenant-Colonel of the Fourth Regiment of Cavalry under Governor Bennett. He was a planter, and on the first day of June, 1820, married Miss Ann Bauskett, a daughter of Major Thomas Bauskett. James Wadlington died October 31st, 1831, and left one son, Thomas B. Wadlington, and one daughter, Caroline J. Wadlington.

Thomas B. Wadlington graduated in the South Carolina College in the class of 1842; read law with his uncle, Col. John Bauskett, and on the 23d of April, 1844, married Miss

Harriet Sondley in Columbia. His wife lived about one year after marriage and he remained a widower the rest of his life, living quietly on his plantation, where he accumulated a large property, most of which was swept away by the war. He died on the 10th of December, 1882, and his earthly remains rest in the family burial ground at Bauskett's Church by the side of his father. He was the last of his name in this county. Those who did not die here moved years ago to Mississippi and Texas. His sister, Caroline J., born in Newberry County November 19, 1831, became the wife of Col. Ellison S. Keitt, of Orangeburg District, January 25, 1853. They lived in Columbia, S. C., until her death, May 4, 1862. Five children were born of this union: Mary Genevieve, who died in infancy; Edward George, who graduated at Wofford College, read medicine and graduated at the College of Physicians and Surgeons in Baltimore, was elected by the faculty assistant surgeon in the hospital of the city of Baltimore where he remained seven months, resigning in consequence of impaired health. He practiced seven months in Newberry County, and died, a martyr to his profession, a loss to science, September 2, 1882. Harriet Ann, married Col. L. P. Miller, of Georgetown, and now lives in Newberry County on Enoree River. Joseph L., served one term in the House of Representatives from Newberry County. In 1890 he was elected State Senator. Thomas W., is a farmer and teacher, living in Newberry County at the old Wadlington place.

During the war between the States Col. Ellison S. Keitt raised and commanded Keitt's Mounted Riflemen and served in and around Charleston during the entire seige of that city —being the last Confederate officer who commanded Sullivan's Island and Mt. Pleasant. Since the war he has lived on his plantation on the Enoree River in Newberry County. He has served two terms as a Representative from Newberry in the State Legislature. The spelling of the family name was changed in 1812 from Kitts to Keitt, by the three sons, Adam, William and George, at the suggestion of William.

—

ANDREW TURNER,

Son of Mary Houston and William Turner, was born in Newberry District on the 25th of July, 1794. At the age of seventeen he enlisted under Captain Gillespie in the war of 1812. On returning from the war he was associated with his maternal uncle, William Houston, in merchandising at a place called "Houston." Near by stood, at that time, Gilder's Creek Church, Presbyterian. Now all is changed; only the cemetery marks the spot.

Some of the best families in the State lived in that section at that time, viz.: Parson Renwick, the Glasgows, the Wrights, the Dugans, descendants of an old Revolutionary family, the Tolands, Andersons and Boyds.

In 1829 William Houston removed with his family to Alabama. Andrew Turner continued to merchandise; and, at the same time, he superintended a small farm. In 1831 he married Maria Marian Dugan, third daughter of Elizabeth Lemon Wright and William Dugan. One child was born to them, Mary Elizabeth, named for her two grandmothers. In 1835 Andrew Turner removed to his residence, "Forest Hill," on Indian Creek, thirteen miles north of the town of Newberry.

In 1837 his wife died at the early age of twenty-four years, leaving an only child, to whom he devoted his long widowed life. He was a man of strong integrity, firm in his friendships, very fond of his home, and had the respect and confidence of all who knew him. He was a director of the Newberry Bank during the "times that tried men's souls."

Andrew Turner died the last year of the war at his residence, "Forest Hill," at the age of three-score and ten, on the 5th of October, 1864. He left an only child, Mary Elizabeth, who in 1853 married William Clement Gilliam, a member of an old Virginia family of English descent. Mr. Gilliam died shortly after their marriage, on August 9, 1854, much beloved by his neighbors, leaving an only son, William Clement, who is now a practicing physician in New York City.

—

Dr. Jacob F. Gilliam

and his wife, Mary Massey, were residents of Newberry District. They had three children to survive them: William Clement, Drucilla Ann and Pettis Wales.

Mary Massey was the only child of her parents. Her mother was a Miss Duncan and married Mr. Massey. They were both Virginians. Dr. Gilliam's mother was Miss Sims. He died in his forty-eighth year; his wife died soon afterwards in her forty-second year. Their daughter, Drucilla Ann, married. James B. Wilson, the only brother of six sisters. Their residence, "Ingleside," was six miles northeast of the town of Newberry. They had six children born unto them, three daughters and three sons. They were a most lovely, lovable and cultured family. In seven years the whole family died, father, mother and six children, from August, 1857, to October, 1864. The oldest was nineteen years old. The names of the children were Mary Rosalie; Sarah Caroline (after her aunt, Mrs. Wilson Caldwell,); William Clement (named for his uncle), killed on the 13th of October, 1864, in Virginia; Gilliam Sims, one of General Ripley's couriers, who died of yellow fever; Josephine Caldwell and Pettus Wales. They all sleep side by side in Tranquil Cemetery, not far from the old homestead, there to await the first resurrection.

PETTUS WALES GILLIAM

Married Harriet Caldwell Wilson, sister to James B. Wilson, both natives of Newberry; resided at "White Oak," seven miles north of the town of Newberry. They had one son, who was named for his uncle, William Clement Gilliam. During the war he and his son, who was then in his sixteenth year, were both in the Southern army. At the close of the war, the following autumn of 1865, he with his wife and son, Roscius Atwood and his family, removed to Arkansas, where two daughters were born unto them, Colin Murchison and Mary Elizabeth. His wife died in Arkansas. He did not survive her many years. They both were buried in their adopted State.

ROBERT GLENN GILLIAM,

Brother of Dr. Jacob F. Gilliam, married Eusebia Blackburn. They resided on Indian Creek in Newberry District. They had one daughter who survived her parents. She is now Mrs. Mary Elizabeth Hinson. Some years ago she lost both her lovely little daughters Mary and Mattie; each had arrived at the age of eleven years. Mary, the eldest, died of diptheria. In two and a half years Mattie died of measles.

WILLIAM DUGAN

Married Elizabeth Lemon Wright. Their residence was situated on Indian Creek, ten miles north of the town of

2   P

Newberry, on the Buncombe Road. They had four daughters, Lucinda, the eldest, married Meredith Freeman, of North Carolina. Mary married Robert Campbell, the father of John B. Campbell, of Jalapa. Maria Marion married Andrew Turner. Frances, the yougest, married John T. Boyd.

ZACCHEUS WRIGHT AND ROBERT GLENN GILLIAM.

In a short sketch (and these that I give are of necessity compelled to be very short) justice cannot be done to the memory of the many good men and women mentioned. Amongst these is Zaccheus Wright, the father of Captain Robert H. Wright, of the town of Newberry, and mentioned lovingly by the one who gives me these sketches as "my sainted uncle." He and Robert Glenn Gilliam were near neighbors, and were truly some of the "salt of the earth." They worshiped together in the same church, "Tranquil," for many years. They both are asleep in Jesus, "blessed sleep." Their bodies are interred in the same cemetery, close by the church, where in life they were so fond of attending, there to await the first resurrection. Rest in peace—with all the faithful in Christ. Amen.

There are a few other families living in close proximity to those already mentioned, whose names must be recalled. Of these is Jacob Duckett, father of Colonel James W. Duckett, who was one of the largest and most successful planters in all that section.

MRS. THOMAS BOND.

Mrs. Thomas Bond left two children. Hugh King Bond, born in Newberry, married Rachel Hunter. They now reside in Laurens County. Laura Bond married Dr. Robert Hunter, of Laurens County. John Bond, brother of Richard Bond, of Laurens County, and his wife Nancy were residents of Newberry. Nathan F. Johnson now owns the place where they lived. They brought up a large and influential family of sons and daughters. Mrs. Smith L. Davis, of Columbia, is the youngest.

CHESLEY AND WM. C. DAVIS.

Chesley Davis and his son, William C. Davis, have both died recently, leaving a good name to their posterity. William C. Davis married Sarah Loftus, and their daughters, Mrs. Dr. Pinckney Johnson and Mrs. W. W. Riser, "will rise up and call them blessed."

WILLIAM PAGE

Married Hester Hancock. They were beloved and respected by all who knew them. With four children they removed to Georgia many years ago.

MARTIN GARY,

Uncle to General Martin Witherspoon Gary, of Edgefield, married Eliza Young, sister of John L. Young, of Union. They resided in Newberry at the "Rich Hill" place, on Indian Creek. Afterwards

STEPHEN BLACKBURN

lived there. He was a brother of Mrs. Robert Glenn Gilliam, married and Elizabeth Gary, sister to Martin and Hillary Gary. They had one daughter born to them, Mary Caroline, and she is now Mrs. Dr. F. F. Gary, of Abbeville. Stephen Blackburn died at Rich Hill. His widow afterwards married Dr. Rook.

WILLIAM DAVIS

Married Lucy Parke Dugan, sister of Col. Robert Dugan. They were highly esteemed and respected by those who knew them. They had two children, William and Mary. The latter survived her parents. She is now Mrs. Mary Caroline Dobbins, beloved and respected by all her friends. She has one son, Ligon.

JOHN B. RICHEY

Married Elizabeth Dillard. They resided in Newberry District and had an interesting family of children: Eunice, now Mrs. Meadows; Lavinia, who married the Rev. J. Emory Watson, who was for twenty-six years a member of the South Carolina Conference of the Methodist Episcopal Church. Curtis Richey and Elam Richey have removed to Florida.

WILLIAM GALLAGHER

Married Mary Grove. They had an interesting family of children: Permelia, James Franklin and Martha. Permelia married Mr. McCullough; Martha married Mr. Swittenberg and moved to Mississippi.

COLONEL B. Z. HERNDON,

a grandson of Col. Benjamin Herndon, of the Revolutionary war, once lived on Little River in Newberry County, on a place now owned by the family of Henry Burton, late deceased. Col. Benjamin Herndon fought at the battle of the King's Mountain. And Mrs. John S. Fair, a descendant of his, now of the town of Newberry, has in her possession a pair of silver spurs that were presented to him for his gallantry in battle. He was once captured by Bloody Bill Cunningham and was about to suffer an ignominious death when he was fortunately rescued by his men. His son Stephen Herndon was born and lived in Newberry. And Newberry gives a hearty welcome to Mrs. John S. Fair and Mrs. Lambert W. Jones, two fair and lovely descendants of Colonel Herndon of the Revolution.

The Reid Family.

David Reid, who lived three and one-half miles east of the town of Newberry, came to South Carolina from County Antrim, Ireland. He landed in Charleston, South Carolina, in 1789 or 1790, and settled in Fairfield County in the neighborhood of Monticello. He remained there two years, then removed to Newberry County and settled on the place three and a half miles from town. He had a family of one and perhaps two children when he came to this country. He raised a family of seven sons and lived to see them all settled around him.

David Reid was highly educated. His education was intended to prepare him for the study of medicine, which he pursued to some extent, but never completed. He was a man of intelligence and of excellent conversational powers. He was fond of reading and had quite a respectable library for that day, and was the first man in his neighborhood who subscribed for and took a newspaper. During the war of 1812 he took the Charleston *Mercury*, which was a week old before it reached Newberry. His neighbors would gather in to hear the news of the progress of the war. About 1810, or thereabouts, he built a mill on Cannon's Creek, which was among the first mills erected in Newberry. A few years later he built a cotton gin to run by water. It was one of the first in the country. It is not now known that he ever held any official position, or had any aspirations in that way. His sons who settled around him were all farmers, and acquired a competency. Daniel Reid, the eldest son, in 1812 was in command of a troop of cavalry, and was held under orders to march at short notice, but was not called into service. When Nullification caused the people to assume a warlike attitude, the men of the county who were over age for active service were formed into companies, and Daniel Reid was assigned to the command of one of those companies.

Samuel Reid, one of the sons of David Reid, was for many years a Justice of the Peace. He was First Lieutenant of a Cavalry Company during the Nullification excitement, Colonel Simeon Fair being Captain. Samuel Reid at his death was an Elder of Cannon Creek Church.

David Reid and four of his sons rest in the churchyard at Cannon Creek Church. All his sons, but one, William, died in this State; and of those who died in the State only one, David, died outside of Newberry County. The sons were Daniel, William, David, John, James, Samuel and Joseph. There was a daughter named Elizabeth, but she died when about twelve years old.

Joseph S. Reid was Lieutenant-Colonel of a Mississippi Regiment during the war of Secession and served with honor in all the campaigns of the West.

LIEUTENANT-COLONEL R. C. MAFFETT,

Son of James Maffett, was born in Newberry County. My acquaintance with Colonel Maffett was quite limited. I only knew him to be a sterling, upright and true man; a farmer, living a few miles below the Court House when the war broke out. He had never sought nor desired any office in the gift of the people, preferring the calm, domestic home life to all other. But when the difficulties between the States culminated in Secession and war he was not slow to offer his services, nor was he backward in doing his best for the success of the cause he espoused. He was elected Captain of Company C, Third Regiment South Carolina Volunteers; was promoted to the rank of Lieutenant-Colonel and serving in that capacity when he had the misfortune to be made prisoner. He was immured in the Union Prison at Fort Delaware, where he died.

At the time of his death he was a young man in the very prime of life between thirty and forty years of age. He left a young widow and child to deplore his loss. The following note was written by him to a lady who was a witness to his capture and who kindly complied with the request therein contained: "Lieutenant-Colonel R. C. Maffett, Address Mrs· R. C. Maffett, Newberry C. H., So. Ca. Tell her that I am a prisoner, am well, have been treated very well so far. Gen. Sheridan received and treated me with great civility; that I think we will be exchanged before long; that I will bear my captivity with as much philosophy and resignation as possible; that I was unavoidably captured, being entirely surrounded and overpowered; that she must bear up under our misfortunes and not become despondent; that I will write just as soon as we arrive at our destination." No date.

Captain James M. Maffett,

Cousin of Col. R. C. Maffett, was a son of Robert Maffett. He was born, I think, in the year 1821, or perhaps 1822. He too was a married man and a successful farmer when our troubles began. He was elected Captain of Company H, Holcombe Legion, and was a brave man and good officer. At the election for Sheriff of Newberry County in 1864 he was the choice of the people, but never lived long enough to see home after the election. He died at Lockhart, Miss., in hospital, on his way home to assume the duties of the office.

Lieutenant-Colonel John C. Simkins,

Whose name appears on our monument as one of the fallen soldiers of Newberry, was a son of Honorable Eldred Simkins, long a member of Congress from Edgefield District, and was born at Edgefield Court House on the 11th day of March, 1827. He attended school at Edgefield and at Greenwood, South Carolina. He was not a graduate of any college or university; in fact, never attended either. But instead, although only about eighteen years of age at the commencement of the Mexican war, he volunteered as a private in Captain Brooks' Company—D—of the Palmetto Regiment. During the campaign he was transferred to the Twelfth United States Regular Infantry, and as Captain in that Regiment distinguished himself at the battle of Churubusco, where he received two wounds. He was recommended to the Government for a brevet "for gallant and meritorious conduct." At the close of the Mexican war he returned to civil life—that of a planter. In 1850 he married Rosalie, daughter of Judge Wardlaw, of Abbeville, and continued to live in Edgefield District until about a year before the war between the States, when he bought from the Chappells a plantation in Newberry District on the Saluda River about a mile above Chappell's Depot. This plantation is part of what is known as Maxwell's Neck.

As soon as the State seceded and war was inevitable, he was amongst the first to offer his services to Governor Pickens. He was immediately appointed Captain in the First South Carolina Regular Infantry. His Regiment was employed largely as Artillery. As Commander of Battery Bee on Sullivan's Island he did good service in the repulse of the ironclads in the naval attack on Charleston, April 7th, 1863, when the *Keokuk* was sunk.

By successive promotions he became Lieutenant-Colonel of his Regiment. On the 16th of July, 1863, he, with three companies of the Regiment, Captains Haskell, Adams and Tatum, was ordered to Battery Wagner, our advanced post on Morris Island. Here he acted as Chief of Artillery, and he and his devoted little band without rest or sleep stood under a terrific bombardment until the night of July 18th, 1863, when the enemy in overwhelming numbers landed and assaulted the works.. They were, however, repulsed with heavy loss. In that night assault, at about 9 o'clock, Col. Simkins fell pierced through the right lung by a minnie ball. Captains Haskell and Tatum were also killed during that engagement and Captain Adams severely wounded. Colonel Simkins was thirty-six years old at the time of his death, and left a widow, four sons and a daughter surviving him.

In his official relations he was strict but just. A born soldier, he was devoted to his profession. Although a good disciplinarian, he was respected and beloved by his comrades. He was very modest and retiring but warm-hearted, frank and true. His purity of heart was shown in his exceeding fondness for children whose company he would seek.

BRIGADIER-GENERAL JOHN GLENN,

Son of Dr. George Glenn, and brother to my old friend Dr. George W. Glenn, a native of Newberry County, though a citizen of Arkansas when the war began, rose to the rank of Brigadier-General in the Army of the Confederate States. He was for a time a Conductor on the Greenville and Columbia Railroad after the war. I had no personal acquaintance with him, but I have no doubt that he was a brave and gallant officer. Being a native of Newberry and a soldier of the Confederacy, he deserves a place here. Where he is now, whether living or dead, I do not know.

COL. WILLIAM DRAYTON RUTHERFORD

Was the son of Dr. Rutherford of Newberry County and a descendant, a great-grandson, of Colonel Robert Rutherford of Revolutionary fame, who removed from Virginia to Newberry about the year 1780. or perhaps just before the American Revolutionary War. Young Drayton was a man of fine promise and liberal education; read law at Newberry; married, in 1862, a daughter of Colonel Simeon Fair, and life was opening before him bright and beautiful, with every promise of a prosperous and happy career. But the trouble between the States having brought on war, he volunteered at an early day, before his marriage, entered the service as a private in the Quitman Rifles; was made 2nd Sergeant, afterwards Adjutant, and finally, after the death of Colonel Nance, was promoted to the rank of Colonel of the regiment, the Third, which position in the service he was holding when he was killed in the battle of Strasburg, Va., October 13th, 1864. He was a brave and gallant youth, and gave his life for his beloved South.

I had not the pleasure of knowing Colonel Rutherford personally, never having met him at any time that I can remember now. He was in Europe pursuing his legal studies when the war began. But I knew his father, and I knew of him as one not likely, by any act of his, to dim the lustre that clung around the name of his illustrious ancestors. He left a widow and one daughter, who still survive.

An incident in the military life of Colonel Rutherford and the history of the Third Regiment has been told me by an eye-witness. It is here given, as nearly as can be remembered, in the words of the witness and narrator:

Colonel Rutherford was promoted Colonel from Lieutenant-Colonel upon the death of Colonel James D. Nance on the 6th of May, 1864—the battle of the Wilderness. On the night of the 7th of May General Grant began his famous flank movement. The rival forces first encountered each other on the "Brock road," leading to Spottsylvania Court House. The cavalry, under General J. E. B. Stuart, held that road. While on the march early in the morning of the 8th of May, an old Virginia gentleman, bare-headed, rode up to General Kershaw and told him that if the Brock road was to be held his troops must do it, as the cavalry under Stuart were being forced to give way by the approach of the United States infantry. General Kershaw responded to this call by directing his old brigade to hurry to the scene. At the double-quick, Rutherford soon had his regiment at the point of danger. He threw his whole soul into the movement, and was enabled to take possession of the rail piles, which had been thrown up by the cavalry as a breastwork, just in time to prevent a strong force of United States infantry from taking the place. Gen. Stuart remained on the ground after his cavalry had retired and assisted, with hat in hand, to stimulate the Third Regiment to stand firm. A very hot fight ensued. The young Colonel was all along his line, giving direction and energy to the fight. The result was a victory over the assaulting forces. The line thus established was the identical line upon which the battles around Spottsylvania Court House were fought on the 8th, 10th and 12th of May.

Late in the afternoon of the 8th Lieutenant-General Stuart and Lieutenant-General Ewell rode up to the Third and called for Colonel Rutherford. After introducing him to General Ewell, General Stuart said: "Colonel Rutherford, I have brought General Ewell down here to show him how you brave South Carolinians can fight." Then turning to General Ewell and pointing with his finger to the piles of Federal dead in the front of the Third Regiment, he said: "General, all these dead are their work."

P. C. CALDWELL.

Patrick Calhoun Caldwell was born in Newberry District March 10th, 1801. He was the son of William Caldwell and brother of John Caldwell.

He graduated from the South Carolina College in 1820, read law, and was admitted to practice in 1822. He was for a number of years the partner of James J. Caldwell. He was married December 13th, 1827, to Frances E. Nance, daughter of

Major Frederick Nance. His married life lasted but a few years, his wife dying March 3d, 1832.

In 1836 Mr. Caldwell was elected to the Legislature from Newberry, a member of the House; re-elected in 1838. In 1840 he was elected to represent the State in the Congress of the United States from the Congressional District then composed of the districts of Laurens, Newberry, Fairfield and Lexington. In the canvass preceding this election he is said to have displayed great ability as a "stump" speaker. His opponents were Colonel James H. Irby, of Laurens, and Mr. Samuel Barclay, of Fairfield.

In 1848 he was elected to the Senate of South Carolina from Newberry District. He was very popular as a man, as a citizen, socially and politically. His career as a public man was entirely satisfactory to his constituents. He died November 22nd, 1855, from the effects of a stroke of paralysis, received three years before.

Major James Graham.

Major James Graham was a native of South Carolina, of Scotch descent. He was Sergeant in active service during the war with Great Britain in 1812-15. He served Newberry District in the State Legislature for two terms.

He married Mary Fair, daughter of William and Elizabeth Fair. By this union four children were born to him, two sons and two daughters.

His son William F. Graham, who was the first Superintendent of the State Military Academy, died in Charleston in the spring of 1844. His other son, Dr. DeWitt C. Graham, read medicine, and after his graduation practiced his profession in Mississippi for a number of years. He returned to Newberry about a year before his death. He died in the fall of 1858, never having practiced medicine in his native State.

The daughters of Major Graham were Harriet, who married Colonel John W. Summers, the builder of the Greenville and Columbia Railroad, and Laura P., who married Dr. David E. Ewart, a notice of whose life and services appears elsewhere in this book. Mrs. Summers left no children. Mrs. Ewart is blest with a son and daughter, William F. and Mrs. Katie Bowman, both living in Newberry.

GENERAL A. C. GARLINGTON

Was a native of Laurens County; graduated at the University of Georgia; read law, and in 1848 came to Newberry to practice, having married in Newberry; where he soon made a fine reputation as a lawyer and orator. He was one of the finest and most eloquent speakers I ever listened to. He was a candidate for the Legislature in 1850, when the whole district and the State were excited on the Bank question. He took the side of the bank, and was elected by a large majority. He was again elected in 1852. In 1854 he ran for Congress against Preston S. Brooks, and was defeated. He was elected State Senator in 1856, and again in 1860. During the War of Secession he served some months as Major of the Holcombe Legion, until his presence was demanded in the Adjutant-General's office, which he also held. In 1865 he was again elected to the House of Representatives—making three terms in the House and two in the Senate, fourteen years of legislative service. After the war he went to Atlanta, Georgia, remaining there a few years, and returned to South Carolina, where he lived the remainder of his life.

He died on the 27th day of March, 1885, having nearly completed his sixty-second year.

He was survived by his widow, who was Sallie L. Moon, daughter of Dr. Peter Moon; one daughter, now Mrs. W. Y. Fair, and three sons, Ernest A., who graduated at West Point, at the head of his class, on June 15th, 1875, and was commissioned as second lieutenant in the United States Army and assigned to the Seventh Cavalry, being promoted to first lieutenant on June 26th of the same year. He commanded the expedition sent to the Arctic Sea in 1882 for the relief of Lieutenant Greeley. He was severely wounded in the right arm in a fight with Indians at Wounded Knee on December 29th, 1890, and shortly afterwards was promoted to the rank of Captain. William M. and Hrrry H., now living in Newberry County.

FRANCIS B. HIGGINS.

A very high but not undeserved compliment is paid to this gentleman in the first part of this work. As Mr. Higgins has passed away since the publication of that part, it is necessary that something more should be added.

As State Senator he represented the county for several terms, always holding an influential place in the councils of the State. The last several years of his life he spent in retirement, having declined re-election in 1844, after serving as Senator for twelve years. As Senator he was always at his post, and kept himself fully informed as to every measure brought up. He once published a statement giving the population and wealth of the different counties of the State. He was a good and useful man, and from 1831 to the time of his death he was a member of the Newberry Baptist Church.

On the 29th of December, 1863, he attended the funeral of Judge O'Neall, and occupied on that occasion, and for the last time, his usual seat in the Baptist Church of Newberry. On the following morning, December 30th, 1863, having already expressed a willingness to go whenever the summons came, he was stricken with apoplexy, and died in a few hours. He was born October 22nd, 1794.

Mrs. Higgins was born July 19th, 1803, at the place where her uncle, Major John Caldwell, was killed by Cunningham in 1781. Her father was William Caldwell. Her mother was Elizabeth Williams, daughter of Major John Williams, member of the Provincial Congress which met in Charlestown on the 11th of January, 1775; who also served in the American army during the Revolution.

Mrs. Higgins' father was also an officer in the army, and was held as a prisoner eighteen months at St. Augustine, in Florida. After the war he was at different times State Senator and Judge of the County Court for Newberry District. Two of her brothers became distinguished men, John Caldwell, member of the Legislature and an eloquent and eminent lawyer, and Patrick Calhoun Caldwell, lawyer, legislator and member of Congress.

She was happily married on the 12th of October, 1820, to Francis Bernard Higgins, of Newberry. In 1835 she joined the Baptist Church at Newberry, having been previous to that time a member of the Associate Reformed Church at Head Spring. It is thought that none are now living who welcomed her into the Baptist Church at that time. Mrs. Elvira Rutherford, who recently died at Newberry, was the last of these.

Mrs. Higgins gave a son to the Palmetto Regiment in the

Mexican War, who was a lieutenant in Captain J. H. Williams' company, and another son to the Confederate army, who was killed during the war. She will long be remembered for the amiable and kindly features of her character. She was a Christian woman. She died on the 2nd of May, 1889, in the eighty-sixth year of her age, in the house at Newberry, now owned by Dr. Jas. McIntosh, in which she had lived continuously for about sixty-five years.

Captain Chesley W. Herbert,

Son of Isaac and Frances Herbert, was born June 10th, 1832. He was prepared for college at the old Cokesbury Conference school, and graduated from the South Carolina College in December, 1855. Was married on January 10th, 1856, to Elizabeth S., eldest daughter of Daniel and Emily Goggans.

When South Carolina seceded he volunteered at the first call for troops, and left home for service in Company C, Third Regiment, South Carolina Volunteers, on April 13th, 1861, the day Fort Sumter surrendered. His regiment was shortly afterwards ordered to Virginia. He was badly wounded at the battle near Gettysburg, July 2nd, 1863. On the retreat to Winchester he was captured by United States cavalry, but was recaptured in a short time and furloughed until again fit for duty. Was again wounded, and this time seriously, by a shot through the left knee at the battle of the Wilderness, May 6th, 1864. He was brought from Virginia to South Carolina on a litter, and after months of suffering returned to the army, and was discharged just previous to the close of the war, because of lameness, which unfitted him for further military service.

His tragic death is briefly described in a letter written by the late General Garlington to Governor Scott: "Did you hear of the murder of the gallant Herbert, by a negro who had stolen his horse, and had been arrested by him, and who was sharing his bread with the culprit by the roadside?" As he was lame, the negro in some way obtained the advantage of him, struck him on the head with a heavy stick, and, while he was insensible, took his pistol from his pocket and shot him through the head, killing him instantly.

The tragedy occurred near the Lexington line, on March 8th, 1866, while the victim was making his way toward his home in this county.

The murderer was afterwards captured, but escaped jail; was recaptured by I. H. Boulware and A. B. Cromer; was tried, convicted and hanged. Before his execution he confessed to having stolen the horse and also to the murder of Captain Herbert.

Captain Herbert was at the time of his death Superintendent of Sunday School at New Chapel Methodist Church, and was and always had been a true friend to the colored race.

He left a widow, who is still living, and four children. The eldest, D. Oscar Herbert, is now (1892) a lawyer in Orangeburg. The eldest daughter, Emma F., married William L. Glaze, Esq., of Orangeburg, S. C., and is still living. One daughter died in infancy, and another, Minnie E., entered into her heavenly inheritance on her birthday, June 25th, 1888, aged twenty-seven years.

THE FOLK FAMILY.

Jacob Folk came to this country from Germany in 1740 or 1741, and settled at Old Granby, three miles below Columbia. He was a tanner by trade, and lived with a man by the name of Cary in partnership for five years. When his term of partnership was up he came to the place at Pomaria and married the daughter of Adam F. Epting, settled there, and commenced the tanning business on his own account. There were born to him seven children, four sons and three daughters. The eldest died in the Revolutionary war; the second son was killed by a tree falling on him; the third son, John Folk, lived at Pomaria until his death in 1844. Jacob Folk died on the 20th of June, 1774, and lies buried at the old Folk burying-ground. From him have sprung numerous and honorable descendants: John Adam, Henry Middleton, W. H. Folk, a lawyer in good practice at Edgefield; Edward H. Folk, also a lawyer at Edgefield; Captain H. H. Folk, of Newberry; David Folk, of Texas; L. E. Folk, of Newberry; Dr. J. W. Folk, of Annandale, Georgetown County; Charley Folk, of Lexington; Christian J. Folk, of Barnwell, and Jacob Folk, who moved to Colleton County in the year 1803, and there left a large family, and J. Wesley Folk, of Pomaria, whose son, Dr. L. B. Folk, is a practicing physician in Columbia, S. C.

No doubt there are many others descended from Jacob Folk, whose names I have not been able to learn.

The Welch Family.

William and Williams Welch, who were brothers, came from Iredell County, N. C., during the first quarter of the present century. They were of Quaker parentage. William was a worthy, guileless man, but of an impatient and restless temper. He died in 1853, aged sixty. Williams was the younger. He was of a generous and impulsive nature; a man of clear judgment and abounding in energy. Though he came to this country a poor boy, he accumulated a fortune in the pursuit of agriculture, besides rearing and educating a family of eleven children. He died in 1874, in his seventy-second year. Professor C. W. Welch, late Principal of the High School, Houston, Texas, and now (1892) Professor-elect in Clemson College, and Williams Welch, the portrait painter, also Professor-elect in Clemson College, both natives of Newberry, are his grandsons.

Mrs. Lucy Sharp was the sister of William and Williams Welch. She came to Newberry from North Carolina in 1850, and died in 1856. She was a woman of unusual industry and very kind and generous in her nature. She left two children, William, one of Anderson's best citizens, and Mrs. Neville, wife of Rev. Mr. Neville of the Methodist Episcopal Church, South.

Jacob K. Schumpert.

Born 26th of October, 1807; died 14th of May, 1885.

He was the eldest son of Frederick Schumpert and Mary Kinard his wife. Jacob K. married, in the year 1833, Harriet Abney, of Edgefield County, who died November 3d, 1884.

They celebrated the fiftieth anniversary of their marriage in 1883, in the presence of their children, three sons and three daughters, and a host of grandchildren, at the old homestead, Elm Grove, seven miles northwest from Newberry Court House. The following children survive them: Dr. John I. Schumpert, who lives in Louisiana; Mrs. E. M. Kingsmore, who lives at Birmingham, Ala., Mrs. C. T. Wells, O. L. Schumpert and F. A. Schumpert, at Newberry, S. C., and Mrs. E. A. Cassity, wife of Rev. Mr. Cassity, Presiding Elder of the Methodist Episcopal Church, South, whose home at present is Mansfield, Louisiana.

Jacob K. Schumpert was a man of vigorous constitution,

strong and evenly balanced mind, and a noble heart; all of which tended to make him one of the finest types of "Nature's noblemen." And in addition to what nature's gifts, experience, observation and a fair education, with their advantages, had done for him, the transforming power of grace had made in him one of the most clearly defined and beautifully symmetrical Christian characters I have ever met. The loss of his wife —a Christian lady of rare excellence—who died a short time after the celebration of their half century of married life, deeply affected him, and left visible traces of the loss of vital power which gave him a presentiment of the early ending of his earthly career. They both lie buried in Rosemont Cemetery. The Revs. Drs. J. Steck and H. W. Kuhns, eminent divines of the Lutheran Church, of which Church both Mr. and Mrs. Schumpert were members, officiated at the burial ceremony.

Mr. Schumpert was a courteous, kind and hospitable gentleman, and both he and his wife were very fond of company, especially of the company of young people, often having a house full for weeks at a time. In their company they seemed to live over the days of their youth and always entered heartily into the most of their sports and recreations. He was also kind and strictly just with his slaves, seldom allowing them to be punished even for gross refractory conduct. He owned a slave, Jack by name, who, though painfully lazy, was a very expert carpenter, and at times pretended to be crazy. He was advised by some of his neighbors to place Jack in the County Jail. This he did, but as soon as he learned that Jack was being flogged with a cat-o-nine tail he immediately took him home; and Jack, it is supposed, in gratitude for his master's mercy never played crazy any more.

In his early youth he had acquired the tobacco habit— both chewing and smoking. This habit he continued in for forty years, yet always persisted in saying that he could quit it whenever he willed to do so. When his oldest son John I. came home from the North, after having finished his medical education, he had also acquired, to his father's intense regret, the tobacco habit. This habit John I. endeavored to conceal from his father, who, catching him in the act one day, without at all scolding him, simply said: "Well, my son, I

John K. Griffin, M. C.

James H. Williams.

Francis B. Higgins

Thos. H. Pope.

B. F. Griffin.

MEMBERS OF CONGRESS AND STATE LEGISLATURE.

see that you are using tobacco. I don't blame you, however, as I set the example and you followed it. A father never should do anything that he would or could reprimand in his son. Now I am going to set you another example; follow it, also." And, suiting the action to the words, he threw from him the quid then in his mouth, and from that day never touched it again. It is useless to say that the son did—*not* follow this example.

Whatever he undertook to do was always done in the most thorough and complete manner. All the buildings on his plantation, from the negro cabin to the mansion house, were models of strength, durability and neatness. "He was a devout lover of the Word of God, a lover of the Church, liberal of his means, peaceable and a peace-maker, progressive, always consistent, a well-rounded man in Christ, whose memory it will always be pleasant to cherish and whose life it will always be safe to hold up for the imitation of others."

Of his other two sons, Osborne Lamar is a practicing lawyer at Newberry and is at present Solicitor of the Seventh Circuit. He was a member of the Legislature in 1884–5. Frederick A. is a merchant at Newberry.

There were many others of this family whose names should not be left out of the roll of the worthies of Newberry.

Amos K. Schumpert, brother to Jacob K., a sketch of whom we have just given, moved to Alabama many years ago. His son Ben was a student in Newberry College when the war broke out; he volunteered in the Quitman Rifles and was killed in battle. His name is on our monument. Amos K. Schumpert, I believe, is still living.

Peter Schumpert, who moved to Edgefield, and left sons and daughters, was well known to the writer.

Sam Schumpert, another most excellent man and good citizen, lived and died near Silver Street, in his native county. He was the father of James Jacob.

George Schumpert, father of Frank, lived for many years on his place between Bush River and Saluda, where he died. His brother John, father of Cal and Bob, lived in the same neighborhood.

There was another John Schumpert, who lived in Edgefield, near Herbert's Ferry, whom I knew many years ago. It was his son Jesse who married Miss Smgley in Newberry. He was running a portable steam engine when the boiler exploded with fatal results. His son has but one arm, but whether the loss of the other was caused by that explosion I am not now sure. John, the father of Jesse, had a brother William, who died many years ago.

Elisha Schumpert, brother of Jacob K., was a mill owner on Bush River; and like his brother, Jacob K., he took great pride in his work and had everything about his mill in perfect order. He made as good flour as it is possible for any mill to make. I know whereof I speak, for I have had wheat ground at his mill.

Of the ladies, members of this family, there is Mrs. Polly Long, widow of my old time friend Jacob Long, and mother of my present time friend Fred Long. Mrs. David Werts, who lived just south and near the Dead Fall, on the Kinard Ferry Road. Mrs. Thomas Carson, of Edgefield, mother of the Rev. James Carson, a minister of the Baptist Church in that county. Mrs. John Paysinger, mother of Ben Paysinger (whose widow lives at the old place), and Jacob J. Paysinger, and Samuel S., and Thomas M., who was once Sheriff, and Fred S.; and another one, Henry, who was killed in battle during the war; and there may have been others whose names I cannot now recall. I know of no other Paysingers in the county, except these, the descendants of John Paysinger. He first settled where Thomas P. Buzhardt, who was married to Miss Emma Paysinger, lived and died.

Mrs. Harriet Schumpert was the daughter of Zachariah Abney (whose father was a Virginian), who was born, lived and died near what is now Kinard's Ferry on Saluda River. He was a baby, if I mistake not, an infant quite small, when his father was killed by the Tories during the Revolution. They found him sick in bed with fever and in spite of the efforts and prayers of his wife they hauled him forth out of the house and killed him even in his wife's arms— the sword that killed him passing through him and entering his wife's body also. House, corn crib, everything was burnt, and the only comfort left the widow was her baby boy. He had crawled away and hid himself in the midst of some tall weeds near by. Long afterwards, nearly fifty years, I was shown by a son of Zachariah Abney the spot where the corn crib had stood, and I there saw, mingled with the soil, the grains of corn burned to a coal that day, still in perfect preservation.

The mother of Mrs. Harriet Schumpert was a Townsend, and her father's father also passed through the fires of the Revolution. His house and premises were sacked and burned, but he escaped, barely with his life. He had time, and just time, to hide himself, without having been seen by his enemies, in a pile of brush near the house. And while the house was burning the heat was so intense where he lay concealed as to be almost unbearable. But he did bear it and so escaped with his life.

The country near the mouth of Tosty Creek, on both sides of the Saluda, had many Tories led by Cunningham and the Turners, especially Ned Turner, and their treatment of the Whigs was sometimes very savage, which treatment some of the Whigs were not slow to return in kind. The compiler of these Annals was born and reared not far from the swamps of Saluda, near the fields which were the scenes of many a bloody conflict. And I remember well when the family of Stewarts and their kinsmen, the Thompsons, were under the ban on account of Revolutionary times. And it was said Alick, or Alexander, Stewart still kept a Red Coat hid away as a Revolutionary relic, preserving and cherishing it as a memento of the good old times.

ABRAM MOORE.

On the 6th day of June, 1889, at a little over the age of ninety-three years, died Abram Moore, having been born on the 18th day of March, 1796. He was a native of this county, and nearly the whole of his long life was passed in a quiet home-life on his farm near Prosperity. When a young man he spent two years with an elder brother in Fairfield.

Of Seceder stock, he was brought up in the admonition and fear of the Lord, and at an early age united with the Church. At the age of twenty-six he was made an Elder, and held that dignified position to the end of his life, sixty-seven years. His attendance at church was so prompt and regular that whenever he was absent people and pastor always thought there was something the matter to prevent his attendance.

On the 21st of January, 1822, he was happily married to Elizabeth Brown. Eight children were born to them, four of whom died before the death of their parents. They lived together in happy wedlock over sixty years. Mrs. Moore died first, about six years before he was called.

His memory ran back to the time when small grain was cut with reap hooks, then with the scythe and cradle, and he lived to see the great reaping machines now in use. He could tell how tobacco, once a staple article in Newberry, used to be hauled to Charleston in a hogshead, and the hogshead itself was the wagon. And when he was a boy the first negroes were brought to that part of Newberry, and their appearance so startled and frightened him that he ran from them as he would from a bear. He remembered when there were no houses at Prosperity, when it was indeed Frog Level, with deep clear ponds of water surrounded by thick woods, and many deer coming down to the ponds to drink. He remembered the war of 1812, and the embargo, and when wagons sometimes went overland to Philadelphia and to bring goods back from that city. So many changes have taken place since his boyhood that to sit and hear him talk was almost like listening to one who lived before the flood.

He died as he had lived, at peace with all men and at peace with God.

JOHN A. MOORE AND JOHN W. CHAPMAN.

These two gentlemen were both natives of Newberry; both read law, and both left the county to practice their profession. Mr. Moore went to Columbia, the other to Kingstree, Williamsburg County. They married sisters, Miss Sarah Arthur and Miss Amanda Arthur, sisters of Edward J. Arthur, Esq.

John W. Chapman left a widow, Mrs. Amanda Chapman, (who once taught the Hartford School,) but no children. She now lives with her nephews, the Killians, about twelve miles above Columbia. Mrs. Moore lives in Columbia, at the place, I believe, where her husband died. Two children live with her, one son and one daughter, Annie, who was a lovely girl and woman, but I have not seen her in a long time. She, too, once taught school in this county, at or near Mr. Cleland's, not far from Silver Street.

Mr. Moore lived at Newberry Village in his boyhood, and

he once told me a story on himself in connection with the Quaker Meeting House on Bush River. That house, as perhaps my readers well know, had the reputation of being a haunted spot; but why, it would be hard to say, as the people, who worshiped there in old days, were certainly a good, quiet folk. But whether haunted or not it had the reputation and that answered every purpose. Mr. Moore said that one Saturday afternoon, having holiday, he thought he would take his gun and walk down to Bush River hunting. The road passed right by the House, which was deeply embosomed in woods. The spot was lonely and he was alone. When he came near the house, looking up he saw high up in a tree, in the edge of the woods, a large owl with its white breast directly towards him. He raised his gun and fired, and the owl, instead of flying off or falling directly down to the earth, came sailing in a straight line towards him. All at once it flashed across his mind that there was something eerie in its performance; that it might be one of the ghosts haunting the place, and he broke and ran towards Newberry for dear life. He ran some two hundred yards or so and finding that nothing caught him he thought he would stop and investigate. He returned to his former standpoint and found the poor owl lying on the ground near where he was standing when he fired, crippled but not dead. He said he picked it up and returned home and hunted no more that day.

Mr. Moore was a good lawyer, a prosperous and energetic man. His eldest son, Arthur, married and settled in Columbia; he was a lawyer, but he too is dead—died a few years ago.

Many of the older citizens of Newberry, no doubt, still remember Mrs. Esther Moore, the mother of John A. Moore. Her neat, quick, bird-like ways were very pleasant. My acquaintance with her was very limited, but I knew her well by sight, and it always gave me pleasure to meet her.

Dear Reader, it is a pleasure, but of a mournful kind, to recall the past and jot down recollections of persons and events long gone. But can an old man, whose active life is over, find better employment than this? There is one danger attending it and that is that the Recorder of past events loses, by degrees, active interest in the present, and comes at lasᵥ to regard passing events and persons as matters giving work, and only this, for the pen of the future historian.

An Old Family Bible.

The Bible belonging to the Chapman family, the family of the compiler of these Annals, was printed in the year 1613, and is at the present time, 1892, two hundred and seventy-nine years old, and, as I have been informed, is in a good state of preservation without a leaf missing.

It appears from the Family Record in it that it belonged in 1664 to Thomas Anderson, of Bridlington, in the East Riding of Yorkshire, England. Thomas Anderson died on the 5th of May, 1683, being the father of three daughters and one son. His daughter, Elizabeth, born 3d of April, 1673, was married to Marmaduke Jackson, on the 14th of February, 1707, at Bridlington. These seem to have had but two children, Nathaniel Jackson, born 20th of April, 1708, and Sarah Jackson, born 27th of December, 1710. Sarah Jackson became the wife of Giles Chapman, who was born January 4th, 1702. These were the parents of six children, Elizabeth, Samuel, Rachel, Joseph, Sarah, Giles—the eldest born January 28th, 1734: the youngest, Giles, June 21st, 1748. This Giles Chapman afterwards became the Rev. Giles Chapman, the grandfather of this writer. He married Mary Summers on the 14th of September, 1775. These were the parents of eleven children, the eldest of whom, Joseph, was born September 23d, 1776, and the youngest, Lewis, was born March 11th, 1800. He died April 13th, 1860. Lewis married Rhoda O'Neall, who was born April 29th, 1802. She is still living, at Appleton City, Missouri, with her son James K. P. Chapman, to whom the old Family Bible now belongs, and who gave me the foregoing information.

It does not appear at what time my great-grandfather, Giles Chapman, left Bridlington, England, and came to Virginia; nor when he left Virginia and came to Newberry, but on "immigrating to this State, first located himself for a season, at the place of our town." He lies buried, if I mistake not, in an old burying ground, two miles east of Newberry, known as the Chapman Graveyard, on a place now belonging to Mr. J. A. Crotwell.

The first edition of the English version, King James', of the Bible now in use, was printed in 1611, only two years before the one of which I have here made record, and I think it doubtful whether there is a Family Bible of King James' version now in the United States older than this.

REV. THOMAS FREAN.

The following sketch of the life of Rev. Thomas Frean was written by Judge O'Neall near the close of his own useful life. Mr. Frean was for many years a citizen of Newberry and in public life, married here, and certainly deserves a place in the Annals of Newberry. I copy from the original manuscript:

"The request of a dying friend is now about to be performed. A friendship of near fifty years pointed to the writer as one better fitted to discharge the duty than any other. It had been, too, the sad privilege of him to write short sketches of the wife and daughters and son of the deceased. He had mourned with him under these sad dispensations. He had witnessed his days of adversity and prosperity, and finally saw the shades gathering over the evening of life. His request, therefore, to do something like justice to his memory in a short sketch of his life, was imperative.

"He was a native of Grange, in the Parish of Lorha, of the County of Tipperary, Ireland. His father was Patrick Frean, of Grange, Parish of Lorha, in the County of Tipperary, Ireland. Thomas Frean was born on the 15th of January, 1793. He received a good education at the home of his birth. He was, on the 7th of March, 1807, bound an apprentice for the term of six years to a merchant, John Cantwell, of the town of Parsonstown, in Kings County, and served some time. Why he left the home of his birth I never certainly knew.

"He was the only child of his parents. From dark hints in a conversation with him, I presume it was from difficulties with a Catholic priest who had the charge of his education. He visited Charleston, S. C., and his relatives, somewhere between 1809 and 1814. His purpose was only a temporary sojourn. The war of 1812, while he was there lingering, occurred, and closed the possibility of an early return. Under the act of Congress, he with an Englishman of the name of Thomas was sent into the interior, and opened a store on Bush River, Newberry District, at the place once known as O'Neall's, then the property of Levi Hilburn.

"The writer has a vivid recollection of his person when he first saw him in the year 1813—his fine Irish youthful complexion, surrounded with natural curled ringlets, has never been forgotten. He was thrown into the society of his wife, Hannah Elmore, the daughter of Mathias and Rebecca his wife. Both were young, he a little over twenty and she approaching eighteen. The grandmother of the latter was an Irish lady, and had a warm regard for all who were from the land of her birth. She used to call Frean her young countryman, and encouraged his addresses. In the year 1813 he returned to Charleston, but kept up the pursuit of his love until the spring of 1814, when he was married by the Rev. Giles Chapman, at the house of his father-in-law. The grandmother of his wife was present, and wished each of her granddaughters an equally good match.

"Subsequent events led her to doubt the propriety of the wish.

"He returned to Charleston, and in a small way embarked in the mercantile business at the lower end of King street, near the South Bay, where I found him and his wife in May, 1814. He did not remain long there. He removed to Newberry District and kept a store at Spear's, now O'Neall's, Mills, Bush River. How long he remained there I cannot tell. Misfortunes and misunderstandings occurred. He abandoned his family, and returned to the lower country. He taught school for a short period in the neighborhood of the Four Holes.

"He was reconciled to his family, and settled on a small tract of land given to his wife near Mendenhall's Mills. Here, in poverty, distress, and the use of intoxicating drinks, he lived a life of suffering. School teaching was his employment. At the death of his wife's grandmother, by her will his wife was entitled to and received a negro girl. After 1820 he accompanied his wife's father and family in a removal to Spartanburg. *There* he lived a life of great poverty. School teaching was his employment. While he lived in Spartanburg his household property was seized and sold under execution and purchased by a friend. More than twenty years after, when the whole transaction was forgotten by his friend, he recalled it and repaid the money. He returned after several years to

Newberry, reoccupied his old place, taught school, abandoned the use of strong drink, and was converted and became a local Methodist preacher. In, perhaps, 1834 he sold his wife's interest in the small tract of land, and purchased the Hendrix tract of land, on which his daughter and son-in-law now reside. By the assistance of a friend who became his surety, he was enabled to pay for the land. This was the turning point of his life. Adversity ceased to haunt his footsteps. In sobriety he sought and found prosperity. In 1838 (the Church record says 1835) he became satisfied that he was wrong in his religious profession. He was baptized (October 24th, 1835, according to the Minutes), by immersion at the fount near Newberry and united himself to the Baptist Church at Newberry. He was soon after licensed and subsequently ordained to preach the gospel.

"He became pastor of the Newberry Baptist Church, of the Rocky Spring Baptist Church, and the supply of other churches in Newberry and Laurens. In 1841 he became a candidate for Surveyor General, and was elected. He entered on the duties of his office in February, 1842, and removed to Columbia. For four years he discharged with great exactness and fidelity the duties of his office; for he was an active and intelligent surveyor of many years' practice. In the latter years of his term of office he was employed to prepare copies of the plats in the Surveyor General's office in Columbia and Charleston. This work he finished with great fidelity and exactness. His charge was supposed to be too high, and the Legislature laid upon his work an unsparing hand and cut down his charges to a most beggarly amount, while they allowed the Secretary of State, for a similar work, a much larger amount. In the beginning this produced unfriendly feelings to him on the part of many good men. It for a time alienated his friend Major Perry. But subsequent examination satisfied him that Mr. Frean had not had justice done him. After many years of trouble an approach to compensation for that and other work was allowed him. He never was satisfied with the justice attempted to be meted to him. It was a source of bitterness to him throughout life, and was not forgotten in his last will and testament.

"For years he discharged the duties of Deputy Treasurer,

and uniformly was praised for the exactness with which he did his duty. His work called "Ten Years in the Treasury" was invaluable to the country.

"During his official terms he preached occasionally in Columbia and its vicinity. His leisure hours he devoted very much to poetry. He wrote many fugitive pieces which were worthy of 'Carolan,' which was the nom de plume under which he usually wrote. He sometimes wrote some pieces of humor under the signature of 'Peter Pheasant.'

"To his children he gave the means of a good education. His son, William Herman Frean, graduated at the South Carolina College, and subsequently attended the course of lectures at the South Carolina Medical College which was to fit him to be a physician. But it so happened in the providence of God that he should be taken away in July, 1855, just as he passed his twenty-first year.

"His daughter Hannah Belton, remarkable for her agreeable character, was next stricken down. She died the 15th of November, 1855. Next followed the wife and mother, Hannah Frean. She died 29th June, 1859. To this gloomy catalogue must be appended his daughter. Abigail Caldwell Southern, who died on the 12th day of November, 1859.

"Thus he was smitten until his house was left desolate, for his only surviving daughter, Bridget Honoria Waldrop, resided in Newberry District. In solitude and sadness he was left to muse on his condition and to prepare for the final end of life. He died at the house of his son-in-law, Wilson W. Waldrop, on Sunday, the 7th of April, 1860.

"He was a fervid, impassioned and impulsive speaker. He was a real *Tipperary man*. He resisted whatever he supposed to be oppression, and he might have on such occasions been excessive in his violence. Generally speaking, he fiulfilled the poet's prayer:

"That mercy which I to others show,
    That mercy show to me."

"He was a perfectly honest man. He became a Temperance man about the year 1838, and scrupulously adhered to the doctrine of total abstinence."

GREGG, SPENCE, McCALLA, TODD.

Near three miles from the town of Newberry, southeast, there stands a tombstone of marble bearing three inscriptions to the memory of three departed relatives, viz.:

"To the memory of William Gregg, Sr., who departed this life on the 10th day of November, 1816, aged seventy-one years."

"Also, of Mary Spence, wife of Samuel Spence and daughter of William and Jane Gregg, who departed this life on the 14th day of September, 1823, in the fortieth year of her age."

"Likewise, of Jane Gregg, who departed this life on the 14th day of September, 1823, aged eighty-four years."

Mrs. Mary Spence, here mentioned as the daughter of William and Jane Gregg, and wife of Samuel Spence, had for her first husband Samuel McCalla, Esq., who came to this country and settled on the land afterwards owned by Major James Graham, then by Chancellor Job Johnstone, now by his son, J. Malcolm Johnstone. Samuel McCalla was compelled to leave Ireland about 1798 because of the part taken by him in some political troubles in that unhappy country. Having to leave the country to avoid arrest, he left his wife and little son Robert, only two or three years old. He seems to have come directly to Newberry and settled on the above-mentioned place, his wife and son Robert not coming to America until 1817. The son he had left a sportive boy was now a young man of about twenty one years. Mrs. Mary McCalla and son Robert sailed from Belfast, Ireland, October 12th, 1817, on the ship Cyrus, commanded by Captain Gassard, and landed at Charleston, S. C., November, 30th, 1817.

Andrew Todd came from Ireland to this country in 1816, and his wife and children came over in the same vessel with Mrs. Mary McCalla in 1817. This family of Todds settled in Laurens County. One of the daughters married Rev. Samuel P. Pressley, who was pastor of the Associate Reformed Church in this county, and lived in the house on Caldwell street commonly known at this time as the Webb house. Drs. Samuel Todd, a brother of Andrew Todd, practiced medicine very successfully in Newberry for a number of years, afterward moved to Laurens C. H., where he died on the 3d of June, 1825, aged sixty-three years.

There is nothing to show the exact date when the Gregg

family came to America, but it is quite probable that they came over prior to the coming of Mrs. Mary McCalla. Nor is it now known what part Samuel McCalla took in the troubles in Ireland; but he was a man of fine intellect, of good education, and qualified in every respect to become a leader. He was ruling elder in the Associate Reformed Church at Cannon Creek, and was for many years a Justice of the Peace for Newberry District. He was well liked and had great influence among his acquaintances. He died not long after being reunited to his family, and was buried at Cannon Creek. His widow married Samuel Spence, who also came from Ireland, but at what time is not known. Mr. Spence was a tailor by trade, and settled and died on a place west from the present Colony Church. Samuel Spence had a brother, James Spence, who was a merchant, but for the last few years of his life taught school.

After the death of his mother in 1823 Robert McCalla, with the Gregg family, some time between 1825 and 1830 removed to Georgia; then to Lincoln County, Tennessee; then to Shelby County, Tennessee, where most of the descendants of Samuel McCalla now live, worthy scions of an honorable ancestry.

Captain John McCalla, son of Robert, was an officer under General Forrest in the war between the States, and it is said that General Forrest would never go into a battle unless he had Captain McCalla at his side.

For the foregoing facts the compiler of these Annals acknowledges his indebtedness to Joseph S. Reid, Esq.

JACOB HUNT.

My old friend Jacob Hunt was a native, I think, of North Carolina; came to Newberry in his youth; married a daughter of Walter Herbert, one of the Quakers of Bush River. Mr. Hunt was a hatter by trade. Some hats of his make were worn by myself when I was a boy. He lived for many years at Newberry, or rather near Newberry, at the place now owned by J. A. Crotwell. He was a good neighbor, citizen and a true friend. One of his sons, I. F., became Colonel of a South Carolina Volunteer Regiment during the war of Secession—now at Greenville, S. C. One, W. H., familiarly known as Herbert, lives at Newberry. A grandson, Walter H., is a successful lawyer in practice at Newberry. One other son, J. H., a successful business man, now in New York City, attained the rank of Major during the war and did faithful service to the Confederacy. Another grandson, I. Hamilton, is now in business in Atlanta, Georgia.

COLONEL JOHN S. RENWICK.

This very excellent man, a native of Newberry County, and who spent his long life as one of its citizens, was of Scotch descent, and a not very remote descendant of James Renwick, the last Scotch martyr. He became a member of King's Creek Church in early manhood and remained in connection with it until the day of his death. The circumstances of his early life prevented him from acquiring a first-rate education, but he knew its worth and he gave his sons and daughters the best that could be obtained. He was the first to suggest to Dr. Bonner, then in charge of the Female Academy at Due West, the propriety of converting that institution into a Female College. He had no political aspirations, but was content to do his duty as a private citizen, a farmer and member of the Church, in which he was a Ruling Elder for nearly the whole of his life. This good man died March 19th, 1889, in the 76th year of his age.

DR. WM. W. MCMORRIES

Died at the home of his daughter and son-in-law, Mr. and Mrs. Cofield, in Union County, S. C., August 22nd, 1883. He was born April 15th, 1803. This date carries us far back in the history of our county. At that time there were only sixteen States in the Union and Jefferson was President, and there were still many surviving soldiers of the Revolution.

Dr. McMorries was a graduate in the Medical School of Philadelphia, but he did not practice long. He united himself with the Associate Reformed Church; was made a Ruling Elder in Thompson Street Church at Newberry in 1858, while Mr. Murphy was pastor. It is said that he took great delight in his office and performed its duties faithfully and well. His family loved him; he was a cheerful and tender father; his life companion was of the same cheerful temper and they made a happy household. He raised seven children, but only three daughters—Mrs. Johnson, of Alabama, Mrs. Dr. Gri r, of Due West, S. C., Mrs. Cofield, of Union, S. C.,—and one stepson, J. C. S. Brown, of Newberry, survive him.

Dr. William H. Harrington

Was a native of Newberry County and was born at Newberry Village on the 17th of November, 1816. He received a good education, read medicine and graduated from the Medical College of Charleston, settled at Newberry and on the 18th of November, 1841, married Miss. Sarah S. O'Neall, daughter of Hon. J. B. O'Neall. After her death, which occurred in August, 1857, he married Mrs. Hollingsworth, *nee* Griffin, in December, 1858. While his home was at Newberry he represented the county in the Legislature for two years. He left Newberry in 1865 and removed to Mississippi, where he died at his home in Crawfordville. His remains have been brought to Newberry and interred in the Calmes Cemetery, where his maternal grand-parents, his own parents and many more of his kindred are sleeping. He was the father of Mrs. Dr. Sampson Pope, the late Mrs. J. Wistar Gary, and the late Young John Harrington, and of Mrs. Thomas J. Lipscomb, of Columbia, S. C. He leaves a son, Dr. Belton Harrington, and a daughter, Mrs. Kier, in Mississippi, and a son, Hugh O'Neall Harrington, in Texas. His widowed sister, Mrs. Nancy Moon, still lives at Newberry. He was a good man.

Major Z. W. Carwile,

The son of the late John S. Carwile, and the last surviving brother of Mr. John B. Carwile, of Newberry, died of apoplexy at the residence of his son Nathan G. Carwile, in Buffalo, Wyoming Territory, on the 30th of November, 1888.

Major Carwile was born in Newberry District in 1818, and came in his early boyhood to Newberry Village. When quite young he went to Columbia, where, with Mr. B. D. Boyd, President of the old Bank of Newberry, he entered the mercantile establishment of his cousin John H. Carwile. After a year or two he returned to Newberry, where he remained until about 1841, when he removed to Edgefield District (now county), of which he remained a citizen until his death. A short time ago he went to Buffalo to visit two of his sons who reside at that place.

He was a member of the House of Representatives from Edgefield for several terms, and was for a good many years Commissioner in Equity for Edgefield County.

Major Carwile was a man of unusual mental powers. Although his school education was limited, by reason of his having at an early age entered into business pursuits, yet he had by reading and observation so cultivated his intellect that he was in the best sense an educated man. His friends remaining in Newberry, who knew him both in times of prosperity and adversity, will bear testimony to his faithfulness as a friend and his unflinching adherence to the right. Major Carwile was at the time of his death, and had been for many years previous, a consistent member of the Baptist Church.

James Packer

Was a native of England. He came to America in 1853 and to Newberry in 1868, where he remained a good and useful citizen until the day of his death. He married here, read law and was a good and reliable lawyer and business man — admitted to the Bar in 1878—had already been appointed Trial Justice by General Hampton in 1877. As a lawyer he was heard in the Supreme Court with marked attention, and was very successful.

I knew him well; he was a good man and a genial and faithful friend, and was a fine example of what patient industry can accomplish in overcoming early disadvantages.

He died on Thursday, 14th day of May, 1885, leaving a widow but no children.

Major James M. Baxter

Was a native of Laurens County; made law his chosen profession; came to Newberry to practice; married one of Newberry's loveliest daughters and made his home here until he died. He was one of the best lawyers that ever practiced at this Bar. His mind was too broad and comprehensive to be trammeled with forms and technicalities, but easily mastered the strong points of his cases, and seized and applied with a masterly hand the broad principles of Law and Equity upon which our judicial system is founded, and which embodies the united wisdom and experience of ages. It was this devotion to principles that gave him his great power with jurors and Judges. He was a man of a large heart and head; kind and courteous to all; and a true and steadfast friend, a patriotic citizen. He was Major of the Third Regiment, South Carolina Volunteers, the first year of the war.

Major Baxter was gifted with rare intellectual powers and endowed with faculties which eminently fitted him for the profession which he adorned so highly. He was not what might be called a popular speaker, abounding in the graces of oratory and possessing the power to sway the thronging multitude. He seldom attempted flights of fancy, but always spoke in language unadorned, but pure and chaste. As a lawyer he was earnest and zealous in whatever business was committed to his charge, and exhibited untiring industry in the cause of his clients, such as is rarely equalled. He was a formidable adversary at the Bar under any circumstances, but most dangerous when his case appeared to be most hopeless—he gathered new strength and rose to the emergency as his case trembled in the balance. He did not know the word fail.

I knew him well for twenty-five or thirty years—had many business transactions with him during that time and always found him prompt, genial and courteous.

For many years he was a member of the Presbyterian Church and died in that communion. He died February 5th, 1881—born September 7th, 1825. He left a widow and three children—one son and two daughters. William, his son, has died since his father; the daughters still survive—the eldest, Lucy, is the wife of Walter H. Hunt, Esq., a lawyer in good practice at Newberry; the latter daughter, Miss Fannie, is a lovely and amiable young lady living at Newberry with her mother.

CHRISTIAN HENRY SUBER.

The hearts of the people of Newberry were made very sad when it was said "Major Suber is paralyzed." And the sadness was deepened when word came: "Major Suber is dead." Small hopes were entertained from the first of his recovery, but it was not thought that he would die so soon. I do not think that any man ever lived in the village or town of Newberry, more personally popular, or more deserving to be so, than Christian H. Suber. In society and at the Bar, with old and young; with the high and low, Mr. Suber was a favorite. He retained his youthfulness, cheerfulness and vivacity of manner to the last.

He was an able and conscientious lawyer, and carefully studied his cases and weighed the evidence both for and

James N. Lipscomb.

Albert C. Garlington.

Christian H. Suber.

Thomas C. Brown.

MEMBERS OF THE LEGISLATURE.

against his side of the case. Besides his ability as a lawyer he was well read in literature generally and was a splendid Shaksperian scholar. In the tone of his mind, and in its evenly balanced make up, he reminded me much of Chancellor Job Johnstone. I thought he would have made a good Judge, and some years ago I said some words to him to that effect. But whether he ever entertained such thought, or had any ambition to be a Judge, I do not know.

To the many beautiful things that were said of him at the Memorial Meeting, to be published in a neat memorial volume, I can add nothing.

The following lines, at the request of a friend, were written soon after his death, but not read at the meeting:

IN MEMORIAM—C. H. SUBER.

I miss him; has he gone away?
  O, who can tell me where my friend has gone?
I saw him, yes, 'twas only yesterday,
  Now he is gone, and I am here alone.

I call him, but he does not hear;
  I speak his name in friendship's tenderest tone.
Is he far off? Far off or very near,
  He answers not and so he must be gone.

Friend of my youth! All miss him here.
  Night came apace and all his work was done;
And now he rests in some far happier sphere;
  But O, I miss him so since he has gone.

Mr. Suber was the son of Solomon Suber, and was born near Pomaria, in Newberry District, on the 4th day of September, 1828, and died at his home in Newberry on the 12th day of March, 1890, from a stroke of paralysis which he received on the 23d of February, 1890.

The house in which he was born is still standing and is occupied by Mr. Wm. Berly at Pomaria.

He entered the South Carolina College in 1845 and graduated in 1848; read law and was admitted to the Bar in 1850, in December—formed a partnership with Silas Johnstone, Esq., and began the practice of the law at Newberry. He continued practice at Newberry until his death, without intermission except the period of the war.

He was elected to the State Legislature in 1858 and was a member of that body for five consecutive terms. And

2   R

again served in the House of Representatives for the term
of 1878–9.

After the election of his partner, Mr. Johnstone, Commissioner in Equity in 1856, he formed a partnership with
Gen. A. C. Garlington, which continued for some years.
After General Garlington's removal to Atlanta in 1869, he
formed a partnership with J. F. J. Caldwell, under the firm
name of Suber & Caldwell. This partnership continued until
Mr. Suber's death.

He was Quartermaster in the Confederate service; sometimes
with the Army of Northern Virginia, and sometimes in Charleston. On several occasions he represented the county in State
Conventions, and was a Delegate at Large to the National
Convention in 1884. He was never married.

JASPER ABRAMS AND ROBERT P. FAIR.

At a meeting of the Quitman Riflemen, held near Fairfax
Court House, Virginia, on the 29th of September, 1862, the
following Tribute of Respect was unanimously adopted:

Although our late friends, Jasper Abrams and Robert P.
Fair, were by sickness forced to obtain a discharge from
the service—and thus to sever their connection with our
Corps—the sad news of their death has excited within us
deeply painful emotions. Nearly all of the last days of their
earthly probation were spent in our ranks, and their labors
were consecrated to the service of their country. Becoming
soldiers at an early age their patriotism glowed with all the
fire of youth. With no vain ambition to gratify, their service
was pure and unselfish—unalloyed with those baser passions
that oftentimes urge men after military fame and glory.
Though they espoused a sacred cause with characteristic
modesty, they yielded to its support their best energies,
their firmest resolve and even life itself; stricken down in
the morning of life, bright hopes have perished and two
brave and youthful spirits have been summoned from this,
we hope, to a better world.

May we not prove indifferent to those oft-repeated warnings,
to prepare for that life which is beyond the grave; "for in an
hour we know not, the Son of Man cometh."

Resolved, That we are deeply pained at the untimely death of our late
friends and fellow-soldiers, Jasper Abrams and Robert Fair; yet, as is our

duty, we bow submissively to the will of our great, good and wise God.

Resolved, That we will cherish their memory and emulate their virtues.

Resolved, That we sincerely sympathise with their respective families in this their sad bereavement, and trust that they may find consolation in Him "who tempers the wind to the shorn lamb."

Resolved, That a copy of this tribute be sent to the families of the deceased, and that it be published in the Newberry papers.

WILLIAM WALTER HOUSEAL.

William Walter Houseal was born in Newberry County (then District) on the 15th day of August, 1818. He died at his home in the town of Newberry on the 1st day of November, 1889. The funeral services were held in the Lutheran Church on November 2nd, and he was buried in Rosemont Cemetery.

His ancestors were German. John Houseal, his grandfather, was one of the original settlers of the "Dutch Fork." John Houseal, his father, was an only son. He married Margaret Counts, the daughter of Colonel John Counts, and by this union there were five children, two sons and three daughters. John Houseal died in 1824, at the age of twenty-seven years, when William Walter was at the age of six years, and was buried on his plantation, which is now owned by Mrs. Jane Barre. The death of his only brother left William Walter the sole male who bore the family name. He often remarked that he owed much in life to the careful training of a pious mother. She died in her fifty-sixth year.

The name was originally spelled Hausihl; then changes were made until it became Houseal. The father of William Walter wrote on the preface page of a text-book—he was a schoolmaster—the following, in a plain, bold hand: "John Houseal, his book: April the 2nd, 1815." This little scrap of paper was the only token of his father that remained to William Walter out of the wreck of time, and it is still preserved in the family as an heirloom.

He was married December 23d, 1841, to Elizabeth C. Barre, daughter of Matthias Barre, who survives him. As a result of this union eight children were born to them, six of whom still survive, four sons and two daughters, namely: John Irving, a machinist in Memphis, Tennessee; James Emlon, a merchant in Cedartown, Georgia; William Preston, one of the publishers of the *Lutheran Visitor* and of the *Herald and News*, and W. Gustave, a physician of Newberry. Of the daughters, Mary E. is the wife of D. Julius Hentz, of Pomaria, and Mattie V., the wife of Rev. J. Q. Wertz, of North Carolina. Frances Cornelia died in her twenty-first year, in 1867, and Edward Julius in his twenty-fourth year, in 1883.

There were thirty-eight grandchildren, twenty-seven of whom are now (1892) living, and one great-grandchild.

He was educated at the Classical Institute, Lexington, S. C., and taught school several years. He united with the Lutheran Church at the age of seventeen, and was confirmed in St. John's, having thus been a church member for fifty-four years.

At the time of his marriage he was living in the Pomaria section, but in 1844 he moved to the Beth Eden neighborhood, being one of the founders of the Beth Eden Lutheran Church. In 1850 he removed to Florida, remaining there a short time. Returning to this county, in January, 1853, he moved to the town of Newberry, where he resided continuously to the time of his death.

He was one of the original members of the Newberry Lutheran Church, and when the congregation was organized, in 1853, he was elected one of the officers of the church, serving as such to the end of his career, being an elder at the time of his death.

In 1855 he was elected Sheriff of Newberry County, after a hotly contested race, defeating his opponent by a large majority. He served one term—till 1859—and was again, in 1863, elected to that office. Under the law at that time a Sheriff could not succeed himself in office. For two years, 1866–68, he held the office of County Assessor.

He had begun merchandizing in Newberry in 1853, and for thirty years he followed that pursuit. In 1862 he volunteered in the Confederate service, but after a short time, his health failing, he was discharged without his request.

Upon the death of Mr. J. K. G. Nance he was appointed Auditor of Newberry, and was recommended at three successive primaries for continuance in that position. In token of his efficiency and acceptability as a public official, and of the esteem and confidence of those among whom he had lived for three score years and ten, in the primary election in 1888 he was nominated without opposition. He was serving his third regular term when his usefulness was estopped by death.

These in brief are the main facts in the public life of William Walter Houseal. Faithful to duty, he performed his life work in a quiet and unostentatious way. But in his private character, in his every day walk and conversation, shone the true nobility of his nature.

His was a life that deserves more than a passing notice, for in it and from it many lessons may be learned that could profit others. He was an affectionate husband, a kind and indulgent father, a faithful member of the Church, and a true and generous friend. He was as gentle as a child and generous to a fault, always more willing to serve others than to be served by them. As a public officer he was faithful and painstaking. As evidence of his fidelity to duty, only a week before he died he got up from his sick bed and came down to assist in drawing the jury. He was faithful to his trust in whatever position he was placed, and went about its performance in a quiet, unobtrusive way. True to his church, he lived the religion he professed; true to his friends, many were his timely acts of kindness; faithful in all things, he was ready when the summons came.

> "When our souls shall leave this dwelling,
> The glory of one fair and glorious action
> Is above all the 'scutcheons on our tomb."

His face we shall see no more. He has passed within the vail. His place at the fireside is vacant. But his life was not lived in vain. Would that we had more such men as was William Walter Houseal!

This tribute, though feeble, must close; and as we drop a tear to his memory we cannot restrain the thought:

> "That man lives greatly
> Whate'er his fate, or fame, who greatly dies."

F. H. A.

> A good man dies: an angel stoops and bears
> His spirit from the dust and stain of earth;
> And death to him is but another birth
> nto a world that knows no fears nor cares!

J. A. C.

The Goggans Family.

About twenty-five years before the Revolutionary war two brothers named Goggans came to Newberry from Virginia. One of these, Daniel Goggans, settled on a place which is now known as Goggans' Old Field, not far from Mount Zion church.

These brothers, with their families, were Whigs, and fought for independence under Marion, Sumter, Pickens, and others. Daniel Goggans was in Marion's command, and once when he was at home on furlough his house was surrounded by a body of Tories commanded by the celebrated and notorious Ned Turner. He knew that his life would be taken in any case, unless he could make his escape, which was impossible; and so he fought them from the house until it was set on fire. He then came out with his arms in his hands, and was instantly shot down. After he was killed the flames were extinguished, and the house stood there for many years, with its scorched and blackened timbers, a monument of the horrors of that war.

All the sons of Daniel Goggans, who were old enough to bear arms in defence of their country, perished in that struggle. His son-in-law, Towles, ancestor of the Colonel Towles who was so long and so favorably known to the people of Edgefield County, was home from the army to see his family—was sick with smallpox—was in hiding in the woods on Saluda, when Ned Turner with a party of Tories went to his house, took two of Towles' little boys up behind them on their horses and compelled them to go with them and show them where their father was hiding. Having found him they killed him at once. It seems that the feud between the Towlses and the Turners was exceedingly and unusually bitter. In an appendix to *Curwin's Journal*, published not long before the war of Secession, there are some interesting circumstances related about the feud told from the other point of view.

Daniel Goggans, of the Revolution, who was killed by Turner as related, left three sons, who were children at the time of his death. These grew up to manhood. One of them, Jerry Goggans, married Elizabeth Peterson, sister of Rev. Jas. F. Peterson, late of Edgefield County, and also sister of Rev. David Peterson, of Newberry, who was the father of John T. Peterson, David Peterson (the father of Warren G. Peterson), and of Captain William Spencer Peterson, who was killed at Atlanta, in one of Hood's great fights, during the war of Secession, in 1864. Hon. John W. Ferguson is a grandson of Rev. David Peterson.

After his marriage to Elizabeth Peterson, Jerry Goggans moved to Ohio, where he soon afterwards died, and was buried at Waynesville in that State. His widow returned to Newberry, bringing with her their only child, Daniel, who was three years old at the time of his father's death, and who had been born in Newberry before the removal of his parents to Ohio. He was named Daniel after his grandfather. He was a man of strong and decided character—of weight and influence.

His children were: E. Jerry Goggans, mentioned in connection with the trouble in Kansas, in 1856 and 1857; Wm. Davidson Goggans, who was Adjutant of the Thirteenth South Carolina Regiment and was killed at the Second Manassas—his name appears on the monument; Mrs. E. S. Herbert, once postmaster at Newberry, S. C.; Mrs. Fannie Dantzler, wife of Rev. D. D. Dantzler, of the South Carolina Conference; James K. P. Goggans and John C. Goggans, now of Newberry.

Capt. E. Jerry Goggans served in the Confederate army through the war of Secession; was at the battle of Fort Sumter as a private; entered the regular service as Third Lieutenant in Capt. David Denny's company, which formed part of the Seventh Regiment; was elected Captain of Company M in 1862; took command of the regiment at Chickamauga after the death of Col. Bland and continued in command until the close of the war in 1865.

Daniel Goggans, of the Revolution, had two other sons. They both removed to Alabama. One of them married a Peterson, a sister to the wife of his brother Jerry. These brothers did well in Alabama and left a numerous progeny; among them may be mentioned Dr. Peterson Goggans, who was surgeon of an Alabama regiment in the Confederate service. Some of the descendants of these two brothers now live in Tennessee.

The descendants of the brother of Daniel who came from Virginia to South Carolina before the Revolution, are now represented by Captain Pickens Goggans, Hogan Goggans and Mrs. Lucy Denny, of Laurens, children of William Goggans, and by Burr F. Goggans, J Gibbes Goggans; Kate, the wife of T. B. Leitzsey; Mollie, wife of A. J. S. Langford; Nora, wife of S. S. Langford, and Lula G , wife of Thos. E. Epting, children of Joseph Goggans, who lived and died in Newberry County.

It may be of interest to note the change that has taken place in the spelling of this name—others have undergone a similar change. This name was originally spelled Goggin. In fact, it is so spelled yet in Virginia. It so appears in the memoirs of William L. and James O. Goggin, of Virginia; and James Goggins, of Gen. McLane's staff, used the same form. In the old family Bible it appears Goggins, and now in Newberry and elsewhere down South it is Goggans, and so let it be.

Daniel Goggans, the father of Jas. K. P. and Jerry, who now lives in Edgefield, and John C., was a man of great force of character and sterling integrity. His opportunities to acquire an education in early life were not great, and yet he made himself a good English scholar; a first rate accountant, and of large and extensive general information. Elsewhere in this history it is mentioned that he was a very good and successful teacher. Starting out in life a poor man he accumulated a handsome fortune, in the use of which he was liberal for all good and proper purposes. He gave his children all the education they would receive, not counting the cost to himself.

THE MARTIN FAMILY.

In writing the history of Edgefield I found a family of seven brothers named Martin, all brave men, and good and true Whigs. Hoping to be able to connect my old friend, J. Newton Martin, with a family so loyal and true, I inquired of him whether he was able to tell me anything about them, or whether they were connected. He said that so far as he knew there was no connection. He then told me that his grandfather, Patrick Martin, with his wife, who was a Miss Gordon, came from County Antrim, Ireland, about the year 1785. The Blairs, who were their neighbors in Ireland, came over at the same time and settled in the same neighborhood in Newberry County.

Patrick Martin's first wife, Miss Gordon, brought him three children: one daughter, who died on the way over and was buried in mid ocean, and two sons, John and Alexander, who settled in Abbeville County. His second wife, Agnes Strait, whom he married in the year 1789, was also from County Antrim. Their first son was born in 1790. William Martin, the father of J. Newton and John B., lived and did business as a merchant at Newberry for many years, where he died. His brother, the father of Mrs. Jane A. Long and Jonathan G. Martin, I never knew. Newton Martin and John were both good soldiers during the war. Patrick Martin died August 24th, 1813; Agnes Martin died February 15th, 1841. John B. Martin died at Newberry, April 18th, 1890. Born June 16th, 1839.

SPENCE—CALDWELL—MONTGOMERY.

Capt. James Spence was the son of William Spence, who, years before the Revolutionary war, came from Ireland with his father, Andrew Spence, and two brothers and two sisters, all children of a first wife. Andrew Spence married again, a Miss Caldwell, sister of the celebrated "Devil" Joe Caldwell, who was one of General Marion's Scouts during the Revolution. Mrs. Esther Spence Montgomery was a daughter of this second marriage—half aunt of Capt. James Spence.

Capt. James Spence commanded a company in the war with the Creek Indians, and was within hearing of the sound of the guns at the battle of the Horse Shoe Bend, where the Creeks were routed and so badly defeated by the Americans under General Jackson. Captain Spence was under a General Milton. After his return from the war he married Betsy Cannon, a half-sister of Abel Cannon and of Mary Wilson, wife of Elder Jimmy. He had only two sons, Milton and Wm. Harrison; the older named for General Milton and the younger for Old Tippecanoe—grandfather of Benjamin—who, at the time he was in the service, was fighting the British and Indians in the Northwest.

Several Spences were in Captain James' company; Robin, an uncle of James, and also John Spence, a cousin. An uncle of the present John Spence was fifer of the company.

William Harrison Spence died early. Milton Spence died in the last year of the war between the States. He served

some time with the State Troops. These were sons of Capt.
James Spence, who died in December, 1864.

Of the family of Captain Spence only two granddaughters
were living in 1892, who owned the homestead of their grandfather, but lived on the place settled by their father, Milton
Spence.

Some of the descendants of "Devil" Joe Caldwell yet live in
Newberry. John F. McCleland and his sister, Mrs. Caroline
Boozer, are his grandchildren. Thomas Q. Boozer and Mrs.
W. T. Jackson are great-grandchildren. "Devil" Joe was dis-
tantly related to the family of Robert T. Caldwell.

--

THE BROWN FAMILY.

From some very interesting papers furnished me by members of two old Newberry families, the Browns and the Risers,
I am able to add the following to the Annals of Newberry:

Among the first settlers of that part of the country which
is now Newberry County was John Brown. He came from
Scotland, landing at Philadelphia, where he then had two
brothers living. While there he became acquainted with Miss
Sarah Sims, and proposed to her that they should marry and
together seek their fortunes in the Southern wilderness. She
agreed to the proposition, as he was a canny Scot and a comely
young man, and she loved him. After marriage they procured
two horses, and, with such equipments packed upon them as
they were able to carry, they bade farewell to their friends
and set out upon their lonely journey through the woods.
Whether tired of traveling, or whether they thought they had
found the garden spot of the world, to this writer is not known.
Be this as it may, they were pleased to make their home nest
on the place now known as the Boozer place, in No. 2 Township, and owned by Rev. E. P. McClintock.

They came about the year 1750, and at that time they were
truly in the woods, their nearest white neighbors being a settlement on Tyger River, not far from Goshen Hill, and one at
Ninety-Six.

There were born to them three daughters and one son, the
son being the youngest. They did not remain alone many
years, as the country about them rapidly filled up. They named

their son Sims. When he was about the age of fifteen years, the Revolutionary war then being in progress, his father took him to Snow Hill, between King's Creek and Kennerly's, and placed him under the care of an old man named Murphy, as a scout in the war. On one occasion, while Murphy was absent, the little fellow made his way into an old Tory's orchard, near by, and partook of the peaches to his satisfaction. It is very probable, however, that if the orchard had belonged to a Whig it would have been all the same to Sims, if the peaches were good. When Murphy returned, and found that his sentinel had left his post, and had stolen peaches besides, he gave him a gentle reminder of his duty as a soldier in the form of a slight flogging with his cane.

At the close of the war he returned home. His father, with his daughters, moved to Spartanburg, but Sims remained at the old home. The daughters married Collins, Miller, Thompson, and lived and died in Spartanburg County. Sims married a Miss Baldreck, of Orangeburg County, with whom he had become acquainted while on a scouting expedition during the war. They settled in Newberry about one mile from the old home, on the place known afterwards as the Reid place, in No. 2 Township. This place remained in possession of some member of the Brown family until just before the War of Secession, when J. C. S. Brown sold it to Thomas J. Price. Sims was appointed Magistrate in early life, and held that honorable and important position for a great many years. He finally gave it up, but was always afterwards known and honored as Colonel or Squire Brown. He grew quite wealthy, and was able to settle his children comfortably. He was the father of six sons and one daughter: James, who read and practiced medicine, married Miss Anna Glasgow, settled near the old home, and died early; John Christopher, Richard Samuel, Sims Edward, Alexander, Thomas Jefferson, and Sarah.

John C. Brown, the second son, was a tanner by trade. He married Miss Jane Caldwell, sister of the late Joseph Caldwell. They settled on the old Brown homestead. Here he taught Joseph Caldwell the art and mystery of making good leather out of raw hides.

To John C. and Jane Brown were born five children, three daughters and two sons, all of whom died in infancy, except one, J. C. S. Brown, who was about six years old at the time of his father's death.

He served as County Commissioner two years, from 1878 to 1880. To him have been born twelve children, six sons and six daughters, seven of whom are living, four sons and three daughters. J. C. S. Brown has lived in this sublunary world about thirteen years longer than any other Brown of the same family. May he live many more.

Richard Samuel Brown, third son of Sims Brown, the Revolutionary scout, married a Miss Law of this county, and settled the Kennerly place, owned in 1892 by his grandson, S. E. Kennerly. He had two sons and one daughter: Dr. James L., Sims E., and Martha.

Dr. James married Miss Glenn, daughter of Dr. Glenn, as his first wife. She brought him two sons, Richard and Glenn. Richard in 1892 was engaged in mercantile business at Anderson, S. C. Glenn went to Texas. After the death of his first wife Dr. James L. married a Miss Bobo, of Laurens. They moved to Mississippi, and soon afterwards to Florida.

Sims E., second son of Richard Samuel Brown, died while in the Senior Class of the South Carolina College.

Martha married Dr. Thomas B. Kennerly, and settled on her father's place.

Sims E. Brown, fourth son of Sims Brown of the Revolution, carried on the mercantile business near Kennerly's, on the old Buncombe road, for a few years, then moved to Newberry C. H., and engaged in mercantile business in a house then standing where the Crotwell hotel building now is. He died early.

Alexander, the fifth son, was a farmer, but lived only a few years after he arrived at man's estate.

Thomas Jefferson, the sixth son, a farmer, married Miss Anna Chapman, of Columbia, S. C., and settled opposite Joseph Caldwell's, on the Buncombe road. They had two sons, Thomas C. and Jefferson E., and three daughters, Sophia, Mary and Sallie. Thomas C. Brown read medicine; during the war was Surgeon in the service of the Confederate States. After the war—when the terrible days of misrule were over—he was elected to the Legislature and to the State Senate. Just in the prime of life he was stricken with paralysis. He partially recovered, but after lingering a few years he quietly passed away. He was a good man, well known to and esteemed by this writer.

Jefferson E. Brown was quite young during the war between the States, but he was a brave and good soldier. For some time, I do not know how long, he acted as courier for General Longstreet, and, being light, vigorous, active and brave, he made a splendid aide. After the war, for a good many years he was engaged in mercantile business at Newberry. He, too, died young. Sophia died young. Mary and Sallie were living in 1892.

Sarah, the only daughter of Sims Brown the Revolutionary scout, ran away from home at the age of twelve years and married Frank Wilson, of this county. Squire Brown was naturally very angry at such a proceeding—angry with his daughter, but more angry with Wilson for persuading one so young to run away with him. After awhile he met Wilson at a barbecue and began to abuse him for stealing his daughter and being too poor to support her. Frank replied by saying he had as many horses, as many sheep, as many cows and as many negroes as the Squire had. "All right," said the Squire; "that settles it."

THE FAMILIES OF MONTS AND FEAGLE.

It is a pleasure, a very great pleasure, to the historian, especially if he is an old man like myself, to look back into the past and record the deeds and fortunes of worthy men and their families. There is no pleasure in life equal to it, especially if we know some of the people of whom we write. It is like clothing in flesh and blood once more the ghosts of the departed and talking with them face to face.

Caspar Monts came from Germany when quite young—time when unknown to this writer. He married a Miss Minnick and settled near where John W. Monts now lives (1892). He reared a family of four sons and two daughters. Two of his sons died early; the other two, John and William, married and reared large families. John's first wife was a Miss Feagle, who brought him one son, Levi, and three daughters, Sallie, Polly and Mary. After her death he married a Miss

Polly Kinard, and to them were born two sons, Adam and G. M. Monts.

Levi Monts married a Miss Bowers and reared three daughters, Mrs. W. C. Sheely, Mrs. John Schumpert and Mrs. J. W. Dominick. Adam married a Miss Mayer and has three sons and one daughter. G. M. Monts married Miss Kate Feagle and has three daughters, Mrs. J. M. Sease and Misses Mary and Bessie.

These three men have all acted their parts nobly. Levi is dead, but he is yet remembered and is often mentioned as an upright, God-fearing man. Adam Monts and G. M. are both what men should be—honest, truthful, upright, and they have, of course, weight and influence in the community in which they live.

William Monts married Miss Sheely and reared six sons and six daughters. Four of these sons lost their lives in the late war; the other two are living—John W. and Jacob.

John W. resides near the old homestead, a successful planter and a courteous and hospitable gentleman. He married a Miss Counts and has four children, Mrs. Johnson, of Kansas City, Mo.; Mamie, Edward and Clarence. One still at the old homestead. Jacob Monts lives in Richland County. Two of his daughters married Derricks, one O. P. Fulmer and another a Swindler. The record of the Monts family has always been good.

The Feagles—Lawrence Feagle, the first of the name in the county, was a German. The time when he came to this country is not known to the writer. He was married twice; first to Miss Leah Quattlebaum, and after her death to her sister Rachel. He reared a family of five sons and four daughters.

Of this venerable man's children I can say nothing, except of his son George and his descendants. George Feagle married a Miss Houseal, a name now almost extinct in that part of the county, but which is well and honorably known in the town of Newberry and elsewhere. From this union there were born three sons, John N., Warren and Irvin; and six daughters, Kate, Mary, Josephine, Elizabeth, Pauline and Leonora.

George Feagle enlisted and entered the Confederate States army in September, 1861, was captured at the battle of Gettysburg in 1863, and was taken to Point Lookout, in which prison he died in 1864, at the age of fifty-five years.

His record is that of a good soldier. He shrank from no duty, but discharged all faithfully, whether as son, husband, father or soldier. His wife died in 1878, and lies buried in the cemetery at St. Paul's. Of his sons, Warren is in Texas, Irvin at Prosperity, and John lives on part of the old homestead. He is a successful planter, and is prominent in the Church and State, having filled the office of Jury Commissioner with credit and honor. He married a Miss Sease, and has a large family of children.

Of the daughters of John Feagle, Kate married G. M. Monts; Josephine, Captain U. B. Whites; Pauline, N. B. Wheeler; Lizzie, A. H. Kohn; Mary, Francis Bobb, and Leonora, J. J. Wheeler. Of these, numerous descendants, children and grandchildren, all take a high stand in the community and with the people amongst whom they live.

This record must not be closed without honorable mention of that venerable lady, Aunt Susannah Houseal, as she loves to be called by the younger people. She is almost a lone survivor of the Houseal family in the Dutch Fork, a name which was once borne by many there. She lives with her niece, Mrs. G. M. Monts, and in her declining years is at peace with her surroundings and with all the world.

—

THE BOLAND FAMILY.

Among the first settlers of the county, not the very first, but of those who came just after the close of the Revolutionary war, were the Bolands, a strong, vigorous and hardy race.

The sire of this great family, John Boland, came from the Vaterland about the year 1784, with Konkle, Schwartz and others.

John Boland was twenty-two when he came to South Carolina. He married a Widow Counts, and settled not far from where Chapin now is. She brought to him one son, Abram. After her death he married a Miss Feltman, who became the happy mother of seven sons and two daughters. The sons were John, Henry, Adam, George, William, Dove and Jacob. The daughters were Barbara and Mary.

Mr. Boland died in the year 1832, at the age of eighty, and ies buried near his old home. He was a thrifty and energetic man, hard working and honest. Seven of his sons, John, Henry, Adam, William, George, Dove and Jacob, went West to seek their fortune. How they succeeded, I know not; but they did not disgrace their ancestry. Abram remained at home, married a Miss Sease, and reared a family of nine sons and one daughter. The daughter, Katie, married Mr. George Shealy. The sons were named William, Frederick, Joe, Adam, Levi, Walter, Middleton, Mark and Osra. All these sons married, and all reared large families, except Levi, who married a Miss Wheeler and died childless.

William and Walter went West, and are still living (1892). Joe, Middleton and Mark, though no longer young, are still faithfully working at their favorite occupation near the place where they were born. The other sons and the daughter are no longer living. Middleton was a good soldier during the war of Secession, and while he was absent from home with the army, Sherman, with the Federal forces, passed through the country, burning everything in the track through which they passed; and when Mr. Boland returned home after the surrender he found nothing but a pile of ruins and one or two of Sherman's "lone sentinels" to mark the spot where once had stood his comfortable home. With unconquerable energy, he went to work and repaired what he had lost. He reared a family of six sons and five daughters, educated them fairly well, and he is to-day living in a comfortable and hospitable home, with a conscience void of offense.

Of his sons, we may mention A. N. and David Boland, two very genial gentlemen, who reside near the old homestead. They are just and upright in their dealings, and men of influence.

Osra Boland died in early life, leaving two sons, D. C. and J. A. Boland. These men began life poor, but have done well, and are now, 1892, extensive mill men.

Joseph Boland still resides where he first settled sixty years ago. He reared a family of three sons and seven daughters. All follow the example of their ancestors and earn their bread by the sweat of their face.

Adam Boland is no more. He has gone to his reward. He

H. H. Kinard.

W. W. Houseal.

John S. Carwile.

James Bonds.

Nathan F. Johnson.

THE SHERIFFS OF "ANTE BELLUM" TIMES.

was a good, jovial old gentleman. His widow still lives and lingers this side the grave. They had two sons and three daughters. The daughter Mrs. George Sheely died a few years ago. Judging from the character of the children she left, she was the best of mothers. Mothers always mould the character of the children.

Uncle Mark Boland is still living.

No member of this family has ever been in public life; no one has ever sought or held any office. Such men are the bone and sinew of the country; they are the strength of the State, and if the country and the State had more like them the country and the State would be infinitely better off.

—

THE KIBLER FAMILY.

As far as I am able to trace the history of this family, it starts with two brothers, John Kibler and Michael, who were living in the lower part of Newberry County; that is, below where the Court House now is. They were members of that great Teutonic family which has done so much to infuse into the other peoples of the world a spirit of sturdy independence and love of liberty.

The father of these brothers was one of the first settlers of the county. John Kibler, the elder of the brothers, married Nancy Farr, by whom he became the father of six sons and three daughters. The sons were: John, Jacob, Andrew, Daniel, William and Levi; the daughters, Polly, Catherine and Ann.

Of these, John married the daughter of Col. John Summer; Jacob married Miss Mary Stack; Andrew and Daniel died unmarried. Levi married Miss Folk, and is still living; has one son, J. D. A. Kibler, living, who also is married and has children grown up.

Of the daughters, Polly married Adam Bedenbaugh, and has two sons, Jacob and Andrew, and two daughters, one of whom married Jacob Singley. Catherine married John Fellers. She and her husband are both dead, but left one son and two daughters, all living. The son John C. lives in Edgefield. One daughter married Captain William Sligh, who is now (1892) on duty in Columbia, S. C. The other daughter married Jerry Wyse, of Edgefield. She is left a widow. Ann married Ivy Busby, and is dead, leaving no children.

2

S

Michael Kibler, the other of the original two brothers, married, and had a family of five sons and five daughters. I am not informed as to the name of the lady he married. He and his wife both lived to a good old age, though she lived in widowhood about twenty years after his death. He died about 1831, and she in 1851. Their sons were Michael, John, David, Adam and Jacob. The names of the daughters I am not able to give. This Michael is said, and it is generally believed in that section of the county, to have had and used the first cotton gin ever employed in the County of Newberry.

Of the sons, Michael married Miss Koon; John, a Miss Eichelberger; David married three times, first, a Miss Fellers, next a Miss Suber, his last wife being Miss Hair. David was the father of nine children, five sons and four daughters, all of whom are dead except three, Drayton (D. W. T.), and Catherine and Amos. The names of the other sons were Godfrey, Middleton and Calvin. Adam married three times, Misses Fellers, Maffet and Kinard. His last wife is still living, a pleasant, genial, comely, good-looking lady. Jacob married Miss Frances Chapman, daughter of Samuel Chapman, Esq. She brought him three sons and three daughters, all of whom are living in the town of Newberry—William, Arthur, John, Elizabeth, Alice and Sarah—none yet married.

Of the daughters of the original Michael Kibler, the names of whom I am unable to give, one married Jacob Sligh, brother of that good old man, Philip Sligh. These left one daughter, who married Lang. Ruff. She is still living, but a widow. One married George Dickert; two became the wives of David Koon. There were two sons of David Koon, both of whom died in the service of the Confederate States. One daughter married John Barre. They left one daughter, who married and died, leaving one child.

THE SHEALYS.

John Windell Shealy was the first of the name that came from the old country to this. A man named John Adam Epting brought over a small colony from the city of Heidelberg, consisting of Shealy, Leitzey, Setzler, Cromer and Myer, in the year 1763. They were all Lutherans, and were among the founders of the present St. John's Church. John Windell

Shealy mar.ied Miss Epting, daughter of Mr. Epting, the pioneer of the colony, in the year 1770, and settled near where W. C. Shealy now lives.

The fruits of this union were twelve sons and one daughter. I can give the names of only eight of these sons; the others I have never learned: Windell, William, Adam, John, Henry, Matthias, David and Andrew. Of these, William, Windell and David married Wertses; Andrew married a Miss Sawyer, and the daughter a Mr. Quattlebaum. Whom the other sons married, if they ever married, I am unable to say.

Mr. Shealy, the pioneer, died in the year 1814, and was buried near the place where he first settled. He lived long enough to see all his sons fully grown; and they were all strong, robust men. They stood six feet in height, and the least and lightest one of them weighed 175 pounds. In those days, when men defended themselves, on all ordinary occasions, with the weapons given them by nature, these twelve brothers, if they felt their rights assailed, could have given any other twelve, or more, a lively tussle.

Mr. Shealy owned all the lands in and around Little Mountain at that time, and settled not a few of his children on them; hence this is the Mecca of the Shealys. Within a few hundred yards of the residence of Mr. W. C. Shealy is the spring of fresh, cool, clear, bubbling water used by the original John Windell Shealy, and it still has in it a portion of the gum placed there by Mr. Shealy over one hundred and twenty years ago. The men of this family, like others who are the salt of the earth, are farmers, cultivators of the soil, and attend to their own business and let others' alone. Some of them are preachers of the gospel, ministers in the Lutheran Church—they are all Lutherans—and one is a teacher of youth, whom I have heard mentioned as a man of large brain and heart, but of small body, like my friend Squire Padgett of Edgefield.

This part of Newberry before, and even after, the war was regarded as the poor portion of the county; but it has been made to bloom as the rose, and is now regarded as the most independent portion. This result has been brought about by hard and strenuous labor. There are Shealys who started after the war without means, who are now independent. Could the original Shealy rise from the grave, and from the tops of the highest hills look over the surrounding country, no doubt he would be filled with wonder at the great and beneficent change. The forests have given place to well cultivated fields; schools flourish; churches are established, and the Word is dispensed to waiting and willing souls; the country is prosperous and happy; and much of this good is due, under divine Providence, to the Shealys and to the example set by them.

—

Thomas Ferguson Greneker.

This past veteran journalist was born in the city of Charleston, S. C., March 2nd, 1827, and died at his home in Newberry on the 3d of December, 1889, in the sixty-third year of his age. He was the eldest son of Captain Thos. Greneker, of the Merchant Marine service. Having the misfortune to lose his parents while quite a boy, with the further loss of a competency that would have given him a classical education, he went into a printing office, after receiving a good English education, as the best means at his command of acquiring that knowledge which he sought and obtained. His bright and retentive mind soon enabled him to master the details of the business and he rapidly rose in the confidence of his employers and the esteem of the craft..

Early in the fifties Mr. Greneker removed to Columbia and took charge of Dr. Robert W. Gibbes' large book and job printing and newspaper office, where he was foreman of the State printing. Some time afterwards he and ·Messrs. Giles & LaMotte published the third daily newspaper ever printed in Columbia. The name of the paper was *The Carolina Times*. Disposing of his interest, he came to Newberry about the year 1858, and was associated with Thos. P. Slider in the *Rising Sun*, which newspaper he published until the Confederate war, when he entered the service as a private in Colonel Edward's Thirteenth Regiment of South Carolina Volunteers. Declining health caused him to return home. He was an invalid to the day of his death, and notwithstanding the intense bodily pain which he almost daily endured, he exhibited great energy and industry in the successful management of the Newberry *Herald* (the successor of the *Rising Sun*), which he conducted with his brother, R. H. Greneker. In

1884 the *Herald* was consolidated with the Newberry *News*. For a number of years this venerable editor was the trusted treasurer of the South Carolina State Press Association, until the wretched condition of his health forced him to resign the position and also, in 1885, to retire from journalism. He wrote with a fluent and facile pen.

Mr. Greneker was twice married; first, in Columbia, on the 30th of December, 1852, to Miss Mary Caroline Fritz. By this marriage three children were born, one son and two daughters. Only one of these, Lula, wife of A. C. Jones, is now living. His second marriage occurred on the 9th of August, 1864, to Miss Corrie G. Sligh, of Newberry County, who survives him. Six children were born of this marriage, four sons and two daughters, three of whom are now living: Sarah, wife of C. C. Davis, Eugene and Claude.

Mr. Greneker was the founder of the *Herald*, and for nearly forty years was identified with the journalism of this county. The best years of his life and his energy and intellect were spent here in our midst in an effort to advance the true interests of his adopted town and county and of his native State. He was one of the organizers of the State Press Association and was a consistent member of the Methodist Church —showing his devotion to Church and State—and died in the assurance of a blissful immortality beyond the grave. He had a large circle of acquaintances and many friends in the county and State.

Mr. Greneker was a genial, kind-hearted and hospitable man, and though a great sufferer from ill-health, had a quiet vein of humor which made him a very agreeable host and companion. Temperate and industrious, he acquired a comforable living for his family and kept a bountiful table in waiting for his friends, who always received a warm welcome to his happy home. He fell peacefully upon his last sleep.

HENRY H. BLEASE.

Henry H. Blease was born at Edgefield C. H., S. C., on the 11th day of May, 1832, and died at his home at Newberry on the 15th day of April, 1892.

His was a strong and vigorous character, the elements of

which were manifested in early life. He had great powers of discrimination in matters involving much investigation, and I have no doubt that he would have made an able lawyer and an ornament to the Bar had his mind been trained in that direction. Other walks in life were his.

In 1849 he left Edgefield and moved to Newberry, and after wards filled, both in time of peace and of war, many places of trust with fidelity. After the war he engaged in farming, but in a short time he moved to the town of Newberry and engaged in business as the proprietor of a hotel and livery stables. For several years he filled the office of Trial Justice at Newberry.

As a friend he was firm and loyal; as a thinker he was clear, and his opinions, once formed, were decided. He was hospitable, and loved social intercourse. To the poor and destitute he was always ready and willing to extend a helping hand, and many acts of kindness were done by him which are known only by the recipients and God.

He was a member of the Methodist Church, loving that Church with a devoted love, as all good Methodists do; but he was no bigot, and could see the spirit of the Master shining through the good people of other churches besides his own.

During several years of the latter part of his life he was a great sufferer; but no one ever heard him lament or complain of his condition. He was patient all through to the last, and when the summons came he had no fears, and only expressed regret that he would be separated from those so near and dear to him.

Mr. Blease was twice married and left several children. Two sons, Harry and Cole L. Blease, are practising lawyers at Newberry. Harry has served as Trial Justice, and Cole L. was elected to the Legislature (House of Representatives) in 1890, and has served one term. There are also several daughters and a younger son. One daughter, Ella, married C. L. Havird; one, Corrie, J. E. St. Amand, of Charleston; one, Leila, T. G. Williams, Newberry. Three children by the last wife; two sons, one daughter.

Rev. William Harmon

Was one of the earliest Methodist local preachers near Saluda Old Town, where he lived so many years. He was twice married. His first wife was Rosannah Summers, by whom he had ten children. His second wife was Honora Bridget Frean, daughter of Rev. Thomas Frean. This union was blessed with two children, Thomas F. Harmon, now living at Newberry, and Sarah Jane, who married Middleton T. Kinard.

The house in which Mr. Harmon lived so many years, and in which he died, is still standing. He was a successful farmer and good and useful citizens. He died in December, 1843, at the age of sixty-four years, and was buried at Moon's Meeting House, the church which he loved and supported. There is no church there now, no house of worship; nothing to mark the spot save the silent tombs around.

MIDDLETON T. KINARD

Lived the latter part of his life on Saluda River and owned what is still known (1892) as Kinard's Ferry. Mr. Kinard, though a brother of General H. H. and John P. Kinard, who for so many years were prominent public men, never sought any office, but preferred to remain in private life and be a successful farmer and a true and honest man.

He married, late in life, Sallie, daughter of Rev. William and Bridget Harmon. He died in the year 1867, in his fifty-fourth year, leaving two children. His wife died in 1865. No man in his neighborhood was more beloved by friends and neighbors than Middleton T. Kinard.

THE BERLY FAMILY.

Gaspar Berly came from Germany and first settled in Charleston; afterwards came to Newberry, some fifteen or twenty years before the Revolution, and settled near Pomaria, where he died and was buried. His first wife came with him from Germany. At her death he married Miss Easter, from Fairfield. By his first wife there were four sons: Syke, Gaspar, Harmon and Martin. By his last marriage there were two sons, John and Frederick, and three daughters, Elizabeth, Mary and Margaret. All the sons moved from Newberry except John. He married Miss Barbara Werts. The children of John Berly were: Rev. William, Adam, Joel A., Elizabeth, Sarah and Jane. Elizabeth married Wm. Riser, Sarah married A. M. Bowers, and Jane married Matthias Barre.

Captain John Martin Kinard,

Of the Twentieth Regiment, South Carolina Volunteers, was a son of General H. H. Kinard. He was born in Newberry County, July 5, 1833. After some preparation at the Winnsboro High School, he attended the South Carolina College, leaving in his Junior year. He was twice married. His first wife, Mary A. Ruff, daughter of Dr. P. B. Ruff, died early in life, leaving a daughter who is now the wife of Elbert H. Aull. His second wife, Lavinia E. Rook, who still lives, bore him two sons, John M., who is now Clerk of Court for Newberry County, and James P., who is a student at Johns Hopkins University, Baltimore.

Captain Kinard enlisted as First Lieutenant of Company F, and became Captain on the resignation of his uncle, John P. Kinard. The regiment was encamped around Charleston in 1862–3. They defended Morris Island during the bombardment. The regiment was ordered to Virginia in 1864. During a fight in the Shenandoah Valley, near Strasburg, and not far from Winchester, Va., Captain Kinard, while acting Lieutenant-Colonel, was shot through the heart, October 13, 1864. After the fight his faithful servant, Ham, secured the body and brought it home.

At the breaking out of the war Captain Kinard was engaged in farming at his home, Kinard's, in the upper part of the county. In his country's call to arms he heard the voice of duty, and resigning the peaceful pleasures of home he poured out his heart's blood in defence of the cause he loved so well. His handsome features and gentle spirit endeared him greatly to his fellow-soldiers. His personal popularity is shown by the loving manner in which the surviving members of his company speak of him.

> "And how can man die better
> Than facing fearful odds
> For the ashes of his fathers
> And the temples of his gods."

—

The Gary Family.

Thomas Gary and West Gary settled in Newberry County about from 1760 to 1770. Thomas Gary was the father of

Captain Jesse Gary, who lived near the place now known as
Gary's Lane, in the County of Newberry. He was a successful planter and grew rich. He married Miss Mary Reeder, a
most excellent lady, one who was earnest in all good words
and works, and who accomplished great good in the community
in which she lived.

Thomas Gary was the father of six children: Thomas R.
Gary; Elizabeth, who married Stephen Blackburn, and Dr.
William Rook; Martin C. Gary; Rebecca, who married Dr. John
F. Gary; Hillary Gary, and Lavinia, who married James
Young.

Dr. Thomas R. Gary, the son of Thomas, moved to Abbeville, and there married Miss Mary Ann Porter. They reared
a large family of children. Among them may be mentioned
the late Dr. F. F. Gary, who married Miss Mary C. Blackburn.
Dr. F. F. Gary was the father of Eugene B. Gary; Frank B.
Gary, of Abbeville; Ernest Gary, of Edgefield, and Mrs. James
M. Eason, of Charleston.

West Gary was the father of Dr. John K. Gary, a practicing physician of Newberry for many years, much loved for his
kindness of heart.

THE CROSSON FAMILY.

The first Crosson who ever came to this country was Alexander, who landed at Philadelphia. His emigration was not
voluntary, having been banished from his home and country
as a punishment for killing his lord's game without license.
He settled in the Shenandoah Valley at Woodstock, Virginia.
Afterwards his father came to this country and landed at
Charlestown. About three years after his arrival he heard
where his son was and went to Virginia and brought him to
South Carolina. Alexander and John were the only children
the old man had. Alex married a Steel or a Smith and
became the father of seven children, viz: Tom, Huey, Robert,
Jane, Ann, Ellen and Mary.

Tom, the eldest son, married Jane Neily in 1800. His
children were James M., Margaret and Jane.

James Crosson's children were J. T. P., H. S. N., David,
Allen, Lizzie and Jane.

THE DOMINICK FAMILY.

Henry Dominick came to Newberry District from Germany about 1760, when quite a small boy. He first married Margaret Fellows (now spelled Fellers), who brought him one son, Henry. His second wife was also a Miss Fellows, a sister of the first, to whom were born George and Andrew. Henry Dominick, Jr., married Mary Paysinger, a sister, if I mistake not, of John Paysinger, elsewhere mentioned; to whom were born John, Frederick, George Wesley, Jacob, Andrew, Catherine, Elizabeth, Polly Stockman, Nancy Kinard, Tena Kinard and Eliza Bowers. John Dominick married Bettie Rikard, who brought him Henry, George, Crayton, Nancy Taylor, Mary Mills and Eva Taylor. Frederick Dominick married Mary Long, who brought him Jacob, Preston, Sidney, Harriet Harmon, Laura Mayer and Alice Johnson. George Dominick married Peggy Nelson, an Irish lady, who brought him John, George, Mary Hunter, Nancy, Fannie Bedenbaugh and Carrie Fellers. Wesley Dominick married Jane Lake, who brought him Fannie Dominick and Trannie Fellers. Andrew P. Dominick married Lucinda Shealy, who brought him Ambrose, Sallie Cook, Cora, Bessie and May. George Dominick married Mary Mack, who brought him Aaron, George, Henry, Lindsey, Mary Warner and Margaret Bowers. Aaron Dominick married, first, Eva Shealy, by whom he became the father of George, Michael, Luther, Lawson, Mary Derrick and Alice Stockman. His second wife was Catherine Cook, who brought him Wesley and Lizzie Monts. George Dominick married Nancy Hunter, who brought him Samuel, Chesley, Lindsey, John Abner and Lizzie Cook. With this happy marriage the old "Dead Line," the line of separation between the Irish and Dutch, became completely obliterated and destroyed. Henry Dominick married Rhoda Banks; Lindsey Dominick married Rosa Cook; George Dominick married Josephine Trotter; Michael Dominick married Lizzie Edwards; Luther Dominick married a Miss Shealy; Wesley Dominick married Mary Dominick; Samuel Dominick married Nancy Stockman; Chesley Dominick married Fannie Dominick; Lindsey Dominick married Carrie Hunter; John Dominick married Thompsie Dawkins; Abner Dominick married Cornelia Bedenbaugh; Simpson Dominick married Frances Moore; Jacob A. Dominick married Eunice Sease.

THE MOSELEY FAMILY.

Absalom Moseley, of English descent, married Mary Richardson, of Irish descent, to whom were born William, Mason, Wiley, Daniel, Sallie, Winnie and Nancy Burckhalter. William, Mason and Wiley Moseley moved to Arkansas in early life. Daniel Moseley married Caroline Bridges, daughter of William Bridges, to whom were born Hanson C., William A. and Nancy C., who married George D. Brown. H. C. Moseley married Carrie Brown, July 30th, 1872. William A. Moseley married Melissa Schumpert, October 22, 1878.

THE BOWERS FAMILY.

Stephen Bowers married a Miss Bates, to whom were born David, Samuel, Andrew, Jacob, Levi, John, Sallie Wheeler, Elizabeth Fellers, Nancy Maffett and Vina Young. David Bowers married Eva Kinard, to whom were born Michael, Levi, Vina Shealy, Katie Shealy, Betsie Frick, Mary Ann Monts and Louisa Swygert. Michael Bowers married Eliza Dominick, to whom were born one son, George, and three daughters. Levi Bowers became a lawyer under Major L. J. Jones' tutorage. He died in the bloom of youth. John Bowers moved to Georgia. Samuel Bowers married, first, a Miss Cook, to whom were born Rebecca Simpson, Elizabeth Werts and Jacob Bowers. His second wife was Margaret Moore, who brought him Levi S., Fletcher M., Emma Nates and Mary Barre. Levi S. Bowers married Mollie Gallman. Samuel Bowers was a magistrate before and during the war between the States; and a most excellent man who held the scales of justice with an even, firm and steady hand. Andrew Bowers married ———— ————, to whom were born George, Jacob, Michael, Levi, John and Nancy Young. John Bowers married Margaret Dominick, who brought him six sons and three daughters, viz: Patrick, George, Lindsey, Luther, Pierce, Nathan, Sarah Stockman, Elizabeth Bowers and Mary Stockman. Patrick Bowers, son of John, married, first, Salome Stockman, by whom he had one daughter, Alice Mitchell. George married Elizabeth Bowers; Lindsey, Mary Bowers; Luther, Golvy Morris; Pierce, Amanda Taylor; Nathan, Bessie Morris; with what further result is unknown to this historian. Of George Bowers, the son of Andrew, I know nothing.

Jacob S. married Sarah, daughter of Samuel Chapman, Esq., who brought him several sons and daughters. One, J. William, engaged in business in Abbeville County; one, Rev. A. J. Bowers, pastor of Lutheran Church in Savannah, Ga.; one daughter, Mary, wife of R. H. Wright, merchant and banker, in the town of Newberry; one, Margaret, wife of McDuffie Sligh, farmer in Newberry County; one, Stevie, wife of George Wright, nephew of Robert H., engaged in business in Texas; one, Elizabeth, who married Rev. H. S. Wingard, but now dead, leaving several children; one, Janie, is unmarried and makes her home with Rev. Wingard, who has married again since the death of his first wife. There was a daughter, Ella, who married a Mr. Mackerell. She is no longer living, but left one or two children. A. Michael Bowers is living and is in business in the town of Newberry. He married Miss Barre, but has long been a widower. He has two children, son and daughter, both grown. Of Levi, the other son of Andrew Bowers, and the daughter, Nancy Young, I can add nothing here.

THE BEDENBAUGH FAMILY.

Adam Bedenbaugh was born near Pomaria, S. C., of German parentage, and entered the Revolutionary war at sixteen years of age. He married a Miss Wertz and settled on Broad River. Afterwards he moved to the Stoney Hills, settling on Little Creek. To him were born nine sons and one daughter, Elizabeth. The sons were named Henry, Adam, Michael, Jacob, Abram, Christian, David, John and William. He lived to be quite aged, his wife living several years after his death. William is still living, his home being in Georgia. Henry settled, after marriage to Elizabeth Brighe, on Big Creek. To him were born four sons, Daniel, John Adam, Simeon and William Pinckney. There were five daughters, Elizabeth, Eve, Melinda, Rachel and Rosanna. He lived to be seventy six years old, his wife living to the age of eighty-one. Daniel died at thirty-one years of age, leaving a wife and two children, who moved to Alabama. John Adam, the next son, now seventy-six years old and living on the old homestead, has a son, Rev. Z. W. Bedenbaugh, and a daughter, Mrs. Mary E. Dennis, both living near him. Two daughters died in 1865.

Simeon, now seventy-four years old, is also living near the old homestead. To him were born five sons, Warren, Jacob, Hawkins, John and Pettus, and three daughters, Amelia, Nancy and Ella. Pinckney died at the age of fifty-eight, without children. Elizabeth died without marrying. Eve was married to Frederick Boozer, and to whom were born two children, a son and a daughter. Melinda was married to Jacob Hawkins, and to them were born four sons and four daughters. Rachel married Mathias Wicker, and to them were born three sons, all now living. Rosanna was married to Allen Nichols. To them were born five sons and four daughters. Adam Bedenbaugh, Jr., settled on Big Creek, near his brother Henry, but afterwards he moved to the Dutch Fork. He married Polly Kibler, and to them were born five sons, Levi, John, Andrew, Jacob and William, and two daughters, Epsie and Nancy. Michael also settled in the Stoney Hills. He had two sons and four daughters. Jacob settled near his father, and to him were born five sons and four daughters. Abram married Sheba Nelson, but left no children. Christian had one son, who moved to Indiana after his father's death. David died early in life. John also settled near his father, marrying Rhoda King. To them were born five sons and four daughters. William, the only surviving son, now living in Georgia at the advanced age of eighty-five years, had four sons and four daughters.

—

THE YOUNG FAMILY.

Abram Young, Sr., came to America from County Down, Ireland, and died here in 1802. He had four sons and seven daughters, viz.: Joseph, Thompson, James and Abram; the daughters' names after marriage being: Nancy Brown, Betsey Fair, Mary Thompson, Hannah Carmichael, ·Jennie Gregg, Abby, or Abia Carmichael, and Esther Boyd, afterward Esther Carr. Abram Young, Jr., married a Carmichael, by whom he had six sons, Thompson, Joseph, Abram, James, Nathan and Arthur. Thompson Young, now living in his eighty third year, married Mary Hunter. To them were born one son, Nathan H., and two daughters, Amanda, now living with her father, and Mary Ann, the wife of James H. Dennis. Nathan was a soldier during the late war, in the Third South Carolina Regiment. He married Nancy Dennis, by whom he had two sons, Thompson and Augustus. All the Youngs, except Thompson and his family, removed to Georgia. Nathan and Arthur died, and lie buried in Prosperity Cemetery. Thompson Young, nephew of Thompson Young just mentioned, has returned to Newberry, and makes his home at the old Ramage place, having married Mary, the daughter of J. J. Paysinger. He returned to Newberry in 1890.

—

THE WHEELER FAMILY.

George Wheeler was born in South Carolina in 1759. At the age of sixteen he entered the American army and fought through the Revolutionary struggle. He married Barbara Addy, by whom were born four sons, John, Simeon, George and Jacob, and one daughter, Polly. John and George died without families. Simeon Wheeler married twice; first he married Elizabeth Mayer (then pronounced Moyer), by whom were born two daughters, Mary, who married Levi Boland, and Elizabeth, who married Frederick Fulmer. His second wife was Elizabeth Shealy, to whom were born six sons, Michael, D. Henry, Simeon, Jacob, Levi and George. D. Henry Wheeler is the only one of the six that ever married. He married Ellen Lorick, to whom were born four sons, Samuel, Jacob, Frank and Martin. D. Henry Wheeler owns large quantities of real estate in the county and the town of Newberry, and is a great friend to the poor. Jacob Wheeler, son of George, married Sallie Bowers, nine sons being born to them, namely, Levi, George, John, Luther, J. Middleton, Daniel B., Andrew H., Nathan B. and James. Four daughters also were born, three of whom died young, the fourth, Emeline, marrying Emanuel Werts, of Edgefield County. Levi Wheeler married Frances Pike, to whom Jacob I., Thompson L. and Alice were born. Levi died in 1861. George is living unmarried. John married Harriet Kempson, and their children were: Marion, Luther, Emma, Alice, John and James (twins). Luther married Anna Kempson, and she brought him one son and one daughter, George and Lizzie. J. Middleton married Nancy Singley, and Sidney, Mary, Pettus, Walton and

Bennie were their children. Daniel B. married Adella Williams, and their offspring are Mallie, Bessie and Sallie. Andrew H. married Elenora Counts, and their children were Nina, Leila and Clarence. Nathan B. married Pauline Feagle, their children being Eugene, Carrie, Albert, Edna, Essie, Ernest, Ellen and Bartow. James married Mary Dickert, having one son, James. James, Sr., died in 1871.

THE HUNTER FAMILY.

Nathan Hunter, a native of County Antrim, Ireland, came to America about 1780. Having married Mary Young in Ireland, they settled in Newberry County, and here were born five sons and three daughters, namely, William, Joseph, George, Nathan, James, Elizabeth Drennan, Jane Thompson and Mary Devlin. William Hunter married Sarah Abernathy, and their children were: Nathan, John, George, Joseph, Rhoda Connor and Mary Teague. Joseph Hunter married Elizabeth Abernathy, their offspring being: James, Nathan, John, William, Joseph, Samuel, Mary Spence, Jane Hawkins, Sarah Lester, Nancy Dominick, Rhoda and Elizabeth. George Hunter married Mary Wellington, and their sons and daughters were: Nathan A., John, William, Elizabeth Leavell and Jane Carmichael. Nathan Hunter married Amanda Mills, granddaughter of Rev. Giles Chapman, and moved to Alabama. James Hunter married, first, Elizabeth Davis, who bore him three sons, Lafayette, James and Calhoun. His second wife was Margaret Bruale, and Mary Sims and Elizabeth McMakin were their children. This family moved to Union, S. C. Nathan Hunter married Frances Reeder, whose children were William and Samuel. John Hunter married Abba Johnson, and moved to Georgia. George Hunter married Mariah Wilson, and became the father of Sarah Davis. His second wife was Elizabeth Starks. She brought him Pennington and two other sons, whose names cannot now be obtained. Joseph Hunter married Ruth Kellar, who became the mother of Isaac, James, William, Hyde, Rachael Bonds, Sarah Drennan, Sue Eddy and Mary Johnson. James Hunter married Sarah Crisel, and moved to Illinois. Nathan A. Hunter married Louisa Aull, and their children are: Joseph H., Alice L., wife of Dr. Peter Robertson;

Julia B., wife of Prof. C. W. Welch; Charles T. and Clarence E. John, William and Joseph never married. Samuel Hunter married Elizabeth Davis, who brought him Chesley D., Joseph, Albert, Bessie, wife of Geo. G. Lane; Rhoda, Belle and Nancy. Nathan Hunter married Susannah Cureton, by whom he became the father of John, James, Thomas, William, Eliza Lake, Mary Young and Susannah Dennis. John Hunter married Rosannah Young, and moved to Florida. James Hunter married Mary Carmichael, and their issue were: John, Robert T. C., Nathan and Eliza Whitman. Thomas Hunter married Juriah Fellers, their children being Jefferson, George, Carrie Dominick, Alma Trotter, Adella and Mary. Joseph H. Hunter married Elizabeth Fant. These have Nathan and Frank. John L. Hunter married Mary Dominick. To these have been born Dr. George Y., Ellie Fellers, Fannie and Maggie. Robert T. C. Hunter married Rebecca Boozer, and he became the father of Thaddeus, James, Joseph, Lafayette, Robert, Allen and Carrie. Robert T. C. Hunter is a prominent man in his section, always taking an active part in public affairs, such as conventions, etc. He served one term in the lower house of the Legislature, after which he declined to be a candidate again. Nathan Hunter married Abbie Boozer, whose sons are Thompson and Rufus.

The Jacob Boozer Family.

Jacob Boozer was of Swiss or Swedish descent. He married Elizabeth Senn about the year 1770, and settled on Twenty-one Mile Creek, at Cherokee Ford, near Fort Granby, and served in the Revolutionary war. By this marriage came Henry, David, William and Jacob. Jacob Boozer married and lived in Lexington. Henry and William, with their families, removed to Alabama. David Boozer married Catherine Rawl, and became the father of Wesley, David L. (dentist in Columbia), and Jacob H., who married, first, Elizabeth Enlow, a niece of Captain Matthew Hall, having by her two sons, Matthew and Luther, and whose second wife was Haphock Lindsey, who brought him also two sons, Lindsey and Jacob. D. Luther Boozer married Emma Moore, nnd has a family who, with him, are now living near Ninety-Six, in Abbeville County.

The P. W. Counts Family.

(THIS NAME WAS ORIGINALLY KOUNTZE.)

Henry Counts, Sr., the grandfather of P. W. Counts, Esq., was born and married in South Carolina, near Pomaria, his father being one of the earliest settlers of the county. He married a Miss Fellows (now spelled Fellers). They had four sons, Henry, Jr., Jacob, Frederick and John. Henry Counts, Jr., married Sallie Hair, the issue of this union being two sons, one of whom died in infancy, and P. W. Counts, the subject of this sketch, who is now eighty years old, having been born in 1812. He married Martha Harmon, and to them were born four sons and two daughters, all of whom are living. One son, J. Henry Counts, lives in Lexington, and has served two terms in the Legislature from that county. J. Calhoun Counts is a Methodist minister. Walter I. and George Counts live near the old homestead. P. W. Counts lives on the identical place where he was born. It has been in the family for one hundred and twenty-seven years. He filled acceptably the office of magistrate, or "Esquire," for a number of years before and during the civil war, and is the only magistrate on record in the county as having pronounced the death sentence upon a murderer; and at the appointed time the man was hanged. He was a slave belonging to a Bobo, and the murdered man was white and an overseer.

—

The Wise Family.

John Wise moved from Lexington District to Newberry District, on Saluda River, about the year 1800. He married Betsey Kelly, by whom he had six sons and six daughters, viz.: George, David, Jesse, Jeremiah, Joel, Levi, Elizabeth, who married, first, John Derrick, then Jacob Caughman; Christiana, who married Frederick Kinard; Margaret, who married Michael Shealy; Jemima, who married George Addy; Nancy, who married John McNeary, and Sallie, who married Jacob Singley. George Wise married, first, Mary Roberts, the issue of this union being Solomon, Charlotte, who died young; Betsy, who married Michael Shealy; Margaret, who married Henry Jennings; John A. and Patrick E. His first wife having died, he married Mary Shealy, and their children were Walter, Jacob, Pickens, James and Lemuel. The last four died without

2   T

families. P. E. Wise married Christiana Aull, by whom he had five sons, George, Lawson, Allen, James and Bachman, and two daughters, Elizabeth, who married John B. Lathan, and Sallie, who married F. N. Calmes, all of whom are living. John A. Wise married Martha Schumpert, the fruits of their union being James, Pickens, Mary Shealy, Savannah Epting and Della. These are all living. John A. Wise was killed at the second battle of Manassas, in 1862. Walter M. Wise married Martha Roberts, by whom were born five sons, John, Lemuel, James, William and Eddie, and one daughter, who died young.

The Lester Family.

Charles Lester, a native of Virginia, of English descent, came to Newberry District, S. C., about the year 1760, and served through the Revolutionary war in the American army. He married a Miss Musgrove, the happy mother of Allen, Smith, Alfred, Mibray Gilbert, Susie Havird and Mariah Boozer. Smith and Alfred moved to Alabama. Allen married Martha Dennis, who filled his house with joy and was the mother of William, James, Charlie, Alfred, George, Martha Connelly, Prudence Rodgers, Phoebe Kirkland and Jane Rikard. William Lester (Colonel) married, first, Sallie Hunter, to whom were born Rhoda Boozer, Mary Havird and Hattie Whitman. His second wife was Hannah Young, who became the mother of Young, Marcus, Thompson, Marcellus, Abbie Dominick and Estelle. At the beginning of the Civil war Col. Wm. Lester raised a company of soldiers, over which he was elected Captain. His company was attached to the Thirteenth Regiment, South Carolina Volunteers, Infantry, of which regiment he was promoted to Colonel. He served through the war with distinction and marked bravery. In the troublesome days of 1876, with a company of old soldiers, he went to Columbia and tendered his services to Governor Hampton, where he remained as long as it was necessary. James Lester married, first, Elizabeth Boozer, to whom were born Allen, George and Amanda Nichols. His second wife was Polly Boozer, to whom were born Newton, Elizabeth Boozer and Fannie Boozer. George Lester married Harriet Rikard, who brought him Willie,

Ella Merchant, Lillie and Mary. George Lester lost a leg in the Civil war. Young Lester (a mute from sickness) married a mute at Cedar Springs. This couple became the parents of two children, who are being taught to speak. The mute, Mrs. Lester, has passed to that country which is sometimes called the Silent Land; but in her case we hope that her tongue has been loosened, that her ears have been unstopped, so that she can hear and take part in the melodies of heaven. Thompson Lester married Elizabeth Hawkins. Allen M. Lester married Mrs. Rose Kibler, *nee* Rose Ridgell. George B. Lester married Sue Kempson. Willie Lester married Anna Hawkins.

—

THE ROBERT BROWN FAMILY.

Robert Brown was born in County Antrim, Ireland, May 20, 1762. He came to Newberry District, S. C., and married Nancy Young on April 8, 1794. By this marriage were born James, George, Young, Mary Russell and Elizabeth Moore. James Brown married Melvina Haynes, and moved with his family to Georgia. Young Brown married, first, Rhoda Schumpert, and, second, Ann Russell, and then moved to Georgia. George Brown was born December 8, 1810, and on April 10, 1834, he married Lucinda Cureton, to whom were born Sarah C. Brown, Jas. R. Y. Brown, J. W. P. Brown, L. Carrie Brown and G. D. Brown. Sarah C. Brown died a maiden. James R. Y. Brown volunteered in the 13th South Carolina Regiment and was killed at the second battle of Manassas. J. W. P. Brown married Carrie Hawkins. L. Carrie Brown married H. C. Moseley and G. D. Brown married Mrs. Nancy Maffett, *nee* Nancy Moseley.

—

THE HAWKINS FAMILY.

Peter Hawkins and wife came from Virginia and settled in the southern part of Newberry District. They were of English extraction, and to them were born Jacob, Edward, Peter, William, Prudence Dennis and Elizabeth Rankin. Jacob Hawkins married Jane Ganter, by whom were born Peter, George, Eliza and Sallie Young. Edward Hawkins married Rebecca Pearson, to whom were born Mark, Allen, Martha Young, Prudence, Phœbe Pugh, Polly Boozer and Anna Whitman.

Peter Hawkins and family moved to Alabama in 1820. William Hawkins married and moved to Greenville, S. C. Mark Hawkins married Jane Hunter, to whom were born Drayton, Pressley, Pierce, Miles, Harriet Boozer, Mary Boozer, Rebecca Boozer, Minta Sheppard and Anna Conwill. Allen Hawkins married Lavinia Fellers, who became the mother of George, Hayne and Carrie Brown. Drayton Hawkins married Nancy Boozer, to whom were born S. Berly, Bates, Paul, Reuben, Laura Nichols, Fannie Ham, Amanda Moore and Ella. Pressley Hawkins married and moved to Florida. Pierce Hawkins married, first, Lucinda Schumpert, who brought him Pressley, Luther and several other children. His second wife was Mary J. Swindler. Miles Hawkins married Hattie Nichols and has a family of several children. Peter Hawkins married Mary DeVall and moved to Tennessee. Rev. Jacob Hawkins, D. D., an eminent Lutheran divine, who now lives in Orangeburg County, is a son of this Peter Hawkins who moved to Tennessee. George Hawkins married Mary Harmon. A. Hayne Hawkins married Rhoda Hunter.

—

Hentz.

About the year 1760 Matthias Hentz lived near the mouth of Cannon's Creek on Broad River. There is a tradition in the family that his father, who lived in the lower German Settlement, was accused of witchcraft and suffered the penalty of death at the hands of fanatical neighbors by being smothered between feather beds. If this be true, and even this is doubtful, it is the only case of the kind where the penalty of death for witchcraft was ever inflicted in South Carolina, by authority of law or without it;—while in enlightened New England, in the Province of Massachusetts. between the years 1645 and 1695 many persons were put to death after due process of trial at law. In 1640 four persons were put to death in Massachusetts, in 1688, one woman was executed for witchcraft in Boston. "Then," says the historian, "commenced at Salem that dreadful tragedy which rendered New England for many months a scene of bloodshed, terror and madness, and at one time seemed to threaten the subversion of civil society. In the year 1692, the frenzy of the colonists reached the highest pitch of extravagance. Suspicions and accusations of witchcraft became general among them; and on this fanciful charge many persons were put to death." . . . . (One historian says as many as twenty.) "Persons accused of the imaginary crime of witchcraft were imprisoned, condemned, hanged, and their bodies left exposed to wild beasts and birds of prey. . . . . Children ten years of age were put to death; young women were stripped naked, and the marks of witchcraft sought for on their bodies with unblushing curiosity. . . . . The prisons were filled, the gibbets left standing, and the citizens were appalled. Under this frightful delirium the miserable colonists seemed doomed to destruction by each other's hands. The more prudent withdrew from a country polluted by the blood of its inhabitants, and the ruin of the colony seemed inevitable." The reader will please bear in mind that none of these victims were burned at the stake, they were only hanged. The New Englanders are very touchy on that point.

To return to Hentz. It is probable that the father of Matthias Hentz was the man who was murdered by the fanatic Weaver and his followers on the Saluda. The story is told by Dr. Hazelius, and also by Bernheim in his history of the Lutheran Church. Weaver was arrested, taken to Charleston, tried, convicted of murder and was hanged.

After the murder of her husband the widow left the Saluda and removed to near the mouth of Cannon's Creek on Broad River, where she became the mother of Matthias Hentz. This is related as a probability only. Matthias married and became the father of two sons: David and Michael. Michael moved to Georgia where he left numerous descendants, among them John, the husband of Caroline Lee Hentz, the celebrated authoress. John is the only one of the name, who ever sought or obtained public office. He served as County Sheriff and a member of the Legislature.

David Hentz left two sons, Wm. R. and H. M., and three daughters, Mrs. John Adam Folk, of Pomaria; Mrs. Wm. Reid, of Cannon's Creek; and Mrs. George Sondley, of Bull Street.

H. M. Hentz died in 1852, leaving an infant son, Wm. J. Wm. R. Hentz died in 1877, leaving four sons, D. J.; T. M.; Wm. A., and Dr. E. O.; and one daughter, Mrs. P. M. Derrick.

The male descendants of David Hentz are all now living on lands he owned and within five miles of them—except one great-grandson whose home is in Texas.

I take pleasure in adding that so far as is known no Hentz has ever been arraigned before a court or sued on a debt.

—

CROMER.

Philip, Christian and Jacob Cromer, brothers, lived on Second Creek, Newberry County. It is not known what became of Philip and Christian, further than that they have some descendants in North Alabama. Jacob Cromer, who was a gunsmith by trade, married a daughter of Jacob Folk, of Pomaria, by whom he left three sons, Abraham, Adam and David. David moved to Georgia, leaving one son, Andrew, the father of James and Pressley; and one daughter, Mrs. Millekin. Abraham died early, but left one son, A. Barham Cromer, and one daughter, Nannie, the wife of Capt. W. J. Lake, who now lives in the town of Newberry. Adam, who married Fannie Hoard, (whose parents, with the Haynies and Buchanans, all closely related, came from Prince William County, Virginia,) left two sons, Thomas Hoard and Adam F., and one daughter, Mrs. William R. Hentz,—Thomas Hoard Cromer, who lived in the Mollohon section, reared a large family, viz.: Capt. W. Philander, who fell at Gettysburg; James L., now deceased; Jno. A.; W. C., present County Auditor; Walter, now in Arkansas; Charlton; George B., a lawyer of high standing and in good practice at Newberry; Buchanan; and two daughters, Mrs. Bridges, of Union, (who is the mother by her first husband of J. P. Glasgow, of Gainesville, Texas, and of Bachman Glasgow, of Newberry,) and Mrs. Dr. Geo. A. Setzler. Adam F. moved to Anderson; has three sons and one daughter and is still living.

Adam Cromer, who was unusually well informed for his day, took a partial course in mathematics and astronomy under Mr. Haynie, who was his wife's uncle.

Besides this, the Cromer family has several branches, all from the same original stock. At one time they seemed almost indigenous to the soil and lived united and content; but now they are somewhat scattered. They are now, as they have always been, honest, industrious and economical; living true and upright lives and fearing no man.

James H. Williams.

James H. Williams was born in Newberry County, S. C., October 4th, 1813, and died at his home, Rocky Comfort, Ark., August 21st, 1892, in the 80th year of his age.

His father was James Williams, a native of Newberry. The family was Welsh and immigrated to America with Lord Baltimore's colony. His mother was Isabella Shuttleworth of English parentage. His grandfather was killed at the seige of Ninety-Six, in the War of the Revolution. His father was a captain in the war of 1812.

Col. Williams was an entirely self-educated man: not having had in his youth the advantages of a High School or Collegiate education. He seemed to have taken naturally to military life, as he enlisted in Col. Caldwell's Regiment of nullifiers in 1831. He served in 1836 three months in the Indian War in Florida, belonging to Col. Goodwin's Regiment of Cavalry.

In 1837 he was elected Major of the 38th Regiment, South Carolina Militia—resigned in 1843, and in the same year was elected Captain of the McDuffie Artillery at Newberry C. H. In 1846, January 29th, he organized a company for the Mexican War for one year; afterwards organized an independent company for the same war, and was mustered into the service of the United States on the 20th of January, 1847, as Company L of the Palmetto Regiment. Took part in the seige of Vera Cruz and fought at Madelon Bridge, and at the capture of Alvarado. He marched with the army to Puebla and was engaged in the skirmish at the Pass of El Penal. August 8th he moved with Quitman's Division from Puebla in the advance on the City of Mexico. Fought at the battle of Contreras and captured General Mendoza and staff in their retreat. On the same day he was in the heat of the battle at Cherubusco. Leading in the storming of Chupultepec and Garita de Belen his troops were the first Americans to make lodgment. He was wounded in this assault. He was amongst the first of the American officers to enter the City of Mexico.

Soon after the capture of the city the war with Mexico closed and Colonel Williams returned home. He left Mexico in May, 1848, and was discharged from service in July of the same year at Mobile, Ala.

After his return home he was elected Brigadier-General and then Major-General of Militia. He served four years as Mayor of the town of Newberry; four years as Commissioner of Equity and was a member of the Legislature, House of Representatives, for several terms.

At the beginning of the war between the States he was elected Colonel of the 3d South Carolina Regiment of Volunteers, which regiment went to Virginia in June, 1861, and was engaged in the battle of Bull Run or First Manassas. He served on the Potomac and in the Peninsula until the reorganization of the regiment in 1862. He afterwards commanded the 4th and 9th Regiments, State Troops, and was on duty in Charleston during the seige. He was at Florence and finally surrendered his command as part of Gen. Joe Johnston's Army.

After the war he was one of the delegates from the State to ask a Provisional Government for South Carolina. He was a member of the State Senate, elected in 1865, until Reconstruction became the order of the time.

In 1867 he left Newberry and moved to Arkansas, where he engaged in planting, but soon again entered into public life. He was a member of the Constitutional Convention of 1874, and assisted greatly in bringing order and prosperity out of chaos and commercial degradation.

General Williams was a lawyer by profession. He was married in Newberry in 1844 to Miss Jane W. Duckett. He was the father of eight children, three of whom are living. One son, P. B. Williams, graduated at the Virginia Military Institute as 1st Lieutenant, Company A. Another son, J. C. Williams, has held several offices of trust. He, like his father, is a successful planter.

BURR JOHNSTONE RAMAGE

Was a native of Newberry County and was born on the 2nd day of December, 1817, three miles south of the town of Newberry. He was the eldest son of John Ramage from his marriage with Mrs. Lucy Kelly Henderson, who was then also married for the second time. His half-brothers and sisters loved him as a brother. His education was good, but limited to an academical course. Arriving at manhood he read law with Col. Simeon Fair—after admission to the Bar he en-

tered into partnership with his tutor and soon became one
of the best office lawyers in Newberry—Colonel Fair always
conducting the cases in Court. Upon the death of Mr. Y. J.
Harrington, in 1850, who had been Clerk of the Court since
1808, Mr. Ramage was elected to that office. He was a most
admirable officer, and was again and again re-elected to that
office, only once, however, without opposition. It is probable
that during that period he was the most popular man that
Newberry ever had. During the war the Courts being virtually
closed he declined re-election and accepted the situation of
Agent of the Greenville and Columbia Rail Road at the Newberry Station. He served in that situation until 1870, when
he resigned and retired to private life.

Loving learning he gave all his children as good an education as possible, sparing no pains nor expense to that end.
He was himself a close observer of nature and took great and
especial delight in the study of Botany. This writer has
gone to him more than once with plants which seemed strange,
but which Mr. Ramage could always elucidate.

His wife was Sarah Ann Wilson, daughter of William Wilson,
Judge of the Court of Ordinary for Newberry. He married in
the year 1846. The fruits of this happy union were eight
children; and it was said to be the happiest family in Newberry. To their intimate friends, those who knew them well,
their home always seemed to be the perfection of peace and
content. His wife died in 1879, leaving him and his home
desolate. One son and three daughters also preceded him to
the grave. He was survived by one daughter and three sons,
who are still living. One daughter, Miss Fanny, and one son,
John, who is in business, live in Newberry; Bartow B., who is
an Episcopal minister, resides at Nashville; and Burr J., a
lawyer, is also resident at Nashville, Tenn. None are married.

Burr J. Ramage died October 28, 1890, and his body was
interred the day following at the family burying ground, less
than a half mile from the house in which he was born.

—

James N. Lipscomb.

Col. James N. Lipscomb was born at White Hall, in Abbeville County, April 11, 1827. His father was John Lipscomb.
He received his academical education at Edgefield Court House

and at Greenwood Academy in Abbeville County. He graduated from the South Carolina College in December, 1847.

Colonel Lipscomb was aide to General Bonham and Captain of the College Cadets at eighteen years of age. In January, 1848, he was married to the eldest daughter of Gov. F. W. Pickens. He was thrice married. His second wife was a Miss Simmons, and his third Miss Ella Motte; all of whom preceded him to the grave.

In 1849 he removed to Florida, but returned to South Carolina in 1855 and settled in Newberry County. He was elected to the Legislature in 1860, being chairman of the delegation.

In 1861, he was Adjutant-General on the Staff of Major-General M. L. Bonham, who commanded the military forces raised by Act of the Legislature in 1860. After the surrender of Fort Sumter, he went to Virginia with the first brigade that entered the Confederate service, with a commission as 1ts Lieutenant of Cavalry, as aide to General Bonham, in which position he served during the campaign of 1861. He joined the Second South Carolina Cavalry, and served seven months as acting Quartermaster. He was afterwards Assistant Adjutant-General to Gen. M. C. Butler with rank of Captain, and was afterwards promoted to the rank of Lieutenant-Colonel on Major-General Butler's staff, where he remained until the close of the war. He then returned to his home near Chappell's Depot where he engaged in farming.

He was one of the original advocates of the nomination of Hampton and contributed largely to the success of the party. Few men were more effective in their appeals to the Democracy than he. He was elected State Senator from Newberry County from 1877 to 1880. He was elected Secretary of State in 1882—re-elected in 1884.

He was made Master of the State Grange in 1874 or 1875, which position he held continuously—re-elected year after year—until his death.

He has one brother, M. B. Lipscomb, living at Ninety-Six, and another, Col. Thos. J. Lipscomb, who was several years Superintendent of the State Penitentiary, living in Columbia. He has several children living. He died at the home of his son-in-law in Bryson City, N. C., June, 1891.

He was a good and useful man and died regretted by all who knew him.

———

THE RISER FAMILY.

The Risers came to this country from Germany before the Revolutionary war. The name was originally Roiser. They settled in the lower section of this county, and the place where Mr. James A. Riser now lives (1892) is part of the old homestead. The father, who came from the old country, and his oldest son were both soldiers in the Revolution. He had five sons and three daughters. The sons were Adam, Martin, John, George and Jacob. They all left Newberry except Martin, from whom has descended a large progeny. Of the three daughters, one married a Sease and one a Copeland. They all moved to Barnwell County, and so did John. Adam and Jacob moved to Mississippi.

Martin Riser, who remained in Newberry County, was married three times, first to a Miss Sease. Their children were John, Martin, Christina, Eve and Lizzie. His second wife was a Miss Rikard, and to them were born Adam, George, Jacob, Mary, Harriet, Sallie and Susie. His third wife was a Mrs. Summer. All his children grew up and married and reared large families.

Martin Riser, Jr., married, first, Mahala Cannon, and then Hannah Suber, and there were several children. Christina married a Dickert. Of her descendants I know nothing. Eve married, first, a Werts, and they had several children; one of whom, Susan, married Solomon P. Kinard, and one, Sallie, married Michael Fellers (whose first wife was Sallie Riser, an aunt), and one, Wm. M. Werts, is now (1892) a successful farmer of this county. At the death of Mr. Werts, Eve married Rev. Herman Aull, and to them were born two children, Mrs. Louisa C. Hunter, now living in Newberry, and Jacob Luther Aull, now living in Edgefield County. Lizzie married a Rhinehart. Adam moved to Louisiana, and in 1892 was living, hale and hearty, in his eighty-third year, for he says, in a letter written to his nephew, Judge Jacob B. Fellers, April 23, 1892, "I work my garden and Irish potatoes and keep my orchard in trim and grape vines." He writes with a steady hand, the letters showing no tremulousness whatever. George went to Alabama. Jacob also went to the West. Mary married Thomas Cannon, and, at his death, Henry Koon. By the last union were born several children—Mrs. Thos. V. Wicker, who is still living, and two sons who were killed in the war. Harriet married Anderson Leitzsey. Sallie married Michael Fellers, the father of Jacob B. Fellers, now Probate Judge of Newberry, Mrs. G. F. Long, Mrs. J. D. Bowles, S. H. Fellers, and possibly others. Susie married Samuel Cannon.

John Riser, the son of Martin Riser, Sr., married Barbara Ann Zeigler, and to them were born ten children: William, John, Hartwell, George, Adam, James A., Walter, Elizabeth, Anne and Lavinia. Of these, William married Elizabeth Berly and was the father of eleven children, six of whom are now (1892) living: Luther P. W. (in Newberry), John F. (Greenville), William Wallace, for eight years Sheriff of Newberry County and elected for a third term—the only man who was ever chosen Sheriff in Newberry for three successive terms—George C. (Laurens), Thomas B., and Cornelia, wife of the Hon. Jno. W. Scott; Mary J. married Jno. L. Blackburn, both now dead—two children living; and Sallie, the first wife of Wallace C. Cromer, now Auditor of Newberry County; she is also dead. John married Elizabeth Rikard, and to them were born nine children, all of whom are living except Rev. Sidney T. Riser, who died in Staunton, Va., in the prime and vigor of young manhood. He was a minister of the Lutheran Church and a young man of great promise. Hartwell married a Miss Kinard and moved to Edgefield County and is still living, and only a short time ago celebrated his Golden Wedding. George married a Miss Peaster and was killed in the last battle of the war in North Carolina; he has two children still living. Adam is living in Columbia. James A. married a Miss Busby and lives in this county, near Pomaria, on the old homestead. Walter died young. Elizabeth married Adam Berly and is now dead. Anne is the wife of Alfred W. Bundrick and is living in Newberry County. Lavinia married Belton Kibler, who was killed in the war. She still lives in this county.

BARRE.

Jacob Barre, the father of Matthias Barre, of whom and his descendants I wish to write, was a son of Colonel Barre, who served in the Revolution. It is thought that he came to this country from the southern side of the Rhine, and settled in the Dutch Fork. Jacob Barre's wife was Mary Quattlebaum; their sons were John, Michael, Jacob and Matthias; there was one daughter, who died in childhood. Matthias Barre first married Mary Magdalene, daughter of Captain Henry Werts, and settled near where he was born. The other sons moved to Lexington County and one subsequently to Florida. There were ten children of Matthias Barre. All except one, Catherine, lived and were given in wedlock.

The only son now living is D. Walter, a prosperous farmer and respected citizen. He married, first, Amanda Barre, of Lexington, and those of this union who are living are W. Matthias, himself twice married; Eloise, wife of Eugene L. Leavell, and Veda. Two daughters are dead, having been paired to good and honest men.

Jacob, the eldest son, married Elizabeth, a sister of W. W. Houseal, and they settled in Lexington County, at Barre's. One of their daughters, Mrs. W. B. Aull, now lives in Newberry. The other children live near the old home, except Mrs. D. L. Boozer, of Columbia. William A., the third son of Matthias Barre, married Hulda C. Goree. He has been dead several years, his widow and two daughters, Alice and Olive, surviving. Eliza Caroline, the eldest daughter, married Wm. Walter Houseal, elsewhere mentioned in these biographies. Martha became the wife of David Holman, and they moved to Mississippi in 1866. Both wife and husband are dead. There were twelve children, but their names I do not know. Harriet, the third daughter, and Frances, the sixth daughter, married, subsequently, A. Michael Bowers, and left one child each, Olivia and James M. Julia A. married D. W. T. Kibler, whose oldest son, Calhoun, died suddenly in early manhood. The daughters—Mary, wife of Wm. Johnson; Lizzie, wife of Wm. A. Kinard; Alma, wife of Robert F. Bryant, of Orangeburg; Lilla and Gussie—and the sons, Dr. James M., Robert and Lawson, now live in Newbery, and Trannie, wife of Dr. Jno. A. Simpson, in Prosperity.

Mary E., the youngest of the children, married, in 1892, Jesse A. Rawls, of Haralson, Ga.

Matthias Barre's second wife was Jane Berly, who is still living. Their children were John J., Sallie, and Lillie, who became the devoted wife of B. F. Griffin. She has passed into the rest of the pure and good.

John J. Barre met a tragic death in Florida, whither he had gone to the home of his uncle, to avoid the Ku Klux persecutions in 1872. He was a brave man, tall and stalwart, and a universal favorite in the town of Newberry. It was while endeavoring to prevent a difficulty, as he thought, at Ellisville, Florida, between Charles Carroll and Daniel Wingate, two brothers in-law, on Saturday afternoon, November 23d, 1872, that he and his cousin James Barre were shot down by the two brothers-in-law with shotguns loaded with buckshot. The young men were entirely unsuspicious of an attack from the brothers-in-law—who left the store of James Barre in apparent great anger, presumably to settle with arms the difficulty between themselves. One of the brothers in-law, Carroll, had a spite against James Barre, and it was plain after the assassination of the two young men that the difficulty between Wingate and Carroll was simply a decoy to get the cousins to follow them out of the store. No word of quarrel had ever passed between them and Wingate and Carroll, the latter of whom carried the double-barrelled shotgun and did the shooting, John Barre receiving seven buckshot in the left breast and James Barre seven buckshot in the right breast just as they started out of the store. The body of John J. Barre was brought to Newberry and buried in Rosemont Cemetery after funeral services in the Lutheran Church on Saturday afternoon, December 13th.

Matthias Barre died on Sunday morning, April 27th, 1873, in his 74th year. He had been for nearly twenty years a citizen of the town, having removed from his Bush River plantation to Newberry in 1854. No more useful citizen, or one more beloved for his many estimable qualities, ever lived. In the sudden, untimely death of his son John J., it might be said he received his death-stroke, for he never recovered from it. He was a devout member of the Lutheran Church, to whose support he contributed liberally of the means with which he had been abundantly blessed.

WERTS.

The brothers, Henry Werts and John Werts, the ancestors of the Wertses of Newberry, Egdefield and Orangeburg, at the age of eighteen and sixteen years respectively, were brave and ardent Whigs in the Revolutionary War. They were of German descent. One incident related of these two brothers shows how much the Tories desired their capture in order to wreak their vengeance upon them. While the two brothers were at home one day in the summer of 1780, a party of Tories heard of their presence in the neighborhood and endeavored to capture them. Their coming was a surprise to the young soldiers and they barely had time in which to escape. They selected as a hiding place, unique and novel, the hollow banks of Crim's creek, and there took refuge behind the luxuriant grass and the thick overhanging undergrowth of briar. The Tories searched up and down the creek, thrusting swords and bayonets into the undergrowth, endeavoring to strike the two brave brothers with mortal wounds. Their search was all in vain. The young soldiers had a narrow escape, however, for several times the Tories' swords pierced through the undergrowth in uncomfortable proximity as they crouched in their hiding place beneath the banks of the creek. The brothers afterwards did valiant service in the Revolution, and were made captains in the early days of the militia.

Captain Henry Werts had five sons, Henry, John, David, Michael and Adam, who all settled on Bush River, and four daughters, Elizabeth, Mary Magdalene, (who became the wife of Matthias Barre), Catherine and Tena. Henry, the eldest son, never married. John married Eve Riser, and their children were Tena, Sarah, Susan, John and William M. Tena married Peter Rikard and Sarah married Michael Fellers. Susan married Solomon P. Kinard, who was appointed postmaster at Newberry in 1852. He held the office under the Confederate Government, being also reappointed after the war. His surviving children in Newberry are James H. M., one of the proprietors of the Newberry *Observer*, Melissa, wife of B. H. Lovelace; William A.; Thomas Edward, an engineer, lives in Georgia; John A., eldest son, died in 1887; Mary, eldest daughter, wife of W. H. Blats, died in 1892. William M. Werts, twice married; first Elizabeth, the daughter of Squire

Samuel Bowers; of their three sons, James, Samuel and William, James and Samuel are living. The daughters are Lavinia, wife of John Mathis, Leonora Alice, wife of J. W. Hartman, Sallie Eve, wife of Andrew M. Counts, and Bettie, the youngest, dead. The second wife of William M. was the widow of Levi Wheeler. Edward S., son by this union, is a teacher in Knoxville, Tenn. Another son, William, died in infancy.

David Werts married Mary Lever. One of their sons, John A., a good man esteemed by all his neighbors, died in 1891, leaving a widow and three children. Of the family of J. Belton, who has moved away, I know but little. A daughter is the wife of Braxton B. Davis, who lives in Newberry.

The sons of Michael (who married Susan, daughter of Col. John Summer of the Dutch Fork), were Michael, who now (1892) is a successful farmer and true citizen, living at Silver Street; Henry, Jonathan, Elizabeth, Caroline, and Susan. It appears almost an interminable labyrinth in the ties of the relationship which the compiler endeavors to trace out in these biographies. Michael married Elizabeth, daughter and only child of David Stephens, a man noted for independence of thought and more than ordinary intelligence. Their children now living are Alice, wife of J. Fred. Schumpert; Emma, wife of Dr. Jas. M. Kibler, whose grandfather, Matthias Barre, was the husband of her great aunt—an instance of the aforesaid labyrinthal tie that binds humanity together; Fannie, wife of James L. Morehead; Maggie, Clarence and Florence. Henry and Jonathan married sisters, Nancy and Drucilla Spearman, and their descendants form a thrifty element in the Silver Street section. Eliza was the wife of John Elmore of Newberry. Caroline was the wife of William B. Reagin, and their living children are James B., John W., Robert T., G. Burton, and Elizabeth C. One son, Henry W., was killed in the war; one daughter, Susan, wife of J. D. Suber, is dead. Susan married George Long and survives him. Their children were Latimer W. and several others dead, and Geo. M., living, in Florida.

The elder Michael Werts was thrice married; Adelaide, only child of the second union, was the wife of Thos. M. Paysinger.

Adam Werts married Elizabeth Hope and left two sons who moved to Edgefield, and another, David, living near Deadfall.

Captain John Werts reared two sons and three daughters, William, Henry, Barbara, Tena and Catherine. William, the eldest of his sons, married Elizabeth Bowers. One of their sons, the Rev. J. H. W. Wertz (final s changed to z) was a Lutheran minister and died in 1883. One of his sons, Joseph Quincy Wertz, is also a Lutheran minister and lives in North Carolina. Several sons of John Werts settled in Edgefield.

Henry, the second son of Capt. John Werts, married Elizabeth Lever; of their sons, Dr. D. H. Werts now lives near Slighs, G. Paul, living at the old home place; Edward and W. Anderson, dead; Henry Middleton and Wesley, killed in the war. Barbara, eldest daughter of John Werts, married John Berly, who is elsewhere mentioned in these biographies. Tena married William Kinard and their children were Adam, Keren-Happoch, wife of Capt. H. H. Riser, of Edgefield; Catherine, wife of W. A. Hipp, whose sons are Moses Q. Hipp and J. J. Hipp; Elizabeth, wife of Major Jacob Epting, whose children are L. Irænius, Bunyan O., Julius J., Nannie, wife of G. M. Ables, Dr. Berly R., a physician of Greenwood, Monroe J., a Lutheran minister, Thomas and Charles.

In the biography of the family of Captain John Werts I find that five of his desendants became ministers of the Gospel. First, his grandson, that consecrated man, earnest student and powerful preacher, Wm. Berly; then his great-grandson, J. Eusebius; contemporary with the elder Berly came another grandson, Rev. J. H. W. Wertz, who was a pioneer of the Lutheran Church in building up the waste places, and his son, Joseph Quincy; and in the third generation, Rev. Monroe J. Epting. Truly they had godly fathers and consecrated mothers.

COUNTS.

John Counts, a descendant of the original Kountze family of Germany, married Elizabeth Eichelberger on May 15, 1810. They both died while their son George was yet a child, and he was reared by Philip Sligh, a man whose life was full of many similar noble acts. This son is now known as George A. Counts, Jr. He married Harriet Cromer, and they have quite recently celebrated their goldren wedding, at which all their children were present—five sons and six daughters, as

2

follows: Elizabeth, wife of John W. Monts; Fannie, wife of Isaiah Haltiwanger; Mary, wife of A. D. Haltiwanger; John A.; Lenora, wife of A. H. Wheeler; Texanna, wife of Capt. John F. Banks; Janie, wife of G. Burt. Reagin; Walter P.; Ernest O., principal of the Prosperity High School; Henry P., a Lutheran minister at Haralson, Ga.; William A., now principal of the Mt. Tabor High School. All the sons have also married.

George A. Counts, Sr., now familiarly known as "Little George" Counts, to distinguish him from Geo. A. Counts, Jr., came to Newberry from Lexington County. He also descended from the German family, Kountze. The baptismal name of his wife was Susannah Singley. Of their children the marital names of the daughters are Caroline Long, Mary Miller, Louisa Sheely. Two sons, Jacob C. and Andrew M., are also married. J. Luther, the eldest son, is dead—a widow and several children surviving him.

—

Rev. Herman Aull,

One of the most beautifully significant features in the incipient declaration of the Gospel is the selection for that purpose of a few unlettered men, some of whom were laboring for their living in the humblest of occupations, namely, that of fishermen—the most notable among them being, as that class of laborers have ever usually been, addicted to coarse, irreligious behavior. Only Divine Wisdom could perceive under their uncouth exteriors the more excellent way waiting to be shown to them. We have reason to believe that two of them, James and John, were turbulent, vindictive men before such showing; and that a third one, Peter, was a fickle boaster and profane swearer. Yet there was in their rugged natures seed which in the former, under spiritual culture, sprang up into faithfulness unto death, and love the purest for God and fellow-man; while the Holy Ghost caused to flourish in the vacillating heart of the latter the very enthusiasm of constancy to the cross. It is true, there was one who, before he was called to preach the Gospel, had acquired much learning at the feet of a great teacher; and he was chosen to disseminate among the learned what had been declared to the simple by the unskilled in worldly wisdom; but before he could be fitted for his office he had to be prostrated physically and morally and be continually buffetted afterwards by the messenger of Satan, until he became wise through the foolishness of preaching.

My memory reaches back to some unpretending men whose devotion to the cause of Christ may somewhat illustrate the meaning of the above introduction; and serve also to show, that Zion is now-a-days, as she ever has been, upheld by the pure, simple energy of the humble.

Along an extent of perhaps ten miles up and down the Saluda River there stepped forth from the rustling corn fields some half-dozen men of mature age and sound judgment—of little liability to be deceived—honest and inflexible, who felt assured that they were called to preach the Word. They were men of very limited book-learning, and knew not how to convince themselves or others of the truth by process of reasoning—that is to say, by logic. They did not all come forth at the same time. From the year 1824, when the Synod of South Carolina was organized, to 1831 or '35 it became known, from time to time, that Jost Meetze and Michael Rauch, between Lexington Court House and the Saluda, had ventured to proclaim the great Glad Tidings to their neighbors, and between the Saluda and Newberry, Jacob Moser, Godfrey Dreher and Herman Aull stood up to show the people their transgressions and the only way of escape from the consequences of them. There were others, but these whose names are here mentioned were seen and heard by myself; and it is of the last named, Herman Aull, I propose to write a short account, because I knew him, and because he was a citizen of Newberry County (District); and, indeed, because some of his numerous descendants, I think, are my warm friends.

Herman Aull (or as he was more frequently called Harmon Aull) was not born in the Dutch Fork, that is, in the area of country irregularly laid off, by a radius varying from five to ten miles long, around a centre fixed at Pomaria Depot on the Greenville and Columbia Rail Road. He came into this neighborhood from one of the most southern counties—probably Beaufort. It is impossible to ascertain any facts relating to his parentage or to the colony of immigrants from which he became separated to seek his better fortune further on in the interior of South Carolina. From the fact that he was bound to one

Mr. John Sultan, as an apprentice to learn the carpenter's trade, he must have been a boy when he came into the community where he lived and died. At the time of his arrival in the Dutch Fork, the German language was the mother-tongue in every family. It comes within my easy recollection how the Dutch Fork people struggled against the encroachment of the English language. They soon became completely surrounded by settlements of Irish and Scotch who of course spoke English destined, at it was easily foreseen, to supplant the German; which really did come to pass, in the course of a half century. The change from one language to the other, however, was very gradual, and brought about a *patois*, or dialect which was called, *"Broken English."* Well-marked traces of this can be recognized at the present time on both sides of the Saluda from Prosperity to Columbia. Herman Aull's mother-tongue was undoubtedly the German. I was young when I for the first time heard him preach, and this *"Broken English"* was plainly perceptible in his utterance. For instance, such phrases as *"The Grace of God," "Come hither, souls,"* he pronounced, *"De crace of Cot," "Come heeder, souls."* This was also the manner of Mr. Meetze, Mr. Rauch and others. I was about sixteen years of age when I heard these pioneer preachers, and fifty-six years have not obliterated my remembrance of the pensive emotion excited by the tender persuasiveness this *"Broken English"* gave to their preaching; —similar to the charm given to the Waverly Novels by the dialect of the Scottish Highlanders.

Sixty years ago, the young men of the Dutch Fork retained many of the wild, frolicksome habits which their forefathers brought with them from the Fatherland. Perhaps the wildest of these customs was, to ramble throughout the night of Christmas Eve, in companies of a dozen persons, from house to house, firing heavily charged guns, and having thus aroused the family they would enter the domicile with stamping scramble to the blazing fire, greedily eat the *praetzilies* and *schneckilies*, imbibe, with many a rugged joke and ringing peal of laughter, heavy draughts of a compound liquor made of rum and sugar, butter and alspice stewed together, and then,

"With monie an eldritch screetch an' hollo,"
rush out into the night to visit the next neighbor.

It was narrated by people of old, that Herman Aull, in the vivacity of youth, was easily led to participate in all the jovialty which marked the behavior of the young in his day. He, however, did not permit the vagaries of youthfulness to encroach upon the soberness of manhood. I could mention other names of men in the Dutch Fork besides Herman Aull whose follies in the first half of their lives served as contrasts by which the beauty of holiness in their latter days shone with brighter lustre.

What caused Mr. Aull to change his ways I am unable to state; but a change did take place in his mind and conduct, to the extent of urging him to apply, in 1831, to the Synod of South Carolina for license to preach the Gospel of Jesus Christ. Before this, he married Miss Christina Rikard, and had combined the occupation of the farmer with that of the carpenter. There can be, I think, no labor of the hands so suggestive of the duty to meditate long and prayerfully upon the claims of Christianity,—so persuasive to the spirit of man to yield obedience to the Spirit of Christ, as the tilling of crops and the building of homes. That must be a dull husbandman who can cast forth his seed over his field without calling to mind the parable of the sower, and dwelling upon its simple but searching applications. That must, likewise, be a dull carpenter, who while "planing his wood" does not feel a thrill of delight in the thought that his Lord and Master "was the same trade as he." I cannot refrain from inserting here the pathetic ballad so well recited by Dr. Alleman in his baccalaureate sermon, delivered some years ago, before the students of Newberry College:

"SAME TRADE AS ME."

Isn't this Joseph's son? Aye, it is He,
Joseph the carpenter—same trade as me;
I thought as I'd find it, I knew it was here,
　　But my sight's getting queer.

I don't know right where, as His shed must ha' stood—
But, often as I've been a planing of my wood,
I took off my hat, just with thinking of He
　　At the same work as me.

He warn't that set up, that He couldn't stoop down
And work in the country for folks in the town;
And I'll warrant He felt a bit pride, like I've done,
　　At a good job begun.

The parson, he knows that I'll not make too free
But Sunday I feels as pleased as can be
When I wears my clean smock—bran new,
  And has thoughts a few.

I think of as how, not the parson his sen [self]
As is teacher and father and shepherd of men,—
Not he knows as much of the Lord in that shed,
  Where He earned His own bread.

And when I goes home to my Missus, says she,
"Are you wanting your key?"
For she knows my queer ways, and my love for the shed,—
  (We've been forty years wed.)

So I've come right away by myself with the book,
And I turn the old pages and has a good look
For the text as I've found, as tells me as He
  Was the same trade as me.

"Why don't you mark it?" Ah, many says so,
But I think I'd as lif with your leave let it go;
It do seem that nice, when I fall on 't sudden you see;
  "Was the same trade as me."

Now, whatever might have been the circumstances impelling
Herman Aull to abandon his ways of carelessness,—whether
of sudden or gradual influence, it is not remembered,—he did
turn earnestly to his Saviour, and in him became a new
creature. In 1831 he was licensed to preach, and four years
afterwards in 1835, he was fully orda'ned. His field of work
was mostly at St. Paul's, in those days called Kibler's Church;
though he often preached beyond the Saluda in Lexington
and Edgefield. It was in St. John's Church, near the Pomaria
homestead, where I heard him, for the first time. Though
young, I was old enough to notice, and I have retained firmly
in my memory some remarkable features of his person and
manners. He was small of stature, and quick in his movements. His hair was black and strait, and his eyes were
brown and bright. In the pulpit he would frequently depress
his chin upon his breast, and glancing his gaze from under
his eye-brows pause and bestow over his congregation looks
of sternness tempered with pity. The hymn he gave out at
that time was one which I believe must have been his favorite
—his song of repentance. In the Book of Worship it is
numbered 369. From the feeling manner of his reading, it
seemed that every stanza must have recalled the days of his
waywardness.

> Jesus my all to heaven is gone
> He whom 1 fixed my hopes upon ;
> His tracks I see, and I'll pursue
> The narrow way, 'til him I view.

I felt sure, from the slow movement of his head to the right and to the left, that the third and fourth stanzas affected him with sorrow.

> This is the way I long have sought
> And mourned because I found it not ;
> My grief a burden long has been,
> Because I could not cease from sin.

> The more I strove against its power
> I sinned and stumbled but the more ;
> 'Til late I heard my Saviour say,
> Come hither, soul, for I am the way.

In his "Broken English," he pronounced the word, "hither," "*he-e-der*," with a tremulous and prolonged emphasis that was truly touching.

The Rev. Herman Aull labored as a preacher from 1831 to the time of his death, in 1852—twenty-one years. I think he might have truly said to the people, whom he endeavored to instruct in the way of salvation, that he eat no man's bread for naught; but wrought with labor and travail that he might not be chargeable to any of them. I, myself, when visiting his house professionally in 1842 saw him coming from his field to greet me. His face was moist with the sweat of labor and his shirt-sleeves were rolled above his elbows. As I took his hand, and felt the palm hardened by contact with the plough-handles, I could not help admiring the old man.

Two sons, John P. Aull and Calvin W. Aull, and several daughters were born from the marriage with Christina Rikard. After her death he married a widow Werts whose baptismal name was Eve Riser. From this union came Jacob Luther Aull and Louisa, the widow of the late Nathan A. Hunter.

These preachers of the Lutheran Church in the interior of South Carolina ought to be retained in honorable and affectionate recollection. They were the short, massive, unpolished pillars upon which rest the arches of the temple of Lutheranism along the Saluda River. Let some others, possessed of facts, and inclined to honor the worthy dead, write brief chronicles of Meetze, Rauch, Dreher, and the rest of these early farmer preachers, to hold them up for somewhat longer remembrance in the Church of their upholding, as I have attempted to do for Herman Aull, whose heart was not the weakest among theirs in love and zeal for the cause of Christ.

O. B. M., SR.

John P. Aull, one of the sons of the Rev. Herman Aull, was a man who was long and favorably known to the people of Newberry County, as a man of sterling integrity of character, enterprise and industry. He was the organizer, and for many years the president and manager of the Newberry Steam Mill Company. He took pride and pleasure in his work and made his institution second to none of the kind in the country. It is in this way that true nobility of character is shown. Measured by this standard John P. Aull was of gentle, even noble birth. This writer knew him for many years—had some business transactions with him and found him always a true man. Mr. Aull, brought up in the Lutheran Church, lived and died in that communion. He was born February 22, 1822; married first Caroline McQuerns; second Eugenia L. Smith; and died at his home by the Steam Mill, January 1st, 1879, leaving several sons and daughters, who, we hope and believe, are worthy descendants of Rev. Herman Aull, who was rated by my old friend, Dr. Mayer, as one of the best of men. There are two children, James H. and Carrie, by the first marriage; and by the second mariage there are William B.; Edward P., and Henry P., in Florida; Drucilla, wife of D. C. Lake, now in Texas; S. Beauregard; Leila E., wife of A. J. Sitton, of Pendleton; John I. H. and Anna Bachman.

William Calvin, another son of Rev. Herman Aull, married Nancy Stockman. He died of wounds in the war in 1863. His children are John M., George B., now County Commissioner of Newberry County; Lizzie, married a Taylor; Mary, wife of J. M. Werts; Adam L. Aull, and Fannie, wife of David Cromer.

NOTE TO PAGE 622.—In sketch of Riser family, Mary, who married Thomas Cannon, had one child by the union with Cannon, and that child is ow the wife of Col. J. C. S. Brown. Mrs. Wicker was not Mrs. Cannon's child as stated. Her children after her marriage with Koon were Mrs. Thomas M. Lake, Mrs. J. Benson Suber and John O. Koon.

Conclusion of Biographical and Family Sketches.

Human life is embosomed in mystery. Its conscious existence begins with a struggle; a gasp; a cry, whether of sorrow, or pain, or surprise, who can tell? It ends with struggles growing feebler and feebler, until they terminate in a gasp, longer than that with which it began, and then darkness. Whither has the life fled?

Of very few of us can more be said after we have left here, than that he was born, he lived and he died. Even of those called great; of those who made some noise and stir while passing through life, only a pale, dim shadow after awhile is left, and the succeeding generations soon begin to call in question the fact, and to doubt whether such and such a man ever lived at all. The glory departs from the name and the name fades away. Many deny the existence of William Tell, and the Swiss mountains that were made memorable and holy by his deeds of heroic resistance to the tyranny of Austria, now hesitate to tell the story, for fear that they will be said to repeat that which was only a lie from the beginning. In low and murmuring tones only, do they tell the tale to the peasants of the hills and valleys of the Alps, for they know that the story is not false which says that Tell shot the apple from the head of his son, leaving an arrow in his belt to shoot the heart of the tyrant Gessler, if the first had killed his son. But the world now is fain to believe that Tell never lived.

In our humble record of the lives and families of the men whose names are written here, there may, perhaps, be few Tells; but here are men and women who lived heroic lives and died heroic deaths. We have found that Newberry, blessed by a genial climate and grateful soil, without the awe-inspiring Alps, has produced sons and daughters worthy of any land. Even they whose names are entirely obscure, of whom it can only be said that they lived and died—even they did their duty faithfully in the sphere in which they moved;— and of no man nor woman can a greater word be said than that he, or "she hath done what she could."

The writer of these brief biographical sketches of the men and women and the families of Newberry, begs his readers to believe that he has tried to write truthfully, so as to make a faithful and just record of the times and of the men. Whenever he was able to write words of praise, it was always to him a source of deep, the very deepest, joy. To write words of blame is no pleasure. The pen of the historian—the pen of the annalist, should have, and should exhibit no animosity in recording the lives and actions of even the vile and the base. But the words of the recorder should glow and burn with an ardent fire of love and admiration, when he writes the lives of the pure and good.

If, in the judgment of the reader, this record falls short; if some names are not mentioned which should have been; if some brave deeds remain still unrecorded, we can only beg our readers to believe that we have done our best under the disabilities and environments by which we have been surrounded and bound. The work is not perfect; nor is there anything perfect in this world except God.

Hereafter, when the writer and compiler of this book shall have passed away, another scribe will take up and carry on the work.

Some pessimistic poet sums up his views of human life in the following lines:

> "A moment's halt, a momentary taste
> Of being from the well amid the waste,
> And lo! the phantom caravan has reached
> The nothing it set out from—O, make haste!"

Another poet, not quite so pessimistic, writes thus of the approaching end of the career of one of his heroes:

> "To this conclusion we must come at last,—
> That he was born, he lives and soon will die;
> The last sands of his life are ebbing fast;
> Soon will his soul mount upwards to the sky;
> Soon will his body sink into the tomb,
> Its final rest—nought can avert that doom."

X.

THE CHURCHES.

LUTHERAN.

I have elsewhere stated that the Lutheran Church has a larger number of communicants in the county than any other church or denomination. They were the first settlers, came in greater numbers and, all being members of the different branches of the great Teutonic family, naturally flocked together. From Bernheim's "History of the German Settlements and the Lutheran Church in the Garolinas," and other sources I glean the following facts as to the Church in Newberry County:

The Newberry County Germans were mostly all descendants from the original German settlers in Saxe-Gotha Township, with an occasional addition from the German settlements of North Carolina and Virginia. It received its Teutonic element previous to the year 1740, and the descendants of those settlers are still there and the Lutheran Church is firmly established amongst them. The Swiss element largely predominated over the other German nationalities, though there were Germans from the Palatinate, Austria, Wurtemburg and Holland.

On the 29th of February in the year one thousand seven hundred and eighty-eight was incorporated the "German Protestant Church of Bethany on Greene Creek," which is supposed to have been in Newberry County; but its location cannot now be found, nor any trace of the church. Does the map of Newberry show a Green Creek anywhere? Or does anybody know a creek by that name now?

There were other Lutheran Churches in Newberry in 1788, incorporated by the same Act, namely: "The German Lutheran Church of Bethlehem on Forest's (Fust's) Ford; the German Lutheran Church of St. Jacob's on Wateree Creek, and the German Lutheran Church of St. Martin's." St. Martin's was organized after the Revolutionary War; when the others were is not known, but the probability is that they had no pastor before that war. The first pastor they are known to have had was the Rev. Frederick Joseph Wallern, but the date of his arrival in Newberry is not now known.

Rev. R. J. Miller, in his Missionary Report under date of November 19, 1811, speaks very highly of the Saluda congregations, as follows: "From Hollow Creek Church, called Salem, I preached through all the German congregations in the neighborhood until the 28th. It is a pleasure to labor here; the people love the Gospel of Jesus and his servants."

Rev. Wallern labored as pastor in Newberry District; and a Rev. Mr. Winckhouse, who afterwards preached occasionally in the Saluda charge made vacant by the death of Rev. C. E. Bernhardt, was also a resident of the same district; but when he commenced and ended his labors in Newberry is not known to the writer. It is possible that some of these churches in the Saluda charge were in Lexington County. By means of the labors of Revs. Wallern and Winckhouse the Newberry churches were preserved from annihilation, although Rev. Wallern was a worldly-minded man and attended industriously to his planting and other worldly interests, as is still reported of him, and at which Rev. R. J. Miller hints, when he said in his Missionary Report: "I went to the Lutheran minister, Wallern; found him about his farming business; conversed that evening and the following day much with him on the state of the Church, of religion and on other subjects, and found him a man acquainted with the world. Sunday, the 8th, I preached in his church. He accompanied me also the following day to a funeral, where I addressed the people on the subject of death and preparation; he preached from Ps. 37:18. On the following day I preached to a small, but to all appearance serious, people, and therewith finished my missionary tour for this year."

At the meeting of Synod on the 16th of October, 1814, at Organ Church, Rowan County, North Carolina, among other congregations received in connection with Synod was one from Newberry District, South Carolina, of which Michael and Peter Rickard, Andrew Wecker and Martin Kinard were elders. This church is believed to have been St. Paul's. At that meeting of Synod in accordance with a written communication from Brother John Dreher, of South Carolina, and upon his desire, it was "Resolved, That negro slaves be instructed in our holy religion, and be received into our Church as members; and that congregations should make proper arrangements in their houses of worship to give the slaves also the opportunity to hear the Gospel. It was also Resolved, That all our ministers unite themselves to labor against the pernicious influence and consequences of dancing and seek to prevent it in every possible way."

St. Paul's Church in Newberry District was dedicated on the third Sunday in June, 1830, by Rev. Messrs. Rauch and Schwartz. But a church had been in existence here for eighty years, or more. It was a new church building dedicated in 1830. A revived state of religion had been visible for some time past, and soon after the dedication of the church thirty-seven persons were added at one time by confirmation.

Rev. William Berly, a graduate of the Theological Seminary at Lexington, was licensed to preach in 1836; labored for a time in Newberry District; was for several years Principal of the Female Academy at Newberry, and was elected the Second Professor of the Theological Seminary at Lexington, whereupon he removed to that place. After the removal of the Seminary to Newberry he established a Female Academy near Lexington, of which he was Principal until a short time before his death. He died April 18th, 1873, at his home in Lexington Village.

Rev. Herman Aull, with others, was licensed by Synod in 1831, before the Theological Seminary went into full operation. He lived, labored and died in Newberry District. A grandson of his, E. H. Aull, Esq., is (1892) editor of the Newberry *Herald and News*. Many other worthy descendants of his are also living in the county.

Rev. Elijah Elmore was licensed to preach November 24th, 1848. He labored in Georgia until his death. He was a grandson of Rev. Giles Chapman, mentioned in Judge O'Neall's Annals, and was born about three and a half miles south of the town of Newberry, at the place now (1892) owned and occupied by the Nobles family. He was a member of the infantry volunteer company that went from Newberry to Florida in 1836 during the Seminole War for three months. He has one son, Rev. J. S. Elmore, who is also a Lutheran preacher now living and laboring in Georgia.

Mount Zion Church having been organized under the pastoral care of Rev. J. Moser, their church edifice was dedicated on the fifth Sunday in August, 1840.

Bethlehem Church, incorporated in 1788, was dedicated in 1816 by Revs. G. Dreher and Miller, and has been served by Revs. Rauch, Schwartz, Hope, Berly, G. Haltiwanger, Jr., J. B. Anthony and T. S. Boinest—by the latter for many years. The remains of Boinest and Schwartz lie buried in the graveyard of this church. Since Mr. Boinest's death the church has been served by Rev. G. W. Holland, Rev. S. S. Rahn, Rev. S. T. Hallman and at present by Rev. J. H. Wyse.

The congregation at Luther Chapel, Newberry, was organized in 1853 by Rev. T. S. Boinest, and through his labors money was raised and a house of worship was built in 1854 and dedicated in December of the same year. Mr. Boinest was the first pastor. After his resignation, which he was compelled to make, having so many churches under his care, Rev. William Berly became the pastor and served two years, 1856–58. Revs. Theophilus Stork, D. D., and J. A. Brown, D. D., were joint-pastors* in 1858-60. Rev. J. P. Smeltzer, D. D., took charge as pastor in 1861 and served in connection with the Presidency of Newberry College until 1868, when he removed with the college to Walhalla. Rev. Jacob Hawkins, D. D., supplied the congregation with preaching in 1869. The church was struck by lightning in 1869, demolishing the tall steeple. Rev. H. S. Wingard was pastor in 1870–71, A call was then given to the Rev. H. W. Kuhns, D. D., of Omaha. He took charge in 1872 and served nearly seven years. Since his resignation in 1878 the church has had as pastors Rev. S. P. Hughes, Rev. J. Steck, D. D., Rev. A. B. McMackin, deceased, and Rev. W. C. Schaeffer.

Mount Pilgrim and Mount Tabor, in Pastorate No. 11, were built in the year 1880; and Ridge Road, in the same pastorate, was built in 1888.

St. Luke's was organized in 1828 or 1829, by Rev. Schwartz, then on a missionary tour. In 1830 or 1831, the first church building was erected, with Mr. Schwartz as pastor. Mr.

---

*In connection with their duties respectively as President and Professor in Newberry College. Dr. Brown, however, served some time after Dr. Stork returned to Pennsylvania.

Schwartz did not live long. He was succeeded by Mr. Berly, who was pastor for many years. Then followed Rev. J. Moser. About 1845 the old house was taken down and a new one, which still stands, was built in its place; served by Rev. J. C. Hope for a short time; then by Rev. T. S. Boinest for nearly eighteen years, assisted by Rev. Smithdeal occasionally; then by Revs. Jacob Hawkins, D, D., H. S. Wingard, J. D. Bowles and M. J. Epting.

Colony was organized in 1845; house built in 1846; dedicated by Revs. Hope and Berly. First pastor was Mr. Berly, since served by Margart, Bailey, Sligh, Jacob Hawkins, H. S. Wingard, J. D. Bowles and G. W. Holland. Colony was rebuilt in 1884.

Newville at Prosperity was organized in 1859, and church built same year and dedicated by Rev. Berly. Rev. Smithdeal first served them. Revs. J. P. Smeltzer, W. Eichelberger and J. A. Sligh officiated occasionally, (Rev. J. A. Sligh was regular pastor for two years,) also H. S. Wingard while a student in the Seminary. Jacob Hawkins was pastor in 1871 for one year. He removed to Virginia and Rev. H. S. Wingard was invited and took charge. In 1874 this church was separated from Pastorate No. 12 and made a separate and distinct charge with H. S. Wingard as pastor. Mr. Wingard was pastor in 1875, but has since removed to Georgia and is now, 1892, in the old Salzburger colony of Ebenezer near Savannah. Newville was rebuilt as Grace Church in 1878. It has since been served by Revs. J. E. Bushnell, C. A. Marks and T. O. Keister.

Beth Eden congregation was organized in 1843. House of worship was built the same year and dedicated by the Revs. Brown, Hope and Aull. Membership at first not more than 20; now over 100. The first pastor was Rev. Brown. The church has been served since by Revs. Berly, Bolles, Fink, Anthony, Sheppard, Hungerpeler,* Moser, Hawkins, Schreckhise, Shirey, Bedenbaugh. Now, 1892, supplied by Prof. W. K. Sligh.

---

*This was Hungerpeler's only charge, his first and last. While pastor here he died in 1855 or 1856, and while here he was mainly instrumental in inducing three of his members to study for the ministry: Revs. J. D. Bowles, J. T. Bowles, (deceased,) and J. A. Sligh.

St. Matthew's, near Ashford's Ferry on Broad River, was organized in 1827 or 1829 by Rev. J. D. Sheck, while on a missionary tour, and he became the first pastor. He has been succeeded by Revs. Moser, Hope, Sheppard, Berly, Anthony, Boinest, Hugerpeler, Hawkins, Bedenbaugh, Shirey, Julian, Wyse. Membership was very small at first, but has increased to 90 or 100. About nine miles distant once stood Zion's Church, which was burnt down and never rebuilt. Most of the members united with St. Matthew's. St. Matthew's was destroyed by the tornado of 1884 and rebuilt and rededicated in 1885.

Liberty Hill was erected in 1840, and dedicated in 1841 by Revs. Hope, P. A. Strobel and Aull. The membership is small. The church has been supplied by Revs. Moser, Hope, Aull, Brown, D. J. Dreher, Anthony, Hungerpeler, Hawkins, Bailey, Schreckhise, J. D. Shirey. In 1869 a new building was erected and dedicated. In 1890 this church was removed to Jalapa and rebuilt. It was dedicated the same year by Rev. W. C. Schaeffer, pastor of Luther Chapel, Newberry.

St. Philip's was built and dedicated in 1887 or 1888 through the efforts of Rev. H. S. Wingard, who was its first pastor. It has since been served by Revs. Hallman and Wyse.

The history of St. Paul's, the old Mother Church, evidently the oldest Lutheran congregation in the county, has not been well preserved. The name does not appear among the Lutheran Churches of the State incorporated by an Act of the Legislature in 1778. But from the fact that Rev. Frederick Joseph Wallern was for many years pastor of this congregation and became a member of the Corpus Evangelicum in January, 1789, while he was a pastor in Newberry County, and from the testimony of some of the oldest persons residing in the community, it is evident that this old congregation had an existence prior to 1787.

The building now used for worship by this congregation was built and dedicated in 1830, the services on the occasion being conducted by Revs. Moser, Rauch and Schwartz. The congregation previous to this had two church buildings, the first one was a log house which stood about 150 yards from the present building.

How long Pastor Wallern served the congregation is not known, but he owned a plantation upon which he lived which is about one and a half miles from the church, and within a few hundred yards of his then residence, where his remains now rest, a marble slab standing at the head of his grave. He died in 1816. Since his death the congregation has been served by the following pastors: Revs. Metts, Herscher, Rauch, Anthony, Berly, Stingley, Margart, Blackwelder and Sligh. The latter is now the pastor.

As early as 1845, when Colony congregation was organized, the old congregation of St. Paul's began her work of colonization, giving off to this congregation the principal part of her membership at its organization. St. Luke's also contributed in membership in building up this little colony.

Mt. Tabor, near Little Mountain, now numbering about 150 members, is also a colony from St. Paul's. The new congregation (Mt. Tabor) was organized and the church built through the efforts of its present pastor, Rev. J. A. Sligh.

Mt. Pilgrim, near by, brought into existence by the labors of Rev. J. D. Bowles, received at its organization a number of members from St. Paul's. Both of these churches were dedicated in 1880.

The organization of Bachman Chapel was effected through the efforts of Rev. J. A. Sligh, the membership coming from St. Paul's and Colony, principally from St. Paul's.

Mt. Olivet was dedicated in 1891, and was built through the efforts of Revs. Marks, Epting, Bowers and Sligh.

Mt. Tabor and St. Paul's, the daughter and mother, constitute a pastorate. Mt. Pilgrim's first pastor was the Rev. J. D. Bowles, and has since his removal, been served by Revs. Bushnell, Marks, Epting and Julian. Bachman Chapel was cared for by Revs. Sligh and J. D. Shealy and Prof. W. K. Sligh until arrangements could be made to secure a regular pastor. Mt. Pilgrim, Bachman Chapel, Mt. Olivet, and Macedonia in Lexington County constitute a pastorate.

Notwithstanding there has been a heavy drain made on St. Paul's congregation in giving off her membership to other organizations, she is still strong and healthy and now numbers about 250 members. From this old congregation the following persons have entered the Lutheran ministry: Revs. Herman Aull, (deceased), Wm. Berly, (deceased,) G. A. Hough, J. E. Berly, (deceased), S. T. Riser, (deceased), M. J. Epting and H. P. Counts. Rev. M. M. Kinard was also brought up in this church, but had moved his membership to Grace Church, Prosperity, before entering the ministry. Prof. W. K. Sligh and Robtert E. Livingston, both of whom it is expected will in a short time be ordained and set apart to the work of the ministry, were brought up in this church, the former, however, of whom is now a member of Mt. Tabor Church. It might be added here to the credit of this church that from her many students have entered Newberry College, among whom are some of her best educated and most useful graduates.

Of Rev. J. A. Sligh I must add that he has been pastor of the same congregation, St. Paul's,—it is his first charge,—for twenty-seven years. That he also has been a member of the Legislature, of which body he was a working and a useful member, taking an active part in all the business. He is now an energetic, useful public man, of sterling integrity and loved by his people.

—

ASSOCIATE REFORMED PRESBYTERIAN.

From the years 1763 to 1775 the elements of Cannon's Creek and King's Creek Churches, from which grew Prosperity and Head Spring, came from County Antrim, Ireland, and settled in the fertile region between Enoree and the Dutch Fork, centreing near the creeks from which the churches took their names. In the year 1767 a portion of Rev. John Renwick's congregation came from Ireland and settled in Newberry County. In 1770, a larger portion, with their pastor, came over and settled near the others; and in 1772 there came a third colony. We thus see that the first Associate Reformed preacher and pastor of the churches in Newberry was the Rev. John Renwick, born in Ireland of Scottish ancestry. His son, Rev. John Renwick, was born at sea on the passage over, December 31st, 1770. The Lord's Supper was first administered to these Christians in Newberry, in Patrick Carmichael's barn, near what is now known as Boyd's Crossing between Newberry and Prosperity. This Rev. John Renwick is believed to have been a descendant of the family of Rev. James Renwick, the last martyr of Scotland, who suffered February 18th, 1688.

Rev. James Renwick preached at Cannon's Creek and King's Creek Churches, which were founded at the same time, in 1772. He died August ?0th, 1775. After his death there was little preaching, owing to the troublous times, until the year 1790. In that year, or the year before, the Revs. David Bothwell and James Rogers arrived, and they were both present at Cedar Springs, February 24th, 1790, at the organization of the Presbytery of the Carolinas. There were also present at that time Revs. Thomas Clark, Peter McMullen and John Boyce, ministers, with James McBryde and William Dunlap, elders.

Mr. Rogers became pastor of Cannon's and King's Creek Churches on the 23d of February, 1791, and served in that capacity for twenty-four or twenty-five years; for though the pastoral relation had been formally dissolved in 1801, yet they having no settled pastor, he continued to serve them, in so far as he was able, until the year 1814.

In 1802 Prosperity Church was built and the congregation organized, with Abram Carmichael and Abram Young, elders.

Rev. John Renwick, son of the first pastor, and who, as has been already mentioned, was born at sea, December 31st, 1770, was licensed to preach January 1st, 1807—missionated two and a half years and settled at Gilder's Creek—was five years pastor, and continued to preach there and elsewhere as long as he was able, until he was superannuated a few years before his death, which occurred about the close of the year 1836.

In 1814 Rev. Joseph Lowry received a call from the Newberry Churches, but failing to secure his services they made further efforts and succeeded in obtaining the services of that great and good man, Rev. Charles Strong. He was installed pastor of Cannon's Creek, King's Creek and Prosperity in 1816, a position which he held for eight years, doing good, and faithfully executing his Master's work. Under his administration assisted by his zealous elders, the churches grew and prospered. The names of some of the elders were, John Caldwell and Capt. Brice at Cannon's Creek; John Dugan, at least, at King's Creek, and Messrs. Carmichael and Young at Prosperity; and also James J. Sloan, Robert Drennon and Samuel McQuerns at Cannon's Creek, and Capt. James Spence and James Wilson at King's Creek; Robert Brown at Prosperity.

Other good men, private members of the churches helped greatly in the good work, among whom may be mentioned, Flemings, Fairs, Reids, Caldwells, McConnells, Youngs, Thompsons, Spences, Enlows, Neels, Hunters, Neeleys, Calmes, Martins, Peasters, Johnstones, Chapmans, from which family I think my old friend Richard C. Chapman sprang, and many others. The pastoral relationship between Mr. Strong and his churches was closed by his death, which took place July 20, 1824.

About this time a commodious church building was erected at Head Spring and on the first Sabbath after the death of Mr. Strong the first sermon was preached in this house by Rev. William Blackstocks. The organization was effected soon after, James J. Sloan and Capt. James Chalmers, elders.

Rev. Samuel P. Pressly, of whom it has been said that he never had a superior in the Presbytery, became pastor of the four united congregations of Newberry in 1826 or 1827. He made his home at the village of Newberry, was Principal of the Academy at that place and preached regularly in his several churches for nearly eight years. Being a man of popular manners, fine address and an able preacher, large congregations waited on his ministry and very many were added to the church. Mr. Pressly's ministry was highly successful and the churches fully maintained their high position and influence among the sister churches of the land. But more liberal measures being advocated and sometimes practiced by Mr. Pressly, occasioning earnest and sometimes heated discussions in the sessions and among the members, the churches were destined to receive a severe shock in the removal of Mr. Pressly and the consequences which ensued. A wider field of usefulness having opened up before the young and talented pastor on his election to a professorship in the Franklin University, Athens, Georgia, at a meeting of Presbytery held at Long Cane, March 28th, 1834. Mr. Pressly asked and obtained a dismission to connect himself with a sister denomination, leaving his congregations vacant and somewhat torn and distracted with internal dissensions. While the eldership and the great majority of the membership adhered to their former faith and practice, yet some good, prominent and influential men followed the example of their pastor. Among these may be mentioned Chancellor Johnstone, Dr. Glenn, Esquires Keller, David Cleary, George Boozer, Dr. Alexander Chambers, the Footes and others with their families, through whose instrumentality and influence sprung Aveleigh Church, now the Presbyterian Church of Newberry, and Smyrna above Bush River; Gilder's Creek seemed also to be revived, and subsequently Mount Bethel was called into being. Hence these churches of Cannon's Creek, King's Creek, Prosperity and Head Spring may be regarded, in a great measure, as the parent of all the Presbyterianism now known in Newberry.

The Presbytery met for four successive years towards the close of Mr. Pressly's pastorate in one of the Newberry churches. At Head Spring, November 5th, 1829; at Prosperity, November 3d, 1830; at Cannon's Creek, November 10th, 1831; at King's Creek, November 8th, 1832. Rev. Jonathan Galloway succeeded Mr. Pressly as pastor of these churches and was installed by Presbytery at Head Spring, April 16th, 1836, pastor of these united congregations, having been found sound in doctrine and consistent in practice. After some years the people of his charge began to desire more preaching and so by mutual consent and arrangement Rev. J. O. Lindsay preached one year, 1848, at Cannon's Creek and King's Creek Churches. The next year King's Creek was supplied one-third of the time by Rev. D. F. Haddon, and two years subsequently by Rev. A. Ransom. In the meantime Elder James Wilson having ceased to act in the capacity of elder, Patrick Martin was added to the eldership at King's Creek—Capt. Spence still surviving to discharge the duties of the office which he had long held.

An Associate Reformed Presbyterian Church was organized in the town of Newberry in the year 1850. Dr. Thomas W. Thompson gave the lot, and the friends of the cause generally assisted in erecting a very neat and substantial edifice. Dr. Wm. McMorries and Dr. Thomas W. Thompson were ordained elders, to whom Prof. Wm. Hood was subsequently added. This church, known as the Thompson Street Church, united with King's Creek in calling Rev. H. L. Murphy. He accepted the call and was duly installed as paster at Newberry in 1853. Here he labored with great acceptance until the close of the war in 1865. Becoming discouraged after the war on account of the death and removal of some good men, Capt. Spence, Patrick Martin and Dr. Thompson—Dr. McMorries moved to the country—Mr. Murphy surrendered his charge and removed to West Tennessee.

Mr. Galloway continued his labors at Cannon's Creek, Prosperity and Head Spring until October, 1855, when through failing health he was compelled to demit his charge. From this time to November 1st, 1858, a period of three years, the word was preached and ordinances administered by different members of Presbytery, when Rev. J. C. Boyd was installed as pastor. He had been licensed by the First Presbytery September 8th, 1857, and was pastor of Prosperity, Cannon's Creek and Head Spring Churches until 1889.

Rev. E. P. McClintock began to preach regularly at Thompson Street and King's Creek Churches in May, 1870, and was installed pastor in May, 1871. That pastorate continued until 1883. At that time Mr. McClintock removed to the town of Newberry and became pastor of Thompson Street Church exclusively, which mutually pleasant relation continues to this day. The officers now are: J. N. Martin, J. C. Wilson, M. A. Carlisle, Geo. S. Mower, ruling elders; James F. Todd, E. C. Jones, Foster N. Martin, S. B. Jones, deacons.

In September, 1884, Rev. W. W. McMorries was installed pastor of King's Creek and Cannon's Creek Churches, and he is still serving these two churches with a full corps of active officers.

To sum up—King's Creek and Cannon's Creek were founded in 1772; Prosperity in 1802; Head Spring in 1824; Thompson Street Church at Newberry in 1850.

The following sketch of the church at Prosperity is condensed from one written by Mr. A. E. P. Bedenbaugh:

The first church was built in 1802 by James Young and others. The second one about twenty-five years later. For eighty-seven years there has been preaching and the ministration of the ordinances at that place. The church was organized by Rev. James Rogers in 1802, and he became pastor and served for several years James Young, Samuel McQuerns and Robert Drennon were first elders. Charles Strong became pastor in 1816—died in August, 1824. The elders at that time were Abram Young, Abram Carmichael and Robert

Young. Robert Brown was born in Ireland, May 20th, 1762; came to America and was an elder in King's Creek Church; married Nancy Young, April 8th, 1794; moved within bounds of Prosperity Church and became an elder there. After Mr. Strong's death, Rev. S. P. Pressly became pastor. In 1832 he was elected to a professorship in Franklin University at Athens, Georgia, and left the church without a pastor. Prosperity was then without a pastor until 1835, when Rev. J. Galloway was called—was installed in 1836, and served for twenty years. The church grew rapidly under the ministry of Strong, Pressly and the first part of Mr. Galloway's ministry, but towards the latter part it declined somewhat. Rev. J. C. Boyd preached his first sermon at Prosperity on the fourth Sabbath of February, 1858. He was ordained as a minister at Head Spring the first Sabbath in November, 1858, and began as pastor of Prosperity, Head Spring and Cannon Creek Churches, and was pastor of Prosperity all the time to 1889. During his pastorship Abram Moore, James Fair, Robert Carmichael, George Brown, Dr. Thompson Young, Col. William Lester, John B. Fellers, J. T. P. Crosson, H. C. Moseley, J. H. Hunter and C. F. Boyd have been elders,—Fair, Brown, Lester and Moore are dead. Capt. Matthew Hall, Dr. A. A. Kibler and A. P. Dominick were made deacons in 1867. Matthew Hall has passed away—gone to his reward. Mr. Boyd was pastor thirty one years. Only two survive of the members of the church, who were there when he took charge, Abram Moore's daughter Esther and Dr. Thompson Young.

—

PRESBYTERIAN.

On the 8th of August, 1806, Josiah P. Smith, of Mount Bethel Academy, which was in the neighborhood of Indian Creek and Gilder's Creek, where there had always been a considerable Presbyterian population since the first settlement, applied to the Second Presbytery for supplies for that place. The application was granted, and Revs. John B. Kennedy, Hugh Dickinson and James Gilliland were appointed to preach there. But the supposition is that the arrangement was not at all permanent.

The church at Indian Creek at the beginning of the century was still the scene of Robert McClintock's labors, as it had been for a good many years. But it does not appear on the minutes of the Second Presbytery, nor was Mr. McClintock a member of that body. His baptismal register contains the names of 2,080 persons baptized by him. One hundred and fifty-nine of these were baptized between the 1st of January, 1800, and June 5th, 1803. The names of the parents are given and a large share of these were persons living in this portion of Newberry District. He baptized two of his own children, John and Robert, on the 23d of April, 1803. He baptized only two others afterwards, as he died some time during the year 1803.

Grassy Spring, in the neighborhood where Maybinton now is, was under the charge of Rev. Wm. Williamson until 1802, who had preached to it one-fourth of his time, but now withdrew from it as pastor. From this time it was supplied by Messrs. Williamson, Montgomery and Rev. John B. Kennedy until August 8th, 1806, when David Gray was ordained and became its pastor, preaching there one-fourth of his time, giving to other churches in Union and Laurens the balance of his time. This arrangement continued until 1810.

A portion of Little River congregation was in Newberry and a portion in Laurens, Rev. John B. Kennedy, pastor, giving part of his time to Duncan's Creek in Laurens,—from 1800 to 1810,—continued till 1820.

Rev. Daniel Gray continued as pastor of Grassy Spring until the 2nd of April, 1811, when he was dismissed from this portion of his charge on account of ill health. He died some time between the April and November meeting of Presbytery in 1816. After being supplied for some time during 1811 and 1812 as a vacant church, by Revs. John B. Kennedy, Daniel Gray and Hugh Dickson, Grassy Spring ceased to exist and disappeared from the records of the Presbytery.

Indian Creek had applied to the original Presbytery of South Carolina for supplies as early as October 11th, 1786, and Francis Cummins was appointed to supply it. In 1787 Rev. Thomas H. McCaule and Francis Cummins—again in 1789. It was reported among the vacancies unable to support a pastor in 1799, when the Presbytery was divided into the First and Second Presbyteries; and it no longer appears on the minutes. As it had been served by Rev. Robert Mc-

Clintock, and he was a member of the old Scotch Presbytery of Charleston, it may have been regarded as disconnected from this Presbytery and so was no longer mentioned in the records. Gilder's Creek is its probable successor. We have seen in the sketch of the Associate Reformed Church that Rev. John Renwick once preached in the church now known as Gilder's Creek. The original site of this church was quite near the stream so called, and at some distance from Indian Creek. In point of fact, about half a mile from Gilder's Creek and a mile and a half from Indian Creek. The building has been moved to a location upon Indian Creek where it now is. Gilder's Creek and Little River in Laurens sent a contribution by Rev. John B. Kennedy of five dollars to Presbytery in 1822; and again, in connection with Little River and Rocky Spring, the same amount. The people now living in that vicinity have no recollection of any one preaching there earlier than 1820, and the preacher then was John B. Kennedy.

With the assistance of Mr. Zaccheus Wright, father of Robt. H. Wright of the town of Newberry, a Sunday-school was organized at this church in 1821. This was then something new and was much talked of in the community. And when the leaders went to Columbia to buy books the people of Columbia did not know what was meant by a Sunday-school. Not all the people of Columbia, however, were so ignorant of Sunday-schools, for a Sunday-school Union, embracing the several denominations, and a number of schools dated back to 1820.

In 1825 the membership of Gilder's Creek numbered sixty-seven; in 1826 there were seventy communicants; in 1827 no report; in 1828 under pastoral care with seventy-five members. This church was originally in connection with the Associate Reformed, but how it came to change connection is not clearly known. It may have been through the change of pastor from Mr. Renwick to Mr. Kennedy. Mr. Kennedy was pastor *until* 1839—during that year the church had no pastor—and several succeeding years. In the fall of 1845 Rev. E. F. Hyde was called to this church, and to Aveleigh and Smyrna. Mr. Hyde continued pastor until the summer of 1848. The three churches were then left vacant until

October, 1849, when a call was given to Wm. B. Telford, a young licentiate. He was ordained and installed on the 8th of June, 1850. The elders in 1845 were William Mars, Wm. Beard and Hiram Glasgow. The membership in 1840 was eighteen; in 1845, seventeen; in 1878, eighteen. The Presbytery of South Carolina met in this church on the 25th of April, 1845. Rev. E. F. Hyde was at that time ordained to to the ministry.

Smyrna Church is located five and a half miles west of Newberry, directly on the high road leading from Newberry to old Cambridge or Ninety-Six. It was organized September 25th, 1838, by the Revs. R. C. Ketchum and M. D Fraser, with seventeen members, George Boozer, Esq., and David Clary were elected and ordained to the eldership. The church was supplied in part by Revs. R. C. Ketchum, Geo. Boggs and P. H. Folker, with perhaps a few sermons from others, until the year 1840. In that year the Rev. John McKittrick received a call from the churches of Aveleigh and Smyrna during the session of Presbytery. At an adjourned meeting of Presbytery held at Smyrna November 11th, 1840, his ordination and installation took place, and he took his seat as a member of Presbytery. In 1845 Rev. E. F. Hyde was stated supply of Smyrna in connection with Aveleigh and Gilder's Creek. The Rev. Bobert McLees became pastor for half his time in 1856 and so continued until his death. During the war and after, until 1872, this church was supplied by different ministers. John and James Senn and David Boozer became elders after those already mentioned. George Boozer, Esq., was always regarded as the leading man, as well as ruling elder in the church. His influence was great, both in the church and out of it. He was the father of Rev. J. I. Boozer, who died in Arkansas before the war, and four of his sons were elders in four different churches. One of his daughters married the first pastor the church ever had.

"The following facts," says Dr. Howe in his history of the Presbyterian Church in South Carolina, "with reference to the first movements toward the organization of a Presbyterian Church at Newberry I have obtained from Chancellor Job Johnstone. I simply make a quotation from a letter which I received from him on this subject: 'My former wife informed me that there was formerly as far back, perhaps, as 1822, a Presbyterian Church organized in this village. I remember there was a meeting of Presbytery held about that time in the old Male Academy, then taught by the Rev. Joseph Y. Alexander, and that he received ordination at its hands. And I find by a memorial in my family Bible that he baptized my son Silas, at my wife's request, on the 18th of January, 1822, at my house, being the first baptism by that minister. Yet so stupid was I that I never for a moment suspected, until years afterwards, that there ever had been any Presbyterian organization at Newberry. Mrs. Johnstone, when she gave the information, stated that her sister, Mrs. Harrington, and her sister-in-law, Mrs. Dr. Johnstone, had all been members, and that Mr. Thomas Boyd, of Bush River, had been an elder. All that I noticed was, that there was very regular preaching in the Court House while Mr. Alexander taught our school, and that there was less of shooting and kite flying in the streets on Sabbaths than formerly. On the removal of that excellent man, Mr. Alexander, to Georgia, I suppose the church fell through, for on the 15th of July, 1832, I find that my wife had three of our children baptized at Head Spring (Seceder) Church, by the late Samuel P. Pressly, subsequently a professor in Athens College, Georgia, but at that time pastor of Cannon's Creek, Prosperity, Indian Creek and Head Spring Churches. By the three children being baptized at the same time, I suppose that was the day she herself joined Mr. Pressly's church. In 1833 or '34 Mr. Pressly went to Georgia, by which his churches were for a time left vacant. He was a very liberal man, and under his administration his churches relaxed the rigor of close communion. All the Presbyterians in the neighborhood united as members with him, and in the course of the few years he was minister here, his churches had more than doubled the number of their communicants. On the 14th of September, 1834, I united with the church at Cannon's Creek, at a communion administered by the Rev. Mr. Boyce, of Fairfield, acting as a temporary supply. I stated at the time that on the first convenient opportunity I should unite with the Presbyterian Church, and that I should exercise the privilege of open communion. I united on this condition, expressed at the time, for after Mr. Pressly's removal, neither I nor the other Presbyterians in his late churches were pleased with the rigor we anticipated in them. On the 30th of November, 1834, Mr. Pressly, on a farewell visit to his churches, administered the sacrament of the Lord's Supper at Head Spring. I remember that there was an eclipse of the sun during the communion. Mr. P. spent a night at my house during the meeting. He was then about to transfer his connection to the Presbyterian Church, and we had a conversation about the prospects of a Presbyterian Church here. On Monday, after the communion at Head Spring, being December 1st, 1834, and saleday, I drew a subscription paper for the building of the church, subsequently called Aveleigh. The necessary amount was soon subscribed. Mr. Robert Boyce conveyed five acres of land as a lot for the church to be built on, at Hunt's Cross Roads, one mile and a half from the village of Newberry. On the advice of those interested, I wrote to Dr. Moses Waddell, Rev. S. B. Lewers and Rev. John Kennedy, of the South Carolina Presbytery, and to Rev. Robert B. Campbell, of Harmony Presbytery, to preach for us as they could, and, also, to Mr. Gladney, then of Columbia, a licentiate. They all generously aided us.'"

A congregation was organized May 30th, 1835, by Rev. Moses Waddell and Rev. S. B. Lewers and entered into a congregational covenant as members of the Presbyterian Church, believing that the Confession of Faith of that Church conformed most nearly to the system of faith and order as taught in the Gospel. Isaac Keller and Alexander Chambers were first elders.

The church was occasionally supplied by Rev. Moses Waddell, D. D., Rev. Isaac Waddell and Rev. S. B. Lewers until the meeting of Presbytery in March, 1836, when application was made for supplies. Supplies were granted two or three times each year and the sacrament of the Lord's Supper was administered at each meeting. At that time, that is in 1838, the church numbered forty-four communicants. In March, 1839, two more ruling elders were ordained, John Johnson and G. W. Glenn. In January, 1838, Rev. R. C. Ketchum was ordained and installed by Rev. Isaac Waddell and Rev. S. B. Lewers. But in the fall of 1839 the pastoral relation between this church and Mr. Ketchum was dissolved, which was a pity, as the church had prospered under his ministration. But Smyrna Church was organized in September, 1838, which no doubt weakened Aveleigh somewhat, as that church was at first composed of members from Aveleigh.

The next pastor was Rev. John McKittrick, for about three years, when the church was again vacant until the fall of 1845 when, in conjunction with Smyrna and Gilder's Creek, the services of Rev. E. F. Hyde, who had already been supplying them, were secured. Mr. Hyde was in charge till the summer of 1848, when the three were again left vacant with only occasional supplies till 1849, when Mr. Telford was called. Rev. W. B. Telford was installed June 8th, 1850.

Meantime the church had dwindled away until there were only about twelve members, and very few persons besides the members attended preaching. The fact is the church was neither a town church nor a country church. The country people regarded it as a town church and would not go to it, and being a mile and a half from town it was too far for many of the town folks to attend. So after due consideration it was thought best to erect a new church edifice in the town, and in due season this end was accomplished. The old house and lot were sold and a new house was erected on a lot given by Mr. E. Y. McMorries for that purpose. The new house was dedicated on the 17th day of December, 1852. After its removal to town some of the country members transferred their membership to Gilder's Creek and Mount Bethel. The church then numbered only about twenty members. The church immediately began to prosper and at almost every communion there were some additions. There were but three ruling elders in this church, Chancellor Job Johnstone in the town and Dr. G. W. Glenn and Mr. Isaac Keller in the country. The *name* of the church was not changed.

For the foregoing sketch of the Presbyterian churches in the County of Newberry I am indebted to the History of the Presbyterian Church in South Carolina by Rev. George Howe, D. D.

The pastors who have since served Aveleigh Church and the dates of their installation are as follows: Rev. A. D. Montgomery, June 29, 1856; Rev. E. H. Buist, June 6, 1862; Rev.

R. A. Mickle, November 30, 1866; Rev. R. A. Fair, October, 1874, being the pastor for eleven years. Rev. J. S. Cozby, D. D., the present pastor, entered upon the work on the 15th of October, 1886. The church edifice has been enlarged and modernized during 1892 at a cost of $3,500.

BAPTIST.

The Baptist Church is the oldest in the town of Newberry, having been organized in the year 1831; and, in the county at large, if it does not take precedence of all others in point of age, yet it is nearly as old as the oldest, running up to over one hundred years. But it matters not which is the oldest, the Baptist Church has always shown an aggressive spirit against all the powers of evil in every form and shape. As in the case of the other denominations I have tried to find a history of the Baptist Church in this State, or in the county; but I have not succeeded, as it seems there is no such book or pamphlet to be had. I have found a history of the Church at Newberry by Rev. Luther Broaddus, but that is all. I give a condensation of that history and such other facts as I have been able to gather in regard to the others.

In September, 1831, Revs. N. W. Hodges, J. M. Chiles, Josiah Furman and John M. Barnes began preaching at a stand in a large oak grove, then and afterwards known, I think, as the Academy Grove, on the southern outskirts of the village. At that time there were only four or five church members in the village; but on the 30th of September, the same month the preaching began, a church was organized with forty-two members. The Presbytery which constituted the church was composed of the following ministers: N. W. Hodges, Jonathan Davis, S. Worthington and Daniel Mangum. John S. Carwile was first deacon and John M. Barnes first pastor. Mr. Barnes was pastor only three months. In December Mr. Hodges was called and began his pastorate in January, 1832, and continued until the close of 1834. At the end of 1833 the church numbered 113 members. The first communion service was held on the fourth Sunday in May, 1832. At that meeting a communication was received from Rev. S. P. Pressly proposing inter-communion with other churches agreeing in their views of the Lord's Supper, though differing on other points. The proposition was declined. At a meeting in July, however, of the same year, the use of their house of worship was offered to other evangelical denominations whenever the pulpit was not occupied by the pastor. The house of worship was completed early in the year 1832. The church and parsonage lots were given by Y. J. Harrington and John L. Young and the bell by Hon. Kerr Boyce of Charleston.

In the year 1835 Daniel Mangum became pastor and was assisted by Rev. E. Lindsay. From 1836 to 1850 the church was served by Mr. Hodges, Thomas Frean, who was ordained in 1837, J. A. Chaplain, Samuel Gibson of Greenville and J. G. Landrum and M. C. Barrett of Spartanburg. In February, 1850, Rev. J. J. Brantley was called and entered upon his pastorate in May of that year and continued as pastor until 1866, when he resigned and preached his farewell sermon on the 6th of January, 1867. Rev. J. T. Zealy was called and entered upon his duties at once. He resigned in September, 1868, and Dr. Richard Furman was called and entered upon the duties of the pastorate the last of that year. But his health failed in the spring of 1869, and the church was supplied from the Theological Seminary, especially by Dr. William Williams, who continued to preach in 1870. Early in that year Rev. John Stout, a student in the Seminary, was asked to take charge, and did so, but continued his studies in the Seminary until May, 1871, when he removed to Newberry. He resigned and left in December, 1873, and was succeeded, July 1st, 1874, by Rev. F. W. Eason, and he, on the 1st of January, 1878, by Rev. Luther Broaddus, whose removal by death in 1885 was mourned as a calamity by the whole community, for he was a godly, noble, true, whole-souled man. He was succeeded by Rev. C. P. Scott, who served until April 1st. 1890. Rev. George A. Wright supplied the church in the summer of 1890, and regularly became pastor in 1891.

In 1869 William Hayne Leavell (son of my old friend Jno. R. Leavell), then a member of this church, was ordained to the work of the ministry. He is now an eloquent and able divine of the Presbyterian Church in Mississippi.

From the very beginning the Newberry Baptist Church has always had amongst its members some of the very best of the citizens of Newberry; among whom I may mention Mendenhall, Pratt, Higgins, Carwile, Hunt, Harrington, O'Neall, G. T. Scott, a strong, noble, upright man, and W. T. Wright. But I must mention no more; and those whose names I have written have all passed away. Those who are now living must show by their lives that they are worthy successors of those who have gone before. Was there ever a better man than Luther Broaddus?

I believe the church at Bush River is the oldest Baptist Church in the county.

I give here some extracts from a poem, bearing date February 1st, 1842, written on a visit to the burying ground of this church. The writer is Mr. David Jones of Ohio. I hope my readers will agree with me that the lines are worthy of presentation here:

Sure 'tis a solemn thing to tread
  Upon that hallowed spot of ground,
The sacred precincts of the dead
  Where many a little yellow mound
    To every eye each spot discloses,
    Where frail mortality reposes
  In slumber so profound;
That fancy ne'er affects the brain
With dreams of pleasure or of pain.

    ✻   ✻

Here closely dwell the young and old,
  The brave, and those who were afraid,
And he who toiled and heaped up gold
  Perchance is by a beggar laid;
    And comely youths who once were vain
    And did less favored ones disdain
  Have with them here decayed;
And learned and ignorant and wise
Are equal in this monarch's eyes.

  * * ✻ ✻ *

But many graves I here behold
  Not even honored by a stone,
With letters traced thereon, to unfold
  The name of him or her alone,
    But shapeless stones are there to tell
    How little love the living feel
  For their departed friends unknown,
As if it was not worth the cost
To keep their names from being lost.

Though it recks nothing to the soul
  When it has from the body passed,
If it should sleep at either pole
  Or to the winds of heaven be cast;
    Yet still humanity will say
    (And should ye not her voice obey?)
  Write o'er the grave at last
The name, that all who come may know
Whose dust it is that sleeps below.

  * ✻ ✻ *

And yonder is the grave of one
  Who died while he was in his prime,
Ah! little thought he that his sun
  Would set within so short a time.
    Buoyant with youthful hopes no doubt
    He had his hopeful plans laid out

The highest mount to climb,
But in a most unlooked for hour
He fell beneath the monarch's power.

    ✻   ✻

Hard by a lovely maiden sleeps,
  A being wrought of finest mould,
Here soft affection often weeps
  As it has done in days of old:
    And that she had an angel's face
    An angel's innocence and grace
  Is often, often told.
But grace and beauty could not save
The victim from the hungry grave.

  * * ✻ ✻ *

A little infant's buried there,
  The youngest inmate of a tomb,
Oh death! couldst thou not deign to spare
  That tender plant to bud and bloom?
    Why pluck it thus and rob the bed
    Where it was sweetly nourished,
  And soon had shed perfume;
'Twas well withall, it did not grow
To feel the bitter tempests blow.

  ✻ * ✻ *

"I once had life and health like thee
  Who now dost on the surface toil,
But mortal know that thou like me
  Must lay thee down beneath the soil;
    I charge thee then by all that's good
    Bring not into this dark abode
  A lamp that has no oil;
Or everlasting wrath and gloom
Will surely be thy dreadful doom."

Enough—this awful voice I've heard,
  'Tis time to hie me now away;
And oh! may I heed every word
  My conscience speaks within—obey
    The Lord! that I without a fear
    May at his holy bar appear
  At the great judgment day,
And with the holy choirs sing
Hosannah to the heavenly King.

PHILOM.

Newberry. S. C., February 1st, 1842.

The Mount Zion Baptist Church, located on the west prong of Beaver Dam, near Silver Street, seven miles west of the

town of Newberry, was organized in July, 1832. The officiating ministers were Revs. Daniel Mangum and N. W. Hodges,
aided by a number of brethren from Bush River and Cross
Roads Churches.

The church was organized by enrolling the names of the
following twenty-six members, adopting the Church Covenant
and ordaining Brother Isaac Kelly as a deacon. Names of
members: Sarah Ann Davenport, Mary Toland, Matilda Kelly,
Emily Davidson, Sarah Wright, Elizabeth Hunt, Charlotte
Richardson, Isaac Davenport, Samuel Davidson, Martha Waldrop, Mary Spear, Jane Stephens, William Adams, John
Goulding, Andrew Andrews, Isaac Kelly, Susan Kelly, Elizabeth Stewart, Nancy Wright, Sarah Davidson, Lucinda Galloway, Mary Andrews, Anna Kelly, Elizabeth Waldrp, John F.
Glenn and Edna Glenn.

Rev. Daniel Mangum, having been chiefly instrumental in
forming and organizing Mt. Zion Church, was called to preach
to them once a month and served them as pastor for eighteen
years. The next pastor was James F. Peterson, whose labors
were eminently blessed. During his pastorate of fifteen years,
one hundred and thirty-eight members were added to the
church. Mount Zion grew strong! Well might she contribute
to his needs in age and to his monument at Red Bank Church
in Edgefield County. He died June 10th, 1881, aged 85.

The third pastor was Rev. James K. Mendenhall—commenced 1865, lasting to 1870, during which time he baptized
sixty-six. He was an earnest laborer for our Master. In the
beginning of the year 1871 the church called to ordination
and to the pastorate, for his entire time, the Rev. A. W.
Lamar, who was ordained January 15th, 1871, by Rev. W. W.
Williams and Rev. Thomas H. Pope. After a pastorate of
one year he was called to act as Secretary and Treasurer of
the Baptist State Convention of South Carolina.

In 1872 Rev. T. W. Smith ministered to the church once
a month, alternated by Rev. Wm. Williams.

Sixth Pastorate, 1873.—In the spring of this year Mount
Zion and Bush River Churches united in calling Rev. W. D.
Rice. He was succeeded in 1878-79 by Rev. James C. Fur-
man, D. D., of Greenville.

In 1880 the church called Rev. Wm. B. Elkins indefinitely

2   W

to its pastorate—a faithful, earnest worker, who, on account of ill health, resigned after a pastorate of three years.

In December, 1883, Rev. W. J. Langston, who was a student at the time in the Theological Seminary at Louisville, Ky., was called to the pastorate indefinitely, to commence as soon as he returned from the Seminary, which was in June, 1884. Rev. Luther Broaddus filled the interim stately until Rev. Langston's return, and he has been pastor since June, 1884, to the present time, now 1892. A more zealous and devoted pastor never served the church.

The church passed through a terrible ordeal in 1888. In a little over six months she lost three of her deacons—all— viz., J. C. Stewart, J. R. Spearman and G. H. Werts, and some of the best female members, which gave her a backset from which she has not entirely recovered. But the present Board of Deacons are working energetically to revive and build up the church. During the year 1892 Mr. James Spear, another of the old Board of Deacons, died. The former deacons have all passed to their reward, except J. S. Floyd, who took his letter, and is now living in Walhalla, S. C. The present Board of Deacons is composed of Michael Werts, J. R. Spearman and J. S. Spearman.

Enoree Baptist Church is one of the oldest churches in the county of Newberry. It was organized in the year 1768. But little is known of the early history and struggles of this church. The first pastor of whom any knowledge now remains was Rev. Jacob King, but there must have been others preceding him. In 1822 a new house of worship was built, which was dedicated by Elders Thomas Ray, J. Davis and Alexander.

The written record begins with the year 1832; there is nothing beyond that. At that time Rev. N. W. Hodges was pastor. In 1836 Rev. Keener was pastor, assisted by Revs. Brooks, A. Ray and Abner. In 1837 Rev. E. Lindsay was pastor, assisted by Revs. Thomas Frean and G. W. Brooks. In 1838 Rev. G. W. Brooks became pastor and continued to serve the church for ten years. In 1849 Rev. J. A. Hill was pastor. In 1850 Rev. G. W. Brooks was again pastor. During the years 1851–2 there was no regular pastor. In 1853 Rev. E. Lindsay was pastor; in 1854, Rev. G. W. Brooks; in 1855–6,

Rev. F. C. Jeter, assisted in '56 by Rev. Spruell; in 1857, Rev. G. W. Brooks; in 1858–9, Rev. W. H. Martin, assisted by Rev. R. R. Vann. In the same year, that is in 1859, the present house of worship was built, and dedicated by Rev. J. J. Brantley, D. D.

In 1860 Rev. W. D. Mayfield was pastor, assisted by Rev. Mulinax. In 1861 the church was supplied by Revs. Mayfield and G. W. Brooks, but not as pastors. In 1862 Rev. James K. Mendenhall was pastor. During the year 1863 there was no record kept, as the Clerk was with the army otherwise engaged.

In 1864 Rev. F. C. Jeter was pastor; in 1865, Rev. James K. Mendenhall; in 1866–7, Rev. W. D. Mayfield; in 1868, Rev. William Young. During 1869 there was no settled pastor—Rev. B. F. Corley preached occasionally. In 1870 Rev. Thomas H. Pope was pastor; and in 1871, Rev. W. H. Leavell, assisted by Revs. J. Stout and W. B. Elkins. In 1872 Rev. W. T. Farrow was pastor; in 1873–4, Rev. F. C. Jeter; in 1875, '76 and '77, Rev. M. E. Broaddus; in 1878, Rev. G. W. Carter; in 1879, Rev. W. A. Gaines; in 1880, '81, '82, '83, '84 and '85, Rev. Harrison Fowler; in 1886, Rev. J. D. Huggins, and also in 1887–8; in 1889, Rev. J. S. West, and also part of 1890. The latter part of the year 1890, through 1891 and part of 1892, Rev. H. T. Smith was pastor.

At this time, August, 1892, the church is without a settled pastor.

Bethel Baptist Church was organized September 29th, 1840, by Revs. Daniel Mangum and Thomas Frean. This church is on the Holley Ferry Road, six and a half miles south of the town of Prosperity, in Newberry County. It was supplied with preaching by Rev. D. Mangum and other ministers, as missionaries, irregularly, until about the year 1852. At that time Revs. A. W. Asbill and A. P. Norris held a protracted meeting and received several members, when the church called Rev. A. W. Asbill as pastor, the duties of which office he faithfully discharged until the year 1867—sixteen years in succession.

Since 1867 the church has been supplied by the following named ministers as pastors: Revs. John Barry, W. T. Farrow, N. N. Burton, J. M. Norris, L. O'Neall, M. D. Padgett,

W. B. Elkins, R. W. Seymour, Joab Edwards, N. B. Williams, J. D. Huggins and H. T. Smith.

Many other preachers have served this church, from time to time, but not as pastors. This church has set apart four of her members to exercise their gifts in the ministry. This church has elected only three clerks, viz., Mark Waites, who served to 1848; D. R. King, to 1874, and A. J. Long, who is now Clerk, August, 1892.

A church, Mount Olive, near by, was an older church, constituted as far back as 1792, and was succeeded by the Fairview Baptist Church in Newberry County, situated one mile from the line between Newberry and Laurens Counties and thirteen miles northwest of the town of Newberry, and organized the 22nd of August, 1859, Rev. A. C. Stepp being Moderator of the Presbytery and W. D. Mayfield Secretary. The following named brethren constituted the Presbytery and approved the Constitution of the Church: Elders E. Lindsay, of the Hurricane Church; John Gibbes, of New Prospect; John J. Jones, of Mount Paran; C. Felder, of Fellowship; A. C. Stepp, of Rabun's Creek, and W. D. Mayfield, of Chestnut Ridge; Deacons, Henry Johnson, J. N. Meadors, Lewis D. Jones, of Hurricane, Dr. J. K. Gary, Geo. S. Cannon, of Bush River; and Laymen, James Copeland, John Horton, of Hurricane; Chesley Davis, Geo. Speake, of Bush River; Ring. Duckett, J. G. Duckett, Isaac Duckett, of Lower Duncan's Creek.

The following named ministers have served this church as pastors: Revs. W. D. Mayfield, A. C. Stepp, Thos. H. Pope, Z. T. Leavell, W. B. Elkins, M. E. Broaddus, G. H. Carter, W. R. Gains, J. D. Huggins, J. S. West, H. Fowler.

Prosperity Baptist Church, at the town of Prosperity, was organized the fourth Sunday in April, 1884. Sermon by Rev. Luther Broaddus, of Newberry, S. C. At the time of the organization of this church Rev. N. B. Williams was State Missionary at Prosperity. One month after the organization the church decided to build a house of worship, and as soon thereafter as possible a small, but comfortable and substant'al "concrete" building, with baptistery under the rostrum, was erected. On the 2nd of January, 1887, Rev. N. B. Williams bade farewell to this church, and on the 20th his successor, Rev. W. B. Elkins, arrived and took charge.

In 1888 the first meeting held was a "Baptist Union Meeting," which began on Friday before the fifth Sunday in April. On the fourth Sunday in May was the first baptism in this church. A large congregation, many of whom had never witnessed the ordinance of baptism by immersion, gathered to witness the immersion of Mr. Carwile Hussa. The first celebration of the Lord's Supper was on the first Sunday in June, 1888. On the first Sunday in August a Sunday-school was organized with thirty-four members. In October following their Sunday-school literature was received and distributed.

Rev. J. D. Huggins was pastor during the year 1889. The house of worship was dedicated October 13th, 1889—sermon by Rev. C. P. Scott, of Newberry. Rev. N. B. Williams; Rev. J. C. Boyd, of the A. R. P. Church; and the pastor, Rev. J. D. Huggins, also took part in the services. Rev. J. D. Huggins preached his farewell sermon on the 22nd of December, 1889. The church then called Rev. T. J. Smith, who did not accept. The call was then extended to Rev. H. T. Smith, January 16th, 1890. He accepted and served as pastor, 1890–1.

At the request of the Lexington Church, this church ordained Mr. S. J. Riddle to the ministry of the gospel, December 27th, 1891. The sermon was preached and the prayer offered by Rev. G. A. Wright; the charge delivered and the Bible presented by Rev. H. T. Smith.

At the first of the year 1892 Rev. J. W. Blanton, as missionary pastor, took charge of this church. The membership in April was thirty-one.

METHODIST.

For the following history of the Methodist Church in Newberry County I am indebted to Rev. J. B. Traywick and his daughter, Miss Mary Traywick:

The early history of the Methodist Church in Newberry County has not been preserved with any degree of accuracy, except in a few instances. This is accounted for by the fact that Methodism was not introduced into the States by immigration from Europe, as in the case of the Lutheran and

Presbyterian Churches, but by the evangelical labors of itinerant preachers; and, also, the early Methodist churches were
generally organized in private houses, and were not served by
resident pastors, but by itinerant preachers, who were usually
changed annually, and who served large numbers of preaching
places. Then the early churches had no record except class-
books for societies; hence we have lost much of the valuable
history of Methodism in the first half century of its existence
in this county.

The first Methodist society in Newberry County could not
have been organized sooner than 1784. The following year
the Broad River Circuit was formed, which circuit extended
from Dutch Fork to Pacolet, in Spartanburg District. The
Broad River Circuit did not include all Newberry District.
A few years later Saluda River Circuit was formed, and those
churches on the Saluda side of the district were included in it.
This arrangement continued until 1794, when Bush River Circuit was organized, and most of the churches in Newberry
Distric', except the churches on Enoree River, which were in
Enoree Circuit, were included in Bush River Circuit, and continued in this circuit until 1820, when Newberry Circuit was
organized, the territory of which included all Newberry County
except Ebenezer, near Maybinton, and Mt. Tabor; also all of
Lexington Fork, and Hopewell, Salem and Sardis, in Laurens.

The churches in Newberry District, from the beginning in
1784, had enjoyed the ministerial service of many of the
leading preachers of that day, beginning with James Foster,
and Stephen Johnson as junior for that year. Bishop Asbury
often preached in Newberry District, as did Bishops Coke and
Whatcoat.

Coleman Carlisle was in charge of Newberry Circuit its first
year, 1820. He was the grandfather of Dr. R. C. Carlisle and
M. A. Carlisle, Esq., of our county. His body sleeps in Salem
Graveyard, in Laurens County, S. C. The preachers on Newberry Circuit for 1821 were: James Mullinnix and Daniel Riley;
1822, Henry Bass and M. McPherson; 1823, Robert Adams;
1824-5, Joseph Holmes; 1826, to be supplied; 1827, Barnett
Smith; 1828, Samuel Dunwoody; 1829-30, - David Derrick;
1831-2, John Watts; 1833, John Compton; 1834, Jacob Ozier;
1835, H. W. Ledbetter and W. C. Ferrill; 1836-7, Frederick

Rush; 1838-9, David Derrick, and in 1839 also John Tarrant; 1840-1, Geo. W. Moore and John Tarrant; 1842-3, J. H. Zimmerman and D. Byrd; 1844, Samuel Dunwoody and L. M. Little; 1845, Samuel Dunwoody and A. B. McGilvary; 1846-7, Ira L. Potter and W. A. Connor; 1848, C. A. Crowell and S. H. Brown; 1849, W. A. McSwain and J. J. Harris; 1850, P. G. Bowman and S. H. Dunwoody; 1851, J. H. Zimmerman and Jas. W. Bouchelle; 1852, C. Murchison and E. J. Pennington; 1853, C. Murchison and W. E. Boon; 1854, C. H. Walker and A. B. McGilvary.

In 1854 the church in Newberry was set off as a station. But we follow the circuit in its preachers to the present. In 1854, Samuel Townsend; 1855, M. Puckett and J. T. Dubose; 1856, M. Puckett and D. D. Byars; 1857, Thos. Raysor and James Cline; 1858, Thos. Raysor and Wesley Graham; 1859-60, J. T. Kilgo and Wm. Bowman; 1861-2, John W. Wightman and ——; 1863-4, M. A. Connelly and J. M. Boyd; 1865-68, J. H. Zimmerman was in charge with W. A. Hodges as junior in '65, J. B. Traywick in '66-7, and Robert M. Harrison in '68. In 1869, W. H. Lawton and J. M. Boyd; 1870, A. J. Cauthen and G. T. Harmon; 1871, A. P. Avant and J. C. Counts; 1872, A. P. Avant and H. W. Whitaker; 1873, J. L. Shuford and D. D. Dantzler; 1874, J. L. Shuford and J. C. Counts; 1875-6, Thos. G. Herbert and L. F. Beaty; 1877, Thos. G. Herbert and James W. Ariail; 1878, Thos. G. Herbert and W. P. Meadors; 1879, Jno. W. Kelly and W. P. Meadors; 1880, J. W. Kelly and Jas. S. Porter; 1881, A. J. Stokes and Thos. W. White; 1882, A. J. Stokes and J. W. Neeley; 1883, M. Brown and W. H. Hodges; 1884, M. Brown and G. R. Whitaker; 1885, M. Brown and G. H. Waddell; 1886, M. M. Brabham and J. M. Steadman; 1887-8, M. M. Brabham and A. W. Attaway; 1889, M. M. Brabham and W. C. Mouzon; 1890, W. H. Lawton; 1891-2, Coke D. Mann; 1893, W. L. Wait.

Newberry as a station had as its first pastor, in 1854, Jno. R. Pickett; 1855-6, W. A. McSwain; 1857-8, A. W. Walker; 1859-60, M. A. McKibbin; 1861-2, Bond English; 1863, Thos. J. Clyde; 1864, J. E. Watson; 1865-6, J. W. Humbert; 1867-8, W. S. Black; 1869-70, O. A. Darby; 1871-2, J. A. Mood; 1873-4, M. Brown; 1875, R. P. Franks; 1876-7,

C. H. Pritchard; 1878, A. M. Chrietzberg; 1879–81, J. B. Campbell; 1882–3, R. D. Smart; 1884–5, J. A. Clifton; 1886, H. F. Chrietzberg; 1887–8, J. L. Stokes; 1889–90, W. S. Wightman; 1891–3, W. W. Daniel.

At the Conference of 1875 North Newberry Circuit was formed, consisting of Tranquil, Tabernacle and Sharon, in Newberry County, and two churches in Laurens, and E. T. Hodges appointed as pastor for 1876; in 1877, J. W. Humbert; 1878–9, M. L. Banks; 1880–1, A. C. Legette; 1882–3, A. A. Gilbert; 1884, W. H. Ariail; 1885, R. R. Dagnall; 1886, M. H. Pooser; 1887–8, T. P. Phillips; 1889, E. P. Taylor; 1890, E. A. Wilkes, 1891–2, O. N. Rountree. This circuit now bears the name of Kinards.

At the Conference of 1889 Prosperity Circuit was set off, consisting of Prosperity Church, Zion, Mt. Pleasant and New Hope, and J. B. Traywick was appointed pastor for 1890–92. For 1893, D. D. Dantzler has been appointed.

Thus, at some length, I have given the pastors who have labored in Newberry County. Among this long list, there are many who have distinguished themselves as able preachers, and as a rule they have been faithful and earnest pastors.

Newberry has furnished the Church and County with a long list of faithful, self-sacrificing local preachers, who, while supporting themselves, have done a vast amount of ministerial labor without pecuniary compensation. I mention most of them as they occur to my mind: John McCartney, Philip Cromer, Dr. M. W. Moon, George Clark, Nathan Boyd, Samuel Neil, William Harmon, Warren Kilgore, Henry Cloy, Stephen Shell, William Curry, Dr. James Kilgore, S. H. Dunwoody, Mark M. Boyd and W. Walter Summers.

Newberry has also furnished a goodly number of itinerant preachers: George Dougherty, J. W. Lee, M. D., Thos. G. Herbert, J. Marion Boyd, Geo. M. Boyd, D. Pettus Boyd, B. M. Boozer, J. C. Counts, E. T. Hodges and J. Matthew Henry. While all these sons of Newberry have reflected honor on their native county, yet the first named deserve special notice.

Geo. Dougherty was born about 1772, in Newberry District, near the Lexington line (the place now unknown). His life was short– only about thirty-five years—his opportunies for education limited; he lost one eye, and was greatly disfigured by smallpox. His burning thirst for knowledge led him to attain a marked position as a scholar, as a logician, theologian and orator. He was far in advance of any contemporaries, according to the accounts given us of his great preaching by Drs. Pierce, Flinn, Chrietzberg and others. No South Carolinian has ever excelled him. Newberrians should hold his name in precious remembrance. He died in Wilmington, N. C., in 1807.

Dr. J. W. Lee went out into the itinerant ministry from New Hope Church. He labored a number of years, first in the South Carolina Conference and later on in the North Carolina Conference. He was a theologian of no mean ability. He died a few years since in North Carolina.

B. M. Boozer went out from Zion Church, and joined the South Carolina Conference in 1875. He was a pure, gentle Christian; was very useful, and died in 1882, in Spartanburg County, S. C. As to the others mentioned, they are still living and highly esteemed by the entire Conference.

As to the local preachers named, they not only contributed largely to the development of the Methodist Church in the county, but were true and patriotic citizens of the county. I may be permitted to write more fully of one of them, though living: Mark M. Boyd ("Uncle Mark"), now in his eighty-seventh year. He was reared in the New Hope community, but has lived many years in the New Chapel. He has been a member of the Church for sixty-seven years, and a local preacher for fifty. No man, dead or living, has exerted a greater influence on the moral and spiritual life of Newberry County than he. His whole record is without a blot or stain; he is universally loved wherever known and his name is a household word well nigh throughout the entire State. His coming to the homes of the people is hailed as a benediction. He is justly proud of the fact that all of his children are true Christians, and his three living sons are influential members of the South Carolina Conference. His father was Rev. Nathan Boyd. So as preachers the name *Boyd* has been continued for a whole century in Newberry County.

While Newberry County has given the Church so many Methodist preachers, perhaps her richest offering has been in

preachers' wives. Not only have most of the local preachers
mentioned above married Newberry women, but the following
itinerant preachers have married wives among Newberry's fair
daughters: W. B. Curry, John Watts, S. H. Dunwoody, J. W.
Lee, J. M. Boyd, G. M. Boyd, J. E. Watson, J. W. Humbert,
Fred Auld, T. H. Edwards, J. B. Traywick, J. C. Counts,
D. P. Boyd, B. M. Boozer, H. W. Whitaker, D. D. Dantzler,
A. Coke Smith, A. M. Chrietzberg, W. W. Jones, J. S. Porter,
L. F. Beaty, J. E. Rushton, G. H. Waddell, A. A. Gilbert,
M. M. Brabham and A. W. Attaway. The greater number of
these marriages have occurred in the past twenty-five years.

It becomes necessary to go back and give a brief account
of the origin and history of each church in the county. This
will not be according to dates in every instance.

It is quite probable that the first Methodist Church in New-
berry County was organized in the house of Edward Finch.
Bishop Asbury held a Quarterly Conference here in 1788.
This was near where Mt. Bethel Academy was built and dedicated by Bishop Asbury in 1795. Its first rector was Rev.
Mark Moore, who was in charge for six years, assisted by
Messrs. Smith and Hammond. Mr. Hammond succeeded Mr.
Moore. He was the father of Gov. Hammond. Mt. Bethel
had a large patronage and gave to South Carolina some of
her most distinguished men. This school continued until
about 1820, when it was superceded by Tabernacle Academy,
in Abbeville District. Annual collections were taken by the
Church for the support of this institution.

Mt. Pleasant was built about 1822, and is five or six
miles from the site of old Mt. Bethel. The first house was a
plain, unpretentious building, but the present commodious
building was erected about 1862. Micajah Suber, who joined
this church late in life, left in his will a gift of $1,000
toward its erection. Among the first members of this church
I mention the Goodwins, Oxners, Lyleses, Gilliams, Hattons.
Dr. Thos. Rutherford, of this church, was mainly instrumental
in building and gave large aid in supporting "Rutherford's
Camp Ground," which was located near the present residence
of Thos. W. Keitt. He also contributed largely to the building
of the church, as did Dr. McCants and many others. Among
the official members of this church, the present and past gen-

eration, I mention the Grahams, Eptings, Adamses, Cromers and Willinghams. J. H. Smith, R. P. Cromer and Thos. W. Keitt are stewards at this time, with E. W. Reese secretary.

Salem was located on Second Creek, near the late residence of Felix Graham. It was built about 1800, but in 1835 was merged into New Hope, which church was organized in 1795. Rev. Nathan Boyd was a leading spirit in its early history. He was zealously aided by the Tygerts, Lakes, Cromers, Grahams, Thompsons and others of that day. The present church building was built about 1831, about two miles from the site of the old church. The church has recently been greatly improved. Among the names connected with this church later on I mention the Glymphs, Bishops, Hugheys, Cannons, Wickers, Kinards, Cromers, Crookses, Lanes, Setzlers, Slighs, Hattons, Hentzes, Woods, Adamses, Grahams, Lakes, etc.

New Chapel, or rather Old Chapel, was built in the first decade of this century. It stood one mile south of the present building. In 1830 the old log church was abandoned and a neat frame building was built. This was accomplished mainly through the liberality of Isaac Herbert. This church gave way in 1879 to the beautiful church which now stands in its place. Among the first members of this church may be mentioned the Herberts, Gibsons, Lakes, Jenkinses, Montzes, etc. From 1840 to 1850 this church had large gains by conversions and transfers: the Boyds—Joshua and Mark M.—with their families, Lakes, Adamses, Morgans, Boulwares, Schumperts and others. The name of Isaac Herbert stands most prominently in Newberry County, and especially in his Church. No man has exerted a greater influence in developing a liberal and progressive spirit in the Church. He died in 1875, leaving a lasting influence for good. One of his sons, Thos. G. Herbert, is a prominent member of the South Carolina Conference, and his children and grandchildren are numbered among the choicest citizens of our State. New Chapel community for the past fifty years has been noted for the sobriety, integrity and hospitality of its citizens.

Stockmans–Bethel was built about 1796; it was located near the residence of the late Dr. J. A. Berly. Among the leading members were the Stockmans, Dickerts and Folks. In 1840 a new church was built near Pomaria and the name changed to Bethel. Only a few white families were connected with it, but the Gospel was here preached to a large number of slaves. After the emancipation of the slaves and the death of John Folk, and the removal of his sons, the church was abandoned.

King's Church stood near the present site of St. Luke's Lutheran Church. It was built in the early part of this century, mainly by John King. It was a plain log house. After the death of John King the church was abandoned. Jacob Bedenbaugh went to Harmon's Church and many of his descendants are members of Zion Church at this time.

Many years after King's Church was given up, in 1845, another church, named Nebo, was built in this community, near the residence of J. Wesley Boozer. His father, John Boozer, was the leading spirit in its erection. David Harmon became a member of this church late in life. Some years after the death of John Boozer, this church was merged with Zion (1871), and the old house disposed of. By this means Zion received some excellent members, mostly descendants of John Boozer.

Harmon's (Zion) was organized and the first church built in 1813. Among its first members were the Harmon brothers—John, Jacob, Thomas, William and James—Daniel Taylor, Matthias Hair and Rev. James McCartney. Some years after, Thomas T. Cureton became a member. He was Ordinary of Newberry District eight years, 1819-27. Dr. Geo. Lester also became a member. The old church was located about a mile from where Zion now stands, and on the east side of Holly's Ferry road. In 1829 the congregation moved and built a neat frame church where Zion now stands, and named it Zion, giving the Baptists the use of the old church, which was the beginning of Bethel. In 1853 Zion was blessed with a great revival under the ministry of Rev. G. W. M. Creighton, and a large number of persons joined. Col. Henry Stockman and 'Squire P. W. Counts were among the number. Col. Stockman was a leading and active member until his death a few years since. 'Squire Counts still lives in age and affliction. His deep piety, upright life and sunny nature make him a benediction to all. In 1866 this church had another wonderful revival. Ninety persons were converted, and many who joined at that meeting still live to bless the church. Two converts of this meeting became useful ministers—J. C. Counts and B. M. Boozer. This church has enjoyed great prosperity for the past twenty-five years, and has now 250 members, with a large Sunday-school in charge of E. P. Cromer. While large numbers have removed to other sections, building up other churches, I cannot leave Zion without mentioning that venerable man, Christian S. Enlow, the oldest member in this church, who has stood true and faithful for nearly sixty years. The large and splendid church in which this congregation now worships was built in 1880 when Rev. J. W. Kelly was pastor. The late Pierce Harmon took a most active part in its erection. The following family names are now on the roll of the church: Amick, Boozer, Bowers, Bedenbaugh, Barnes, Cromer, Counts, Connelly, Clamp, Cameron, Crompton, Cook, Dominick, Dawkins, Enlow, Fellers, Frazier, Fulmer, Gibson, Hipp, Harmon, Hendrix, Hair, Hawkins, Koon, Morris, Mayer, Moore, Mills, Nichols, Pugh, Rikard, Stockman, Shealy, Taylor, Vaughn and Warner.

Tranquil was first built in 1799, and the first members were Wrights, Shells, Browns, and Seymore families, from Virginia, who had become Methodists in their native State. In 1832 the old log church gave way to a frame church, and in 1859 this second building was superseded by a beautiful church, which building continued to be used until 1890, when it was taken down and moved to Jalapa, still retaining the old name of Tranquil. The once large membership of such choice material, having passed away by death and removal, only a very few remain. For over fifty years this church was a leading one in Newberry District. Among the many excellent members of this church, special mention should be made of Zaccheus Wright, (father of Capt. R. H. Wright), and Robt. G. Gilliam (father of Mrs. Lizzie Hinson). These two noble souls, though diverse in temperament, were one in the work of Christ's kingdom. To this church and community belongs the honor of organizing the first Sabbath-school in Newberry County—in 1827—conducted by Zaccheus Wright and Absalom Glasgow, (Presbyterian).

Tabernacle was organized in 1842. John B. Richie was the leading spirit in its beginning, and continued one of its main supports until his death. The first building was succeeded by a comfortable one in 1856, on land donated by Nathan Johnson, a leading Baptist in the community. Zaccheus Wright and Robert G. Gilliam, from Tranquil, greatly aided in building these houses of worship, and otherwise developing the church. Mrs. Bettie Gilliam, the Oxners, Bishops, Davises, and others are names connected with this church's history.

Sharon was built in 1869, on land donated for cemetery and church by Capt. John Martin Kinard in 1854. Jacob Summers was the leading spirit in the enterprise. The Gorees, Oxners, Harmons, Whittens, and Hinsons are among its first members. Rev. W. Walter Summer is an earnest, useful local preacher in this church. The church membership is not large, but made up of fine material. Near by stands the parsonage of Kinard's Circuit.

In 1838 Col. Samuel Cannon, David H. Buzhardt, Jacob Sligh and John Moore erected a stand near Cannon's Creek Church, known as Pleasant Grove, for preaching by the Methodists. Rev. David Derrick had regular appointments here. A church was built here in 1840. This church was kept up for a few years, but after the death of Col. Cannon, Jacob Sligh and John Moore moved to Ebenezer, and David H. Buzhardt with his family to Newberry, the church was abandoned.

After Pleasant Grove was discontinued, there was no Methodist Church for fifteen miles northeast of Newberry. Preaching services were held occasionally at a stand not far from where Lebanon now stands. J. C. Counts commenced preaching here regularly in 1872, and a church was soon afterward built. Benjamin F. McGraw, D. H. Buzhardt and their families were most active in this enterprise. The membership was small for many years, but it has grown rapidly for the past few years, and is now a prosperous church with a little less than one hundred members. The following are some of the family names: McGraw, Buzhardt, Reagin, Lominick, Wendt, Cromer, Adams, Thomason, Wilson, Harris, Parrott, Hayes, Dickert, Brown, Oxner, and Caldwell.

In the year 1848 a small church was built a mile southeast of the village of Prosperity, then called Frog Level. Those most interested in the church at first were Jesse Dominick,

John Dominick, George Stockman and their families. C. S. Enlow took an active part in building the church, which never prospered greatly. After some changes the congregation removed their place of worship, which was called Bethesda, to Prosperity, and worshiped in halls and school-rooms for a few years until they succeeded in building a small, but neat church, and gave it the name of Wightman Chapel, which was completed in 1881. Special mention should be made of J. Luther Counts, for without his aid the work would have long been delayed. E. P. Cromer and A. J. Kilgore were with him on the building committee. The membership of this church was small during the first decade of its existence, but for the past few years it has grown until there are seventy-five members, with a most excellent Sunday-school, which has been superintended first by D. M. Langford and now by F. V. Capers. This church is made up largely of most excellent material. The members showed an heroic spirit in building up their church and their advanced liberality in its support. The first members of this church were the families of Counts, Boulware, Langford, Dominick, Kinard, Taylor and Amick. Added to these at present there are Bowers, Capers, Hardy, Hodges, Sims, Lake, Ruff, Nichols, Kibler, Hunter, Etheridge and Long.

Mt. Tabor, located sixteen miles north of Newberry, was organized about 1820. It is a frame building, thirty by thirty-six feet, with a gallery across the end for the accommodation of the large number of worshipers in that neighborhood. The gallery was not built for the negroes as is usual with churches erected before the War between the States. The following were prominent members: Andrew Hipp, William Shell, Col. Benjamin Herndon, (at whose home Bishop Asbury was wont to lodge), John Epps, Jacob Hipp, Daniel Epps, Laban Rhodes, John Casey, John Lake, John Anderson, Aldrich Hipp, Thomas Phillips. Benjamin Ogletree and John B. Glenn were local preachers. In the year 1843 a camp meeting was held about one mile to the northwest, and in a year or two thereafter a new church was built there, and it took the place of the one mentioned. The new structure was built by Absalom Shell and John A. Abrams, the former being the first person married in the new edifice. The five acres of land embraced in this location were given by Allen Shell and Nathan Whitmire. The following deceased members were actively associated in the development of the new church: John Sims, George Hipp, Allen Shell, Henry Whitmire, John A. Abrams, James Epps, Thomas B. Kennerly, James Gordon, Solomon C. Hargrove, Samuel Abrams and Mark Shell. The following family names are to be found on the present membership roll: Abrams Abernethy, Andrews, Atchison, Baker, Bishop, Cromer, Dean, Denson, Epps, Enlow, Fant, Hargrove, Hipp, Metts, McCarley, McCrackin, Phifer, Sims, Spearman, Suber, Shannon, Tidmarsh, Whitmire, Wright, Wicker. The church building is commodious, painted, carpeted and supplied with an organ. Large congregations continue to assemble. The church is embraced in the Clinton circuit. For many years it was part of the Goshen Hill circuit.*

Ebenezer (Maybinton) is perhaps the oldest organized Methodist Church in Newberry County. Bishop Asbury, in his journals, spoke of lodging in this neighborhood, in 1800, with Thomas Hardy—grandfather of Hon. W. D. Hardy—who was a leading member of this church. It had been long established then—possibly soon after the Society at Finches (Mt. Bethel). The first building was used as a school-house. The second building was built on land donated by Dr. Burwell Chick. The second was superseded by the present building in 1848. The ground was given by Rev. George Clark, a local preacher who traveled some years in the Conference, but located and lived in this community. In 1876 the church was remodeled and enlarged through the zeal of the ladies of the congregation. In the long and prosperous history of this congregation, as members and laborers, are to be found the names of many of the most excellent citizens of Newberry County. In its early history are to be found the names of Huron, Hardy, Caldwell, Cofield, Brazzleman, Clark, Chandler, Davis, Harris; and later, Moorman, Chick, Maybin, Douglass, Lyles, Oxner, Glenn, Worthy, Bishop, Goudlocke, Murtishaw, Hodges and Sims. The membership is now small, as her sons

---

*At the Conference of 1892 the Whitmire Circuit was established, including Mt. Tabor, the church at Whitmires and possibly one or two in Union and Laurens. The church at Whitmires, a neat frame building, was built in 1892 by Rev. W. A. Betts, then pastor of Clinton circuit. Rev. S. T. Blackman was appointed as the first pastor of the new circuit. The church was dedicated on Sunday, January 1, 1893, by Bishop Duncan.

and daughters have gone out a blessing to other places. Rev.
E. T. Hodges, of the South Carolina Conference, went out
from this church. I have not been able to give the pastors
of this church and Mt. Tabor, as they have been connected
with Enoree, Union and Goshen Hill circuits.

Moon's was located in the forks of Saluda and Little Rivers.
It dates back to the last decade of the last century. Among
its first members was Dr. W. M. Moon, who was a local
preacher and most prominent in its building and support.
Bishop Asbury often rested at his hospitable home. Later on
in its history we find connected with this church, Dr. Peter
Moon, Mrs. Tabitha Atkinson, Rev. William Harmon and the
Boulwares. Mrs. Nancy Boulware and her husband, Robert
Boulware, were active members, then their sons, Andrew and
James R. Boulware. In 1851 this church was disbanded;
Dr. Peter Moon moving to Newberry and the Boulwares to
Soule Chapel in Laurens, and the remaining members to
Trinity.

In 1814 Jacob Gantt sold the lot on which Ebenezer
Church was built to Edward Finch, Stephen Shell and David
Owens, Trustees. The first church was probably built that
year, 1814. We find that in 1830 a new Board of Trustees
was appointed, viz: Daniel Smith, Wm. Watson, Wm. Harmon,
Zachariah Connelly and Jeremiah Morgan. Among those most
prominent in the early years of its history, we find the Wat-
sons, Morgans and Owenses, in 1832. Dr. Jas. Kilgore moved
into this community from Stoney Battery, where he had but
recently become a Methodist at Harmon Church. He at once
became a most liberal and zealous member of Ebenezer. He
was a physician of large practice, and a most successful local
preacher. We find in 1837, through his efforts, the church
lot was much enlarged, and it was about this time the large
frame church was built, which was used by the congregation
until 1880, when the beautiful church now in use was built
higher up the hill. It was about 1835 when camp-meetings
began to be held here annually, and continued to be held
for twenty years,* though camp-meetings had been held here
prior to 1827, and the camp ground had been popularly known

---

*Camp-meetings were begun here again in 1875, and were continued
to be held annually for about seven years.

as Watson's Camp Ground. This church received most valued acqusition in 1851, when Jacob Sligh moved into this community. The name Kilgore has been associated with this church for sixty years, and that of Sligh for forty years. Dr. Kilgore died in 1856, and his son, A. J. Kilgore, was also an officer for many years. Jacob Sligh died in 1885, and his son, G. McD. Sligh, is still a leading member here. Among the names found on her roll in the past are Morgan, Watson, Owens, Moore, Kilgore, Lake and Smith, and later on to these we add Sligh, Swindler, Hipp, Dunwoody, Hair, Goggans, Frazier, Cromer, Alewine, Hayes, Summers, Teague and Maffett. This church sustained a heavy loss in the death of A. J. Kilgore this year, 1892.

Shady Grove was located not far from the residence of the late John T. Peterson, and Kadesh about four miles above, in the Senn neighborhood. I am unable to give the date of the building of these churches, but they were among the first Methodist churches in Newberry County. They were built not later than 1795, and had a separate existence until 1836, when they were united and the name Trinity given the new church. The church built in 1836, on the site where Trinity now stands, continued in use until 1888, when the elegant church now used by the congregation was built. This church is one of the largest and most prosperous churches in the county.

The Methodist Church was organized in the town of Newberry about 1833. Mrs. Higgins once gave the writer an account of a great revival in Newberry in 1831. She said that it was a union meeting largely conducted by Baptists and Methodists, and that the results were the building of the Baptist and Methodist Churches; first the Baptist in 1832, and the Methodist the following year. It is worthy of remark that the town of Newberry was laid out in 1785, and the first church, the Baptist, was not built until 1832—forty-seven years. It is highly probable that the people of the town had had preaching in the Court House frequently.

The building now in use by the Methodist congregation is the same which was built in 1833. Large improvements were made in 1873; and, I am glad to say, at this writing a large subscription has already been raised to build a brick church to cost $8,000.

Among the first members of this church we find Philip Schopert and family, Mrs. Martha Turner, Mrs. Precious Schell, Daniel Boozer, Thos. Pratt, Jr., and Josiah Bishop. One of the original members still lives in Newberry—Mrs. Sarah Pope, *nee* Lorick. In looking over the names of the members, we find those of many of Newberry's choice citizens. Philip Schopert was, for a number of years, Recording Steward of Newberry Circuit. Dr. Geo. F. Epps, Dr. Peter Moon, Gen. H. H. Kinard, Richard C. Chapman, Robt. Moorman, Andrew M. Wicker, Dr. P. B. Ruff, Thos. F. Greneker, and many other devoted men and women. On the roll at this time are to be found the following family names: Blease, Bynum, Bishop, Chapman, Cook, Caldwell, Cromer, Evans, Eddy, Epting, Fair, Fant, Greneker, Gilder, Goodman, Hornsby, Johnson, Jones, Kinard, Lane, Livingstone, Langford, Lake, Moorman, Moore, Metts, Maybin, McWhirter, Merchant, Pope, Pitts, Russell, Riser, Rivers, Salter, Suber, Shockley, Summers, Taylor, Tarrant, Williams, Wright, White, Wallace, Welch, Wicker.

The present pastor, Rev. W. W. Daniel, organized, in 1891, a second church at Factoryville, with sixty members, and J. R. Thornton and Martin Berry as stewards.

Newberry Methodist Church has had continuous prosperity from the beginning; has now about three hundred members. Three sessions of the South Carolina Conference have been held here—1853, 1863 and 1878.

There are at this time fourteen Methodist Churches in the county, divided into four pastoral charges, with four parsonages; one located in the town of Newberry, one at Ebenezer, one at Prosperity and one at Kinards. There are fifteen hundred members in the white churches, with about two thousand in the colored. The colored Methodists of the county have, as a rule, good churches and are well supplied with pastors. They worshipped with the whites until after Emancipation; since then they have gone mostly into the A. M. E. Church. A few have joined the C. M. E. Church.

I have given a meagre account of Methodism in Newberry County. It would require a large volume to tell of the camp-meetings and revivals, of the active workers in her Sunday-schools, and of the great numbers who have gone out to bless other States. But I trust to save from utter oblivion some valuable facts for the future historian.

EPISCOPAL.

There is only one Episcopal Church in the county—St. Luke's, at the corner of Pratt and Calhoun Streets, Newberry. It is a handsome little Gothic edifice, with self-supporting roof, stained glass and tasteful interior design and finish, and was built by Contractor Hamilton, of Charleston, in 1854-5 from a drawing by Architect Walker, of Columbia. The plat was made by Mr. F. B. Higgins.

St. Luke's was consecrated by Bishop T. F. Davis, August 26, 1855. The first officers were: E. S. Bailey and Stiles Hurd, Wardens; Norman Bronson, Wm. B. D'Oyley, Wm. C. Johnson, C. H. Kingsmore and Albert C. Garlington, Vestry.

The first Episcopal Missionary to Newberry was Rev. R. S. Seely, in 1845, and the first minister officiating at St. Luke's was Rev. E. T. Walker, in 1855.

The following is the order in which the church has been supplied: Rev. C. R. Haines, 1859-60; Rev. Lucien C. Lance, 1862 to 1866; Rev. J. Maxwell Pringle, 1867; Rev. E. R. Miles, 1870 to 1873; Rev. P. F. Stevens, 1874; Rev. John Kershaw, 1876 to 1879; Rev. S. H. S. Gallaudet, September, 1879, to June, 1880; Rev. Frank Hallam, October 17, 1880, to December, 1881; Rev. W. F. Dickinson, January, 1882, to close of same year; Rev. W. H. Hanckel, January, 1883, to October, 1892, when in the providence of God Mr. Hanckel was removed from his labors in the Church Militant to the higher duties of the Church Triumphant. St. Luke's is at present without a rector.

The congregation of St. Luke's being small, the church has had but one resident minister, Rev. Dr. Dickinson. It has depended for pastoral work upon stated services by ministers of adjacent parishes. But it has been kept open every Sunday with rare exceptions by its present beloved and devoted lay reader, Capt. N. B. Mazyck. May he be spared for this labor of love for many years to come.

In connection herewith might be mentioned the names of the ministers who in the past have visited this church and held divine services: Rev. J. W. McCullough, Rev. J. Ward Simmons, Rev. Richard Trapier, Dr. A. Toomer Porter, Dr. C. C. Pinckney, Rev. Cranmore Wallace, Rev. Robert Wilson, Rev. E. C. Logan and others.

The following are the present officers of the church: N. B. Mazyck and A. W. T. Simmons, Wardens; R. H. Greneker, J. Newton Fowles, O. McR. Holmes and E. S. Motte, Vestry

---

QUAKERS.

Of the Quakers little more need be said. The last one who clung to the old faith died a good many years ago. The property on Bush River still belongs to the church, and I have heard a rumor that an effort is to be made to revive the church and rebuild the house of worship. I hope it may be done. We need thrifty, God-fearing men. We need those who believe in the direct and immediate movement and quickening and inspiration of the Holy Ghost, and who are men of peace. We need and the world needs more such.

My old friend Lambert J. Jones, Esq., possesses in an eminent degree those staid, quiet, steady habits so characteristic of the Friends. I do not think it will offend him if I class him with the Friends. It certainly would not offend me to be called a Quaker. But the Tunkers, of whom I am one by descent, though elsewhere I call myself a Swedenborgian, are sober, grave and steady as the Quakers. I would there were many of both. I am sure that neither the town nor county would suffer loss if all the inhabitants were as industrious and upright and true as Mr. Jones. A lawyer who has never missed a term of court in fifty-six years' practice, where his business called him, must be steady and true.

THE TUNKERS,

In the beginning of this century, had one church in the county, and that was all, I think. They lived near the Quakers, not far from Bush River, and like them were men of peace, believing it wrong to bear arms or to fight in any cause. I have understood that in parts of Pennsylvania and Virginia they are in considerable numbers. I have never met one, though my ancestors on my father's side were of that persuasion. They are German Baptists. James Howe, the school teacher, mentioned by Mr. David Jones in his contribution to this work, lies buried about the centre of the Tunker burying ground, where rest the remains of many members of the old families of that part of the county. It is on the place and near the house where S. S. Paysniger now lives, and who married a descendant of one of the old original Tunker settlers of Newberry. The oldest inscription I have been able to find on any tombstone there bears date 1811, but there are some much older without date, as it was used as a burying ground before the close of the last century.

THE UNIVERSALISTS,

Some years ago, had several churches or societies in this county. There are none in existence at this time, though there is still one house of worship and lot attached held in trust for the use of the Universalist Church and for a school house. There is, however, a pretty good sprinkling of Universalists in the county. The house of worship, Hartford, is just three miles south of Newberry. This denomination in the neighboring county of Edgefield in the year 1888 built a meeting house and organized a church with about three dozen members.

THE COVENANTERS,

A remnant of those devoted men and women of the Solemn League and Covenant of Scotland, who gave their blood and their lives so freely in the cause of God and human rights, once had a church in this county, about seven miles northwest from the town of Newberry. But as their faith was the same as that of the Presbyterians and Associate Reformed, they naturally became extinct and lost their identity in one or the other of those bodies.

SWEDENBORGIANS.

I believe there are no Swedenborgians in the county except myself. I have been told that J. Wood Davidson is of that faith, but I have never talked with him on religious subjects, and though a native of Newberry, he has not been a citizen for many years.

OTHER CHURCHES.

The Christians organized a church here a few years ago, but I believe they all moved away and their church organization was broken up, so that at this time there are none here.

The Jews have been good citizens of the town for a great

many years, but they have no synagogue here, nor any Rabbi that I am aware of.

The Roman Catholic Church has some very devoted members, but there is here no resident Priest.

The colored people of the county have their own separate organizations—the Methodist and Baptist predominating—the Presbyterians next. I do not think there are any Lutheran churches made up of colored people, though some are members of that body of Christians. They have amongst them two divisions of the Methodist Church, and probably three. I believe the greater number of them are members of some Church, being rather emotional in their nature and naturally religious. They would make good Roman Catholics, and I wonder sometimes why that Church has never established missions amongst them and made an effort to absorb them.

—

SUNDAY SCHOOLS.

In our notice of the Presbyterian Church we have already seen that the first Sunday-school ever in the County of Newberry, was instituted and organizad with the assistance of Zaccheus Wright in the year 1821. *Now* a church without a Sunday-school to train up the children in the faith, would soon lose its hold on the growing youth and become *non est*. Its sole dependence would be upon the extreme of revivalism. and I fear that even that would fail to keep alive an interest in spiritual things. It is better that the young should be trained in the right way than driven into it after coming to years of maturity.

I transcribe here an address read by Mr. Zaccheus Wright before a Sunday-school Convention held at Newberry, in the year 18—:

"DEAR FRIENDS: I would not presume to consume your time, or tax your patience on this interesting occasion, with anything that I might have to say, but for the earnest solicitation of those who have so kindly honored me with a seat in this Convention. This is a time and place to me both pleasant and interesting; pleasant on account of its associations, and interesting on account of the object to be attained; which is no less than that of striving to arrive at the best and most successful way of feeding the lambs of Christ. For more than thirty years I, with others, have been engaged in this great work, and, although our labors have not produced as much fruit and as great a reformation as we could have desired, yet I have great and abundant reasons for heartfelt gratitude to God for His approving smiles on our imperfect labors. A few years ago and we had never heard of a Sunday-school Convention; a little farther back and we had no *Sunday-school Visitor;* no *Child's Paper;* no *Sunday-school Times* or *Banner*, paying to each child and parent their weekly, semi-monthly and monthly visit, making up in all a more lively interest in the Sunday-school cause. Still farther back and we had no well filled Sunday-school Libraries teeming with the memories and biographies of good children, who had learned in Sunday-school to love the Saviour, and are now safely housed in His bosom. In short, forty years ago in all our happy country we had no Sabbath-school. How different then and now. Then, even in our cities and towns no Sabbath-school bell was heard to chime its pleasant notes to call parents and children together for the purpose of prayer and praise. But now, not only in town and villages do you find Sunday-schools, but all over the country, in almost every church and school house, you will find a group of little children anxiously awaiting and eager to hear the story of the cross as it comes from the warm heart of their devoted teacher.

"The first Sunday-school of which I have any personal knowledge was organized in a small school house, about eleven miles North of this place in the year 1827. I, with the efficient aid and assistance of a well tried and faithful friend, Absalom Glasgow, who has long since gone to his reward, were the humble instruments in the hands of God, of putting on foot, I believe, the first Sunday-school that was ever organized in this District. It is true that compared with the schools of the present day it could hardly be called a school. We had many difficulties to labor under that those of the present day know not of. We had no experience, no suitable books, a very uncomfortable house, and all the prejudices that then existed to contend with. Notwithstanding all these difficulties, we succeeded in getting some twelve or fifteen to enroll their names and thus the Sunday-school ship was launched in our community, and, by the blessing of God on our weak endeavors, has continued to float until the present time. And we have good reasons to believe that it has been the means in the hands of God of doing much good. Our statistics was imperfectly kept for some years for the want of an efficient Secretary. The whole number connected with our school since its organization is about three hundred. Out of this number fifty-six are dead, perhaps many more of those who have moved away. I do not know of any that was raised a member of the school and lived to be 21 years of age but what has joined some branch of the church, with one exception, and that one is now a member of the church.

"In looking back over the past I can see many, very many, errors and shortcomings; much remissness of duty and ingratitude to God; yet I trust and humbly pray that He will forgive them all for Christ's sake.

"Brethren, pray for me that God, who has borne with my weaknesses thus far, may not forsake nor leave me.

"Yours truly,

"ZACCHEUS WRIGHT."

XI.

EDUCATIONAL AND LITERARY.

NEWBERRY COLLEGE.

For several years during the history of this State, since the war, colleges known as denominational were the only institutions of higher learning in the State, and they filled an important gap. Many of these have been struggling amidst meagre support, with no endowment and poorly paid faculties, yet withal they are still doing a good work and form an important factor in the educational work in South Carolina.

Newberry College is one of these. It was chartered by the Legislature of South Carolina in 1856, with the following Trustees: John Bachman, D. D., LL.D.; Revs. E. B. Hort, N. Aldrich, T. S. Boinest, J. P. Margart and J. H. Bailey, and Messrs. G. Muller, W. K. Bachman, J. K. Schumpert, M. Barre, Patrick Todd, Henry Summer, N. A. Hunter, A. C. Garlington, J. P. Anll, Simeon Fair and J. P. Kinard.

The corner-stone of the projected new building was laid with imposing ceremonies on the 15th of July, 1857, addresses being made by Rev. J. J. Brantley, Gen. A. C. Garlington and Rev. Dr. J. Bachman. This building when completed was at that time one of the handsomest in the South.

The College was opened in the autumn of 1858 with most favorable prospects, one hundred and fifty students being enrolled during the first session. The catalogue of the second session, 1859–60, showed a roll of one hundred and seventy-five names.

The third year of the College, 1860–61, opened most encouragingly, but before many months the country was involved in the excitement and confusion of an approaching civil war. Students were summoned home and Professors resigned. Early in the spring of 1861 the College was closed for that session.

The first President of the College was Rev. T. Stork, D. D. Rev. J. P. Smeltzer, of Virginia, was the second President of the College, entering upon his duties in the fall of 1862. With much personal sacrifice and under many difficulties the College was kept open for students until the spring of 1865. The condition of the College building was such at this time as to repel students. The approach of the United States army toward Columbia in 1865 led the Confederate authorities to remove their purveying establishment from that city to Newberry. The College building was taken for this purpose. As a matter of necessity the exercises were now indefinitely suspended.

After the war the College was reopened under the Presidency of Rev. Dr. Smeltzer. The College building was so near a ruin in 1868 that it was both unsafe and unsuitable. At this crisis an offer came from Walhalla of a suitable building and grounds, which was accepted by the Lutheran Synod of South Carolina, and in November of that year the College, with the Faculty, a few students and a small amount of movable property, was removed to Walhalla. Here, with varying success, it remained until September, 1877.

An extra session of the Lutheran Synod of South Carolina was held in Newberry, April 3–5, 1877, to consider the question of removing the College from Walhalla. Bids were received from Prosperity, Walhalla, Columbia, Anderson, Lexington and Newberry. Newberry's bid was $15,780 in subscription, together with a gift of ten acres of land, or the privilege of buying the old site at $2,500, valued at $3,750. This generous offer of the old site was made by Mr. Jordan P. Pool, who then owned it. Newberry was chosen on the second ballot by a vote of twenty-five out of thirty-nine, and on motion of Rev. J. A. Sligh, who was a strong advocate for Prosperity, the vote was made unanimous.

It was largely through the efforts of Rev. H. W. Kuhns, who was then pastor of the Lutheran Church at Newberry, that Newberry gave the large subscription that she did and secured the College. Dr. Kuhns is a man of great energy and perseverance, and threw his whole soul and heart in bringing Newberry College back to its original home.

It may be worth while to put on record the fact that the first four months of the session of 1877–78, the first after the return to Newberry, were spent in the rooms now occupied by

Mr. Salter as a photograph gallery, on Pratt Street, which were given, free of charge, by Mr. Geo. S. Mower.

On July 19, 1877, the corner-stone of the new building was laid, and in February, 1878, it was so far completed as to permit of occupancy, and since that time the exercises have been regularly continued.

Since the founding of the College, one hundred and two young men have been graduated, the first graduation being in 1869. Of this number seven are dead. Of the living ninety-seven alumni, twenty-eight are farmers and merchants, sixteen are teachers, ten are physicians, eleven are lawyers and thirty-two are clergymen or in the course of preparation for the ministry.

The College has a well-selected library of 7,500 volumes; a valuable and interesting collection of mineralogical and nat-ural history specimens, known as the Sifley Museum; chemical and philosophical apparatus; two literary societies, which meet weekly in well furnished halls, and other appliances for doing first-class work.

There are two departments in the College—Preparatory and Collegiate. The Preparatory course covers a period of three years, and is designed to fit young men for College or for active life. The Collegiate Department is divided into two courses—the Classical, leading to the degree of Bachelor of Arts, and the Philosophical, leading to that of Bachelor of Philosophy.

This is the list of Presidents, Professors and Tutors of Newberry College from its inception to January, 1893:

1858, 1859, 1860—Rev. T. Stork, D. D., President. Robert Garlington, A. M., Professor of Mathematics and Mechanical Philosophy. O. B. Mayer, M. D., Professor of Chemistry, Mineralogy and Geology. Rev. J. Bachman, D. D., LL.D., Lecturer on Natural History. Rev. J. A. Brown, A. M., Professor of Hebrew and Sacred Greek. Charles A. Stork, A. B., Professor of Greek. Rev. M. Whittle, A. B., Adjunct Professor of Latin and Principal of Preparatory Department. A. P. Pifer, Professor, 1860, 1861.

Under the Presidency of Rev. J. P. Smeltzer, 1861 to 1877—Rev. J. P. Smeltzer, D. D., President. D. Arrington, A. M., Professor of Mathematics and Natural Sciences. O. B. Mayer,

M. D., Professor of Chemistry, Mineralogy and Geology. Rev. J. McNeille Turner, D. D., Professor of Greek, 1869 to 1871. J. E. Houseal, Tutor, Preparatory Department, 1869 to 1872. Rev. J. M. Schreckhise, A. M., Professor of Ancient Languages, 1862–1865. Webster Eichelberger, Principal Preparatory Department, 1862–1864. Rev. J. H. C. Schierenbeck, Professor of German Language and Literature, 1871–1873. E. J. Dreher, Tutor, Preparatory Department, 1872–1875. Rev. G. W. Holland, Professor of Greek and Latin, 1874–1878. John C. Watkins, Assistant Preparatory Department, 1874–1876. Rev. J. F. Probst, A. M., Professor of German, 1876. D. B. Busby, Principal Preparatory Department and Assistant Professor of Latin, 1876.

Under the Presidency of Rev. G. W. Holland, D. D., 1878 to 1892—Rev. G. W. Holland, D. D., President, 1878–1892. Geo. D. Haltiwanger, A. M., Principal Preparatory Department and Adjunct Professor of Mathematics, 1877–1879. George B. Cromer, Professor of Latin, History and Political Science, 1877–1881. Rev. S. S. Rahn, A. M., Professor of Greek and German, 1879–1882. O. B. Mayer, M. D., Professor of Chemistry, Mineralogy, Geology, Physiology and Hygiene, 1878–1892. George G. Sale, A. M., Professor of Mathematics, 1879–1881. R. H. Clarkson, A. M., Princpal Preparatory Department, 1879. B. W. Bittle, A. M., Professor of Latin and History, 1880–1884. C. W. Welch, A. M., Professor of Mathematics, Physics and Astronomy, 1881–1885. E. H. Aull, A. M., Principal Preparatory Department, 1881–1882. Rev. J. Steck, D. D., Professor of History and Political Science, 1883. Rev. Holmes Dysinger, A. M., Professor of Ancient Languages, 1883–1888. Hart Gilbert, A. M., Principal Preparatory Department, 1884. Rev. A. G. Voigt, A. M., Professor Modern Languages, 1885–1889. Rev. J. B. Fox, A. M., Ph.D., Professor Mathematics and Natural Sciences, 1885–1892. Thos. H. Dreher, A. M., Principal Preparatory Department, 1885–1889. W. C. Schott, Principal Business Department, 1890–1891. Rev. A. J. Bowers, A. M., Professor Ancient Languages, 1890–1892. Arthur Kibler, A. B., Professor Latin, 1892. A. S. Laird, Principal Preparatory Department, 1890–1891. G. E. Werber, A. B., Principal Preparatory Department, 1884. Rev. W. K. Sligh, A. B., Principal Preparatory Department, 1891–1892. A. W. Fogle, Preparatory Department,

1891–1892. W. G. Houseal, M. D., Lecturer on Physiology and Hygiene, 1892. Rev. S. P. Hughes, A. M., Professor of History and English Literature, 1877.

Dr. O. B. Mayer, Sr., was a member of the Faculty from the founding of the College, except the few years the College was conducted at Walhalla, until his death in 1891. His son, Dr. O. B. Mayer, Jr., now fills his place.

Rev. Dr. G. W. Holland, the present President of Newberry College, should have been mentioned in that part of this book which records the names of those who served the Confederacy. Though he is a native of Virginia, he has long been a valued and true citizen of Newberry, and now wears an empty sleeve as a constant testimony to service in the times that tried men. At the outbreak of the war he enlisted as a private soldier in the 33d Virginia Regiment, of the "Stonewall Brigade," and served the Confederacy until he lost his left arm at Fairfax Court House, Virginia. He was afterwards commissioned by the Governor of Virginia as Captain of the "Reserves."

He was a brave and true soldier, and has shown fidelity to duty in all the positions to which he has been called in the civil walks of life.

He has been President of the College since its relocation at Newberry, and was several years before one of the Professors. The College is now successful under his administration.   E. H. A.

—

THE OLD NEWBERRY ACADEMY.

In the midst of the Halcyon Grove once stood a long, low, cheap, wooden building, known as the Newberry Academy. It was about a half mile from the Court House, and just south of the Greenville and Columbia Rail Road, and east of the Higgins' Ferry Road. The Newberry Academy was built by voluntary subscriptions and went into operation in 1806. Rev. John Foster and Rev. Charles Strong were amongst the earliest teachers. Chancellor Job Johnstone, F. B. Higgins, John Belton O'Neall and Drayton Nance here received their Academical education. It is elsewhere stated in these Annals that a lottery was authorized to be held for the benefit of the Academy, at two different times. All escheated property was vested in the Trustees.

This Academy was incorporated in 1834, having for Trustees Frederick Nance, John Belton O'Neall, Job Johnstone, Y. J. Harrington, James Fernandes, Thos. Pratt, W. Wilson, Burr Johnstone and F. B. Higgins.

Mr. Silas Johnstone is our authority for stating that the first Academy building stood opposite to where W. T. Tarrant's residence now stands. It was a large two-story wooden house. The first floor was devoted to school purposes; the upper one was used by the Masons as a Masonic Hall. The first floor, according to the same authority, was also sometimes used as a Thespian Hall. The great religious revival of 1830 disorganized the society and caused its discontinuance; many of the Thespians becoming converted and joining the Church. Soon after this revival, and as one of the fruits of it, the Baptist Church was organized and the house of worship built.

The teachers succeeding Foster and Strong were Mr. Mc-Guinnis, Rev. James W. Alexander, then Mr. Corbin. Col. Simeon Fair was a pupil of Mr. Alexander's. Gen. Young Fair, once Minister to Berlin, was also a pupil at this Academy. In 1827 Mr. Parker taught here awhile; then followed Samuel Pressley, assisted by Solomon Pope, John Pressley and Jefferson Fair. In 1828 James Divver was Master. Henry Summer, afterwards a lawyer at Newberry, also taught here.

As pupils at various times at this Academy were Silas Johnstone, Dr. W. F. Pratt, Robert Pratt, Simeon Pratt, Robert and Andrew Jackson Maxwell, John and Henry Fernandes, George Alexander and C. D. Pope, James Henderson, Reuben and John Lyles, J. and W. Caldwell, Robert and David Holman.

In 1834 the Male Academy was transferred to a building on the lot where now stands the Jail, and here Silas L. Heller taught during that year. George Parker succeeded him; and also Dr. D. Dobson.

After the transference of the Male Academy in 1834, another building was erected at Halcyon Grove, which was used as a Female School until 1839. The first teacher was Miss Boyd, sister to D. B. Boyd, President of the old Bank of

Newberry. She was assisted by Mrs. Saxon as a music teacher. The Female Academy in 1839 was moved to a house on Dr. Thompson's place on Pratt Street, and the building at Halcyon Grove was reconverted to the purposes of a Male School under the charge of Rev. Wiley, an Episcopal minister. Mr. Leonard Williams succeeded him, assisted by James M. Baxter. They were followed by James M. Crosson, Principal, and Major George James, Assistant. Then followed Joseph S. Reid; then Wm. Hood, who was the last of the dominies in this venerable institution. It seems to me that W. J. Duffie and Thomas Duckett also taught here, but I am not sure.

I fear that there are several inaccuracies in this sketch, but I have not the data at hand to enable me to do better.

Amongst the many pupils of this School, besides those already named, I may be permitted to mention W. F. Nance, D. C. Suber (Little X) and Henry Suber, John C. McLemore, James D. Nance, W. D. Rutherford, R. C. Maffett, James Stewart and J. A. Rutherford, who have passed to the silent land. And there are many, many others gone.

After the removal of Newberry College to Walhalla in 1868 Capt. A. P. Pifer taught a successful male school in the Baptist Church annex until July, 1869. He was followed by Rev. J. B. Hillhouse for one year at his residence, the place now owned by John C. Wilson.

In 1870 a lot on the corner of Harrington and Crenshaw streets was bought and a new Male Academy building was erected, and here the exercises of the school were begun in January, 1871, with James C. Hardin as teacher, with about one hundred pupils. The names of his successors that I now recall were Wm. M. Brooks, R. H. Clarkson, James P. Kinard, John P. Glasgow and Miss Willie Cozby. And that was the last of the separate existence of the Newberry Male Academy, as it ceased to live upon the establishment of the Graded Schools, and the house and lot were sold.

A brick building, long used as a Female Academy, near the Methodist Church, was built some years before the war, and some able teachers wielded the ferule within its walls, among whom may be mentioned Rev. Wm. Berly, Wm. Hood, Mrs. Susan Anderson, Capt. A. P. Pifer and Miss Octavia Garlington, who were the last.

PROSPERITY HIGH SCHOOL.

In the spring of 1879, the citizens of Prosperity, realizing the importance of education, became concerned in the establishing of an institution in their midst that should yield to them and their children the benefits that always flow from the cultivation of the mind. Accordingly, at a meeting held some time in the month of May, attended by a large number of representative citizens, it was agreed to establish a school to be known as the Prosperity High School. Looking to this end an Association was formed, a charter was obtained, and the books for the subscribing of stock were opened. Maj. P. E. Wise was President of the Association. In a very short time about one hundred shares of ten dollars each were taken, nearly every citizen taking one share or more. The money thus raised was to be used for erecting and equipping a suitable building. It was decided to entrust the management of the school to a board of trustees, consisting of five members of the association. In 1880 the number was increased to nine. Rev. J. C. Boyd, Rev. J. Hawkins, D. D., Maj. G. G. DeWalt, Capt. Henry S. Boozer and B. L. Dominick were the first trustees.

The board, after making a careful survey of all that was to be considered in connection with the opening of the school, decided to begin the regular work of teaching in September following. C. W. Welch, a graduate of Newberry College, class of '79, was elected Principal and Mrs. Jane A. Long, who had been teaching in Prosperity a number of years, was chosen assistant. Until the new building was ready, the exercises of the school were held in a very old, uncomfortable house near the old Prosperity Associate Reformed Presbyterian Church. In this house, during several previous years, J. B. Lathan, a graduate of Erskine College, had taught quite successfully.

At the same time that the association elected a board of trustees, it appointed a building committee. This committee purchased a lot conveniently located, and during the course of the following spring and summer a large, substantial two-room frame building was erected and supplied with modern desks at a total cost of about $1,000.

During the time that the new building was being talked about, planned and erected, many disappointments and heartaches were experienced by those who loved the school for the good it was to do. And when, in the fall of 1880, this new building was occupied for the first time, all felt that a long stride forward had been made toward the goal of their hopes. The town was united in the endeavor to make the school a blessing as well as a pride. About this time there were many whiskey saloons in the town and the friends of the High School realized that, to have a successful school, the saloons must be closed up. Accordingly a vote was taken to decide the matter. All the better class of citizens rallied around the cause of decency and intellectual freedom, and under the battle cry, "Prohibition and the High School," won a decided victory. So marked was the improvement in all respects that Prosperity became a new town, and before the close of its second year the Prosperity High School had enrolled one hundred and thirty-five pupils, about twenty-five of whom were non-residents.

This institution has not been free of troubles, but the great principle for which it has so constantly stood has always been the rallying point of its friends; and to-day, 1892, it gives promise of a long lease of fresh life and renewed vigor.

Scores of young men and women have been prepared for college or the active duties of life during the thirteen years of its existence. It has truly been a blessing to many. In the country districts around the town, other schools of the same character have been organized, and the time is fast coming when the lower part of Newberry County will be one of the leading communities of the country for all that makes for the betterment of mankind. For much of this, the Prosperity High School may truthfully, yet modestly, claim the honor. The work has always been so thoroughly done that graduates of this institution could easily enter the Sophomore class of the best Southern colleges.

As a matter of interest, a list of the principals of the school is subjoined: C. W. Welch, September, 1879, to June, 1881; D. C. Lake, 1881–82; J. S. Perrin, 1882–83; J. C. Cork, 1883–84; J. A. Huffard, 1884–85; A. S. Scheetz, 1885–87; A. J. Bowers, 1887–88; J. E. Brown, 1888–89; *F. E. Dreher, 1889; †J. T. Moore, 1890; E. O. Counts, 1891–92.

---

*Resigned in the winter of 1889, and E. O. Counts elected to fill the unexpired term—the latter declining re-election in 1890.

†Resigned soon on account of ill health, and E. O. Counts was elected.

Mt. Tabor High School.

This school is situated on the Columbia, Newberry and Laurens Railroad, one mile from Little Mountain and one mile from Slighs. The present commodious school building was erected in 1884. There was at that time a school house about a half mile from the present building. This school had been in operation for about eight years prior to the organization of the Mt. Tabor High School, and had been taught by Geo. M. Wilson, P. H. E. Derrick, and others. W. K. Sligh was teaching near Mt. Tabor at the time the new building was erected, and when it was completed he moved into it. The new building had become a necessity, as at that time there were more than one hundred children in attendance upon the school. There are three rooms to the building, and the school is taught by two or three teachers as the attendance may demand. The following have been the principals of the school since its organization: W. K. Sligh, E. O. Counts, E. S. Dreher, Eugene Smith, W. A. Counts—the lattter of whom is now the successful principal of the school. This school has been a great boon to this community, and in addition has prepared many boys and girls for college. The name is taken from the Lutheran Church of the same name, which is located at the same place. The average yearly attendance exceeds one hundred children. It is governed by a Board of Trustees who are elected by the patrons. The public funds are supplemented by tuition charges, and the school is run nine months in the year. Would that we had a school like this in every community in the county.

—

Bethel Academy, Pomaria.

The situation and surroundings of this Academy, near Pomaria, are quite romantic. It is within a half mile of the town, just in the borders of a beautiful grove and near a spring of clear, cool water, which gushes out from among the rocks at the foot of a hill.

Few academies or high schools in the county can make a better showing than this. The citizens of the neighborhood soon after the war, seeing and feeling the great importance of education, united with the Masonic order, the Grange and the Knights of Jericho, and built a school-house sixty by twenty-six feet, with a second or upper story, the latter for the use of the orders mentioned. The lower story was the school room and had blackboards surrounding the entire inside of the building. The several School Commissioners, in their rounds looking after the interests of the schools, have pronounced this house superior to any in the country parts of the County.

According to the best recollection of the writer, the schools at Bethel have been taught in the order named by the following experienced and educated teachers: Miss E. A. Souter, Lexington; Capt. John F. Banks, Newberry; Prof. D. Benjamin Busby, now of Edgefield; J. M. Alewine, lately deceased, Texas; J. B. O'Neall Holloway, now of Orangeburg; Mrs. S. M. B. Wright, deceased; Miss Mattie Steck, now Mrs. Jaynes, of Walhalla; Miss Hennie Boozer, now the wife of Dr. W. D. Senn, of Newberry County; Rev. W. K. Sligh, now Professor in Newberry College; Miss Alma Kibler, now Mrs. R. F. Bryant, of Orangeburg; Prof. Burr H. Johnstone, now teaching at Allendale; W. B. Boinest, of Pomaria; Miss Lula Teague, now of Johnston; Miss Ella Belle Shirey, now one of the leading teachers of Mount Amoena Female Seminary, Mt. Pleasant, N. C.

The following graduates from Newberry College may be mentioned as having been prepared here to enter that institution: L. E. Busby, '75, minister, Leesville; J. B. O'Neall Holloway, '75, farmer, Orangeburg County; J. B. Boinest, '77, since deceased; J. Eusebius Berly, '79, minister, deceased; John F. Hobbs, '79, Australia; C. W. Welch, '79, professor Clemson College; W. W. Berly, '82, farmer, Pomaria; E. O. Counts,' 83, Principal Prosperity High School; Sidney T. Riser, '84, minister, died at Staunton, Va.; Henry P. Counts, '85, minister, Haralson, Ga.; E. O. Hentz, '85, physician, Walton; Monroe J. Epting, '86, minister, St. Luke's.

The following named, prepared at this institution, are now (1892) in the Sophomore class of Newberry College: Richard H. Hipp, Henry C. Holloway, Robert H. Welch.

It is due to Prof. D. B. Busby to say that he taught this school several years, and that he prepared for college all the graduates mentioned to 1886, including also some who were not graduates of Newberry: W. C. Dreher, once Professor in

Roanoke College, and recently engaged in literary work in New York; Paul D. Hyler, who went to Wofford, afterwards studied law and died soon after entering upon the practice of his profession; L. B. Folk, who entered the Junior class in South Carolina College, but left college, read medicine and is now a practicing physician in Columbia. To Prof. Busby is due also the credit for the greater part of the school work done here, and I feel sure that a grateful people will remember him always kindly for the part he took in moulding the minds of their children, not only through the books used and taught, but also for his influence in helping them to a high plane of character and sense of honor.

—

PAGESVILLE ACADEMY.

This institution, which did such good work for awhile and gave promise of many years of usefulness, was established in the year 1848. It was situated on the line now traversed by the Laurens Railroad, about a mile from Gary's Lane and within a quarter of a mile from the present residence of Capt. Thompson Conner, in a lovely grove of oaks to the right or north of the railroad and the public road. The Academy owned one hundred acres of land, held in the name of seven trustees, viz: Dr. John K. Gary, Hilliary Gary, Dr. Rush Gary, J. J. Reeder, J. K. Schumpert, Col. Geo. S. Cannon and a Mr. Davis. On the grounds were one four-room cottage for professors, and also necessary outbuildings for other purposes. The Academy building was about seventy-five by fifty feet, and was divided into two apartments, one for large boys and one for girls and young ladies.

The following eminent educators were successively masters of the Academy; Professor S. E. Graydon; A. H. Little, graduate of the Citadel and gallant member of the Palmetto Regiment during the War with Mexico; Jas. Watson; W. D. Reeder; Dr. Memory Bonner, now of Gaffney City; Robert Pasley and Zachariah C. Wright.

The war closed this school and its labors were never resumed thereafter.

This was a High School, and prepared many well-known citizens of Newberry for entrance into the South Carolina College. Among these may be mentioned Col. R. C. Watts; Maj.

W. T. Gary; Capt. J. W. Gary; Dr. William Williams; O. L. Schumpert, Esq., Solicitor of Seventh Circuit (1892); Dr. John I. Schumpert, of Louisiana, and Dr. Spencer G. Welch.

THE RUTHERFORD SCHOOL.

The people of the Enoree section of Newberry County, realizing the necessity of having better schools, procured the signatures of a majority of the freeholders of the community to a petition asking the Legislature of South Carolina to set off a certain portion of Newberry County into a special school district, to be known as the Rutherford School District. The petition was granted, and on December 22nd, 1888, Rutherford School District was formed. The qualified voters have the power to vote a 3-mill supplemental tax for educational purposes. The following gentlemen were, by Act of the Legislature, made trustees of the school: Joseph L. Keitt, Thomas W. Keitt, Thomas W. Hutchinson, John A. Cromer and F. W. Higgins. Mr. Higgins has since resigned, and J. Owens Turnipseed was elected in his place. The trustees and patrons working together have built a school house costing $400, and have acquired title to two acres of land; thus securing a permanent location and a good building for school purposes. This school was first taught by Thos. W. Keitt and Miss Ellen Suber. Mr. Keitt resigned in 1892, having been elected to the office of School Commissioner for Newberry County, and he was succeeded by J. O. Turnipseed, who is also assisted by Miss Ellen Suber. The school has been quite successful.

About the same time that the Rutherford School District was organized, another district, known as the Broad River District, was also organized, mainly through the efforts of Col. D. A. Dickert. It is also supported by taxation. The common school system of the State is good enough as far as it goes, but in order to realize the full benefit from this fund it is necessary to supplement it by local taxation, or tuition charges.

We have here two cases of additional taxation and one of tuition charges, and in all three the schools are prospering.

The great need of this country is more and better schools of a high order in our rural districts within the reach of all children of school age.

NEWBERRY GRADED SCHOOLS.

Graded schools for both white and colored have been established in the town of Newberry, after a full discussion of the system by the press and the people, and they have proven to be a great and decided success.

The schools are supported by taxation and tuition is free to all children within the corporate limits of the town. There are seven trustees, J. F. J. Caldwell, Geo. B. Cromer, W. H. Wallace, J. K. P. Goggans, J. S. Cozby, Geo. S. Mower and N. B. Mazyck, who are life members, and four trustees who are to be elected annually by the people. L. M. Speers, W. E. Pelham, Alan Johnstone and J. K. Gilder were elected in 1890, and re-elected in 1891 and 1892. The first superintendent was J. Fleming Brown. He was succeeded in September, 1891, by Frank Evans, who is now superintendent for his second year.

The Graded School building is a large three-story structure, and was completed in 1891 at a cost of $16,500, which included furniture and the heating arrangement. The first session of the white school was held in 1890 in the old Female Academy and the Thompson house on Pratt street.

THE LITERATURE.

The literature of Newberry has not been mentioned heretofore, except incidentally, but I think it deserves a page or two of its own.

Besides the Annals of Newberry, Judge O'Neall wrote and published the "Bench and Bar of South Carolina," which is a valuable work of its kind. He also wrote and published in a Southern Magazine some interesting and valuable contributions to Revolutionary History. H. H. Caldwell published two small volumes of poems during his too short life, which gave promise, especially his last work, of ability to do much better work in the future. J. F. J. Caldwell's History of McGowan's Brigade, to which reference has already been made, is a valuable contribution to the history of the war, the merits of which will be recognized some day. Two volumes of poems have been published by the author of these Annals, and he also aided largely in the preparation of Stephens' School History of the United States, which has been adopted as a text-book for schools in some of the States. Mrs. L. M. Sale published a novel, "The Saddest of All is Loving," which I have read and found fully equal to many others of greater reputation. Paul Johnstone's work on the Electoral question showed much ability, and had great influence at the time it was written and published. Silas Johnstone has prepared and published a valuable Equity Digest, if it be proper to include a work of that character under the head of Literature. He has also written many humorous sketches for Porter's *Spirit of the Times*, some of which were published in book form together with stories by other and different writers. My old friend, Dr. O. B. Mayer, with others, has been mentioned in another place. But, so far as I know, Newberry has produced only one man who has made literature a profession, and he is J. Wood Davidson. And he left the County so long ago that he is scarcely known by any man living in it. His book, "The Writers of the South," is a good review of the labors of those who had worked in the literary field of the South at the time it was written and published. His "Poetry of the Future" shows deep study and thought, and to the student of the subject on which it treats, I doubt not, it affords many valuable hints. Mr. Davidson himself, if not a poet, is a good writer of verse. And so is Mrs. Mary A. Evans, though she has never written a book.

John B. Carwile has recently published a very delightful book, "Reminiscences of Newberry," which ought to be in the library of every citizen of the County. The style is admirable, and some of the incidents related are very touching.

John C. McLemore, who was once connected with the Press of Newberry, as associate editor of the *Conservatist*, deserves more than the mere mention of his name. He was a young lawyer of great promise; a graceful and forcible writer; a brave and gallant soldier; and a poet, who might have become eminent in the field of letters. I have heard it said that his verses in W. Gilmore Simms' "War Poetry of the South," published soon after the war, were the best in the book.

One writer who lived for some years at Newberry, though not a native of the town nor of the county, is fully as worthy of notice as an author, a lover of literature and of letters, as any I have mentioned. She has written and published three

books, not large, not great books, of the fame of which the
world is full, but good books. The first, published in 1875,
by J. B. Lippincott & Co., was a little story book for children, called "The Golden Fence." The next "A Sequence of
Songs," was published by W. J. Duffie in 1882. The third,
"A Hero's Last Days," was also published by Mr. Duffie, in
1883. Besides these, this same author has written "Echoes of
Holy Week." "Songs of a New Age," and others, which I
have never seen. These books were all published anonymously,
and it may be that I ought not to mention the name of the
author here. But I feel sure that it will do no harm to make
her name known. Her work is good, and of a quality, in style
and sentiment, of which she need not be ashamed. The author
of the books mentioned is Miss Mary Fowles. I give here a
poem from "A Sequence of Songs":

DEAD CAROLINA.

Methought, erewhile, I saw a funeral pyre,
Like that sad mount that Tyrian Dido reared;
And on the pile were laid full many forms
Of those I knew, all pale and cold in death.
As, in the Niobean group, there showed
One female figure towering o'er the rest,
But with a beauty e'en more terrible
In the awful dignity of death;—
For,—ere by death from worse than death relieved,—
Like Niobe, she saw her children die,
One, then another, till her own turn came.
Yet some were left to mourn, and these stood round
Weeping. And you might see the smoking piles—
Their sacrifices offered at her tomb—
And you might know them by their stricken mien
Among the pitying or the jeering crowd.
And hereupon, methought I saw a maid
With calm and even tread approach the pyre
And lay a wreath upon it. Then I asked,
Who is this maiden with the face unmoved
By the conflicting passions of the crowd?
And one replied: The Muse of History
Bringing her solemn tribute to the dead.
But ah, thought I, no tribute ever can
Wake her to life again. And then I heard
The mournful moving music of the dirge:

Thou liest low to rise no more,
All covered with thy children's gore,
          Carolina !
Thy foes around thee mocking stand,
Thou liest still, nor movest thy hand,
          Dead Carolina !
Thy very soul and life are fled,
No mourning bringeth back the dead,
          Carolina !
O Carolina of the Past !

For thee no resurrection blast
Shall sound.   This sleep shall be thy last,
            Dead Carolina !
And here the children of the dead advanced
And, with a voice all choked with sobs and groans,
Said: Vale, vale, in eternum vale !
Then next methought the hills, dales, woods and streams,
And all the land that once had owned her sway,
But ne'er should own it more, gave back the voice
Of Vale, vale, in eternum vale !
And then the people out of every nation
Who stood around, some mocking and some mourning,
Cried: Vale, vale, in eternum vale !

—

THE NEWSPAPERS.

I may say that the newspapers of the County have always been equal in merit and ability to any published in any County in the State. I give a list of them with names of editors and publishers, prepared by Mr. R. H. Greneker, Sr., who, himself, has labored for many years in that field and is a graceful and pleasant writer:

Newberry was without the light of the Press until 1849, when Mr. James H. Giles began the publication of the Newberry *Sentinel*, with Gen. A. C. Garlington as associate editor during the last two years that he published the paper. It was afterwards sold to James M. Crosson and Thomas P. Slider, who disposed of it to Jos. S. Reid, then publishing the *Weekly Newberrian*, which was started in 1852. Mr. Reid carried out the contracts of the *Sentinel* and discontinued it in 1853. He then changed the *Newberrian* to the *Mirror*. In 1854 the *Mirror* was made a tri-weekly, and a year afterwards Gen. A. C. Garlington was associate editor. In 1856 the *Mirror* was sold to Capt. Wm. F. Nance and John C. McLemore, and the name of the paper changed to *The Conservatist*. This paper passed into the possession of Col. James D. Nance and Silas Johnstone, Esq. Soon after the beginning of the war Col. Nance volunteered and went with the army to Virginia, the paper was discontinued and its publication never resumed, Col. Nance having been killed during the war.

In the year 1855 Thos. P. Slider illuminated the land with the rays of the *Rising Sun*, and later associated Thos. F. Greneker with him in the business. Mr. Slider afterwards sold his interest to R. H. Greneker, who continued it in a diminished size until the close of the war, when it was pub-

lished for a short while as a tri-weekly under the name of the
Newberry *Herald.* The tri-weekly was discontinued and the
paper published for a long time by Messrs. T. F. and R. H.
Greneker. In 1873 the junior partner withdrew from the paper
and Thos. F. Greneker, the Nestor of the Newberry Press,
continued its publication until failing health caused his retirement in 1885. During his sole ownership of the paper, he
had associated with him at different times, Ira B. Jones,
W. H. Wallace, the present editor of the *Observer,* G. B. Cromer,
G. G. Sale and Elbert H. Aull. Mr. Wallace served on the
paper for a considerable length of time.

On the 14th of February, 1873, Thos. P. Slider began the
publication of the *Progressive Age,* a paper devoted principally
to the development of the County. It was soon afterwards
purchased by R. H. Greneker, and changing the character
somewhat, the paper was devoted to ethics in journalism. He
cut short its bright career a few years later, not wishing the
appearance of opposition to his brother, Thos. F. Greneker, of
the *Herald.*

On the 4th of January, 1878, the bonnie Newberry *News,*
by R. H. Greneker, Jr., and Wm. P. Houseal, with John A.
Chapman as editor, made its appearance. Mr. Chapman was
editor for one year only. This paper had a bright staff some
time later in Milledge L. Bonham and Lewis W. Simkins, to
whom the paper was leased, and at intervals later was edited
by G. G. Sale and E. H. Aull. Prior to these later changes
Mr. Houseal withdrew from the paper, and R. H. Greneker,
Jr., was then sole editor (except when Messrs. Sale and Aull
were on the staff) and proprietor until August, 1884, when on
the death of Thomas Edward Greneker, a young man of great
promise, of the *Herald,* the *News* and the *Herald* were
united under the name of the *Herald and News.* The paper
passed into the hands of A. C. Jones in 1885. It was edited
first by G. G. Sale, then by E. H. Aull, and finally by Mr.
Jones himself, who disposed of it in March, 1887, to E. H.
Aull and Wm. P. Houseal.

On the 21st of April, 1881, Wm. P. Houseal began the publication of the *Lutheran Visitor* at Newberry. This paper was
established in 1868 in the interest of the General Synod of
the Lutheran Church in the South. It has been published at

Charleston, Salisbury, N. C., Columbia, and a year prior to its removal to Newberry, at Prosperity. Various eminent Lutheran divines have edited the paper. Rev. J. Hawkins, D. D., the present editor, was appointed in 1878, and he has been assisted since its removal to Newberry by Revs. F. W. E. Peschau, D. D., A. B. McMackin, A. G. Voigt and W. C. Schaeffer. The paper is now controlled by a chartered company, and since 1887 has been published by Aull & Houseal.

January 11th, 1883, the Newberry *Observer*, under the firm name of Wallace, Houseal & Kinard, made its appearance. After awhile Wm. P. Houseal withdrew, and W. H. Wallace and Jas. H. M Kinard have since conducted its publication.

In the spring of 1885 E. H. Aull and M. S. Hallman ventured out in the *Reporter* at Prosperity; but in a short time Mr. Aull withdrew to take charge of the Newberry *Herald and News*. A joint stock company was afterwards formed and the name of the paper changed to the *Press and Reporter*, with F. V. Capers as editor.

Newberry County now has four good weekly papers. They are invaluable aids to a people's prosperity, and in order to be at their best they should be liberally sustained both by subscription and advertising patronage.

XII.

INDUSTRIAL, COMMERCIAL AND BENEVOLENT

THE FAIR GROUNDS AND THE NEWBEERY AGRICULTURAL SOCIETY.

From the year 1840 to the breaking out of the War of Secession, Newberry had her Fair Grounds about half a mile from the Court House in the southern part of the town. These grounds did not belong to the Agricultural Society, but to the Newberry Academy, and by permission of the trustees the meetings of the Society were held there. The Academy building was situated in a beautiful grove of oaks, which was euphoniously called Halcyon Grove. In this then lovely place the annual meetings of the Society were held for many years.

The first officers of the Society were John Belton O'Neall, President; Dr. Geo. W. Glenn, First Vice-President; Simeon Fair, Second Vice-President; Lambert J. Jones, Recording Secretary; Gen. H. H. Kinard, Treasurer. Afterwards Silas Johnstone became Recording Secretary and W. B. D'Oyley, Treasurer.

The grounds extended south and east from where the bridge now is over the railroad cut, far enough to include an area of several acres of land. Never having examined the plat, and not knowing the exact boundaries I cannot give them. The 'grove was a very inviting and lovely spot, shaded by many large and spreading oaks, affording a cool and delightful shade in the hottest weather. A spring of cool, fresh, ever-flowing waters afforded an exhaustless supply. Here every year about the middle of July, the members of the Society, and many who were not members, met together bringing in their domestic animals of all kinds; fine horses, mules, jacks, hogs, chickens of various fancy breeds, turkeys, pigeons, bantams, etc. Specimens of sorghum, wines, oats, wheat, and all the various products of the agriculture of Newberry and the adjoining districts were on exhibition. Among the many exhibitors were S. P. Kinard, who had enormous squashes, and T. F. Greneker, who had mammoth tomatoes. Farm products were exhibited by Henry Burton, Wash Floyd, Col. J. Duckett,

George H. Chapman, A. K. Tribble, Dennis Lark, Pompey Floyd, Maj. P. Hair, Col. John Hair, Maj. John P. Kinard, Gen. H. H. Kinard, Col. Glenn, Dr. Glenn, Daniel Goggans, Matthias Barre, Wesley Folk, H. H. Folk, Frank Moon, John M. Floyd, J. S. Birge, Dr. McKellar, Ellison S. Keitt, Chancellor Johnstone, Gen. Garlington, Gen. Williams, Joseph Caldwell, John A. Cannon, Wm. Ray, Dr. Rutherford, Thomas Henderson, Col. B. Maybin, Jesse Maybin, J. C. Hope, Dr. J. K. Gary, Philip Sligh, Col. B. F. Griffin, R. C. Chapman, Isaac Herbert, Thos. V. Wicker, Dr. Bobo, W. B. D'Oyley, P. W. Chick, R. S. Chick, Jas. Fair, J. J. Kibler, Wm. Boozer, Gen. C. B. Griffin, Gen. James Rogers, W. W. Renwick, J. S. Renwick, Maj. John Sims, Col. G. S. Cannon, Rush Gary, Dr. T. W. Thompson, Dr. R. P. Clark, Col. W. S. Lyles, James Gauntt, J. Adam Eichelberger, B. F. Paysinger, D. L. Wicker, R. S. Phinney, Rev. J. J. Brantley, J. R. Leavell, J. E. Guy, Dr. Herndon, Dr. W. H. Harrington, W. R. Hentz, Bela Mangum, Capt. James Maffett, Wm. Philson, John T. Peterson, Col. W. S. Dogan, Col. J. M. Maffett, Matthew Hall, J. Wistar Simpson, John Hopkins Williams, and many others whose names I cannot call to mind.

The ladies also had many articles of domestic manufacture on exhibition such as blankets, quilts, netting, knitting, crochet work, paintings, preserves, pickles, butter, etc. Among the lady exhibitors were Miss McCoy, Mrs. John Kinard, Mrs. Gen. Kinard, Mrs. Pope, Mrs. Wm. Satterwhite, Mrs. John Coate, Mrs. Robert Stewart, Miss Sallie Barre, Mrs. Col. Fair, Mrs. John Elmore, Mrs. Walter Ruff, Mrs. Dr. E. M. Bobo, Mrs. Lucinda Brown, Mrs. T. W. Holloway, Mrs. Charlotte Gordon, Miss Dallas Boyd, Mrs. C. McLemore, Mrs. E. A. Hall, Misses Counts, Mrs. W. S. Sharpe, Mrs. Wm. Riser, Mrs. F. B. Higgins, Mrs. D. B. Pratt, Mrs. Thomas Pope, Mrs. Lucy Shelton, and others.

There were also exhibited every year some agricultural implements and farmers' tools: Plows, harrows, grain cradles, etc. Reaping machines and mowers were not known here at that time. Jesse Senn always had on hand a grain cradle, and also Samuel Chapman. J. K. Schumpert had beautifully made fly brushes and fans; C. M. Harris chairs, and Wearn & Kingsmore photographs.

At one of the meetings, July, 1857, a short letter was read from Col. J. F Marshall, stating the quantity of wheat raised by himself on two acres of land in the year 1857—signed by Thomas Robinson and J. B. Wilson—37¼ bushels on one acre and 36½ on the other.

After the reading of the reports of the various committees, and the annual speech by the orator chosen for the occasion, came the dinner, a very sumptuous and cheerful repast.

At these meetings might be seen for many years in succession the Founder and President of the Society, John Belton O'Neall; the earnest and honest Drayton Nance; the talented and versatile A. G. Summer; Dr. McKellar; the deep-thoughted Chancellor Johnstone; the practical Robert Stewart, and such men as Dr. Peter Moon, Dr. G. Douglass, John D. Williams, Robert Moorman; Wm. Summer, the horticulturist; George Brown, John R. Spearman, Thomas W. Holloway, and Paul Johnstone, the gentle and the good, whom to know was to love. These were all earnest workers and stood pre-eminent in the cause.

In 1856 the President came to the determination to resign, but so great was the feeling in opposition to his resignation that he was not permitted to do so. The following, signed by many citizens, was sent to him: "To Hon. John Belton O'Neall, President N. A. S.: Dear Sir—With deep regret we have learned your intention of resigning the Presidency of the Society. In all the fulness of our hearts we would most respectfully entreat you not to do so. Respectfully, W. E. Hardy, and others, 17th July, 1856." He then determined to remain President to the end, and so it came about that he was the first and the last President the Society ever had.

The last meeting of the Society was held on the 21st and 22nd of July, 1859. There was a great falling off in attendance and in the number of articles on exhibition; but the display in the Ladies' Department was more than usually fine. On this occasion Col. James N. Lipscomb delivered the anniversary address—a good, practical, farmer-like speech, which was well received. The President manifested considerable anxiety as to the future condition and welfare of the Society. As it turned out, this was the last meeting of the Society. J. N. Lipscomb was the last orator, Silas Johnstone the last

Recording Secretary and W. B. D'Oyley the last Treasurer.

April 18th, 1860, a meeting was held in the Court House, Dr. G. W. Glenn, President; James D. Nance, Secretary. At this meeting measures were adopted to raise subscriptions to purchase a Fair Ground and erect all necessary buildings thereon. J. D. Nance and two others were appointed a committee to select a suitable lot and report. At a meeting held May 16th, 1860, the committee reported that a suitable place had been found about three-fourths of a mile from the Court House, on the Higgins' Ferry Road, on land belonging to Judge O'Neall. They also reported that the owner would sell as many acres as were needed at $100 per acre, and that he would subscribe $100. The committee stated that this was the most liberal offer they had received, and recommended the purchase of eight acres. The report was adopted and $1,300 were subscribed. A new committee was then appointed to buy the lands for the Fair Grounds; to solicit subscriptions and to report on the first Monday in June, 1860. That committee was Washington Floyd, Robert Spearman and J. D. Nance, and twenty-one others from various parts of the District. That committee never reported. The old Agricultural Society, after twenty years of a useful career, closed its existence in the midst of wild and intense political excitement and dreadful anticipation of war.

In the year 1878, the Newberry Agricultural and Mechanical Association was organized as a joint stock company. The officers were elected on August 19th, 1878, as follows: President, John C. Wilson; 1st Vice-President, Thos. W. Holloway; 2nd Vice-President, John McCarley; 3d Vice-President, John R. Spearman, Sr.; 4th Vice-President, W. D. Hardy; Secretary and Treasurer, Geo. S. Mower; Executive Committee, A. J. Kilgore, Alan Johnstone, J. A. Sligh, S. A. Hunter, M. Werts.

The first fair of this new Association was held on November 20th and 21st, 1878, in the buildings and grounds at the corner of Pratt and McKibben Streets. It was a success. The second fair was a greater success. It was held in October, 1879, at the grounds on the eastern end of Pratt Street, which the Association in that year had purchased and fitted up with all necessary buildings. There were nearly one thousand entries at this fair, about one hundred more than the first fair, and six hundred dollars in premiums were awarded.

Good fairs were held each year until October, 1885, which was the last one. It was found that the investment did not pay the investors for the trouble and expense involved and the property was sold, and now there is no Agricultural Fair nor Society in the County. The Farmers' Alliance being composed of farmers, one might suppose it to be somewhat similar in character and purpose to Agricultural Societies, but they appear to be very different. The one is to encourage the production of the best crops and stock; the other is a combination of farmers to protect themselves against others in their warfare in the world.

But I am glad to know that the old fashioned Fairs and Societies still survive, though Newberry has none. The State Agricultural Fair, held annually in Columbia, has for many years been a flourishing institution, and the exhibits every year are very creditable to the State and its advance in agriculture and the various domestic arts. Mr. Thomas W. Holloway, its very efficient Secretary and Treasurer, has held that position for about fifteen years, and it is exceedingly doubtful whether any one in the State could better fill the place. He is a native of Newberry, and it is very pleasant to the historian of the county to be able to speak well of those who have gone from amongst us and have made their homes elsewhere, although in Mr. Holloway's case he still retains his residence at Pomaria in this county.

—

The Banks.

Previous to the year 1853 there were no banking facilities in Newberry. In that year the Bank of Newberry was organized, the capital stock being $300,000, which was increased in (probably) 1856 to $400,000. B. D. Boyd, who is now living at an advanced age in San Fernando, California, was its first and only president. Thomas W. Holloway, of Pomaria, S. C., was its first cashier, and was succeeded in 1856 by Robert L. McCaughrin, of Newberry, who was at the time of his election just twenty-one years of age. Mr. McCaughrin resigned in 1860 and was succeeded by W. H. C. Dudley, who came from Americus, Ga., and when the recent war had about brought the business of the bank to a close he returned to that place, and is still residing there.

The Bank of Newberry did a successful and profitable business until the recent war, by the disastrous termination of which it, in common with all other banks in the State, lost the greater part of its property. It finally paid all its debts and returned to the stockholders about fifteen per cent. ($60,000) of their original stock.

The National Bank of Newberry was organized May 6th, 1871, with the following Board of Directors: R. L. McCaughrin, Jno. B. Carwile, G. T. Scott, Jno. T. Peterson, Robert Moorman, J. N. Martin, W. H. Webb, J. B. Palmer, Y. J. Pope. The officers elected were: R. L. McCaughrin, President; Jno. B, Carwile, Cashier, and T. S. Duncan, Assistant Cashier. Mr. Carwile resigned the office of Cashier in 1884 on account of failing health; T. S. Duncan was elected in his place, and T. J. McCrary succeeded Mr. Duncan as Assistant Cashier. Mr. McCaughrin has been annually re-elected President of the Board. In 1892 Mr. McCrary resigned as Assistant Cashier and was succeeded by J. W. M. Simmons. The present officers are: R. L. McCaughrin, President; T. S. Duncan, Cashier; J. W. M. Simmons, Assistant Cashier; John S. Carwile, Book-keeper; Richard H. Wearn, Collector.

The original capital stock was $100,000, which was, in 1872, increased to $150,000. The charter of the bank having expired, it was renewed May 6th. 1891, and the bank re-organized with the following Board of Directors: R. L. McCaughrin, Jno. B. Carwile, J. N. Martin, J. O. Peoples, J. F. J. Caldwell, R. H. Wright, James McIntosh, M. A. Renwick, R. C. Carlisle. The three first named were members of the board when the bank was first organized in 1871 and have served continuously since.

The condition of the bank on the first day of January, 1892, was as follows: Capital Stock, $150,000; Surplus Fund, $150,000; Undivided Profits, $8,715.47. The bank has paid for the twenty years of its existence an average dividend of nine and one-half per cent. per annum to its shareholders.

The Newberry Savings Bank was organized on the 2nd day of April, 1891, with the following Board of Directors: James

McIntosh, R. H. Wright, R. L. McCaughrin, J. N. Martin, John O. Peoples, R. C. Carlisle, M. A. Renwick, H. C. Robertson, deceased, and J. F. J. Caldwell; with James McIntosh, President, and R. H. Wright, Cashier.

The condition of the bank on the first day of January, 1893, was as follows: Capital Stock, $15,000; Surplus Fund, $2,000.

In the spring of 1888, feeling the need of some banking facilities in the town of Prosperity, J. M. Wheeler, H. C. Moseley and W. A. Moseley, who were conducting a mercantile business, and George D. Brown, of Brown & Moseley, lumber dealers, went to work and organized a private bank under the firm name of Wheeler & Moseley, Bankers. The management of the bank has been in charge of Mr. H. C. Moseley, with Mr. Joseph H. Hunter as cashier and book keeper. The bank is still in operation and has done a successful business. Both the deposit account and the loan and discount business have been as good as the projectors could have expected or even desired, and the enterprise has been a great convenience to the people of Prosperity and the adjacent country, for it has helped greatly in the matter of handling the cotton brought to the town, and in this way made Prosperity a much better cotton market than it otherwise could have been. During the season just closed they managed to handle and pay for about ten thousand bales of cotton. The bank has back of it the firms of Moseley Bros. and Brown & Moseley and J. M. Wheeler, who represent a capital of more than $100,000. It is hoped that this private bank will lead to the organization of a bank on a larger scale, as it no doubt will in the near future.

—

The Newberry Cotton Mills.

The Newberry Cotton Mills was organized May 7th, 1883, with the following Board of Directors: J. N. Martin, R. H. Wright, James McIntosh, W. T. Tarrant, Wm. Langford, James A. Crotwell, George S. Mower, M. A. Renwick, D. H. Wheeler, R. L. McCaughrin, James H. McMullan. R. L. McCaughrin was elected President and Treasurer and Geo. S. Mower Secretary. The handsome and substantial buildings were erected by W. T. Davis & Co., contractors, under the supervision of C. W. Holbrook, the Superintendent of the Mill. The building was completed and the mill began work in January, 1885. Mr. Holbrook was for many years connected with cotton mills both in the United States and Mexico, and was a faithful and efficient officer. He continued in the office of Superintendent until within two years before his death (having resigned on account of sudden loss of health), which occurred on the 8th day of October, 1890. He was a native of New Hampshire.

The mill has at this time (1892) 330 looms, 11,000 spindles, consumes annually 5,500 bales of cotton, and employs 250 hands. It manufactures cloth only. The mill has now: Capital Stock (paid up), $250,000; Surplus Fund, $100,000. The present officers are: R. L. McCaughrin, President; Thos. J. McCrary, Treasurer and General Manager; George S. Mower, Secretary; J. Higgins, Superintendent. George A. Moody, of Massachusetts, succeeded Mr. Holbrook as Superintendent, and filled the position very acceptably for several years, but in the spring of 1892 he returned to his home at the North.

There has been no change in the Board of Directors since the organization of the mill. Robert D. Wright has been the efficient book-keeper of the mill since it has been running.

Mr. Henry C. Robertson came to Newberry from Charleston in 1887 and was Treasurer and General Manager of the Mill from that time until his death on September 9th, 1892. He was a most estimable gentleman, and made many friends during his residence in Newberry.

The houses for the operatives are situated on the western side of the mill, towards Scott's Creek. The operatives have the advantage of church and school, provided by the company.

THE OIL MILL.

The Newberry Cotton Seed Oil Mill and Fertilizer Company was organized on July 8th, 1890, and the following Directors were then elected: Thos. V. Wicker, Thos. M. Neel, O. B. Mayer, L. W. Floyd, G. W. Summer, G. F. Long, H. H. Folk, J. M. Johnstone, Geo. S. Mower. The Directors held a meeting a few days afterwards. J. M. Johnstone was elected President and L. W. Floyd the Secretary and Treasurer and

General Manager.   Work was at once commenced on the necessary buildings, which were located on Caldwell Street, at the junction of the Columbia and Greenville and the Columbia, Newberry and Laurens Railroads.   The mill began running the latter part of December, 1890.   There has been no change in the officers of the company since its organization.   It has a capital stock of $30,000.

SOCIETIES OF NEWBERRY—MISSIONARY, ETC.

The following historical sketch of the Newberry Woman's Missionary Society of the Methodist Episcopal Church South has been kindly given me by Mrs. J. W. Humbert, Corresponding Secretary:

Until within the last decade the missionary operations of the Methodist Episcopal Church South were, as Bishop Pierce stated, like a boat with oars on one side, and made but slow progress.   But since the organization of the Woman's Missionary Society the working power of the boat is complete, and much greater progress has been the result.   In May, 1878, a few "elect ladies" of the Southern Methodist Church assembled in First Church, Atlanta, Ga., to hear the action of the General Conference then in session relative to woman's missionary work in foreign mission fields.   The Woman's Missionary Society of the Methodist Episcopal Church South was organized at that meeting.

The South Carolina Conference met in Newberry December 11–17, 1878.   Bishop W. M. Wightman presided.   Monday afternoon, 16th December, 1878, Dr. A. W. Wilson, Missionary Secretary, now Bishop, addressed the ladies in the Methodist Church on the importance of this great missionary movement and urged them to form a Conference Missionary Society. The names of forty persons from ten charges in the Conference were secured, and the South Carolina Conference Woman's Missionary Society was organized.   The following officers were elected: President, Mrs. Wightman; Vice-Presidents, Mrs. Williams, Mrs. Martin, Mrs. Blake and Mrs. Breeden; Corresponding Secretary, Mrs. J. W. Humbert (daughter of Gen. H. H. Kinard of Newberry); Recording Secretary, Mrs. A. M. Chriezburg, formerly Miss Hattie Kilgore of Newberry; Treasurer, Mrs. F. J. Pelzer.   Thus Newberry furnished two officers and sixteen charter members of the Conference Society. These two officers have been identified with the work ever since—to the present time, 1892.

The Newberry Auxiliary Society was organized by the Rev. J. B. Campbell, March 4, 1879, with the following officers: President, Mrs. Y. J. Pope; Vice-Presidents, Mrs. T. F. Greneker and Mrs. S. F. Fant; Corresponding Secretary, Miss Mary Pope; Recording Secretary, Miss Nellie Chapman; Treasurer, Miss Addie Moorman. This Society has been in successful operation ever since. Mrs. E. S. Herbert was President for several years.

All the other Churches in Newberry have similar Societies, and all active in the prosecution of this great Christian work. And as the years pass on, more and more we can see that the clouds of darkness, ignorance and superstition are lifting from all Pagan lands. Outside barbarians are no longer excluded from China and Japan, and even the Dark Continent of Africa is receiving the rays of light. I cannot doubt that the heroic, the Apostolic efforts of Bishop Wilson and others will yet be crowned with success.

I give here, as the most fitting place, a brief sketch of the life and work of Miss Mary Galloway (Mrs. Giffen), who died in the mission field of Egypt, having devoted her life and all her energies to that work:

Mrs. Mary E. Galloway Giffen, one of the noble and heroic women of the world, was born in Newberry County, S. C., December 8th, 1842. She was the second daughter of Rev. Jonathan and Mrs. Martha Speer Galloway. At the time of her birth her father was pastor of all the Associate Reformed Churches in the County of Newberry, and so remained for fifteen years, when, in consequence of the failure of his health, he gave up his pastoral charge and devoted the rest of his life to the education and religious training of his children.

Mrs. Giffen exhibited in childhood all those characteristics which so marked her in after life—contented cheerfulness and intense activity of mind, body, hands and feet. She early exhibited a great passion for books, especially history; and the wonderful stories and simple narratives of the Bible fascinated her.

During a part of the years 1854, 1855, 1858 and 1859, she

was under the tuition of Prof. Wm. Hood. In the winter of
1859 her father, having surrendered his pastoral charge, removed with his family to Due West, the better to enable him
to accomplish the education of his children. In the College
of Due West Mrs. Giffen remained about sixteen months,
when she graduated with the highest honors conferred by the
institution. At the time of her graduation the country was
overshadowed by the clouds of war soon to burst. She still
devoted herself, however, to the acquisition of knowledge, and
soon turning her attention to the vocation of a teacher she
took charge of a school in Georgia. At the close of the year
she returned home, the country having become so convulsed
that almost all the liberal professions were suspended. On
the 12th of May, 1864, at Spottsylvania Court House, her
brother, Calvin M. Galloway, was killed in battle. Before
this time she had had no deep religious experience, but her
brother's death produced a complete revolution in her feelings.
She became deeply interested in religious subjects, and in her
own salvation that she might join her brother in the better
world. She had a clear apprehension of truth, and she was
soon moved by the new divine life stirring within her to seek to
do something for others, and to bring others into the Master's
kingdom, if it were possible. And soon we find her, in the
latter part of the year 1865, making application to the Board
of Foreign Missions of the United Presbyterian Church. But
they were not able to employ her. She made application to
the Board because, at that time, the Associate Reformed Church
had no Board of Missions. Baffled for the time and foiled in
her efforts to go on a foreign mission, she determined to
devote herself to teaching in this country. Accordingly we
find her teaching French and mathematics in a school in
Middle Tennessee.

In 1873 she is in the interior of Texas for several months,
making a careful study of the people, the country and its
resources; and writing letters for the *Presbyterian*, which were
highly appreciated by the editor and the readers of the paper.
Finally, in December, 1874, Dr. J. B. Dales, Secretary of the
Board of Foreign Missions of the United Presbyterian Church
of North America, wrote to Dr. Bonner, Secretary of the
Board of Foreign Missions of the Associate Reformed Church,

stating that his Board would soon send two young men to
Egypt, and asking if the Church South could not send some
one to co-operate with them in the same field. Dr. Bonner
at once sought Miss Galloway and warmly urged her to offer
herself for the work. She answered if the Board wished she
would willingly go. A meeting of the Board was immediately
called and she was unanimously appointed. The appointment
was heartily endorsed by the Church.

On the 28th of January, 1875, she left her father's house
and passed out over the threshold for the last time, on the
journey to Philadelphia, accompanied by the Rev. Dr. J. I.
Bonner. A series of meetings had been arranged all along
the route to bid her farewell and Godspeed. Every mark of
kindness and of honor was freely manifested at every place
on the way. "In Newberry, the place of her birth, her
father's old friends received her as if she had been their own
child. Her father's old slaves, in procession, escorted her to
the depot on her departure, and overwhelmed her with their
demonstrations of sincere affection, creating a scene rarely
witnessed in the streets."

On the 10th of February Miss Galloway, with the missionary
party to which she was attached, left Philadelphia for Egypt,
never to see her native land again. In a little more than a
year after her arrival in Egypt she was married to Rev. John
Giffen, of the same mission, into whose care she had been
committed by Dr. Bonner on their departure from Philadelphia.
With her husband she lived and labored for nearly six years,
in the effort to give to some of the women and children of
Egypt the Gospel of Christ, and in teaching them the way of
deliverance from sin. No more devoted worker for Christ ever
left America, as all her labors in Egypt and all her letters
from that country show. In a letter to the Ladies' Benevolent Society of Newberry, S. C., she says in conclusion: "So
do not forget to pray for us. Without the spirit of God we
can do nothing, and when we look over our mission station
here, it makes us feel as I have often felt at home when
looking upon a field of corn parching up in a summer
drought: 'O! for the rain!' "

At twenty minutes past ten on Sabbath night, the 16th of
October, 1881, this noble and devoted woman passed to a

better world, having lived only one week after giving birth to her last child. Mrs. Giffen left three children: Bruce Johnstone Giffen, born in Ramle, Egypt, March 5th, 1878; Lulu (Margaret) Speer Giffen, born in Cairo, Egypt, February 24th, 1880; Marion Galloway Giffen, born in Cairo, Egypt, October 9th, 1881. She was not quite thirty-seven years of age at the time of her death.

For a more extended and better account of the life and labors of this good woman the reader is referred to the "Life and Letters of Mrs. Mary Galloway Giffen," compiled by Rev. J. C. Galloway, A. M.

In concluding this brief notice of a good and lovely woman I must be permitted to insert here the following sonnets, tributes to her memory:

Another name is added to the roll
Of noble women, who with faith sublime
A father's house forgot in some strange clime
Beyond the sea, and with undaunted soul
Explore the trackless waste, or forest drear,
Bearding the lion in his very den,
Or tiger fierce, or still more savage men,
To bring the tidings of Salvation near;
Though weak, yet strong, a glorious sisterhood,
In body weak, but strong in faith, and love,
And bright-eyed hope; as when the timorous dove,
Back to the ark, across the raging flood,
Sped like an eagle hastening to the prey,
As in her mouth she bore the olive leaf away.

Not dead, but sleeping ! and the silent power
The world shall own, when yonder stately pile,
Which towers in solemn grandeur o'er the Nile,
Shall vanish like the pageant of an hour;
When she, whose beauty dazzled every eye,
And lured the haughty Roman to his fate,
A willing victim, robbed of all her state,
Shall unlamented and forgotten lie ;*
Then take thy rest, our honored pioneer,
All undisturbed amid the deafening roar
Of hostile guns that shake the neighboring shore,
And blanch the cheek of swarthy Copt with fear;
For thou must sleep until the Bridegroom come,
And open wide for thee thine everlasting home !

E. L. P.

July 24th, 1882.

*Cleopatra, Queen of Egypt.

One Society introduced in Newberry in the year 1888, but which has been in existence several years in other parts of the country, has for me a particular charm and attraction, and always makes a warm and sympathetic feeling in my heart whenever I think of it. That Society is known as the "King's Daughters," and the sole purpose of it is to do good in some way, as it is entirely practical, to visit the sick and the afflicted, and to nurse them back to health if possible, and to comfort them in sorrow. They are true Sisters of Charity. I remember when I was lying sick and suffering in hospital how I longed for the gentle touch of a woman's hand. I asked for the Sisters of Charity, but there were none connected with the hospital, and I had to put up with such nursing as men only could give. They did well, but no man's hand can soothe pain like the soft touch of a pure woman's fingers. My nurses did as well as men can do; and you, Gibbes and Brown, I can never forget; but you, gentle and kind as you were, had not the sympathetic souls of women. May this Society of the King's Daughters never cease its good work, work done in His name, as long as there is work. And we cannot doubt that work will always present itself, for the poor, the sick, and the sorrowful are always here.

Is the *world* growing more Christlike? I do not know. But this I *do* know, that there are men and women in it that are growing more Christlike as the years roll on; as the existence of the Society just mentioned and the one next named proves, I think.

—

The W. C. T. U.

There are other benevolent societies in active operation in Newberry, amongst which the Woman's Christian Temperance Union occupies a prominent place. The society here was under the energetic and effective management of Mrs. C. Mower, who was its head from its organization at Newberry until her death. Since then Mrs. Sophia Mower Redus has taken up the work and has been actively and successfully carrying it on. It has an excellent library of four or five hundred volumes, mostly of a temperance and religious character, and all good. I have read quite a number of the books, not all, and have found some of them of a superior character. Societies of the same name, and for the same purpose, were organized by Mrs. Mower at several places in the county—one at Helena, one at Chappells, one at Prosperity, and perhaps, also, at some other places. Mrs. Mower and her successor in office, Mrs. Redus, and those associated with them, deserve great credit and praise for their active and energetic work for the suppression of the vice of drunkenness; for its suppression, not so much amongst the adults, those already surrendered to the habit, but amongst those of young and tender minds, still plastic; thinking rightly that early impressions, made deep and strong, are apt to be lasting. And thinking, rightly, also, that temperance and sobriety are good auxiliaries to help one to live a Christian life.

I may be permitted to insert here a short sketch of the life of Mrs. Mower, who died suddenly while actively engaged in Christian work.

Mrs. Cynthia Mower was born in the State of Maine on December 22nd, 1829, and was therefore in her 62nd year at the time of her death, which occurred on May 23d, 1892. She was born Allen and was married in 1852 to Duane Mower. In 1854 they decided to come South. They settled at Prosperity in the District of Newberry and engaged in the mercantile business, in which they were successful, and they became entirely identified with the South. In February, 1867, they moved to Newberry, and here they continued the mercantile business until Mr. Mower's death on the 2nd of July, 1872. After the death of her husband, Mrs. Mower continued the business with success; with such success, indeed, as to place her in the front rank of business circles.

But it is not for her success in business only that the writer has, and has long had, so great an admiration for her. She was a woman of true Christian piety and benevolence; and the words as applied to her may be used with the utmost degree of truth, that she was foremost in every good word and work. The church of her choice, the Associate Reformed Presbyterian, never had a more devoted or consistent member, and to all church enterprises and purposes she gave liberally. She was kind and benevolent to the poor, helping them wisely in the best way in which it was possible for any one to be helped, that is, helping them to help themselves.

To her the Woman's Christian Temperance Union was greatly indebted for its planting and success as a living institution at Newberry. She was always in earnest in every work which she undertook. The cause of temperance was very dear to her, and in connection with the W. C. T. U., and as part of her temperance work, she organized Bands of Hope among the children. She rarely missed one of the meetings, which were held during her life on every Tuesday afternoon in the Thompson Street Church. Her annual Christmas treats to the children of the Band of Hope became one of the institutions of Newberry. I had prepared a separate notice of the W. C. T. U. to go with the other societies of the town and county of Newberry, but it is scarcely necessary to separate it from this tribute to Mrs. Mower, as she was the principal mover in the work here, and it may be that without her it would not have been. Though all good women see the beauty, necessity and value of such an organization, yet all good women are not able to do what they always want done; neither are all good men.

The following is the manner of Mrs. Mower's death as related by Rev. E. P. McClintock, pastor of the Associate Reformed Presbyterian Church at Newberry, in a letter to the Rev. Dr. Grier, of Due West, and it will be seen that she died while engaged in her benevolent work. Mr. McClintock says:

"Her death occurred last Saturday, the 23d instant, at Little Mountain, a station eight miles below Prosperity, on the Columbia, Newberry and Laurens Railroad. We were taking the Busy Bees, the missionary society of the children of our church, to spend the day and have a picnic on Little Mountain. We were detained at the station only a little while in arranging to send the baskets in a wagon. We then started to walk to the mountain about half a mile distant. Minnie Todd and Mrs. C. Mower were walking with Mr John B. Lathan, a merchant of that place. Mrs. George S. Mower and I were walking as hort distance in rear of them. The Busy Bees and their guests were a considerable distance ahead of us. We had walked three or four hundred yards, and Mrs. Mower was talking busily to Mr. Lathan about her fondness for children and her temperance work among them. Suddenly she caught his arm, exclaiming, 'Oh! Mr. Lathan,' as if in great pain. He called to me and we let her down gently to the ground, and she was dead. Mr. and Mrs. M. A. Carlisle, Miss Mamie Holbrook and Mr. S. B. Jones joined us at once, but all efforts to revive her were unavailing."

She died while in a good work, a good and useful woman and a Christian. She is survived by an only child, Hon. George S. Mower, a practicing attorney at Newberry. He married Miss Fannie D. Jones, daughter of Maj. L. J. Jones, and they have four children: Mary Helen, Frank Duane, McHardy and Myra.

Y. M. C. A.

And not least amongst the societies for the promotion and doing of Christian work stood the Young Men's Christian Association, which was at work here from the year 1875 to 1889, with some intermissions. There is at this time (January, 1893,) a Y. M. C. A. in active operation in Newberry College.

There is also a Bible Society, auxiliary to the American Bible Society, which has been in existence and active operation for many years. Its sole purpose is to distribute the pure Word of God in the authorized version without note or comment.

—

THE FUTURE PROGRESS SOCIETY.

I am glad to be able to give here a sketch of this Society, which is better than a mere mention.

This Society was organized in Newberry County, S. C., February 9, 1878, by Lewis Duckett, Isom Greenwood, John P. Sims, L. H. Sims, N. C. Duckett and others. The same year a county charter was granted them by the Clerk of Court. After organizing several societies in Newberry County, a charter was granted the corporators by the State Legislature on February 9, 188?. The corporatorss were: David F. Lyles, George W. Starks, Lewis Duckett, John P. Sims, Lafayette H. Sims, Perry W. Greenwood and Wade M. Morgan. The charter was so amended as to allow an insurance policy among its members, and there has been more than four thousand dollars paid to bene ficiaries since March 5, 1885.

The headquarters of this organization are located at Newberry. David F. Lyles was the first President. Then P. L. Spearman served one year. R. E. Williams served one year, and then Rev. F. R. Wallace was elected and is still President, having filled the position four years in succession. W. W. Lazenbury served one year as secretary. The present secretary, George W. Starks, was then elected and has served the past seven years. M. A. Carlisle, Esq., has acted as legal adviser and attorney for the society since its organization.

The objects of the society are good morals, to enlarge the fund of general intelligence, and the general elevation of the colored people by any means it may adopt, but especially by providing a relief fund in case of sickness and a benefit fund in case of death. Much good has been done by this organization.

Lewis Duckett, the father and founder of this organization, and its treasurer from the beginning, was born a slave in Newberry County, and is said to be worth more than five thousand dollars. He is a man that his race seems to be proud of.

From this brief glance at the benevolent Societies of Newberry the reader will perceive that the lovers of good order and right living are not idle in their efforts to check the advance of immorality and to overcome the evil influences that continually assail humanity.

THE FARMERS' ALLIANCE.

How many years the organization known as the Farmers' Alliance has been in existence I do not know; it first took hold in Newberry about six or seven years ago, but no county organization was effected until the year 1888. There had to be five Sub-Alliances in the county before the County Alliance could be organized. On the 30th of October, 1888, the county organization was effected, the body meeting with the Cannon Creek Sub-Alliance. The first officers were: W. D. Hardy, President; W. C. Cromer, Vice-President; John F. Banks, Secretary; W. B. Boinest, Treasurer; J. W. Scott, Lecturer; F. N. Calmes, Assistant Lecturer; Jeff Quattlebaum, Chaplain; H. S. Knight, Doorkeeper; J. M. Werts, Assistant Doorkeeper; P. H. Koon, Sergeant-at-Arms. The officers are elected annually in July of each year. Joseph L. Keitt was the second President, and then J. A. Sligh was elected and is still serving as President. The other officers at present are: W. E. Lake, Vice-President; C. F. Boyd, Secretary; Benjamin Halfacre, Treasurer; John F. Banks, Lecturer; J. B. Fellers, Assistant Lecturer; J. J. Kinard, Chaplain; B. H. Miller, Doorkeeper; J. Perry Cook, Assistant Doorkeeper; R. I. Stoudemayer, Sergeant-at-Arms.

The objects and purposes of this order are no doubt good. The owners and tillers of the soil are the great producers of wealth and subsistence, without which every other industry in the world would perish, even the manufacturing, which should be the ally of the producer, but which, too often, is not. The farmers are the people, the basis, the foundation, upon which at last the real prosperity of the country depends.

The merchant, the mechanic, the manufacturer, should be the allies of the farmer and not seek to grow rich at his expense and make him a mere toiling drudge. To protect themselves against the leeches of the body politic, trusts and speculations of various kinds, the farmers have formed this great Alliance, which is destined to be *the Power*, not only in this State, but in all the States, if they are wise enough to let all their councils be governed by prudence and common sense. The Sub-Treasury Bill originated with them. Whether that bill is wise in its leading features, I cannot say. But it is aiming well; that is, the deliverance of the producers from the fluctuation of prices, and from their thraldom to speculators. If the Alliance continues it is destined soon to become a great political power. In fact it will be *the* party in the United States. And it will do more to abolish and remove all cause of dissension between the North and the South than it is possible for any other party or influence to do.

This Party knows, and can know, no North, South, East nor West, because it is composed of the people, the producers everywhere, and their interests are one. Its tendency is to Union, to make the Union stronger and stronger and to allay all ill feeling. And that tendency is certainly good if wisdom and justice govern the party.

XIII.

SINCE THE WAR.

RECONSTRUCTION, AND EVENTS FOLLOWING.

My heart fails me, my hand trembles and holds the pen unsteadily when I undertake to write, however briefly, of those dark ten years immediately succeeding the war, through which we were compelled to pass. At first it seemed from the friendly advances made by President Johnson that the rehabilitation of the State would not be so very difficult. B. F. Perry, of Greenville, who had been known to be opposed to the measures of the Secessionists and always a consistent Union man, a man of wealth, and of high standing on account of his probity and firm adherence to his convictions of right, was sent for by the President to consult upon the necessary measures for the establishment of good order and good government in the State. Mr. Perry went to Washington where he was received with honor and respect. He was appointed Provisional Governor of the State and immediately set to work for its reconstruction upon the basis agreed upon by the President and other prominent men of the North. An increase of confidence was felt all over the State at his appointment to the Chief Magistracy. Upon the issuance of his Proclamation as Governor, which was well written and well received by all classes, hope was felt that peace and prosperity were once more about to return to the State when absolute ruin had been feared by many. Civil Government was restored; a Convention was held composed of the ablest men in the State; a new Constitution was adopted to meet the new condition of things; members of the Legislature of both houses were elected, and the people of the State fondly hoped that an era of good feeling was about to return and that the State was to take her place in the Union once more with all her sovereign rights and powers unimpaired. But these hopes were rudely dispelled; the President himself became very unpopular with the leading spirits of his party. The opposition went so far that he was impeached, in the hope that he might be deprived of his office and driven in disgrace from Washington. In this his enemies did not succeed, but all his measures for the restoration of the State were despised and trampled upon; the State Government was overthrown as not being radical enough, and our Senators and Representatives were not allowed to take their seats in Congress until after reconstruction under radical regime.

The following named gentlemen were members from Newberry of the Convention which met in September, 1865: Robert Stewart, E. P. Lake and Henry Summer.

Under that Constitution, that is, the Constitution adopted in September, 1865, the members elected to the Legislature, which met at the usual time in November, 1865, from Newberry County were: J. H. Williams, Senator; C. H. Suber, A. C. Garlington and E. S. Keitt, Representatives. By that Legislature, and at the first session, Y. J. Pope, Esq., was elected District Judge of Newberry County, to hold his Court in the Court House once each quarter, that is to say, four times yearly, with certain well defined powers and jurisdiction. At that session was passed what is known as the Black Code, by which, although the rights of person and property of the colored people were declared to be under the shield and protection of the law, yet they were not admitted to the full rights of citizenship and had not the ballot given to them. It was considered right and proper and even necessary that they should be held in a state of pupilage, being considered, and rightly so considered at that time, as unfit to exercise the full rights of citizenship. It was hardly reasonable to suppose that an ignorant people, no matter how well disposed they might be—and these were well disposed as a rule—suddenly freed from the condition of chattel slavery, would or could be competent to vote well and wisely, or to make and execute the laws of the State.

All the members from Newberry voted for the passage of this Act except Mr. Suber. He did not favor it.

This action of our people gave great offence to the ruling party at Washington and all over the North. James L. Orr, who had been elected Governor, was permitted to hold his position, but as Provisional Governor, until 1868, when the reconstruction of the State under radical auspices having been completed, R. K. Scott, of Ohio, was elected Governor. But

Burr J. Ramage.

Jas. Y. McFall.

Young John Harrin,

Thomas M. Lake.

CLERKS OF COURT.

in point of fact the State was under military rule from the close of the war until 1868.

In 1868 Charles W. Montgomery, a native of Charleston, was made Senator from Newberry; J. A. Henderson, J. D. Boston and James Hutson, Representatives. The Representatives were all colored and, I believe, natives of Newberry. In 1870, Boston, Jas. A. Henderson and James Hutson were elected to the House, Montgomery being still Senator. In 1872 Corwin of Ohio was elected Senator, with Boston, S. S. Bridges and Jno. T. Henderson, as Representatives. In 1876 Corwin was again Senator, with Thos. Keitt, W. H. Thomas and S. S. Bridges as Representatives. It was not until 1878 that Newberry ceased to be represented by colored men and aliens. For a complete list of Senators and Representatives the reader is referred to the Appendix.

In 1868 was held the Convention which framed and adopted the present Constitution of the State, which is now the supreme law *under* the Constitution and laws of the United States. Of that Convention the members from Newberry were: B. O. Duncan, Lee A. Nance and James A. Henderson. This Convention met in Charleston, January 14th, 1868.

By that Constitution our present Free School system was established; manhood suffrage without regard to race, color or previous condition was admitted and declared to be a right pertaining to and inherent in every citizen; married women, as to their own property, both real and personal, no matter how acquired, were emancipated from all control of their husbands and were declared to have all the rights and privileges of a *femme sole*.

Whether that Constitution was wisely made, and whether its provisions are altogether wise and good, is still a doubtful question. But be that as it may, over twenty years have passed since it was adopted and no steps have been taken by the people to change it or to modify it in any way. This writer has grave doubts of the utility of the boasted Free School system as it is administered here; and graver still of the Woman's Rights feature in the Constitution; and graver still of the wisdom of that desire that so many strong minded women have in these times for the extension of suffrage to women. But I am very free to say and to admit

3   A

cheerfully that I am somewhat of an old fogy; attached to old things and customs, and especially and very warmly at-tached to the general principles of the old English Common Law, from which our present Constitution is far removed. According to my view of marriage and the relations existing, or which should exist, between the sexes, a man and his wife are one in heart, soul and essence, indissoluble, and therefore any legislation which tends to make them two separate beings, independent of each other, is that far radically wrong. And so the old English Common Law, which merged the being of the wife in that of the husband, was founded in the very "nature, reason and the soul of things." But after all, the nature and the mind of man are so flexible and yielding, that, given any particular set of circumstances, or any particular environment (to use a modern word), they yield and adapt themselves accordingly, so that life at last may be rendered moderately comfortable under almost any condition.

I hope my readers will forgive me if I pause here and insert some thoughts that occurred to me in 1865 soon after the close of the war, as to the proper course to be pursued by the people of the State. My own thought was that the Convention which met in September, 1865, should take no steps towards rehabilitating the State or establishing govern-ment of any kind, but that it should, in a solemn State paper addressed to all the States and the people of the States, set forth the reasons for seeking independence by Secession, and then, after doing this in a manner as able, distinct and dig-nified as possible, make a formal, complete and absolute sur-render of the State with all its rights and privileges as a Sovereign Power to the General Government, asking that Gov-ernment to place the State and its inhabitants under Terri-torial Government and to give such laws and institutions as might be necessary for the securing of good order, peace and prosperity.

What would have been the result of thus proceeding I do not know; but such, I thought, was the proper course to pursue, and I still believe that it would have been better than what was done. We fondly hoped that we could go on and act as a Sovereign State, ignoring the fact that we were con-quered and at the mercy of our conquerors. As we have seen, our first movements gave great offence, and we were placed under military rule and so held until the carpet-bag dynasty was firmly established over us.

Of those dark days I do not wish to say much. It was a period of such confused thought and action that the whole period seems more like a troubled dream than a sad reality of life. A number of deeds of violence were committed by reckless white men. Some negroes were killed, not only in the country around, but in the town of Newberry, even in the day time. One colored man was shot to death near where I was living, not far from the College, while I was eating my dinner. Amos, the barber, was killed in the early evening, July 25, 1866, near the Court House, by some persons unknown. The air was full of rumors of Ku Klux, and one night an attack was made upon the house of Sim Young. The house was on Adams Street, about two hundred yards from where it intersects with Pratt Street, and north of Pratt. Sim Young was too hard for the party; the assailants were driven off, and one poor fellow was seriously wounded and afterwards captured and lodged in jail. He was admitted to bail, I believe, was never brought to trial, but what was his after fate I do not know, though it was rumored that he was hidden and made away with by some of his friends and associates. At any rate he disappeared. Many citizens of Newberry County were arrested and lodged in jail on account of their alleged connection with the Ku Klux Klan; but none here were ever brought to trial, though many from other parts of the country were tried, convicted and severely punished, whether justly or not it is impossible for me to say; though I have little doubt that in many cases harsh measures were meted out to them, judging from the language used by President Grant on the occasion of the Ku Klux arrests. In that message to Congress he said, speaking of the Ku Klux: "It is thought that no innocent person has been arrested," thus prejudging them and condemning them as guilty before investigation and trial; certainly a very unfair and unjudicial mode of proceeding.

I append here a list of alleged Ku Klux arrested in Newberry County, and some few from Laurens County who were put in jail here: Charles Sims, Dr. F. M. Setzler, Dr. E. C.

Jones, John I. Houseal, J. Y. McFall, T. P. Slider, Baxter Chapman, W. I. Harp, J. M. Johnstone, Dr. Wm. M. Kinard, Thomas Wadlington, Adam Berly, Simpson Malone, Charles Franklin, Bennet Hancock, Dr. Wm. Hatton, John L. Epps, Dr. T. C. Brown, Richard V. Gist, Isaac Nance, Wm. Calmes, Duff Odell, Thos. H. Chappell, Jno. F. Watkins, Jno. Wilson, Wm. R. Smith, Dr. J. O. Dickert, Osborne Bishop, J. M. Calmes, Sol. Hubbard, P. H. Hargrove, W. L. Andrews, Jas. R. Irvin, P. M. Denson and M. M. Buford. Mr. Buford was the only man from Newberry who was really put on trial. He and Osborne Bishop were in the Columbia jail. He was put on trial along with four prisoners from Laurens. The jury failed to agree and a mistrial was ordered. The right to the writ of habeas corpus was no longer suspended and they gave bond and were never afterwards brought to trial.

It is nothing more than proper and just to state that after the war the first acts of violence were committed by colored men; but it is not probable that these acts had any political significance, but that they were done rather for purposes of plunder or revenge. In 1866, July 27, Mr. Lemuel Lane was murdered by his former slaves in the lower part of the county. And in 1866 Mr. James Cureton, for purposes of plunder, was killed by colored men in a very atrocious manner.

During all these years from the surrender of Appomatox in 1865, to the Democratic victory in 1876, eleven years, the State was in a continual ferment, feverish and excited; under military and radical carpet-bag rule, with a semblance only of law and order on which none of the old citizens could repose with any sure trust and confidence. A feeling of insecurity and uncertainty pervaded the minds of almost all persons; a feeling as if no horrible nor strange, unnatural deed would be surprising at any time. It is very fortunate for us that we forget; or that we see the horrors through which we are passing and have passed, through a vail of mist that softens their harsh outlines and clothes them in a dress not altogether repulsive, so that looking backwards years after we can view them with a tender and somewhat pleasant melancholy. So those dark days now seem to us, or to me at any rate. I am sure that severe trials, patiently and firmly borne in a high and heroic spirit, raise to a still greater degree of perfection the grandest and purest qualities of man. The hottest furnace is necessary to the perfect refining of gold.

For a vivid picture of carpet-bag rule and of the time of reconstruction in the State, I beg leave to refer the reader to Major Leland's book, "A Voice from South Carolina," published by Walker, Evans & Cogswell in 1879. Major Leland was himself a sufferer, having been arrested as a member of the Ku Klux Klan and in his book he gives a graphic account of the times, of his experience as a prisoner, of the riot at Laurens and the flight of Joe Crews.

Of the actual working of the Ku Klux Klan, or whether there was any such Klan, I know nothing. Or if there were ever such a Klan, the view I have always taken of its object and purpose is, that it was organized as a matter of self-defence, for the purpose of keeping some kind of order by striking the minds of the colored people so lately manumitted and brought face to face with duties and responsibilities of the gravity and magnitude of which they had no adequate conception, with a wholesome and mysterious awe. But like all other similar organizations and secret societies of regulators, there can be little doubt that it speedily degenerated into an engine of wrong and oppression. If the tales told of them be true, of which I know nothing and so cannot repeat them here, the objects of their regard and visitation were colored people and not the carpet-bag leaders of the colored race.

> "It was folly all;
> They struck the negro when they should have struck
> The carpet-bagger under the fifth rib;
> That is if they struck any."

I understand that a gentleman, a citizen of this town, has in preparation a history specially devoted to the Ku Klux period. I have no doubt that his work will be all that it should be to give the reader a just conception of the state of the country at that trying time. The material is not before me to enable me to write as fully as I desired. But even if I had it and used it judiciously this book would soon grow to a size beyond that allowed. So then we will leave the Ku Klux and pass to other matters.

SHERIFFS OF THE COUNTY SINCE THE WAR.

W. W. Houseal was Sheriff during the war and at the close.
J. Middleton Maffett, an officer in the army and while in
service, was elected Sheriff in 1864, but died in hospital while
on his way home to take charge of the office. Next after
Mr. Houseal was Thomas M. Paysinger, who beat Gen. Kinard
in the race for the office in 1866. However, owing to some
Ku Klux, or to some other troubles in which Paysinger became involved, Gen. Kinard, Coroner, acted as Sheriff for
some time. Afterwards Paysinger being relieved of his trouble
acted as Sheriff until the close of his term. Carrington succeeded. After him came Daniel B. Wheeler, who was Sheriff
for eight years, from 1878 to 1886. Mr. Wheeler was succeeded by the present incumbent, W. W. Riser, in 1886, who
is now (1893) serving his third term.

—

CLERKS OF COURT.

The Clerks of Court have been in the order in which they
are here named, as follows: E. P. Lake, Thomas M. Lake,
Jesse C. Smith, H. C. Moses, E. P. Chalmers, J. Y. McFall
and J. M. Kinard, the present incumbent. Mr. Kinard was
appointed to fill the unexpired term of J. Y. McFall, who
died while in office, and having given entire satisfaction to
the Judges and to the people at the general election in 1888
he received an almost unanimous vote for the office. Re-
elected in 189?. Burr J. Ramage was Clerk during the war
and before.

Of the foregoing Clerks E. P. Lake, a native of this county,
was an old man when the war began; H. C. Moses was a
native of Sumter; Jesse C. Smith, a stranger from Ohio;
J. M. Kinard, a boy during the war and too young for service; but his father was a gallant officer and soldier and was
killed during the war in the Valley of Virginia; J. Y. McFall,
a good soldier and captain of a company, was a successful
merchant for some years after the war, retired from business,
was elected Clerk and died in consequence of injuries received
from a fall caused by slipping up on some ice-covered rocks
near his house, when he was on his way to the office. E. P.
Chalmers is still living. Mr. Chalmers has had the honor to

represent his county in the Legislature, having been elected to the House in 1886. Thomas M. Lake is now dead.

For some time during the war and until the close, T. M. Lake was courier for Gen. Longstreet, and while acting in that capacity he had some adventures which were quite romantic. There was one especially so in which my old friends Joe. Cofield and Lieutenant Joe. Culbreath, an old soldier who passed through the Mexican War and revelled in the halls of the Montezumas, were participants. This was a ride on a fast running railway locomotive from Richmond towards the mountains of Virginia during a raging and terrific thunder storm at midnight. Cofield says, "On we went through the pitch darkness with the deep valleys and hills all about us illuminated often by the bright flashes of lightning, revealing momentarily the wild grandeur of the scenery and making us feel almost as though we were about to rush headlong into the deep, black abysm of hell. And all the while Culbreath was lying on his back in a happy way behind Lake and myself telling the story of his love and talking of his sweetheart, Sally, whom he afterwards married."

In 1876, after ten years of Radical reconstruction rule, Gen. Wade Hampton was elected Governor of the State and in almost every county a partial or complete Democratic victory was won. Never in all my life have I looked upon a scene of more enthusiastic joy than I saw in the streets and the square around the Courthouse that day when the result of the election was declared. Men seemed mad with joy. We had gained no victory here, but we saw that the cloud was broken and we hoped, rightly, that the thick blackness would soon roll itself away and let in the light once more. With the passing of that cloud the days of reconstruction passed and within a few years the last carpet-bagger had left the State. And now we have another kind of bagmen, men traveling the country in every direction, here, there and everywhere, peaceable, industrious, jolly good fellows, known as drummers. Long may they flourish. Cæsar commends them and speaks of them as helping to spread the civilization of Rome among the outlying peoples. Cæsar was right, the bagman is a civilizer; the carpet-bagger a locust.

I remember, on the day of election I think it was, or perhaps it was the next day just before the result was declared, I was standing in the door of my bookstore, which was then in Law Range, feeling rather sad and downcast, not seeing into the future and rather despondent generally. While I was standing thus alone looking out upon the moving world, J. C. Leahy, who was then Probate Judge, came up and spoke to me and began talking about the election and the political situation. I did not wish to talk about politics or about any thing with him just then, as I saw that he was considerably under the influence of whiskey, or some other ardent, and begged him to desist. He would not stop, and again, and again, I begged him not to talk as I was not in the humor to discuss any of the exciting topics of the day. Had he been entirely sober I think he would not have gone on, as he was usually very discreet, and he was certainly a man of sound, good sense and judgment and did all the duties of his office faithfully and well. Finally, as he would not desist, I turned upon him and talked to him as I wish never to talk to any man again. I told him all that was in my heart; what I thought of him as regarded his position here; what the people thought of him and all his class, and finally concluded by telling him that he and all his companions were intruders and that we would be justified in doing anything that would drive them out of the country. "What," he says, "assassination?" I replied, "No, sir; not assassination, that is never lawful." He said not much more and soon left me. But when he went to his room, as I was afterwards told, he walked the floor, and stamped his feet and talked and swore and raved like a madman.

Though the Democratic victory in the State in 1876 was decisive, yet in this county the Radicals still retained their hold, Corwin having been elected Senator and Republicans to the House. But since that election the State and the county have both been entirely under the control of the Democratic party.

———

To the foregoing brief picture of reconstruction times must be added some facts and events transpiring in the years immediately succeeding the war. In the first place it is very proper to take into consideration the great losses sustained and the consequent dazed and insecure feeling that naturally pervaded the minds of every body. The loss to the white people of the county in actual valuable property was not less than five millions of dollars through the manumission of their slaves. And through that manumission they lost also, to a very great extent, that direction and command of labor, which, previously, had been almost absolute; and, consequently, the productiveness of that labor was likely to be greatly reduced. However, during the year 1865 the movement amongst the colored people seeking new homes was not very great, as they, too, seemed to be somewhat uncertain as to the future. About the middle of June the first United States troops arrived at Newberry and were stationed under command of Capt. Murray. Under military orders from him all contracts with laborers were to be reduced to writing, and the cultivators of the soil, field laborers, were to receive one-third of the produce as compensation for their labor. Capt. Murray, with his men, was soon removed to another station and Gen. Van Wyck succeeded him. During his stay here Gen. Van Wyck used the college building as barracks for his soldiers, whence they issued, apparently at their own sweet will, and robbed orchards, watermelon patches and made requisitions generally upon the country around. While thus indulging their usual taste they were found one day by Mr. J. S. Hair's manager, a young Kentuckian who had been a Confederate soldier, making rather free with the watermelons and were requested or ordered by him to desist from their amusement and to seek other fields and pastures new. They being very well content where they were refused to accede to his request and continued their pleasant pursuit. The young Kentuckian, feeling, doubtless, somewhat like the old man who found a rude boy up one of his trees stealing apples, thought, that as good words and gentle means did not prevail, he might lawfully use a little force. So he fired upon them and one of the men was slightly wounded. For this offence Hair was arrested by the military authorities, but what measure was meted to him by them, if any, I do not know, (he was absent from home at the time); but the depredating soldiers were never punished for their disorderly conduct. But soon afterwards a party of them went to Hair's place, applied the incendiary torch to the house and burned it to the ground.

CALVIN CROZIER.

Calvin Crozier, a Confederate soldier from Texas, who met death at Newberry, deserves more from the historian of the county than the mere mention of his name. From some cause, I know not what, he was delayed at Newberry—travel was not very expeditious at that time—he had been delayed elsewhere so that it was September, several months after the cessation of hostilities before he arrived at Newberry where he was compelled to remain the night of September 8th, 1865. Some ladies were under his care and they concluded that it would be as well to pass the night in the car, a common box-car, in which they had come from Alston. Late in the night some colored soldiers belonging to the 33d U. S. Regiment, commanded by Col. Trowbridge, which had arrived at Newberry that day on their way to some other station, intruded themselves into the car and made their presence very unpleasant to the ladies. Mr. Crozier requested them to leave and they refusing to do so a difficulty occurred when one of the soldiers was slightly wounded by Crozier with a knife. The regiment to which these colored soldiers belonged was bivouacked in a grove not far from the depot, and it was not long before a number of them assembled at the depot. Not knowing Crozier and mistaking their man they seized upon a railroad employee, Mr. Jacob S. Bowers, who had just come in, and despite his protestations of his innocence, they were about to lynch him, when Crozier, learning that another man was about to suffer in his stead, presented himself and declared that he was the man who had wounded the negro soldier. He was seized at once, tied and taken to the camp in the grove, where he was shot to death by the soldier mob, who danced upon the shallow grave into which they had thrown the body. The white officers of the regiment, before the shooting, were appealed to in vain, and Trowbridge, the Colonel commanding the regiment, was heard to declare after the shooting that he took upon himself all the responsibility for the act.

Too seldom, indeed, do we find such deeds of heroic self-sacrifice as this that is here recorded of Calvin Crozier. He had escaped, and he might have gone entirely free and might have reached his home in safety could he have permitted another man to suffer in his place. What ever he may have been otherwise I know not; but this I know that such a death works forgiveness for many misdeeds and the place where he died and where he sleeps is holy. If any spot on earth is holy surely that is where one freely gives himself to die for another.

Prince Rivers, who was then an officer in Trowbridge's regiment, wishing to save the life of a brave man, went to him after he was bound and helpless and begged him to say that he was not the man who had the difficulty with the negro soldiers, and Mr. Crozier refused to do it saying, "Loose me and I will show you whether I am the man or not."

In 1891 the citizens of Newberry had the remains of Crozier removed from the Village graveyard to Rosemont Cemetery and erected a monument to his memory. The monument is a beautiful one and the citizens of Newberry have honored themselves in erecting this monument to the memory of Crozier.

—-

Murder of Chesley Herbert.

This community was greatly shocked when it was known here that Capt. Chesley W. Herbert, a man much beloved by all who knew him and highly esteemed for his truth, bravery and uprightness of character, had met with the shocking death of murder. Capt. Herbert was born in the county, son of Isaac Herbert and grandson of Walter Herbert, Esq., a member of one of the old Quaker families of Bush River, but who, after the Quaker exodus, united with another denomination of Christians. Chesley Herbert was Captain of a company at the close of the war, a rank well won by his faithful service as a soldier. He was a man of education, a graduate of the South Carolina College, of devoted piety and blameless in all the relations of life. His would seem to have been a sad ending. His death was brought about in this wise: A negro man, whose name I have never heard, stole a horse from him one day at Newberry; he pursued and captured the thief and property some where in the neighborhood of Lexington C. H., and started on his return to Newberry. The next that is known of him his dead body was found near a spring a few miles from Lexington C. H. and near the road leading from Lexington to Newberry. The body was terribly bruised and battered and there was a pistol shot or gun shot through the back of the head. It is not known precisely how the murder occurred, but I have been told that Capt. Herbert had the negro man tied and when they stopped to rest and refresh themselves by the spring, after Herbert had eaten a lunch the negro begged him to free his hands so that he also could eat something without so much inconvenience to himself. Capt. Herbert yielding to the impulse of humanity, granted his request, and then, not being sufficiently wary and watchful, the negro struck him unawares, stunned him, and finally shot him through the head with his own gun or pistol. The assassin was arrested in a short time, tried and convicted of murder at the following, October, term of Court at Lexington, but afterwards broke jail and escaped. He was afterwards captured and hung.

—

In November, 1866, there was an emigration of quite a goodly number of negroes from the United States, and some from Newberry, to the far-off land of Liberia, a Republic of colored people on the west coast of Africa. About one hundred and fifty went from this county, most of most unlettered field-hands. But some few from the town were quite intelligent with some education. Burrell Raines, the tailor, is one who went. But he, with several others, returned the next year, preferring his old home with all its disadvantages to the jungles of the African coast. Raines has done well since his return and has always been a quiet, orderly and well-behaved man. The others I know nothing of.

Field labor during the year 1866 had been very poor and inefficient, much worse than in 1865, and the crops were, in consequence, both of food stuffs and cotton, very scant. The fields had less tillage than I have ever known them to have during any year before or since the war. But cotton brought a high price, and from the rich lands of the West and North-west a great deal of corn and flour was sent here and elsewhere to be distributed among the needy without price.

At the close of the year there was a little light low down on the political horizon as if day were about to break. But on the 11th of April, 1867, Gen. Sickles, military commander, in fact, military and civil Governor and Legislature of the State all in one, issued his celebrated order, known as order No. 10, which became the supreme law of the State, superceding all others, and regulating all the business affairs of the people in every particular; regulating all affairs, both civil and criminal, all proceedings of Courts both law and equity; touching and regulating every thing but the subject of religion; and that I suppose the Governor-General did not think about, as he probably had none of his own, and so, even if the subject occurred to him he dismissed it as a matter of no importance. This order was confirmed by act of Congress and the State was thus placed entirely under military rule. By military order an election was held for county officers in June. In October of the same year the same power ordered an election to be held for delegates to frame a Constitution. It has already been stated that the Convention met in 1868, and a Constitution was framed and adopted which is still the Constitution of the State, so that we are now, whether we will or no, under the rule and management of affairs arranged and set going by the military and carpet-baggers. Meantime Gen. Canby had been appointed military Governor in place of Gen. Sickles, who had been sent elsewhere. It was he who removed Judge Aldrich because he refused to permit colored men to serve as jurors; it was he who ordered the election for delegates to the Constitutional Convention; and it was he, or R. K. Scott, after he was elected Governor, who appointed County Commissioners for Newberry, ignoring an election that had been held by his own order for that purpose. D. R. Phifer was one of his appointees, 1871.

On the 17th of October, 1868, a quarrel arose between Sam. Dogan, a colored man, who had been somewhat conspicuous for some time, a man of sufficient courage but not of sufficient brain capacity to become the leader he aspired to be—at the time County Commissioner, one of the appointees above mentioned—and a young white man named Murtishaw, a native and citizen living in the northeastern part of the county. That afternoon as Murtishaw, D. M. Ward and some other young men were riding out of town they were fired upon by a concealed party near Main Street within the cor porate limits of the town, not far from the Episcopal Church. Ward's horse was killed and Ward himself was so seriously wounded that he has been lame ever since and must continue so during life.

On Monday following Murtishaw and Clarence Fitzgerald, a Tennesseean by birth, but who had married and was living in this county, a neighbor of Murtishaw's, believing, from all the circumstances connected with the affair, that armed men had been seen that Saturday evening coming out of Lee Nance's house and from other suspicious matters, that he was cognizant of, if not an instigator of the assault, went armed into his little retail store, which he kept on Main Street, and shot him dead while he was behind his counter. The Sheriff as soon as possible got a squad of soldiers from the military commandant at this place and went in pursuit of the young men, but failed to capture them. Of their fates since then I know nothing. Whether living or dead, they have vanished. Where are last year's flowers, last year's leaves, last year's joys? Vanished.

And yet just after writing the above I received a letter from my old friend, Dr. P. B. Ruff, sending me a cheerful anecdote of which he knew so many, in the conclusion of which he said : "There are periods in most lives when care, and sorrow, and perplexity seem to declare a truce and leave the man to the unmixed enjoyment of the delights of living. My situation pretty much." Happy, good old man ! The exuberant joys of youth and manhood may evaporate and vanish, but when care and sorrow and perplexity have declared a truce, does not life become more beautiful than ever before? So then it is not always true as the poet sings:

"The Beautiful has vanished and returns not."

So the State continued under military reconstruction rule until the adoption of the Constitution of 1868, then under Radical domination until the Democratic victory of 1876, just one hundred years after the Declaration of Independence of the United States (Colonies) at Philadelphia in 1776.

Peace and prosperity have followed the people of the State and the people of Newberry from that day to this. And if we take a survey of the county to-day, January 1st, 1893, and look at the well-tilled fields and the abundant crops of cotton and corn which have just been harvested, we must conclude that never before was it more prosperous. And, notwithstanding the several disastrous fires since the war and the heavy losses consequent thereon, the town has continued to grow and prosper, and at no time has business been more safe or given a better return for the investment of capital. From the very first Newberry has had a steady and sure growth, indicative of solid prosperity, never jerky and spasmodic.

——

On the night of June 18th, 1866, was the first great fire at Newberry after the war. It swept through the town from northwest to southeast, burning everything in its way almost without let or hindrance, as there was no fire engine and no organized fire department, or fire company, here at the time. Ten or twelve stores were burned and several dwelling houses. Loss estimated at not less than one hundred and fifty thousand dollars, with very little insurance. All was done that could be done to save property from destruction. The colored people on this occasion were rather slow to help, but they have long since corrected the backwardness that they then showed, and now the hook and ladder company, composed entirely of colored men, is frequently first upon the field in time of danger and alarm and always does efficient work. This great fire of 1866 was supposed to have been the work of an incendiary, and immediately thereafter was formed a volunteer patrol company for the purpose of guarding the town and securing it from suffering an infliction of a like calamity. But everything continuing entirely quiet and there being no indications of danger of any kind, after a very brief existence the volunteer patrol company died a natural death, and that there ever had been such an organization was soon almost entirely forgotton.

On the 8th of March, 1877, about 4 o'clock in the afternoon, the old Hotel building, which had been standing ever since the year 1820, was discovered to be on fire. The weather had been dry for some time and soon the whole building was in flames. In a short time all the adjoining buildings on Main Street to the next corner were on fire, together with those on both sides east of Adams Street.

The wind was blowing briskly from the south or southwest and soon the sky became evercast with clouds with every indication of rapidly approaching rain. Early in the evening after sunset the rain began to fall in very copious showers and the fire rapidly subsided, and the next morning all that central part of the town was a mass of smoldering, smoking ruins. If Providence had not sent the rain the fire must have swept through to the extreme northeastern limit of the town, for there was nothing to prevent it. The loss was at least $150,000, with insurance of $60,000.

Since the great fire of March 8th, 1877, there have been several others in the central business part of the town that did a great deal of damage. One on February 17th, 1879, which occurred early in the night, and which burnt Julius Smith's large two story building at the corner where once stood his celebrated Tupper House, and also J. D. Cash's new two story building adjoining, and others on Main or Pratt Street, south of and near the Courthouse. The Courthouse itself was saved with difficulty as it was on fire more than once. I saw Mr. Gilliland make trial after trial to out the flames, that seemed as though they would not be put out, but he at last succeeded and the Courthouse was saved. The wood work was on fire just under the roof at the southeastern corner of the building. One on July 19, 1883, that burnt the buildings on Mollohon Row, which had withstood the great fires of 1866 and 1877, besides a fire in 1883 that destroyed three stores in rear of it on Pratt Street. The fire department had just been organized, but there was no water supply. A small quantity of water from Mower's cistern was thrown by the engine on the front of the buildings on Boyce Street and saved them just in the nick of time. The water in the cistern being soon exhausted, the engine was moved to Scott's creek and water thrown through one thousand feet of hose to the roof of the Crotwell building, then being rebuilt, whence it was caught in buckets as it flowed down the gutters and dashed upon the flames. The Newberry Hotel was saved by keeping blankets thoroughly wet with water carried in buckets upon the roof. The building was also protected by a row of shade trees on the street, just thirty feet wide, from the fierce flames. The loss by this fire was $100,000, with insurance of $44,500.

There have been some other small fires with very slight damages. But, speaking of fires, I think it probable that the 9th day of March, 1855, was one of the most fiery days ever known in South Carolina, scarcely excepting General Sherman's fiery trail that he left trailing behind him in 1865 as he marched through the State. If Sherman had been a man he would have owned up to having burnt Columbia and say that he did right.

I do not know that the loss of property was very great on the 9th of March, 1855, except in the way of fences around farms and plantations. But a great deal of fencing and of timber in the woods was destroyed. I remember the morning and the day, as though it were only yesterday. I was then living on what is known as the Ramage Place, two and a half miles south of Newberry. The morning was mild and pleasant and the air was as still and quiet as October's balmiest weather. I walked up to Newberry, and stopped at Mr. Henry Summer's law office, at, I suppose, about half past 9 o'clock. The wind was still when I went in, but soon began to rise and when I left the office it was blowing a perfect gale. But still there was no indication of fire anywhere about. On my way home I called at a neighbor's and remained to dinner. Still no appearance of fire. While we were eating dinner a servant came in and told us that there was fire towards the Ramage Place. I did not stay to finish my dinner, but immediately left for home. When I came out of the house and looked around I saw fires in every direction, some near and some far off. The whole county was ablaze and the wind was blowing with great violence. Before I got home the fire had already swept through the place, burning fences and timber, but no buildings, as they, fortunately, were not in its course. The whole country was burnt over, on that day, from the mountains to the seaboard, and in woodland portions of the country many buildings were destroyed. I have had many fights with fire, but that fire could not be met in front.

———

SKY GLOWS, CYCLONES, EARTHQUAKES, FRESHETS.

About the first of November, 1883, began those wonderful morning and evening sky glows, which attracted the attention

3   B

of the world for so long a time, and for which no satisfactory explanation has ever been given. Some have supposed that the earth became enveloped in an immense cloud of cosmic or star-dust. Others suggested that the terrific volcanic eruptions of the preceding year in the East threw up so much earthy material in exceedingly fine particles, that the whole atmosphere of the earth became completely filled with it through the long continued dry weather, so that of mornings and evenings the sky would glow with an unwonted lustre, the beams of the sun being reflected from the fine particles of dust. Whatever may have been the cause, it was, at first, high up in the atmosphere far above the region of the clouds and gradually sank lower until it came to the surface of the earth and was absorbed. During the following winter the air was more heavily charged with electricity than I had ever known it to be at any previous time. On February 19th, 1884, and for some time following, came those wonderful cyclones, that swept over this whole State, and other parts of the world, with unprecedented violence.

The cyclone that swept over the State in the afternoon and night of February 19th, 1884, doing so much damage in places, destroying Chappell's Depot and the village around it, and St. Matthew's Church, in this county, did not touch the town of Newberry. It struck Chappells about seven o'clock with terrific force. Wash. M. Boazman had a leg and arm broken which crippled him for life; C. D. Shuford, a railroad man from North Carolina, there at work on the new depot, was killed; Will Smith had his arm badly hurt. These men were in the second story of Geo. T. Reid's store, which was totally wrecked and his goods blown entirely away. Mr. Reid's loss was $9,000. His residence was also destroyed, and Mrs. Reid and the children miraculously escaped death. A little negro child was also killed. The residences of D. M. Dickert and Mrs. Rosalie Simkins were blown down. Mrs. Dickert had her skull slightly fractured and Mrs. Simkins had an arm broken. There were other casualties and destruction of property at Chappells. Six out of eight freight cars were blown forty feet and their contents scattered to the winds. The storm next struck on the other side of the county and its havoc there was just as great. Every building on Capt. D. A. Dickert's place was demolished except his residence, making a loss of $2,000. The residences of Charles P. Dickert, Wm. Heller and others in that section were blown down. Some of the peculiar evidences of the force of the cyclone was shown in blowing a scantling through a bale of cotton at Chappells and a shingle through a pine tree near St. Matthew's Church. There were other like instances. An observer near Chappells, who was not in the cyclone, but about a mile away southward on the Edgefield side of Saluda, in a letter written to me a short time after it passed, thus describes the appearance of the cyclone: "The upper part of the cloud was jet black; the lower and southern side was startling in its brilliancy—not of a reddish color, but precisely that of flame, so luminous and glowing that I could see objects in the yard distinctly. I then said 'it must be a cyclone,' which thought made me watch it more closely. It seemed to be pointed, or funnel-shaped, the point down and whirling, just as I imagine a maelstrom. I saw no lightning, that is, flashes of lightning, in the cloud—it was too bright. Every one I have spoken to about it who saw the cloud agrees as to its luminous appearance."

From this description I conclude that the cloud shone with a steady flame. It must have been a most magnificent sight.

From other sections of the county I learn that rooms in houses in which persons were, in some instances seemed to be on fire, or to have flames or balls of fire playing and rolling about. In one instance an old gentleman thought of trying to put the fire out with a bucket of water, but concluded it was useless to try it.

From these data and from my own observations of clouds and the lighting, especially of those clouds that throw down quantities of hail, I conclude that electricity is a very important agent in the production of cyclones and hailstorms. I conclude also that a hail-bearing cloud *is* a cyclone in the upper air. All observers tell us that cyclones, after sweeping the surface of the earth for some distance, frequently bound upwards and pass high up through the air without touching the tops of even the highest trees. The one near Jalapa on the morning of March 9th, 1884, touched the earth for a short time and distance only, and as it rose it tore off the tops of trees in its passage and passed away doing no further hurt. That cloud, too, was intensely electrical, throwing out angry flashes of lightning and hail in considerable quantities.

On the 13th of September, 1892, there were two terrific tornadoes in Newberry County about three o'clock in the afternoon,—one in the lower part of the county and the other in the upper. One of the greatest sufferers in the lower section was Mr. John A. Shealy, whose residence was a mass of ruins, and whose stables, barns and outhouses were razed to the ground. Mr. and Mrs. Shealy were both absent from home, but hearing the roaring and seeing the approach of the storm, they hastened homewards. The children were playing in the lot, not thinking of danger. Mr. Shealy was in time to get them into the house. Mrs. Shealy was caught a short distance from the the house. The telegraph wire came down with a crash and she was caught and entangled in its clutches. The house was lifted from its pillars, and the roof was torn to fragments and carried with the winds. The whole house was a ruin in less time than it takes me to write it. No one was hurt physically. A large piece of timber was driven through the ceiling of the room in which Mr. Shealy and the children had taken refuge. John Riddle's dwelling house was blown to pieces, but the family were fortunately from home on a visit. In the middle of his corn field, which was about the centre of the storm track, there were found large piles of rock, as if they had been hauled there by human hands. The farms of Mike Bowers, H. P. Dominick, D. L. Long, Adam Hartman, M. D. Long and others were in the path of the storm. Bales of seed cotton were blown away and the growing crops destroyed. Locust Grove school house was torn to pieces. Large trees were seen sweeping through the air, curling and twisting about, and a large one lodged in front of G. M. Shealy's store; whence it came no one knows. The town of Newberry helped the sufferers with a liberal subscription of money.

The storm in the upper portion of the county occurred about the same hour, 3 P. M. It was almost as violent, and did considerable damage. It first struck L. P. W. Riser's place, near the Laurens line, destroying cotton and corn, and passed to the plantation of John W. Scott, blowing down tenants' houses and breaking the arm and leg of one child and the arm of another, and scattering furniture and clothing. All the houses on the Thos. F. Ray place were demolished except the gin-house and part of the dwelling house. Several houses on Wade Anderson's place were demolished, and the storm passed thence in the direction of Avery's ford on Enoree River.

The general direction of both these storms was from south-west to northeast. The lower one passed near Mount Tabor Lutheran Church, and the upper one not far away from Mount Tabor Methodist Church.

In the year 1886 there was a great freshet throughout the South. The downpour of rain began in Newberry County about the middle of May, and continued almost without inter-mission until the first of June. Railroad tracks and bridges were washed away and Newberry was completely cut off about a week from communication with the outside world, and then only by way of Laurens and Augusta, whence supplies of food for man and beast were obtained. Our condition was critical, as the supply of provisions in the stores grew small indeed before a train could come through. The damage to the Co-lumbia and Greenville Railroad along Broad and Saluda Rivers amounted to $100,000. It took a large construction force three weeks to repair the damages before trains could run through between Columbia and Greenville. On the 21st of June, just as the trains had begun their regular schedules, the rains again came down and the tracks were washed away for the second time within six weeks. The rain finally ceased about the first of July, and railroad and mail connections were restored in about ten days.

On the 31st of August, 1886, came the earthquake that devas-tated the city of Charleston and left many of its fine build-ings in ruins. Newberry suffered but little; some few chim-neys and weak walls were injured, but the damage was not great. The firm granite rock that underlies this part of the country is not liable to very great volcanic disturbance.

Since 1886 the rainfall has been unusually great. In the great freshet of September, 1888, the water in Saluda, to say nothing of other streams, rose to a greater depth than had ever been known before. The high water mark at Chappells marks now, since that freshet, five feet higher than ever be-fore. In Broad River, however, the freshet was not as great as that of 1886.

It seems to me that all these phenomena are connected together, one with the other, and indicate that the deep interior
forces of nature are at work preparing for some great change.
And that change, whatever it may be, will be for good.

—

DEDICATION OF THE OPERA HOUSE.

The Opera House being quite an institution of Newberry
and a prominent feature of the town, the following account of
the dedication, with a copy of the Dedication Ode read on
the occasion by Mr. Jaeger, the author, will, I hope, be
acceptable to the readers of these Annals. I take the following from the Newberry *News* of February 24th, 1882:

"The Newberry Opera House, finished and complete in all its
parts and appointments was dedicated last Monday night. On
the stage were Mayor J. P. Pool, Aldermen J. Y. McFall,
D. W. T. Kibler, Geo. A. Langford and D. M. Ward;* President Holland of Newberry College, Capt. A. P. Pifer of the
Female Academy, Capt. O. L. Schumpert of the Thespian
Club, Gen. Y. J. Pope and Mr. C. G. Jaeger. The interesting ceremonies were begun by Gen. Pope, who represented
the Mayor and Aldermen, and who spoke in fitting words of
the gentlemen who had erected the builing by their money,
brain and brawn; and he likewise expressed the appreciation
of the citizens at having so magnificent and serviceable a
structure. Then followed a varied entertainment, consisting
of very sweet and beautiful music and singing by Mrs. F. O.
Bailey, of Newberry, and Mrs. Warren Davis, of Charleston,
and remarks by Profs. Holland and Pifer and Capt. Schumpert; the former expressing thanks for the use of the building for commencement and other exercises, the latter for school
exhibitions, and Capt. Schumpert spoke in behalf of the Thespian
corps; at the close of which Mr. Jaeger, whose brilliant mind
is recognized wherever he is known, read the following poem
composed by him for the happy occasion:

> This stately fabric by noble spirits planned,
> Designed with art and reared by skillful hand;
> This radiant hall where light with beauty vies,
> Whether the brighter shine is from jets or eyes;
> These scenes that shift from town to forests hush,

—

* The Opera House was built under the administration of this City
Council.

That sprung thus lifelike from the artist's brush;
The far-seen tower that greets the coming guest
And tells him, "Stay! for here 'tis well to rest";
This noble pile from ground to heaven's blue,
Was planned, was built and was adorned for you;
For you, to here forget the daily strife,
Strip off the care, the turmoil of this life;
To here commune with spirits of the past
And learn that nothing but the good will last;
To leave behind this mighty lust of pelf,
And to forget this little selfish self.
Let music tremble through your willing breast,
And feel for one short hour that you are blest;
Let merry laughter chase your cares away
And gather vigor for another day.
Behold the world! between these narrow slides
There lives and moves what here on earth abides.
No phantom he whom on these boards you see,
The only man, the real man is he.
He opes his heart, truth through his lashes beams;
He shows you what he is, not what he seems.
We build this world, destroy it with a crash,
But with the passing of the lightening flash
We build it up anew.
For king, for peasant, valiant knight or knave,
For all, here stands the cradle—there the grave.
We plant the seed; at once burst leaf and flower,
And here a life is lived within an hour.
What we create can never know decay,
It lives and moves and moves and lives for aye;
Forever with immortal laurel wreathed,
And Hamlet lives, though Hamlet never breathed.
Here may be heard what often has been told
Of fiery tongues, the magic tongues of old;
Where eloquence has taught the Right to do.
To strengthen Virtue and enforce the True.
Listen! the air with distant music filled,
You cannot understand—but you are thrilled;
The strains that tremble on your willing ear,
They swell from yonder and they echo here—
Subduing hatred and to kindle love,—
Perhaps they're messengers from spheres above.
And over all there hovers Beauty's sheen,
The vesture of a presence felt, not seen;
A veil of grace that o'er this world is thrown,
Revealing, as it hides, a world unknown.

We've done! and now we dedicate this Hall
For you, for those to come—for one, for all—
And may its spell and fragrance ne'er depart!—
To Beauty, Music, Eloquence and Art.

"The programme closed with a charming chorus by Mrs. Bailey's large singing class, assisted by several gentlemen in appropriate costumes. And thus pleasantly ended the dedication of the Newberry Opera House."

Charles Gustav Jaeger, the writer of the foregoing Ode, was born in Germany, and was a student in the University of Heidelberg at the same time with Dr. O. B. Mayer. But they never met until long after their student life had closed and Mr. Jaeger had come to this country. Mr. Jaeger, like many of the German youth, and especially the youth of the Universities, when quite a young man became deeply imbued with republican principles and in 1848, when almost all Europe was in a blaze of revolution, took part with the people who wished to remove the old order of things and establish a new and, they fondly hoped, a better in a form giving to the people a larger degree of liberty than they had ever known. A reaction, however, took place, the revolution was quickly suppressed and many of the revolutionists had to flee for their lives from a country which they then found entirely too hot for them. Mr. Jaeger escaped from the city in which he was at that time through the connivance of the lieutenant commanding the guard at the gate, they having been fellow-students at the University in former years.

Mr. Jaeger is, or was, a fine musician and for some time gave lessons at the Female School at Cokesbury, in Abbeville County. He was also professor and teacher of music at the Laurens Female College; and while there on some occasion read a lecture on music which was afterwards printed. It is one of the finest compositions I ever read, and is like a strain of music pure and ethereal, breathing the highest and tenderest sentiments possible for heart to conceive or pen to write. But like the poet Shelley, Mr. Jaeger wanted one thing without which it is impossible for genius, no matter how great, to be consistent throughout and to do a perfect work.

XIV.

SHIFTING SCENES AND CHANGES.

I feel that I cannot better close my labors on this work than by briefly noting some of the changes that have taken place in family names, the disappearance of some and the incoming of others, since the publication of O'Neall's Annals. I have long observed, with a great deal of interest and curiosity, the continual change that is going on in the component parts of the crowds of men and women that fill the streets from day to day. Always the same movement and bustle going on; the same kind of anxious look on the faces passing continually; the same stir and push in business; the same buying and selling; success and failure treading on each other's heels. But when I look closely and examine the individuals that compose the crowd of fighters and strugglers and bargainers, I find that familiar faces are vanishing every day and new ones taking their places. Some seek other fields for the exercise of their energy, and some, the larger number, vanish from earth by the ever-lasting process of death. To me it seems as though it were only yesterday when Robert Stewart, McMorries & Brother, William Martin, S. T. Agnew, Walker & Glenn, W. G. Mayes, and many others, whose names I cannot now call to mind, were active business men here and men of power in their spheres.

Then there was Julius Smith, the dispenser of the ardent at the Tupper House down here at the corner, and who kept a clean house, if it be possible for a house of that kind to be so kept. He and all those named have vanished. I believe there are no tailors here now except Burrell Raines. In those old days there was O'Connor, whose shop was on Caldwell Street, opposite the present front of the Newberry Hotel. Joseph Mooney's shop was at the corner of Adams and Main Streets, where now stands a brick house, owned by G. S. Mower and occupied by Eddy Brothers. Mr. Mooney's dwelling was a brick house standing on ground now covered by the Crotwell Hotel. James Guy was also a tailor here once, a native of Newberry, and a good and worthy man and a most inveterate smoker. He worked, I think, with Mr. Mooney for a time, or was a partner of his, or perhaps both. And Harrington & Guy once kept a ready-made clothing store on Main Street, in a room on the ground floor of the old hotel building that stood where the Newberry Hotel now is. Patrick Scott was also a tailor for many years from 1858 to his death; his place of business was on the corner of Friend and Caldwell Streets. All these with their works, their cares and their anxieties have passed away. But the world's work goes on as earnestly as ever. There is no abatement, no rest, no cessation. And men went to law then as eagerly as now. They joined issue and fought sometimes to their very last dollar about matters that they might have settled much better and much more satisfactorily without resort to law than with it. The eloquent tongues of those old lawyers are now silent in death. Jack Caldwell and Jemmy J. Caldwell, as they were always familiarly called, I never knew. The first had died and the other had been made Chancellor and had gone to Columbia to live before I knew much about Newberry.

As an instance of the great physical strength and activity of Mr. Jack Caldwell, as my old friend called him, I was once told by Mr. David Stephens, of the Dead Fall section, that he had seen Mr. Caldwell put a horse at full gallop and dismount and mount twice in the distance of one hundred yards without checking the speed of the horse. He must have been a man of wonderful endowments both of mind and body. I do not remember ever seeing him. His brother, the Hon. P. C. Caldwell, I saw on several occasions. James J. Caldwell I never knew. My father knew and loved him.

I remember Thomas H. Pope—his brother Charles was for a few months a schoolmate of mine. Ah, what a boy Charley was. Henry Summer, Simeon Fair, A. C. Garlington, James M. Baxter, I knew well—all good lawyers, and one of them, A. C. Garlington, grandly eloquent sometimes, and having the finest and most melodious voice of any public speaker that it was ever my good fortune to hear. These are all gone, but the Bar is still full.

As it is with the business men and lawyers of the town, so also is it with those who look to the spiritual welfare of the people and physicians of the body. And as it is with these, so is it with the great body of the people over the country.

Names and families disappear and others come in and take their places. Some names mentioned by Judge O'Neall in his Annals have entirely passed away and those who bore them are well nigh forgotten. The name O'Neall itself is no longer borne by any one in Newberry; the blood is here still, but the name is gone. And many others that were once names of power and influence have clean vanished. Some, however, seem to be perennial and to cling to the soil as firmly as ivy to an old castle wall. And though they may send off many shoots and branches to distant lands, they retain firm hold upon the soil where they first took root after their transplanting across the sea.

It is my purpose in this section to mention the names of some of those old families and settlers enumerated in O'Neall's Annals, now never, or seldom, heard, and then the names of new comers, as far as I may be able to do so.

This movement of men, nations and families has been going on from the very earliest ages. Like bees swarming from a hive. the superabundant inhabitants of a country overflow its bounds and seek less densely populated regions, or regions inhabited by -weaker races, whom they can dispossess and drive out, or conquer. So the Goths and Vandals overflowed Southern Europe on the decline of the Roman power, penetrated even into Africa, and wasted themselves in the equatorial regions of upper Egypt and Abyssinia. So the Tartars and Turks swept down from Middle and Northern Asia, overcame the empire of Persia, planted themselves in Southern Europe on the ruins of the Greek Empire, where, becoming stationary, they entered upon a slow but sure decay. So the people of Europe in modern times, moved by the spirit of adventure and seeking new worlds to conquer, passed the deep sea, which was once thought impassable, found a new world, dispossessed the Red man of his home in the wilderness, civilized him off the face of the earth, and planted a mighty nation, or family of nations, in the Western world. And there is still no rest. The movement still goes on. Migration follows migration in one eternal flow without end. Even Newberry, which is "the garden spot of the garden spot of the world," is insufficient to still the restless spirit and keep its children at home. And this no doubt is well.

Strong, energetic movement is life, or is indicative of a great and superabundant supply of life. Repose, stillness, save for temporary and necessary rest, end in a stagnation of all the vital currents and forces, which is death. As long as the people of this country give manifestations of strong and energetic life, we need have no fears of the speedy approach of decay. It is not always progress but *movement* that the world wants. Stagnant water becomes corrupt and loathesome; stagnant air breeds pestilence and death. Earthquakes, storms and tempests free the soil, water and air, from poisonous matter, which would ultimately destroy all life did they not occur. Even war acts as a corrector and stimulator, and, through the agencies of bloodshed and slaughter, gives new life to the peoples and nations engaged. Even where and when one nation fails and is blotted out it is only exemplifying that great law of nature, "the survival of the fittest."

Taking this philosophic view of the subject, it is no sufficient ground of sorrow or regret that names, which were once names of power here, are now heard no more. Nor should we lament that so many of our talented and energetic young men are seeking to better their fortunes in Texas, in California, or elsewhere in the far West. Some of my own ancestors, in the old time, came from Saxony to England, and long afterwards some came with William of Normandy. Long afterwards they passed from England to Virginia and Maryland, thence to the region and place now covered by the town of Newberry. And now their descendants are everywhere from Canada to California, and perhaps in every part of the world. It is all right.

Amongst the many citizens of Newberry who left for the West, I must mention here the name of my old friend James M. Crosson, Esq., who has proved himself a worthy representative of his old home. There are Crossons still here—good people. Col. Jim is far West.

I did hope that some one would do for me in regard to the Southwest what Mr. David Jones has done as to the Northwest; but my hope was not fulfilled; and I have done the best I could. But I must not pass unmentioned Jonathan Martin, John I. Houseal and his brother, J. Emlon Houseal, who have left Newberry since the war to better their fortunes in

the West. There are a number of other young men who have
gone West in the past few years, amongst whom I now recall
the following: J. Lawson Long, John P. Glasgow, G. Ernest
Folk, Nathan E. Aull, J. Thornwell Boozer, D. C. Lake—all engaged in teaching. Mr. Lake married in Newberry before he
left, and only last summer Mr. Glasgow returned to Newberry
and took back with him a Newberry girl to share his fortunes.
Mr. Lake married Miss Drucie Aull and Mr. Glasgow Miss Mallie
Wheeler. Miss Carrie Aull, one of Newberry's accomplished
daughters, has also gone to Texas and is engaged in teaching.
F. L. Schumpert, Charles T. Hunter, Clarence E. Hunter, Daniel
Maffett, R. A. Welch, Jr., W. M. Feagle and George P. Wright
are also in Texas engaged in the mercantile business and are
all doing well. Mr. Wright returned to Newberry, also, for his
life partner, and was married to Miss Stevie Bowers. John G.
Piester and family, J. W. Singley and family, and W. S. Birge
and family, are in the Lone Star State and engaged in farming.
Mr. Birge has died since leaving Newberry. Jas. B. Wheeler
settled in California. Prof. C. W. Welch was, also, in Texas for
several years engaged in teaching, but has recently returned
to South Carolina.

Among those who have gone to Florida, I can now recall
Samuel and Frank Teague, E. L. Chalmers, Forrest Lake, Robert E. Leavell, Wm. Reagin, and, no doubt, some other worthy
young men. Also Dr. John M. Thompson and family and Dr.
and Mrs. J. D. Bruce. S. P. Sligh has been in Florida for a
number of years. All these, so far as I am informed, are
doing well for themselves. Wherever you find the sons and
daughters of Newberry settled, as a rule, you are going to
find a thrifty and prosperous population.

If it be true, as Mr. David Jones says, of the great Northwest, that Newberry County, S. C., has furnished more men,
women and children to people and develop that section than
any other county or district in the United States, I am very
sure that the same may be said of the great Southwest.
From the great Northwest, as far as Dakota, down the Mississippi to Texas, to the orange groves of Florida, go where you
may you will meet Newberrians whom you knew here, acting,
moving and at work—useful and elevating work.

Newberry was first settled by thrifty and industrious Germans, Quakers, Scotch Covenanters and Scotch-Irish; and many scions from the old stock are here yet.

The following names have vanished from the records of the county entirely. Thier blood, however, still flows in the veins of their descendants of other names; but their names are now only matters of history or tradition, and some of them are but dimly remembered and are almost forgotten: Casey, Manning, Means, Hampton, Wadlington, Cates, McElduff, Tune, Eichelberger, Gray, Cappleman, Wallern, Staley, Souter, Miles, Furman, Frost, Patty, McCoole, Hollingsworth, Gilbert, Galbraith, Insco, Spray, Pemberton, Inman, Steddam, Crumpton, Jay, Hasket, Kirk, McQuerns, Drennan, Carmichael, Gregg, Cameron, Fleming, McCalla, McCreeless, Madigan, Boyce, Myrick, Marshall, McKee, McConnell, Gaskins, Malone, Gordon, Littleton, Flanagan, Herndon, Starkes, Tinney, Heuston, Grasty, Crenshaw, Finch, Shell, Parks, Cole, Crow, Crosswhite, Eastland, Parnell, Dun, Allison, Caradine, Hatcher, Worthington, Riley, Cothran, Musgrove, Bemount, Ganter, Rial, Spillers, Bieler—was a physician—Presnell, Cain, Baldres, Cox, Larger, Thwett, Barrett, Cureton, Farnandis, O'Neall, Hammond, Clark, Downs, Ker, Schoppert, Sherman. These names are all extinct in Newberry County and there may be others.

And the name Coate, though not entirely gone is very nearly so. I believe that Boliver Coate, a descendant of John Coate, the first owner of the land upon which the town of Newberry stands, or of a brother of his, left a family of sons and daughters in the lower part of the county. I knew him slightly many years ago. He married a daughter of Luke Nichols, and is long since dead. His brother, John Coate, who married a Miss Sims, left only one son, Sims Coate, who I believe read medicine, but of this I am not sure, and went to Mississippi many years ago.

John Coate was a very useful man in his day, and was for many years a merchant in Newberry in partnership with Robert Stewart, under the firm name of Stewart & Coate. He was County Treasurer or Auditor of the county in the year 1866, or 1867, or perhaps both. I know that he held some official position, as I remember making returns of property to him, and also receiving pay from the county through him for taking care of a sick negro, whom I picked up at my front gate in the street one night. I must say, however, that I took care of him against my will, for I made diligent search for the police and for the marshal of the town, and being unable to find any of them had the sick man on my hands. I also called on some negroes who lived near by, but they refused to have any thing to do with him or to help him.

John Coate died at Newberry and was buried in Rosemont Cemetery. It is perhaps worthy of note that it was *John* Coate, who first owned the land here, and the last of his descendants, or the last of the name, who has lived and died here was *John* Coate. I received a letter, July 16th, 1889, from O. S. Coate, whose home is at Wilmington, Clinton County, Ohio, and he says that there are quite a number of the family near that place, descendants of those who went from Newberry to West Milton, Miami County, many years ago; and who, Mr. David Jones, of West Milton, says, "Are an honor to Miami County and no discredit to Newberry District." A fact which I take great pleasure in recording; as I and every other citizen of Newberry must be pleased to know that every one who goes from this county does it no discredit.

W. J. Duffie, a native of Chester County—none of the name now in Newberry—was for some years bookseller and stationer at Newberry, is still living and selling books and publishing in Columbia, S. C. E. S. Bailey preceded Mr. Duffie in that business—was a watch-maker and jeweller also—son of Amity Bailey, whose name, "Amity," was given to the Masonic Lodge here; none of the family are now in the town or county. Mr. Townsend was also bookseller at Newberry before the war, but before Secession he had removed to Columbia and was selling books there during the war in partnership with Mr. North, under the name of Townsend & North. He died while in business there. Mr. Douglas was the first bookseller at Newberry and began business here not long after the railroad was completed to this place. I believe there is no one bearing the name of either Douglas or Townsend in the county. At any rate not doing business in the town.

J. A. Chapman sold books and stationery for many years

in the town of Newberry, beginning the first of the year 1861 and leaving the business early in the year 1889—making a total of twenty-eight years, having lost, however, the years 1864 and 1865 by the war, leaving twenty six years devoted to bookselling. His son, J. W. Chapman, was owner and proprieter of the business two or three years at the close. During this time Cofield, Petty & Co., of Spartanburg, started the same business at Newberry—continued one year and sold to Caston and Hunt, who carried on the business for two years, when Mr. Caston sold his interest to Mr. Hunt, who continued for two years and sold out to Z. F. Wright, who also bought out J. W. Chapman; so that at this time, January, 1893, Mr. Wright is the only bookseller at Newberry.

It is impossible for me to trace and record all the changes in business that have taken place here in the last thirty years, or even since the war. Some have grown up quickly and vanished speedily. Others seem to have taken deep root, as if they were fixed like the oak to stay in one place until they died. Many new names have come in since the war. George McWhirter, Wooten and McWhirter, Wooten from Edgefield and McWhirter from Georgia; names not borne by any persons living in the County. C. & G. S. Mower, W. T. Tarrant, Thomas F. Tarrant, Peoples & Johnson—Peoples came from North Carolina many years ago. John O. and his brother, W. C. Peoples, were saddle and harness makers by trade. When I first knew them they were engaged in business on Main Street near where Gary & Cook's store is. Johnson was born in Newberry and has lived here ever since his birth, and married here. His father was an Englishman and a good man. Peoples & Johnson are engaged in the hardware and cutlery business on Mollohon Row. S. P. Boozer, then S. P. Boozer & Son, natives of Newberry, were in the same line of business. Many years ago there was a firm of Duncan, Peoples & Co., Silas Johnstone was the Co. T. S. Duncan is now an officer in the National Bank of Newberry. Mr. Duncan may not be aware of the fact, but he is a man for whom I have long had, even from the very beginning of our acquaintance, the very highest regard and esteem, though in social life we have seldom met. A short time before the war, for a few years I was engaged in farming a few miles from town. Mr. Duncan at that time was buying cotton and my partner, who was also manager of the farm, sold to him part, or perhaps the whole of the crop at a given price. In that transaction appeared the strict integrity and honor of the man in business. And now, unless he has sadly deteriorated in all these years, I would rely upon his word as soon, and as much as I would upon the bond of any man. In giving Mr. Duncan this high praise I do not want to be understood as wishing to disparage any other business man. Far from it. Many other business men I know to be good and true. In fact, a business man to succeed well must not be tricky. But this particular transaction touched me very deeply.

Was the first drugstore kept by Pratt & James, or was it W. F. Pratt alone? I first met William Pratt at school at Mount Enon, in Edgefield County, in the year 1835. James F. Harrington was at the same school at the time. There were also some boys and young men from Edgefield C. H. Preston S. Brooks was one of them, and the first sight I ever had of him he was on the roof of a house just built by Dr. R. G. Mayes for a dwelling-house, and a number of boys, amongst them Bart. Blocker, on the ground below, were pelting him with pine cones, some of which were hard and heavy, and he was swearing and pelting them back with all his might. If there were any other Newberry boys there at that time I do not remember them. Charley Pope was there the next year.

W. F. Pratt continued in the drug business until his death. For a time Motte & Tarrant (H. P.) were druggists at Newberry. Also Grierson & Brother, or Grierson & Ferguson. The combinations I do not accurately remember. But Dr. Ferguson was in business here, and so was Grierson. And now the name of Pratt is extinct in Newberry. There is no James, nor Grierson in the county. Maybin & Tarrant (H. P.) also had a drug store for a few years; afterwards Johnstone (Dr. Theodore) & Maybin. Dr. L. A. East kept the last drug store at Pratt's old stand. Dr. W. K. Griffin, now living in Georgia, was a druggist here before the war, also R. H. Land and J. D. Bruce about the year 1860; and Dr. Sampson Pope a few years since the war. Dr. S. F. Fant conducted the drug business for a long time, and was succeeded after his death by Cofield (Dr. J. E.) & Lyons. At the death of Dr. Cofield, Mr. Lyons retired

3   C

from the business and they were succeeded by Dr. Peter Robertson and Dr. James K. Gilder. Dr. Robertson is a native of Charleston. Dr. Gilder was born in this county, and is a grandson of Dr. James K. Gilder, so long and so favorably known as the advocate and practitioner of the botanic, or rather, the eclectic system of medicine. Dr. Robertson was in business before the death of Dr. Cofield; and after he and Dr. Gilder formed their partnership, Drs. Belcher, Houseal & Kibler went into business together at the stand just vacated by Dr. Robertson. Dr. W. E. Pelham is also in business here as a druggist, —at first as Pelham & Wardlaw (J. C.)—and has been for a number of years. He came from Columbia, and is a son of C. P. Pelham, Esq., once editor and publisher of the *Guardian*, an able and influential paper during Mr. Pelham's management of it. He died in 1879. These names Pelham, Robertson and Belcher are all new in the county. Dr. Belcher is now in business alone. Pope (Dr. D. S.) & Wardlaw were also in the drug business after Pelham & Wardlaw dissolved partnership.

Many other changes have taken place here since the war; some even that I knew nothing of at the time. But I must mention W. H. Webb, who once did quite a large business here. He came here during the war and was agent of the Confederate Government for the purchase of leather and rawhides. Near the close of the war, being unfit for field service, the present writer was assigned to light duty under Capt. Webb, who was then at Newberry. After the war he carried on several kinds of business for some years quite largely. Finally he quit business and moved with his family to Texas, where he has recenly died. I think he came from Georgia here. I think there are no Webbs living in the county, though there are some living not far away in the adjoining County of Edgefield. Just after the war B. H. Lovelace and D. B. Wheeler were associated with W. H. Webb. The firm was Webb & Lovelace; then it became Lovelace & Wheeler; then D. B. Wheeler & Co., W. W. Houseal being connected with the two last named. D. B. Wheeler succeeded all of these, and his successors were Floyd & Purcell (Lou Wash and C. J.), and now the firm is Purcell & (M. L.) Spearman.

W. G. Mayes and Brother, before the war—they are both gone—Mayes & Martin after the war, did a general mercantile business, especially in hardware and family groceries—sold also cotton gins. Since the death of W. G. Mayes, J. N. Martin has continued a business of much the same character. His brother John was associated with him for a while, but he sold buggies after the firm was dissolved, and is now dead.

J. Y. McFall, long and favorably known as a dry-goods merchant, was Clerk at the Court of the time of his death and had retired from all other business. He at one time was associated with Robert B. Holman (now dead, January, 1893,) and with Tench C. Pool, and then also with D. S Satterwhite. And J. D. Cash, for some years, I know not how many, was an active, energetic and successful merchant. I have heard it said of him that he was one of the most public spirited men that Newberry ever had, and that he helped very greatly in re-establishing Newberry College here. He married Miss Langford, daughter of Stanmore B. Langford of this town—died leaving a wife and two children. He too was a newcomer, and the only persons now bearing the name of Cash in the county are his two children. His widow married again, Mr. Burr F. Goggans, who has also done business here. A. C. Jones, who came from the County of Laurens, and married the eldest daughter of my old friend, Thos. F. Greneker, also did quite a large dry goods business here for some years, the firm being Jones & Satterwhite. He is now traveling salesman for a wholesale house and is quite an active and energetic business man. Jas. F. Todd, another Laurens man, has conducted the grocery business here at different times, and his brother Proctor is now in that line, and Jas. F. the Southern Express Company's agent.

I must not neglect to mention the old and well known firm of Carwile & McCaughrin. These two, John B. Carwile and Robert L. McCaughrin, left the mercantile business long ago and went into the Bank, where Mr. McCaughrin still is—he is also the President. But Mr. Carwile, on account of ill health resigned his position in that institution and now devotes himself to letters, and the writing of personal reminiscences, and the recording of recollections of persons and places, and the many scenes and incidents that he has witnessed during his life. Long before these pages are printed and published I have no doubt that the people of this county and elsewhere will have read with much pleasure his delightful Recollections.

Nor must I pass by without mention the names of Marquis J. Jenkins and Jenkins & Riser, who were in business here long ago. Jenkins is in Orangeburg—I believe he was a native of Newberry, but Orangeburg having greater attractions he left us. A daughter of his, Mrs. Cuttino, who is a widow, was on a visit here during the summer of 1889. She is now dead—died in 1890.

Another institution of long standing occurs to me now and must not be passed by unmentioned. And that is the Baltimore Corner, kept going for so many years for the dispensing of candies and confectioneries by Andrew Wicker. I believe that A. M. Wicker was one of the gentlest and most guileless souls that I ever knew. He was entirely transparent, as simple as a child, and the evil in him, if any, was as plainly perceptible as the good. He once dispensed the ardent as a clerk for old Gilbal, who was a character in his day, but I did not know him; afterwards he sold liquor on his own account, and it has been told of him that soon after his conversion he was strongly moved to empty the whole of his stock into the streets, considering the traffic in liquor as inconsistent with the religious life, but was persuaded by friends to sell his stock and business to another not so scrupulous, which he did. He remained the balance of his life, which lasted a good many years, a consistent and zealous member of the Methodist Church. Andrew Wicker died as he had lived—trusting The last words that he was ever heard to murmur as he passed away, were these: "Love is the fulfilling of the law."

Who does not remember Dr. T. Gouin, who was a Frenchman, and kept the "French store,"—confectioneries and many other delicacies. His store was always as neat as a well-kept parlor. His wife sleeps in Rosemont Cemetery, and he went back to France many years ago.

M. Barre & Son, R. Moorman & Co., Houseal & Jones (John I. and Dr. E. C.), Wilson & Wicker, Chapman & Crawford (Junius E. and Jas. M.), B. J. and Alex. Singleton, Fellers & Gallman (J. B. and J. J.), Girardeau & Kettlebahd were all in active business during the years succeeding the war. Junius E. Chapman was indeed a good man and true.

He removed to Florida in 1884, and died several years ago. L. R. Marshall, once here in business, now lives in Columbia.

The scenes continue shifting and the changes keep going on. I cannot fix them. Even while I write and since I began writing of the changing scenes, many deaths have occurred; many partnerships have been dissolved and many new ones have been formed. They change almost as fast as the shadows in a dream, and dreamlike they pass before the eyes of the scribe who has lived to see many of them come and go. S. P Boozer became Boozer & Goggans; and now S. P. Boozer, who has been a merchant at Newberry for many years, is no longer one, but an insurance agent, which he had been some time before. His successors are Goggans & Fant—John C. Goggans, who has been in Newberry only a few years; Wm. A. Fant, son of O. H. P. Fant and a member of O. H. P. Fant & Son, which firm is *non est.*

Col. J. R. Leavell's marble works were in existence before the war, and are now conducted at the same place by his son R. Y. Leavell and Leland M. Speers, who also conduct the furniture and undertaking business. Mr. Speers was in business alone for a few years. C. M. Harris was a splendid cabinet maker in years gone by. He was also an undertaker, and has himself been borne to his last rest. Robert T. Caldwell is the successor of R. C. Chapman as an undertaker.

To-day while I write, the old Chapman workshop is being torn to pieces to make room for a dwelling house for his son-in-law, Thos. Cook, and daughter, who have sold the house built by Richard Chapman, and in which he lived and died. The town eastward towards the fair grounds of since the war is new and splendid, and growing newer and splendidior every day of its life. The fact is, in that direction it is beginning to put on airs, and the buildings threaten to grow more and more elegant all the time. Aveleigh Church of the old primitive times, when it was out in the woods as it were, would not know the Aveleigh Church of to-day with its stained glass windows, its fine organ, and groined arches and gothic roof. And at College Place the professors' houses, built by the contributions of the Lutherans of the State and Savannah, add to the beauty of that classic eminence.

But to come back to business changes—there have been

some small failures, not many. The changes have mostly been made, not from outside pressure, but for the convenience of the parties in business.

The contractors and builders of Newberry at this time are W. T. Davis & Co. and the Shockley Bros. In former years, from 1850 to 1880, W. A. Cline was a fine builder. The old Newberry College was built by him and the woodwork of the one now in use. J. L. Aull & Son were builders here for a time. Amongst the contractors of the past must be mentioned Thos. W. Blease and his brother J. Hart. Blease. Matthias Miller was also a contractor here.

Many years before the war a shoe store was kept here by Goveneur Thompson, and in 1858–60 by Metts & Land. The shoe house of I. M. Suber & Co., after the war, was suc-succeeded by Abrams, Griffin, (B. F.) & Hargrove. McDuffie Metts was the leading salesman for both of these firms. He was in the business longer than any man in Newberry, and was a travelling salesman for a wholesale house at the time of his death in 1888. After the war for some years, Robt. F. Phifer, a brother to D. R., did business in that line. He sold out and returned to North Carolina. W. H. Diekert & Son manufactured shoes and had a shoe store for awhile, but they closed out the business and have moved away. There is now no shoe store in town, though shoemaking and repairing is carried on by Wm. H. Blats, who succeeded Peter Rodelsperger and J. D. Hornsby, who for many years carried on a fine and successful shoemaking business.

Some of the dry goods merchants before the war were R. H. Marshall, W. W. Houseal, W. M. Hatton, W. D. Goggans, Smith, Coppock & Boozer. E. S. Coppock began the clothing business in 1858, and Geo. D. Smith kept on in dry goods. W. H. Hunt conducted an extensive grocery business at different times with his brothers J. H. and I. F. Hunt, styled Hunt & Bro.; so did Walker & Glenn, also Jas. Y. Harris and R. C. Wright; and Johnson & Hill; Stiles Hurd in carriages and buggies; B. M. Blease in saddles and harness; Geo. Larsen in confectionery; A. M. Riser in dry goods; also A. Harris, who left here after the war; Morgan & Floyd in general stock.

Wright, (R. H.) Coppock (E. S) & Co. (Henry Whitmire) were clothiers just after the war; then for fifteen years the firm was

Wright & Coppock, when it changed to Wright & J. W. Coppock, which was succeeded by Blalock & Green (L. W. C. and Jordan R.); then Mr. Blalock alone; and he has now been succeeded by Brown & Smith (S. E. and Robt. G.) E. A. Scott was in the clothing business up to about 1883. Cloud & Smith, also clothiers for a number of years, have been succeeded by Smith (R. D.) & Wearn (R. H.). Minter & Jamieson, merchants and clothiers, have been succeeded by O. M. Jamieson, at whose place of business, the old Stewart corner, once flourished the firm of P. W. & R. S. Chick, a name now extinct. In rear of the old Stewart building the postoffice was located for forty years, where Solomon P. Kinard, the postmaster, collected the penny contributions along in 1840–50 for the monument to the "Father of his Country" at Washington.

Kingsmore & Wearn (E. H. and Richard) were photographers for a good many years. Kingsmore was a good portrait painter besides. I have seen portraits painted by him that were very good. W. C. Wiseman was a good photographer. Andrew Chapman worked a while in that line and did very good work. William H. Clark, now in Missouri, was succeeded by J. Z. Salter, who does excellent work.

William T. Wright was long and favorably known as a dealer in stoves and tinware and also as a tinner. He was a devoted member of the Baptist Church, and I am very sure that that church here never had a more strict and conscientious member, nor a warmer friend to the temperance cause. At the time of his death he was a little over fifty years of age. His wife, who was about five years younger than himself, was not quite forty-nine at the time of her death. She was Mary Blease. They sleep together in Rosemont Cemetery, and resting near them in the same enclosure, lie six children, ranging in age from one month to twenty-fours years. Two still survive.

Henry H. Blease was once in the stove and tinware business with Mr. Wright as Blease & Wright. He was also in the grocery business before and the tinware since that time. The tinware and stove business is now conducted by M. J. Scott and J. W. White. A. J. Sproles, now of Greenwood, was in this line here several years.

There is only one business house in which no change has taken place in twenty-five years—that of W. T. Tarrant. In

1866–67, the firm was Young & Tarrant, who succeeded Geo. D. Smith, agent for Wm. Young, in the dry goods business. R. C. Shiver & Co., and Thos. F. Harmon once conducted the dry goods business extensively in the building now occupied by Mr. Tarrant. "M. Foot, established 1857," was the sign of an extensive business for nearly thirty years. The firm was afterwards M. Foot, Jr., & Co. Mr. Foot and his entire family moved to Atlanta in 1889. At his old stand are now Evans & Reeder, (Everett M. and Jno. W.) and recently Jas. A. Mimnaugh. O. Klettner is in the same neighborhood. He deals in dry goods and groceries, also, as I have been told, in the ardent. He is active and energetic. What effect the Dispensary law may have upon his business, and upon A. M. Bowers & Co. (J. H. Ruff), D. M. Ward & Co. (Geo. W. Pearson), E. Y. Morris, Thos. Q. Boozer and the others, I cannot tell, and therefore cannot note at present.

The saddle and harness business was carried on after the war by John Boyle; afterwards more extensively by Webb, Jones & Parker, who added to it carriages and buggies, the same kind of business that F. A. Schumpert & Co. now conduct. Jno. W. Taylor & Co. are now the carriage makers of Newberry. This business was followed just after the war by C. M. Jones, whose son S. B. Jones is in the confectionery business; another son, Ira B. Jones, is a lawyer in Lancaster, and now for his second term Speaker of the House of Representatives; another son, William, lives also in Lancaster. His eldest son is the dentist, Dr. E. C. Jones. Dr. Theodore Johnstone and Dr. Jno. R. Thompson are also dentists in Newberry. Dr. W. B. McKellar, successful and generous, had a large practice in dentistry. Dr. R. S. Whaley was another good dentist. Both have passed from life's changing scenes.

I find that I have not yet mentioned among the business men of the olden time John and Summerfield Montgomery. John is here still and in business—jeweler and watchmaker. Summerfield died long ago—left a widow and daughter and son. All have gone West. They had a brother, Charles W. Montgomery, who was a member of the Legislature after the war. I once visited that august body while he was a member, and F. J. Moses was in his glory as presiding officer—many members were colored people.

C. B. Buist, a new name for Newberry, was once in business here and was at the time of his death Coroner. His name appears among those of the soldiers of the Confederacy. Another new name must be added, Eduard Scholtz. He is a native of Germany—was watchmaker and jeweler here for several years, but having married North returned there in 1889, and is now living in Washington.

Leavell & Spearman were in the mercantile business for a long time where Jos. Mann now keeps store. Next door was the firm of Brown, Wilson & Co., John C. Wilson being now in the fertilizer business. J. J. Lane, a newcomer, is also in this business. Andrew J. McCaughrin conducted a large fertilizer business for a number of years. He has now retired and delights in the cultivation of roses, of which he has a fine collection. Eddy Bros., R. C. Williams, John L. Ramage, Paul Johnstone, J. W. Kibler & Co., Summer Bros., are all new men in business and must be noted in the changes. F. B. McIntosh has just left the Baltimore corner and is succeeded by T. J. Hayes. Wm. A. Kinard also conducted business at that familiar place. The racket store, now Gary & Cook (I. N. and Thos.), is quiet and prosperous. J. D. Davenport, a newcomer in the dry goods business, has just formed a life-long partnership with one of Newberry's loveliest daughters. The firm of Wooten & McWhirter is, comparatively speaking, a new one. C. L. Havird is in the mercantile business in the street with those just named. J. O. Havird was a merchant there, but is now dead. The death of Mrs. C. Mower made a change there necessary and the house is now known as the C. & G. S. Mower Company. The business itself is unchanged. But I cannot keep up with the changes. Were I to note down to-day the name of every business house in Newberry, to-morrow would find a change.

> " Life's but a dream at best;
>   A strange, bewildering scene,
> In magic colors drest;—
>   What is and what hath been,
> All mingled like a gorgeons show
>   That flashes, moves and passes, but don't go."

Joseph Brown, who is now, and for some years has been, doing business as a merchant at Newberry, was a good soldier of the Confederacy and a member of the 10th South Carolina Regiment. He was wounded and taken prisoner at Missonary

Ridge, near Chattanooga, Tenn., in the fall of 1863, and was in prison at Rock Island, Illinois, for six months and probably a longer time. He suffered much in prison as the winter was very cold and the allowance of food was only half of full ration, in retaliation, as the Federal authorities said, for the cruel treatment of the prisoners at Andersonville.

From my own personal knowledge and observation I know nothing of the treatment the Federal prisoners received at Andersonville. But it is matter of history that the United States government refused to make exchange of prisoners. Why was this? If they knew that their soldiers were suffering unnecessary hardships and cruelties at Andersonville, or elsewhere, were they not, by refusing exchanges, making themselves parties to the crime? They ought in mercy, if not in justice to their soldiers, to have relieved them of all useless suffering. They well knew that the care of many thousand prisoners was a great burden to the Confederacy in every way, and that they *must* suffer even when the Confederate authorities did their best to prevent it. So knowing, they were criminal, and deeply criminal, in not extending relief to their men whenever they could. They did it to throw odium upon the government of the Confederate States, callous to the suffering caused, or that might be caused, by their own deliberate cruelty. When on my way home in 1864 from Forsyth, Georgia, at which place and at Atlanta previously, I had been lying in hospital for ten weeks, I stopped at Macon very nearly twenty-four hours, trains not making proper connection, and while there I heard from rumor that the prisoners were dying rapidly at Andersonville; but I heard nothing said of any specially cruel treatment they were receiving. But, admitting that they were cruelly treated, Major Wurz, the commandant, was hung for it afterwards, being made to suffer for his own sins, and bearing as a scapegoat the sins of the Confederacy and of the United States. Well, I hope they got absolution. It was the duty of the Federal authorities to give every possible relief to their suffering soldiers and they refused to do it when it was in their power. They deliberately made themselves parties to a great crime.

Of the cruel treatment of Confederate prisoners in Federal prisons, in some of them at least, all doubt must vanish when we read a letter written in July, 1891, for the Prosperity *Press and Reporter*, by Rev. J. B. Traywick, who had the misfortune to be a Confederate prisoner confined for some time in the Federal prison at Point Lookout, Maryland. If Federal prisoners fared worse and suffered more at Andersonville or anywhere else in the South, their condition must have been awful indeed. But that is simply impossible. Hell, itself, is no worse than Point Lookout was; but that is believed to be eternal and Point Lookout has ceased.

While at Macon I saw Stoneman and his men, who had just been made prisoners a short time previous, pass through the streets on their way to the depot to take the cars for Charleston, at which place they were to be imprisoned. Just before their capture they had cut the railroad and burned the bridge near Macon, hoping to cut off our communications. It was a very daring enterprise, a little too daring, and not quite as successful as they had anticipated, but really a serious damage to the railroad. Just after their raid and capture, my friend Smith Livingston, who was then in hospital at Forsyth, having been shot through the thigh in one of the battles near Atlanta, was furloughed for home for sixty days. I begged him not to go so soon, telling him that he would have to walk on crutches for about half a mile, and that in his condition it would kill him. "Well," said he, "I'll risk it anyhow, if it does kill me. I must go home." I was very uneasy about him, but learned nothing until I got home myself in August; when I inquired and was told that he did not quite die but came very near it.

I have mentioned the name of A. P. Pifer more than once, but have I spoken of him as a soldier? A native of Virginia, at the outbreak of the war he was teacher or professor in Newberry College. After Virginia seceded he returned to that State, entered the service of the Confederacy and was appointed by Gen. Lee commander of his body guard with the rank of Captain, which he was holding at the close of the war. After the war he returned to Newberry, having been elected Professor in the College. He remained with the College some time and after its removal to Walhalla he taught a boys' school for awhile—was elected by the Board of Trustees Principal of the Newberry Female Academy, which institution he conducted with great success until 1888, when he resigned.

Mr. A. Singleton, who is now living at Newberry, and his brother B. J. Singleton, who died here some years ago, were both soldiers in the armies of the Confederacy, and did their duty as such.

The town of Newberry itself is almost entirely new. All the central, business part, has been burnt and reburnt and rebuilt since the war. Out from the centre there are still some few houses as landmarks and relics of the olden time. Part of the house now occupied by J. D Hornsby is quite old, but he has added to it and so transmogrified its outward appearance that it does not look like the same house. The Pratt house and the Graham house are both quite old, and there are a few others. But not many of the houses first built are standing now. Like their builders and the gay young people, who once filled them with mirth and laughter, they have passed away.

Passing out into the country towards Saluda we find that the Worthingtons, Jenkins and others, who once lived and flourished on Bush River are all gone. No one bearing those names now live in that section of the county. But I have already given a list of names no longer borne by any now living here.

I do not think the white population of the county is as great as it was fifty years ago; the increase not having kept pace with the loss by death and emigration. But indeed, I have no means just now of knowing, as I have not the statistics before me. The *town* has greatly increased in population, but the *country* around has not; as the tendency has been to move to the town and leave the cultivation of the soil to the colored people, some few of whom have shown themselves to be good managers and successful farmers. Lewis Duckett is a good example of what an industrious, intelligent colored man can do. And he, as I have been told, is not alone as a successful farmer.

In the list of family names that have disappeared from the county I find that I did not mention that of Hilburn. There may be others also. Hilburn's Mills, lying next below Mendenhall's on Bush River, was once a valuable property as a flouring and grist mill. The mills are no longer in existence, but the lands that once belonged to the Hilbrun estate are still of considerable value. They are now the property of Mr. F. Werber's estate, who married the daughter of Dr. John E. Bobo, who was the owner of the land at the time of his death, he having married the widow Hilburn. There is neither a Hilburn nor a Bobo in the county. Werber, a new name, takes the place of both. Mr. F. Werber was a native of North Germany and was a most excellent man. He died in February, 1891. His widow still lives here. His two sons, F. and G. E. Werber, are in Washington. It would be well for the county if there were more like him.

My friend, Dr. G. W. Glenn, died recently, and he was a good man! What man, young or old, now lives in the county to represent that family name? He left daughters, but no son. We have James F. Glenn, but I suppose the families are entirely distinct. But is he not also nearly entirely alone?

Among the new names, that is, names not of the original settlers though they have been in the county a long time, we have the names of Cline, Blease, Bangle and Mazyck. Cline came from North Carolina near the town of Lincolnton. Wallace A. Cline was a prosperous, energetic, good man; one of the kind that gives solid prosperity to any country in which his citizenship may be. The death of such men is always a real loss, not only to their families, but to the State. Bangle's name is extinct as he left no legitimate children. My old friend Mathias Miller came also from the neighborhood of Lincolnton—has no descendants here—left sons, but they are dead. His daughter, Mrs. Boag, is a clerk in the Treasury Department at Washington. N. B. Mazyck came here from Charleston, brought his family here during the war—he, himself, was in the Confederate service, doing his duty as a soldier should. At the close of the war he remained and was railroad agent at the Newberry depot for many years. E. S. Keitt, who also gives a new name to the county, came from Orangeburg, and succeeds to the Wadlingtons and Bausketts, whose names, once so familiar, are no longer heard. Osborne Wells came from near Lincolnton, N. C., married here and has taken, I hope, firm root in Newberry soil. He has made several valuable inventions which have been patented. Z. L.

White is also from North Carolina, the man who prides himself, and it is an honest pride, upon having grown and fattened and slaughtered the largest hog ever raised in the County of Newberry. Its weight was over eight hundred pounds. Capt. Speck, also from North Carolina, was for a while an active business man here—a watchmaker and jeweller. He remained just long enough to appropriate to himself one of Newberry's lovely daughters when he returned carrying her with him. In 1889 he returned to Newberry and was in business until the first of January, 1893, when he removed to Florida.

I have no doubt that there are other new names, newcomers, both in town and county, unknown to me. They must not think that I have left them out purposely. I write from my recollection of persons and changes without reference to the Treasurer's or Auditor's books.

And now in closing these labors and reviewing them, this January 28, 1893, I find that much more might be added about persons of whom nothing has been said. Many events have transpired in the county unknown to me, which, if properly told, would be of interest to the reader and carry a healthful moral. Many persons, both men and women, have lived noble lives and died heroic deaths, not known to me, whose names cannot be recorded here, but are recorded in a book from which they can never be erased, the Book of God. So I must beg my readers, when they find, if they should so find, that something has *not* been that should have been written, to cover the omission with the mantle of charity and to believe that the writer has done what he could. Some names dear to me have been omitted, or only casually mentioned, and the reader must know from this fact that the pen that traced these words has been absolutely impartial.

Hereafter another volume of Annals must be written and so the record must be kept up, and *that* volume must be made to supply the defects of this.

HAIL AND FAREWELL ALL!

APPENDIX.

THE WAR WITH THE SEMINOLES, 1836.

In the first part of this work, I believe that no mention is made of the war with the Seminole Indians in Florida, nor of the actors in that war, except of Nicholas and John Summer, of Capt. Hargrove's Company. Heretofore some few of the actors have only been casually and incidentally mentioned in the Second Part. There having recently come into the hands of the writer the roll of a Mounted Company of Volunteers who went from Newberry County, and also a daily record of the movements of the company until their arrival at Tampa Bay, from the time of their leaving home, kept by the Captain of the Company, we have thought it well to make here a record of that roll, and also some extracts from the diary of the Captain, as a part of the Annals of Newberry.

I find on the roll names of privates, 58; non-commissioned officers, 7; commissioned officers, 4. Total, 69.

S. C. Hargrove, Captain; James T. Sims, 1st Lieutenant; James V. Lyles, 2nd Lieutenant; Robert Dugan, Ensign; G. Ashford, Sergeant; Nicholas Summer the first; H. T. Clark, Sergeant; E. F. Williams, Sergeant; H. Martin, Corporal; J. K. Jenkins, Corporal; D. Lewis, Corporal; L. Suber, Corporal.

Privates—J. Hunter, J. M. Henderson, T. J. Stewart, J. L. Kenner, James Caldwell, J. Summer, D. Simmons, H. Oxner, E. Prewit, R. Cotes. No. 2—D. Jinkins, H. Roberts, M. McClure, B. Whitmire, A. Aughtry, W. McCracking, J. Boyd, S. Stark, J. F. Williams, J. McMorris. No. 3—L. Lane, M. Ruff, J. Miller, G. Harris, R. Dawkins, J. Floyd, W. Adams, B. Felkman, M. Goree, I. Davidson. No. 4—M. Chambers, I. Prewit, O. Simmons; — Walker, O. Towles, J. Motes, N. Johnson, J. Baker, T. Livingston, G. Smith, T. D. Chambers, H. Suber, P. Suber, — Stribbling, S. Vessels, E. Harris, J. W. Bird, J. O. Bedsil, W. H. Allen, W. Smith, L. E. Horton, P. Philips, L. Culbreath, Harvey Suber, B. Durrett, T. Morris, D. Alewine, A. M. Nembil.

The Captain begins his diary by saying: "Received orders from Col. Neal on Friday, 5th February, 1836, to have my company warned to meet at Teague's Old Field on Monday, the 8th, stand a draw to go against the Seminole Indians in Florida. Met agreeable to orders, but did not stand a draw; patriotism was too high. They volunteered rapidly and made up a company of seventy-four men, and then they had the right to elect their officers and I was chosen Captain of the respectable company."

The roll I have copied gives only 69 names, rank and file, add Nicholas Summer makes 70, what became of the other four does not appear. Orders were now received from Gen. Caldwell to rendezvous at Newberry C. H. on Wednesday, the 10th. On the 11th the horses of the company were appraised and the men dismissed until 2 o'clock, when they paraded and made ready for the march. While on the old field Brig.-Gen. Bull arrived and gave orders for the company to march to Purysburg without baggage wagon. Marched to J. Paysinger's and camped. The night was cloudy with some rain and there was considerable confusion in camp about the baggage wagon, and the Captain says: "I hired P. P. Gilder's wagon to haul baggage for my company at my risk."

Before proceeding with the Captain's journal I must revert to the roll of the company. In the memorandum book which I have, there are three rolls, and I copied that in which I found most names recorded, thinking that it would have all to be found in the others, but it does not. The one I copied gives George Ashford as Orderly or 1st Sergeant, but in the first roll the name N. Summer appears as 1st Sergeant. I suppose Geo. Ashford must have received the appointment in Florida after Sergeant Summer received his fatal wound.

To proceed—On Friday, 12th, they crossed Saluda at Lee's Ferry, the day's march being fifteen miles—the night cloudy and looked like rain. On Saturday, 13th, they started at 8 o'clock and marched for the Edisto. Had some trouble in getting corn and fodder from Mr. Phelps, but threatened if he did not let us have it that I would take the boys and have it any how, and he fetched them. Passed through Aiken on Saturday, 14th —stopped about thirty minutes while the steam cars were run up the hill, and when we mounted we were saluted with three rounds of six pounders and were highly complimented as the finest troop they ever saw. After various ups and downs and inconveniences, but nothing very serious, they find themselves on the evening of the 20th of February, the tenth day after leaving home, at the city of Savannah. Here he says the Quartermaster did not know where to station us for the night, but at length put us in the old Barrack, the water bad and no wood at all, and rations late coming out—much dissatisfaction among the men—many of them went to town for supper. I had to curse the Quartermaster that night before we could get ration or wood. *February 21st.*—Sold Mr. P. P. Gilder's wagon and team to the Quatermaster for the use of the Government to haul our baggage on, as it was all the chance, for $600. Here the other battalion of mounted men came up and we marched out about two miles and camped. Crossed the Ogechee River late in the afternoon of February 22nd—went about three miles and camped—much complaint about the corn being rotten. Wm. Walker's mare was snagged in the side and died this morning.

February 23d.—Went on by Riceborough to Jonesville where they stayed all night. It rained all night, but got houses to stay in. The men much displeased with the Quartermater and spoke harsh to him and about him. Poor fellow ! I suspect he must have had a hard time of it with the cussing and abuse he got from the Captain and the men. *February 24th.*—Started for Barrinton—road nothing but a cow path—went four or five miles and was compelled to retreat, for perhaps it was the worst road that was ever seen. Returned and took the road to Darien. Arrived at Darien next afternoon at 7 o'clock—part went across the Altamaha—part camped out. On the 26th, paraded early and went to the boat landing, but stayed all day waiting for the boat, which did not come—it set in to raining, the evening was cold and we were invited to take shelter in the city hall. Being interrupted by a drunken soldier I ordered him to be taken to jail and it was done. We went to the Matron House for supper, say eight or ten of us—had to wait some time for it, and when we got to eating we could eat faster than they could cook until we cleaned the table and all they could fetch us. The price was fifty cents for the cold scraps. On the 27th, they went up the Altamaha and landed about 12 o'clock—found part of Capt. Matthews' Company—got a snack for breakfast and set out on their unknown march without anything for selves or horses. Went a few miles and came up with Capt. Matthews' Company with provisions for themselves and horses—they would not divide with us—went on about a mile and found a good old Virginian named Lyles, who gave them plenty for themselves and horses. On the 29th, they were at Jeffersonville where they found Col. Butler and the rest of the troops that were ahead of us. Struck camp. Some boys went to town, found lying in the street an old cannon—they got some powder and charged the piece quite heavy—took an old empty hogshead and laid before it and fired off the piece into the hogshead, which bursted all to pieces and wounded one of the boys on the foot. When they returned to camp Col. Goodwyn sent out for them to be sent for and to be kept in camp. And the same set were sent back for themselves, but returned without a prisoner as they were the offenders themselves.

March 1st, 1836.—Started about 10 o'clock—went through a cold rain to a station on the St. Mary's River—ordered to clean arms and put them in order for fighting, for we begin to get near the hostile land. Camped and drew rations for selves and horses to last to Jacksonville. The bread we drew was made of rye meal, and made in the year 1825, or stamped so, and was full of worms, and was thrown out by the boys. I do not think the boys were to be blamed for throwing it away, for bread eleven years old, made of rye meal and full of worms must have been rather so-so. So they went on through mud, rain and swamps, crossing rivers, but in spite of mud, accidents and bad bread they arrived at St. Augustine about 3 o'clock of the afternoon of March 8th—marched through the town and about two miles passed by a camp of South Carolina Militia Volunteers, and formed our camp in the worst thicket that ever was seen—had to clean a place to hitch our horses and to lay on ourselves. On the 11th, got permission to go to see the old fort at St. Augustine. Beautiful scenery—fort very strong and built with shell, &c. *Saturday, March 12th.*—Dress parade—many citizens out to see us on that occasion. *Sunday, 13th.*—No regard paid to the Sabbath. *Monday, 14th.*—Left camp near St. Augustine and on Tuesday night camped at Col. Hernandes' plantation, which had been destroyed by Indians and all waste and destruction. Found Capt. Denny, of Edgefield, with his company there. *Wednesday, the 16th.*—Passed three sugar mills that were burnt down and destroyed—last two miles nothing but mud and water—wagons mired down, men had to go in up to the waist to get them along—pitched tent at 12 o'clock at night—men so tired and sleepy they went to bed without supper. *Thursday, 17th.*—Started for Volusia, marched through mud and water from ankle to waist deep the most of the day, but late in the day came to a beautiful pine barren where we camped for the night. Here we came up with Col. Huiet with his command, who camped with us for the night. Reached Fort Volusia at 10 o'clock at night of the 18th, tired almost to death; appointed officer of the day and had command of the guard of mounted men, and slept none that night. Late in the evening of Sunday, March 20, one man came into camp and said he had seen an Indian. A detail of men was ordered out to see if his statement was true. When they returned they brought an opossum with them, but no Indian. Ordered to prepare for a scout on the next day; all ready.

Monday, 21st.—Started for Orange Grove by way of Spring Garden; about 12 o'clock in the day had a drive for Indians; Col. Brisbane's Battalion drove while the mounted men stood, but saw no Indians. We then passed through Col. Read's plantation and saw some of the finest land I ever saw. It seems that they got lost on the way to Orange Grove, the guides not knowing the way perfectly, and on Wednesday, March 23d, the men became so much displeased that they threatened to shoot the guides if they did not find the way; they became very shy; all at once, however, after passing through a hammock, they came in sight of Orange Grove; went into the houses and found plenty to eat for selves and horses, and Col. Butler gave orders to eat as much as they could and to feed the horses as much as they could eat; but they had not pots, pans nor kettles to cook in; soon got old hoes, pieces of saws, etc., and went to cooking and eating with all their might, and what was better than all, the Captain says, we found some whiskey. *March, 24th.*—Stayed at Orange Grove all day, cooking and preparing tomarch back again.

3   D

Friday, 25th.—Went back to the old camp at Spring Garden; R. Dugan and W. Allen both sick with the measles; saw some signs of Indians; rained all night and all got wet to the skin.

Saturday, March 26th.—Started in the rain; went on our way and met some of our hunting forces; some had been sent out the day before looking for us, and fell in with some Indians and had a scrimmage in which one of our men was wounded, but would have succeeded in killing all the Indians if Lieutenant Arnold, who was in command, had not called off the men and commanded them to return to the army. About 12 o'clock we got to Volusia, all wet and cold, where we found Colonel Goodwyn and all the mounted regiment, and all the rest of the left wing of the army. Heard of a battle that had taken place between our men and the Indians on the other side of the River St. Johns, when they commenced crossing, in which three of our men of Capt. Thrip's and Capt. Ashley's companies were killed and several wounded. Found one dead Indian that was said to be a chief by the name of Ochey Billy; suppose they killed several others from the signs. Army under orders to march, but we knew not where, as Gen. Eustus did not let that be known. Left seventeen of our men at the fort sick.

Forty-sixth day, Sunday, March 27.—Made ready for the march. Drawed four days' rations for ourselves and horses, and had to take that on horseback; did not get across the river until late that evening; marched about two miles and camped on bad ground; had to build a brush heap to lie on that night to keep out of the water. On Wednesday, the 30th, came to Oclawahha River about 12 o'clock; it was swimming. The river runs out of a lake of its own name, which was beautiful. Built a bridge for footmen and baggage wagons. Col. Butler's Battalion of mounted men were detached to scour the country for Indians and cattle; found thirteen head of cattle and came up with some Indians running to make their escape—Gen. Shelton with a party of men put after them and came within shooting distance, and Shelton fired on him with his double-barrel shotgun and the Indian fell to his knees. Shelton rushed up to him and snapped a pistol at his breast, and the Indian balanced his gun across his arm and shot Shelton in the hip, and the Indian was then shot down by a Mr. Gibson of Capt. Smith's Company of mounted men.

Thursday, March 31st.—Started with Col. Butler's Battalion in front; saw signs of Indians; found some ponies; front guard saw an Indian run into a hammock. Lieut. McVigh with a party of men were sent by Col. Goodwyn to see where he went; as soon as they got near enough they were fired on by the Indians; fire kept up for some time. Col. Butler's Command rushed in and kept up a brisk fire on them for a minute or two and then dismounted, rushed up on foot but could not get at them. By this time the whole command was up. Col. Brisbane's Battalion of footmen was commanded to follow them. They did so for about a mile and fired two rounds after them without effect. If there were any Indians killed we did not know it. There were five of the whites wounded—among the rest was N. Summer, my Orderly Sergeant; got his thigh broke. There was shot at Col. Butler about twelve or fifteen steps, but missed him and hit Jackson in the thigh; the Indian hit his breast and yelled. When the troops all got back to camp they took up the line of march again and camped about two miles from the battle ground.

On Friday, the 1st of April, the fifty-first day, started at 5 o'clock; came to an Indian town, fired it and caught some ponies and about one hundred head of cattle; pursued on a few miles and camped for the night, fired two guns for a sign but got no answer; sent an express to Gen. Scott; killed some calves and had some fresh beef to eat. I commanded the right wing guard that night and Col. Huiett was officer of the day; had the cowpen close to the guardhouse, the worst fuss with cattle I ever had in all my life.

Fifty-second day, Saturday, 2nd April.—Stayed in camp until 10 o'clock; fired two guns for a signal; but got no answer; marched one mile, halted and camped for the remainder of that day. One company was detailed to see if they could find the Tampa Bay road. They returned and said it was within two miles of us. The express that was sent off the evening before returned with the news from Fort Kane that Gen. Scott had left for the Withlacooche for some time, and had not been heard from. Now out of rations for our horses, and had not had any since we left Fort Volusia, but what we carried on our horses. Much dissatisfaction on account of it—the men murmuring.

Fifty-third day, Sunday, 3d April.—Started at 6 o'clock; struck the Tampa Bay road; did not travel far before, we came to the place of the Dade massacre. There were human bones lying about on the ground. Had to build a bridge over the Withlacooche. *Tuesday, April 5th*—Started at half past four in the morning; came to Fort Alabama on the Hillsborough River. Some volunteers there from Alabama. They told us that the Indians had attacked them a few days before and they had a severe fight. They were of opinion that they had killed fifteen or twenty of the Indians. There was but one of the whites killed and one wounded. They supposed there were 150 or 200 Indians, from all appearances,—and some negroes were seen with them in the fight. Before we left that place there came a friendly Indian with an express from Gen. Scott to Gen. Eustis. We went on eight miles further and camped. *Wednesday, 6th April.*—All the mounted men were ordered to Tampa Bay. The footmen, sick and wounded were left there in camp under Gen. Bull. This is the first command he has had since the army has been together. The mounted men went on with their poor horses, for they had been six days· without corn, or anything else but grass, and in looking over this you can see that there was not much chance for that. My company was ordered to the front guard. The order was to walk and lead. I pursued on. After awhile Gen. Eustis came along. Some of the men had mounted unbeknown to me, and were riding. He scolded and threatened to courtmartial them for it; and that displeased them very much with him. Col. Goodwyn came up after him, and he told them to mount and ride half the time. We reached Tampa Bay about 3 o'clock in the afternoon. Our horses had been starving so that they scarce would eat.

Captain Hargrove's diary thus abruptly ends with the arrival of his company at Tampa Bay. Elsewhere he gives a list of fifteen men who lost their horses in the United States service in Florida in 1836.

There was another company, an infantry company from Newberry, but that roll the Compiler has never seen. I suppose it may be found in the records of the War Office at Washington. It is not in the archives of the State in Columbia.

—

SOLDIERS OF THE CONFEDERACY.

George A. Lewie, of Lexington County, at present a citizen of Newberry, was Major of the 2nd Regiment of State Troops; called into service in September, 1863, for six months. This regiment was commanded by Col. Wm. Fort and was stationed at Pocotaligo, S. C.

F. M. Lindsay, our present Coroner, was a soldier of the Confederacy, and was a member of Co. I, 1st Regiment, from Charleston County, and lost an arm at the battle of Seven Pines.

Thomas J. Rook, of Co. F,—Capt. Kinard's Company—20th Regiment, was captured at Strasburg, October 19th, 1864. When surrounded by the enemy and resistance was hopeless, he raised his hatchet (which he used for culinary purposes and carried in his belt) and told the enemy if they did not stand back, "I will split your head open with my axe." His captor, speaking of it soon afterwards, enjoyed the joke hugely, and pointing to him and remarking on his white head, pronounced him the bravest man he had ever seen. Carried to Point Lookout.

William H. Sloan was a member of Co. F, 20th Regiment, Jno. M. Kinard, Captain; entered the service in the fall of 1861 and served through the war; wounded at the battle of Strasburg.

27TH S. C. INFANTRY.

I find the following volunteers from Newberry in the 27th Regiment, S. C. Infantry:

Co. B—John C. Hammett, age 30; killed at Secessionville. Andrew J. Sullivan, age 37.

Co. F—W. W. Long, age 23. James Thomas, age 16; transferred. D. R. Thomas, age 17; transferred.

Co. G—J. K. Blakely; captured at Petersburg, June 24, 1864, and prisoner of war.

LAST SAD TRIBUTE TO THE PRESIDENT OF THE SOUTHERN CONFEDERACY.

Jefferson Davis died in New Orleans on December 6th, 1889, and memorial meetings were held throughout the South on Wednesday, the 11th. The Newberry *Observer* of December 12th, 1889, published the following account of the meeting in Newberry:

The people of Newberry, as in every portion of the South, loved Jeff. Davis with a patriotic devotion. The announcement of his death, therefore, while not unexpected, caused a feeling of sadness in all hearts. It was felt that something should be done to testify the love and respect cherished for the dead chieftain; and accordingly a meeting was held on Monday to take the matter into consideration. Capt. R. H. Wright was elected Chairman and Dr. James McIntosh, Secretary. The following Committee on Arrangements was appointed: J. B. Fellers, J. N. Martin, Capt. J. W. Gary, D. B. Wheeler, W. T. Tarrant—and, on motion, the Chairman was added to the committee. The following were appointed a Committee on Resolutions: R. L. McCaughrin, J. B. Fellers and M. A. Carlisle.

The Committee of Arrangements decided that the city bell, in the Opera House tower, should be tolled from 11.30 to 12 M. on Wednesday, and at that at 12—the hour of Mr. Davis' funeral—the people of the city should assemble in the Opera House for exercises appropriate to the occasion.

The hall of the Opera House was elaborately draped for the occasion, under the direction of the following committee of ladies: Mrs. Fannie N. Baxter, chairman; Mrs. N. B. Mazyck, Mrs. Jas. A. Burton, Mrs. O. McR. Holmes, Mrs. Y. J. Pope, Mrs. O. L. Schumpert and Mrs. J. N. Martin.

The big bell in the tower was tolled from 11.30 to 12. At 12, a large congregation, filling the spacious hall and stage, had assembled. The Confederate veterans marched in under command of Capt. J. W. Gary. Mayor Cromer, in language beautiful and thrilling, stated the object of the meeting, and then called the meeting to order. On motion of Capt. Wright, Dr. James McIntosh was called to the Chair and Mr. C. F. Boyd was requested to act as Secretary. The exercises were then opened with prayer by Rev. G. W. Holland, D. D., after which followed addresses by J. F. J. Caldwell, Esq., Rev. E. P. McClintock and Rev. J. S. Cozby, D. D. Judge J. B. Fellers then read the following resolutions, in behalf of the Survivors' Association of Newberry County. They were seconded by Jas. Y. Culbreath, Esq., in a few words and were unanimously adopted:

"The Confederate Survivors' Association of Newberry County, South Carolina, deploring and lamenting the demise of their beloved and illustrious Chieftain, the Hon. Jefferson Davis, ex-President of the Confederate States, do in assembly resolve

"First. That death has removed from time to eternity, and from the presence of those who esteem and love him, one of the most notably conspicuous heroes that has ever adorned the annals of American history, and we deeply and sadly join in the universal grief which has stricken the Southern heart.

"Second. That from which he added to the Southern Confederacy; the lustre which adorned his name; the valor which crowned his arms; the splendor with which his intellect shone in the councils of the nation; the statesmanship which he at all times displayed; the unselfish devotion which always characterized his life; the patience and forbearance with which he bore defeat; the Christian virtues he exhibited in passing through the fiery ordeals of life, and his unswerving fidelity to the great principles which he advocated, challenge as well our unbounded admiration as that of the civilized world; and they are a sweet heritage which we cherish and hold dear, and the memory of which shall never fade from our hearts, but shall be always treasured by us as jewels in his glorious but now ended earthly career.

"Third. That it is the unanimous desire that an engrossed copy of these resolutions be transmitted by the Secretary of this Association to the widow of the illustrious dead, as a small token of our sincere sympathy and profound grief in this her great loss."

The benediction was pronounced by Rev. W. S. Wightman.

The stores and public buildings in Newberry were nearly all heavily draped in mourning, and were closed from 11.30 A. M. to 2 P. M.

OFFICERS OF NEWBERRY COUNTY.

LEGISLATIVE, JUDICIAL AND EXECUTIVE.

1785–1892.

MEMBERS OF CONGRESS.

1802—Levi Casey.   1830-38—John K. Griffin.   1840-42—P. C. Caldwell.
1890-92—George Johnstone.

STATE JUDICIARY.

Chief Justice:	*Associate Justice:*
1850-63—John Belton O'Neall.	1891— Y. J. Pope.*
Chancellor:	*District Judge:*
1828-50—John Belton O'Neall.	1865-68—Y. J. Pope.
1831-62—Job Johnstone.	*Solicitor:*
1846-50—James J. Caldwell.	1836-46—James J. Caldwell.
Judge Seventh Circuit:	1846-68—Simeon Fair.
1871-76—Montgomery Moses.	1888-92—O. L. Schumpert.†
*Unexpired term of Henry McIver.	†Re-elected in 1892 for second term.

STATE OFFICERS.

Lieutenant-Governor:	*Adjutant-General:*
1808-10—Frederick Nance.	1862-64—A. C. Garlington.
Secretary of State:	*Superintendent of Penitentiary:*
1882-86—Jas. N. Lipscomb.	1877-90—Thos. J. Lipscomb.
Attorney-General:	*Regent of Lunatic Asylum:*
1890-91—Y. J. Pope.*	1883-89—John C. Wilson.†
Railroad Commissioner:	
1892— J. A. Sligh.	
*Resigned.	†Resigned 1892 at reorganization of Board.

STATE SENATE.

1788		1832	Francis B. Higgins.	1876	H. C. Corwin.
1792		1836	Francis B. Higgins.	1877	Jas. N. Lipscomb.‡
1796	John Hampton.	1840	Francis B. Higgins.	1880	Thos. C. Brown.
1800	Levi Casey.	1844	John P. Neel.	1884	J. A. Sligh.
1803	Wm Caldwell.*	1848	P. C. Caldwell.	1888	Y. J. Pope.
1804	John Hampton.	1852	Robert Moorman.	1890	Joseph L. Keitt.‖
1808	John McMorries.	1855	John P. Kinard.†	1892	J. A. Sligh.§
1812	Frederick Nance.	1856	A. C. Gárlington.		*Clerk:*
1816	Frederick Nance.	1860	A. C. Garlington.	1890	Sampson Pope.
1820	John K. Griffin.	1864	J. H. Williams.	1892	Sampson Pope.
1824	John K. Griffin.	1868	C. W. Montgomery		*Seargeant at Arms*
1828	John K. Griffin.	1872	H. C. Corwin.	1888	J. D. Smith.

*Unexpired term of Levi Casey, elected member of Congress.
†Unexpired term of Robert Moorman, resigned.
‡Unexpired term of H. C. Corwin, resigned, whose seat was contested.
‖Unexpired term of Y. J. Pope, elected Attorney-General.
§Elected Railroad Commissioner, December 22, 1892, and resigned.

HOUSE OF REPRESENTATIVES.

1788		1792	Jacob R. Brown.	1796	William Dunlap.
			Levi Casey.		Lewis Saxon.
			Philemon Waters.		John Simpson.
1790	Mercer Babb.	1794	John Davis.	1798	Jacob R. Brown.
	James Mayson.		William Hunter.		Levi Casey.
	George Ruff.		James Saxon.		Jno. Adam Summer.

HOUSE OF REPRESENTATIVES.—*Continued*.

1800	Jacob R. Brown.	1828	Thomas Bauskett.	1860	Jas. N. Lipscomb.
	William Calmes.		John Caldwell.		C. H. Suber.
	George Herbert.		James Graham.		J. H. Williams.
1802			Walter Herbert.	1862	J. H. Williams.
		1830	John Caldwell.		Robt. Stewart.
			James J. Caldwell.		C. H. Suber.
1804	William Calmes.		John Graham.	1864	A. C. Garlington.
	Frederick Gray.		B. F. Griffin.		Ellison S. Keitt.
	George Herbert.	1832	James J. Caldwell.		C. H. Suber.
1806	Jacob Beiler.		Walter Herbert.	1866	A. C. Garlington.
	Samuel E. Kenner.		S. L. Heller.		Ellison S. Keitt.
	James McKibben.				C. H. Suber.
1808	James Dyson.	1834	Hugh K. Boyd.	1868	Joseph D. Boston.
	Samuel E. Kenner.		James J. Caldwell.		Jas. A. Henderson.
	James McKibben.		Walter Herbert.		James Hutson.
1810	Samuel Cannon.			1870	Joseph D. Boston.
	James Dyson.	1836	James J. Caldwell.		Jas. A. Henderson.
	Charles Griffin.		P. C. Caldwell.		James Hutson.
	James Williams.		James H. Maffett.	1872	Joseph D. Boston.
1812	John Caldwell.		John P. Neel.		S. S. Bridges.
	John Henderson.	1838	P. C. Caldwell.		Jno. T. Henderson.
	Samuel E. Kenner.		James H. Maffett.	1874	Joseph D. Boston.
	A. Crenshaw.		John P. Neel.		S. S. Bridges.
1814			John H. Williams.		Isom Greenwood.
		1840	Simeon Fair.	1876	S. S. Bridges.
			C. B. Griffin.		Thos. Keitt.
			Thos. H. Pope.		W. H. Thomas.
1816	Samuel Cannon.	1842	James Graham.	1877	S. S. Bridges.†
	George W. Glenn.		C. B. Griffin.		Y. J. Pope.‡
	John K. Griffin.		J. H. King.		George Johnstone‖
	John B. O'Neall.	1844	Simeon Fair.	1878	W. M. Dorroh.
1818	Samuel Cannon.		Isaac Herbert.		George Johnstone.
	John K. Griffin.		J. H. King.		C. H. Suber.
	Walter Herbert.	1846	Matthew Hall.	1880	George Johnstone.
	George McCreleys.		Henry Summer.		J. A. Sligh.
1820	John Counts.		Benjamin Waldo.		John C. Wilson.
	Abram Dyson.	1848	Robert Moorman.	1882	W. D. Hardy.
	Reuben Flanagan.		R. Pitts.		George Johnstone.
	Benjamin Maybin.		Henry Summer.		J. A. Sligh.
1822		1850	A. C. Garlington.	1884	W. D. Hardy.
	John Bauskett.		John P. Kinard.		Sampson Pope.
	Reuben Flanagan.		Robert Moorman.		O. L. Schumpert.
	John B. O'Neall.	1852	J. M. Crosson.	1886	E. P. Chalmers.
			A. C. Garlington.		Joseph L. Keitt.
1824	John G. Brown.		Reuben G. Pitts.		Sampson Pope.
	John Caldwell.	1854	J. M. Crosson.	1888	R. T. C. Hunter.
	Benjamin Maybin.		W. H. Harrington.		J. M. Johnstone.
	John B. O'Neall.*		Lambert J. Jones.		Geo. S. Mower.
1826	Robert Dunlap.	1856	G. G. DeWalt.	1890	Cole. L. Blease.
	George W. Glenn.		Lambert J. Jones.		W. D Hardy.
	Peter Moon.		T. B. Rutherford.		John W. Scott.
	John B. O'Neall.*	1858	Lambert J. Jones.	1892	Cole. L. Blease.
			C. H. Suber.		John T. Duncan.
			J. H. Williams.		W. D. Hardy.

* Speaker of the House·
†63d member sworn in the "Wallace House," making a quorum.
‡Elected July 26, 1877; seat of W. H. Thomas having been declared vacant.
‖Elected January 9, 1878; seat of Thos. Keitt—convicted of bigamy.
1868-76—Negro domination and carpetbaggers' misrule.

CLERK OF COURT.

1785	William Malone.	1859	Burr J.Ramage.	1876	Thos. J. Clayton.‖
1794	Frederick Nance.	1863	Burr J. Ramage.‡	1877	E. P. Chalmers.
1807	Y. J. Harrington.*	1866	E. P. Lake.	1880	E. P. Chalmers.
1850	John S. Carwile.	1868	Thos. M. Lake.	1884	Jas. Y. McFall.₴
1851	Burr J. Ramage.†	1872	Jesse C. Smith.	1888	Jno. M. Kinard.
1855	Burr J. Ramage.	1875	H. C. Moses.	1892	Jno. M. Kinard.

*Appointed by the Legislature; predecessors by County Court Judges; died in office.
†First election by the people. ‡Resigned February, '66. ‖Failed to give bond.
₴Died in 1877; Jno. M, Kinard appointed for unexpired term.

SHERIFF.

1785	Thomas Gordon.	1819	William Gilliam.	1859	N. F. Johnston.
1787	Robert Gillam.	1823	Samuel Cannon.	1863	Jas. M. Maffett.*
1889	Richard Speake.	1827	John S. Carwile.	1863	Wm. W. Houseal.
1791	Richard Watts.	1831	Robert R. Nance.	1867	Thos. M. Paysinger
1795	Wm. Satterwhite.	1835	Reuben Pitts.	1872	J. J. Carrington.
1799	PhilemonB.Waters	1839	H. H. Kinard.	1877	D. B. Wheeler.†
1803	Benj. Long.	1843	John P. Kinard.	1880	D. B. Wheeler.
1807	James Caldwell.	1847	H. H. Kinard.	1884	W. W. Riser.
1811	Thos. T. Cureton.	1851	James Bonds.	1888	W. W. Riser.
1815	William Caldwell.	1855	Wm. W. Houseal.	1892	W. W. Riser.

*Elected while in the army and died before reaching home. W. W. Houseal elected.
†Contested election (1876) of J. J. Carrington, ousted by decree of court.

ORDINARY.

1800	Samuel Lindsey.	1841	Hugh K. Boyd.*	1853	E. P. Lake.
1815	Jas. Fernandis.	1845	Hugh K. Boyd.	1857	E. P. Lake.
1818	Thos. T. Cureton.	1849	Hugh K. Boyd.	1859	E. P. Lake.
1829	William Wilson.	1851	E. P. Lake.†	1863	John T. Peterson.

*First election by the people. The duties of County Ordinary were discharged by
the County Courts, 1785-1800, when elections for life or during good behavior were made
by the Legislature. †Unexpired term of Hugh K. Boyd, died while in office.

JUDGE OF PROBATE.

1868	Jno. T. Peterson.	1876	J. C. Leahy.	1884	J. B. Fellers.
1870	J. C. Leahy.	1878	Jo. J. B. Fellers.	1886	J. B. Fellers.
1872	J. C. Leahy.	1880	J. B. Fellers.	1888	J. B. Fellers.
1874	J. C. Leahy.	1882	J. B. Fellers.	1890	J. B. Fellers.

COMMISSIONER IN EQUITY.

1818	Francis B. Higgins.	1834	Drayton Nance.	1852	James H. Williams.
1822	Francis B. Higgins.	1838	Thos. H. Pope.*	1856	Silas Johnstone.
1826	Drayton Nance.	1840	Lambert J. Jones.	1860	Silas Johnstone.
1830	Drayton Nance.	1844	Lambert J. Jones.	1864	Silas Johnstone.†

*Resigned second year of term. †Office abolished 1868.

MASTER.

1878–Silas Johnstone.	1882–Silas Johnstone.	1886–Silas Johnstone.
	1890–Silas Johnstone.	

TAX COLLECTOR.

——	Chas. Crenshaw.	1824	Robert R. Nance.	1848	Jacob Kibler.
1812	Ker Boyce.*	1832	Alex. Chambers.	1852	John T. Peterson.
1815	John S. Carwile.*	1836	Hugh K. Boyd.	1856	M. M. Boyd.
1820	Jas. W. Tinsley.	1840	Hugh K. Boyd.	1860	John R. Leavell.
1824	Jas. W. Tinsley.*	1844	James Bonds.	1864	J. B. Fellers.

*Resigned;—J. W. T. at beginning of his second term.

TREASURER.

1868	Jos. M. Ward.	1877	U. B. Whites.*	1884	A. H. Wheeler.
1869	T. P. Slider.	1878	U. B. Whites.	1886	A. H. Wheeler.
1872	D. R. Phifer.	1880	U. B. Whites.	1888	A. H. Wheeler.
1874	D. R. Phifer.	1882	A. H. Wheeler.†	1890	C. F. Boyd.
1876	Jesse C. Smith.	1882	M. H. Gary.	1892	C. F. Boyd.

*Appointment of Hampton Government. †Unexpired term of U. B. Whites.

AUDITOR.

1868	S. Montgomery.	1878	L. E. Folk.†	1886	Wm. W. Houseal.
1870	H. C. Corwin.	1880	Jas. N. Lipscomb.‡	1888	Wm. W. Houseal.
1872	Jas. W. Haywood.	1880	John K. Nance.	1889	W. C. Cromer.‡
1874	R. E. Williams.	1882	John K. Nance.†	1890	W. C. Cromer.
1876	R. E. Williams.	1884	Wm. W. Houseal.‡	1890	W. C. Cromer.
1877	L. E. Folk.*	1884	Wm. W. Houseal.	1892	W. C. Cromer.

*Appointment of Hampton Government. †Died while in office. ‡Unexpired term.

SCHOOL COMMISSIONER.

1868	Wm. Summer.	1878	J. C. Boyd.	1888	Arthur Kibler.
1870	Jesse C. Smith.	1880	H. S. Boozer.	1890	Arthur Kibler.
1872	M. S. Long.	1882	J. C. Boyd.	1892	Thos. W. Keitt.
1874	H. B. Scott.	1884	G. G. Sale.		
1876	M. S. Long.	1886	G. G. Sale.		

CORONER.

1842	John S. Carwile.	1866	H. H. Kinard.	1878	E. C. Longshore.
1846	N. Sligh.	1871	Wm. Summer.	1884	John N. Bass.
1848	Wm. W. Houseal.	1870	M. S. Long.	1888	C. B. Buist.*
1855	Wm. B. D'Oyley.	1872	Jas. A. Henderson.	1892	John W. Reagin.†
1857	Henry Halfacre.	1874	Jas. Eichelberger.	1892	F. M. Lindsay.

*Died while in office. †Unexpired term, appointed.

JURY COMMISSIONER.

1870	W. G. Mayes.	1877	J. S. Hair.	1886	John R. Leavell.
1872	Simeon Young.	1878	J. S. Hair.	1888	John R. Leavell.
1874	A. L. Snead.	1880	J. S. Hair.	1890	J. N. Feagle.
1876	A. L. Snead.	1882	J. S. Hair.	1892	J. N. Feagle.
1877	Jos. M. Ward.	1884	John R. Leavell.		

COUNTY COMMISSIONERS.

1868		1877	Henry Kennedy.	1868	S. B. Aull.
			L. B. Maffett.		John J. Kinard.
			Simeon Young.		P. B. Workman.
1870	A. Gregory.	1878	Wm. Lester.	1888	J. C. Perry.
	David Hailstock.*		A. J. Livingston.		J. H. Smith.
	Simeon Young.*		J. C. Swittenberg.		Silas Walker.†
1872	Thos. Keitt.	1880	J. C. S. Brown.	1889	Osborne Wells.‡
	Dennis Moates.		A. J. Kilgore.	1890	John J. Kinard.
	Allen Rice.		Wm. Lester.		J. H. Smith.
1874	Henry Kennedy.	1882	Jacob Epting.		Jno. W. Smith.
	Simeon Young.		A. J. Livingston.	1892	Geo. B. Aull.
	Wesley Brown.		J. D. Smith.		J. C. Dominick.
1876	Henry Kennedy.	1884	John A. Cromer.		Irby D. Shockley.
	Simeon Young.		A. J. Livingstone.		
	Wesley Brown.		E. C. Longshore.		

*Convicted of official misconduct, June, 1871; Wm. Lester and J. N. Martin elected on August 8, 1871, but Gov. Scott refused to issue their commissions, and he afterwards appointed W. P. Harris, Dennis Moates and D. R. Phifer for unexpired term.
†Resigned. ‡Unexpired term.

MAGISTRATES.

1841	A. Summer.	1858	Jos. S. Reid.	1868	I. McC. M. Calmes
	W. M. Armstrong.		Wm. F. Nance.		Wm. Summer.
1842	F. C. Ruff.		J. Elvin Knotts.	1869	C. C. Chase.
1843	F. C. Ruff.	1860	Sampson Pope.		G. M. Girardeau.
1847	A. P. Brolley.		Sam'l R. Chapman		L. B. Maffett.
1851	V. B. Pope.		C. W. Herbert.		J. P. Kinard.
1852	Jno. C. Stewart.		Sam'l Bowers.		Josiah Stewart.
1857	Wm. K. Blake.	1868	Jas. E. Peterson.		A. M. Riser.
	Robt. Garlington.		H. H. Kinard,		M. S. Long.
					Sam'l Dogan.

TRIAL JUSTICE.

1870	Matthew Gray.*	1879	Jno. L. Epps.	1885	Jas. H. Irby.
	Jesse C. Smith.*		Jas. Packer.		Jno. B. Campbell.
	M. S. Long.†		B. S. Golding.		W. W. Wallace.
	Sam'l Dogan.		M. A. Carlisle.		Chas. P. Dickert.
	Wm. Summer.		Jno. T. Bynum.		Jos. S. Reid.
	A. M. Riser.*	1880	Jas. R. Irwin.		J. L. Epps.
	J. T. Henderson.*		Jno. S. Fair.		B. B. Hair.
	L. B. Maffett.		M. A. Carlisle.		Jno. S. Fair.
	J. B. Heller.	1881	A. H. Wheeler.‡		C. P. Dickert.
1871	J. T. Peterson.‡		Jas. Packer.	1886	Jas. H. Irby.
	J. D. Pitts.		Jas. R. Irwin.‡		Jos. L. Keitt.‡
	F. H. Whitney.		M. M. Buford.	1887	H. H. Blease.‡
	Sam'l Furman.‡		M. J. Boyd.		W. G. Peterson.
	Jesse C. Smith.‡		B. H. Maybin.		Jno. B. Campbell.
	A. R. Gantt.		J. B. Heller.		Chas. P. Dickert.
	Wm. Summer.		J. L. Epps.		H. S. Boozer.‡
	G. P. Jacoby.		W. G. Peterson.	1888	B. B. Hair.
1872	Simeon Young.		Jas. N. Lipscomb.‡		Harry H. Blease.
1873	C. C. Chase.		Jno. B. Campbell.		W. G. Peterson.
	F. C. Aldridge.	1882	J.B.O'N.Holloway.		Jno. B. Campbell.
	Wm. H. Thomas.		J. B. Heller.		Chas. P. Dickert.
1874	A. R. Gantt.		P. E. Wise.	1889	G. M. Girardeau.
	G. P. Jacoby.		W. W. Wallace.		B. B. Hair.
	M. L. Louis.	1883	Jas. Packer. ‡		Geo. P. Hill.‡
	R. W. Boone.		Jno. S. Fair.		J. W. D. Johnson.
	W. H. Thomas.		W. G. Peterson.		Jas. H. Irby.
1875	D. R. Phifer.		M. M. Buford.		W. G. Peterson.
	Thos. P. Slider.		J.B.O'N.Holloway.		Chas. P. Dickert.
	Jas. F. Kilgore.		J. B. Heller.	1891	P. E. Wise.
	F. C. Aldridge.		W. W. Wallace.		R. C. Maybin.
	J. B. Heller.		Jno. B. Campbell.		W. G. Peterson.
1876	Dennis Moates.		J. L. Epps.		N. W. Gregory.
	J. F. Sims.		Jos. S. Reid.		Wm. C. Sligh.
1877	D. M. Ward.		B. H. Maybin.‡		J. B. Heller.
	Jones Lowman.		R. S. Davidson.		Jas. S. McCarley.
	Jas. Packer.		A. H. Wheeler.	1893	H. H. Evans.
	M. A. Carlisle.		Chas. P. Dickert.		S. L. Fellers.
	Jno. T. Bynum.		H. H. Blease.		Jas. S. McCarley.
	Jno. W. Riser.	1884	Jas. H. Irby.		J. W. D. Johnson.
	Jas. N. Lipscomb.	1885	H. H. Blease.		W. G. Peterson.
	Jacob B. Fellers.		T. L. Schumpert.‡		M. J. Longshore.
	Thos. W. Holloway		R. S. Davidson. ‡		L. W. Etheridge.
1878	A. H. Wheeler.		J.B.O'N.Holloway.		G. M. Singley.
1879	M. M. Buford.		W. G. Peterson.		J. B. Heller.

SUPERVISOR OF REGISTRATION.

1882	Wm. Y. Fair.	1886	A. H. Kohn.	1890	D. M. Langford.‡
1884	Wm. Y. Fair.	1888	A. H. Kohn.	1892	B. B. Schumpert.‖

*Not confirmed. †Removed. ‡Resigned.   ‖Also unexpired term, 1891.

POPULATION OF NEWBERRY COUNTY.

Townships.	1880	1890	Increase.	Decrease.
Newberry (including the town)	4482	4881	399	. .
Caldwell.	1556	1635	78	. .
Maybinton	1504	1181	. .	323
Cromers	2681	2223	. .	458
Reeders	2244	2120	. .	124
Floyds	2830	2639	. .	191
Moons.	2102	2265	163	. .
Mendenhall	2230	2123	. .	107
Stoney Battery.	2628	3526	898	. .
Cannons.	1840	1658	. .	182
Hellers	2400	2195	. .	205
Totals	26497	26446		51

	1880.	1890.
Population of Town of Newberry	2342	3034
Population of Town of Prosperity.	357	*582

These figures show that a large number of people are moving to towns—the population of the County, outside of the towns, having fallen off nearly one thousand, and the towns having increased in the same ratio during 1880-90.   *Estimated.

THE COLUMBIA, NEW BERRY AND LAURENS RAILROAD.

When Judge O'Neall wrote his Annals the Columbia and Greenville Railroad was just about completed. That, with the branch to Laurens, was the only railroad Newberry had for nearly forty years.

In 1884 there was talk of a narrow guage being built from Augusta to Newberry, and No. 1 Township voted $40,000 and No. 8 Township $10,000 in bonds to this enterprise. The road was graded, and then it was turned over to the Charleston, Cincinnati and Chicago Railroad, and was to be extended to Blacksburg, where it touches the main line of this system.

Nothing has been done on this enterprise for the past two or three years, but it is only a matter of time when this road will be completed.

Another system which the town has missed and ought to have secured is the Georgia, Carolina and Northern. It passes through the northern edge of the county and strikes Clinton. Newberry should have secured this system; but it is gone now.

The building of the Columbia, Newberry and Laurens Railroad was first agitated by Mr. H. C. Moseley and Rev. J. A. Sligh, of Prosperity, and Messrs. G. S Mower and M. A. Carlisle, of Newberry, in the spring and summer of 1885. This railroad was incorporated by Act of the Legislature in 1885, and the Act was amended at the session of 1886. The corporators from Newberry were: J. A. Sligh, H. C. Moseley, G. G. DeWalt, L. S. Bowers, J. M. Wheeler, R. L. Luther, A. G. Wise, G. S. Mower, J. P. Pool, Y. J. Pope, O. B. Mayer, Jr., M. A. Carlisle, Wm. Langford, O. L. Schumpert and Geo. S. Cannon.

A meeting of the corporators was held on 14th January, 1886, and appointed a sub-committee to procure $20,000 in private subscriptions.

In the spring of 1886 the first meeting of the stockholders was held at Newberry to see what had been done in the way of securing subscriptions. The $20,000 had to subscribed be before an organization could be effected, and Mr. J. O. Meredith was appointed solicitor to raise this amount in Newberry, Lexington Fork and Columbia.

After that a meeting was held in Columbia and an organization effected as follows: H. C. Moseley, President; R. S. Desportes, Vice-President; C. J. Iredell, Secretary and Treasurer; M. A. Carlisle, Attorney. The other Directors elected were: G. S. Mower, A. G. Wise, J. A. Sligh, M. Chapin, G. R. Shealy, G. Leaphart, W. B. Lowrance, T. T. Moore. After that, township subscriptions were secured as follows:

In Newberry, No. 9 gave first $15,000; No. 1, $10,000. In Lexington, Saluda, $10,500; Broad River, $15,000; Fork, $14,500; and Columbia, $40,000. Rev. J. A. Sligh and H. C. Moseley, M. A. Carlisle and Geo. S. Mower were largely instrumental in securing the township subscriptions.

Some persons who opposed the township subscriptions carried the matter into the Courts, and the Supreme Court decided they were unconstitutional. This gave the enterprise a black eye, but the Legislature passed a validating Act and the bonds were placed.

Through the influence of the promoters of the scheme a Construction Company was organized in May, 1889, and took the contract to build the road to Newberry.

Mr. H. C. Moseley resigned as President in October, 1889. He had served in that capacity from the beginning of the enterprise three years before, and by the signal ability and skill with which he discharged the difficult work of his position, demonstrated the wisdom and discrimination of those who had placed him at the head of the enterprise. The grading was nearly completed to Newberry; the rock piers for the bridge at Columbia had been built, and the rails were on the ground. He gave up the presidency because of the urgent demands of his private business upon his time. The stockholders at their meeting on October 1st, 1889, adopted unanimously the following resolution offered by Dr. James Woodrow:

Whereas, our former President, Capt. H. C. Moseley, having declined re-election on account of the increased labors now required of that office and the demands of his private business upon him; and, whereas, the zeal and fidelity displayed by him in his efforts, on behalf of the enterprise now about to be achieved, have been of the highest order, and it is in a great measure due to them that the Columbia, Newberry and Laurens Railroad is now a thing of the near future, be it

Resolved, That we, the stockholders, extend to him our heartfelt thanks for his services so energetically and unselfishly rendered, and hope that his labors in the future may always be, as they have been in the past, crowned with an abundant measure of success.

Mr. Moseley was complimented by the directors by being unanimously elected Vice-President, which position he still holds.

Mr. W. G. Childs, a successful financier and business man of Columbia, was elected his successor, and is still President of the road.

Capt. C. J. Iredell, as Secretary and Treasurer, was active and rendered valuable assistance in the building of the road.

The road was completed to Newberry 1st July, 1890, and opened for business 15th July, 1890. It was then built to Clinton, and completed to that point May, 1891. Mr. C. J. Ellis was the Civil Engineer of the road until it was completed. The first year it was operated by the South Carolina Road, but in June, 1892, a deal was made with the Atlantic Coast Line, and now it is operated in connection with that road and the Sea Board Air Line. Capt. C. O. Little is the Superintendent, and the road is doing a good business; and it is increasing, thereby demonstrating the wisdom of its friends in projecting the enterprise. It is the connecting link between two great systems.

The first train on this road was in charge of Capt. P. C. Gaillard, who has identified himself more fully with Newberry by securing a life partner from among her daughters—Miss Eoline Merchant.

The telegraph line on the Columbia and Greenville Railroad was completed to Newberry on Wednesday, July 5th, 1871. The first dispatch was a congratulatory message sent by President Bush to Thos. M. Paysinger, then Sheriff of the County. Before the war there was, however, a line run several miles towards Columbia from one of the newspaper offices, with the intention of its completion and the publication of a daily newspaper, which was never accomplished.

BIOGRAPHICAL.

NANCE.

Of the descendants of Major Frederick Nance, who was the first settler at the County Seat of Newberry County, there are many of whom this writer has never heard and knows nothing. Besides those living in recent times—Maj. W. F. Nance, Col. J. D. Nance, Capt. J. K. G. Nance, and others, whoss names appear in the body of this work—I feel that I must mention Col. F. W. R. Nance, now Sheriff of Abbeville County.

Capt. J. K. G. Nance, at the time of his death, in December, 1884, was Auditor of the County of Newberry, and was at the time the only one in the county bearing the name who was the head of a family. He left several sons, two of whom are now happily married, one to Miss Sease, daughter of G. L. Sease, and the other to Miss Sease, cousin to the former and daughter of J. L. Sease.

SIMEON PRATT.

Simeon Pratt was one of the writers of Newberry. He never wrote and published a book, but his contribntions to the papers, especially for a few years after the war, would have made a volume of respectable size. His sketches of the war and of his personal experiences during that time were of considerable interest. He called himself the "Queer Recruit," a name that was given to him by some of his comrades soon after he joined the army. Simeon Pratt was never engaged in business here, nor was he ever married. He died in Mississippi in 1890. He was a member of the Baptist Church, and was an amiable and pleasant gentleman. His father was Thomas Pratt, who, for many years in old days, was an active, energetic and useful merchant of this town. The house in which he lived and died, and which, I believe, he built, still stands at the corner of Friend and Nance Streets, facing neither street, but towards the corner.

CROSSON.

The Crossons were among the earlier settlers of Newberry. Before the Revolutionary War they came from the North of Ireland and settled in the Shenandoah Valley in Virginia. Branches of the family are to be found in Illinois, Arkansas, Texas and South Carolina.·

Thomas Crosson moved to Newberry, prior to the Revolution, with his two sons, Alexander and John, and some daughters. Thomas was the son of Alexander. John Crosson was a lad during the Revolutionary War. He settled near Jalapa upon what was known as the Beasley road. He died about 1829, leaving one child, David. They were both Covenanters and were buried in the old Covenanter graveyard. After the Reformed (Covenanter) and Associate Presbyterians united and formed the Associate Reformed Presbyterian Church, David became a member of that Church, as did his warm friend James Sloan (Long Jimmie), and together they with others were instrumental in building the Head Spring Church. In 1821 David married Isabella Spence. Some one told his mother he was going to marry a Scotch lass that could not speak English. "Well," the old lady replied, "it is Davy that marries—not me." She was the daughter of James Spence and H. Murray, and the niece of Samuel Spence (spoken of in O'Neall's Annals), and whose remark to his grand nephew is worth remembering: "Jamie, there's no harm in a joog if you don't take the stapper out too aften." Isabella was well educated, having graduated in a Moravian school at Ballymena, Ireland. Her parents came from Scotland to Newberry in 1820. David after his first marriage lived about a mile from Jalapa and at the time of his death in the town of Newberry. He was a man of strong religious convictions, kind and generous, a friend to the poor, and was by them much lamented. He believed that slavery was a sin, and hence set his negroes free.

Out of his five children, John Wylie and Eliza sleep in the Covenanter

Churchyard. Sarah married S. S. Gaillard, a Presbyterian minister, now dead. She, with her sister Mary, lives in Griffin, Ga.

Jas. M. is a lawyer and lives in Runnels County, Texas. He represented Newberry twice in the Legislature and was probably the first to introduce a bill to create an agricultural professorship. The bill failed. He was Colonel of 10th Regiment, Cavalry. In 1848 he married Helen Maria James, daughter of Jno. Stobo James and Elizabeth Pope, at the house of her uncle-in-law, Judge O'Neall. She is the sister of Capt. Geo. S. James, who fired the first gun on Fort Sumter, and a descendant of Archibald Stobo, the first Presbyterian preacher in Charleston. James M. went to Texas in 1857. He has filled the office of Judge and District Attorney, and has had a very extensive legal practive there. Although opposed to the policy of Secession, he entered the Confederate Army in 1861 and was Major of the 4th Texas Cavalry. He has four daughters, who have all married energetic, successful business men who are Christian gentlemen. His son Thomas T., born in Newberry, is District Attorney,—a fine lawyer and forcible and eloqnent speaker.

Samuel J. Red was an early settler of Newberry, and probably came from Abbeville. At the time of his death, about 1836, he lived on Bush River, at what is now known as Piester's Mill. He and his wife were Covenanters and set their negroes free. He was a good man. He left a son, Dr. Geo. W., and several daughters, one of whom married Thomas Henderson of Abbeville. They all moved to Texas. Dr. Geo. W. is dead, leaving three children—one a Presbyterian preacher, one a very promising young physician in Houston, and the daughter, Lil Purcell, is at the head of the Stuart Female Institute in Austin—one of *the* schools in Texas. All of S. J. Red's daughters are dead. Mrs. Henderson left three sons—John, who lost an arm in Virginia, is Judge; Thomas is a member of the Legislature, and Sam'l J. a prosperous financier. The danghter, Mrs. Alice Fowler is a remarkably intelligent woman.

STILES HURD

Was born in Brookfield, Conn., 17th April, 1814. He came to Newberry in 1842 and engaged in business, it is believed, with his brother-in-law, David Jennings. who was a member of the firm of Jennings, Tomlinson & Co., of Charleston, and of Condict, Jennings & Co. of New York, wholesale and retail dealers in saddlery and harness. In the latter part of the year 1843 Mr. Hurd, having been encouraged by his success in business, brought his family, then consisting of his wife and three daughters, to Newberry, and made this town his permanent home until 1866, when he removed to Stratford, Conn., where he died 13th December, 1891.

The Bridgeport (Connecticut) journals, on the morning after his death, paid a just tribute to his memory. There was a remarkable unanimity in their estimate of his genuine worth. He was pronounced by these journalists as a man of sterling integrity, upright and honorable in all his dealings, kind and charitable to all men, and possessed of a gentleness of disposition that won for him the esteem and love of all who knew him. This is entirely true, bnt it is bare justice. In one of these notices —that of the Bridgeport *Standard*—there was an error, however, which should be corrected. After a very kind tribute, the editor makes this statement: "At the breaking out of the rebellion he came North with his family and engaged in business in Bridgeport, his family residing in Stratford. About fifteen years ago he retired from business, and has since lived very quietly at his home. His property at the South had been confiscated, but was restored to him after the close of the war."

Mr. Hurd was thoroughly American—loved the whole country. Attached to the place of his birth, he also loved the home of his adoption, and was a thorough South Carolinian by choice. He was a Statesright Democrat. Living amongst us, he soon saw that slaveholders were not the cruel task-masters that fanatics represented them, and that the so-called downtrodden negro slaves were a happy people, and he became a slaveholder himself. He was attached to the political principles of the State, and was always on the side of the right and the good. Unassuming, he was never a partisan, but was unflinching in what he thought his duty. He was a Secessionist, that is, he believed that a State had a right to secede, but possibly that the exercise of that right might be inexpedient. He did not regard the war between the States as a rebellion, for he could not be convinced that it was possible that one sovereign could rebel against another; but, like all true Carolinians, believed the late Civil War was a war of invasion. And though a Northern man by birth, and having all of his kinsmen, possibly without a single exception, living in New England, he could not take part with the North in this crusade. South Carolina stood in need of his services, and he did not withhold them, although he was over the age of conscription. He was not in active service in the field, but served well in some quartermaster's department.

One morning it transpired, without Mr. Hurd's knowledge, that his household in Newberry—by whom the weary, worn soldiers were entertained—had accommodated, on the night before, eleven poor, fatigued privates with food and lodging. This aroused the citizens to a sense of their duty, and then it was that our people undertook to care for them, and regularly every day had tables spread for the passing soldiers.

It sounds strangely to the Northerner, where whole households were not personally acquainted with a single person engaged in the Federal Army, when told that there was scarcely a hearthstone in the South that was not saddened by the loss of some loved one of the household Every able-bodied white man in South Carolina was in the Confederate Army. Husbands and sons all in the army, wives and children of the inhabitants of the sea coasts sought refuge in the middle and upper counties of the State. Hundreds and hundreds of them came to Newberry. A year or two after the war some young persons of the town were endeavoring to recall the names of the refugees at this place, and they numbered over five hundred of different patronymics. These people for the most part were unaccustomed to country life—were in the habit daily of marketing for their wants, and knew nothing of foraging. Here was an opportunity for the unselfish of our community to do kindness. Mr Hurd, who was always doing good, soon saw this chance; and he was so active and so successful in procuring supplies for the refugees, that he aroused the suspicions of some few persons to whom he was not well known, who charged him with engrossing these articles of food with a view to speculation. A public meeting was called for the purpose of denouncing him. A number of his friends, hearing of the call, attended the meeting, and indignantly refuted the charge. They disclosed the true purpose of this benevolent man and made manifest the good deeds that he was doing in secret; and the whole matter resulted to his credit, and to the satisfaction of his accusers, who were convinced of their mistake. But so mortified was he at being so charged, though falsely, and so great was his sensitiveness, that he could not dismiss it from his mind, and as soon as he was able, after peace was declared, he left the home of his adoption, never to return or revisit it. So Newberry lost one of her best citizens—one unsurpassed in moral excellence—who had spent the prime years of his life in this community.

It seems that he was the first Episcopalian who ever resided in Newberry, and to 1846, when that Church was organized at this place, his immediate family, with one exception, were the only members now remembered. He was largely, if not solely, instrumental in its permanent organization, and was one of its Wardens until his removal from the State in 1866. But now for him

"———— is o'erpast
The needless fret, the strife,
The troubles and the weariness
That crush this mortal life."

THE CONFEDERATE DEAD.

As a matter of interest to the people of Newberry, as well as to the people of the whole State, I think it well to give a copy of the inscription on the monument to the memory of the "Confederate Dead," in Columbia, S. C. The inscription was written by Hon. William C. Preston, and is as follows on the obverse sides:

THIS MONUMENT
Perpetuates the Memory

of those who,
True to the instincts of their birth,
Faithful to the Teachings of their Fathers,
Constant in their love for the State,
Died in the performance of their duty,
Who
Have glorified a fallen cause
By the simple manhood of their lives,
The patient endurance of suffering,
And the Heroism of Death,
And who,
In the dark hours of imprisonment,
In the hopelessness of the hospital,
In the short, sharp agony of the field,
Found support and consolation
In the belief
That at home they would not be forgotten.

LET THE STRANGER,
Who may in future times,
Read this inscription,
Recognize that these were men,
Whom power could not corrupt,
Whom death could not terrify,
Whom defeat could not dishonor;
And let their virtues plead
For just judgment
Of the cause in which they perished.
LET THE SOUTH CAROLINIAN
Of another generation
Remember
That the State taught them
How to live and how to die,
And that, from her broken fortunes,
She has preserved for her children
The priceless treasure of their memories,
Teaching all who may claim
The same birthright,
That TRUTH, COURAGE AND PATRIOTISM
ENDURE FOREVER.

ROSEMONT CEMETERY.

Of quiet, holy Sabbath days it sometimes gives me a calm, though a melancholy, pleasure to walk and meditate and rest in the Silent City adjoining our town; to muse there upon the brevity of human life. How soon we are forced to migrate from this to another country; to a better, we hope. That city is peopled, like our own noisy one, with inhabitants of all ages, from the wee babe, whose eyes were just opened into this world, to the old, who have passed their three-score years and ten. One corresponds to the other in all particulars—this is a city of bustle and activity—that, as far as we can see and know, is one of stillness and repose. Eternal peace broods over it.

Once when attending a burial service there I heard, or thought I heard, —I do not believe it was a fancy, but a reality,—in response to the singing at the grave of the dead child, ethereal voices far up in the air, making the sweetest, most angelic music that ever fell upon my ear save only in dreams. No, it was no fancy. A friend once told me, who now himself sleeps there, that riding past there one afternoon alone he heard, floating far up above the City of the Dead, music, for sweetness and happiness of tone, indescribable. He said he had never before mentioned it to any one for fear of being laughed at. I told him that he need not hesitate on that account, for I had heard the same. But I have never been so happy as to hear those ethereal tones, at that place since, the burial of that little child.

It is in a very solemn spirit that I read the many and varied tributes to the departed upon the stones erected to perpetuate their memory. One upon the headstone of the grave of a little child impressed me much, a good many years ago, as being exceedingly beautiful. Mother and child are both gone, and, if our hopes are well-founded, they are together now, and the child is no longer a child, but a bright and lovely youth blooming in eternal beauty. I do not know the author of the lines, never having seen them before I found them engraved upon that rock:

"Full short his journey was, no dust
Of earth unto his sandals clave;
The weary weight that old men must,
He bore not to the grave."

Then a little further on, and near the highest part of the cemetery, we come to the grave of one who was very dear to me. She was as a daughter, her father being for a number of years a neighbor and true friend. And she herself, during the brightest years of her maidenhood and early womanhood, was daily with my own children. The inscription upon the marble column that marks the spot where she sleeps was written by Maj. William F. Nance, and is as follows:

ELIZABETH MOORMAN WARDLAW!
Her happy life was distinguished
By a constant, innocent joyousness,
By a uniform sweetness of temper,
By a wide benevolence of heart,
By an upright gracefulness of conduct,
Governed always by purity of motive;
Always sustained
By a pure, unostentatious piety,
By an unfaltering trust in Jesus Christ,
She calmly passed to the higher life
June 27th, 1877.

And then not far away there is a stone upon which we read these words:

"Pretend not that I am of saintly fame,
Let mercy save me!
Sufficient for my epitaph the name
My mother gave me."
Born Dec. 16th, 1859, Died April 12th, 1887.
Only 27 years old, Johnnie had already made a
Record for himself for intellectual ability,
Fidelity to duty, honesty,
Uprightness of purpose, and as being
"Fearless of danger,
To falsehood a stranger;
Looking not back
Where there's duty before."

The last time I saw John B. Jones in health was the morning of the day in which he received his fatal wound, as he rode past in front of my Bookstore, on that ambling white horse, as he was in the habit of doing almost every day on his way to his office. I could but think of him then as a young man of much promise, in robust health, just entering upon a long career of usefulness in active life. I knew nothing of any impending difficulty; knew not that he had any misunderstanding with any person in the world, but saw him ride by, bouyant and full of health, and thought of him as of one whom I might envy, if I could ever envy any one. In a little while I heard of his fatal hurt. He has passed, I hope, to a country where there is no fighting.

Let us stop a little while at one other grave before we leave Rosemont. She who sleeps here was a good child. The stone tells not the date of her birth nor death, but only this:

ANNA MORTIMER.
O she was good!
So pure! if ever mortal form contained
The spirit of an angel, it was hers.

Reader! it is time that I close this book. It is already too large. There are other works that I want to accomplish before I go hence. But if Time tells the truth it cannot be many years before I give you, and it may be that I *now* give you, the last

HAIL AND FAREWELL!

INDEX.

PART FIRST.

PART SECOND.